Also from the Hound

VideoHound's® Golden Movie Retriever®

VideoHound's World Cinema:
The Adventurer's Guide to Movie Watching

VideoHound's Epics:
Giants of the Big Screen

VideoHound's Complete Guide to
Cult Flicks and Trash Pics

VideoHound's Horror Show:
999 Hair-Raising, Hellish, and Humorous Movies

VideoHound' s Vampires on Video

The St. James Film Directors Encyclopedia

St. James Women Filmmakers Encyclopedia:
Women on the Other Side of the Camera

To my parents
Boyd Wayne Mayo
and Betty Jo Mayo,
World War II veterans
and movie fans

VideoHound's WAR+MOVIES

CLASSIC
CONFLICT
ON FILM

Mike Mayo

Foreword by
Capt.Dale Dye,
USMC(Ret.)

VISIBLE INK PRESS

DETROIT • SAN FRANCISCO • LONDON • BOSTON • WOODBRIDGE, CT

"You can't show war as it really is on the screen, with all the blood and gore. Perhaps it would be better if you could fire real shots over the audience's head every night, you know, and have actual casualties in the theater... But when I do a war film, I want the story to be about real war, not just action. Many of the incidents in my stories have to do with the emotions of men in war. This is every bit as important as the actual fighting...."

— Sam Fuller. *Film: Book 2.*

Edited by Robert Hughes. Grove Press. 1962.

Copyright © 1999 by Visible Ink Press

Published by Visible Ink Press ®, a division of Gale Group, Inc.
27500 Drake Rd.
Farmington Hills, MI 48331-3535

Visible Ink Press, *VideoHound*, the VideoHound logo, and A Cunning Canine Production are registered trademarks of Gale Group, Inc.

Most Visible Ink books are available at special quantity discounts when purchased in bulk by corporations, organizations, or groups. Customized printings, special imprints, messages, and excerpts can be produced to meet your needs. For more information, contact Special Markets Manager, Gale Group, Inc. 27500 Drake Rd., Farmington Hills, MI 48331-3535.

Art Director: Martha Schiebold
Photos: The Kobal Collection and Del Valle Archives
Cover Photos: The Kobal Collection

Library of Congress Cataloging-in-Publication Data

Mayo, Mike, 1949-
Videohound's war movies : classic conflict on film / Mike Mayo ; foreword by Dale Dye
     p.   cm.
    Includes indexes.
    ISBN 1-57859-089-2 (softcover)
    1. War films--Catalogs.   I. Title.
PN1995.9.W3M39   1999
016.79143' 658--dc21

99-40600
CIP

ISBN 1-57859-089-2
Printed in the United States of America
All rights reserved
10 9 8 7 6 5 4 3 2 1

A Cunning Canine Production®

CONTENTS

Mike Mayo

Mike Mayo is the author of *VideoHound's Video Premieres* and *VideoHound's Horror Show*, and is a proud contributor to *Cult Flicks and Trash Pics* and *Sci-Fi Experience*. He has written about film and video for the *Roanoke Times* and the *Washington Post*. From 1981 to 1996, he was Book Editor for the *Roanoke Times*. His occasional column, *Hidden Video*, appears on picpal.com.

Capt. Dale Dye

Capt. Dale Dye is a former Marine with two tours of duty in Vietnam and one in Beirut, Lebanon. Among his numerous decorations are the Bronze Star and three Purple Hearts for his service in Vietnam. Since retiring from the military, Capt. Dye has starred in and served as military/technical advisor for over 40 films. His credits include *Platoon*, *Born on the Fourth of July*, and *Saving Private Ryan*.

Somewhere in the HTO (Hollywood Theater of Operations)...24 June 99

As I sit here in my beleaguered Command Post—surrounded by clueless liberals and pounded mercilessly by Big Buck artillery registered on the bottom line—I'm forced to wonder if the war can be won. The enemy is brutal, well armed, and constantly resupplied, while we are forced to fight back with only bayonets, small arms, and the occasional smart weapon. Fanatical Divisions of Directors—led by Assault Sections of Screenwriters, and whipped into a frenzy by their Political Commissar Producers—attack our outposts day and night. Casualties have been high and hurtful, particularly in the Military Image area.

Interrogations of the few dazed and confused POWs we've been able to capture reveal the pervasive and insidious nature of this conflict. Specifically, our Intelligence Section has discovered the following significant points about the enemy's mind-set and motivation:

1.) Soldiers are almost always mindless drones duped by nefarious politicians with an evil agenda, or...

2.) They are overweight, unkempt, ill-disciplined, and ignorant Southerners or ethnic minorities motivated by brainless blood-lust or a violent libido.

3.) Reality is a crutch which will not support a successful operation, and has no bearing on public acceptance.

4.) They almost always need a haircut.

Faced with these horrid misconceptions, we have no choice but to continue the battle. Vastly out-numbered and out-gunned—often powerless and fighting a subversive, guerilla-style war from within—my small band of Warriors, reinforced by a few right-thinking Panavision Commandos, will fight on for a fair shot and our just place in the public opinion sector.

Believe it. Fighting the good fight for truth, justice, and the American way out here in the Hollywood Theater of Operations is brutal in the extreme. You lose more than you win, and are regularly forced to sacrifice important details in daily firefights to give yourself a chance of winning the war over The Big Picture. As a professional military man most of my life (military schools starting at age 10 and never looked back), there are times when I wonder why I continue to assault the barricades.

The fact that both of the conflicts in which I fought (Vietnam and Beirut, Lebanon) over a 20-year active duty career were losers going in might have something to do with it, but there's more to the story. And here's the short version.

After the 1983 tragedy in which we lost 241 of America's finest fighting men in Beirut as a result of ridiculous, politically motivated Rules of Engagement and a single fanatical truck-bomb attack on the barracks housing my old outfit—the 24th Marine Amphibious Unit—I decided perhaps it was time to seek gainful employment elsewhere. I had worked my way up through the enlisted ranks in the United States Marine Corps, with my eyes always on the prize of eventually becoming an officer. On the day I was commissioned at Quantico, Virginia, after 12 years of enlisted service in war and peace—following some incredible leaders and struggling to please others who never should have gotten beyond college ROTC—I vowed that I would not quit as a leader until the day came when I could no longer look into the beady eyeballs of my Marines and honestly proclaim our sacrifices were just and necessary. When that day dawned in October of 1983, shortly after I had returned to the States from service in Beirut, I submitted the paperwork to retire from active duty.

In the summer of 1984—for the first time in my memory—I was a man without a plan...and not a whole hell of a lot of marketable skills either. The Mafia wasn't hiring just then, and I'd been shot enough times to realize I didn't want to be a cop on America's mean streets. That led to a long night of fuzzy-headed navel-gazing, during which I listed my assets versus my liabilities as a potential employee in the mysterious world of civilians. Not surprisingly, the latter list was about four feet longer than the former. Clearly I was bound either to dedicate my second career to researching lethal levels of alcohol consumption among former military men, or to invent a job that would keep me motivated. There was also some vague notion that I should find something that might benefit the good batch of men and women I left behind serving their nation on active duty.

High on my short list of assets was the fact that I had always been a movie fan, particularly war movies, which demonstrates how little of value I had available in my seabag to lay before the job market for inspection. Anyway, I got to thinking about it and decided that one of the main reasons I avidly consumed each and every war or military film to hit the bricks was so I could sit there and criticize Hollywood's take—in general and specifically—on my world and the world of other military people. Every good Marine understands that where there is room for criticism, there is room for improvement. The key is to spot the problem, make a plan, and then beat the bastard until it goes away or submits to your will.

That's the Marine Corps way. A dim bulb began to glow, which led me to an airport where I bought a cheap ticket to Los Angeles.

Fatefully, the $4 matinee on that airborne bone-crusher was a military movie. I don't recall the title, and it's not important. What's significant is that I noticed a line in the final credit crawl that named the movie's "military advisor." This epic—even allowing for ham-handed airline editing and small-screen distortion—had a lot in common with the jet engines whining out there on the wings. It both sucked and blew. That dim bulb began to glow a little more brightly.

By the time we were chocked and chained at LAX, I had thought it through sufficiently to believe that either the guys who worked as Military Advisors in the film industry were incompetent boobs, or they were brilliant former soldiers and the incompetent boobs in the film industry simply refused to pay any attention to their advice. Turns out it was a little of both.

Mainly because I had neither the business acumen nor the necessary tact to deal with civilians on their terms, I launched an investigation on Hollywood turf that involved such *faux pas* as barging in on major Producers sans appointment, berating powerful Executive Assistants as if they were shiftless lance corporals, and generally making it known that, in my opinion, practically every military movie they made stunk out loud. Why they put up with it, I'll never know. Maybe my approach was unusual and therefore entertaining. Hollywood is, after all, about entertainment.

At the end of that ugly reconnaissance mission, I was able to draw some simple conclusions. Most filmmakers who bothered to seek military advice searched for some old soldier who was willing to make script notes about technical details, or sit quietly on the set and answer questions if and when they were asked. "Listen, pal…just tell us which side the ribbons go on, OK? We've been doing this for a while, you know? We know what plays in Peoria…and you don't. It's wrong, huh? Yeah, well, who cares? Who's gonna know the difference? Go get some lunch, OK? And don't talk to the actors…you'll only confuse them."

That's painting with a fairly broad brush. There were some gritty, veteran filmmakers, such as Sam Fuller (himself a WWII combat vet), who cared deeply about the message they sent in war films, but these guys were clearly an exception that proved the rules I was discovering. By the time I got to Hollywood back in 1985, finding a producer, director, or screenwriter who had served in combat—or in the military at all—was about as likely as finding a PFC in the Pentagon.

Military Advisors to movies and television were reactive. They fought in defense. Fine, I concluded, but the art of war is in the offense. War...art? Was there a practical connection here? More research, conducted by volunteering my services as an unpaid fetch-boy on sets, revealed that motion picture companies were organized—in fact if not in fancy—along basic military lines, complete with commanding officers, senior NCOs, staff sections, administrators, logisticians, and line troops. Given proper motivation and a proactive approach to the battle, they just might be swayed to care a little bit more about the military image and attention to detail.

Here's where I was forced to become more philosophical and academic than I tend to be when stumbling through life on a day-to-day basis. It was time to confront the three major attitudinal obstacles on the path to helping Hollywood make better military movies:

1.) If it's ugly or unsettling, people won't come to see it;

2.) Nobody cares about details; and

3.) Nobody knows the difference anyway.

"Think about this," I said, when I could get someone to listen. Hemingway had it right. "War is man's greatest adventure." That's why novelists, screenwriters, and other storytellers keep coming back to the well. It features, totally unfettered, the full gamut of human emotions. Bad guys can be good and good guys can be bad under pressure of combat. Hell, anything can happen—and usually does—in war. The war format is heroin for the imaginative. In moviespeak, war's got legs.

On the other hand, Gen. William Tecumseh Sherman was also on the mark when he said: "War is cruelty and you can't refine it." What that means, I try to explain, is that when you mine this fertile format for movies, you've got to graphically communicate the cruelty. If you polish it or pull back, you're lying, and that's a recognizable farce that will put people off your efforts to collect their money at the boxoffice.

Prove it? Tough task...but ponder this. Globally we are a media-saturated society. At no time in mankind's turbulent history have we ever had more consistent war-like conflicts around the world, or more immediate exposure to the brutal images of those conflicts. When people start pumping ammo at each other, people who are not interested, or only peripherally involved, get inundated with bloody reality through TV, radio, newspapers, and magazines. My theory was, is, and remains that you can't show reasonably intelligent people that kind of stark reality and then expect them to accept a different, sanitized version in a movie theater without a certain amount of what the shrinks call cognitive disconnect. And that's bad for business.

So what you've got to do, I told those few still listening, is pay attention to the details. Make what they see on the Evening News compare visually with what they see in the theater later that evening. It lends credence. It gives you a head start on suspending disbelief. Tossing around terms like that got me a few more listeners, so I expanded on the theme.

Furthermore, you can't expect young actors (old actor is a Hollywood oxymoron) to perform effectively without giving them some sort of baggage they can dig into when a role requires them to plumb the character of a trained soldier or portray the physical and emotional roller coaster he rides in combat. Yeah, yeah, I know, it's about acting and that's why they get the Big Bucks, but effective acting is about finding the truth, and communicating it on stage or screen. The truth will, indeed, set you free...but you've got to know it first. My recommendation was that I be allowed to take actors on a little trek to hell and back prior to the start of principal photography on military films, thus filling their physical and emotional rucksacks with real world experiences on which they could draw to bring a ring of truth in their posture, movement, expression, emotional reaction, and physical performance.

At that point, I stepped over the start-mark into a minefield sown with whining agents and sniveling gate guards who could not imagine having their star-studded cash-cow mistreated, or required to sleep in a filthy hole for days on end without cell phones or go-fers to make life comfortable. Fortunately, as I was struggling to probe my way through this explosive terrain, I met a brilliant, visionary, and virulent filmmaker named Oliver Stone who, like me, had fought through extended tours in Vietnam. Understandably, as combat vets, we spoke the same language. Oddly, as men from opposite ends of the political spectrum, our views on verisimilitude in films were also the same. Oliver understood, and I will be forever grateful to him for that, as well as for giving me the first chance to test and prove my theories.

By the time we finished making *Platoon*, on a relative shoestring, and exorcising many of our wartime demons on screen, I knew my methods had merit. By the time we became contenders for the Academy Awards, I was refining a method for the madness. By the time we won four Oscars, including Best Picture of 1986, I had a fair-sized bloc of True Believers in Hollywood.

So, now I'm a man with a mission again and at last. Given success with *Platoon*, and leading over the course of about 40 military films to my contribution on Steven Spielberg's monumental *Saving Private Ryan*, I'm in a position to influence images a bit. When I say that America's military men and women are the ultimate example of dedicated and selfless public servants, the message is at least heard, if not always heeded. When I say that the realities of military life are quite often more colorful and dramatic than fiction, images of those realities often reach the motion-picture or TV screen. When I plead for honor and gratitude in our images of the people who have fought our wars and sacrificed so much to keep us free to enjoy things like movies, sometimes my plea is answered. That's better than stars on my shoulders or an Oscar on my mantle.

As a film reviewer and fan, I love a well-told story—one with clearly delineated conflicts, characters involved in exciting situations, settings that show me something new or present familiar territory in new light. At their best, war movies can do all of those things. From historical epics to contemporary dramas, they have a universal appeal that cuts across national boundaries. And so, despite the inherent ugliness and horror of real war, people love movies about it. As I watched these 201 war films (more about that number later), I came to a new appreciation of the form, and at times was able to see beyond the explosions and the gunfire and the politics to find more basic human truths.

War movies deal in strong stuff—destruction on a vast scale, heroic adventure, the most grotesque horror, noble sacrifice, cowardice, loud pyrotechnics, men and women in perilous straits where death can arrive on a butterfly's wing or a whistling artillery shell. When made properly, these films have a legitimate reason to present human conflict in its most extreme dramatic conditions, and so when you watch the best ones, you really want to know what's going to happen next. To misquote Samuel Johnson, the immediate prospect of being blown up concentrates the mind wonderfully. War films give viewers a tiny vicarious fraction of that experience, and the adrenaline hit that comes with it accounts for much of their popularity. But in the good ones, something more serious is at work.

That's what this book tries to reveal, though it is just as interested in celebrating worthwhile escapism.

First though, my credentials: I am a film reviewer, not a warrior. My experience with the military is limited to two disastrous semesters of NROTC at the University of North Carolina where I amassed a number of demerits that might still be unsurpassed. Three years later in the first draft lottery, I drew 339, a number that effectively ended my active association with the military. I got married instead. Since 1975, I've been writing about movies for various media.

After all those years of watching films and talking to veterans, I am convinced that even the most accurate movie cannot come close to re-creating the realities of war. As Dale Dye explains in his foreword, the great majority of Hollywood war films play fast and loose with the details of combat to serve their narrative purposes. They don't let facts, logic, or common sense get in the way of a good visual. Viewers should not look to war movies for objective historical truth. Actually, any adult who expects to find historical accuracy in a Hollywood movie deserves to be lied to.

Viewers can demand reasonably accurate *emotional* truth. That's what movies are good at. And when filmmakers do find the emotional truth in war, it's often complicated and hard to resolve. Most of the time, though, filmmakers mean only to entertain. Hollywood movies are a business. War movies, like all movies, are largely financed by producers who are interested in profits, and so repeat the formulas that have been successful in the past. Because of that, war films can be divided into seven categories:

- Unit pictures
- Resistance movements and spies (often combined in World War II films)
- Homefront stories of domestic life and/or women in non-traditional jobs
- Action adventures that stress heroics and gunplay
- Anti-war combat films that stress waste and destruction
- Re-creations of actual battles
- Service comedies

Each of these seven types is represented here, though only one service comedy (*Mister Roberts*) made our final list of 201. Also included are seven documentaries, including *Battle of Midway*, *Memphis Belle: A Story of a Flying Fortress*, *The War at Home*, and *The Guns of August*.

Creating the list was difficult. Editor Jim Craddock and I began with what we thought would be simple criteria. The first was availability on video. We decided not to deal with films that had never been distributed on tape or disc. (Then we promptly broke that rule when we learned that William Wellman's *The Story of G.I. Joe* was rumored to be in negotiation for a video release.) We also tried to avoid titles that are out of print and exceptionally hard to find. When we discussed the films that would be included, we took into account historical importance, critical reputation, boxoffice success, and our own favorites. We tried to cover the proven audience favorites—*Braveheart*, *The Great Escape*—while saving room for the lesser-known titles—*Come and See*, *The Siege of Firebase Gloria*, *Fires on the Plain*, *The Winter War*—that have developed passionate followings over the years. We wanted to include the older important films—*All Quiet on the Western Front*, *Sands of Iwo Jima*—and the current crop—*Saving Private Ryan* (for which director Steven Spielberg has been awarded the Defense Dept. Public Service Award, the highest honor the U.S. military can confer on a civilian), *The Thin Red Line*, and *Life Is Beautiful*. The book is weighted toward World War II because "the last good war" has been the most popular one for filmmakers. Of course, we tried to include work from other wars and other countries, striking the best balance we could find to represent the remarkable breadth of the genre.

We understand that these 201 will not suit everyone. Given the physical limitations of the book, we tried to include as many filmmakers and stars as we could. So David Lean's seriously underrated *Ryan's Daughter* was left out, though he is represented by *In Which We Serve*, *Bridge on the River Kwai*, *Lawrence of Arabia*, and *Doctor Zhivago*. Much of John Wayne's career is based on war films and we've included his best work (and some that's not his best) but still had to leave out *Back to Bataan* and *Flying Tigers*. So, if our final choices do not satisfy everyone, we hope that most readers will find something new here, or, at least, will be reminded of a forgotten favorite.

Why 201? 200 was the original limit but when, some months into the project, we learned of some fine older foreign films, we made in-flight adjustments and compromised on 201.

Though technological changes and the public appetite for graphic violence have made recent war movies more realistic, the earliest efforts are shocking and moving and often starkly cynical. In many cases they were made by directors who had served in World War I and did not want to glamorize the experience. William Wellman drove an ambulance for the French Foreign Legion and then flew for the Lafayette Escadrille when America entered the war. Howard Hawks also flew and trained pilots. Rex Ingram, director of the 1921 *Four Horsemen of the Apocalypse*, served in the Canadian Royal Flying Corps. Lewis Milestone was in the Army Signal Corps.

The aerial sequences in the Wellman and Hawks movies are magnificent, but whenever the directors look into the trenches, the adventure stops cold. The Great War devastated a generation, and the men who made movies about it tried to show all of the waste and horror. Decades later, such veterans as Sam Fuller and Oliver Stone would translate their wartime experiences to the screen with varying degrees of realism and success, while "noncombatant" filmmakers like Francis Ford Coppola and Stanley Kubrick would be accused of making "imagist" war films when they addressed the same subject. (*Violent Screen*. Stephen Hunter. 1995)

(By the way, war films may be the last bastion of male dominance. Female filmmakers have never had an easy time of it in the American movie business and, for practical purposes, the war movie is an all-male enterprise. No woman has had much of an influence in any key creative capacity. Conventional wisdom also holds that men are the primary audience for war movies, but that is simply not true. Women also appreciate good war films, perhaps because they often show men in their most vulnerable, honest, and open moments. Admittedly, though, women do seem to lack a taste for really loud, stupid films filled with explosions from beginning to end, while guys understand them implicitly.)

As memories of World War I faded farther into the past and Nazism arose in Germany, the movies lost their bitter, realistic edge. The studio system that evolved in the 1930s was built upon light entertainment, and war again became a grand adventure in *Beau Geste*, *Gunga Din*, and dozens of others. By the time America entered World War II, Hollywood was ready to sign on. In fact, the entertainment business had been so enthusiastically anti-fascist that American isolationists were up in arms. In September 1941, Sen. Gerald Nye of North Dakota called for hearings to investigate radio and motion picture propaganda. The discussion ended on December 7, but everyone realized that the film industry was going to play an important role in the war effort.

In the years just before the war, "out of a population of 120 million, 90 million went to the movies every week." (Film historian Greg Black, *Cartoons Go to War*. A&E. 1995) The studios produced a polished product and controlled every step of the process, from the conception of story ideas to ownership of the theaters where the finished film was shown. Soon after the war started, President Franklin Roosevelt ordered the formation of the Bureau of Motion Pictures as a division of the Office of War Information. Its purpose was to review screenplays, suggest ideas for films that would support the war effort, and facilitate technical support. Despite Hollywood's fondness for combat pictures, the Bureau actually requested more musicals, and 75 were produced in the first two years of the war. Throughout the war years, the government and the film industry seldom disagreed. After all, the administration merely wanted Hollywood to keep on doing what it had been doing—to provide inspirational, positive entertainment. Though a few movies might be mildly critical of the armed services, the film business was resoundingly pro-military until the 1950s. The screen adaptation of James Jones's *From Here to Eternity*, for example, virtually eliminated the novel's portrayal of ambitious, self-serving officers and institutional rigidity. Instead, it presented the Army as an essentially benign, intelligent, and fair organization that removed bad apples as soon as they were revealed.

Cracks began to appear in the symbiotic Hollywood–Washington relationship when conservative forces resurfaced after the war and the anti-Communist House Un-American Activities Committee witch-hunts intensified. At around the same time, 1949, the Supreme Court fundamentally changed the economic nature of the industry with the Paramount Consent Decree, which ordered the studios to divest themselves of their theaters. That breakup opened the way for independent producers with more controversial ideas. It was not until Stanley Kubrick made *Paths of Glory*, about World War I, and his Cold War comedy *Dr. Strangelove* that mainstream films specifically criticized Washington and the Pentagon.

In American movies, though, political considerations are less important—much less important—than individual characters. Until World War II, the American war film is almost always about a divided country with conflicting loyalties that place friends and family on opposite sides of important issues. Even at its most patriotic, the serious American war film, from *Sergeant York* to *Saving Private Ryan*, revolves around a reluctant warrior—a man who simply wants to do a job and go home. As John Wayne says in the otherwise soapy *In Harm's Way*, "All battles are fought by scared men who'd rather be somewhere else."

After Pearl Harbor, however, that reluctant warrior became more enthusiastic, and the "unit" picture emerged as the dominant form of war film. Those stories are about a group—almost always men—who enter the armed service as self-centered individuals with varying degrees of motivation. Through training and combat they become an effective fighting unit. Some or all are sacrificed for the greater good of the cause they're fighting for.

The unit picture is a retelling of the basics of any military indoctrination. Most armies use some form of "boot camp" in which the new recruits' existing loyalties to family, religion, and community are broken down by harsh physical and mental conditioning, and then are replaced with a new allegiance to the military and the military's goals. The World War II unit picture typically paints that process in the most flattering tones. Stanley Kubrick presents it as a nightmare in the brilliant first act of *Full Metal Jacket*. Other unit films take the formula a step farther and literally turn the military organization into a family. The story of the individual who finds a home in the service is a familiar one, from *All Quiet on the Western Front* to *To Hell and Back* and *China Beach*. That equation of the military and the family is a second major theme in modern American war movies. In bringing the two together, the movies really abandon their propaganda role for a simple truth: Family is more important that politics—in war films, in all films, in real life.

It's impossible to determine exactly how significant a role the movies have played in various war efforts—either in support or opposition. In general, films don't so much change people's minds as validate opinions they already hold, knowingly or not. When movies do that well, they can be profoundly important. Though the years have heightened their flaws, films like *Mrs. Miniver* and *The Deer Hunter* capture the national mood of their moment so profoundly that they become cultural touchstones.

In his excellent book, *The Hollywood History of the World* (Beech Tree Books. 1988), historian, novelist, screenwriter, and veteran George MacDonald Fraser writes at length about *Immortal Battalion* (a.k.a *The Way Ahead*) and the other English war films of the early 1940s. He takes issue with the critics who dismiss them as mere flag-waving propaganda and then go on to suggest that viewers at the time were somehow tricked by the filmmakers into a false sense of victory.

"The British public were well aware of the score," Fraser writes. "They had a fair idea of what was true and what was false and what was glamourised and what was slanted; nobody ever sold them anything, except hope. The so-called propaganda of the wartime films was the equivalent of a pat on the back, and a reminder that what they were doing was worthwhile, in the short term at least. Indeed, they didn't even think of it in terms of 'worthwhile'; it was just plain stark necessity. Most important, they could see the point of propaganda. Does it ever occur to modern cinemagoers that *Dirty Harry* and *Animal House* and *Full Metal Jacket* and *Kramer vs. Kramer* may be propaganda, too, whether their makers know it or not?"

Fraser's right. It's easy enough now to see the manipulation in *Casablanca* and *Sands of Iwo Jima*. The creators of *Born on the Fourth of July* and *Hamburger Hill* are no less subtle, really. Today's propaganda is much more sophisticated technically, and today's viewers ought to cultivate an equally sophisticated degree of skepticism.

The writing of this book certainly honed my own skepticism. I saw a lot of propaganda in all its forms—effective, sly, obvious, silly. But that's only one side of the war film and overall, the good far outweighs the bad in the ones considered here. I remain a true fan, and I hope that this book will enhance other fans' enjoyment of the form. As I said earlier, war movies generally tell fast-paced, lively stories. At their worst they can be entertaining. At their best they can give viewers some insight and appreciation of experiences they will never know directly. At least, that's what my favorites do. A top-ten list was impossible, so here are my own top 21 in chronological order:

All Quiet on the Western Front (1930)
Gunga Din (1939)
The Story of G.I. Joe (1945)
The Best Years of Our Lives (1946)
Battleground (1949)

From Here to Eternity (1953)

Seven Samurai (1954)

Fires on the Plain (1959)

The Guns of Navarone (1961)

Zulu (1964)

Dr. Strangelove (1964)

Cross of Iron (1976)

Go Tell the Spartans (1978)

The Big Red One (1980)

Das Boot (1981)

Platoon (1986)

Hope and Glory (1987)

Glory (1989)

The Siege of Firebase Gloria (1989)

When Trumpets Fade (1998)

Saving Private Ryan (1998)

My top 21 is an eclectic list with some titles that are probably unfamiliar to many readers. Its diversity is a testimonial to the many variations of the war story. It is my hope that *VideoHound's War Movies* will inspire similar video exploration and a richer understanding of these films. Suggestions, questions, and comments can be forwarded to me at:

Visible Ink Press
27500 Drake Road
Farmington Hills, MI 48331-3535

Or by e-mail at videohound@galegroup.com

—Mike Mayo
Chatham, NJ

This book would not be possible without the help of many people. First, **Steve Mormando** of Belle and Blade Home Video, **Jim Olenski** of Thomas Video, and **Irv Slifkin** of Movies Unlimited kindly provided rare tapes, encouragement, and opinions.

The tireless reference and inter-library loan department of the **Chatham Borough Library** also helped to locate documentaries and books.

Bob Cosenza at the Kobal Collection and **David Del Valle** at Del Valle Archives provided the excellent photographs.

Marco Di Vita at the Graphix Group was again tireless and speedy with the typesetting.

At Visible Ink Press, **Marilou Carlin, Marty Connors, Julia Furtaw, Kim Marich, Betsy Rovegno**, and **Lauri Taylor** were never shy about speaking up for their favorite war films.

Sarah Chesney and **Maria Franklin** capably handled the photo permissions.

Randy Bassett, Imaging Database Supervisor; **Robert Duncan** and **Michael Logusz**, Imaging Specialists; and **Pamela A. Reed**, Imaging Coordinator, prepared the photos for publication.

Cindy Baldwin and **Martha Schiebold** designed the book under sometimes difficult circumstances and time constraints.

Wayne Fong came up with the programming that made it all work.

Carol Schwartz made valuable contributions every step of the way.

Finally, editor **Jim Craddock** made sure that the reviews came in on time and the deadlines were met.

To all, thank you, thank you, thank you.

WAR VIDEO SOURCES

The home video revolution of the 1980s brought us a profusion of cable and satellite channels and tape distribution outlets. War films and documentaries have carved out a sizeable niche within the marketplace. Here is a short list of the sources I'm familiar with. I've dealt with all of them in various capacities, and recommend them without hesitation.

With more than 1,000 titles, **Belle and Blade Home Video** has the most complete listing of war and war-related films you'll find in one place. Prices are standard for the marketplace. This is the first place a serious collector would check for hard-to-find titles, particularly those from Europe. *The Bridge*, *The Siege of Firebase Gloria*, *The Winter War*, and *Zulu* were reviewed from Belle and Blade tapes.

Belle and Blade Home Video
124 Penn Ave.
Dover, NJ 07801
(973)328-8488
(973)422-0669 (fax)
www.belleandblade.com

Antiquary Video is more focused on public domain documentaries, with an emphasis on aviation. It carries the best version of William Wyler's *Memphis Belle* that I've seen.

Antiquary Video
P.O. Box 61
Milltown, NJ 08850-0061
(732)828-70218
airwar@antiquaryvideo.com
www.antiquaryvideo.com

Movies Unlimited handles essentially everything that is available on tape and disc. The catalogue is exhaustive, witty, and fun.

Movies Unlimited
3015 Darnell Rd.
Philadelphia, PA 19154
1-800-4-MOVIES
www.moviesunlimited.com

For tape and disc rentals by mail, try **Thomas Video** and **Facets Multimedia**.

Thomas Video
122 S. Main St.
Clawson, MI 48017
(248)280-2833

orders@thomasvideo.com
www.thomasvideo.com

Facets Multimedia
1517 W. Fullerton Ave.
Chicago, IL 60614
1-800-532-2387

On cable and satellite TV, **The History Channel** and the **Arts and Entertainment** network produce and air hundreds of documentaries and films. Almost all of their programs are available for sale. To order from either directly, call 1-800-423-1212.

A&E
235 E. 45th St.
New York, NY 10017
www.AandE.com
www.Biography.com

The History Channel
235 E. 45th St.
New York, NY 10017
www.HistoryChannel.com

For older films, the best cable and satellite sources are **American Movie Classics** and **Turner Classic Movies**. (Working on this book, I benefitted from both.)

American Movie Classics
111 Stewart Ave.
Bethpage, NY 11714
(516)364-2222
www.amctv.com

Turner Classic Movies
1010 Techwood Dr., NW
Atlanta, GA 30318
(404)885-5535
www.tcm.turner.com

INSTRUCTIONS FOR USE

Alphabetization

Titles are arranged on a word-by-word basis, including articles and prepositions. Leading articles (A, An, The) are ignored in English-language titles; the equivalent foreign articles are not ignored (because so many people—not you, of course—don't recognize them as articles); thus, *The Big Red One* appears within its chapter in the Bs, but *Das Boot* appears within its chapter in the Ds. Acronyms appear alphabetically as if regular words; for example, *M*A*S*H* is alphabetized as "MASH." Common abbreviations in titles file as if they were spelled out, so *Dr. Strangelove, or: How I Learned to Stop Worrying and Love the Bomb* will be alphabetized as "Doctor Strangelove, or: How I Learned to Stop Worrying and Love the Bomb." Movie titles with numbers, such as *84 Charlie MoPic*, are alphabetized as if the number were spelled out—so this title would appear within its chapter in the Es as if it were "Eighty Four Charlie MoPic."

---

(1) DR. STRANGELOVE, OR: HOW I LEARNED TO STOP WORRYING AND LOVE THE BOMB

(2) Ripper's Folly

(3) 1964 (4) Stanley Kubrick (5) ♪♪♪♪

(6) Seen from the perspective that only time can give, *Dr. Strangelove* now seems almost inevitable. During the coldest days of the Cold War, someone simply had to satirize the paranoia that drove it. But Stanley Kubrick and writers Terry Southern and Peter George did it so brilliantly that their work has improved with repeated viewings over the years. The ultra-deadpan humor and carefully controlled acting have lost nothing, and the three-sided plot could serve as a model for the well-built screenplay….

(7) Cast: Peter Sellers (Group Capt. Lionel Mandrake/President Merkin Muffley/Dr. Strangelove), George C. Scott (Gen. "Buck" Turgidson), Sterling Hayden (Gen. Jack D. Ripper), Keenan Wynn (Col. "Bat" Guano), Slim Pickens (Maj. T.J "King" Kong), James Earl Jones (Lt. Lothar Zogg), Peter Bull (Ambassador de Sadesky), Tracy Reed (Miss Scott), Shane Rimmer (Capt. G.A. "Ace" Owens), Glenn Beck (Lt. W.D. Kivel), Gordon Tanner (Gen. Faceman), Frank Berry (Lt. H.R. Dietrich), Jack Creley (Mr. Staines); **(8) Written by:** Stanley Kubrick, Terry Southern, Peter George; **(9) Cinematography by:** Gilbert Taylor; **(10) Music by:** Laurie Johnson. **(11) Technical Advisor:** Capt. John Crewdson; **(12) Producer:** Stanley Kubrick, Victor Lyndon, Leon Minoff, Columbia Pictures. **(13) MPAA Rating:** R **(14) British. (15) Awards:** American Film Institute (AFI) '98: Top 100; British Academy Awards '64: Best Film, National Film Registry '89; New York Film Critics Awards '64: Best Director (Kubrick); Nominations: Academy Awards '64: Best Actor (Sellers), Best Adapted Screenplay, Best Director (Kubrick), Best Picture. **(16) Budget:** 1M. **(17) Boxoffice:** 10M. **(18) Running Time:** 93 minutes. **(19) Format:** VHS, Beta, LV, Letterbox, DVD.

Sample Review

Each review contains up to 19 tidbits of information, as enumerated below. Please realize that we faked a bit of info in this review for demonstration purposes.

1. **Title**

2. **Alternative title (we faked it here)**

3. **Year released**

4. **Director(s)**

5. **One- to four-bone rating, four bones being the ultimate praise**

6. **Description/review**

7. **Cast, including cameos and voice-overs, with corresponding character names**

8. **Writer(s)**

9. **Cinematographer(s)**

10. **Music composer(s)**

11. **Technical/Military advisor(s)**

12. **Producer(s)/Production company**

13. **MPAA Rating (we faked it here, too)**

14. **Country of origin (where it was produced, if other than U.S.)**

15. **Awards, including nominations**

16. **Budget**

17. **Boxoffice**

18. **Length in minutes**

19. **Format(s), including VHS, DVD, Laservideo/disc (LV), letterbox, and others**

AMERICAN WARS

American Wars on Screen

When American filmmakers look at wars fought in their own country, they tend to be more interested in reconciliation than in victory. Their reasons are primarily commercial; they don't want to offend part of their potential audience by making them the enemy, as foreigners so often are. But historical distance plays a part, too, and relatively few films have been made about the Revolution. Today, the tactics, weapons, and costumes of the Colonial period make the films look like vaguely silly period pieces, and so it's difficult for audiences to invest much passion or involvement in the conflict. Michael Mann's *Last of the Mohicans* comes close, but it is still most effective as a star-driven historical romance. D.W. Griffith's *America* repeats the basic structure and themes of *Birth of a Nation* in a colonial setting.

John Wayne's preachy *The Alamo* suffers under a double load of heavy political baggage and a poorly written role for the leading man. Wayne was trying to turn the story of the siege into a Cold War allegory, and the combination of history and propaganda never really works.

Historical distance begins to diminish in the Civil War films. The ones chosen here differ widely in their attitudes and depiction of the conflict. That war is the central event of American history, and still capable of inspiring fiery arguments. The first important film to deal with it is a perfect example. The racist *Birth of a Nation* presents a false revisionist portrait of the Civil War and Reconstruction that was instrumental in the maintenance of state-sponsored segregation in the first half of the 20th century, and is still accepted by some. The unbridled romanticism in *Gone with the*

Wind masks a less virulent racism, but the film is not much closer to the truth of the times. Sergio Leone turns the conflict into a mythic backdrop for his ambitious and violent anti-war epic, *The Good, the Bad and the Ugly*. John Huston, like John Wayne, attempts to make political points in *The Red Badge of Courage*, but they tend to be lost in that troubled production's inability to illustrate its psychological concerns.

When directors try to stick more closely to historical fact, the results are mixed. The most successful is Edward Zwick's *Glory*. Despite an undeniable stiffness and slow pace, the film brings the passions and hatreds of the era to life with a reality that few films match, and the depiction of combat is as emotionally moving as any war film. *Gettysburg* is an accurate overview of the three-day battle, and though the various generals and officers look right, they never emerge as fully fleshed characters. Jeff Daniels's Chamberlain is a notable exception. John Ford paid as little attention to history as possible in *The Horse Soldiers*, despite the fact that he was working with a remarkable true story.

Of course, anyone who really wants to understand that war should go first to Ken Burns's masterful PBS series, *The Civil War*. (See sidebar.)

Most of the films that deal with the country's westward expansion in the 19th century are more properly categorized as westerns than as war films, even when they deal with the armed encounters that took place between Indian tribes and settlers. *She Wore a Yellow Ribbon* represents John Ford's cavalry trilogy. *They Died with Their Boots On* is such a revisionist version of the Battle of Little Bighorn that it can be enjoyed only as Hollywood escapist entertainment.

The films that deal with America's ambiguous colonial aspirations—another rarely visited subject—form a lively trilogy: *The Real Glory* (Philippines) , *The Sand Pebbles* (China), and *The Wind and the Lion* (a minor incident in Morocco).

Finally, the comedies in this section are two of the finest films covered in the book. Everyone knows Kubrick's *Dr. Strangelove*, and everyone should watch it again at regular intervals. Though the immediate prospect of Mutually Assured Destruction through nuclear weapons may have abated for the moment, the Cold War mentality that Kubrick and writer Terry Southern so deftly parody is still out there and still dangerous. Buster Keaton's *The General* is America's great "lost" comedy—a brilliant Civil War film that young fans of Jackie Chan and Roberto Benigni would love if they'd give a silent movie a chance.

THE ALAMO

1960 John Wayne

John Wayne's first turn in the director's chair is not his finest moment. For a novice filmmaker—even for a 53-year-old novice—it's not a bad debut, but the director-producer-star lacks sensitivity to the more realistic, human moments on which true epics are based. The large-scale battle scenes work well enough, but the characters never rise above the level of historical caricature. Equal blame on that count must be shared by writer-associate producer James Edward Grant, whose script does no one any favors.

The year is 1836 and the film establishes its political point of view before the action begins with a foreword that refers to the "tyrannical rule" of Generalissimo Santa Anna. Some "Texicans," as the film calls them, do not want to be a part of Mexico, and Sam Houston (Richard Boone) is leading the fight. "I've been given command of the Armies of Texas," he says, "but the fly in the buttermilk is there ain't no armies in Texas." The closest thing he's got is two groups of volunteers, one led by Jim Bowie (Richard Widmark) and a smaller contingent under the command of William Travis (Laurence Harvey). The two men don't like each other to begin with, and when Houston promotes Travis over Bowie, the friction becomes even more intense. Houston orders them to make a stand at a mission called the Alamo while he raises a larger force.

Enter Davy Crockett (Wayne) with a "colorful" crew of Tennessee volunteers, including Beekeeper (Chill Wills, who, incredibly, received a Supporting Oscar nomination) and Thimblerig (Denver Pyle). Crockett maintains an uneasy peace between the other two commanders while other plot elements are introduced, only to be dropped or inconclusively ended. Emil Sande (Wesley Lau), for example, first appears to be a quisling villain but just when he could be developed, he disappears. His only real function is to threaten the lovely Flaca (Linda Cristal), so that Crockett can defend her, but then she makes an early exit, too. In the meantime, Bowie delivers a patronizingly pro-Mexican speech and a few minutes later, Crockett comes up with a variation on the "Domino Theory" to convince his men that if they don't stop Santa Anna there, he'll soon be in Memphis.

It takes two full hours of that malarkey before the film arrives at the actual attack and defense of the mission. The battle scenes involving cavalry, cannon, and musket are clearly laid out and properly paced, but they can't generate any real energy for several reasons. First, the characters simply aren't real. All of them carry soapboxes upon which they stand every time they open their mouths. As often as not, they make campaign speeches. As the situation becomes more intense, their noble self-sacrifice is pretty hard to stomach, and when they hold forth about the one true God, the film turns into a cranky religious tract.

Given that level of writing, it's unfair to be too harsh on the cast. Suffice it to say that singer Frankie Avalon, as the juvenile Smitty, isn't out of place, and Laurence Harvey's Anglo-Southern accent is whimsically bizarre. Hidden deep beneath the gallons of political posturing and the ill-concealed racism—when Jim Bowie frees his slave Jethro (Jester Hairston), Jethro elects to stay and die beside his Massa—lies a decent John Wayne western. During the final attack, he actually knocks down a horse, eerily predating Alex Karras doing the same thing 14 years later in *Blazing Saddles*.

In the end, though, *The Alamo* ought to be much better. The battle occupies an important place in American history and it deserves an equally important dramatization.

Col. William Travis (Laurence Harvey) takes a stand at *The Alamo.* The Kobal Collection

Cast: John Wayne (Col. Davy Crockett), Richard Widmark (Col. James Bowie), Laurence Harvey (Col. William Travis), Frankie Avalon (Smitty), Richard Boone (Gen. Sam Houston), Carlos Arruza (Lt. Reyes), Chill Wills (Beekeeper), Veda Ann Borg (Blind Nell Robertson), Linda Cristal (Flaca), Patrick Wayne (Capt. James Butler Bonham), Joan O'Brien (Mrs. Dickinson), Joseph Calleia (Juan Sequin), Ken Curtis (Capt. Almeron Dickinson), Jester Hairston (Jethro), Denver Pyle (Thimblerig, the Gambler), John Dierkes (Jocko Robertson), Guinn "Big Boy" Williams (Lt. Finn), Olive Carey (Mrs. Dennison), William Henry (Dr. Sutherland), Hank Worden (Parson), Ruben Padilla (Gen. Santa Anna), Jack Pennick (Sgt. Lightfoot), Wesley Lau (Emil Sande); **Written by:** James Edward Grant; **Cinematography by:** William Clothier; **Music by:** Dimitri Tiomkin, Paul Francis Webster; **Technical Advisor:** C. Frank Beetson Jr., Jack Pennick. **Producer:** John Wayne, John Edward Grant, United Artists. **Awards:** Academy Awards '60: Best Sound; Golden Globe Awards '61: Best Score; Nominations: Academy Awards '60: Best Color Cinematography, Best Film Editing, Best Picture, Best Song ("The Green Leaves of Summer"), Best Supporting Actor (Wills), Best Original Dramatic Score. **Budget:** 12M. **Boxoffice:** 2M. **Running Time:** 161 minutes. **Format:** VHS, Beta, LV, Letterbox, Closed Caption.

THE ALAMO

5

AMERICA
Love and Sacrifice
1924 D.W. Griffith 🦴🦴🦴

In many ways, D.W. Griffith's attempt to use the American Revolution the same way he had used the Civil War in *Birth of a Nation* is a better film. It lacks the blatant racism, excessive sentimentality, and religiosity; the important scenes are neatly built and suspenseful. But *America* also lacks the scope and the energy of the earlier film, and, most importantly, it lacks the originality.

Again, Griffith shows the war through the eyes of a couple on opposite sides of the conflict. Nathan Holden (Neil Hamilton) is a Massachusetts messenger, like his friend Paul Revere (Henry O'Neill), a rider who carries important correspondence between colonists who favor rebellion. On one trip south to Virginia, he meets Miss Nancy Montague (Carol Dempster), daughter of a wealthy Tory family. Though the Montagues are close personal friends of George Washington (Arthur Dewey), they're loyal to King George III (Arthur Donaldson). Despite their political differences, and the fact that she is far above his station, Nancy falls for Nathan, basically because he's a hunk who writes poetry for her. Nancy, however, has also caught the eye of the treacherous Capt. Walter Butler (Lionel Barrymore), who plans to side with the British in the upcoming revolution, then to betray them and set himself up as emperor of the continent.

> "Stand your ground. If they mean to have a war, let it begin here."
>
> **Jonas Parker (James Milady) at the battle of Concord Bridge**

To do that, he works with the Mohawk chief Joseph Brant (Riley Hatch) and Capt. Hare (Louis Wolheim), who also lusts after the fair Nancy. Butler even persuades Nancy's patrician father (Erville Alderson) to help him. Meanwhile, as the war progresses, Nathan rises through the ranks, giving Griffith and writer Robert W. Chambers license to hit all of the historical high points—Revere's ride, the battles of Lexington and Concord, Bunker Hill, the signing of the Declaration of Independence, Valley Forge, and the surrender of Cornwallis at Yorktown.

Griffith worked with four cinematographers to re-create the battles, and they did reasonably accurate work, making effective use of high wide-angle shots. Most of those large-scale action scenes look more like the work of present day re-enactors than conventional Hollywood heroics. Even if the bad guys are broadly drawn lechers, Butler is based on a real character and the fictional conflicts have a foundation in fact. Changes in acting style, characterization, and tinted scenes (blue for night, red for anger) have dated the film, but the melodramatic structure is sound, and its blend of fiction and history has been copied hundreds, perhaps thousands of times since. On a more cinematic level, Griffith uses Revere's ride and the first battles to generate suspense, and he's even better with the big finish, where, again echoing *Birth of a Nation*, two storylines converge. Also, those unfamiliar with films made before the Hayes office applied its strict guidelines will be surprised by how violent and leeringly sexual it is at times.

A true Anglophile, Griffith had done propaganda films for the English during WW I and he did not want to cast them as villains. In fact, he edited a separate version of the film under the title *Love and Sacrifice* for distribution in England. Griffith also needed permission from the War Department to use troops and cavalry in the battle scenes, and he wanted the good wishes of such patriotic organizations as the Daughters of the American Revolution. Accordingly, this is very much an "official" version of history, with no hint of error or failing in any of the real figures.

See also
Birth of a Nation
Battleship Potemkin
Alexander Nevsky

AMERICAN WARS

American colonists prepare to battle the British in _America_. The Kobal Collection

Cast: Neil Hamilton (Nathan Holden), Carol Dempster (Miss Nancy Montague), Lionel Barrymore (Capt. Walter Butler), Erville Alderson (Justice Montague), Charles Bennett (William Pitt), Arthur Donaldson (King George III), Charles Mack (Justice Charles Montague), Frank McGlynn (Patrick Henry), Henry O'Neill (Paul Revere), Ed Roseman (Capt. Montour), Harry Semels (Hikatoo), Louis Wolheim (Capt. Hare), Hugh Baird (Maj. Pitcairn), Lee Beggs (Samuel Adams), Downing Clarke (Lord Chamberlain), Sydney Deane (Sir Ashley Montague), Arthur Dewey (George Washington), Michael Donavan (Maj. Gen. Warren), Paul Doucet (Marquis de Lafayette), John Dunton (John Hancock), Riley Hatch (Joseph Brant, Chief of the Mohawks), Emil Hoch (Lord North), Edwin Holland (Maj. Strong), W.W. Jones (Gen. Gage), William S. Rising (Edmond Burke), Frank Walsh (Thomas Jefferson), James Milady (Jonas Parker); **Written by:** Robert W. Chambers; **Cinematography by:** Marcel Le Picard, Hendrik Sartov, Billy Bitzer, H. Sintzenich. **Running Time:** 141 minutes. **Format:** VHS, DVD.

Long, involving, and poisonously racist, D.W. Griffith's tale of war and reconstruction is the archetypal "flawed masterpiece." As a landmark of world film, its importance cannot be overstated. It's the first American epic, and it was such a smashing commercial success that it essentially created the film industry as we know it now. That's easy to understand.

Politics and racism not withstanding, the film succeeds as popular entertainment. Griffith created a thumping potboiler of a plot that's been copied many times since, and despite some slow stretches, he ends it with a swiftly paced double conclusion. The protagonists are the Stoneman family of Pennsylvania and the Camerons of Piedmont, South Carolina. Before the war, the sons of both families are friends. Ben Cameron (Henry Walthall) actually falls in love with a photograph of Elsie Stoneman (Lillian Gish) before he meets her. When the war comes, it divides the friends and ironically brings them together in combat and in a hospital. After the war, Austin Stoneman (Ralph Lewis), Elsie's father and a rabid reformer, takes political control of Piedmont and turns things over to the vile mulatto Silas Lynch (George Seigmann). After suffering a host of indignities, insults, and crimes at the hands of the occupying forces, Cameron and the other noble Confederate veterans are forced to form the Ku Klux Klan to protect themselves.

As Cameron puts it in a moment of typically purple oratory, "Brethren, this flag bears the red stain of the life of a Southern woman, a priceless sacrifice on the altar of an outraged civilization."

Seen today, the film's attempts at political manipulation are laughably blatant, but to leave it at that misses the point. Griffith, son of a Confederate officer who made many dubious claims of heroism, passionately believed in the rightness of his ideas and was hurt by the accusations of racism that were raised in the wake of the film's astonishing popularity. The truth is that Griffith was a product of his times and his values were not uncommon. The film wouldn't have been such a commercial success if it had diverged too far from the mainstream of American culture.

Seen specifically as a war film, *Birth of a Nation* transformed the way armed conflict was portrayed on screen. Griffith perfected a cinematic language that audiences were just beginning to understand in 1915 and still respond to. The battle scenes—mostly filmed with a combination of high panoramic shots of battlefields and more mobile close-ups of individual action—still hold up. They're ambitious attempts to convey the scope and feel of the fighting, though historical accounts make it clear that this fiction doesn't come close to capturing the massive horrors of that war. Again, the point is that Griffith was the first. Viewers watching the film for the first time will be astonished when they realize how often Griffith has been copied. Several historical "re-creations" are set apart from the fictional narrative and they've aged well. In fact, the techniques that Griffith developed to stretch time and enhance suspense during Lincoln's assassination are still used today. (Unfortunately, Joseph Henabery, the actor playing Lincoln, wears such heavy makeup that he appears to have a box on his head.)

"John Whedon, who was writing screenplays for Disney at the time I was beginning to write a biography of D.W. Griffith . . . helpfully described for me the hoopla attending the New York premiere of *Birth of a Nation* when he was a boy—mounted men, dressed in Ku Klux Klan regalia, thundering down Broadway drawing crowds toward the Liberty Theater on 42nd St."

Richard Schickel,
Film Comment Sept./Oct. '98

Title card quotes from *Birth of a Nation*:
"For her who had learned the stern lesson of honor we should not grieve that she found sweeter the *opal gates of death*."

Stoneman eulogizing
a suicide (original emphasis)

"Former enemies of North and South are united again in common defense of their Aryan birthright."

Editorial comment near conclusion

**Members of the Ku Klux Klan
attack a group of black soldiers
in** *Birth of a Nation.* The Kobal Collection

AMERICAN WARS

Though some of the acting is a bit fevered, much of it is still effective. Lillian Gish and Henry Walthall are quite good. Griffith's portrayal of his villains is troubling. He uses white actors in blackface to indicate mulattos, and, for the filmmaker, they are the true source of evil. He sees black people with that patronizing, paternalistic condescension so typical of some Southerners, but when races are mixed, he finds true evil and villainy. His attitudes toward war itself are equally contradictory. On one hand, the film claims to be passionately anti-war, to deplore the devastation that armed conflict causes to individuals and the nation. On the other, it celebrates the terrorism of the cowardly Klan. To contemporary audiences, Griffith's attempt to equate the war itself and Klan activities is the most troubling part of the film.

As for the film's historical liberties, Griffith was prescient. He was among the first to demonstrate that in popular filmmaking, you can get away with almost anything if you're entertaining enough, a lesson not lost on Oliver Stone. That entertainment aspect is dated now, but as a milestone of American and world cinema, the film's place in history is undiminished.

DidyouKnow?

In the summer of 1916, the standard price for a movie ticket was 25 cents. For *Birth of a Nation* that was increased to $2.00, an increase of 700%. The film was originally titled *The Clansman*, after the novel and play it is based on. But author Thomas Dixon was said to be so impressed by a preview screening of the film that he told Griffith the title should be changed to *Birth of a Nation*. The story may well be apocryphal, because the longer title had already appeared in the trade press, but Griffith never denied it.

Fact:

V.I. Lenin, who understood that "Of all the arts, the cinema is the most important for us," was a devoted fan of *Birth of a Nation*.

Cast: Lillian Gish (Elsie Stoneman), Mae Marsh (Flora Cameron), Henry B. Walthall (Col. Ben Cameron), Ralph Lewis (Austin Stoneman), Robert "Bobbie" Harron (Ted Stoneman), George Siegmann (Silas Lynch), Joseph Henabery (Abraham Lincoln), Spottiswoode Aitken (Dr. Cameron), George Beranger (Wade Cameron), Mary Alden (Lydia Brown), Josephine Crowell (Mrs. Cameron), Elmer Clifton (Phil Stoneman), Walter Long (Gus), Howard Gaye (Gen. Robert E. Lee), Miriam Cooper (Margaret Cameron), John Ford (Klansman), Sam De Grasse (Sen. Sumner), Maxfield Stanley (Duke Cameron), Donald Crisp (Gen. Ulysses S. Grant), Raoul Walsh (John Wilkes Booth), Erich von Stroheim (Man who falls from roof), Eugene Pallette (Union Soldier), Wallace Reid (Jeff, the blacksmith); **Written by:** D.W. Griffith, Frank E. Woods; **Cinematography by:** Billy Bitzer; **Music by:** D.W. Griffith. **Producer:** D.W. Griffith, Epoch. **Awards:** American Film Institute (AFI) '98: Top 100, National Film Registry '92. **Boxoffice:** 3M. **Running Time:** 175 minutes. **Format:** VHS, LV, DVD.

DR. STRANGELOVE, OR: HOW I LEARNED TO STOP WORRYING AND LOVE THE BOMB

1964 Stanley Kubrick 🎬🎬🎬🎬

"Well, boys, I reckon this is it. Nuclear combat toe-to-toe with the Russkies."

Maj. T. J. "King" Kong (Slim Pickens)

"I got a fair idea of the kind of personal emotions that some of you fellas may be thinking. Heck, I reckon you wouldn't be human beings if you didn't have some pretty strong personal feelings about nuclear combat."

Maj. T. J. "King" Kong (Slim Pickens)

"Mr. President, I'm not saying we wouldn't get our hair mussed, but I do say no more than 10 to 20 million killed. Tops! Depending on the breaks."

Gen. "Buck" Turgidson (George C. Scott)

"Gentlemen! You can't fight in here. This is the War Room!"

President Merkin J. Muffley (Peter Sellers)

Did you Know?

At one point in the filming, Kubrick considered ending the film with a huge pie fight in the War Room. Stills from the scene exist. Some say the reason it was not used can be traced to the assassination of John F. Kennedy.

Seen from the perspective that only time can give, *Dr. Strangelove* now seems almost inevitable. During the coldest days of the Cold War, someone simply had to satirize the paranoia that drove it. But Stanley Kubrick and writers Terry Southern and Peter George did it so brilliantly that their work has improved with repeated viewings over the years. The ultra-deadpan humor and carefully controlled acting have lost nothing, and the three-sided plot could serve as a model for the well-built screenplay.

At Burpelson Strategic Air Command base, Gen. Jack D. Ripper (Sterling Hayden) has gone completely mad. Convinced that all-out war is the only way to defeat an insidious Communist conspiracy—which he explains with chilling mad logic—he has closed the base and ordered his planes to attack the Soviet Union. Gen. "Buck" Turgidson (George C. Scott) is forced to cut short an assignation with his secretary (Tracy Reed) to meet with President Merkin J. Muffley (Peter Sellers) in the Pentagon War Room to deal with Ripper. All the while, with the jaunty strains of "When Johnny Comes Marching Home" in the background, Maj. T.J. "King" Kong (Slim Pickens) pilots his fully loaded B–52 over the arctic wastes in search of his primary target. The wild card is the Soviet's secret "Doomsday Device," a massive bomb enriched with "Balthorium-G," which will eliminate all life on the planet for 93 years.

Virtually the entire story is told from those three stages—the base, the bomber, the War Room—and all of them are remarkably realistic. The details of the plane, from the codebooks to the communication equipment and the systems checks, could have been taken from training manuals, and the interior of the bomber feels authentic. In the same way, the attack on the SAC base is filmed with strict realism. The grainy, soft-focus, hand-held black-and-white camera work, reportedly divided between Kubrick himself and cinematographer Gilbert Taylor, could have come from a World War II documentary.

That severe understatement is carried over into the acting, too. The ensemble plays these grandly bizarre characters with their crazy names without cracking a single smile. The only overt joke—a brief one involving a Coke machine—seems so horribly out of place that it may have been a comedic beauty mark, included intentionally for contrast. Virtually all of the casting was done against type, and it works. Sterling Hayden lets Ripper's mania unfold slowly and never overplays his hand, not even when he reaches into his golf bag and pulls out a .50 caliber machine gun. At that point in his career, George C. Scott wasn't known as a comedic actor, and though he is much more demonstrative as Gen. Turgidson, he doesn't go for any easy laughs either.

Star Peter Sellers was nominated for an Academy Award and his work has certainly held up as well as, if not better than, the winner's (Rex Harrison for *My Fair Lady*). He plays President Muffley as a quietly desperate Adlai Stevenson–school liberal who carefully tucks his handkerchief into his coat sleeve. As Gen. Ripper's executive officer, Group Capt. Mandrake of the RAF, he's the film's real hero—the one character who may be able to stop things. Finally, as the ex-Nazi Presidential advisor Dr. Strangelove ("He changed it

from Merkwürdigliebe," another character mutters), he embodies the rationalization of nuclear madness. His final speech about the necessity of stocking mineshafts with nubile young women for political and military leaders to repopulate the earth is brilliant, and a perfect conclusion for the sexual undercurrent that runs throughout the film.

Perhaps the most remarkable aspect of the satire, though, is the way it combines comedy and suspense. The pace tightens in the third act as the three plotlines converge, and it's difficult not to become involved with the story, no matter how familiar it is. In the end, it's easy to see *Dr. Strangelove* as a more successful companion piece to Kubrick's *Paths of Glory*. Both films question authority; both are profoundly anti-military; neither comes to a conventional ending.

Dr. Strangelove (Peter Sellers) struggles to control his errant hand while addressing the President of the United States.
The Kobal Collection

Cast: Peter Sellers (Group Capt. Lionel Mandrake/President Merkin Muffley/Dr. Strangelove), George C. Scott (Gen. "Buck" Turgidson), Sterling Hayden (Gen. Jack D. Ripper), Keenan Wynn (Col. "Bat" Guano), Slim Pickens (Maj. T.J. "King" Kong), James Earl Jones (Lt. Lothar Zogg), Peter Bull (Ambassador de Sadesky), Tracy Reed (Miss Scott), Shane Rimmer (Capt. G.A. "Ace" Owens), Glenn Beck (Lt. W.D. Kivel), Gordon Tanner (Gen. Faceman), Frank Berry (Lt. H.R. Dietrich), Jack Creley (Mr. Staines); **Written by:** Stanley Kubrick, Terry Southern, Peter George; **Cinematography by:** Gilbert Taylor; **Music by:** Laurie Johnson; **Technical Advisor:** Capt. John Crewdson. **Producer:** Stanley Kubrick, Victor Lyndon, Leon Minoff, Columbia Pictures. **British Awards:** American Film Institute (AFI) '98: Top 100; British Academy Awards '64: Best Film, National Film Registry '89; New York Film Critics Awards '64: Best Director (Kubrick); Nominations: Academy Awards '64: Best Actor (Sellers), Best Adapted Screenplay, Best Director (Kubrick), Best Picture. **Running Time:** 93 minutes. **Format:** VHS, Beta, LV, Letterbox, DVD.

DR. STRANGELOVE

THE GENERAL

1926 Clyde Bruckman, Buster Keaton ♫♫♫♫

Buster Keaton is the forgotten genius of American silent films and this Civil War comedy is his masterpiece. In terms of plot, execution, pace, humor, and philosophy, it is as relevant and enjoyable now as it was when it was made in 1927. Viewed simply as a war film, it is the polar opposite of *Birth of a Nation*. Where Griffith's picture is long, sentimental, and historically dubious, Keaton's is short, skeptical, and relatively accurate. At least, it's based on a real event and its anti-war sentiments are much more deeply felt.

In the pre-war South, Johnnie Gray (Keaton) has "two great loves in his life." One is his railroad engine named "The General"; the other is Annabelle Lee (Marion Mack). The problem is that the girl is a dewy-eyed romantic Southern belle while Johnnie is a down-to-earth sort who's a terrific engineer. When they learn the news about Fort Sumpter, her brothers and father immediately enlist, and she demands the same of Johnnie. He agrees and hightails it to the recruiting office, but is turned down when the Confederates realize how important his current work is. But Johnnie doesn't know that key piece of information. Annabelle Lee concludes he's a coward and Johnnie thinks that somehow, he doesn't measure up. Those misunderstandings generate the rest of the comedy.

> "He was nicknamed Buster by Harry Houdini, who admired the way Keaton, at the age of six months, survived unharmed a fall down a flight of stairs at a boardinghouse for show people."
>
> **Ephraim Katz, *The Film Encyclopedia***

Some years later, with the war at its height, the despicable Yankee spy Capt. Anderson (Glen Cavender) steals The General and tries to sabotage the South's railroad system. He also kidnaps Annabelle Lee, and Johnnie sets off in pursuit. The resulting chase is an extended series of brilliantly choreographed comic set pieces. It's carefully timed, intricate physical humor, which will not be revealed here—that's why you want to watch the film—but it's not giving away too much to say that many of the jokes and gags in the first half are repeated with extra twists in the second half. Underlying both the comedy and the plot is Keaton's deadpan, apolitical approach.

Though Southerners are the nominal heroes, the film's real point of view is antiauthoritarian. The generals, officers, and true believers on both sides are the real buffoons. The engineers—both Union and Confederate—are the heroes, intentional or not. They're the common men who pay attention to the work that needs to be done and go about it, often oblivious to the vast destruction that's taking place around them. In Keaton's world that makes them heroic clowns.

Don't forget that Buster Keaton was the Jackie Chan of his day. The man did all of his own stunts—and many of them were genuinely dangerous. Notice the way the engine's wheels lose traction and spin on the rails after the train has been stolen. It's not an uncommon sight. Now remember that just a few minutes before, Keaton was sitting on the drive shaft between those steel wheels when they started moving. He could have been killed in the scene. (Keaton actually broke his neck while taking a fall in another film, *Sherlock Jr.*) His efforts to achieve realism on the screen extend to the famous conclusion, which is accomplished without special effects. What you see on screen really happened.

For various reasons, Keaton's films have never been as popular or as influential as those of his contemporary, Charlie Chaplin. Somehow, they don't seem as polished. *The General* has a particularly raucous, free-wheeling quality when compared to Chaplin's work. It's tempting to say

that the film has aged well, but that's not really the case. Viewers have caught up to Keaton. We've experienced even more destructive wars than the one he is describing, and so his ideas hit even closer to home. And his clear-eyed, unsentimental approach to comedy ought to find a much larger and more receptive audience today.

Of all the silent and early sound films mentioned in this book, *The General* is the one that ought to be restored and re-released theatrically. It really is that good.

Buster Keaton is southern railroad engineer Johnnie Gray in *The General*. The Kobal Collection

Cast: Buster Keaton (Johnnie Gray), Marion Mack (Annabelle Lee), Glen Cavender (Capt. Anderson), Jim Farley (Gen. Thatcher), Joe Keaton (Union General), Frederick Vroom (Southern General), Charles Smith (Mr. Lee), Frank Barnes (His son), Mike Donlin (Union General); **Written by:** Clyde Bruckman, Al Boasberg, Charles Henry Smith, Buster Keaton; **Cinematography by:** Bert Haines, Devereaux Jennings. **Producer:** Buster Keaton, Joseph Schenck, United Artists. **Awards:** National Film Registry '89. **Running Time:** 78 minutes. **Format:** VHS, Beta, LV, 8mm.

GETTYSBURG

1993 Ronald F. Maxwell ♪♪♪♩

This overachieving mini-series turned theatrical release may be the most historically accurate depiction of a Civil War battle ever put on film. It's also long and deeply flawed, but still worth watching. Based on Michael Shaara's Pulitizer Prize–winning novel *The Killer Angels*, it tells the story of the three-day battle from the point of view of the key officers involved. Though more than 5,000 re-enactors and excellent battlefield locations provide verisimilitude, none of the foot soldiers even have names. Appropriately then, writer-director Ronald F. Maxwell films the battle scenes in medium and long shots that emphasize relationships between conflicting masses of soldiers over individual emotion and action. Also, each important part of the battle is explained in detail more than once before it occurs. That clears up any confusion but also slows an already languid pace.

Further distancing the viewer from an appreciation of the physical realities of the events of July 1863, each of the major characters makes at least one impassioned political or philosophical speech that's longer than Lincoln's Gettysburg Address (and says considerably less). Man's nobility vs. his baser nature; states' rights; Darwin vs. the Bible; the rationale behind secession—each is commented upon while the plot stops dead. Many historical films are guilty of this cinematic sin, but that doesn't make it any more forgivable.

Did you Notice?

Ken Burns, creator of the PBS series *The Civil War,* appears briefly as Gen. Hancock's aide. Media mogul Ted Turner is a Confederate soldier who yells "Let's go, boys!" right before he gets one in the brisket at Pickett's charge.

The film's dedication to authenticity is made clear during the opening credits, where photographs of the real historical figures are paired with the actors playing them in almost identical makeup, even when that calls for some extremely styled beards and mustaches. As the strengths and positions of the armies are set up, it's clear that key aspects of the battle are matters of luck and coincidence, not planning.

Early on, as the Confederates approach, Union General Buford (Sam Elliott) realizes that he is facing a much larger force than anyone on his side had suspected. He commits his men to hold high ground in a little Pennsylvania town where nobody had planned to fight. In that act, he changes everything that follows. Robert E. Lee (Martin Sheen) would have preferred another time and place. For the first time in his successful career, Lee faces a larger force that holds better ground. His most trusted general, Longstreet (Tom Berenger), advises that they fight somewhere else, but Lee is determined to end the war there.

The film divides the battle by key engagements on the three days over which it was fought. First is the attack on Buford's position. It's followed by the defense of Little Roundtop by Col. Joshua Chamberlain (Jeff Daniels)—hands down the most gripping and exciting part of the story—and, on the third day, Pickett's (Stephen Lang) charge.

The most compelling of the characters are Berenger's Longstreet and Daniels's Chamberlain. As presented here, Longstreet is a tragic figure, a man who understands that he is ordering his men into disaster but cannot disobey his beloved commander. Moreover, he is also pictured as a man who cares little about the causes he's fighting for. Beneath his devotion to the cause is the realization that "We Southerners...would rather lose a war than admit a mistake." Chamberlain, on the other hand, is shown as a true idealist, a Christian humanist who believes in the Union and treats his men with respect. He's also the hero of

See also

Charge of the Light Brigade (1968)

Glory

The Civil War

the story, a citizen soldier who fights bravely, and at one pivotal moment changes the course of the battle and of American history. Daniels plays him with a perceptive mixture of humor and courage, and so is able to make even his high-flown rhetoric sound true. Lee, however, eludes the filmmakers. Though Sheen looks the part and even manages a fair accent, the man behind the myth is missing. This Lee has just stepped down from a pedestal. Though he's dignified and courtly, he's also a bungler who willfully ignores the obvious. Historical arguments can be made to defend those interpretations of the man and his decisions. But the figure in the film is never fully human and does not demonstrate the strength of character which, even then, had earned Lee such respect. Perhaps so many myths have been wrapped around Lee that the real man is forever lost.

Within such a long work, even such a key flaw is not fatal. *Gettysburg* does capture the scope of the battle and its importance as the central event of this country's most important war.

Pickett's Charge is depicted in great detail in *Gettysburg*. The Kobal Collection

Cast: Jeff Daniels (Col. Joshua Lawrence Chamberlain), Martin Sheen (Gen. Robert E. Lee), Tom Berenger (Lt. Gen. James Longstreet), Sam Elliott (Brig. Gen. John Buford), Richard Jordan (Brig. Gen. Lewis A. Armistead), Stephen Lang (Maj. Gen. George E. Pickett), Kevin Conway (Sgt. "Buster" Kilrain), C. Thomas Howell (Lt. Thomas D. Chamberlain), Maxwell Caulfield (Col. Strong Vincent), Andrew Prine (Brig. Gen. Richard B. Garnett), James Lancaster (Lt. Col. Arthur Freemantle), Royce D. Applegate (Brig. Gen. James L. Kemper), Brian Mallon (Maj. Gen. Winfield Scott Hancock), Cooper Huckabee (Henry T. Harrison), Bo Brinkman (Maj. Walter H. Taylor), Kieran Mulroney (Maj. G. Moxley Sorrel), Patrick Gorman (Maj. Gen. John Bell Hood), William Morgan Sheppard (Maj. Gen. Isaac R. Trimble), James Patrick Stuart (Col. E. Porter Alexander), Tim Ruddy (Maj. Charles Marshall), Joseph Fuqua (Maj. Gen. J.E.B. Stuart), Ivan Kane (Capt. Thomas J. Goree), Warren Burton (Maj. Gen. Henry Heth), MacIntyre Dixon (Maj. Gen. Jubal A. Early), George Lazenby (Brig. Gen. J. Johnson Pettigrew), Alex Harvey (Maj. Hawkins), John Diehl (Pvt. Bucklin), John Rothman (Maj. General John F. Reynolds), Richard Anderson (Maj. Gen. George G. Meade), Bill Campbell (Lt. Pitzer), David Carpenter (Col. Thomas C. Devin), Donal Logue (Capt. Ellis Spear), Dwier Brown (Capt. Brewer), Mark Moses (Sgt. Owen); **Cameo(s):** Ken Burns, Ted Turner; **Written by:** Ronald F. Maxwell; **Cinematography by:** Kees Van Oostrum; **Music by:** Randy Edelman; **Technical Advisor:** Brian Pohanka. **Producer:** Robert Katz, Moctesuma Esparza Productions, Turner Pictures; released by New Line Cinema. **Budget:** 25M. **Boxoffice:** 10.7M. **MPAA Rating:** PG. **Running Time:** 254 minutes. **Format:** VHS, Letterbox, Closed Caption.

GLORY

1989 Edward Zwick ♪♪♪♪

Writers Kevin Jarre and Marshall Herskovitz and director Edward Zwick cleverly disguise a basic formula of the American war movie, apply it to real events and produce the finest depiction of the Civil War ever to appear on the big screen. They leave themselves open to charges of historic revisionism, and their work is unbalanced, with many of the strongest moments held back until the second half, but *Glory* is still a masterpiece.

Their chosen formula is the World War II "unit" picture, where young men from diverse backgrounds are brought together in one regiment (or platoon or squad). After considerable conflict among themselves, and with the rough guidance of a gruff sergeant and the wise counsel of their commanding officers, they submerge their individual identities to form a coherent fighting group and are tested under fire. With many variations, the same story has been told from *Sergeant York* to *Saving Private Ryan*.

In this case, it's based on the truth, and most of the men are black. The 54th Massachusetts Voluntary Infantry is to be a regiment of escaped slaves and free black men commanded by white officers. Col. Robert Gould Shaw (Matthew Broderick) is the son of abolitionists, and even though he'd been wounded at Antietam, he is still something of an idealist when the 54th is created and he takes command. At first, when the focus is on Gould and the problems he faces with his friend and fellow officer Lt. Forbes (Cary Elwes), the action tends to move slowly. The stories of his recruits are more interesting.

Rawlins (Morgan Freeman) is a grave digger who becomes an NCO. Searles (Andre Braugher), another childhood friend of Shaw, is the intellectual. Sharts (Jihmi Kennedy) is a sweet-natured, baby-faced kid who's a dead shot. Trip (Denzel Washington in an Oscar-winning performance) is a bitter escaped slave.

Zwick and Oscar-nominated art directors Keith Pain and Dan Webster aim for strict authenticity in costumes, equipment, and sets, and even in the pervasive racism that the 54th faced from other parts of the Union Army. Col. Montgomery (Cliff DeYoung), an equal opportunity bigot who hates Southerners and Jews with equal ferocity, sums it up when he says of Shaw's troops, "They're little children, for God's sake. They're little monkey children, and you've just got to know how to control them."

The first two-thirds or so are about the creation of the 54th as an effective force and the transformation of the group—the gradual, halting, imperfect understanding that comes to white officers and black enlisted men. For all of Shaw's protestations of abolitionist enlightenment, he has a lot to learn, and so do his men. All of them are facing a new world with changing rules. For a war film, that learning process is unusual because it is not accomplished through big action scenes. The opposition to the 54th comes from within the Union bureaucracy, not from the Confederates. When those battle scenes do occur, *Glory* is transformed. The concluding attack on Fort Wagner is emotionally powerful and wrenching. The incredible bravery of the men who fought and the incredible waste and horror of the war itself have seldom, if ever, been brought to the screen with such emotional power.

> "Any Negro taken in arms against the Confederacy will immediately be returned to a state of slavery. Any Negro taken in a federal uniform will be summarily put to death. Any white officer taken in command of Negro troops shall be deemed as inciting servile insurrection and shall likewise be put to death."
>
> **Col. Robert Gould Shaw (Matthew Broderick), reading a Confederate proclamation to his troops.**

> "The portrayal of this attack on Fort Wagner in *Glory* is the most realistic combat footage in any Civil War movie."
>
> **James M. McPherson, *Past Imperfect: History According to the Movies* (Henry Holt. 1995)**

See also
The Civil War
All Quiet on the Western Front

The entire film is one of those rare Hollywood productions where every element is given the full Hollywood treatment, and they all work toward a single goal. James Horner's powerful score adds the same inspirational dimension that he gave to *Titanic*.

Though the casting of Broderick may seem odd, he does perhaps his best screen work, and his resemblance to the real Shaw is remarkable. Along with Washington, veteran cinematographer Freddie Francis and soundmen Lon Bender, Donald O. Mitchell, and Elliot Tyson also won Academy Awards.

One of the greats.

The 54th Regiment of Massachusetts Volunteer Infantry storms a Confederate fort in *Glory*. The Kobal Collection

Cast: Matthew Broderick (Col. Robert Gould Shaw), Morgan Freeman (John Rawlins), Denzel Washington (Trip), Cary Elwes (Lt. Cabot Forbes), Jihmi Kennedy (Sharts), Andre Braugher (Thomas Searles), John Finn (Sgt. Mulcahy), Donovan Leitch (Morse), John Cullum (Russell), Bob Gunton (Gen. Harter), Jane Alexander (Mrs. Shaw), Raymond St. Jacques (Frederick Douglass), Cliff DeYoung (Col. Montgomery), Alan North (Gov. Andrew), Jay O. Sanders (Gen. Strong), Richard Riehle (Quartermaster), Ethan Phillips (Hospital steward), RonReaco Lee (Mute drummer boy), Peter Michael Goetz (Francis Shaw); **Written by:** Kevin Jarre, Marshall Herskovitz; **Cinematography by:** Freddie Francis; **Music by:** James Horner. **Producer:** Pieter Jan Brugge, Freddie Fields, Tri-Star Pictures. **Awards:** Academy Awards '89: Best Cinematography, Best Sound, Best Supporting Actor (Washington); Golden Globe Awards '90: Best Supporting Actor (Washington); Nominations: Academy Awards '89: Best Art Direction/Set Decoration, Best Film Editing. **Boxoffice:** 26.8M. **MPAA Rating:** R. **Running Time:** 122 minutes. **Format:** VHS, Beta, LV, 8mm, Letterbox, Closed Caption.

GLORY

GONE WITH THE WIND

1939 Victor Fleming, George Cukor

Hollywood's most lavish and popular epic is really overrated. As escapism based on the Civil War, its romanticism is thick, sticky and unashamed. The on-screen crawl states as much before the film begins:

There was a land of Cavaliers and Cotton Fields called the Old South. Here in this pretty world Gallantry took its last bow. Here was the last ever to be seen of Knights and their Ladies Fair, of Master and Slave. Look for it only in books for it is no more than a dream remembered . . . A Civilization gone with the wind.

That purple prose is a fitting introduction of a big fluffy mass of celluloid cotton candy. Deliberately or not, it's also an admission of the film's biases. It sees antebellum Georgia, the war itself, and reconstruction through the eyes of a wealthy white Southerner and never goes beyond that. As such, it may be fairly accurate in its portrait of the Southern aristocracy as a starry-eyed lot who simply could not believe that large numbers of men and weapons would be a match for their "fighting spirit" because God was on their side. The filmmakers never mention the more pertinent issue of the states' right to secede from the union, and understandably so. That's a difficult question with several answers. Who wants to deal with it? Fiddle-dee-dee. We'll think about that tomorrow.

And as for slavery, in this cinematic South, the "darkies" really don't mind it much. They're basically happy. In fact, they enthusiastically join in to help dig trenches for the Confederate troops, and after the war, they don't want to leave the plantation. Those who do leave, like Big Sam (Everett Brown), return as soon as they're shown the error of their ways. The film's racist attitudes are essentially identical to those of *Birth of a Nation*, though without the more bitter aspects. Without ever mentioning the Klan by name or showing its terrorist violence, one key scene tacitly endorses those tactics.

When director Victor Fleming (and uncredited George Cukor) turn their attention to the war and its immediate effects, they create the most involving and memorable scenes in the film. Those are the ones set in the hospital, the long newspaper list of the names of the men killed in action at Gettysburg, the burning of Atlanta, and the famous shot of Scarlett crossing the train tracks where the camera pulls back to reveal the thousands of dying and wounded.

Though the portrait that is painted of the destruction and devastation left in the wake of Sherman's march through Georgia isn't quite as rosy as the rest of the film, it's not exactly hard-bitten, either. Given the film's romantic underpinnings, that part of it probably shouldn't be too explicit. Scarlett's (Vivien Leigh) lone encounter with a Yankee deserter (Paul Hurst) is over almost before it begins. (If only he hadn't holstered his pistol . . .)

Even though it is Hollywood's most famous look at the Civil War, *Gone with the Wind* finally fails as a Civil War film because it misses the central fact of the pivotal event in American history, and that is the bitter divisions that the war left between individuals and between

> "Melanie Hamilton is a pale-faced mealy-mouthed ninny and I hate her."
>
> **Scarlett O'Hara (Vivien Leigh)**

> "Kathleen, who's that? That man looking at us and smiling? That nasty dog!"
>
> **Scarlett O'Hara (Vivien Leigh) on seeing Rhett Butler (Clark Gable) for the first time**

> "I don't know nothin' about birthin' babies."
>
> **Prissy (Butterfly McQueen)**

> "You still think you're the belle of the county, don't you? That you're the cutest little trick in shoe leather."
>
> **Rhett Butler (Clark Gable) to Scarlett O'Hara Kennedy (Vivien Leigh)**

See also

Glory

The Good, the Bad and the Ugly

Jezebel

The Civil War

states. For all of its flaws, *Birth of a Nation* comes much closer to that inescapable truth. This film and its many fans are more interested in the characters, as relentlessly one-dimensional as they are, than in the war and what it did to America. And even a critic who dislikes the film as much as I do has to admit that as a big, gaudy, superficial soap opera, it's a fine one to wallow in.

Rhett (Clark Gable) and Scarlett (Vivien Leigh) are surrounded by retreating Confederate soldiers in *Gone with the Wind*.
The Kobal Collection

Cast: Clark Gable (Rhett Butler), Vivien Leigh (Scarlett O'Hara), Olivia de Havilland (Melanie Hamilton), Leslie Howard (Ashley Wilkes), Thomas Mitchell (Gerald O'Hara), Hattie McDaniel (Mammy), Butterfly McQueen (Prissy), Evelyn Keyes (Suellen O'Hara), Harry Davenport (Dr. Meade), Jane Darwell (Dolly Merriwether), Ona Munson (Belle Watling), Barbara O'Neil (Ellen), William "Billy" Bakewell (Mounted officer), Rand Brooks (Charles Hamilton), Ward Bond (Tom), Laura Hope Crews (Aunt Pittypat Hamilton), Yakima Canutt (Renegade), George Reeves (Stuart Tarleton), Marjorie Reynolds (Guest at Twelve Oaks), Ann Rutherford (Careen O'Hara), Victor Jory (Jonas Wilkerson), Carroll Nye (Frank Kennedy), Paul Hurst (Yankee deserter), Isabel Jewell (Emmy Slattery), Cliff Edwards (Reminiscent soldier), Eddie Anderson (Uncle Peter), Oscar Polk (Pork), Eric Linden (Amputation case), Violet Kemble-Cooper (Bonnie's nurse), Fred Crane (Brent Tarleton), Howard Hickman (John Wilkes), Leona Roberts (Mrs. Meade), Cammie King (Bonnie Blue Butler), Mary Anderson (Maybelle Merriwether), Frank Faylen (Doctor's aide), Everett Brown (Big Sam); **Written by:** Sidney Howard; **Cinematography by:** Ray Rennahan; **Music by:** Max Steiner; **Technical Advisor:** Susan Myrink. **Producer:** David O. Selznick, MGM. **Awards:** Academy Awards '39: Best Actress (Leigh), Best Color Cinematography, Best Director (Fleming), Best Film Editing, Best Interior Decoration, Best Picture, Best Screenplay, Best Supporting Actress (McDaniel); American Film Institute (AFI) '98: Top 100, National Film Registry '89; New York Film Critics Awards '39: Best Actress (Leigh); Nominations: Academy Awards '39: Best Actor (Gable), Best Sound, Best Special Effects, Best Supporting Actress (de Havilland), Best Original Score. **Budget:** 3.9M. **Running Time:** 231 minutes. **Format:** VHS, Beta, LV, Closed Caption, DVD.

The Hound Salutes: Clark Gable

When World War II began, Clark Gable was the reigning "King of Hollywood." He was the most popular mature male star in the movie business. During the years when his career was at its peak, he shared the top spots on the popularity list with Shirley Temple, Sonja Henie, Mickey Rooney, and Abbott and Costello. The gossip columnists had given Gable the crown, and the ticket-buying public had made *Gone with the Wind* a record-breaker at the box-office. His personal life was equally rosy, with a new marriage (after two that had gone bad) to Carole Lombard.

Then in January 1942, she was killed in a plane crash while taking part in a War Bond drive. According to his friend David Niven, Gable's grief was crushing. He made the funeral arrangements, and retreated to a mountain fishing camp for three weeks of alcohol and mourning. He came back to finish the picture he had been working on and enlisted in the Air Force the day he was finished with it. Eventually, he became an officer. Stationed in England, he flew several bombing runs over Germany, and narrated a War Department documentary, *Combat America*, about the 351st Bomb Group. He ended the war as a Major with a Distinguished Flying Cross and an Air Medal. His professional career never returned to its previous heights.

Gable was able to bring an undeniable air of authenticity to his role as an Air Force General forced to make hard choices in *Command Decision*, but it wasn't enough to energize an essentially static plot. In *Run Silent Run Deep* (1958), he fares much better as a submarine captain who breaks the rules and must face down another officer (Burt Lancaster). It's something of a reversal, on a much smaller scale, of the roles Gable and Charles Laughton played in 1935 in *Mutiny on the Bounty*. In *Betrayed* (1954), he's a spy against the Nazis. In the soapy *Homecoming* (1948), he's a doctor in the Medical Corps. *Band of Angels* (1957) is a Civil War story.

If David Niven is to be believed—and his affection for his friend is undeniable—Gable never completely recovered emotionally from Carole Lombard's death, and so The King can be seen as an early casualty of the war.

THE GOOD, THE BAD AND THE UGLY
Il Buono, Il Brutto, Il Cattivo
1967 Sergio Leone ♫♫♫♪

Unlike the other two films in his "Man with No Name" trilogy, Sergio Leone's Civil War tale is a full-blown epic. Using some of the same cast members, narrative ideas, and musical and visual themes, he mythologizes both the war and the West. Like all of Leone's work, the film should not be seen as realism. It's not based on any "real" America, but instead on images of America. As such, the film is an Italian interpretation of an American war with absolutely no regard for historical fact. When Leone—the quintessential 1960s filmmaker—looks at war, he sees only waste and destruction. Politics, religion, and morality count for next to nothing.

To anyone unfamiliar with Leone's imaginative use of conventional narrative techniques, the opening scenes are virtually incomprehensible. More than 10 minutes pass before the first word is spoken. But while he may be confusing viewers, Leone is also setting out all the information they need to understand his three-sided conflict among Angel Eyes (Lee Van Cleef), the "Bad" of the title; Tuco (Eli Wallach), the "Ugly"; and Blondie (Clint Eastwood), the "Good." Angel Eyes is hired by a bedridden, wizened Confederate to find a man who tells him that a fortune in rebel gold has been hidden, and that another man who goes under the name Bill Carson knows where it is. Meanwhile, Blondie runs a scam where he turns in Tuco to collect the bounty on his head and then rescues him as he's about to be hanged. Coincidence leads Blondie and Tuco to learn where the gold is, but Union and Confederate forces are in the way.

At first glance, the plot appears to be almost episodic, wandering off pointlessly for long digressions. But the truth is that Leone and his four co-writers never lose sight of their main themes. Every scene adds something, pushing the plot forward, while Leone uses the rest of his vast canvas to create a richly textured mythic amalgamation of the Old West and the war. The big set pieces are ambitiously staged and beautifully photographed by Tonino Delli Colli. From the shelling of the town, to the gun shop, crossing the desert (an allegorical descent into hell), the prison camp, the battle on the bridge, and, most memorably, Tuco's delirious run through the cemetery, they're instantly recognizable moments.

Seen strictly as a war story, the film gains another level of bitterness. For example, every military character who has even a word of dialogue is wounded or injured: the bedridden old man who hires Angel Eyes, a legless "half-soldier," the camp commandant with a gangrenous leg, the massive corporal with a milky eye, the drunken captain at the bridge, and finally the dying Confederate boy who provides Blondie with his signature poncho. The only exception might be Angel Eyes, who assumes the role of sergeant for a time, but in the final shootout, it's revealed that he's missing the tip of one finger.

Though the film is undeniably part of the Eastwood "No Name" trilogy, stylistically and thematically, it fits easily with Leone's next film, *Once Upon a Time in the West*, another extravagant history. In these two films, Leone seems to be most comfortable with the touches for which he has become so famous—the extreme closeups, the extended conclusions (the final gunfight here is more than five full minutes of twitchy fingers and cutting eyes), the leisurely pace, and, perhaps most important, the fine acting he elicits from his cast. Though he gets third billing, Eli Wallach has as much screen time as his co-stars and his none-too-subtle clowning steals the film.

> "You see, in this world, there's two kinds of people, my friend—those with loaded guns and those who dig . . . You dig."
>
> **Blondie (Clint Eastwood) to Tuco (Eli Wallach)**

See also
The General
Where Eagles Dare

Tuco (Eli Wallach) does the dirty work while Blondie (Clint Eastwood, right) and Angel Eyes (Lee Van Cleef) look on. The Kobal Collection.

In the end, historical flaws notwithstanding, *The Good, the Bad and the Ugly* remains a valuable addition to the comparatively small body of Civil War films. If nothing else, it shows Americans how the war can be translated by a European imagination.

Cast: Clint Eastwood (Blondie, the "Good"), Eli Wallach (Tuco Benedito Pacifico Juan Maria Ramirez, the "Ugly"), Lee Van Cleef (Angel Eyes Sentenza, the "Bad"), Chelo Alonso, Luigi Pistilli (Padre Ramirez), Rada Rassimov (Maria, the prostitute), Livio Lorenzon (Baker), Mario Brega (Wallace); **Written by:** Sergio Leone, Sergio Donati, Furio Scarpelli, Luciano Vincenzoni, Agenore Incrocci; **Cinematography by:** Tonino Delli Colli; **Music by:** Ennio Morricone. **Producer:** Alberto Grimaldi, United Artists. **Italian.** **Boxoffice:** 6.1M. **Running Time:** 161 minutes. **Format:** VHS, Beta, LV, Letterbox.

This is the only feature-length film John Ford made about the Civil War, and it's far from his best work. Even so, it has some worthwhile moments and is based, however loosely, on two historical incidents, Grierson's Raid and the Battle of New Market.

As the story begins, Gen. Grant (Stan Jones) is unable to take Vicksburg because the Confederates have it so well defended. Col. John Marlowe (John Wayne) comes up with a plan to take a small brigade of cavalry from Tennessee, ride 300 miles into Confederate territory and destroy the railroad at Newton Station, Mississippi, thereby cutting the supply line to Vicksburg. To do it, he will have to avoid all contact with Rebel forces until he has reached his target.

The first problem Marlowe encounters is Maj. Hank Kendall (William Holden), a doctor who will be accompanying the force. For reasons that are explained late and unpersuasively, Marlowe hates doctors. His plans for taking care of the wounded are simple: "Those too badly shot up to carry on will be left to the clemency of the enemy, civilian or military." The next problem is Marlowe's second in command, Col. Secord (Willis Bouchey), who makes no secret of his plans to use his military career to further his craven political ambitions. The third problem is Southern belle Hannah Hunter (Constance Towers). The Yankee soldiers stay at her plantation soon after they cross into the Confederacy. When she learns of Marlowe's plans, she must be taken along as a prisoner.

That's a tenuous premise for any film, particularly one made by Ford. Throughout his career, he was attracted to historical and military subjects, and he was cavalier about rewriting history to suit his dramatic purposes. Given a choice between shooting the truth and shooting the legend, he admitted that he always went for the legend. But this material is hardly legendary.

The conflict between the hard-headed Marlowe and the humanist Kendall seems particularly forced. Even when the cause of his dislike for physicians is revealed, Marlowe comes across as a dim-witted bully. Kendall is a much more sympathetic and moving character, and Holden is much more at ease with the role. In most of his confrontations with Marlowe, Kendall is placed in a secondary position—smaller, farther from the camera, to one side of the screen—but he still comes across as the wiser and more important of the two.

The relationship between Marlowe and Hannah Hunter Is equally unsatIsfactory. They are meant to be another variation on the battling lovers Ford created in *The Quiet Man*, *Donovan's Reef*, and so many others, but the chemistry just isn't there. That cannot be blamed solely on the actors, though. They're saddled with one ludicrous moment after another. At their first dinner, for example, she passes him a platter of chicken. As she leans over, threatening to spill out of her plunging decolletage, she coos, "Oh come now, Colonel, a man with a great big frame like yours can't just nibble away like a little titmouse. Now what was your preference, the leg or the breast?" Yes, the scene is funny, but not the way Ford means it to be.

Ford handles the political issues even-handedly, though his treatment of black characters is patronizing, and casting track star Althea Gibson as Hannah's maid is blatant tokenism. The bat-

> "Well, you think there's no Confederate army where you're going? Do you think our boys are asleep down there? Well, they'll catch up with you and they'll cut you to pieces, you nameless, fatherless scum!"
>
> **Hannah Hunter (Constance Towers), upon being captured after trying to escape.**

Fact:
John Ford's only other dramatization of the Civil War was his part of *How the West Was Won*. The other parts were directed by Henry Hathaway and George Marshall. It was one of the first of the few films that were made in Cinerama.

John Wayne leads *The Horse Soldiers* deep into Confederate territory. The Kobal Collection

tle scenes, the destruction of the railroad, and the relatively realistic medical scenes are the best moments. As for the truth behind the fiction, Ford would have been well advised to stick closer to the facts. Marlowe is based on Col. Ben Grierson. He was a music teacher and bandmaster from Jacksonville, Illinois, who had "an acquired mistrust of horses dating back to a kick received from a pony in childhood, which smashed one of his cheekbones, split his forehead and left him scarred for life." (*The Civil War*, Shelby Foote.)

His raid roughly followed the route Ford lays out in the film, covering more than 600 miles in 16 days. It was more successful than anyone could have imagined. He suffered only a handful of casualties while capturing and burning two locomotives and 36 freight cars, some containing artillery ammunition. At Newton Station, his men ripped up miles of track and cross ties, burned trestles and bridges, tore down telegraph wires, and burned a small building filled with small arms and new uniforms—all in about two hours. During their retreat, the Union forces burned two more trains, which ignited nearby buildings. In both cases, the soldiers helped the Southern townspeople put out the fires.

Late in the film, young cadets from a military school attack the raiders who turn and run, but not before they spank some of the adolescents. Apparently, that is based on the participation of Virginia Military Institute cadets at the battle of New Market, where they fought bravely and won, suffering considerable casualties against a much larger Union force.

Cast: John Wayne (Col. John Marlowe), William Holden (Maj. Hank Kendall), Hoot Gibson (Brown), Constance Towers (Hannah Hunter), Russell Simpson (Sheriff Henry Goodbody), Strother Martin (Virgil), Anna Lee (Mrs. Buford), Judson Pratt (Sgt. Maj. Kirby), Denver Pyle (Jagger Jo), Jack Pennick (Sgt. Maj. Mitchell), Althea Gibson (Lukey), William Forrest (Gen. Hurlbut), Willis Bouchey (Col. Phil Secord), Bing Russell (Dunker), Ken Curtis (Wilkie), O.Z. Whitehead (Otis "Happy" Hopkins), Walter Reed (Union officer), Hank Worden (Deacon Clump), Carleton Young (Col. Jonathan Miles), Cliff Lyons (Sergeant), Stan Jones (Gen. Grant); **Written by:** John Lee Mahin, Martin Rackin; **Cinematography by:** William Clothier; **Music by:** David Buttolph. **Producer:** Martin Rackin, John Lee Mahin, United Artists. **Running Time:** 114 minutes. **Format:** VHS, Beta, Closed Caption.

LAST OF THE MOHICANS

1992 Michael Mann 𝄞𝄞𝄞

"Their kids would have such great hair!"

That's what a publicist spontaneously said of stars Daniel Day-Lewis and Madeleine Stowe after a preview screening of this historical romance. The remark explains to a large degree the film's huge boxoffice success, and it remains as much a love story as a war story. So is *Casablanca*. But the movie is also an exciting, if historically fanciful, depiction of early Colonial wars.

It's 1757, the third year of the French and Indian War, somewhere on the frontier west of the Hudson River (actually the North Carolina mountains at their most scenic). There, Hawkeye (Day-Lewis), aka Nathaniel Poe, Chingachgook (Russell Means), and Uncas (Eric Schweig) roam the forest and make a living as trappers. (This being an exceptionally polite and "correct" retelling of history, we never actually see them trapping small furry creatures. In fact, they even apologize to a deer they shoot.) They have nothing to do with the war until they come upon the vengeful Magua (Wes Studi) and his Huron war party as they attempt to kill Cora (Stowe) and Alice (Jodhi May), daughters of the English Col. Munro (Maurice Roeves). Eventually, our heroes find themselves in Fort William Henry under siege by the French forces of Gen. Montcalm (Patrice Chereau) and his Huron allies. Then they've got to take sides in the war, but it's not a clear-cut choice.

"The French haven't the nature for war. Their Latinate voluptuousness combines with their Gallic laziness and the result is they'd rather eat and make love with their faces than fight."

Gen. Webb (Mac Andrews)

The Brits, stereotyped as mindless authoritarian bullies, demand that the settlers, stereotyped as rugged individualists, obey their orders and serve in the militia. Hawkeye foments sedition while swapping smoldering glances with Cora.

The siege is a grand affair of roaring nighttime cannon and mortar attacks. It and other aspects of the plot are loosely based on fact, but director Michael Mann plays fast and loose with history and his source material. He and writer Christopher Crowe streamline James Fenimore Cooper's novel, paring it down to a few big scenes and letting the glamorous cast do the rest.

Viewed simply as highly polished escapist adventure, the film is virtually perfect. Unlike the stiff characters in so many historical dramas, these people look comfortable, like they're wearing clothes, not costumes. This Hawkeye is a Samurai warrior in buckskins, and Cora's heaving bodice is ready to rip. Magua is a strong, vibrant villain with the curious flaw that screenwriters so often ascribe to Indians. Even though Magua is fluent in English, French, and Huron, he sometimes lapses into pidgin, and he hasn't grasped the concept of the first person singular pronoun. The words "I," "mine," and "my" are not in his vocabulary. Magua always speaks of himself in the third person.

Because the film is so relentlessly stylish—Mann is still best known for the TV series *Miami Vice*—it's pointless to criticize either the historical or emotional accuracy. The real inspiration here is the exotic romanticism of such '30s adventures as *Charge of the Light Brigade*, *Gunga Din*, and *Lives of a Bengal Lancer*, where stalwart heroes never waver in the face of savage foes.

See also

Birth of a Nation
America

Daniel Day-Lewis is Hawkeye
in Michael Mann's romance-
intensive retelling of *Last of the
Mohicans.* The Kobal Collection

Cast: Daniel Day-Lewis (Hawkeye), Madeleine Stowe (Cora Munro), Wes Studi (Magua), Russell Means
(Chingachgook), Eric Schweig (Uncas), Jodhi May (Alice), Steven Waddington (Maj. Duncan Heyward), Maurice Roeves (Col. Edmund Munro), Colm Meaney
(Maj. Ambrose), Patrice Chereau (Gen. Montcalm), Pete Postlethwaite (Capt. Beams), Terry Kinney (John Cameron), Tracey Ellis (Alexandra Cameron), Dennis
Banks (Ongewasgone), Dylan Baker (Bougainville), Mac Andrews (Gen. Webb); **Written by:** Christopher Crowe, Michael Mann; **Cinematography by:** Dante Spinotti; **Music by:** Trevor Jones, Randy Edelman; **Technical Advisor:** Dale Dye. **Producer:** Michael Mann Company, Inc., Hunt Lowry, James G. Robinson, 20th Century-Fox. **Awards:** Academy Awards '92: Best Sound. **Boxoffice:** 72.45M. **MPAA Rating:** R. **Running Time:** 114 minutes. **Format:** VHS, LV, Letterbox.

THE REAL GLORY

1939 Henry Hathaway

Director Henry Hathaway and star Gary Cooper don't really remake their hit *Lives of a Bengal Lancer* with this overlooked sleeper. It's more accurate to note that Hathaway cheerfully pillages his favorite plot elements, gives them a few twists, and relocates them in the Philippines. Cooper plays another soldier who's less flamboyant, more intelligent, and just as engaging as he was before. Together, they come up with another enjoyable entertainment, one that has acquired some unintentional historical resonance.

Army doctor Bill Canavan (Cooper) is newly arrived at Fort Mysang in 1906 just as the brass has decided that it's time for the locals to defend themselves from the murderous Moro rebels. Yes, the good doctor is about to join a small group of American advisors in an Asian civil war. The crafty rebel leader Alipang (Tetsu Komai) plans to lure the foreign devils out into the jungle where he will pick them off. But the Americans stay inside their compound and train the Philippine Constabulary (to whom the film is dedicated).

That group, led by Capt. Hartley (Reginald Owen), consists of Lt. McCool (David Niven), an alleged "one man army," and Lt. Larson (Broderick Crawford), who's more interested in orchids than ordnance. Though Canavan lobbies for a psychological approach that will teach the people not to fear the Moro, Hartley is a by-the-book type who believes that drilling and marching and marching and drilling are the answer. As Alipang intensifies his efforts, Hartley's lovely daughter Linda (Andrea Leeds) arrives, setting off a flurry of competitive courtship among his officers.

That's a fairly standard premise, but it becomes considerably less predictable and more lively as it develops. The action takes several odd turns, some verging on the silly. (You won't believe what they do with the palm tree catapults.) Well-written characters and an attractive, talented cast keep the excesses in check. Hathaway directs with his customary unobtrusive, economical style. The main difference between *The Real Glory* and *Lives of a Bengal Lancer* is grittiness. This is a dirtier, sweatier adventure that's interested more in peasants than in officers. Though it's tempting to draw parallels between this story and the Hollywood films that came out of the Vietnam era, that's unproductive. Despite the fact that World War II was beginning in Europe when the film was made, it has no propaganda objectives, either overt or hidden. It's an entertainment without historical or political baggage.

Perhaps the reason the film remains relatively unknown is due to the timing of its release. It came out in 1939, Hollywood's famous golden year that also saw the releases of *Gone with the Wind*, *Mr. Smith Goes to Washington*, *Stagecoach*, *The Wizard of Oz*, and *Dark Victory*. No wonder *The Real Glory* was elbowed into the background. Any fan of the period should take a look.

See also
Beau Geste
Gunga Din
Lives of a Bengal Lancer
The Wind and the Lion
The Sand Pebbles

Army Doctor Canavan (Gary Cooper, second from right) returns to his Philippine army post with a captured Moro killer, as members of the unit, including David Niven and Broderick Crawford (left) look on in *The Real Glory*. The Kobal Collection

Cast: Gary Cooper (Dr. Bill Canavan), David Niven (Lt. McCool), Andrea Leeds (Linda Hartley), Reginald Owen (Capt. Hartley), Broderick Crawford (Lt. Larson), Kay Johnson (Mabel Manning), Russell Hicks (Capt. Manning), Vladimir Sokoloff (Datu), Rudy Robles (Lt. Yabo), Tetsu Komai (Alipang), Roy Gordon (Col. Hatch), Henry Kolker (The General), Soledad Jiminez (Old native woman); **Written by:** Robert Presnell, Jo Swerling; **Cinematography by:** Rudolph Mate; **Music by:** Alfred Newman; **Technical Advisor:** Col. William H. Shutan. **Running Time:** 95 minutes. **Format:** VHS.

THE RED BADGE OF COURAGE

1951 John Huston 🎖🎖🎖

John Huston's adaptation of Stephen Crane's novel is one of Hollywood's most famous cases of studio interference in a film that might have been great, or at least very good. As it is, the story of fear and bravery has some striking moments that remain mired in a story that lacks focus and clarity. It's difficult to say exactly where blame should be placed. (See sidebar.)

Henry Fleming (Congressional Medal of Honor–winner Audie Murphy) is a young, untested Union soldier who chaffs at the constant drilling his army undergoes. Like the other men in his unit, he complains and argues and claims to be hungry for a real battle. At the same time, the idea of war terrifies him, and Henry is afraid that he will disgrace himself when the shooting starts. His doubts and uncertainties are handled with believable complexity. War hero Murphy is able to make those universal emotions seem absolutely real. It's not so much a question of cowardice as of imagination and involvement in a war that is anything but absolute.

In a telling early moment before the fighting starts, Henry wanders away from his camp one night and comes close to the Confederate lines. A nearby unseen rebel picket then advises him to move out of the moonlight unless he wants to wear the "little red badge." How does someone muster up anger and hatred at such an enemy?

Other touches of dialogue and the details of a soldier's life have a similar ring of authenticity. The entire cast is filled with veteran character actors whose faces are more familiar than their names—John Dierkes, Royal Dano, Whit Bissell, Arthur Hunnicutt. Cartoonist Bill Mauldin, another semi-professional actor, acquits himself well as Henry's friend Tom, who is just as afraid as he is. The battle scenes are realistically staged and paced. Legendary photographer Harold Rosson (*The Wizard of Oz*, *The Asphalt Jungle*) certainly deserves an equal amount of the credit there. The confrontations begin with easily identifiable forces moving slowly against each other. Then as the action intensifies, it becomes increasingly chaotic until Henry's panic is a natural reaction.

The point of the story, however, is Henry's transformation from frightened tyro to flag-waving hero. Within the context, both extremes are credible, but the middle ground between them is less so. Henry's long dark night of the soul wrestling with his own inner angels is never completely real to the viewer, and that is the core of the story. Another part of the film's problems becomes evident in the voice-overs that were added after preview audiences reacted negatively. Narrator James Whitmore states that his text is taken from Stephen Crane's text, implying that it's holy writ and that this is a serious high-minded film and anyone who doesn't appreciate it ought to be ashamed. That kind of cinematic eat-your-vegetables approach has never worked, and it is doubly offensive here. The often unnecessary narration gives a pompous tone to the pared-down simple images and story.

Those flaws notwithstanding, *The Red Badge of Courage* is still one of the better Civil War films. The performances are first rate; the characters are believable; the political and historic elements aren't romanticized. Though it falls far short of greatness, this one is well worth watching.

Dear Mr. Mayer: We read the script for your proposed production of *THE RED BADGE OF COURAGE*, and beg to report that the basic story seems to meet the requirements of the Production Code. Going through the script in detail, we call your attention to the following minor items. Page 1A: Here, and throughout the script, please make certain that the expression "dum" is pronounced clearly, and does not sound like the unacceptable expletive "damn." Page 21: The expression "damn" is unacceptable. Page 41: The same applies to the exclamation "Lord," the expression "I swear t'Gawd." Page 42: The exclamation "Good Lord" is unacceptable. Page 65: The expression "hell to pay" is unacceptable.

Joseph Breen of the MPAA in a letter to Louis B. Mayer (quoted in *Picture* by Lillian Ross, p. 38)

Did you Know?

Screenwriter Albert Band went on to become a successful producer and director of action-exploitation films, and so is his son Charles Band, the head of Full Moon Studios.

Union soldiers take the Stars
and Stripes from the fallen flag
bearer in *Red Badge of Courage*.
The Kobal Collection

Cast: Audie Murphy (Henry Fleming—the Youth), Bill Mauldin (Tom Wilson—the Loud Soldier), Douglas Dick (The Lieutenant), Royal Dano (The Tattered Soldier), Andy Devine (The Cheerful Soldier), Arthur Hunnicutt (Bill Porter), John Dierkes (Jim Conlin—the Tall Soldier), Richard Easton (Thompson), Tim Durant (The General), Whit Bissell (Wounded officer); **Written by:** Albert Band; **Cinematography by:** Harold Rosson; **Music by:** Bronislau Kaper. **Producer:** Gottfried Reinhardt, MGM. **Running Time:** 69 minutes. **Format:** VHS, Beta.

The Red Badge of Courage— "Borrowed Imagination"

Conventional Hollywood wisdom has it that John Huston's *The Red Badge of Courage* was a "great" war film that was taken from him and hacked to pieces by studio executives. That idea is based mostly on Lillian Ross's brilliant 1952 book, *Picture* (Modern Library. 1997), compiled from a series of articles she wrote for *The New Yorker* magazine. But a closer examination of that book and other sources suggests that Huston may not have been completely blameless.

By all accounts, the film was at or near the center of a struggle in the early 1950s between Louis B. Mayer, head of MGM, and Dore Schary, vice-president in charge of production. At stake was control of the studio. Mayer, a traditionalist who believed that movies should be light escapism, disliked the idea of a realistic examination of the Civil War told without stars and—more importantly—without women. Schary understood that with the emerging importance of television, movies had to change. He saw this film as part of the industry's maturation. After considerable argument and discussion, and with the intervention of Nicholas Schenck—president of Loew's Consolidated Entertainment, MGM's parent company—Mayer gave his grudging consent.

Then Huston, his assistant Albert Band, and producer Gottfried Reinhardt went to work on the script. That's also when Lillian Ross started following the production, sitting in on meetings, following the key participants, and learning the intricacies of studio politics. As she describes the production, it was in trouble from the beginning. The film's central problem is one that has always plagued Hollywood. After a long fight to get the project approved, Huston still didn't have a satisfactory script. As rehearsals were about to begin, he was still rewriting with Reinhardt and Band. Reading Ms. Ross's account, one doesn't have to search too far between the lines to see that throughout the shooting, important changes were being made. No one, not even Huston, was happy with the way that the protagonist—called The Youth in Ms. Ross's book and Henry Fleming in the film—makes his change from coward to hero. Key scenes were written and re-written, and the filmmakers still asked each other questions about them.

The filming was relatively uneventful. Some of it was actually done at Huston's ranch. Throughout the process, everyone worried about how it was going, how the scenes looked. With her fussy *New Yorker* prose, Ms. Ross captures the overarching insecurity of Hollywood, the way that film people constantly thank each other and compliment each other so effusively and insincerely, in much the same way that the devoutly religious bless each other and pray. It's a constant and necessary affirmation of the validity of their chosen pursuits. And because Ross attempts to be so objective, the John Huston she portrays can be seen in two very different ways.

The first John Huston is a director who struggles with complex psychological material, attempting to make real and visible the workings of one man's mind. The second John Huston is a director who is looking forward to his next film—*The African Queen*—one that is already much more important to him, with bigger stars and potentially, a much bigger payoff. (He mentions it first on page 10 of her book.) Because of that preoccupation, he's never fully engaged with *Red Badge*. For example, he's late to his first meeting with his star Audie Murphy, and blithely blames a secretary for letting him oversleep. Later, when filming is well underway, he doesn't show up for a rewrite session with Reinhardt and goes fishing instead. As soon as Huston completes his contractual duties as director, he's off to England and Africa to make *African Queen*, leaving Reinhardt to fight for *Red Badge*.

So, who gets credit or blame? Whatever the truth of the matter, this film, and several others in Huston's career, prove that as a director, he was no better than his script, and, if Ross is to be believed, he did not particularly like the work of writing, preferring instead to dictate. Whatever the truth, Huston was out of the country when the first preview audiences saw the film and gave the studio their exceptionally negative comments. When the executives realized the depth of public antipathy, they scrambled to make changes. They re-edited battle sequences and added narration. It didn't work. Though the film took very good reviews, the audience stayed away in droves.

Late in Ms. Ross's book, Howard Dietz, an ad man for Loew's, identifies the problem with *The Red Badge of Courage*, summed up in the phrase "no stars and no story." He goes on, with the wisdom of a Hollywood professional to say, "The phony talk I've had to listen to about this picture! 'It's a classic.' 'Art.' Nonsense. A novel is a novel. A poem is a poem. And a movie is a movie. . . . What stops you is the equity that goes with the classic. It's borrowed imagination."

THE SAND PEBBLES

1966 Robert Wise 🎵🎵🎵

Robert Wise's anti-imperialist epic is a sort of blue-collar *Lawrence of Arabia*. When it was made in 1966, its implicit criticism of American participation in the Vietnam war was more significant than it is today, but the film remains entertaining, complex, and notably lacking in propaganda. At one point, the film seems to finger communists as the villains, but before it's over, everyone has a share of the blame for a violent, tragic situation.

The setting is China, 1926, "a country of factions trying to unite to become a nation through revolution." Freshly arrived Navy machinist Jake Holman (Steve McQueen) wants nothing to do with politics. He's had a hard-luck career and wants nothing more than to settle down and work on the engine of his new assignment, the gunboat *San Pablo*. But, as another character tells him, "American gunboats in Central China are a painful local joke, Mr. Holman, and the most painful is the *San Pablo*. I think she is something you chaps inherited from Spain after the Spanish-American War."

When Jake finally arrives, he finds that Capt. Collins (Richard Crenna) runs a strange ship, operating under a military-civilian caste system that mirrors the larger colonial-political organization of the country. Much of the work is done by local Chinese who actually live on board. Instead of doing their assigned jobs, the sailors' main duty is to maintain a presence, to present a brave front. In short, their role is as much political as it is military. If Jake is to do his job properly, it means "breaking someone else's rice bowl" and nobody wants to upset the delicate balance of power.

Of course, it is upset, first by Jake, then by his friend Frenchy (Richard Attenborough), who falls in love with Maily (Marayat Andriane). At the same time, Jake begins a tenuous romance with Shirley Eckert (Candice Bergen), a missionary. But Jake's first love is his engine, and that's the strongest emotional relationship in the film. The long scenes in which he learns about the machines and then teaches his assistant Po-Han (Mako) about them are touching and memorable.

Did you Know?

According to the Internet Movie Database, Marayat Andriane, who plays Maily, is also Emmanuelle Arsan, author of the novel *Emmanuelle*, the source material for the famous soft-core film starring Sylvia Kristal. Ms. Andriane also appears in *Forever Emmanuelle*.

But director Robert Wise and writer Robert Anderson mean to show that the world has become too complex for such simple answers. Jake may retreat to the safe confines of his engine room, but he cannot escape what's going outside—the deepening conflicts between Chinese and American, between officers and enlisted men, between military and civilian, between men and women, between insiders and outsiders.

The first half of the film is fairly slow, as all of those relationships are established, but the action picks up sharply in the second half. Chaotic political unrest on land sets the stage for a superbly staged and very violent naval battle between the *San Pablo* and a barricade of junks. That, in turn, sets up the long conclusion in an open courtyard. The film ends with a famous line—"What the hell happened?"—that has been taken as a comment on American intervention in Vietnam. That's exactly what it means and the line becomes even clearer when you realize that it's used twice in the film, both times in the same circumstances.

See also

Zulu

The Wind and the Lion

From Here to Eternity

The General

Lawrence of Arabia

Today, *The Sand Pebbles* might be nothing more than an interesting period piece if the performances weren't so strong. McQueen's role is letter perfect for a young actor who's establishing a rebellious image, and he plays it to perfection. In the right moments he seems gawky, stiff, and uncomfortable, just as he should be. (This was the only time he'd be nominated for a Best Actor Academy Award.) Richard Crenna's slightly unhinged Captain should have been nominated, but wasn't. For her part, Candice Bergen is mostly called upon to look beatific and she does. In this role, she's got beatitude down cold.

More importantly, though, the film's politics have aged gracefully and well. Without resorting to preaching or comfortably "correct" positions or easy villains, Wise and Anderson stress the human costs of war and revolution.

Jake Holman (Steve McQueen, left) and Frenchy Burgoyne (Richard Attenborough) stay on the alert for trouble in 1920s China in *The Sand Pebbles*. The Kobal Collection

Cast: Steve McQueen (Jake Holman), Richard Crenna (Capt. Collins), Richard Attenborough (Frenchy Burgoyne), Candice Bergen (Shirley Eckert), Marayat Andriane (Maily), Mako (Po-Han), Larry Gates (Jameson), Gavin MacLeod (Crosley), Simon Oakland (Stawski), James Hong (Victor Shu), Richard Loo (Maj. Chin), Barney Phillips (Chief Franks), Tommy Lee (Chien), Ford Rainey (Harris), Walter Reed (Bidder), Gus Trikonis (Restorff), Joe Turkel (Bronson), Glenn Wilder (Waldron); **Written by:** Robert Anderson; **Cinematography by:** Joe MacDonald; **Music by:** Jerry Goldsmith. **Producer:** Robert Wise, 20th Century-Fox. **Awards:** Golden Globe Awards '67: Best Supporting Actor (Attenborough); Nominations: Academy Awards '66: Best Actor (McQueen), Best Art Direction/Set Decoration (Color), Best Color Cinematography, Best Film Editing, Best Picture, Best Sound, Best Supporting Actor (Mako), Best Original Score. **Running Time:** 193 minutes. **Format:** VHS, Beta, LV.

SHE WORE A YELLOW RIBBON

1949 John Ford ♪♪♪

Despite a nearly non-existent plot, the second installment of John Ford's "cavalry trilogy" is the strongest part. It is the only one of the three films made in color and Ford gets superb work from two of his favorite collaborators, John Wayne and Monument Valley.

A voice-over prologue sets the scene: "Custer is dead and around the bloody garden of the immortal 7th Cavalry lie 212 officers and men. The Sioux and Cheyenne are on the warpath. By military telegraph the news of the Custer massacre is flashed along the long lonely miles to the Southwest. From the Canadian border to the Rio Bravo, 10,000 Indians—Kiowa, Comanche, Arapaho, Sioux, and Apaches—under Sitting Bull and Crazy Horse, Gall and Crow King are uniting in a common war against the United States Cavalry." Ford sticks to that tone and point of view for the rest of the film. This is not a dispassionate view of the settlement of the West. It's about a war; it's about the winners of the war.

Capt. Nathan Brittles (John Wayne) is six days from retirement at Fort Stark when he's sent out on patrol with about 100 troopers. His mission is to reconnoiter Indian activity and to escort young Olivia Dandridge (Joanne Dru) to the stagecoach so she can leave the increasingly dangerous area. During the patrol, the conventional villains—the Indians and the greedy connivers who sell them rifles and whiskey—are dispensed with in short order, almost disdainfully. To Ford, they're unimportant. He's much more interested in showing the cavalry engaged in its everyday work. Though a few scenes revolve around whooping, hostile Indians chasing the heroic Sgt. Tyree (Ben Johnson), many more are simple shots of the column of riders crossing Monument Valley, Utah.

That incredible landscape is displayed with all the drama that its changeable light and weather can provide. The complex relationship between the land and the sky crowded with massive thunderheads makes the backdrop as important as the human characters. (Having seen Monument Valley go from bright sunlight to snow, hail, and sleet in less than half an hour, I can vouch for the accuracy of Ford's vision.) Director of photography Winston Hoch won a well-deserved Oscar for his work.

When the filmmakers do turn to other aspects of the traditional plot, their efforts are less than inspired. Though it's part of the title, a romantic triangle involving two younger officers is a weak subplot, and the concluding barroom brawl feels obligatory. The scenes of Brittle at his family's graves where he talks to his dead wife are much more authentic and moving. The emotion behind them is real and it's reflected in the theme of reconciliation between North and South within the cavalry ranks. That's what Ford really cares about, as the final voice-over narration makes clear: "So here they are, the dog-faced soldiers, the regulars, the 50-cents a day professionals riding the outposts of a nation from Fort Reno to Fort Apache, from Sheridan to Stark. They were always the same—men in dirty-shirt blue and only a cold page in the history books to mark their passing. But wherever they rode and whatever they fought for, that place became the United States."

See also
Hondo
Zulu
The Searchers

John Wayne as Capt. Nathan Brittles in *She Wore a Yellow Ribbon* The Kobal Collection

Cast: John Wayne (Capt. Nathan Brittles), Joanne Dru (Olivia Dandridge), John Agar (Lt. Flint Cohill), Ben Johnson (Sgt. Tyree), Harry Carey Jr. (Lt. Pennell), Victor McLaglen (Sgt. Quincannon), Mildred Natwick (Mrs. Abby Allshard), George O'Brien (Maj. Mac Allshard), Arthur Shields (Dr. O'Laughlin), Noble Johnson (Red Shirt), Harry Woods (Karl Rynders), Michael Dugan (Sgt. Hochbauer), Jack Pennick (Sgt. Major), Paul Fix (Rynder's partner), Francis Ford (Barman), Cliff Lyons (Trooper Cliff), Tom Tyler (Cpl. Mike Quayne), Chief John Big Tree (Pony That Walks); **Written by:** Frank Nugent, Laurence Stallings; **Cinematography by:** Winton C. Hoch, Charles P. Boyle; **Music by:** Richard Hageman. **Producer:** John Ford, Merian C. Cooper, RKO Radio Pictures, Argosy. **Awards:** Academy Awards '49: Best Color Cinematography. **Running Time:** 93 minutes. **Format:** VHS, Beta, LV.

SHE WORE A YELLOW RIBBON

SHENANDOAH

1965 Andrew V. McLaglen 🎵🎵🎵

In many important ways, this is one of Hollywood's more accurate attempts to show what the Civil War was like, both on the battlefield and at home. But director Andrew McLaglen and writer James Lee Barrett never let strict adherence to accuracy get in the way of their historical soap opera, and that's why the film has been such an enduringly popular hit. It is also the basis for a hit Broadway musical.

In the fictional community of Shenandoah Gap, widowed patriarch Charlie Anderson (James Stewart) rules his clan of six sons and one daughter and is determined not to pay any attention to what is happening beyond the boundaries of their 500-acre farm. "This war is not mine and I take no note of it," he states without hesitation or doubt. Anderson does not believe in slavery and has no thoughts on the preservation of the Union. He's more concerned with the raising of his children and the running of his farm. It takes almost an hour to limn in the details of that world—the conflicts with neighbors and authorities, and the romance between daughter Jennie (Rosemary Forsyth) and Sam (Doug McClure), a young Confederate officer.

About half way through, Anderson is forced to take action, and the pace quickens. Well-timed coincidences keep things moving briskly, but the whole tone of the film takes on a sad quality as the family comes to understand how badly the war is going for Virginia. By far the best scene is an encounter between Anderson and Col. Fairchild (George Kennedy), a Union officer whose war-weariness seems absolutely authentic. In that moment, the film has the tough-mindedness associated with the James Stewart–Anthony Mann westerns of the 1950s. But McLaglen quickly reverts to the sentimental melodramatics and action scenes that were always his strong suit. If the battles lack the sweeping scope of some Civil War epics, they are true to the individual combatants and the tactics of smaller engagements. As such, they're believable, though in appearance and sensibility, the film is almost a western. (At the time *Shenandoah* was made, the TV series *Bonanza* was at the peak of its popularity, and any similarity between the two is intentional.)

For the most part, McLaglen wisely keeps the camera on his star, and Stewart carries the film. While several of his younger supporting cast adopt unfortunate Southern accents, he sticks to the voice that everyone knows. That's a very good thing, because he's called upon to deliver many long, weighty, and wise monologues. Actually, this may be the most pontificatory role in his long career. The speeches work because they're grounded in a believable sense of reality. The Oregon locations are similar to the Shenandoah Valley. Slavery was not as prevalent there as it was in other parts of the South; smaller farms were prevalent. (They grow a lot of turkeys there now.) Finally, the film's refusal to take sides in the war also serves it well. This is a sentimental, tear-jerking Hollywood melodrama that means to entertain while remaining fairly faithful to history. It does that.

See also
Birth of a Nation
Gone with the Wind
The Good, the Bad and the Ugly
The Searchers
Pharaoh's Army

ast: James Stewart (Charlie Anderson), Doug McClure (Sam), Glenn Corbett (Jacob Anderson), Patrick Wayne (James Anderson), Rosemary Forsyth (Jennie Anderson), Katharine Ross (Ann Anderson), George Kennedy (Col. Fairchild), Phillip Alford (Boy Anderson), James Best (Carter), Charles Robinson (Nathan Anderson), James McMullan (John Anderson), Tim McIntire (Henry Anderson), Eugene Jackson (Gabriel), Paul Fix (Dr. Tom Witherspoon), Denver Pyle (Pastor Bjoerling), Harry Carey Jr. (Jenkins), Dabbs Greer (Abernathy), Strother Martin (Engineer), Warren Oates (Billy Packer); **Written by:** James Lee Barrett; **Cinematography by:** William Clothier; **Music by:** Frank Skinner; **Technical Advisor:** D.R.O. Hatswell. **Producer:** Robert Arthur, Universal. **Awards:** Nominations: Academy Awards '65: Best Sound. **Running Time:** 105 minutes. **Format:** VHS, Beta, LV.

James Stewart is Charlie Anderson, stern patriarch of a large family who wants nothing to do with the Civil War in *Shenandoah*. He speaks to Col. Fairchild (George Kennedy, back to camera.) The Kobal Collection

THEY DIED WITH THEIR BOOTS ON

1941 Raoul Walsh ♪♪♪

> And so was born the immortal 7th U.S. CAVALRY which cleared the plains for a ruthlessly advancing civilization that spelled doom to the red race.
>
> **Supertitle on screen after the 7th Cavalry adopts *The Garry Owen* as its song**

> "I think it was an idea that made them, an idea and a song. You should have seen them the day they were first mustered in—derelicts, outcasts, criminals of every kind who'd just joined up because they couldn't make a living any other way. But wait till you see them now, Mr. Commissioner. Wait till you see what discipline, devotion to duty and a little human understanding can do! You'll see men who aren't afraid to look death in the face with pride in their eye. And not for any measly $13 a month but because they've got pride in their regiment!"
>
> **Gen. George Custer (Errol Flynn) in a typically florid moment**

Raoul Walsh's sprawling and hugely inaccurate biopic is also contradictory. On one hand, star Errol Flynn makes Gen. George Armstrong Custer a dashing, attractive hero. But behind the glamour, the character is a vainglorious, publicity-hungry idiot whose success comes from dumb luck and a wife whose family is well connected politically. In short, this Custer is a 19th century media whore. Though there appears to be at least a grain of truth to that interpretation of the man, other historical facts fare poorly here. Director Walsh and writers Wally Kline and Aeneas MacKenzie play fast and loose in their creation of villains and in the Civil War scenes, which are pure Hollywood eyewash.

The story begins with Custer's arrival at West Point in 1857, where nasty upperclassman Ned Sharp (Arthur Kennedy) takes advantage of the dim-witted newcomer. Even without Sharp's interference, Custer manages to accumulate such an impressive number of demerits that his military career is saved only by the South's secession. Most of the staff officers in Washington realize how incompetent he is, but Custer ingratiates himself with Gen. Winfield Scott (Sydney Greenstreet), is given an assignment, and steals a horse to get to the Manassas battlefield. A clerical error results in his promotion to Brigadier General and he's off to Gettysburg, where he disobeys orders and defeats Jeb Stuart's cavalry. That sequence sets the tone for the rest of the film.

To the accompaniment of Max Steiner's rousing score, Custer leads his men in repeated cavalry charges. The cannons thunder, the music rises up, Errol brandishes his saber, hundreds of horsemen gallop from left to right across your screen and into a cloud of dust. Seconds later, a few of them return. Reinforcements are brought up and Errol valiantly leads them in another charge. Cue cannon, cue music, cue smoke. Not one single Confederate is even seen, much less engaged in combat. But Custer has saved the Union single-handedly, so he can go back to Michigan and marry the lovely Elizabeth Bacon (Olivia de Havilland).

Presently, they're off to the West, where they meet Crazy Horse (Anthony Quinn) and Custer promises him that the Great White Father will honor all of his promises, etc., etc. The film's portrayal of black and Indian characters is casually, paternalistically racist, though the pidgin-spouting Indians are treated with a degree of sympathy. In fact, the final reels resort to lawyer- and government-bashing to set up the Battle of Little Big Horn. Sharp reappears as a villain who sells whiskey to the cavalry and repeating rifles to the Indians, and by the time they meet again, Custer and Crazy Horse are almost on the same side.

The battle itself is handled well by second-unit director "Breezy" Eason, who performed an identical job on *Charge of the Light Brigade*. The tactics and the landscape may not have anything to do with reality, but the scene is a fine piece of energetic filmmaking. And throughout, Flynn and Olivia de Havilland radiate enough pure star power to make the proceedings thoroughly entertaining. They're abetted by some superb characters, including Hattie McDaniel. Kennedy is at his nasty best, and Greenstreet's

See also
Zulu
Charge of the Light Brigade
Birth of a Nation
She Wore a Yellow Ribbon

AMERICAN WARS

Errol Flynn is Gen. George
Custer in *They Died with Their
Boots On.* The Kobal Collection

garrulous General brings to mind his work in *The Maltese Falcon*. They make the film first-rate escapism, and an important part of Hollywood's mythologization of the West.

Cast: Errol Flynn (George Armstrong Custer), Sydney Greenstreet (Gen. Winfield Scott), Anthony Quinn (Crazy Horse), Hattie McDaniel (Callie), Arthur Kennedy (Ned Sharp), Gene Lockhart (Samuel Bacon), Regis Toomey (Fitzhugh Lee), Olivia de Havilland (Elizabeth Bacon Custer), Charley Grapewin (California Joe), G.P. Huntley Jr. (Lt. Butler), Frank Wilcox (Capt. Webb), Joseph Sawyer (Sgt. Doolittle), Eddie Acuff (Cpl. Smith), Minor Watson (Sen. Smith), Tod Andrews (Cadet Brown), Stanley Ridges (Maj. Romulus Taipe), John Litel (Gen. Philip Sheridan), Walter Hampden (William Sharp), Joseph Crehan (President Grant), Selmer Jackson (Capt. McCook), Gig Young (Lt. Roberts), Dick Wessel (Staff Sgt. Brown); Written by: Wally Kline, Aeneas MacKenzie; Cinematography by: Bert Glennon; Music by: Max Steiner; Technical Advisor: Lt. Col. J.G. Taylor. Producer: Robert Fellows, Hal B. Wallis, Warner Bros. Running Time: 141 minutes. Format: VHS, Beta.

THE WIND AND THE LION

John Milius's rousing adventure is a direct cinematic descendant of *Gunga Din* and *Charge of the Light Brigade*, refracting history through a severely distorted cinematic prism. Think of it as a Republican historical fantasy inspired by real events. As such, it is escapism, not American History 101, and it is particularly well-crafted escapism.

In 1904, the reigning superpowers (to use a thoroughly anachronistic term), France, Germany, and the United States (apparently there wasn't room in the film's budget to include the British), are jockeying for influence in Morocco. For political reasons of his own, the Berber chieftain Mulay el-Raisuli (Sean Connery) kidnaps an American woman, Eden Pedecaris (Candice Bergen) and her two children, and demands an outrageous ransom. For political reasons of his own, Theodore Roosevelt (Brian Keith) adopts a get-tough policy. "Pedecaris alive or Raisuli dead!" he thunders at campaign whistle stops. His Secretary of State John Hay (John Huston) thinks it's an excellent strategy, though he's afraid that his candidate may believe his own bluster.

While all of that is working itself out in the background, Mrs. Pedecaris is redefining "feisty" in her dealings with her charismatic kidnapper, and her kids are having a dandy time, particularly William (Simon Harrison) who thinks that this is about the coolest thing that could ever happen to a 10-year-old. The opening scene, where the Raisuli's men come galloping through the streets of Tangiers on their beautiful horses, trampling the French flag, and leaping through latticework, is grandly staged. The scene is matched later with an equally impressive march by U.S. Marines through the same streets. The two other big action scenes are a mounted "rescue" at the midpoint, and a climactic shoot-out based on the end of *The Wild Bunch*. Throughout, however, the levels of violence are kept well within the limits of a PG rating, and that is a mistake. The story would have been better served with a more direct and honest approach.

As long as he's dealing with physical action, director Milius is on solid footing. He makes excellent use of Spanish exteriors to turn his deserts into magical places, and the equestrian scenes are among the best ever put on film. He also gets excellent performances from his leads. Connery and Keith seem to be having a splendid time. In her Gibson Girl hairdo, with seldom more than a strand or two out of place no matter how dreadful the situation, Candice Bergen is every bit the equal of her male co-stars. While those central characters are sympathetically, if cartoonishly drawn, the rest of the Arab characters are treated as gibbering, lecherous, predatory stereotypes.

As a writer, Milius gives the political discussions a combination of seriousness and humor, at least near the beginning. But as the story progresses, Milius appears to accept his sophomoric Manifest Destiny flapdoodle as genuine insight. (Years later, he would let his right-wing fantasies run wild in the abysmal *Red Dawn*.) The director is careful to compare and to equate the two leaders in ways that are both obvious and subtle. In two campsite scenes, for example—one in Morocco and one in Yellowstone—Milius unobtrusively places the same hand-operated barbecue spit. Again, that is dubious history but fine entertainment.

> "NOW I don't know who you are or what you want with us, but I will tell you that I am no coward and if you or any of these men should dare to lay a hand on me, I will try with all the strength in me to kill you, and with my last breath I shall curse you to God. AND GOD WILL LISTEN!"
>
> **Eden Pedecaris (Candice Bergen) to the Raisuli (Sean Connery) after being kidnapped**

> "You know as well as I do that we can't have Arab desperados running around kidnapping American citizens."
>
> **Theodore Roosevelt (Brian Keith) to John Hay (John Huston)**

Fact:

Vladek Sheybal, who plays the Moroccan Bashaw, also co-starred with Sean Connery as Kronsteen, the SPECTRE chess master in From *Russia with Love*.

Sean Connery is the Raisuli and Candice Bergen is his American kidnap victim Eden Pedecaris in *The Wind and the Lion.* The Kobal Collection

It's easy enough to ignore the posturing and inaccuracies—the real Pedecaris was a middle-aged man who was released almost immediately—and to enjoy the film on its own lightweight merits.

Cast: Sean Connery (Mulay el-Raisuli), Candice Bergen (Eden Pedecaris), Brian Keith (Theodore Roosevelt), John Huston (John Hay), Geoffrey Lewis (Gunmere), Steve Kanaly (Capt. Jerome), Vladek Sheybal (The Bashaw), Nadim Sawalha (Sherif of Wazan), Roy Jenson (Adm. Chadwick), Larry Cross (Henry Cabot Lodge), Simon Harrison (William Pedecaris), Polly Gottesmann (Jennifer Pedecaris), Marc Zuber (The Sultan); **Written by:** John Milius; **Cinematography by:** Billy Williams; **Music by:** Jerry Goldsmith. **Producer:** Herb Jaffe, Phil Rawlins, MGM/UA Entertainment Company. **Awards:** Nominations: Academy Awards '75: Best Sound, Best Original Score. **MPAA Rating:** PG. **Running Time:** 120 minutes. **Format:** VHS, Beta, LV, Letterbox.

The Civil War Documentary Series

"We have shared the incommunicable experience of war. We have felt—we still feel—the passion of life to its top. In our youths, our hearts were touched with fire."

With those words of Union veteran and Supreme Court Justice Oliver Wendell Holmes, Ken Burns's brilliant depiction of America's costliest war begins. Though the long work is a documentary, it is more moving than most Hollywood fiction. Producer-writer-director Burns uses a few simple techniques to tremendous effect. He overcomes the central limitation of any film about that war—the lack of moving pictures—by creating the illusion of movement within still photographs and paintings. He pans his camera over the surface of carefully chosen images of faces, bodies, battlefields, towns, and rivers, and weaves that footage into pastoral shots of unpopulated contemporary landscapes and cemeteries over the natural sounds of insects, birds, and weather. The primary musical accompaniment is Jay Ungar's poignant, and now familiar, "Ashokan Farewell" and Jacqueline Schwab's understated solo piano.

The series is roughly framed with historical newsreel footage shot at President Franklin Roosevelt's speech at Gettysburg in 1938 and the 1913 50th Gettysburg reunion, where aging veterans re-enact the battle. The main body of the narrative comes from narrator David McCullough and the comments of Shelby Foote, with accompaniment from historians Ed Bearrs, Stephen B. Oates, and Barbara J. Fields. For about 11 and a half hours they and writers Geoffrey C. Ward and Ric Burns tell about what happened in this country between 1861 and 1865. Though some action takes place in the West, the focus stays east of the Mississippi.

The filmmakers follow the successful approach that Shelby Foote took in his three-volume *The Civil War*. They see the material as a vast novel, an epic of America filled with so many reversals and twists that they need no embroidery. First, they sketch in the growth of the anti-slavery movement in the 1850s and the rise in Southern militias after John Brown's Raid. They pause to note that both Stonewall Jackson and John Wilkes Booth were present at John Brown's hanging, and in the following episodes, they continue to mine the rich vein of irony and contradiction that runs throughout the war. Whenever possible, they let the participants speak for themselves in carefully chosen quotations.

Mary Chesnut (voiced by Julie Harris) is a South Carolinian who knows Jefferson Davis and keeps a diary throughout the war. In the north, New York lawyer George Templeton Strong (George Plimpton) serves much the same purpose, adding his often dyspeptic observations on the conduct of the war. Frederick Douglass (Morgan Freeman) is the conscience of the nation who stresses the importance of slavery as an issue. Elisha Hunt Rhodes (Chris Murney), from Pawtuxe, Rhode Island, enters the war as a private and rises to the rank of colonel. Walt Whitman (Garrison Keillor) manages to be at several critical events. Robert E. Lee (George Black) remains an aloof, mysterious, and finally unknowable figure, particularly when compared to his principal adversaries, Ulysses Grant (Jason Robards Jr.) and William T. Sherman (Arthur Miller), a pair of cold-eyed realists who tell the truth as they see it.

If the story can be said to have a hero, two figures share the billing. Abraham Lincoln (Sam Waterston) is a fully human President who is forced to make difficult choices time after time, and does not always make the best choice. On the battlefield, Col. Joshua Lawrence Chamberlain (Paul Roebling), of the 20th Maine, is the college professor who becomes a sort of warrior-poet and then a hero, first at the battle of Fredericksburg, and again at Gettysburg where, arguably, he saves the nation.

At first, nearly everyone is shocked by the suddenness of the Southern states' secession. All of them (except Sherman) believe that it will be a short war which their side will win, and so they approach it with naive enthusiasm. When the battles begin at Manassas, the numbers of casualties are appalling, and they become even more appalling at Antietam, Shiloh, Chickamauga, Fredericksburg, and Vicksburg. But the series is not a dry recitation of place names, numbers, and maps, with blocks and arrows. Burns and company want to show the viewer what it feels like to be on the ground in the middle of a battle, and what it feels like to be a civilian back home.

The filmmakers create that you-are-there sense of immediacy and believability with a series of fascinating details:

• By 1860, one out of every seven Americans belonged to another American.

• When the first battle of Manassas was fought on his farm in 1861, Wilmer McLean decided to move. He went to Appomatox Courthouse, where the surrender between Grant and Lee would be signed four years later.

• In the Shenandoah Valley of Virginia, the town of Winchester changed hands 72 times during the war.

• 85% of the black men eligible to fight for the North signed up.

• In the North, any man who could come up with $300 or find a volunteer to replace him was exempt from conscription. In the South, any man who owned 20 Negroes did not have to serve.

• The Minie ball, invented by Claude Minie, is a huge, slow-moving .53 caliber bullet made of soft lead. It did not pierce a limb, it destroyed it, accounting for the horrific number of amputations. One year after the war, a fifth of the state budget of Mississippi went for artificial limbs

• The photographs of emaciated prisoners kept at the Confederate prison camps of Andersonville and Belle Isle frighteningly presage the Holocaust. Henry Wirz, commandant of Andersonville was hanged for war crimes.

• At Little Round Top in Gettysburg, "farmers from Taledega, Alabama, fought fishermen from Presque Isle, Maine. Both towns are 650 miles from Gettysburg, almost on a line between them."

• For every soldier killed in battle, two died from disease.

In the end, though, the series has been so popular because it makes clear the deep, heart-felt emotions of that war, the passionate beliefs that people on both sides died for and that people still, to this day, quarrel over and debate. Serious scholars of the war will not find much new here. That's not the point. For everyone else, *The Civil War* is fierce, strong entertainment with a serious purpose. It's even more rewarding on a second viewing.

BRITISH WARS

British Wars on Screen

The British war film can trace its roots straight back to Shakespeare. One of the most famous and most honored is Sir Laurence Olivier's version of *Henry V*, which was made, miraculously, while German bombs were falling on the country. That courageous, ambitious spirit is at the heart of the best of the English efforts. (Since this category is limited to civil and colonial wars, the fine propaganda work done for World War II is covered elsewhere.)

The films that look realistically at the various facets of the British Empire have generally been even-handed. Bruce Beresford's *Breaker Morant*, for example, questions the morality of tactics when the military and civilians are involved in a guerrilla war, and can find no comfortable answers. *Zulu*, which could have degenerated into jingoism, is instead a classic combat film because it refuses to demonize the African enemy. It is an apolitical examination of one engagement where a small, well-equipped force defends an outpost against a larger force trying to remove it. The reasons behind the conflict and the race of the combatants are studiously ignored.

Brits also make great villains. In movies, almost every other nationality takes at least one shot at those red-coated rascals. Such a role comes with the empire-building they pursued so energetically for so many centuries. The most obvious recent examples are King Edward I, Longshanks (Patrick McGoohan) in Mel Gibson's *Braveheart*, and Cunningham (Tim Roth) in Michael Caton-Jones' *Rob Roy*. Both are morally corrupt, duplicitous Royals who inspire impassioned rebellions.

But the British, either playing themselves or being impersonated by Americans, are at their most entertaining in the light-hearted escapist adventures of the 1930s. The trend begins in '35 when Gary Cooper and Franchot Tone save India for England in *Lives of a Bengal Lancer*. A year later, Errol Flynn and David Niven would do the same in *Charge of the Light Brigade*, where most of the action takes place in the province of Suristan, not the Crimea. Cary Grant, Douglas Fairbanks Jr., Victor McLaglen, and Sam Jaffee do it a third time in George Stevens's wonderful *Gunga Din*. It's up to John Clements to subdue the Dervishes in Khartoum and rescue his pals in *The Four Feathers*. Gary Cooper, Ray Milland and Robert Preston go toe to toe to toe to toe with the sadistic Brian Donleavy in *Beau Geste*.

Tony Richardson takes a decidedly different approach with his 1968 version of *Charge of the Light Brigade*. The film wears its anti-war sentiments on its sleeve, but still manages to make the debacle at Balaklava appallingly real.

Finally, Kenneth Branagh goes back to the source for his 1989 *Henry V*. It is a tribute to the Olivier version that surpasses the original in some regards. Branagh's bloody battle scenes may not be any more realistic in a historical sense, but they are more visceral, and Branagh gives his interpretation of King Harry different shadings, making him a more uncertain monarch. Saying that, though, I do not mean to disparage the Olivier film. I re-watched the films back to back over two days. It was one of the most enjoyable experiences in the creation of this book.

BEAU GESTE

1939 William A. Wellman ♫♫♫♩

Novelist Percival Christopher Wren (1885–1941) is one of the founders of the war-as-grand-adventure school of fiction. Though director William Wellman has worked with more serious war themes in his career, he does a fine job of bringing Wren's juvenile heroics to the screen. In this case, he has a top-notch ensemble cast to work with. Together, they create one of Hollywood's most enduring and memorable genres. The mention of the three words "French Foreign Legion" is enough to conjure up the necessary images of sand, khaki uniforms, kepi caps, rifles, oasis, more sand, lonely fort, a lot more sand.

Though the entire premise of the film—not to mention the plot, acting style, and point of view—are so completely dated that younger viewers will laugh themselves silly. They'll also find that the film is enjoyable for precisely the same reasons. The first half is slow because it's setting up a complex narrative structure built on three layers of flashbacks. In the film's "present," the Legionnaires at Fort Zinderneuf have already been attacked and seem to have been massacred. But how? Under what circumstances? At least one of the dead men may have killed one of his comrades. The newly arrived reinforcements have no idea how it happened. And what about the mysterious disappearance among their own ranks?

"The love of a man for a woman waxes and wanes like the moon . . . but the love of brother for brother is steadfast as the stars and endures like the word of the prophet."

Arabian proverb used as preface for *Beau Geste*

Then the first flashback takes us to the three Geste brothers as children in an idyllic English manor house, where they play involved make-believe games under the leadership of the eldest, Beau. After tossing in assorted complications involving their guardian, Lady Brandon (Heather Thatcher), household finances, and a fabulous but cursed sapphire called "Blue Water," we flash forward a few years. Beau (Gary Cooper), John (Ray Milland), and Digby (Robert Preston) join the Foreign Legion. The reasons why are too baroque, unrealistic, and embarrassing to explain. They just do, all right?

They find all the adventure and high-flown rhetoric they could want. As Maj. Beaujolais (James Stephenson) tells the new recruits, "We're here on the desert as guardians of 20 millions of natives. They look to us for the protection and justice that is the tradition of the Foreign Legion. Yours is a high duty and a hard one. The odds are great. It is our allegiance to France and our debt to civilization to uphold that tradition." The doughty brothers also meet the sadistic Sgt. Markoff (Brian Donlevy).

To reveal anything more would spoil the fun, because the plot is nothing if not surprising. It charges right along from one preposterous turn to another that's even more ridiculous, and soon the craziness of it all becomes quite reasonable. Much of the film's success is due to two people who seldom receive the credit they deserve in the collaborative effort of filmmaking: art directors Hans Dreier and Robert Odell, who created the grand sets for Fort Zinderneuf. They gave the film that indelible look that's been copied so many times since.

Of course, an ensemble cast filled with familiar faces and voices deserves credit for handling the material with absolute conviction. Donald O'Connor is the young Beau; a lovely Susan Hayward

See also

Titanic

The Last Remake of Beau Geste

March or Die

The Good, the Bad and the Ugly

The Lost Patrol

appears briefly as Isobel, the love interest. J. Carrol Naish, Broderick Crawford, and Albert Dekker show up as fellow Legionnaires. All of them are excellent, particularly Gary Cooper. But the film belongs to Donlevy, who received a Supporting Actor nomination. He provides most of the gleefully villainous energy that drives the story. About 30 years later, Lee Van Cleef would take a similar approach to a similar role in *The Good, the Bad and the Ugly*.

The result of their efforts is an unashamed appeal to the 12-year-old adventurer in all of us.

The Geste brothers: Digby (Robert Preston), John (Ray Milland), and Beau (Gary Cooper). The Kobal Collection

Cast: Gary Cooper (Michael "Beau" Geste), Ray Milland (John Geste), Robert Preston (Digby Geste), Brian Donlevy (Sgt. Markoff), Donald O'Connor (Beau at age 12), J. Carrol Naish (Rasinoff), Susan Hayward (Isobel Rivers), James Stephenson (Maj. Henri de Beaujolais), Albert Dekker (Schwartz), Broderick Crawford (Hank Miller), Charles T. Barton (Buddy McMonigal), Heather Thatcher (Lady Patricia Brandon), James Burke (Lt. Dufour), G.P. Huntley Jr. (Augustus Brandon), Harold Huber (Voisin), Harvey Stephens (Lt. Martin), Stanley Andrews (Maris), Harry Woods (Renoir), Arthur Aylesworth (Renault), Henry Kleinbach Brandon (Renouf), Nestor Paiva (Cpl. Golas), George Chandler (Cordier), George Regas (Arab Scout); **Written by:** Robert Carson; **Cinematography by:** Theodor Sparkuhl, Louis Clyde Stouman, Archie Stout; **Music by:** Alfred Newman. **Producer:** William A. Wellman, Paramount Pictures. **Awards:** Nominations: Academy Awards '39: Best Interior Decoration, Best Supporting Actor (Donlevy). **Running Time:** 114 minutes. **Format:** VHS, Beta.

BRAVEHEART

1995 Mel Gibson

Big-budget American movies are driven by star power, and this overachieving sword-and-kilt epic has so much celestial wattage that its many lapses and cliches are almost covered up. But despite all the awards and honors, *Braveheart* is still a cold-climate gladiator flick—an expensive and ambitious gladiator flick, to be sure—that is built on a stereotyped structure and an over-reliance on cinematic cliches in the clinches. That's not to say it isn't entertaining as a classy guilty pleasure.

Writer-producer Mel Gibson also stars as William Wallace, folk hero and savior of 14th century Scotland, which suffers under the cruel yoke of Longshanks, King Edward I (Patrick McGoohan), who seduces the local aristocracy with grants of land in England and installs his own nobles in the Highlands. In a genuinely chilling opening scene, the young Wallace sees the results of Longshanks's treachery after he kills a number of rebellious Scots. But when Wallace grows up, he turns his back on politics. Instead, he wants only to settle down with the lovely Murron (Catherine McCormack), until those plans are ruined by the rapacious invaders. At the same time, Longshanks's son Edward (Peter Hanly) is a mincing homosexual who finds himself unhappily married to Princess Isabelle (Sophie Marceau) of France. When Wallace raises an army to challenge the Brits, Robert the Bruce (Angus MacFadyen) has to scramble to maintain his carefully balanced power base between the other Scottish lords and the King.

> "Uncompromising men are easy to admire. He has courage. So does a dog."
> **Leper (Ian Bannen) about Wallace**

Gibson and writer Randall Wallace embellish the story with unrestrained romanticism. Every emotion is larger than life, and the graphic physical violence is splashed across the screen with equal enthusiasm. From Wallace's mystic psychic visions, to the decaying leper (Ian Bannen) who advises Robert the Bruce, to McGoohan's wonderfully reptilian interpretation of Long-shanks, the film revels in excess. And it works well enough. Mostly.

Before the first big battle, Gibson declaims, "I am William Wallace and I see a whole army of my countrymen here in defiance of tyranny. You have come to fight as free men and free men you are. What will you do with that freedom? Will you fight?... They may take our lives but they'll never take our freedom!" Yes, it's a far cry from Henry V's St. Crispin's Day speech, but Gibson brings it off, and he follows it with a spectacular battle that begins with a "heavy horse" charge and brutal hand-to-hand combat. With the assistance of hundreds of extras provided by the Irish army, Gibson spins a stirring, if fanciful, approximation of medieval warfare.

Other moments are less successful. For example, during his first confrontation with the English, while he's being pursued by dozens of soldiers, Wallace drags one of them into a hut and then emerges with the man's tunic, helmet, and spear. Of course, the clever trick fools his adversaries. Why not? It worked for the Tin Man, Scare-crow, and Cowardly Lion when they needed to get into the Witch's castle, and Bugs Bunny used it effectively countless times. But when an Oscar-quality film resorts to such easy gimmicks, can anyone take it seriously? Not really.

See also
Spartacus
Gallipoli
The Vikings
Rob Roy
Star Wars
Henry V
The Adventures of Robin Hood
Macbeth

BRITISH WARS

For escapism, *Braveheart* is rousing, energetic stuff. The political elements provide a little welcome complexity. James Horner's score gives the emotional moments a gravity they'd otherwise lack, and Scottish locales are a superb setting. In theatrical release, the film was a huge commercial success, and it has been just as popular on the small screen. Millions enjoy it as entertainment; no one should look for any real insight or historical understanding.

William Wallace (Mel Gibson), flanked by his captains Hamish (Brendan Gleeson) and Stephen (David O'Hara), leads the Scottish into battle against the British forces of King Edward I.
The Kobal Collection

Cast: Mel Gibson (William Wallace), Sophie Marceau (Princess Isabelle), Patrick McGoohan (King Edward I—Longshanks), Catherine McCormack (Murron), Brendan Gleeson (Hamish), James Cosmo (Campbell), David O'Hara (Stephen), Angus McFadyen (Robert the Bruce), Peter Hanly (Prince Edward), Ian Bannen (Leper), Sean McGinley (MacClannough), Brian Cox (Argyle Wallace), Stephen Billington (Phillip), Barry McGovern (King's Advisor), Alun Armstrong (Mornay), Tommy Flanagan (Morrison); **Written by:** Randall Wallace; **Cinematography by:** John Toll; **Music by:** James Horner. **Producer:** Mel Gibson, Alan Ladd Jr., Bruce Davey, Stephen McEveety, Icon Productions; released by Paramount Pictures. **Awards:** Academy Awards '95: Best Cinematography, Best Director (Gibson), Best Makeup, Best Picture; British Academy Awards '95: Best Cinematography; Golden Globe Awards '96: Best Director (Gibson); MTV Movie Awards '96: Best Action Sequence; Writers Guild of America '95: Best Original Screenplay; Broadcast Film Critics Association Awards '95: Best Director (Gibson); Nominations: Academy Awards '95: Best Costume Design, Best Film Editing, Best Original Screenplay, Best Sound, Best Original Dramatic Score; British Academy Awards '95: Best Director (Gibson), Best Score; Directors Guild of America Awards '95: Best Director (Gibson); Golden Globe Awards '96: Best Film—Drama, Best Screenplay, Best Score; MTV Movie Awards '96: Best Film, Best Male Performance (Gibson), Most Desirable Male (Gibson). **Budget:** 72M. **Boxoffice:** 202.6M. **MPAA Rating:** R. **Running Time:** 178 minutes. **Format:** VHS, Beta, Closed Caption.

BREAKER MORANT

1980 Bruce Beresford ♪♪♪♪

Few plays make the transition from stage to screen as fluidly as Kenneth Ross's courtroom drama. Though its subject is an incident in England's Boer War in South Africa, the film is really about war as it has evolved in the 20th century, where the lines between combatant and non-combatant have become so blurred as to be meaningless. They're meaningless to the soldier who's supposed to identify and defeat the enemy, but can they be meaningless to his superiors?

In Pietersburg, Transvaal, South Africa, 1901, the British and their Australian troops are involved in a war against Dutch immigrants, the Boers. It's a guerrilla war, with small groups of Boers staging hit-and-run attacks. (The word *commando* was originally applied to units of Boer militia and raiding parties.) Lt. Harry "Breaker" Morant (Edward Woodward) of the Bushfeld Carbiniers and his men are sent out after an ambush kills his friend, Capt. Hunt (Terence Donovan). Morant does find the men responsible and he executes them, but exactly why were they killed, and by which orders? And how did a German missionary come to die at the same time?

Morant, Lt. Peter Handcock (Bryan Brown), and Lt. George Witton (Lewis Fitz-Gerald) are accused of murder and brought before a court martial. Prosecuting is Maj. Bolton (Rod Mullinar). Their attorney is another Aussie, Maj. J.F. Thomas (Jack Thompson), who argues that the men were following direct instructions from the highest levels of the British command. "New orders from Kitchener," Hunt had told Morant, "Col. Hamilton's confirmed it to me himself. No prisoners. The gentleman's war is over." Another officer says, "This is a guerrilla war, not a debutante's ball. There are no rules here." But the British also want to placate the Germans to keep them from entering the war on the Dutch side.

Within the framework of the trial, director and co-writer Bruce Beresford flashes back to the events that take place out in the field. Those revelations are deftly layered, changing subtly with each new fact and added nuance. Even though the filmmakers are clearly on the side of the accused men, they never let the story become pure anti-British propaganda. They're interested in degrees of complicity, not pure guilt and innocence. No single individual or group emerges completely untainted. Visually, Beresford emphasizes the contrasts between the softly rolling hills of the Transvaal (actually Australia) and the measured confinement of courtroom and stockade cell. The film seems to have been made almost entirely on location, in real rooms with echoing hard floors and stone walls. That gives it an unusually authentic atmosphere. Accurate or not, it feels right.

> "It's a new kind of war, George. It's a new war for a new century. I suppose this is the first time the enemy hasn't been in uniform. They're farmers. They're people from small towns and they shoot at us from houses and from paddocks. Some of them are women. Some of them are children, and some of them are missionaries, George."
>
> **Lt. Morant (Edward Woodward) to Lt. Witton (Lewis Fitz-Gerald)**

> "War changes men's natures. The barbarities of war are seldom committed by abnormal men. The tragedy of war is that these horrors are committed by normal men in abnormal situations, situations in which the ebb and flow of everyday life have departed and been replaced by a constant round of fear and anger, blood and death. Soldiers at war are not to be judged by civilian rules."
>
> **Maj. Thomas (Jack Thompson) in summation**

So do the performances. Woodward's tightly controlled bearing and stiff-legged walk are perfect for a professional soldier who's got a bit of Kipling in his heart. Brown's amiable manner plays well against him, and the two have one perfect moment toward the end. It's a simple gesture that's beautifully touching and unexpected. The whole film builds to that moment, and the conclusion falls away from it.

See also

The Caine Mutiny

Paths of Glory

A Time to Love and a Time to Die

When *Breaker Morant* was released in 1980, its immediate connections to Vietnam were perhaps too apparent. Today, the film stands on its own as a clear-eyed examination of the difficult moral questions posed by war. In its refusal to accept easy answers, it remains relevant, compelling, and not at all dated.

Lt. "Breaker" Morant (Edward Woodward) is defended during his court-martial by Maj. Thomas (Jack Thompson). The Kobal Collection

Cast: Edward Woodward (Lt. Harry "Breaker" Morant), Jack Thompson (Maj. J.F. Thomas), John Waters (Capt. Alfred Taylor), Bryan Brown (Lt. Peter Handcock), Charles Tingwell (Lt. Col. Denny), Terence Donovan (Capt. Simon Hart), Vincent Ball (Col. Ian Hamilton), Ray Meagher (Sgt. Maj. Drummond), Chris Haywood (Cpl. Sharp), Lewis Fitz-Gerald (Lt. George Witton), Rod Mullinar (Maj. Charles Bolton), Alan Cassell (Lord Kitchener), Rob Steele (Capt. Robertson); **Written by:** Bruce Beresford, Jonathon Hardy, David Stevens; **Cinematography by:** Donald McAlpine; **Music by:** Phil Cunneen; **Technical Advisor:** Stan Green. **Producer:** Matt Carroll, South Australian Film Corporation. **Australian Awards:** Australian Film Institute '80: Best Actor (Thompson), Best Film; Nominations: Academy Awards '80: Best Adapted Screenplay. **MPAA Rating:** PG. **Running Time:** 107 minutes. **Format:** VHS, Beta, LV, 8mm.

CHARGE OF THE LIGHT BRIGADE

1936 Michael Curtiz ♪♪♪

Hollywood has seldom taken more liberties with history than it does with this depiction of the most famous battle of the Crimean War. Since it's based on Alfred Lord Tennyson's patriotic poem, that artistic license is to be expected. But who could have guessed that the writers would set virtually all of the action in India?

That's probably a smart move. Most movie audiences probably don't know what, or even where, the Crimea is anyway. India has elephants, leopards, evil potentates, and scenic mountains, and all those find their way into this gorgeous bit of heroics. The film was made during the studios' "Golden Age," and so has all of the polish and glamour of a big-budget Hollywood production. The cruel, grotesque side of the studio system is also evident—far too evident.

> " I sometimes think, Sir Charles, that a great government resembles a beautiful woman who, intoxicated with the power of her own beauty, is apt to withdraw from a sincere suitor the favors she has always granted, and when she finds this suitor console himself with another beauty, regrets her coldness. "
>
> **Surat Khan (C. Henry Gordon, who, miraculously, makes that tortured syntax understandable, and even humorous, when he delivers the lines)**

The story begins in the fictitious Indian province of Suristan, ruled by the shrewd Surat Khan (C. Henry Gordon, who gives his villain a dry sense of humor). Early on, Surat Khan's life is saved by Maj. Geoffrey Vickers (Errol Flynn) of the 27th Lancers, but Vickers and his commanding officer, Sir Benjamin Warrenton (Nigel Bruce) fear that the Indian ruler is ready to ally his forces with the Russians. Before much can be done with that plotline, we learn that Geoffrey's fiancee Elsa Campbell (Olivia de Havilland) is in love with his younger brother Perry Vickers (Patric Knowles). It takes the better part of the film's first 90 minutes to sort out the romantic triangle, and that sorting-out is slow. Several supporting characters, most notably Lady Warrenton (Spring Byington) take center stage then. The romantic angle is also needlessly drawn-out and passionless, with considerable doing-the-right-thing self-sacrifice on all sides. Geoffrey is far too noble to be believed, and there's a peculiar lack of "screen chemistry" between him and Ms. de Havilland.

If co-star David Niven is to be believed, the anti-romance between the two was the same off-camera. Niven plays the best friend, Capt. Randall, and the camaraderie between the two saves the first part of the film. The famous cavalry charge at Balaklava is the point, however, and when, at length, the scene finally shifts to the Crimea, it is an incredible sequence. In purely visual terms, the conclusion rates comparison to the battle on the frozen lake in *Alexander Nevsky*.

Credit for it goes to second-unit director B. Reeves "Breezy" Eason, not director Michael Curtiz. Eason specialized in such big action scenes. He was also responsible for the chariot race in the silent version of *Ben-Hur* and the burning of Atlanta in *Gone with the Wind*.

Fact:

Director Michael Curtiz was a Hungarian emigre who was famously uncomfortable with the English language. "Bring on the empty horses" was his way of calling for riderless horses.

In this beautifully edited sequence—which gains nothing with the addition of superimposed lines of Tennyson's poetry—wide-angle shots establish the dimensions of the battlefield, the famous "valley of death," while mobile cameras follow the advancing horsemen, hundreds of them. It begins slowly, with the ranks of riders moving at a walk. Then the speed increases along with the cannon fire. Unfortunately, the intensity came at a high price. In his fine book, *Bring On the Empty Horses*, David Niven says that one man was killed during the filming of the scene, and countless horses had to be destroyed because stunt-

See also

Alexander Nevsky

Charge of the Light Brigade (1968)

Waterloo

She Wore a Yellow Ribbon

Errol Flynn is Maj. Geoffrey Vickers in the 1936 version of *Charge of the Light Brigade.* The Kobal Collection

men used the infamous "running W" tripwire to make the animals fall at the right spot before the cameras. "Flynn led the campaign to have this cruelty stopped," Niven writes, "but the studio circumvented his efforts and completed the carnage by sending a second unit down to Mexico, where laws against maltreating animals were minimal, to say the most."

As for the "truth" behind the giving of the orders for the Light Brigade's charge, the film presents a complete whitewash. In this version, it was all done intentionally, for the most courageous and heroic of reasons. But to criticize the film on historical grounds misses the point. Remember that it was made in 1936. Hitler had been in power for three years and threats of war were growing daily. Though the film contains no overt propaganda, the one Russian character, Count Igor Volonoff (Robert Barrat) bears an unmistakable resemblance to Stalin. In short, the filmmakers did not want to question authority; they wanted to celebrate gallantry, whether it existed or not, and that's precisely what they did.

Cast: Errol Flynn (Maj. Geoffrey Vickers), Olivia de Havilland (Elsa Campbell), David Niven (Capt. James Randall), Nigel Bruce (Sir Benjamin Warrenton), Patric Knowles (Capt. Perry Vickers), Donald Crisp (Col. Campbell), C. Henry Gordon (Surat Khan), J. Carrol Naish (Subahdar-Major Puran Singh), Henry Stephenson (Sir Charles Macefield), E.E. Clive (Sir Humphrey Harcourt), Scotty Beckett (Prema Singh), G.P. Huntley Jr. (Maj. John Jowett), Robert Barrat (Count Igor Volonoff), Spring Byington (Lady Octavia Warrenton), George Regas (Wazir); Written by: Michael Jacoby, Rowland Leigh; Cinematography by: Sol Polito; Music by: Max Steiner; Technical Advisor: B. Reeves Eason, Maj. Sam Harris, Capt. E. Rochfort John. Producer: Hal B. Wallis, Samuel Bischoff, Warner Bros. Awards: Nominations: Academy Awards '36: Best Sound, Best Score. MPAA Rating: PG-13. Running Time: 115 minutes. Format: VHS, Beta, LV, Closed Caption.

The Hound Salutes: David Niven

David Niven will be remembered first for his light touch with sophisticated comedy. He'll be remembered second for his books about his Hollywood experiences—*The Moon's a Balloon* and *Bring On the Empty Horses*—two of the funniest, most insightful and enjoyable ever written on the subject. War films will place third, at best, and then as much for his real service as for his screen work.

Coming from a family of soldiers, Niven attended Sandhurst, the British equivalent of West Point. He was stationed with the Highland Light Infantry in Malta before he decided that the military wasn't for him, and set off to seek his fortune, as they say. He found it in Hollywood, 1934, where he worked his way up through the ranks. Niven had just been promoted to starring roles in 1939 when England declared war on Germany. He went back home and eventually wound up in a commando unit, but later was transferred from that outfit to work as a liaison officer with American forces during the D-Day invasion. Twice during his service, he was given four-weeks "special duty" to make propaganda films—*Spitfire*, about the fighter planes, with Leslie Howard, and *The Immortal Battalion* (see review) with Peter Ustinov.

Before the war, though, Niven had made an impression as Errol Flynn's friend in *Charge of the Light Brigade*. Two years later, in 1938, he and Flynn teamed up again, even more successfully, in *Dawn Patrol*. Their on-screen camaraderie reflects their real friendship and is the key to both films. A year later, he helped Gary Cooper pacify the Philippines in Henry Hathaway's sleeper, *The Real Glory*.

After the war, Niven returned to romantic drama and comedy and did not try a war film until 1946, in Michael Powell's fantasy *Stairway to Heaven*. *Soldiers Three*, from 1951, is a *Gunga Din–Bengal Lancers* adventure where Niven shares top billing with Stewart Granger and Walter Pidgeon. (It is not available on home video.) Then in 1961, Niven enjoyed one of his biggest commercial hits with *The Guns of Navarone*. In later decades, he would appear in *The Extraordinary Seaman*, *Escape to Athena*, and *Sea Wolves*, but none of them would approach the success of his early career. His easygoing, affable personality was more suited to lighter roles, particularly when war films became more graphically violent.

CHARGE OF THE LIGHT BRIGADE

1968 Tony Richardson 🎬🎬🎬

Tony Richardson's version of the key events at the battle of Balaklava is very much an answer to the 1936 film. Where director Michael Curtiz and writers Michael Jacoby and Rowland Leigh find high adventure, Richardson and writer Charles Wood see incompetence, petty jealousy, and lies. Though they stick much closer to historical fact (and historical supposition), the "truth" of their story is every bit as suspect as the earlier work.

Richardson uses Richard Williams's animation in the opening credits to set the scene. A cartoon Russian bear attacks a fez-wearing Turkey, and the British lion puts on a policeman's hat and steps in. Part of the reality behind that English threat is Lord Cardigan's (Trevor Howard) 11th Hussars. But when Capt. Nolan (David Hemmings), recently arrived in England from service in India, joins the Hussars, he finds that the outfit is virtually a sham. Despite their handsome uniforms, with the famous tight red trousers, the officers are idiots— empty-headed noblemen who have bought their commissions. Richardson and Wood spend the first three-quarters of the film castigating the British upper-class and military. Though they certainly have some historical basis for their charges, they are so heavy-handed that they undermine their own efforts.

> "That young man, Nolan, I don't really like him. He rides too well, knows a lot, and he has no heart. It'll be a sad day when England has her armies officered by men who know too well what they're doing. Smacks of murder."
>
> **Lord Raglan (John Gielgud)**

Nolan is presented as caring, thoughtful, patriotic, intelligent, and kind to animals. Cardigan is an ignorant, lecherous, vain, racist bully, and he's no better or worse than his superiors. Lord Lucan (Harry Andrews) petulantly refuses to take part in the war against the Russians until he is guaranteed a higher rank than his brother-in-law Cardigan. Lord Raglan (John Gielgud) is a doddering, one-armed old man who puts forth an early version of the "domino theory" as a reason for fighting the war to begin with.

While the staff officers stumble toward confrontation in the Crimea, Nolan is reunited with his best friend and fellow officer Capt. Morris (Mark Burns) on the eve of Morris's marriage to Clarissa (Vanessa Redgrave). The wedding scene is strongly reminiscent of the gathering for the famous hunt scene in Richardson's masterpiece, *Tom Jones*. The romantic subplot involving the relationship between Nolan and Clarissa attempts to put a modern spin on the triangle from the 1936 film, but it has an unfinished feel. In any case, it has little to do with the film's main plot and, at the earliest moment, is simply abandoned. At that point, a supporting character, Mrs. Duberly (Jill Bennett), takes center stage. Like Lucan, Cardigan, and Raglan, she was a real figure—she actually wrote a book about her experiences, *A Journal Kept During the Russian War, 1856*— and she receives the same shabby treatment.

When the filmmakers turn to the famous charge itself, their work is remarkably clear. The carnage is captured in all its bloody horror, sparing neither horse nor man. The credits make special note of the Turkish Presidential Cavalry, and the riders do tremendous work. If the scope of the engagement isn't as sweeping as the 1936 film, the sense of realism is even greater. The conclusion means to leave the viewer with an intense sensation of waste and needless destruction, and it succeeds far too well.

See also

Charge of the Light Brigade (1936)

They Died with Their Boots On

The Horse Soldiers

Despite the filmmakers' ham-fisted politics, the acting is excellent, with one exception. Trevor Howard's apoplectic portrayal of Cardigan is one of the best in his varied and underappreciated career. "If they can't fornicate, they can't fight," he thunders about his men. "And if they don't fight hard, I'll flog their backs raw for all their fine looks." Though they don't have as much to work with, Gielgud and Andrews are just as good. Hemmings and Vanessa Redgrave never come close to the edgy chemistry that they found in *Blow Up*. Her simpering performance is easily the worst of the ensemble.

In the end, like the 1936 film, this one is a product of its time, and the conflicts of the late 1960s were essentially generational. As such, it's more concerned with youth vs. age than with history.

Trevor Howard is the pompous, inept Lord Cardigan in the 1968 version of *Charge of the Light Brigade*. The Kobal Collection

Cast: Trevor Howard (Lord Cardigan), John Gielgud (Lord Raglan), David Hemmings (Capt. Nolan), Vanessa Redgrave (Clarissa), Harry Andrews (Lord Lucan), Jill Bennett (Mrs. Duberly), Peter Bowles (Paymaster Duberly), Mark Burns (Capt. Morris), Alan Dobie (Mogg), T.P. McKenna (Russell), Corin Redgrave (Featherstonhaugh), Norman Rossington (Corbett), Rachel Kempson (Mrs. Codrington), Donald Wolfit ("Macbeth"), Howard Marion-Crawford (Sir George Brown), Mark Dignam (Airey), Ben Aris (Maxse), Peter Woodthorpe (Valet), Roger Mutton (Codrington), Joely Richardson; **Written by:** Charles Wood; **Cinematography by:** David Watkin; **Music by:** John Addison. **Producer:** Neil Hartley, United Artists. **British. MPAA Rating:** PG. **Running Time:** 130 minutes. **Format:** VHS.

THE FOUR FEATHERS

1939 Zoltan Korda ♪♪♪

Younger moviegoers tend to think of anything that's more than a few years ago as somehow dated and slow, not really on a par with today's entertainment. They're wrong. They've simply become accustomed to cookie-cutter vehicles for overpaid stars in replaceable plots. A glance at something as maniacally original as this adventure ought to change their minds.

A.E.W. Mason's novel has been adapted to the screen several times, but this lavish production is by far the best. It was released in 1939, Hollywood's "golden" year, and stands up well against its contemporaries, *Gone with the Wind*, *Stagecoach*, *The Wizard of Oz*, *Mr. Smith Goes to Washington*, and *Beau Geste*. The film's blithe racist tendencies are off-putting, but in that regard, it's simply a product of its times. The story of heroism begins with Dervishes ripping down the Union Jack over Khartoum, 1898. Back in England, four young upper-class friends are members of the Royal North Surrey Regiment. Harry Faversham (John Clements) and John Durrance (Ralph Richardson) are competing for the hand of the lovely Ethne Burroughs (June Duprez), and she has chosen Harry. When the Regiment is assigned to the Sudan, Harry's doubts about his chosen career rise to the surface. He's in the Army because that's what generations of men in his family have done. For various reasons, he's unsure about that course for himself and so he resigns his commission. Everyone who knows him is scandalized.

> "The memories will be the best because they'll be right out of reach of uncertainty and care. Memories just float about on their own with no shadows upon them. Dance music, the moon and evening primroses, that's all."
>
> **Ethne Burroughs (June Duprez), in a particularly dreamy moment before Harry announces his plans**

Durrance, Ethne's brother Peter (Donald Gray), and their pal Arthur Willoughby (Jack Allen) send Harry three white feathers, thereby branding him a coward and telling him that they want nothing to do with him. Ethne adds the fourth feather. After that comes one of the most astonishing and indescribable plot twists in the history of the movies. For those who don't know what's coming, it's a real jaw-dropper. Of course, it will not be revealed here.

Did you Know?

Lone Pine, California, provided some of the African locales. Lone Pine was also India in *Gunga Din* and the Sahara in *Beau Geste*.

The rest of the film revolves around a military campaign in Africa against "The Khalifa's Army of Dervishes and Fuzzy Wuzzies on the Nile," as one supertitle puts it. The battle scenes, pitting Africans on horses and camels against British infantry, are dramatically staged. Director Zoltan Korda takes pains to see that the various positions and movements of the forces are clearly drawn. He was assisted by Capt. Donald Anderson, technical and military advisor, and second unit director Geoffrey Boothby. Despite the sweeping scope of those "big" moments, they lack the attention to individual engagements that add a human element.

That human element comes in other areas. June Duprez, for example, has a very slight lisp, so slight that it's unnoticeable in most scenes. It is, unfortunately, revealed at her most dramatic moment fairly late in the film, when she says, "You think I behaved bwutally to him, doctor? I did behave bwutally! I failed to help him when he was so tewibbly in need of help!" It's a completely charming moment. Most of the dramatic heavy lifting, though, falls on John Clements and Ralph Richardson. They manage to make preposterous situations and events seem credible, and they make us believe the characters.

See also

The Razor's Edge
The Big Country
Zulu
Lawrence of Arabia
Bridge on the River Kwai
Any John Ford western

BRITISH WARS

The film was photographed in the original "three-color" Technicolor process, and so the tape is still unusually—some might say unnaturally—vivid. Reds and blacks seem almost three-dimensional. The desert scenes are bright and lush, while some of the day-for-night scenes (recognizable for their strong shadows) have an unusual look. The film was shot by Jack Cardiff, one of the finest Technicolor cameramen of his day.

Compared to other "exotic" adventure films of the late 1930s, *The Four Feathers* is more polished and serious, and it was certainly one of the most expensive. Its combination of exotic locales with troubled British military men is an obvious influence on the films of David Lean that would follow. Its mad plotting, though, still stands on its own.

Cast: John Clements (Harry Faversham), Ralph Richardson (Capt. John Durrance), Sir C. Aubrey Smith (Gen. Burroughs), June Duprez (Ethne Burroughs), Donald Gray (Lt. Peter Burroughs), Jack Allen (Lt. Arthur Willoughby), Allan Jeayes (Gen. Faversham), Frederick Culley (Dr. Sutton), Hal Walters (Joe), Henry Oscar (Dr. Harraz), John Laurie (Mahdi), Clive Baxter (young Harry Faversham), Robert Rendel (Colonel), Derek Elphinstone (Lt. Parker), Norman Pierce (Sgt. Brown), Amid Taftazani (Karaga Pasha), Archibald Batty (Adjutant), Hay Petrie (Mahdi Interpreter), Alexander Knox; **Written by:** R.C. Sherriff, Lajos Biro, Arthur Wimperis; **Cinematography by:** Osmond H. Borradaile, Georges Perinal, Jack Cardiff; **Music by:** Miklos Rozsa; **Technical Advisor:** Capt. Donald Anderson. **Producer:** Alexander Korda, United Artists. **British. Awards:** Nominations: Academy Awards '39: Best Color Cinematography. **Running Time:** 99 minutes. **Format:** VHS, Beta, LV.

THE FOUR FEATHERS

GUNGA DIN
1939 George Stevens ♪♪♪♪

George Stevens's adaptation of a short Rudyard Kipling poem is one of Hollywood's great comic adventures. It's a completely frivolous work, so lacking in substance that its inherent paternalistic racism is rendered mostly harmless. In these more sensitive times, some will take offense at the very idea of white actors in "brown-face" playing Indian characters, but that kind of criticism should be reserved for films that are trying to say something. This one is trying simply to entertain.

Writers Ben Hecht, Fred Guiol, Joel Sayre, and Charles MacArthur took a standard Western plot and moved it from the prairie to the subcontinent. (All right, most of the exteriors were filmed in the California Sierra Nevadas, but those sure *look* like Indian mountains.) They turned the U.S. Cavalry into the British Army and exchanged Apaches for Thuggees (worshipers of the goddess Kali, who . . . oh, never mind).

> "You're looking
> very regimental, Din!"
>
> **Sgt. Cutter (Cary Grant) to
> Gunga Din (Sam Jaffe)**

> "If you mention gold temples
> to me again, I'll tear the
> back right off you with a
> shovel!"
>
> **Sgt. McChesney (Victor McLaglen)
> to Sgt. Cutter**

> "Look here, I'm a soldier of
> Her Majesty, the Queen. I
> don't grovel before any
> heathen!"
>
> **Sgt. McChesney to Guru (Eduardo Ciannelli)**

The immediate problem facing Sgt. Cutter (Cary Grant) and Sgt. McChesney (Victor McLaglen) is that their pal Sgt. Ballantine (Douglas Fairbanks Jr.) is about to leave the Army and marry his sweetheart Emmy Stebbins (an underused Joan Fontaine). They want him to stay and help them in barroom brawls and boozing and all the other fun stuff that guys do in movies like this. Of course, there's also the little matter of a rebellion against British colonization being led by Guru (Eduardo Ciannelli), but that shouldn't present much of a problem for three such splendid chaps. And they certainly are splendid in their tailored uniforms, shiny boots, pencilthin mustaches, and natty pith helmets. It's no wonder that Gunga Din (Sam Jaffe), a regimental waterboy, wants to join up and be a soldier just like them. When he tells Sgt. Cutter that he knows where to find a golden temple, a few Thuggees aren't going to stop him. From the midpoint on, the film charges on to a conclusion that's 24-karat Hollywood hokum. Throughout, the sets and locations have an exotic look that's somehow enhanced by excellent black-and-white cinematography from Joseph H. August.

Taken at the schoolboy level it's aiming for, this is derring-do that's daringly done. It's like a summer camp where they let you play with real guns. The violence is almost tongue-in-cheek, and the broader comic moments—particularly the punch bowl scene—are really funny. After all, producer-director Stevens got his start directing Laurel and Hardy short films, and he brings their chaotic irreverence to this crowd-pleaser.

Gunga Din received only one Academy Award nomination, and in another year, that would be unusual for such a finely crafted, big-budget picture. But in 1939, the competition was fierce. It was up against *Gone with the Wind*, *Mr. Smith Goes to Washington*, *The Wizard of Oz*, *Stagecoach*, *Wuthering Heights*, and several others.

See also

The Three Musketeers

The Man Who Would Be King

Indiana Jones and the Temple of Doom

The Party

Help!

Sergeants Three

Sgt. Cutter (Cary Grant), Sgt. McChesney (Victor McLaglen), and Sgt. Ballantine (Douglas Fairbanks Jr.) fight off the Thug cult with the help of waterboy *Gunga Din* (Sam Jaffe). The Kobal Collection

Cast: Cary Grant (Sgt. Archibald Cutter), Victor McLaglen (Sgt. McChesney), Douglas Fairbanks Jr. (Sgt. Ballantine), Sam Jaffe (Gunga Din), Eduardo Ciannelli (Guru), Montagu Love (Colonel), Joan Fontaine (Emmy Stebbins), Abner Biberman (Chota), Robert Coote (Higginbotham), Lumsden Hare (Maj. Mitchell), Cecil Kellaway (Mr. Stebbins), Roland Varno (Lt. Markham), George Regas (Thug Chieftain), Reginald Sheffield (Journalist), Clive Morgan (Lancer Captain); **Written by:** Fred Guiol, Joel Sayre, Ben Hecht, Charles MacArthur; **Cinematography by:** Joseph August; **Music by:** Alfred Newman. **Producer:** Pandro S. Berman, George Stevens, RKO. **Awards:** Nominations: Academy Awards '39: Best Black and White Cinematography. **Boxoffice:** 1.91M. **Running Time:** 117 minutes. **Format:** VHS, Beta, LV.

HENRY V
1944 Laurence Olivier ♪♪♪♪

Shakespeare's are the most challenging and tempting plays for a filmmaker to adapt to the screen. They're filled with action—often confusing action—and far too much dialogue—dialogue often used to describe events and actions that film can show directly. How does the director streamline the weighty works so that the public will be attracted without losing the richness? Laurence Olivier managed that and much, much more on his first try. In some ways, his acting-directing debut is as impressive as Orson Welles's *Citizen Kane. Henry V* is an ambitious, demanding film that gracefully transcends its roots as a piece of expensive propaganda.

> "And the men are like the mastiffs. Give them great meals of beef and iron and steel. They'll eat like wolves and fight like devils."
>
> **French nobleman on the English**

The famous opening shot is of a playbill fluttering down from a blue sky. It advertises a Globe Theater production of "Henry Fift." The camera pans down to reveal an aerial view of Shakespeare's London, ships on the Thames, and then into the theater itself. As the orchestra strikes up and signals curtain time, the theatergoers slowly find their places, some sitting onstage. The performance begins, and after a few minutes, the camera prowls backstage to the actors, some already in costume, some getting ready. The first 30 minutes or so are rough Skakespearian sledding, as characters discuss the young King Harry's (Olivier) decision to invade France, and broadly overplay all of the comic elements. Within those opening scenes, the confines of the Globe Theater slowly dissolve, and the action takes place on larger sets, with elaborate backdrops somehow reminiscent of the Emerald City in Oz, finally moving to full exteriors for the battle of Agincourt. Seen purely as stagecraft—or should that be filmcraft?—the transition is remarkable. Olivier uses the play's unwieldy structure to his advantage.

The action shifts from the haughty French ambassador's dismissal of Henry's claim on French territory, to Henry's boyhood pal Pistol (Robert Newton), to the French court, to Henry's future wife Katharine (Renee Asherson), to the Channel crossing and the first battle. Though Olivier completely eliminates two key subplots, the story doesn't find its emotional center until the night before the battle of Agincourt, "a time when creeping murmur and the poring dark fills the white vessel of the universe." That's when the film settles down, too. Olivier puts aside his bag of tricks and focuses on the young, uncertain king who walks in disguise among his men, equally uncertain but willing to follow him. To grossly oversimplify, Olivier the actor takes over from Olivier the director, and he makes the final stage of Harry's coming-of-age seem completely real. That is also the moment when Olivier invented what has been called "the oblique close-up," where he sits thoughtfully and his character's soliloquy is delivered in voice-over.

Fact:
Olivier agreed to direct the film only after William Wyler and Carol Reed had passed on the project.

The battle itself is a grand piece of epic filmmaking that's set up by Olivier's stirring delivery of the famous St. Crispin's Day speech. Following it, the charge of the French knights across the field is a colorful, gaudy romp... until the arrows fly. If the sequence lacks the violent hand-to-hand intensity of some other cinematic combats, it's still superbly paced and choreographed, and it's photographed in bright, vibrant tones. Comparisons to *Alexander Nevsky* and *Charge of the Light Brigade* are not out of place.

See also

The Adventures of Robin Hood

Battleship Potemkin

Alexander Nevsky

Chimes at Midnight

Henry V (1989)

BRITISH WARS

Finally, though, perhaps the most incredible thing about the production are the circumstances under which the film was made. In 1943 and '44, German bombers were attacking England every night. Art directors Paul Sheriff and Carmen Dillon had to work with what they could find. All the crowns are made of papier-mache; the chain mail is woven wool sprayed with aluminum paint. It's easy to say that the "blood and toil and sweat and tears" spirit of the times informs the film itself, but Olivier is never that obvious. Yes, *Henry V* is patriotic and courageous. It's also an exciting portrayal of a pivotal historical event that never loses sight of the humanity of the people involved, kings and yeomen alike.

HENRY V

Cast: Laurence Olivier (King Henry V), Robert Newton (Ancient Pistol), Leslie Banks (Chorus), Esmond Knight (Fluellen), Renee Asherson (Princess Katharine), Leo Genn (Constable of France), George Robey (Sir John Falstaff), Ernest Thesiger (Duke of Berri), Felix Aylmer (Archbishop of Canterbury), Ralph Truman (Mountjoy), Harcourt Williams (King Charles VI of France), Max Adrian (The Dauphin), Valentine Dyall (Duke of Burgundy), Russell Thorndike (Duke of Bourbon), Roy Emerton (Lt. Bardolph), Robert Helpmann (Bishop of Ely), Freda Jackson (Mistress Quickley), Griffith Jones (Earl of Salisbury), John Laurie (Capt. Jamie), Niall MacGinnis (Capt. MacMorris), Michael Shepley (Capt. Gower); **Written by:** Alan Dent, Dallas Bower, Laurence Olivier; **Cinematography by:** Robert Krasker; **Music by:** William Walton. **Producer:** J. Arthur Rank, Laurence Olivier. **British. Awards:** National Board of Review Awards '46: Best Actor (Olivier); New York Film Critics Awards '46: Best Actor (Olivier); Nominations: Academy Awards '46: Best Actor (Olivier), Best Interior Decoration, Best Picture, Best Original Dramatic Score. **Running Time:** 136 minutes. **Format:** VHS, Beta.

Kenneth Branagh boldly challenges Lord Laurence Olivier's screen interpretation of Shakespeare's great History. If his version of the play isn't as technically innovative, it is tighter. It takes different risks and—for my money—it's even more moving. Branagh cuts to the core of the story and finds a coming-of-age tale about a young man who is not at all sure about what he is doing and finally realizes that he has involved two nations in that decision.

Like Olivier, Branagh takes an unconventional approach to the translation from stage to screen. The famous opening line, "Oh, for a muse of fire," is spoken by a Chorus (Derek Jacobi) in modern clothing. In a long tracking shot that will be echoed later, he walks through a soundstage, then throws open two tall doors. There, in a heavily shadowed room slouches young King Harry (Branagh), surrounded by older clerics and lords who tell him that he has every right to invade France. As they interpret history, it belongs to him, but when the French ambassadors show up, they have a different opinion and are scornfully disrespectful of him. In fact, they piss him off big time.

Meanwhile, Sir John Falstaff (Robbie Coltrane) is dying. Flashbacks taken from *Henry IV, Pt. 1* reveal the wild times that he and Harry shared with Ancient Pistol (Robert Stephens), Mistress Quickly (Judi Dench), and Bardolph (Richard Briers). But they're no longer part of his life. Instead, Harry has found the bear-like Lord Exeter (Brian Blessed) and Fluellen (Ian Holm) for military advice and guidance.

Though Branagh liberally cuts lines of dialogue to their essence, and even rearranges scenes, he leaves in two key elements that Olivier cut out. The first involves three treacherous aristocrats; the second has to do with crimes committed by one of his old pals. Both are key moments in Harry's maturation, and they set the stage for the film's final act, which is made up of the night before the Battle of Agincourt and the battle itself. Those long wonderful scenes are the point of the play and of both screen versions. The moment begins with the king in disguise, walking among his men, listening to them, and coming to understand their fear and their sense of duty. His long dark night of the soul ends with the literary equivalent of a prayer made in a foxhole.

When the sun comes up, Harry realizes that it is St. Crispin's Day. As the French knights ready themselves, thinking that they're prohibitive favorites, King Henry delivers the most rousing, kick-ass stem-winder in the English language. Branagh, the actor, wrings every drop of emotion out of the words. Branagh, the director, backs himself up with Patrick Doyle's stirring score, and from there, without missing a beat, the dramatic momentum sweeps into the battle itself. Unable to re-create the wide, panoramic fields that Olivier used for the charge, Branagh takes Kurasawa's *Seven Samurai* for his model. The Battle of Agincourt is staged in mud and rain, where the focus is on individual fights, not sweeping masses. It's brutal stuff, and it ends with a scene of true horror—the massacre of the boys accompanying the English army. In the Olivier film, that act ends the battle. Branagh takes it a step further to a more fitting conclusion with his famous 3-minute 48-second tracking shot. Though it can be dismissed as showing off, the

See also
Henry V (1944)
Platoon
Seven Samurai

"Banish plump Jack and banish all the world."

Falstaff (Robbie Coltrane) to Harry (Kenneth Branagh)

"We few, we happy few, we band of brothers.
For he to-day that sheds his blood with me
Shall be my brother; be he ne'er so vile,
This day shall gentle his condition;
And gentlemen in England now a-bed
Shall think themselves accurs'd they were not here,
And hold their manhoods cheap whiles any speaks
That fought with us upon Saint Crispin's day."

Harry to his troops

shot is the right way to end the scene—actually to end the film—with a moment that stretches and heightens the emotions. If the director couldn't add words, he could add the right image, and that is the primary difference between the stage and the screen.

In the end, after questions in style and audience expectations are accounted for, the main difference between the two films comes down to Olivier and Branagh's interpretations of Henry. To Lord Olivier, he's a king who is forced by circumstances to lead his people in a just war. To Branagh, he's a much less confident figure, a young man—by turns hot-tempered and fearful—facing the first tests of maturity and leadership.

Both interpretations are completely justified and both result in masterful films that are worth watching more than once.

Cast: Kenneth Branagh (King Henry V), Derek Jacobi (Chorus), Brian Blessed (Duke of Exeter), Alec McCowen (Bishop of Ely), Ian Holm (Fluellen), Richard Briers (Lt. Bardolph), Robert Stephens (Ancient Pistol), Robbie Coltrane (Sir John Falstaff), Christian Bale (Falstaff's boy), Judi Dench (Mistress Quickly), Paul Scofield (King Charles IV of France), Michael Maloney (Dauphin), Emma Thompson (Princess Katherine), Patrick Doyle (Court), Richard Clifford (Duke of Orleans), Richard Easton (Constable of France), Paul Gregory (Earl of Westmoreland), Harold Innocent (Burgundy), Charles Kay (Archbishop of Canterbury), Geraldine McEwan (Alice), Christopher Ravenscroft (Mountjoy), John Sessions (Capt. MacMorris), Simon Shepherd (Duke of Gloucester), Jay Villiers (Grey), Danny Webb (Capt. Gower); **Written by:** Kenneth Branagh; **Cinematography by:** Kenneth Macmillan; **Music by:** Patrick Doyle. **Producer:** Bruce Sharman, David Parfitt, Stephen Evans, Samuel Goldwyn Company. **British. Awards:** Academy Awards '89: Best Costume Design; British Academy Awards '89: Best Director (Branagh); National Board of Review Awards '89: Best Director (Branagh); Nominations: Academy Awards '89: Best Actor (Branagh), Best Director (Branagh). **Boxoffice:** 10.6M. **Running Time:** 138 minutes. **Format:** VHS, LV, Letterbox, Closed Caption.

Though it was hailed by some as the greatest war film ever made, this rousing adventure really doesn't attempt to be a realistic account of British colonial rule in India, and should not be judged as such. The movie's real importance—beyond its undiminished entertainment value—lies in its evocation of the exotic. If a *National Geographic* magazine from the 1930s could have been put on a theater screen, it would have looked like this. Yes, most of the exteriors were filmed in California mountains but they still feel somehow right. The plot combines blood-and-thunder military bravery with a two-sided look at male bonding that's much more serious than most of the "buddy" pictures that have followed.

The setting is somewhere on the northern frontier of India, sometime during the British "Raj." The 41st Bengal Lancers keep the peace there, though for years they have been trying to capture the wily Mohammed Khan (Douglass Dumbrille, who almost steals the film). Lt. McGregor (Gary Cooper) is an old hand assigned to show two new officers the ropes. Lt. Forsythe (Franchot Tone) is a transfer from a fashionably tony regiment, "the Blues," while young Lt. Stone (Richard Cromwell) comes to the Lancers straight from the military academy. He wouldn't be there at all if it weren't for Maj. Hamilton (C. Aubrey Smith), who knows that the gruff commander, Col. Stone (Guy Standing), is about to retire and wants to keep the Stone name alive in the history of the Lancers. Lt. Stone is his son, but the Colonel is far too much of a by-the-book soldier to show any favoritism, or even any emotion.

So it's up to the hot-tempered Mac and the smart-alecky Forsythe to set things right between father and son while, at the same time, extinguishing the flames of revolution, saving the Empire and all that. The story is so loosely basted together that it could easily have fallen apart, but the film never falters. Director Henry Hathaway, a thorough professional whose work has never been fully appreciated outside the industry, handles the material with precisely the right combination of humor and seriousness. Despite the adolescent fantasy aspects of the plot, Hathaway and his cast don't make light of the characters. Cooper and Tone are particularly complementary, each playing off and reacting to the other in unexpected ways. The relationship between father and son isn't as important, but it isn't neglected, either, and though the action is often talky, it's not slow.

The film was nominated for seven Academy Awards—including best picture, director, screenplay, and art direction—and the glossy look that a studio could give to a big-budget production is still impressive, even in something as simple as costuming. When these guys aren't decked out in khaki, jodhpur, and pith, they're spiffed up in ice cream suits and snap brim hats, or they're dolled up in their fancy dress uniforms, complete with plaid turbans that would make Carmen Miranda envious. That attention to appearance is an important part of the picture's appeal.

> "It has none of the panoramas of the real India and its peoples to be seen in *Gandhi* and *The Drum*; but it does have bungalows and tents just like the ones I lived in, and dusty maidans, (parade grounds), and long-tailed puggarees (turbans), and glittering lance-heads like those of the lancer barracks where we drilled, and what looks awfully like waitabit thorn but probably isn't, and the actors (even the Americans) seem truer to type than those of other films. Perhaps I remember India in black and white; I can only say that *Bengal Lancer* has an atmosphere that still strikes me as true."
>
> **George MacDonald Fraser.** *The Hollywood History of the World* **(Beech Tree Books. 1988)**

See also

Gunga Din
The Four Feathers
Beau Geste

As a serious comment on war, *Lives of a Bengal Lancer* may not have much to say, but as sophisticated lightweight adventure, it's hard to beat.

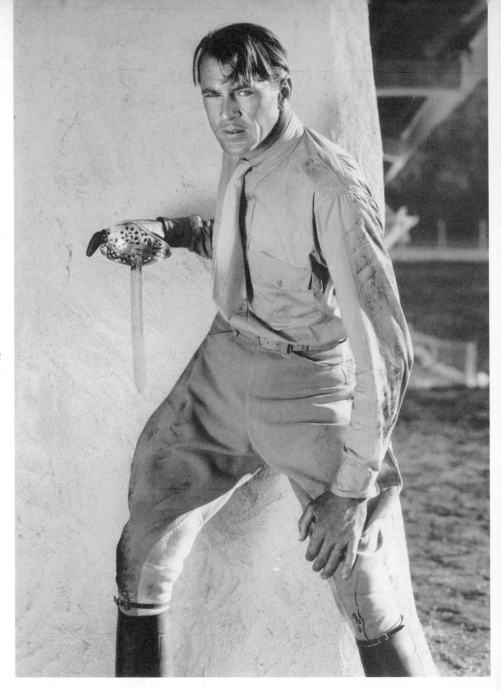

Gary Cooper is Lt. Alan McGregor in *Lives of a Bengal Lancer.* The Kobal Collection

Cast: Gary Cooper (Lt. Alan McGregor), Franchot Tone (Lt. John Forsythe), Richard Cromwell (Lt. Donald Stone), Guy Standing (Col. Stone), Sir C. Aubrey Smith (Maj. Hamilton), Douglass Dumbrille (Mohammed Khan), Kathleen Burke (Tania Volkanskaya), Noble Johnson (Ram Singh), Lumsden Hare (Maj. Gen. Woodley), Akim Tamiroff (Emir of Gopal), J. Carrol Naish (Grand Vizier), Monte Blue (Hamzulla Khan), Ray Cooper (Assistant to Grand Vizier), Leonid Kinskey (Snake charmer), George Regas (Kushal Khan), Reginald Sheffield (Novice), Mischa Auer (Amdi), Charles Stevens (McGregor's assistant), James Warwick (Lt. Gilhooley), Clive Morgan (Lt. Norton), Colin Tapley (Lt. Barrett), Rollo Lloyd (The Ghazi, a prisoner), Maj. Sam Harris (British officer); **Written by:** Waldemar Young, John Lloyd Balderston, Grover Jones, William Slavens McNutt; **Cinematography by:** Charles B(ryant) Lang; **Music by:** Milan Roder; **Technical Advisor:** Maj. Sam Harris. **Producer:** Louis D. Lighton, Paramount Pictures. **Awards:** Nominations: Academy Awards '35: Best Director (Hathaway), Best Film Editing, Best Interior Decoration, Best Picture, Best Screenplay, Best Sound. **Running Time:** 110 minutes. **Format:** VHS, Beta.

ROB ROY
1995 Michael Caton-Jones 🦴🦴🦴

Michael Caton-Jones's Scottish period piece will probably always be known as the other Men in Kilts movie of 1995. That may be unfair, but it does bear many similarities to Mel Gibson's over-sized *Braveheart*, telling essentially the same story of provincial resentment of overbearing English landlords. Director Caton-Jones and writer Alan Sharp pare Sir Walter Scott's massive novel down to a more recognizably human story that seldom strays from the formula for a contemporary action melodrama.

Robert Roy MacGregor (Liam Neeson) is a sort of overseer for the effete Marquis of Montrose (John Hurt) in 1713. The opening scene establishes the spectacular Scottish highland setting as Rob and his men hunt down a group of Tinkers (i.e. gypsies) who have stolen several head of His Lordship's cattle. Alan MacDonald (Eric Stoltz) sagely sniffs, and then nibbles a cow patty to deduce that the thieves are about two hours ahead of them. Soon enough, Montrose shows up with his villainous associate Cunningham (Tim Roth).

As that introduction suggests, the filmmakers are anything but subtle. Rob is a lusty husband to his equally lusty wife Mary (Jessica Lange), and a devoted dad to their kids. When he enters an ill-advised business arrangement with Montrose, he innocently leaves himself open to the schemes of Montrose's man Killearn (Brian Cox) and Cunningham. The unfolding of their treachery is the most original and enjoyable part of the film, though it takes a nasty turn with a violent rape. When Rob is finally forced to rebel against the redcoats, the action becomes more conventional, ending with the predictable duel between him and Cunningham. William Hobbs (see sidebar) is responsible for the fights. If Neeson and Roth don't have the graceful athleticism of Tyrone Power and Basil Rathbone in *Mark of Zorro*, they make the swordplay exciting in a more measured and calculated fashion.

> "One must never underestimate the healing power of hatred."
>
> **Montrose (John Hurt) to Cunningham (Tim Roth)**

Within the wildly baroque and improbable plot, the filmmakers try to achieve a degree of historical realism. Details of weapons, tactics, and clothing have rough edges that appear to be authentic whether they are or not. The crooked yellow teeth sported by most of the characters are probably true to the times, too, though they are a distraction. The film works best, though, through the male leads.

Neeson brings an oversized Gary Cooper presence and gravity to Rob. He gives the character heroism without the swagger. Roth's Cunningham dismisses himself as "but a bastard abroad" and dryly underplays the more outrageous characteristics. He really does steal the film from the good guys with a performance that earned him a Best Supporting Actor nomination. Hurt brings his usual deft touch with character roles to make Montrose something more than a bewigged pouf. All of them, and the supporting cast, boast such mush-mouthed accents that much of the dialogue in incomprehensible, though the simple plot doesn't suffer irreparably. Its conflicts pit the stereotyped inconsiderate British imperialist against the stereotyped sensitive native, and, of course, those conflicts arrive at a stereotyped Hollywood conclusion.

See also

Last of the Mohicans
Braveheart

Rob Roy MacGregor (Liam
Neeson) and the Duke of Argyll
(Andrew Keir) lead a charge in
Rob Roy. The Kobal Collection

Cast: Liam Neeson (Rob Roy MacGregor), Jessica Lange (Mary MacGregor), Tim Roth (Cunningham),
John Hurt (Marquis of Montrose), Eric Stoltz (Alan MacDonald), Andrew Keir (Duke of Argyll), Brian Cox (Killearn), Brian McCardie (Alasdair), Gilbert Martin
(Guthrie), Vicki Masson (Betty), David Hayman (Sibbald), Jason Flemyng (Gregor), Shirley Henderson (Morag), Gilly Gilchrist (Iain), John Murtagh (Referee),
Ewan Stewart (Coll); **Written by:** Alan Sharp; **Cinematography by:** Karl Walter Lindenlaub, Roger Deakins; **Music by:**
Carter Burwell. **Producer:** Richard Jackson, Peter Broughan, Larry DeWaay, Michael Caton-Jones, Talisman Films; released by United Artists.
Awards: British Academy Awards '95: Best Supporting Actor (Roth); Nominations: Academy Awards '95: Best Supporting Actor (Roth); Golden Globe
Awards '96: Best Supporting Actor (Roth). **Budget:** 28M. **Boxoffice:** 31.6M. **MPAA Rating:** R. **Running Time:**
144 minutes. **Format:** VHS, LV, Closed Caption, DVD.

The Hound Salutes: William Hobbs

Very few movie fans know the name William Hobbs, but nearly all of them have seen his work.

Hobbs is a fight and battle director, and he literally wrote the book on the subject. *Fight Direction for Stage and Screen* (Heinemann. 1980 and 1995) is a guide for fellow professionals, but any war film fan will find it fascinating. Hobbs began his work in the early 1960s with the British naval film *Damn the Defiant!* Over the decades, he has developed a distinctive rough-and-tumble style of screen swordplay that is immediately recognizable. Probably his most famous work is Richard Lester's Musketeer trilogy. He has also contributed to Shakespeare productions and Monty Python films.

As he explains in the book, his primary aim is to make physical action part of the narrative. At their best, his fights do not exist in a vacuum; they reveal character and move the plot forward. He has also realized that, just as acting styles have changed, fighting styles must change, too. The graceful gymnastics of Tyrone Power and Basil Rathbone in *The Mark of Zorro* are still enjoyable, but contemporary audiences have different expectations of action.

To understand that, take a look at the conclusion of Michael Caton-Jones's *Rob Roy*. In his book, Hobbs devotes four pages of notes and illustrations that explain the characters' movements and reactions in two fights. Diagrams block out the action for the director and the actors, and the results are two of the most important scenes in the film. Just as important to Hobbs, though, are preparation and safety. He believes in using actors, not stuntmen, whenever possible, and that calls for extra work. As Hobbs puts it, "The thing is, that an actor can act through the fight, something a stunt double may not be trained to do, and the acting of the fight and those particular moments within it is vital."

In one foreword, director Roman Polanski is quick to praise Hobbs's abilities as a teacher and coach to both actors and stunt people, and his ability to get the most out of their performances. He also notes Hobbs's creativity, the "new reality" that he has developed. Though Hobbs does not go into much detail in his book, it appears that he was a drama student who began studying fight techniques for use on the British stage, where he is still active, and then refined his ideas for the screen.

A selected videography includes Ridley Scott's *The Duellists*, *Robin and Marian*, John Boorman's *Excalibur*, Terry Gilliam's *Brazil*, Polanski's *Macbeth* and *Pirates*, *Dangerous Liasons*, Mel Gibson's *Hamlet*, *Cyrano de Bergerac* (1990), *Shakespeare in Love*, and *The Man in the Iron Mask* (1998). While you may not remember everything about those films, you probably remember the fights. I do.

Seen as an accurate depiction of a real historical event, this is one of the finest war films ever made. Though serious historians and military buffs will find fault on a few details, the film deals with such dramatic material that the conventional fictional excesses are unnecessary.

It opens on January 23, 1879, at the aftermath of a massacre. Several thousand Zulu warriors have attacked and destroyed a 1,500 man British column at Iswandhlwana. Word soon reaches the small outpost of Rorke's Drift, where about 100 British soldiers have a small hospital. Though Lt. Bromhead (Michael Caine) is in charge, Lt. Chard (Stanley Baker), an engineer whose men had been part of the column, actually has seniority. After some niggling disagreements about what they should do, Chard takes over and decides to defend the outpost. His first problem is a drunken pacifist preacher (Jack Hawkins) and his blonde daughter (Ulla Jacobsson). Then the Zulus appear on the horizon. Four thousand strong, they're determined, disciplined, and besides their short spears, they're armed with captured rifles.

The Brits are a mixture of committed soldiers and grumbling malingerers. To a man, they're fully believable characters who go beyond the stereotypes that they appear to be. Hook (James Booth) is the guy who can always find a reason to check himself into the hospital, though he knows that he's not going to get any sympathy from Surgeon Reynolds (Patrick Magee). The real power inside the compound is Colour Sgt. Bourne (Nigel Green). (Though those names may not be familiar, the faces are; these are some of the best of a fine generation of British character actors. Baker, also a co-producer, cast the film perfectly.)

Once the waves of attack begin, director Cy Endfield sets out the action skillfully. You always understand where the forces are in relation to each other and what each must to do defeat the other. At the same time, Endfield and writer John Prebble layer in the important details—how ammunition is packaged and distributed, how the troops line up and then are rearranged to face the attackers from various directions. "Mark your target when it comes," the Colour Sgt. barks repeatedly to his men. "Look to your front."

More significantly, Endfield, Prebble, and Baker strictly circumscribe the limits of the film, reducing it to the essential elements. It is about one battle and nothing more. A large group of men are trying to take a particular piece of ground. A smaller group is determined to hold it. Though the viewer's sympathies are clearly with the defenders, the attackers are not demonized or demeaned in any way. The film makes no mention of politics, history, or background. The legitimacy of the British presence is not an issue. Neither is race.

The fighting is shown in realistic detail, though it may not be as graphic as younger audiences have come to expect. The hand-to-hand grappling will seem a bit slowly paced and lacking in bloody flourishes to those weaned on high-octane action films. The emotions are real, though, and that's what matters. You believe

> "Brandy's for heroes, Mr. Hook. The rest of you'll make do with boils in your skin, flies in your meat, and dysentery in your bellies."
> **Surgeon Reynolds (Patrick Magee) to Pvt. Hook (James Booth)**

> "If it's a miracle, Colour Sergeant, it's a short-chamber box of Henry .45 caliber miracle."
> "And a bayonet, sir, with some guts behind it."
> **Lt. Chard (Stanley Baker) and Colour Sgt. Bourne (Nigel Green)**

Fact:
Director Cy Endfield was fingered as a Communist before the House Un-American Activities Committee in 1951. Blacklisted, he was then forced to work in England under pseudonyms.

See also

Bridge on the River Kwai
The Siege of Firebase Gloria

Michael Caine defends his small outpost against a large contingent of angry natives in *Zulu*. The Kobal Collection

those characters in that place—impressively filmed on location by cinematographer Stephen Dade. (Letterboxed, widescreen edition is the *only* one to see on video.) The final part of the cinematic equation is one of John Barry's best early scores.

Zulu is one of the greats.

Cast: Michael Caine (Lt. Gonville Bromhead), Jack Hawkins (Rev. Otto Witt), Stanley Baker (Lt. John Chard), Nigel Green (Colour Sgt. Bourne), Ulla Jacobsson (Margareta Witt), James Booth (Pvt. Henry Hook), Paul Daneman (Sgt. Maxfield), Neil McCarthy (Pvt. Thomas), Gary Bond (Pvt. Cole), Patrick Magee (Surgeon Reynolds), Dickie Owen (Cpl. Schiess), Larry Taylor (Hughes), Dennis Folbigge (Commissary Dalton), Ivor Emmanuel (Pvt. Owen), Glynn Edwards (Cpl. Allen), David Kernan (Pvt. Hitch); **Written by:** Cy Endfield, John Prebble; **Cinematography by:** Stephen Dade; **Music by:** John Barry. **Producer:** Stanley Baker, Cy Endfield, Paramount Pictures. **Running Time:** 139 minutes. **Format:** VHS, Beta, LV, Letterbox, Closed Caption.

FRENCH WARS

The Battle of Algiers

Napoleon

317th Platoon

Waterloo

French Wars on Screen

To most American moviegoers, the words "French film" imply a certain air of delicacy and intellectual snobbery, possibly mixed with sex—everything that the French war film is not. From the 1960s on, these movies have been notable for their hard, semi-documentary approach and tightly controlled emotions. They've also been based on a sophisticated political awareness that's seldom seen in similar American films.

The first major work is Abel Gance's 1927 epic *Napoleon*, restored to a version approaching its full length by Kevin Brownlow in the early 1980s. The massive work begins with Napoleon's childhood, touches briefly on the Revolution and the Terror that follows, and then ends as Napoleon's Italian campaign is beginning. The big battle scenes are impressively staged, and were a significant influence of D.W. Griffith's *Birth of a Nation*. Though the film is not to all tastes, and suffers somewhat on video, it is a remarkable work.

Russian Sergei Bondarchuk works with the end of the Corsican's career in *Waterloo*. Like the Gance film, it is worth watching mostly for the battle scenes. They are some of the most historically accurate ever put on film. The same cannot be said of Rod Steiger's maniacal interpretation of Napoleon. It, however, is easily overlooked within the impressively staged cavalry and infantry charges. The proverbial cast of thousands (some of them members of the Red Army) has never been choreographed so well.

The French involvement in Vietnam is the subject of Pierre Schoendoerffer's grim *317th Platoon*, the sadly prophetic story of a small group of Foreign Legionnaires trying to make a retreat after the battle of Dien Bien Phu. It's a rough black-and-white look at a nasty little war.

Gillo Pontecorvo takes a documentary approach to the French occupation of Algeria and resistance to it in *The Battle of Algiers*. Both films are implicitly critical of the government's actions, but neither can be reduced to propaganda. Without taking sides, they are about the human costs of guerrilla and terrorist campaigns.

And those films were not created out of nothing. The French tradition also goes back to Jean Renoir's 1937 *Grand Illusion*; Robert Bresson's fact-based POW drama *A Man Escaped*, from 1965; Schoendoerffer's second Vietnam film, *Anderson Platoon*; and Louis Malle's autobiographical *Au Revoir les Enfants*. All are discussed in different sections. Seen together, they reveal just how significant the French contribution to the genre has been.

THE BATTLE OF ALGIERS
La Bataille d'Alger
La Battaglia di Algeri
1966 Gillo Pontecorvo ♪♪♪♪

In the mid-1960s, while Truman Capote was creating his "non-fiction novel" *In Cold Blood*, Italian writer-director Gillo Pontecorvo applied the same techniques to film. *The Battle of Algiers* has been just as popular with critics and audiences as Capote's work, and, if anything, it has grown more impressive with age. Pontecorvo's *cinema verite* style has often been copied, but his ability to combine passionate political belief with cold professional style is rare. His subject is three critical years in the Algerian rebellion against French colonial occupation.

> "Why are the liberals always on the other side?"
>
> **Col. Mathieu (Jean Martin), answering a reporter's question about Jean-Paul Sartre's public support of the F.L.N.**

He begins the story in 1957, with a stunning scene. French soldiers have just finished the successful torture of an Arab prisoner. None of the horror is shown; the man's shattered reaction is enough to tell us what has happened, and his captors' solicitous reaction to his confession makes the scene even more unnerving. As the French close in on their real target, Ali La Pointe (Brahim Haggiag), the scene shifts to 1954. Ali's transformation from street hustler to revolutionary leader parallels the growth of the F.L.N. (Front de Liberation Nationale) as a significant opposition force to the French. Through assassination and intimidation, the group spreads its message of Islamic fundamentalism. Eventually, Col. Mathieu (Jean Martin) is brought in to deal with them. That's where the film begins to confound expectations and conventions.

Did you Know?

Producer Yacef Saadi also plays an F.L.N. leader on screen. He was acting from experience, having been part of the F.L.N. uprising in the Casbah.

Mathieu, who should be the villain, is an attractive figure—Martin is the only professional actor in the cast—who's simply there to do a job. If anything, he is in agreement with the aims of the F.L.N., but that doesn't change his tactics. And while Pontecorvo is clearly sympathetic to the Arab cause, he takes pains to show the human cost of terrorism. Perhaps the finest sequence follows three Arab women as they alter their appearances and identities, then are given bombs in handbags to plant in public places. At the time the film was made, it was criticized as an instruction manual for terrorists, and was banned in France. Today, the methods that it details are commonplace. Anyone who has followed the news has seen the same scenario played out from Belfast to Beirut. In 1965, it was more exceptional.

Pontecorvo, however, handles the distribution of the bombs with matter-of-fact realism. He and cinematographer Marcello Gatti use hand-held cameras, grainy black-and-white film, and long lenses to give the action a depersonalized quality. The characters deliberately lack identities, too. The audience is not meant to empathize with any of them on an individual basis. Instead, like Eisenstein's sailors in *Battleship Potemkin*, they're part of history in the making, replaceable figures who either advance or retard inevitable political tides. Despite that emotional detachment, the film is remarkably involving. Pontecorvo knows how to create and sustain suspense, and so he engages the audience on a voyeuristic level, if not an emotional one. You want to know what's going to happen next.

In fact, the film so deftly captured the tumultuous politics of the time that it was nominated for a Best Foreign Language Academy Award in 1966, and two years later, Pontecorvo was nominated as Best Director.

See also

In Cold Blood
317th Platoon
Is Paris Burning?
Anderson Platoon

French paratroops, led by
Mathieu (Jean Martin, with
bullhorn), try to persuade
cornered rebel leader Ali La
Pointe to surrender in *The
Battle of Algiers*. The Kobal Collection

Cast: Yacef Saadi (Kader), Jean Martin (Col. Mathieu), Brahim Haggiag (Ali La Pointe), Tommaso Neri (Captain), Samia Kerbash (One of the girls), Fawzia el Kader (Halima), Michele Kerbash (Fathia), Mohamed Ben Kassen (Petit Omar); **Written by:** Gillo Pontecorvo, Franco Solinas; **Cinematography by:** Marcello Gatti; **Music by:** Gillo Pontecorvo, Ennio Morricone. **Producer:** Antonio Musu, Yacef Saadi, Casbah Igor Films. **Algerian, Italian. Awards:** Venice Film Festival '66: Best Film; Nominations: Academy Awards '66: Best Foreign Film; Academy Awards '68: Best Director (Pontecorvo), Best Story & Screenplay. **Running Time:** 123 minutes. **Format:** VHS, Beta, LV.

Judged by any standard, Abel Gance's silent epic is a masterpiece, but the word carries with it images of a dry, high-minded, frowningly serious work, and that is certainly not true of this one. *Napoleon* is inventive, playful, screwy, and, almost a century after its creation, still surprising. It's also a film that challenges viewers with its length, loose structure, and some less than completely successful innovations.

The opening, which introduces our hero (Vladimir Roudenko) as a child in boarding school, sets a Dickensian tone. It's a snowball fight where Napoleon and his friends are surrounded by vicious attackers. Through sheer will and refusal to surrender, the boy perseveres. The scene itself establishes the strong visuals that Gance finds at every turn for the next four hours. (Different versions of the film, some meant to be viewed in serial installments, run even longer. Others, also edited by Gance, are shorter. The most readily available in America is the 1981 Francis Ford Coppola/Zoetrope edition of the Kevin Brownlow restoration.)

As Napoleon grows, the scene shifts to Paris, with the Revolution approaching its peak. As the city is subjected to incredible political upheaval, Napoleon (now played by Albert Dieudonne) undergoes his own transformations on Corsica, and then leads French forces in a successful battle. In that long central section, it's easy to see why a filmmaker like Coppola would be attracted to the film. Many of the techniques that were used so successfully in *The Godfather* films appear here. The most obvious is Gance's brilliant use of editing to synthesize disparate events into an emotionally complete whole. In the film's second most famous sequence, the movement of a camera swinging above the revolutionaries gathered at the Paris Convention matches the ocean's effect on a small boat in which Napoleon is escaping.

The influence of D.W. Griffith's *Birth of a Nation* is most apparent in the chaotic, graphically violent combat scenes. And like Griffith, Gance often includes other historical events—the assassination of Marat, for instance—even though they may be only tangential to his central story. Also, Gance's use of a symbolic eagle will strike modern viewers as intrusively overt.

Discounting differences in cinematic conventions and acting style, this Napoleon remains a fascinating character. As envisioned by Gance and Dieudonne, he's a driven, half-mad genius who's more than a little frightening. Amazingly, they manage to make him believable both as a historical figure and as a human being.

The film ends with the beginning of Napoleon's Italian campaign and Gance's most famous innovation, Polyvision. It's a precursor of Cinerama from the 1960s, with three images projected onto a wide screen, sometimes meant to create one wide panoramic view and sometimes framing a central image with a second mirrored image. To re-create the process on video, the image is suddenly

> **"I** have given myself three months to conquer Italy."
>
> **Napoleon (Albert Dieudonne)**

> **"If the Revolution does not spread beyond our frontiers, it will die here. Will you lead it into Europe?"**
>
> **The Spirits of the Revolution speaking to Napoleon**

Did you Know?

In the Corsican scenes, Napoleon is forced to flee the authorities in an extended chase on horseback. They're some of the most exciting scenes in the film and, according to Kevin Brownlow's fine book *Napoleon* (Knopf. 1983), they were exciting for the star, too. Bijou, the horse he rode, was obtained from a local bordello and had a nasty habit. In rehearsals, he would do everything asked of him flawlessly. But during the actual filming, he tended to be spooked by the sound of the cameras and would break into a run the moment he heard them. In one shot, he dashed under an olive tree when he was supposed to walk. Dieudonne was injured and unable to work for eight days.

See also

Birth of a Nation
The General
Waterloo
Charge of the Light Brigade (1936)

Napoleon (Albert Dieudonne) addresses his troops before the march into Italy. The Kobal Collection

and radically letterboxed and the overall effect is considerably less successful than it would be on a large screen. In fact, it's irritating. When Gance uses the process to layer superimposed images upon each other to reveal strong emotions, he's on firmer footing. Gance's pioneering use of lightweight mobile cameras does much more to involve viewers with the story. One long carriage ride, the rise of the Terror in Paris (where Gance himself plays Saint-Just, "the most awe-inspiring figure of the Terror"), and the "Thermometer of the Guillotine" are indelible moments.

Another important difference clearly separates Gance from Griffith. In looking back at the bloodiest and most violent moments in his country's history, Gance did not let romantic sentimentality color his vision. He doesn't gloss over the horrors of mob rule, and though he presents Napoleon as a heroic figure, he's also a dangerous deeply flawed man, and Dieudonne's performance captures those less-flattering aspects of his personality.

In the end, home video is not the preferred medium to experience *Napoleon*, but the film is such an important landmark that any serious fan should see it in any form.

Cast: Albert Dieudonne (Napoleon Bonaparte), Antonin Artaud (Jean-Paul Marat), Pierre Batcheff (Gen. Lazare Hoche), Gina Manes (Josephine de Beauhamais), Armand Bernard (Dugommier), Harry Krimer (Rouget de Lisle), Abel Gance (Saint-Just), Georges Cahuzac (Vicomte de Beauharnais), Annabella (Violine Fleuri), Georges Lampin (Joseph Bonaparte), Max Maxudian (Barras), Maurice Schutz (Paoli), Marguerite Gance (Charlotte Corday), Conrad Veidt (Marquis de Sade), Edmond Van Daele (Robespierre), Alexandre Koubitzky (Danton), W. Percy Day (Adm. Hood), Yvette Dieudonne (Elisa Bonaparte), Nicolas Koline (Tristan Fleuri), Vladimir Roudenko (Napoleon as a boy), Suzy Vernon (Mme. Recamier), Robert Vidalin (Camille Desmoulins), Paul Amiot (Fouquet Tinville), Suzanne Bianchetti (Marie Antoinette), Louis Sance (Louis XVI); **Written by:** Abel Gance; **Cinematography by:** L.H. Burel, Roger Hubert, Jules Kruger; **Music by:** Carmine Coppola, Arthur Honegger, Carl Davis. **Producer:** Abel Gance, Kevin Brownlow, WESTI/Societe Generale de Films. **French. Running Time:** 235 minutes. **Format:** VHS, Beta, LV.

Timeline—Important Dates in the History of War, Film, and Video

c. 8000 BC—The city of Jericho is fortified. Who's that knockin' at the door?

c. 900 BC—Samurai class emerges in Japan.

c. AD 750—Chinese invent gunpowder.

1220—Chinese develop shrapnel bombs.

1250—Moors use cannon.

1290—European artillery uses gunpowder.

1297—William Wallace defeats English at the Battle of Cambuskenneth. (*Braveheart*)

1299—English defeat Wallace at Falkirk. (*Braveheart*)

Oct. 28, 1415—English defeat French at Agincourt. (*Henry V*)

c. 1485—Leonardo da Vinci sketches multi-barreled machine guns.

1588—Dutch use explosive artillery shells.

1757—French and Indian forces attack Fort William Henry. (*Last of the Mohicans*)

1775–81—American Revolution. (*America*)

July 4, 1776—Second Congressional Congress passes Declaration of Independence.

1789–1810—French Revolution. (*Napoleon*)

1793—Eli Whitney invents the cotton gin and makes Southern slavery economically viable. (*Gone with the Wind*)

1800—Eli Whitney builds muskets with interchangeable parts on an assembly line and helps make Northern military superiority possible. (*Gone with the Wind*)

1815—English and European armies defeat Napoleon. (*Waterloo*)

Mar. 6, 1836—Mexican Gen. Antonio Lopez de Santa Anna takes the Alamo. (*The Alamo*)

1849—Conical bullet invented.

Oct. 25, 1854—Battle of Balaklava. (*Charge of the Light Brigade*)

Apr. 1861—Confederates attack Fort Sumter. (*The Civil War*)

May 1863—Grierson's Raid. (*The Horse Soldiers*)

July 1–3, 1863—Battle of Gettysburg. (*Gettysburg*)

July 18, 1863—54th Massachusetts attacks Fort Wayne. (*Glory*)

Apr. 15, 1865—Lincoln assassinated. (*Birth of a Nation*)

June 25, 1876—Crazy Horse and Sitting Bull defeat Custer at Little Bighorn. (*They Died with Their Boots On*, *She Wore a Yellow Ribbon*)

Jan. 22–23, 1879—Battle of Rorke's Drift. (*Zulu*)

1887—French inventor Louis Aime Augustine Le Prince produces moving images on perforated film.

1891—Thomas Edison develops Kinetograph camera and Kinetograph viewer.

1894—Kinetograph parlors open in America.

1902—Melies' *A Voyage to the Moon* released.

Dec. 1903—Wright brothers fly at Kitty Hawk, N.C.

1904—John Fleming invents the diode tube, making the cathode ray tube and television possible.

1905—Russian workers revolt. (*Battleship Potemkin*)

1907—Lumiere brothers develop color photography.

1914—Archduke Ferdinand assassinated at Sarajevo. (*Guns of August*)

Apr. 25, 1915—Australian and New Zealand forces attack Turks. (*Gallipoli*, *The Lighthorsemen*)

1915—*Birth of a Nation* premieres.

1915—German Zeppelins bomb England. (*Hell's Angels*)

1916—Arab forces take Aqaba. (*Lawrence of Arabia*)

1917—Russian Revolution. (*Dr. Zhivago*)

1920—Licensed radio broadcasts begin in U.S.A.

1921—Mussolini takes power in Italy.

1925—*Battleship Potemkin* released.

June 13, 1925—Inventor Charles Francis Jenkins broadcasts images from a Navy radio station to his laboratory five miles away on Connecticut Ave. in Washington, D.C. Television is born. (Scottish inventor John Baird performs a similar experiment either a few months later or a few months earlier, depending on which source you believe. Jenkins also patented the conical paper drinking cup, so I give him the nod.)

1927—*The General* and *Wings* released. Sound comes to the movies.

1930—*All Quiet on the Western Front* released.

1933—Nazis take over in Germany.

1935—Radar invented.

1936–39—Spanish Civil War. (*For Whom the Bell Tolls, Land and Freedom*)

1939—*Gone With the Wind* released.

Sept. 3, 1939—England declares war on Germany. (*Hope and Glory, Mrs. Miniver*)

Nov. 30, 1939—Russia invades Finland. (*The Winter War*)

1939—Hitler and Stalin sign a Non-aggression pact. Sergei Eisenstein's anti-Nazi propaganda film *Alexander Nevsky* is taken out of distribution.

1940—Luftwaffe attacks England. (*Battle of Britain, Hope and Glory, Mrs. Miniver*)

June 23, 1941—Hitler breaks the Non-aggression pact and invades Russia. *Alexander Nevsky* is re-released.

Dec. 7, 1941—Japan attacks Pearl Harbor, Hawaii. (*Air Force, From Here to Eternity, In Harm's Way, So Proudly We Hail, Tora! Tora! Tora!*)

Jan. 20, 1942—Nazi officials meet to discuss "the Final Solution." (*The Wannsee Conference*)

1942—*Casablanca* released.

Aug. 1942–Jan. 1943—Americans defeat Japanese on Guadalcanal. (*The Gallant Hours, Guadalcanal Diary, The Thin Red Line*)

1943—Germans massacre Jews in Warsaw Ghetto. (*Schindler's List*)

June 6, 1944—Allied forces land at Normandy beach. (*The Longest Day, The Big Red One, Saving Private Ryan*)

1944—Ballistic missile invented.

Dec. 1944—Germans counterattack Allies. (*Battle of the Bulge, Battleground, Hell Is for Heroes, A Midnight Clear, When Trumpets Fade*)

1945—Atomic bomb dropped on Hiroshima. (*Above and Beyond, Empire of the Sun*)

1945–6—Nuremburg trials. (*Judgment at Nuremburg*)

1952—Hydrogen bomb invented.

1953—Korean Peace Talks. (*Pork Chop Hill*)

1954—Viet Minh defeat French at Dien Bien Phu. (*317th Platoon*)

1956—Videotape recorder invented.

1956—Robert Adler of the Zenith Radio Corporation develops the "Space Command," the first practical wireless television remote control device.

1959—Lasers invented, making laserdiscs, CDs, and DVDs possible.

Jan. 30, 1968—North Vietnamese launch Tet Offensive against South. (*The Boys in Company C, Full Metal Jacket, Platoon, Siege of Firebase Gloria*)

1973—Helicopters evacuate the American embassy in Saigon, soon to be Ho Chi Minh City. (*The Deer Hunter*)

c. 1988—Home video revolution begins.

Jan–Feb., 1991—Persian Gulf War (*Courage Under Fire*)

c. 1998—DVD moves into the marketplace.

Sources:

American Spectrum Encyclopedia. Michael D. Harkavy, editor-in-chief. American Booksellers Association. 1991.

Larousse Desk Reference. 1995.

Museum of Broadcasting Encyclopedia of Television. Edited by Horace Newcomb. Fitzroy Dearborn. 1997.

Past Imperfect. Marc C. Carnes, general editor. Holt. 1995, 1996.

Watching: Four Decades of American Television. By Harry Castleman and Walter J. Podrazik. McGraw-Hill. 1982.

317TH PLATOON

1965 Pierre Schoendoerffer ♪♪♪♪

Pierre Schoendoerffer's fatalistic 1965 view of the French involvement in IndoChina can be seen as a preview to the American experience. The trappings, the characters, and the dramatic rise and fall of the plot have all been repeated both in reality and on film. Schoendoerffer scrupulously avoids any overt political statement, and so his film's relevance to what happened immediately after it was made is cast in sharp focus.

The setting is May 1954. An introduction explains that after nine years of fighting, the Viet Minh is on the verge of victory. The battle of Dien Bien Phu is in its second month, and various national delegations are about to meet in Geneva where, two months later, an armistice will be signed. The French Command has ordered the 317th Platoon to abandon its post in Luong Ba in Northern Cambodia, destroy what equipment they can't carry out, and withdraw 100 miles south to Tao Tsai. Under the leadership of Lt. Torrens (Jacques Perrin) and the veteran NCO Wilsdorf (Bruno Cremer), a few Frenchmen and their Cambodian allies make ready to leave. At the last minute, they decide that, because they like to drink their Pernod cold, they'll take the refrigerator. They become more serious when they meet the first of the advancing Vietnamese.

With location filming and rough black-and-white photography, the film has a familiar look. The weapons, uniforms, and jungle settings have been seen in hundreds of other films and countless hours of news footage. More significantly, the characters and their attitudes are ones that audiences know all too well. These French "advisors" display a superior disdain for the indigenous people while they indulge their taste for the local opium. They booby-trap bodies and, weather permitting, call in air support when things get tight. What may strike American audiences as strange (and will certainly put off many viewers) is the overall harshness of these personalities. These are not sympathetic characters; they're not meant to be. They're professional soldiers—one a veteran of the *Wehrmacht*—who enjoy war and killing. For reasons of their own, they're involved in a conflict that has nothing to do with them. It's hard to summon up much empathy for them, then, as the faceless Viet Minh come ever closer.

That coldness makes it difficult to maintain much emotional interest in the film, too. It is exceptionally well made, with a maturity that few American films of the mid-'60s possessed. Schoendoerffer, who directed from a script he'd written from his own novel, makes no effort to smooth over the characters' rough edges. To do so would undercut his larger historical point—that such wars are doomed. In *317th Platoon*, the idea is understated but unmistakable.

See also

The Siege of Firebase Gloria
Go Tell the Spartans
Platoon
The Boys in Company C
Anderson Platoon

FRENCH WARS

Jacques Perrin in *317th Platoon*.

The Kobal Collection

Cast: Jacques Perrin (Le Sours-Lt. Torrens), Bruno Cremer (L'Adjudant Wilsdorf), Pierre Fabre (Le Sgt. Roudier), Manuel Zarzo; **Written by:** Pierre Schoendoerffer; **Cinematography by:** Raoul Coutard; **Music by:** Gregorio Garcia Segura, Pierre Jansen. **French. Running Time:** 100 minutes. **Format:** VHS, LV.

WATERLOO

Sergei Bondarchuk ♫♫♫

To appreciate this realistic re-creation of one of Europe's most important battles, fans of war films must ignore the first hour. (Don't forget, every VCR has a fast forward button.) That part of the movie is devoted to Rod Steiger's maniacal portrayal of Napoleon. It may be his most apoplectic performance in a career not noted for restraint, and it is difficult to take him or the character seriously. As his antagonist, Wellington, Christopher Plummer makes the most of a less-flattering character, but neither of them is really that important to the battle itself, and that's a stunner. It takes up all of the second hour and is widely regarded as one of the most accurate depictions of a major battle ever put on film.

Novelist, historian, and screenwriter George MacDonald Fraser devotes several pages of his fine book, *The Hollywood History of the World* (Beech Tree Books. 1988) to *Waterloo* and flatly states that it is "quite the best battle film ever made, both as a motion picture and as a piece of history."

The story begins at Fontainbleu on Wednesday, April 14, 1814, with Napoleon having been driven back to Paris by armies of Austria, Russia, Prussia, and England. (Throughout the film, director Sergei Bondarchuk uses subtitles to identify place and time. Though the device seems intrusive at first, he is establishing its importance for the second half, when it keeps the action clear during the battle.) At the insistence of his advisors— chief among them Marshal Ney (Dan O'Herlihy)—Napoleon abdicates his throne and is sent in exile to Elba with his most trusted soldiers. Ten months later, he's back and a corpulent Louis XVIII (Orson Welles) dispatches Ney to get rid of him. Meanwhile, Wellington is in Brussels and knows that he'll have to fight again.

"Gin is the spirit of their patriotism."
Wellington (Christopher Plummer) on his troops

"I saw this ground a year ago and I've kept it in my pocket."
Wellington on his choice of Waterloo as a battlefield.

In that first half, the influence of Italian director Sergio Leone is hard to miss. The film is structured like a spaghetti western, with extended preparations for conflicts and long silent closeups. Alas, Napoleon isn't silent enough. He bellows, he rants, he convulses, he scowls, a single tear pools in the corner of his eye. Steiger leaves toothmarks on every stick of scenery. For his part, Plummer plays Wellington as a stiff-backed upper-class Brit with a certain roguish zeal. Though Bondarchuk, again like Leone, constantly intercuts between the two men, they never appear in the same frame.

Once Bondarchuk settles on the fateful clash of armies, the tone and look of the film change dramatically. The battle is fairly simple in strategic terms. The two armies face each other on hillsides with a shallow valley between them. It's a mostly open field, so each general can observe the other's tactics and troop movements. That's where *Waterloo* comes into its own. Seldom have so many extras been organized into marching and mounted units and then choreographed with the accompaniment of spectacular artillery barrages and roaring walls of flame. Bondarchuk goes far beyond the conventional crane and tracking shots of a few hundred horsemen or infantry moving across a flat plain. He uses high-angle aerial camerawork to show off thousands of extras (many of them members of the Red Army) moving in complex formations. In the most impressive of those, a tidal wave of French cavalry breaks against huge "squares" of British troops. No other comparable film comes close to the scope of Waterloo.

Glory
Zulu
Gettysburg
Birth of a Nation
Battleship Potemkin
Napoleon

The only criticism that can be leveled at the battle scenes concerns the lack of recognizable common characters. We never experience the action from the point of view of the guy on the ground with a rifle in his sweaty hands. Perhaps it's asking too much for one film to provide both perspectives, and Bondarchuk's sweeping overview is an impressive achievement.

Napoleon (Rod Steiger) stares down Marshal Ney (Dan O'Herlihy, back to camera) in *Waterloo*. The Kobal Collection

Cast: Rod Steiger (Napoleon), Orson Welles (Louis XVIII), Virginia McKenna (Duchess of Richmond), Michael Wilding (Ponsonby), Donal Donnelly (O'Connor), Christopher Plummer (Arthur Wellesley, Duke of Wellington), Jack Hawkins (Gen. Thomas Picton), Dan O'Herlihy (Marshal Michel Ney), Terence Alexander (Uxbridge), Rupert Davies (Gordon), Ivo Garrani (Marshal Soult), Gianni "John" Garko (Gen. Drouot), Ian Ogilvy (William De Lancey), Andrea Checchi (Sauret), Jean Louis (Oudinot), Willoughby Gray (Capt. Ramsay), John Savident (Gen. Muffling), Adrian Brine (Capt. Normyle), Jeffrey Wickham (Sir John Colborne), Sergei Zakariadze (Marshal Gebhard Blucher), Richard Heffer (Capt. Mercer), Aldo Cecconi (Charles X), Peter Davies (Lord Richard Hay), Eugene Samoilov (Vicomte Pierre Cambronne); **Written by:** Sergei Bondarchuk, H.A.L. Craig, Vittorio Bonicelli; **Cinematography by:** Armando Nannuzzi; **Music by:** Nino Rota. **Producer:** Dino De Laurentiis, Mosfilm, Columbia Pictures. **Italian, Russian. MPAA Rating:** G. **Running Time:** 122 minutes. **Format:** VHS, Closed Caption.

JAPANESE WARS

The Hidden
Fortress

Ran

Seven Samurai

Yojimbo

Japanese Wars on Screen

The four films in this section are the work of one man—Akira Kurosawa. It is completely unfair to limit one country's contribution to the genre to so narrow a cross section, but Kurosawa's films are the most widely known and available of the serious Japanese war films. And he always had an international audience in mind, even when it made his life and work difficult at home. In an article for *Look Japan* magazine, Nishizawa Masafumi outlines the difficulties that Kurosawa had with his own country. Those were largely a result of Kurosawa's refusal to compromise on expensive budgets and stories which studios were reluctant to back. As his career was beginning, the Japanese film industry had created a system that was meant to grind out large numbers of B-movies, not to realize individual artistic visions.

The most obvious example is *Seven Samurai*. It had a budget of 370 million yen, at a time when the studios were used to spending only two to three million yen per picture. And even though *Seven Samurai* eventually made a profit, many of Kurosawa's films lost money. Working within that environment, then, his achievement is even more astounding. As the Japanese say of themselves, the nail that stands up is the one that's hammered back down.

Kurosawa, who was born in 1910, uses his country's medieval past as a setting for tales of heroic figures who are often trying to create some order in a time of chaotic violence, where the old social structure has disintegrated. *Seven Samurai* (1954) can be seen as a variation on the American World War II unit picture. The tough sergeant is transformed into an unemployed warrior who recruits the men to fill out his squad and defeats a much larger enemy force. *The Hidden Fortress* (1958) is a more light-hearted adolescent adventure about two comic heroes caught in the middle of a three-sided civil war. Just as important as the characters and plot is the exotic fairy-tale landscape where the action takes place—steep mountain slopes, foggy forests, flooded dungeon.

In *Yojimbo* (1961), the wandering swordsman hero is looking out only for himself in a corrupt town ruled by dueling gangs. Again, the cold autumnal setting cuts across cultural and national lines, and gives the archetypal story universal appeal. (That's why it has been remade so often.) *Ran* (1985) is Kurosawa's mature masterpiece, an amalgam of *King Lear* and *Macbeth* that contains some of his most striking battle scenes.

Opinions will differ on this point, but these four titles are the high points of a great filmmaker's career. If, as Masafumi suggests, Kurosawa was more Western than Japanese, so be it. His films speak for themselves.

THE HIDDEN FORTRESS

Kakushi Toride No San Akunin • Three Rascals in the Hidden Fortress • Three Bad Men in the Hidden Fortress

1958 Akira Kurosawa ♪♪♪

Akira Kurosawa's lighthearted adventure is best known in the West as an inspiration for George Lucas's *Star Wars*. Lucas translates characters, situations, themes, and even landscapes from feudal Japan to a galaxy far far away, but Kurosawa wasn't working in a vacuum, either. It's easy to see the Hollywood influence on his work.

His two heroes—Tahei (Minoru Chiaki) and Matakishi (Kamatari Fujiwara)—come from a long line of mismatched cinematic comic squabblers such as Laurel and Hardy, Abbott and Costello, Sylvester and Tweety. (Sergio Leone and Eli Wallach might have found some inspiration for Tuco in *The Good, the Bad and the Ugly* in these scheming peasants, too.)

As the film begins, these two guys, whose greed is matched only by their stupidity, have just escaped from a grave-digging detail and are wandering across a sandy landscape as they try to get back home. They're farmers who sold everything they had to seek their fortune in war. Alas, they backed the wrong side, but they have figured out that if they can slip unnoticed into the Hayaka territory, they might then be able to go back to the Akizuki territory without attracting the attention of the Yamano guards. All this is necessary because Lord Yamano has placed a bounty of 10 pieces of gold on the head of Princess Yuki Akizuki (Misa Uehara). Our heroes would turn her in and collect the reward (they'd probably rat out their own mothers for the right price), but by then they've been tossed into the slammer.

They escape in an astonishing slave rebellion, reminiscent of the Odessa steps sequence in *Battleship Potemkin*. Eventually, that bit of business leads them to Gen. Rokurota Makabe (Toshiro Mifune), last remaining defender of the Princess and guardian of a cleverly disguised fortune in gold. Matakishi and Tahei would happily steal it, but Rokurota keeps them on a tight leash. Further complicating matters are hidden identities, warring armies, a resourceful young woman (Toshiko Higuchi) who's saved from bondage, and a princess who's lippy, bitchy, and sexy.

Just as important as the plot, however, are the rugged landscapes where the action is set. Kurosawa makes his steep mountains and fog-shrouded forests exotic and magical; places where anything might happen. The few interiors are just as impressive, most notably a flooded dungeon and the prison where the guys are held. The two best scenes are a long, almost ritualized duel with lances between Rokurota and his old opponent, Gen. Tadokoro (Susumu Fujita), and the ceremonial fire dance. Along with the escape of the slaves, they are the kind of big, carefully staged scenes that Kurosawa handles so well. But those larger-than-life moments work only because the individual characters are so strongly drawn. As the brief synopsis indicates, these are immediately recognizable transcultural archetypes—scheming peasants, regal princess, valiant warrior—and the film has a strong fairy tale quality.

The Hidden Fortress lacks the emotional power of *Seven Samurai* and the fast-paced action of *Yojimbo*, but it's about essentially the same subject—how an individual or small group survives when surrounded by larger warring forces—and it may be the most entertaining of Kurosawa's black-and-white films of that period.

See also

Yojimbo
Star Wars trilogy

Gen. Makabe (Toshiro Mifune) stares down an enemy solider in *The Hidden Fortress.* The Kobal Collection

Cast: Toshiro Mifune (Gen. Rokurota Makabe), Misa Uehara (Princess Yukihime), Kamatari Fujiwara (Matakishi), Susumu Fujita (Gen. Hyoe Tadokoro), Eiko Miyoshi (Lady-in-waiting), Takashi Shimura (The old general, Izumi Nagakura), Kichijiro Ueda (Girl-Dealer), Koji Mitsui (Soldier), Minoru Chiaki (Tahei), Toshiko Higuchi (The farmer's daughter), Shiten Ohashi (Samurai); **Written by:** Akira Kurosawa, Shinobu Hashimoto, Ryuzo Kikushima, Hideo Oguni; **Cinematography by:** Kazuo Yamazaki; **Music by:** Masaru Sato. **Producer:** Akira Kurosawa, Masumi Fujimoto. **Japanese. Awards:** Berlin International Film Festival '59: Best Director (Kurosawa). **Running Time:** 139 minutes. **Format:** VHS, Beta, LV, Letterbox.

THE HIDDEN FORTRESS

RAN

1985 Akira Kurosawa

Akira Kurosawa's mature masterpiece is an adaptation of Shakespeare's *King Lear*, with strong elements of his own *Throne of Blood*, itself a version of *Macbeth*. Such comparisons apply only to specific plot elements. In every respect this is one of the most significant achievements of world cinema—an epic of war, betrayal, madness and family.

As an old man, Lord Ichimonji (Tatsuya Nakadai) has consolidated a vast kingdom out of the confusion of feudal Japan. (The title refers to a Japanese character which translates, in part, as "chaos.") One afternoon after a tiring hunt, he decides that he will turn over his authority to Taro (Akira Terao), the oldest of his three sons. Jiro (Jinpachi Nezu), the middle son, agrees, but Saburo (Ryu Daisuke), the youngest, says no, claiming that the old man is sowing the seeds of discord among them. Enraged, Ichimonji banishes Saburo and divides his kingdom among the other two. Of course, he'll keep his personal guards, his concubines, his titles, his honors, etc. etc.

The only people who remain faithful to him are the sturdy vassal Tango (Masayuki Yui), and Ikoma (Kazuo Kato), the wise fool. The two sons immediately begin to plot against each other, though it's immediately apparent that Lady Kaede (Mieko Harada), wife of Taro, is the most Machiavellian, and perhaps the most powerful force in the kingdom. As their various schemes are spun out, the depths of Ichimonji's own cruel history is slowly revealed. At the same time, he could reverse his folly and atone for his sins if he only chooses to do so. But this is a classical tragedy—the story of a powerful man brought down by his own failings, even when he is given every chance to redeem himself.

Though the cast members are probably unfamiliar to most Western viewers, they manage to give these potentially stiff, cold characters believable personalities. The most memorable of them is Meiko Harada's Lady Kaede, who makes Lady Macbeth look like a Girl Scout.

Shakespeare purists may be put off by Kurosawa's vision of the Bard, but it's absolutely true in spirit. Instead of attempting to bring the poetic language directly to the screen, he translates it into image. Ichimonji's madness and terror are as real and as heartfelt as Lear's, and the reasons behind them are even more horrible.

Kurosawa carefully balances the incredible natural beauty of the Japanese mountains and its historic castles with the destruction of war. He tells the story in long, slow, virtually motionless takes, usually involving no more than two or three characters. When the wars begin, the action becomes graphic, bloody, beautiful, and terrible, with huge forces coursing against each other in vast tidal surges. The proverbial cast of thousands has seldom been put to better use. Kurosawa's mastery of the heavily populated panoramic shots is the equal of Eisenstein's in *Battleship Potemkin*. The first big battles are presented without sound, heightening the power of Toru Takemitsu's evocative score. The more limited scenes of violence are stomach-churningly realistic and frightening, though the passion of the concluding battle in *Seven Samurai* has been replaced by an older master's calm precision. That lack of conventional emotionalism is a criticism that could be extended to the entire film, but Kurosawa is looking for a deeper, more profound reaction from the audience. He deliberately

See also

Seven Samurai
Throne of Blood
Bridge on the River Kwai
Henry V (1944)

distances the viewer from much of the action, often presenting it as a stylized ritual, not as a realistic narrative. That's completely appropriate to the universal themes he is dealing with—characters and conflicts that rise above cultural and nationalistic differences. He succeeds so brilliantly that, for all practical purposes, *Ran* is a great film that's above criticism.

Cast: Tatsuya Nakadai (Lord Hidetora Ichimonji), Akira Terao (Tarotakatora Ichimonji), Jinpachi Nezu (Jiromasatora Ichimonji), Daisuke Ryu (Saburonaotora Ichimonji), Meiko Harada (Lady Kaede), Hisashi Igawa (Kurogane), Peter (Kyoami), Kazuo Kato (Ikoma), Takeshi Kato (Hatakeyama), Jun Tazaki (Ayabe), Toshiya Ito (Naganuma), Yoshiko Miyazaki (Lady Sue), Masayuki Yui (Tango), Norio Matsui (Ogura), Takashi Nomura (Tsurumaru); **Written by:** Akira Kurosawa, Hideo Oguni, Masato Ide, Masato Ide; **Cinematography by:** Asakazu Nakai, Takao Saito, Masaharu Ueda; **Music by:** Toru Takemitsu. **Producer:** Serge Silberman, Masato Hara, Herald Ace. **Japanese, French. Awards:** Academy Awards '85: Best Costume Design; British Academy Awards '86: Best Foreign Film; Los Angeles Film Critics Association Awards '85: Best Foreign Film; National Board of Review Awards '85: Best Director (Kurosawa); New York Film Critics Awards '85: Best Foreign Film; National Society of Film Critics Awards '85: Best Cinematography, Best Film; Nominations: Academy Awards '85: Best Art Direction/Set Decoration, Best Cinematography, Best Director (Kurosawa). **Boxoffice:** 3.52M. **MPAA Rating:** R. **Running Time:** 160 minutes. **Format:** VHS, Beta, LV, Letterbox, Closed Caption, DVD.

Big Screen vs. Small Screen

I remember seeing *Lawrence of Arabia* for the first time on the huge screen of a theater built for Cinerama in Charlotte, North Carolina. It was 1962. That's when I began to understand how powerful and moving a film can be. I remember, even more vividly, seeing the 30th anniversary restoration at the wonderful Uptown Theater in Washington, D.C. That 70mm image, beautifully projected on a wide screen, is the way the film was made to be seen and heard. To shrink it down to fit a conventional television, and then to lose even more of the size when it is "letterboxed" to re-create the original dimensions, diminishes the film's power by at least half.

Among war films, *Lawrence* is the most extreme example, but much the same holds true for most of the major studio releases from the 1950s until now. The reasons are simple. When television came into its own in the early '50s, Hollywood experienced an immediate drop in popularity. To give audiences something they couldn't see on those small black-and-white screens, filmmakers experimented with all sorts of techniques and gimmicks. The most common were the various widescreen processes—CinemaScope, Todd-AO, etc. And the studio heads who dreamed them up were essentially right. Those films do offer an experience that the best home theater systems still cannot reproduce. As we enter the digital future, that may change, but for now, the best combination of image and sound is still to be found in theaters.

Video, instead, gives us access to films that most of us would never have a chance to see otherwise. And the war films of the 1930s and '40s actually lose very little in the transition. In some respects—most noticeably sound—they may actually gain clarity on video. With the popularity of older fare on the cable channels *American Movie Classics* and *Turner Classic Movies*, many of the better black-and-white war films look better now than they have in decades. *Gunga Din*, *Lives of a Bengal Lancer*, *Wake Island*, *Bataan*, *Sahara*, *Five Graves to Cairo*, *Battleground*, and *The Third Man* are particularly impressive.

Of the "big" films that lose something on home video, *Bridge on the River Kwai*, *Dr. Zhivago*, *The Guns of Navarone*, *The Blue Max*, *The Good, the Bad and the Ugly*, *Apocalypse Now*, and *Glory* probably suffer the most. When a good director composes a shot and tries to fill the entire screen with information, some of it is going to be sacrificed in the traditional "pan and scan." That process trims the edges of the image and then tries to pick out the most important bits in the middle. When the image is letterboxed, with dark horizontal strips at the top and bottom of the screen, anything less than the largest monitor can make the result unwatchably small. Younger viewers who haven't seen these films should not avoid them on tape or disc, but they shouldn't be too critical if the video doesn't live up to what they've heard and read.

Of course, in a few years, we'll all have High Definition TVs, DVD machines, and really good microwave pizza. Until then, try to find the best copies available of your favorite movies in theaters or on home video.

SEVEN SAMURAI
Shichinin No Samurai
The Magnificent Seven
1954 Akira Kurosawa ♪♪♪♪

Ignore labels. Call it a war film, an adventure, a period piece—Akira Kurosawa's early master-piece is one of the few films that genuinely deserves to be called "great." Though the setting is 16th century rural Japan, the film's emotions and conflicts are universal.

Like so many of Kurosawa's works, this one is set in a time of civil war, when established law and order have mostly disappeared. The countryside is terrorized by groups of roving ex-soldiers who have been reduced to banditry. A small mountain hamlet has already been the target of a particularly fierce band when one of its citizens overhears the bandits plotting to return there after the next harvest. When he goes home with the news, the villagers are distraught. "Farmers are born to suffer," one of them wails, "Let's greet them meekly and give up our crops!" After con-siderable discussion, much of it along the same hysterical lines, four men are dispatched to a nearby city on a desperate mission to find unemployed samurai (or ronin) who will agree to defend the town for nothing more than three squares a day and the chance to fight.

The men's first efforts are met with derision, but then they find Kambei Shimada (Takashi Shimu-ra), a grizzled veteran who doesn't like the deal but knows it's the best he's likely to get. He finds the rest. The first is right at hand, Katsuishiro (Isao Kimura), a handsome young man of some means but no real experience. At first, Gorobei Katayama (Yoshio Inaba) isn't interested, but his fatalistic sense of humor leads him to reconsider. For Heihachi Hayashida (Minoru Chiaki), the choice is much easier. He's been reduced to chopping firewood, so even this job sounds good to him. Shichiroji (Daisuke Kato) is Kambei's old right-hand man, so he signs on right away. Finally, there is Kyuzo (Seiji Miyaguchi), the master swordsman who personifies lethal dignity.

But that's only six, isn't it? The drunken, boastful Kikuchiyo (Toshiro Mifune) fills out the group's ranks. He isn't really a samurai at all, but he so desperately wants to be one that he tags along, ignoring all the jokes and insults the others bait him with. Kikuchiyo manages to prove himself, too, though not as he had expected.

Almost the first half of the film covers that recruitment process, and it's beautifully paced. The slow duel that introduces Kyuzo stands alone as a brilliant set piece. The middle section moves back to the village and is focused on tactics, training, and the social turmoil sparked by the arrival of the samurai. Superficially, the relationship between helpless victim and valiant defender ought to be simple enough, but Kurosawa knows better. After conflicts have erupted in several areas, Kikuchiyo launches into a bitter soliloquy about farmers that encapsulates Kurosawa's views of Japanese social contradictions: "They pose as saints but are full of lies. If they smell a battle, they hunt the defeated! Listen! Farmers are stingy, foxy, blubbering, mean, stupid, and murder-ous! (Expletive deleted.) Damn! But then, who made them such beasts? You did! You samurai did it. You burn their villages! Destroy their farms! Steal their food! Force them into labor! Take their women! And kill them if they resist! So what should farmers do? Damn . . . Damn."

In the third act, the bandits return and the battle is joined. Those long scenes contain some of the most memorable action footage ever put on film. Kurosawa subtly uses a few moments of slow and fast motion to emphasize different types of violence. He also mixes

See also
Henry V (1989)
The Magnificent Seven
Yojimbo

the quick cutting that has become typical of large-scale action with several long, complex single takes in the middle of battle scenes. Still, the camera work is unobtrusive. He's not showing off when he follows Kikuchiyo through an intricate series of moves as he taunts the enemy, then retreats, climbs up a log and moves off it. That's simply the best way to tell that part of the story. The confrontation ends with the famous battle in the rain where the village becomes such a morass of mud that the black-and-white almost seems to bleed into sepia.

Throughout the film, but most notably in the last third, Kurosawa integrates the rugged mountain landscape with the action and the characters. In the same way, the sexual and social questions that have been raised earlier are brought to conclusion with the addition of several levels of irony as the physical action intensifies. Kurosawa is justly famous for his ability to create strong visceral action scenes and to deal with complex moral issues. His ability to work with actors hasn't been as highly praised, but he finds sterling performances in all the key roles here, particularly the three leads. Seiji Miyaguchi's laconic warrior who has nothing to prove crosses all cultural divisions. Takashi Shimura's rough-edged tactician is an engaging, likeable leader. They're both commanding performances by mature actors, but Toshiro Mifune owns all of his scenes. His character is the wise fool, equal parts clown and tragic hero, and Mifune plays him with such animated spirit that he becomes the film's core. But he does not define the film. All the parts that comprise this ambitious picture fit together so well that it's pointless to praise one over the others.

The *Seven Samurai* who protect a village of farmers from marauding bandits in Kurosawa's epic. The Kobal Collection

SEVEN SAMURAI

Like David Lean, Akira Kurosawa understands that the epic—and despite its relatively narrow limits, this is an epic—must be based on believable characters caught up in larger circumstances completely beyond their control.

Seven Samurai is one of the best by any measure. Watch it again.

Cast: Toshiro Mifune (Kikuchiyo), Takashi Shimura (Kambei Shimada), Yoshio Inaba (Gorobei), Kuninori Kodo (Gisaku), Isao (Ko) Kimura (Katsushiro), Seiji Miyaguchi (Kyuzo), Minoru Chiaki (Heihachi Hayashida), Daisuke Kato (Shichiroji), Bokuzen Hidari (Yohei), Kamatari Fujiwara (Manzo), Yoshio Kosugi (Mosuke), Yoshio Tsuchiya (Rikichi), Jun Tatara (Coolie), Sojin (Minstrel), Kichijiro Ueda (Bandit Leader), Jun Tazaki (Doomed, arrogant samurai), Keiji Sakakida (Gasaku), Keiko Tsushima (Shino), Gen Shimizu (Masterless Samurai); **Written by:** Akira Kurosawa, Shinobu Hashimoto, Hideo Oguni; **Cinematography by:** Asakazu Nakai; **Music by:** Fumio Hayasaka. **Producer:** Shojiro Motoki, Kingsley International, Toho Films. **Japanese. Awards:** Venice Film Festival '54: Silver Prize; Nominations: Academy Awards '56: Best Art Direction/Set Decoration (B & W), Best Costume Design (B & W). **Running Time:** 204 minutes. **Format:** VHS, Beta, LV, DVD.

Though some sources give mystery writer Dashiell Hammett partial credit for the script to this seminal adventure tale, it really belongs to Akira Kurosawa. He may have borrowed the concept of a lone man playing two opposing forces off against each other, but he simplified and streamlined the story so effectively that it owes little to Hammett. Variations on the theme show up in many of his other films, too, but he has seldom approached it with such single-minded diligence.

Title cards set the scene: "The time is 1860. The emergence of a middle class has brought about the end to power of the Tokugawa Dynasty. The samurai, once a dedicated warrior in the employ of Royalty, now finds himself with no master to serve other than his own will to survive . . . and no devices other than his wit and sword."

Such a samurai is Sanjuro Kuwabatake (Toshiro Mifune). His given name translates to "Mulberry Field," but he's such a hardcase that nobody laughs at him. Ever. Sanjuro is a twitchy, itchy, no-nonsense kind of guy who, when we meet him at a crossroads, doesn't know what to do with himself. In one of the movies' most famous establishing shots, he walks into a desolate small town, where he sees a dog running down the street with a human hand in its mouth. This, he realizes, is his kind of place. It's run by two warring gangs of gamblers, one controlled by Seibei (Seizaburo Kawazu), the other by Ushi Tora (Kyu Sazanka). As Sanjuro tells his first ally, the local bartender (Eijiro Tono), "I get paid for killing. Better if all these men were dead. Think about it. Seibei, Ushi Tora, gamblers . . . pretty nice to get rid of them."

He would have no problem taking care of things straightaway if it weren't for Ushi Tora's younger brother, Nosuke (Tatsuya Nakadai), who has a revolver.

> "Stop it! I hate pathetic people! I'll kill you if you cry."
>
> **Sanjuro (Toshiro Mifune) to people he has just saved from a fate worse than death**

The rest of the plot is a series of neatly duplicitous tricks and lies that Sanjuro uses to keep his opponents off balance. By comparison, the scenes of violence are short, explosive, and surprising. The first swordfight, where Sanjuro dispatches three opponents, is finished in five seconds. In part, at least, contemporary action films can trace their roots directly to *Yojimbo*. Sergio Leone remade the film as the spaghetti western *A Fistful of Dollars*, where more graphic depictions of explosions and gun violence gained some of their first mainstream acceptance. In Kurosawa's hands, however, that kind of action is only one part of the film, and not the most important part.

Working with his longtime collaborators, production and costume designer Yoshiro Muraki and director of photography Kazuo Miyagawa, he tells the story within a few blocks of this small town, giving the film a self-contained reality. That quality is reinforced by the chilly autumnal atmosphere. Most of the characters keep their arms tucked inside their kimonos for warmth, and the streets are often scoured with blowing dust and dry leaves. To keep the grim environment and the largely unsympathetic characters from becoming too oppressive, Kurosawa lightens the film with broad stripes of comedy. Even though Mifune turns in one of the screen's greatest macho kick-ass performances, he gives Sanjuro a self-mocking quality, and he gets scene-stealing support from moon-faced Daisuke Kato, who plays

See also

Seven Samurai
A Fistful of Dollars
For a Few Dollars More
Last Man Standing

Toshiro Mifune is a mercenary
samurai working both sides of a
war in *Yojimbo*. The Kobal Collection

the henchman Ino as the fourth Stooge. Finally, Masaru Sato's music, clearly inspired by Nino Rota, sets the right unpredictable but elegiac tone.

As the opening title cards suggest, this is a story about a warrior who has outlived his era. His sword is an anachronism in a time of firearms. The social order he once fought to uphold has vanished. To overcome his opponents he must rise from the dead, both literally and symbolically. The single act of mercy that he shows almost gets him killed, and at the end of the film, he's no better off than he was at the beginning. None of the remakes has come close to capturing that bleak vision.

Cast: Toshiro Mifune (Sanjuro Kuwabatake), Eijiro Tono (Gonji the sake seller), Isuzu Yamada (Orin), Seizaburo Kawazu (Seibei), Kamatari Fujiwara (Tazaemon), Takashi Shimura (Tokuemon), Tatsuya Nakadai (Noosuke), Daisuke Kato (Inokichi), Yoshio Tsuchiya (Kohei), Susumu Fujita (Homma), Hiroshi Tachikawa (Yoichiro), Kyu Sazanka (Ushi Tora), Ko Nishimura (Kuma), Ikio Sawamura (Hansuke), Yoko Tsukasa (Nui); **Written by:** Akira Kurosawa, Hideo Oguni, Ryuzo Kikushima; **Cinematography by:** Kazuo Miyagawa; **Music by:** Masaru Sato. **Producer:** Akira Kurosawa, Ryuzo Kikushima, Tomoyuki Tanaka, Seneca International Films. **Japanese. Awards:** Nominations: Academy Awards '61: Best Costume Design (B & W). **Running Time:** 110 minutes. **Format:** VHS, Beta, LV, 8mm, Letterbox.

RUSSIAN WARS

Alexander Nevsky

Battleship Potemkin

Chapayev

Doctor Zhivago

War and Peace

Russian Wars on Screen

The Soviet government of the 1920s controlled all aspects of Russian filmmaking. The medium that was just beginning to learn how to entertain mass audiences in Europe and America was appropriated by the Soviets to teach and indoctrinate, and so those first Soviet films are of limited appeal—mostly historic—to today's videophiles. That said, the early Russian filmmakers invented or perfected many of the basic techniques that are still in use today. The most famous example is editing. An acute shortage of film stock during the Revolution forced students at the Moscow Film School to experiment with what they had on hand. They learned how to take short pieces of film, which had nothing to do with each other when they were shot, and combine them to create a coherent narrative.

The result of the Russian work came to the attention of a worldwide audience with Sergei Eisenstein's *Battleship Potemkin*. The Odessa steps sequence is one of the most famous examples of early audience manipulation. That baby carriage is as indelible an image of the silent era as Chaplin's Little Tramp and Griffiths's Klansmen.

Eisenstein would attempt more conventional propaganda—conventional by Western standards—in *Alexander Nevsky*. There he translates Russian legends into a flag-waving anti-Nazi polemic that ends with another famous scene, the Teutonic Knights fighting on the frozen lake. It's a moment that demonstrates the enduring power of film. Despite some absolutely ridiculous costumes and dialogue that have gone before, the big finish is an involving, well-choreographed battle scene.

Sergei and Georgi Vasilyev are more realistic, but no less ideological, in *Chapayev*, the heroic tale of a peasant warrior of the revolution. The 1934 film casts White Russians as Nazi invaders.

The 1956 King Vidor *War and Peace* certainly owes more to Hollywood than to the Moscow Film School, and its main value now lies in an attractive, youthful cast led by Audrey Hepburn and Henry Fonda. The same might be said of Julie Christie and Omar Sharif in *Doctor Zhivago*, but David Lean treats the Russian Revolution seriously. Despite the fact that it was made during the coldest years of the Cold War, the film is remarkably even handed.

ALEXANDER NEVSKY
1938 Sergei Eisenstein

At the risk of making light of an acknowledged masterpiece of world cinema, it must be said that Sergei Eisenstein's second great piece of unashamed flag-waving propaganda (after *Battleship Potemkin*) has aged artlessly. Given the film's checkered genesis, that's almost inevitable. It's obvious that Eisenstein is uncomfortable with the basic premise, and though the film was made at the beginning of the sound era, he never accepted sound as a useful part of film. While the big frozen lake scene is still studied and imitated by filmmakers, the whole work lacks enthusiasm and life. Today, *Alexander Nevsky* is most notable for its impressive battlefield orchestration, big crowd scenes, pneumatic heroines, and stiffbacked heroes. Actually, its most obvious successors are those lumbering historical epics that Hollywood cranked out in the 1950s. In fact, a young Troy Donohue in a blond Prince Valiant wig would have been perfect as the lead.

> "If you died for Russia, you died a noble death!"
>
> Song sung by the Spirit of the Motherland as the dead and wounded are collected after '"The Battle on the Ice" in "Alexander Nevsky.

But the title role went to square-jawed Nikolai Cherkasov. As the opening credits explain, "13th Century Teutonic Knights were advancing upon Russia from the west. Russia's vast lands and riches attracted the invaders. The Germans expected an easy victory." The rest of the film is equally blunt and blatant. As the Germans approach, Russian nobles and peasants implore Alexander (Cherkasov), a hero in the last war, to raise an army and lead them. A few traitorous aristocrats disagree, advocating immediate capitulation to the invaders. Meanwhile, the Teutonic Knights, whose crucifix symbol is reminiscent of a swastika, are literally throwing children into a bonfire. With their armor, tall helmets, white capes, and robed horses, they're as visually impressive as D.W. Griffith's Klansmen in *Birth of a Nation*. (Virtually identical robed riders and horses would reappear in the 1970s as supernatural monsters in Armando de Ossorio's *Blind Dead* horror films.)

In a laborious subplot, two young men vying for the hand of the same girl decide that the most valorous in battle will win her. Another young woman disguises herself as a man so she can join the fight. During the extended preparations, the characters who aren't making speeches tend to speak in fortune cookie aphorisms. "What makes a sword strong? The arm that wields it."

Modern viewers who can get past those excesses will find that the famous sequence on the frozen Lake Chudskoye is still one of the finest medieval battle scenes ever put on film. Whether it's accurate or plausible, the tactics of the engagement are clearly choreographed and the whole thing is played out in fine dramatic fashion. The icy landscape is an eerie setting for the knights and their horses, all in white. (At the same time, some of the other costumes and the bowl haircuts give the action a dated, silly quality.) The battle itself is filled with exciting moments and Prokofiev's rousing score is one of the finest pieces of film music ever written. Eisenstein actually conceived the work more as a "cinematic symphony" (*A Short History of the Movies*, Gerald Mast) than as a conventional narrative. Even so, nothing here matches the visual complexity of *Potemkin*.

Throughout the film, it's apparent that the central theme of the individual hero-redeemer was not to Eisenstein's liking. As a dedicated communist, he didn't agree with that kind of cinematic storytelling. But he was also a filmmaker who wanted to work. During the course

See also
Battleship Potemkin
Birth of a Nation
Waterloo

Nikolai Cherkasov is medieval
Russian warrior Prince
Alexander Nevsky. The Kobal Collection

of his career, political realities had changed. *Battleship Potemkin* was made in 1925 under Lenin, when the ideals of the Russian Revolution were still fresh and vital. When *Alexander Nevsky* was made in 1938, Stalin was in power and Hitler was an immediate military threat to the Soviet Union. The film was conceived and executed as propaganda to rouse the Soviet citizenry, to move them to action without making the Germans seem invincible. Judged then as propaganda, it succeeds brilliantly—so brilliantly that it didn't survive the next change in political reality. A year later, in 1939 when Hitler and Stalin signed a Non-aggression Pact, *Alexander Nevsky* was abruptly withdrawn from distribution. But, as we know, what goes 'round comes 'round. On June 23, 1941, the day after Hitler broke the treaty and German forces invaded Russia, the film found itself back in favor.

ALEXANDER NEVSKY

Cast: Nikolai Cherkasov (Prince Alexander Nevsky), Nikolai P. Okhlopkov (Vasili Buslai), Andrei Abrikosov (Gavrilo Oleksich), Alexandra Danilova (Vasilisa), Dmitri Orlov (Vasili Buslai), Vera Ivasheva (Olga Danilovna), Sergei Blinnikov (Tverdilo, Traitorous Mayor of Pskov), Lev Fenin (Archbishop), Vladimir Yershov (Von Balk, Master of the Teutons), Nikolai Arsky (Domash Tverdislavich), Naum Rogozhin (Black-Cowled Monk), Varvara O. Massalitinova (Mother Buslai), Vasili Novikov (Pasha, Governor of Pskov), Ivan Lagutin (Anasias); **Written by:** Sergei Eisenstein, Pyotr Pavlenko; **Cinematography by:** Eduard Tisse; **Music by:** Sergei Prokofiev. **Russian. Running Time:** 110 minutes. **Format:** VHS, LV, DVD.

BATTLESHIP POTEMKIN
Potemkin
Bronenosets Potemkin

1925 Grigori Alexandrov, Sergei Eisenstein 𝄞𝄞𝄞𝄞

Sergei Eisenstein's unembarrassed propaganda is one of the silent screen's first international hits. Short and swiftly paced, it remains a remarkably watchable work, too, for at least part of its running time. Contemporary audiences new to the film will be astonished at how often its big scenes have been copied and borrowed. Though the film was commissioned by the Soviet government and is very much an "official" version of history, its politics don't get in the way.

In 1925, the Soviets ordered an eight-part series of films about the glorious revolution of 1905. This is the only section that was ever produced. It tells a simple five-act story of the mutiny of the crew of the battleship *Potemkin*, the reaction of the citizens of Odessa when the ship docks there, and finally, its encounter with the rest of the Russian Navy. The immediate inspiration for the mutiny is rotten meat that the sailors refuse to eat. That act precipitates a tense confrontation between the crew and their officers, dramatically staged on the ship's foredeck beneath massive cannon barrels.

The scene that everyone knows is the justly famous six-minute massacre on the Odessa steps where Cossacks attack the citizens who are supporting the mutineers. Boots, baby carriage, umbrella, woman carrying her son's body, lady with the glasses, horrified lions' reaction. The fact that the images have become cinematic cliches is an affirmation of their power. But the sequence has been reworked so often that now it seems somehow unfinished or unsatisfying. The most obvious example is the woman and the boy. If the film were made today, we'd know more about them before they arrived at the steps and we would see their deaths. But times have changed and so have audience expectations of cathartic violence. The intent of the scene has not changed. It means to involve viewers on one side of the action and to show that side in the most sympathetic light possible. If imitation really is the most sincere form of praise, Eisenstein succeeded beyond any expectations.

> "Kill the brass mounted tyrants! Shoot them down!"
> — **Mutineer**

In a larger historical sense, it may be more useful to think of *Battleship Potemkin* as a young nation's first image of itself, the cinematic equivalent of *The Spirit of '76*, Archibald Willard's famous painting of the three American Revolutionary War veterans marching with fife, drum, and flag. At the painting's debut, a gallery owner called it "an embodiment of the hardships of the Revolution" and the filmmaker probably wouldn't have been too disappointed with that blurb, either. Eisenstein was a believer, a son of the revolution who was trying to tell a different kind of story, one largely without individual characters. His stated purpose was to make "the proletariat" the hero of the piece. The single named protagonist, Vakulinchuk (Alexander Antonov, who eerily resembles football coach Mike Ditka when he calls for "direct action") makes an early sacrificial exit. Tellingly, the officer-villains do have sharply etched, mustachio-twirling personalities. Even if Eisenstein wanted his audience to identify with the heroic masses, he gave them an individual enemy with a recognizable face to hate.

See also
The Untouchables
Mutiny on the Bounty
The Caine Mutiny
Birth of a Nation

The rest of the story is told through the masses. Almost all of the big scenes are built around carefully orchestrated shots of large groups of people. Judged by any standard of any era, these are really complex, large-scale crowd scenes, almost always involving

BATTLESHIP POTEMKIN 117

The famous, often-imitated Odessa steps scene from *Battleship Potemkin*. The Kobal Collection

opposing or bidirectional mass movements on different planes. Whatever one thinks of the film's politics, the screen is often filled with striking shapes and movements.

In the second half, the film loses its strong kinetic energy when the action involves ships instead of human beings. At the same time, Eisenstein allows his politics to undercut the drama and the film comes to a comparatively weak conclusion. Today, the film's importance is historical and political. Eisenstein's ideas about characters and dramatic structure have proved to be about as popular and enduring as Marxist economics.

The Republic Pictures tape retains the Russian title cards with English translations. Some others do not.

Cast: Alexander Antonov (Vakulinchuk), Vladimir Barsky (Capt. Golikov), Grigori Alexandrov (Chief Officer Gilyarovsky), Mikhail Gomorov (Sailor Matyushenko), Sergei Eisenstein (Ship's Chaplain), I. Brobov (Sailor), Beatrice Vitoldi (Woman with baby carriage), N. Poltavseva (School teacher), Alexandr Levshin (Petty Officer), Repnikova (Woman on the Odessa steps), Korobei (Legless veteran), Levchenko (Boatswain); **Written by:** Nina Agadzhanova Shutko, Sergei Eisenstein; **Cinematography by:** Eduard Tisse; **Music by:** Dimitri Shostakovich. **Producer:** Goskino. **Russian. Running Time:** 71 minutes. **Format:** VHS, Beta, LV, DVD.

If this piece of revolutionary propaganda had been made in America, it might well have been directed by John Ford and starred John Wayne. The film is unashamed hero-worship of a rough-hewn common man who bravely steps forward in a time of trouble and becomes a reluctant leader. In this case, though, he's a card-carrying Soviet member of the Red Army.

As portrayed here, Chapayev (Boris Babochkin) is one of nature's noblemen, a genuine folk hero who has risen through the ranks and inspires everyone he comes in contact with to stand firm against the White Russians. The war between the Reds and Whites has been going on for some time as the story begins, without explanation. Soviet audiences of the 1930s would not need any background. Contemporary viewers, however, will at first be mystified by this figure who comes charging into a village on a horse-dawn cart towing a large-caliber machine gun on a trailer. With all the jingling bells on the harness, he's a sort of mythic warrior-Santa who rallies his dispirited countrymen . . . and countrywomen. Anna (Varvara Myasnikova) wants to learn how to operate the machine gun and she's not about to stand for the crude moves that one soldier tries to put on her when she asks for instruction.

"In war everything is allowed."

Unnamed soldier's rationale for stealing a pig from a protesting peasant

The rambling first half establishes civilian-military conflicts and Chapayev's bona fides as a peasant, someone who understands both sides. He's a self-taught soldier whose ideas about tactics are explained in a wonderfully bombastic demonstration with potatoes. When young Furmanov (Boris Blinov) is assigned as the region's new commissar, making him Chapayev's superior, trouble appears to be eminent. At about the same time, though, the White Army arrives. With their black uniforms and death-head flag, they're none-too-subtle stand-ins for Nazis, and that is the point. Though they are somewhat dated, the battle scenes are the most vigorous parts of the film. The obvious comparison here is Eisenstein's *Alexander Nevsky*, made four years later, though *Chapayev* is so much more realistic that the two films have little to do with each other.

Directors Georgy and Sergei Vasilyev—who were called brothers even though they were not related—worked for the state film company and their real objectives here are never in question. This is inspirational propaganda; the story of a brave, seasoned hero and the sympathetic bureaucrat who loves the older man and tries to help him adjust to changing times. The Vasilyevs also try to smooth over internal civilian-military conflicts. Seen today, the political manipulation is so transparent that it's never offensive and the whole disjointed tale is made more palatable by a quirky sense of humor. *Chapayev* is too rough, too "foreign" for most audiences today, but it's also engagingly unsophisticated and passionate.

See also

Seven Samurai
Alexander Nevsky
The Red Badge of Courage
Come and See

Chapayev (Boris Babochkin)
leads the Bolsheviks against the
White Russians. The Kobal Collection

Cast: Boris Babochkin (Gen. Chapayev), Leonid Kmit (Petka), Boris Chirkov, Varvara Myasnikova (Anna), Illarian Pevzov (Borosdin), Stephan Shkurat, Boris Blinov (Furmanov), Vyacheslav Volkov, Nikolai Simonov, Georgi Zhzhenov; **Written by:** Sergei Vassiliev, Georgy Vassiliev; **Cinematography by:** Aleksander Sigayev, Alexander Xenofontov; **Music by:** Gavriil Popov. **Producer:** Lenfilm. **Russian. Running Time:** 101 minutes. **Format:** VHS, Beta.

Though it doesn't equal *Lawrence of Arabia*, David Lean's epic wartime romance may be his most accessible film. It tells a simple love story in a complex setting and, for the most part, avoids easy resolutions to messy emotional relationships. Even though the focus is squarely on those relationships, everything in the film revolves around the Russian Revolution. The vagaries of both World War I and the prolonged struggles among the various Bolshevik factions are the driving forces behind the plot.

In adapting Boris Pasternak's novel to the screen, writer Robert Bolt tells the story in flashback, with the powerful Gen. Yevgraf Zhivago (Alec Guinness) questioning a teenaged girl (Rita Tushingham) about her past. He thinks she might be the daughter of his brother Yuri (Omar Sharif) and Lara (Julie Christie). Flashback to their youth and the first time that Yuri and Lara's paths cross on a streetcar. He's a promising, prosperous medical student and poet, engaged to his childhood sweetheart Tonya (Geraldine Chaplin). Lara is the daughter of a dressmaker who has a long-term "arrangement" with Komarovsky (Rod Steiger), a well-connected lawyer who understands the political changes that are coming. Lara's fiance Pasha (Tom Courtenay) is an idealistic revolutionary who is part of that change. Komarovsky's interest in Lara is not platonic.

> "There are two kinds of women and you, as we well know, are not the first."
> **Komarovsky (Rod Steiger) to Lara (Julie Christie)**

> "People will be different after the revolution."
> **Pasha (Tom Courtenay)**

As those relationships are being sorted out, protesters are marching in the streets and the Czar's troopers are taking them seriously. In the first big confrontation between a demonstration and a cavalry charge on snow-covered streets, Lean avoids the inevitable comparisons to Eisenstein's Odessa steps scene in *Battleship Potemkin*, but he can't help but make a few references to it. The clash in the streets also serves as a counterpoint to Komarovsky's seduction of Lara, and the two elements are deftly interwoven. The combination of the personal and the political has seldom been so seamless or effective as it is in that long sequence.

The most memorable scenes, however, take place during World War I and the revolution: a mass of deserters meets a mass of replacement troops on a lonely road; Yuri and family embark on a long grim rail journey from Moscow to the Urals and negotiate territory controlled at times by Red Guards and at times by White Guards; a machine gun attack on an unseen enemy across a field; Yuri's being dragooned into service and then his long trek back home through the snow.

The Cold War being what it was in 1965, Lean was denied permission to make the film in the Soviet Union, but Spain, Finland, and Canada are more than adequate substitutes. They give the film an impression of stark, beautiful expanse. Lean's canvas is the full-width Panavision screen. He and cinematographers Freddie Young (who won an Oscar) and Nicolas Roeg use all of it in both interior and exterior scenes. Ideally, the film should be seen in a theater. Failing that, find a letterboxed tape or disc. Ignore pan-and-scan editions.

See also
Lawrence of Arabia
Ryan's Daughter
Battleship Potemkin
War and Peace

On the other hand, some of Lean's devices—the use of mirrors and windows, lighting that isolates eyes in shadowed faces, Guinness's voice-overs to bridge narrative gaps—are overused. In a film of this size, those are minor flaws. Finally, like all love stories, this one

Dr. Zhivago (Omar Sharif) and Lara (Julie Christie) tend to wounded soldiers. The Kobal Collection

depends on viewers' involvement with the characters, and these work very well. The two leads are attractive, but not in conventional Hollywood terms, and their supporting cast could not be better. Courtenay was nominated for a Supporting Actor Oscar, but Steiger's Komarovsky is an indelible archetypal survivor.

Doctor Zhivago remains one of the most ambitious and watchable of the "big" '60s films, and one of the best depictions of a civil war's terrible human costs.

Cast: Omar Sharif (Yuri Zhivago), Julie Christie (Lara), Geraldine Chaplin (Tonya), Rod Steiger (Komarovsky), Alec Guinness (Gen. Yevgraf Zhivago), Klaus Kinski (Kostoyed), Ralph Richardson (Alexander Gromeko), Rita Tushingham (The girl), Siobhan McKenna (Anna), Tom Courtenay (Pasha/Strelnikov), Bernard Kay (Bolshevik), Gerard Tichy (Liberius), Noel Willman (Razin), Geoffrey Keen (Prof. Kurt), Adrienne Corri (Amelia), Jack MacGowran (Petya), Mark Eden (Dam engineer), Erik Chitty (Old soldier), Peter Madden (Political officer), Jose Maria Caffarell (Militiaman), Jeffrey Rockland (Sasha), Wolf Frees (Comrade Yelkin), Lucy Westmore (Katya); **Written by:** Robert Bolt; **Cinematography by:** Frederick A. (Freddie) Young, Nicolas Roeg; **Music by:** Maurice Jarre. **Producer:** Carlo Ponti, MGM. **Awards:** Academy Awards '65: Best Adapted Screenplay, Best Art Direction/Set Decoration (Color), Best Color Cinematography, Best Costume Design (Color), Best Original Score; American Film Institute (AFI) '98: Top 100; Golden Globe Awards '66: Best Actor—Drama (Sharif), Best Director (Lean), Best Film—Drama, Best Screenplay, Best Score; National Board of Review Awards '65: Best Actress (Christie); Nominations: Academy Awards '65: Best Director (Lean), Best Film Editing, Best Picture, Best Sound, Best Supporting Actor (Courtenay). **Budget:** 11M. **Boxoffice:** 111.72M. **MPAA Rating:** PG-13. **Running Time:** 197 minutes. **Format:** VHS, Beta, LV, Letterbox, Closed Caption.

The Hound Salutes: David Lean

Fair or not, David Lean will always be identified with the big-budget, widescreen epic. It's a cinematic style that's dated now—more dated than many films of the 1940s—and it does not translate well to video. Those epics of the '50s and '60s were produced as competition to television, and Lean, of all the practitioners, made full use of his massive canvas.

Actually, his first war film is relatively modest, and it's one of his best. Lean worked his way up the British film industry to the director's chair, beginning as a "tea-boy" in 1927, then learning other jobs until he became a film editor. Noel Coward gave him his first shot behind the camera on his top-drawer propaganda, *In Which We Serve*, and the two men share director's credit.

After the war, Lean turned to Dickens, with adaptations of *Great Expectations* and *Oliver Twist*, and romance with *Brief Encounter*, which received his first Oscar nomination. It was the next three films, though, that set his reputation in stone. He became the director of choice for expensive, prestigious productions with an exotic locale and a backdrop of armed conflict.

First was *Bridge on the River Kwai*, a smash hit that dominated the Academy Awards and the boxoffice. Hidden beneath the sheer scope of the film is a simple story of a contest of will between two men—Alec Guinness and Sessue Hayakawa—who are more alike than different. Five years later, Lean topped himself with *Lawrence of Arabia*, considered by many to be the finest "epic" war film ever made. The combination of stunning desert photography with a carefully shaded character study is really more than home video can handle. (See Big Screen vs. Small Screen sidebar.)

Though *Dr. Zhivago* may suffer in comparison to *Lawrence*, it's a superb love story with some of Lean's most evocative location work. After it, he made *Ryan's Daughter*, an attempt to comment on the Irish "troubles." Unlike the other three, it was poorly received by critics and viewers but, to my mind, it is an underrated and enjoyable film, really more successful than his final work, *A Passage to India*.

Perhaps public tastes did move beyond Lean's inclinations as a filmmaker, but he should not be judged harshly. He created indelible images and characters for the wide screen.

WAR AND PEACE
1956 King Vidor ♪♪♪

"You're over 30. By the time a man's over 30, life should be sad, meaningless, and hopeless."

Prince Bolkonsky (Wilfrid Lawson)

"Finally, he will bleed to death from this victory."

Gen. Kutuzov (Oscar Homolka)
on the battle of Borodino

Fact: Of the 600,000 men in Napoleon's army who invaded Russia, only about 50,000 returned home. The rest were killed, captured, or deserted.

If truth in titling guidelines had been followed, this lumbering epic would have been called *Peace and War*. Most of the military side of the story takes place in the second half, and it seems slow to arrive. When the subject does turn to Napoleon's (Herbert Lom) disastrous invasion of Russia, however, the action becomes more impressive and interesting. But before the battle of Borodino can be fought and Moscow can burn, other matters must be settled. More to the point, who marries Natasha Rostov (Audrey Hepburn)?

Natasha has been friends with Pierre Bezukhov (Henry Fonda), whose "heart is pure and good," forever, but after Pierre's father dies, he falls under the spell of the buxom Helene (Anita Ekberg) and marries her even though everybody knows that she's fooling around on him with Dolokhov (Helmut Dantine) and they fight a duel while Pierre's friend Prince Andrei (Mel Ferrer) is worried that his wife Lise (Milly Vitale) won't have a doctor when their baby is due because he (Pierre) will be off at the battle of Austerlitz and then when Lise does die, he's heartbroken and doesn't come around until he meets Natasha and she likes him too but his nasty old dad (Wilfrid Lawson) says they should wait a year before they get married and they do, but then Helene's creepy brother Anatole (Vittorio Gassman) gloms onto Natasha and she's swept off her feet until Pierre tries to straighten her out but by then it's too late because Natasha has told Prince Andrei that she doesn't love him anymore and he sends back all her letters and she's heartbroken and Pierre would step in but he's still married to Helene and all of that is just so unfair.

By that point, Tolstoy's novel has been reduced to a soap opera by seven writers (including an uncredited Irwin Shaw), but Audrey Hepburn is so fetching and Fonda is so earnest that the breathless folderol is more fun than it ought to be. The film picks up energy whenever Gen. Kutuzov (Oscar Homolka) appears on screen. As Napoleon's adversary, he is a realist who understands that he has to take the long view against an opponent who has a larger, more efficient force. The battle of Borodino is fairly well handled by second unit director Mario Soldati and directors of photography Jack Cardiff and Aldo Tonti. They focus on one part of the battle as observed by Pierre and make it seem real and explosive enough. Later, the filmmakers do good work with long shots of the invading and retreating French troops over Kutuzov's famous "scorched earth," particularly the latter stages which, again, are seen through Pierre's eyes.

Though *War and Peace* is faithful to the larger historical events, its heart is really with the romantic side and so it's most successful as a period melodrama.

See also

Gone with the Wind (if you must)

Waterloo

Napoleon

Love and Death

A Shot in the Dark

A Time to Love and a Time to Die

Andrei (Mel Ferrer) rallies the
fleeing Russian troops at the
Battle of Austerlitz in *War and
Peace.* The Kobal Collection

Cast: Audrey Hepburn (Natasha Rostov), Mel Ferrer (Prince Andrei Bolkonsky), Henry Fonda (Pierre Bezukhov), Anita Ekberg (Helene), Vittorio Gassman (Anatole), John Mills (Platon Karatsev), Oscar Homolka (Gen. Kutuzov), Herbert Lom (Napoleon), Helmut Dantine (Dolokhov), Tullio Carminati (Kuragine), Barry Jones (Count Rostov), Milly Vitale (Lise), Maria Ferrero (Mary Bolkonsky), Wilfred Lawson (Prince Bolkonsky), May Britt (Sonya), Jeremy Brett (Nicholas Rostov), Lea Seidl (Countess Rostov), Patrick Crean (Denisov), Sean Barrett (Petya Rostov), Richard Dawson; **Written by:** King Vidor, Bridget Boland, Mario Camerini, Ennio de Concini, Ivo Perilli, Irwin Shaw, Robert Westerby; **Cinematography by:** Jack Cardiff, Aldo Tonti; **Music by:** Nino Rota. **Producer:** Dino De Laurentiis, Paramount Pictures. **Awards:** Golden Globe Awards '57: Best Foreign Film; Nominations: Academy Awards '56: Best Color Cinematography, Best Costume Design (Color), Best Director (Vidor). **Running Time:** 208 minutes. **Format:** VHS, Beta, LV.

WORLD WAR I

World War I on Screen

"**W**aiting! Orders! Mud! Blood! Stinking stiffs! What the hell do we get out of this war anyway! Cheers when we left and when we get back! But who the hell cares . . . after this?" Jim Apperson (John Gilbert) *The Big Parade* (1925)

The movies as we know them—the system of studios and stars—were born in the aftermath of the Great War. The first depictions of it on screen were created by men who had experienced it, and those films were meant for an audience that still held clear memories of the subject.

The first big commercial hit to deal with the war is *The Four Horsemen of the Apocalypse* (1921). Though the film is primarily a vehicle for star Rudolph Valentino, director Rex Ingram had served with the Canadian Royal Flying Corps. He handles the combat scenes with a strong sense of realism that is somewhat at odds with the rest of the ambitious, sprawling story. In *The Big Parade*, made four years later, King Vidor uses the experiences of three young Americans in the trenches as the basis for a strong anti-war statement. William Wellman's *Wings*, the first Academy Award winner, made in 1927, presents the air war as a more adventurous enterprise, but when he turns the cameras to the struggle on the ground, he stresses sheer scope of the destruction in cratered landscapes.

Lewis Milestone's *All Quiet on the Western Front* is the most famous film to come out of the war. It's an unequivocal condemnation that has influenced virtually every realistic war film that has been made since. It was also a commercial and critical hit, but producers realized that more money is to be made in glorifying the adventure of war than in revealing the horror. Millionaire Howard Hughes certainly understood that when he made *Hell's Angels*. He began the project as a silent film, then reworked it for sound. The basis of the picture's appeal, though, lies in its combination of spectacular aerial combat footage and an equally spectacular Jean Harlow, usually wearing as little as possible. Variations on that formula have been repeated countless times over the decades.

Just as influential in its own way is *The Lost Patrol*, one of John Ford's first sound films. It tells an elementally simple story of soldiers who are stuck in the desert without an officer and must struggle against a largely unseen enemy. Again, with only a few variations, the plot would be adapted to fit different circumstances and different wars.

Jean Renoir's *Grand Illusion* combines ideas about war, society, and class in a prisoner of war setting. Virtually all of the conventional action scenes are absent. Instead, Renoir uses the genre to more intellectual ends. That is precisely not the case with *Dawn Patrol*. In the 1938 film, a remake of the 1930 original unavailable on video, Errol Flynn and David Niven are at their youthful best. So is Basil Rathbone as their commanding officer, but the airplanes are the real stars.

By 1940, when *The Fighting 69th* was produced, America was getting ready for another war, and the story of the "Rainbow Division" is high-flown propaganda. It unsubtly stresses the need for men to submerge their individuality within a group to work for a higher purpose, indeed a holy purpose. A year later, Howard Hawks's *Sergeant York* would do the same, though with a much more heroic tone. On the eve of World War II, nobody wanted to think about the horrific realities of World War I.

It wasn't until 1957, in the brief lull between Korea and Vietnam, that a filmmaker would look back at the "War to End All Wars." Stanley Kubrick's angry *Paths of Glory* can be seen as an anti-unit picture, one that shows what happens when leaders, and the military organization itself, fail the men who serve. It's a grim story, superbly acted by producer-star Kirk Douglas, and marred only by a weak ending.

David Lean is more respectful, but not uncritical, in *Lawrence of Arabia*, by far the best of the '60s epic war films. John Guillerman's *The Blue Max* returns to Hughes's proven formula with some of the best color aerial sequences ever filmed, and an often-undressed Ursula Andress.

In the 1980s, the Aussies were finally heard from, with two fine films detailing their contribution. Peter Wier's *Gallipoli* could almost be a companion piece to *All Quiet on the Western Front*, as it follows a group of young men who approach battle with varying degrees of enthusiasm and understanding of what they're doing. Simon Wincer's *The Lighthorsemen* works with more conventional heroics, and features superb equestrian action scenes.

Finally, Nathan Kroll's adaptation of Barbara Tuchman's *The Guns of August* is a fair introduction to the whole subject of World War I. If it misses the emotional, human costs of the war, it does do a good job of sorting out the complex causes of the war, presenting the tactics, and counting the dead.

ALL QUIET ON THE WESTERN FRONT

1930 Lewis Milestone ♫♫♫♫

"This story is neither an accusation nor a confession and least of all an adventure, for death is not an adventure to those who stand face to face with it. It will try simply to tell of a generation of men who, even though they may have escaped its shells, were destroyed by the war."

That's the preface to the first great war film, which is also the first great anti-war film. In adapting Erich Maria Remarque's novel, director Lewis Milestone creates many of the conventions and archetypes that virtually all other serious war films acknowledge. The contemporary viewer discovering the film will recognize every key scene, character and conflict. They've been copied and transformed countless times.

The story begins in a nameless German town in the first year of World War I. Young Paul Baumer (Lew Ayres) is an impressionable high school–age student who believes his professor's fervent patriotic sales pitch. "You are the life of the Fatherland, you boys," the teacher declaims before the all-male class. "You are the Iron Men of Germany! You are the great heroes who will repulse the enemy when you are called upon to do so!" Spontaneously, Paul and several of his classmates enlist in "The Great War." Everybody's doing it—even the postman (John Wray). The boys are simply afraid that it'll all be over before they've had a chance to taste glory. Their first disillusionment comes early.

> "Three years we've had of it—four years and every day a year, and every night a century. And our bodies are earth and our thoughts are clay and we sleep and eat with death. We're done for because you can't live that way and keep anything inside you."
>
> **Veteran Paul Baumer (Lew Ayres)**

Given an officer's uniform, the friendly hometown postman is transformed into a strutting, self-important little tyrant. Their training is brutal, dirty, and painful. Despite some stage-bound cinematic techniques—Milestone tends to create a proscenium arch to frame many of his interior scenes—the film deftly captures the speed and ease with which the individual becomes one small cog among many in the military machine. Once the young men move toward the front, the pace picks up. That's where they meet the scrounger, Katczinsky (Louis Wolheim, with a wonderful catcher's mitt of a face), and his pal Tjaden (Slim Summerville), a couple of seen-it-all veterans who take the youngsters under their wings.

After that, the film turns to the horrors of trench warfare—incessant shelling, rat infestation, claustrophobic underground barracks. The only area where the film might be accused of a rose-colored vision is in the depiction of hospitals and medical procedures. It's a bit antiseptic there, and makes no mention of the diseases that claimed so many lives, but that is a niggling criticism. Instead, Milestone focuses directly on combat and the daily life of a soldier, and he creates some indelible images: hands on barbed wire, the boots, the beans, the French soldier (Raymond Griffith) in the crater, and, of course, the famous "swimming scene" with the French girls. Milestone's use of the shadow of a bed frame to indicate sexual intimacy may seem dated and coy to today's audiences, but it certainly captures the emotional importance of the scene with a lightness that a more explicit approach would miss.

Finally, Milestone and Remarque make their point with simple, unrefined eloquence. When Paul returns home for a brief visit on leave and stands beside the same windy professor who talked him into enlisting, he describes the reality of his experience to a new

See also

Saving Private Ryan

A Time to Love and a Time to Die

Battleground

A Walk in the Sun

generation of boys: "I can't tell you anything you don't know. We live in the trenches out there. We fight. We try not to be killed but sometimes we are. That's all."

That's where the filmmakers leave it. Because they're telling the story from a German point of view, virtually all politics and nationalism have been stripped away. It really doesn't matter which

Paul Baumer (Lew Ayres) contemplates the miseries of war in *All Quiet on the Western Front.* The Kobal Collection

side the soldiers are on. Their experience is the same. Steven Spielberg restates the idea in *Saving Private Ryan*, but he has little beyond a second world war to add to Milestone and Remarque.

Cast: Lew Ayres (Paul Baumer), Louis Wolheim (Katczinsky), John Wray (Himmelstoss), Slim Summerville (Tjaden), Russell Gleason (Muller), Raymond Griffith (Gerard Duval), Ben Alexander (Kemmerick), Beryl Mercer (Mrs. Baumer), Arnold Lucy (Kantorek), William "Billy" Bakewell (Albert), Scott Kolk (Leer), Owen Davis Jr. (Peter), Walter Rodgers (Behm), Richard Alexander (Westhus), Harold Goodwin (Detering), Pat Collins (Lt. Bertinck), Edmund Breese (Herr Meyer); **Written by:** Maxwell Anderson, George Abbott, Del Andrews; **Cinematography by:** Arthur Edeson, Karl Freund; **Music by:** David Broeckman. **Producer:** Carl Laemmle, Universal. **Awards:** Academy Awards '30: Best Director (Milestone), Best Picture; American Film Institute (AFI) '98: Top 100, National Film Registry '90; Nominations: Academy Awards '30: Best Cinematography, Best Writing. **Budget:** 1.2M. **Running Time:** 103 minutes. **Format:** VHS, Beta, LV, DVD.

ALL QUIET ON THE WESTERN FRONT

The Hound Salutes: Lewis Milestone

Lewis Milestone's reputation pegs him as a filmmaker who never lived up to the promise of his early work. To a degree, that's a fair assessment. A Russian emigre and veteran of World War I who learned about filmmaking in the Army Signal Corps, Milestone was responsible for the first great anti-war film. He began his Hollywood career as an assistant editor and worked his way up the food chain to win the first (and only) Oscar for Comedy Direction in the Academy's debut year, 1927, for *Two Arabian Knights*. Two years later he was named Best Director, and *All Quiet on the Western Front* was Best Picture.

Though some of the conventions have become dated, it remains one of the screen's most impressive statements. Milestone translates Erich Maria Remarque's novel about young Germans who answer calls to patriotism into a universal examination of the horrors of war. Those ideas were not lost on a 1930 audience that remembered all too clearly the sacrifices that a generation of young men had made.

As the years passed, though, and a re-energized, militaristic Nazi Germany appeared, Milestone and others were unable to maintain their philosophical opposition to all war. In the years between wars, Milestone made some memorable films—*The Front Page* (1932), *Of Mice and Men* (1940)—but when America entered the conflict, he joined many of his fellow directors working on both conventional propaganda features and documentaries. *The Edge of Darkness* with Errol Flynn was about the brave Norwegian resistance; *The North Star* lionized our brave Russian allies; *The Purple Heart* showed what fiendish beasts the Japanese were.

Milestone came close to his previous success with *A Walk in the Sun*, adapted from Harry Brown's acclaimed short novel. It's a more serious work than his other World War II films, one that attempts more realism in its story of a short patrol in the Italian campaign. As an ensemble unit picture, it's one of the best, but Milestone also experimented unsuccessfully with sound, including an incessant theme song that comments on the action.

Milestone's third important work in the genre presents different problems. *Pork Chop Hill* (1959) is set in the Korean War, and attempts to show the absurdity of war, while at the same time indulging in the anti-communist, anti-Chinese rhetoric of the day. In the same vein, Milestone is quick to point out various examples of American military incompetence, and then, just as quickly, to forgive or excuse them. The result is a combat film with admirable complexity that's somehow not what it ought to be. The director cited studio interference.

Without denying or diluting any of those criticisms, it should be said that from World War I to Korea, Milestone could put the viewer into the middle of a battlefield, and make the hellish confusion of it seem all too real to the viewer. Steven Spielberg noted as much when he credited Milestone's work as partial inspiration for *Saving Private Ryan*.

So, whether or not he lived up to those first expectations, Lewis Milestone made significant contributions to the war film.

King Vidor's epic silent film would have a better reputation today if its major themes hadn't been stated so much more forcefully and memorably five years later in *All Quiet on the Western Front*. As it is, this one is still a landmark of the silent era, but some of its conventions are dated, and Vidor lets sentimentality soften the horror of his subject. When novelist Erich Remarque and director Lewis Milestone look at World War I from a foot soldier's point of view, romance is a brief and realistic subplot. In Vidor's work, based on a play by Joseph Farnham, the romantic relationship takes up the first half of the film.

The two films begin identically, though on opposite sides of the conflict, with young men answering the call to enlist at the declaration of war. As a title card puts it: "What a thing is patriotism! We go for years not knowing we have it. Suddenly—Martial music! . . . Native flags! . . . Friends cheer! . . . and it becomes life's greatest emotion!"

> "This dump is lousy with Heinies! I could chuck my hat across to where they are."
>
> **Bull (Tom O'Brien), during the first attack**

Jim Apperson (John Gilbert) is the spoiled son of a wealthy family. Slim Jensen (Karl Dane) is a New York construction worker. Bull O'Hara (Tom O'Brien) is a Bowery bartender. The three join up and find themselves in the same unit. After disappointingly brief training scenes, they're in France, billeted in a farmhouse where Jim meets Melisande (Renee Adoree), a cute gamine. Their flirtation is tentative at the outset and runs into all of the expected obstacles, and a few of the unexpected. It leads up to the famous "farewell" scene that has been copied many times since. The moment builds beautifully, riding on the energy that's going to carry the second half. But changes in audience expectations have made the conclusion of the scene unintentionally comic.

Fact:
King Vidor "discovered" comedienne Zasu Pitts, who would appear in European versions of All Quiet on the Western Front. (Her character is cut out of American prints.)

Some of the film's humor has aged poorly, too. Slim is meant to be something of a horse-faced buffoon, but he's such a grotesque, slobbering caricature with exaggerated features that he actually becomes frightening at inappropriate moments. Once the film moves to the war itself, those criticisms are forgotten. The title refers to troops heading for the front, "An endless column surging forward over roads that were never retraced." The battle scenes are intense, focused more on individuals than on mass attacks. Specifically, the focus is on Gilbert, and he's excellent. This role made him an international star. If they'd given Oscars when the film was made, he'd certainly have been a strong contender. His portrayal of the changes that a young man goes through in the transition from callow layabout to disillusioned veteran has lost nothing. Toward the end, he says, "Waiting! Orders! Mud! Blood! Stinking stiffs! What the hell do we get out of this war anyway!—Cheers when we left and when we get back! But who the hell cares . . . after this?" His expression says much more. Years later, in World War II, it would be called "the thousand yard stare," a haunted unfocused look. In the last reels of *The Big Parade*, Gilbert makes it seem completely real.

See also
All Quiet on the Western Front
The Fighting 69th
Sands of Iwo Jima
Paths of Glory

Cast: John Gilbert (James Apperson), Renee Adoree (Melisande), Hobart Bosworth (Mr. Apperson), Claire McDowell (Mrs. Apperson), Claire Adams (Justyn Reed), Karl Dane (Slim), Robert Ober (Harry), Tom O'Brien (Bull), Rosita Marstini (Melisande's Mother); **Written by:** Harry Behn; **Cinematography by:** John Arnold; **Music by:** William Axt, David Mendoza. **Producer:** Irving Thalberg, MGM. **Awards:** National Film Registry '92. **Running Time:** 141 minutes. **Format:** VHS, LV.

THE BLUE MAX
1966 John Guillermin 𝄞𝄞𝄞

John Guillermin collects all of the conventions of the early 1930s flying adventures and adds an unmistakable mid-1960s spin to create an enjoyable but understandably uneven entertainment. Many parts of the film work beautifully. In fact, the flying scenes are among the best ever put on screen. But whenever sex-starlet Ursula Andress shows up, the illusion of 1918 reality evaporates. Her appearance is completely at odds with everything else around her. She's decorous and undeniably sexy—that's what the cinematic marketplace of 1966 demanded—but she's also as anachronistic as a thong bikini in a stagecoach.

In 1916, Bruno Stachel (George Peppard) is fighting for the Fatherland on the Western Front (actually Ireland). Exhausted in the midst of battle, he takes refuge in a muddy crater and looks up to see two biplanes soaring high and slowly above him. Flash forward two years. The foot soldier has managed to transfer out of the Army and into the Air Corps, where he's a newly minted pilot. Ruthlessly ambitious, Bruno dreams of getting 20 kills. For those, he'll be rewarded with a medal, the Blue Max, and that will make him the equal of anyone. Heidemann (Karl Michael Vogler), Bruno's new squadron leader, already has a Blue Max, and the veteran flyer Willi von Klugermann (Jeremy Kemp) is closing in on his. More importantly, Willi and Heidemann are members of the aristocratic "officer corps." Bruno, son of a hotel keeper, really doesn't fit in.

At least, he doesn't fit in until Count von Klugermann (James Mason), Willi's uncle and a high-ranking officer, realizes Bruno's potential value. "If this young man lives long enough," the Count reasons, "he could be useful to our propaganda department. The common people of our country are war-weary, restive. They need to be provided with a hero of their own. Von Richthofen and Willi are of our class. Now, this fellow Stachel is common as dirt. He's one of them!"

The film's central conflict boils down to a competition between Heidemann's old-school, chivalrous knight-of-the-air approach and Bruno's pragmatic survival-of-the-fittest tactics. The more interesting relationship, though, is between Bruno and Willi. It always is in this sort of movie. While Peppard has enough screen presence as a movie star to carry the lead, he's not a good enough actor to make Bruno's obsessive ambition seem fully real. Jeremy Kemp's slyly comic cynicism is a welcome balance, and he walks away with all of his scenes, both on the ground and in the air.

Credit for the aerial work is shared by director Guillermin, aerial director Anthony Squire, and director of photography Douglas Slocombe. Together they manage to integrate the flying sequences into the larger narrative. It's not simply a matter of dogfights between British and German fighters; conflicts on the ground are settled or expanded in the air. Toward the end, when the Germans are attacking ground forces, the scenes are as tense and explosive as those in *Wings*, *Dawn Patrol*, or any of the "classics."

> "Look at Willi. Doesn't he look splendid. The Blue Max will go so well with his eyes."
> **Kaeti von Klugermann (Ursula Andress)**

> "He's wounded, isn't he? A mentionable wound? . . . Good. The people like soldiers to be shot in the right places."
> **Count von Klugermann (James Mason) on his potential hero, Bruno Stachel (George Peppard)**

See also
Dawn Patrol
Wings
The Manchurian Candidate
Catch-22

**George Peppard is German pilot
Bruno Stachel in *The Blue Max*.**

The Kobal Collection

Guillermin attempts to keep the ground-based action as interesting as the rest and he's generally successful. To use the Hollywood cliche, this is a big budget picture and every penny is on the screen. Note the lavishly staged state dinner with an impressive crane shot at the center. Guillermin also deserves credit for historical accuracy in the hospital scenes, and civilian life in 1918 Germany, complete with horses and road apples in the city streets.

In the end, *The Blue Max* is more enjoyable as simple escapism than as a serious war film, but those magnificent aerial sequences are enough to recommend it to fans. Jack Hunter's novel is a much more carefully observed portrait of those times. More appropriately but less cinematically, it ends with Stachel meeting a young Herman Goering.

This is a CinemaScope film, and Guillermin makes use of the whole screen. On video, the widescreen version is preferable to the sometimes clumsy pan-and-scan.

Cast: George Peppard (Bruno Stachel), James Mason (Count von Klugermann), Ursula Andress (Kaeti), Jeremy Kemp (Willi von Klugermann), Karl Michael Vogler (Heidemann), Anton Diffring (Holbach), Harry Towb (Kettering), Peter Woodthorpe (Rupp), Derek Newark (Ziegel), Derren Nesbitt (Fabian), Loni von Friedl (Effi); **Written by:** Ben Barzman, Basilio Franchina, David Pursall, Jack Seddon, Gerald Hanley; **Cinematography by:** Douglas Slocombe; **Music by:** Jerry Goldsmith. **Producer:** 20th Century-Fox, Christian Ferry, Elmo Williams. **Running Time:** 155 minutes. **Format:** VHS, Beta, LV, Letterbox.

DAWN PATROL

1938 Edmund Goulding ♪♪♪♪

It's a cliche in the restaurant business that the key to success is three things: location, location, location. In this remake of a 1930 film, the key is casting, casting, casting. Three actors in their youthful prime make *Dawn Patrol* a thoroughly enjoyable, if undemanding, aerial adventure.

The setting is France, 1915, where the Royal Flying Corps stages daily flights across enemy lines. Their biplanes are rickety crates held together with chicken wire and spit, and they're shot down so often that new replacements are sent up with virtually no training. Maj. Brand (Basil Rathbone) hates the way the war is being conducted. He'd rather be flying, but he has to play his part and so he delivers the unpopular orders. His best pilot, Capt. Courtney (Errol Flynn) detests him and is barely able to hide his contempt when the names of the dead are erased from the blackboard where missions are assigned, and new names of green pilots are chalked in. For the most part, though, Brand and his best friend Lt. Douglas Scott (David Niven) make the best of it. They hide their fear, have their first brandy of the day at 10 in the morning, and join in for a rousing chorus of their favorite drinking song, "Hurray for the Next Man That Dies!"

> "That's just about what it is—a great big noisy rather stupid game that doesn't make any sense at all. None of us know what it's all about or why."
>
> **Capt. Courtney (Errol Flynn) on war**

Writer John Monk Saunders makes the unsettled relationship of the three characters so interesting that the film is just as intense when it's on the ground as it is when the scene shifts to flying. Saunders, also responsible for the story of the original *Wings*, served in the Army Airs Corps. Even when the physical action is far-fetched—and some of it fetches about as far as it possibly can—the characters' emotions ring true.

Did you Know?

In his book, *The Moon's a Balloon*, David Niven claims that the scene in which his character, Scotty, is shot down in his pajamas is based on a real WWI incident. He also says that he met the pilot to whom it happened, and he believes that *Dawn Patrol* was the movie that made him a star.

As for the flying scenes themselves, many were repeated from the 1930 version and some of the process special effects are much too obvious. (Though this film was made five years after *King Kong*, the effects don't even come close to that masterpiece. Saunders, by the way, was married to Fay Wray.) Those criticisms aside, two long aerial sequences, one in the middle and another at the conclusion, are imaginative and fast-paced. By the time they occur, we care enough about the characters that the effects' shortcomings aren't too important.

Flynn, Niven, and Rathbone are simply superb. The conflicts they must resolve don't have any easy answers and the characters are engagingly flawed. In a way, Rathbone has the most to work with because Maj. Brand is more serious. Courtney and Scott can get by on good looks and easy charm, while he has to take care of the dramatic heavy lifting. They find able support in veteran character actor Donald Crisp, as Phipps, the adjutant. His rambling speech to Brand about an imaginary dog is a small gem. In that scene, the characters virtually cut a template for the roles that Nigel Bruce and Rathbone would create a year later when they played Dr. Watson and Sherlock Holmes in *Hound of the Baskervilles*.

See also

The Blue Max

Wings

Air Force

Hell's Angels

Twelve O'Clock High

Capt. Courtney (Errol Flynn) prepares to take off in *Dawn Patrol*. The Kobal Collection

Cast: Errol Flynn (Capt. Courtney), David Niven (Lt. Douglas Scott), Basil Rathbone (Maj. Brand), Donald Crisp (Phipps), Barry Fitzgerald (Bott), Melville Cooper (Sgt. Watkins), Carl Esmond (Von Mueller), Peter Willes (Hollister), Morton Lowry (Donnie Scott), Michael Brooke (Capt. Squires), James Burke (Flaherty, the motorcycle driver), Stuart Hall (Bentham); **Written by:** Seton I. Miller, Dan Totheroh; **Cinematography by:** Gaetano Antonio "Tony" Gaudio; **Music by:** Max Steiner. **Producer:** United Artists, Warner Brothers. **Running Time:** 103 minutes. **Format:** VHS, Beta.

THE FIGHTING 69TH
1940 William Keighley ♫♫♫

Rule number one of reviewing states that films should be judged by how well they do what they set out to do. This early piece of pre-war propaganda means to prepare 1940 audiences for an imminent war by lionizing a World War I regiment. It does just that without shame or subtlety, so to criticize the film as a false representation of that terrible war misses the point. It begins with a pious introduction and ends on an even higher moral note, pleading with God to bless and embolden America.

The title refers to the 69th New York regiment, and the studio states its reverential aims right up front: "In gratitude to all those millions of young men who served and fought in the fighting forces of the United States in the last war . . . to the Rainbow Division, which most nearly represented in its ranks all of our States and Territories . . . to the 69th New York Regiment (165th Infantry, A.E.F.) which was the average, yet the epitome of our national courage . . . and to the memory of Fr. Francis P. Duffy, a beloved Chaplain and a truly great humanitarian . . . Warner Bros. respectfully dedicates this film."

> "Amid the turmoil and angry passions, when all worthwhile things seem swept away, let the tired eyes of a troubled world rise up and see the shining citadel of which these young lives form the imperishable stones— America, the citadel of peace. Peace forever more. This I beg of you through Christ Jesus, our Lord, Amen."
>
> **Father Duffy's (Pat O'Brien) closing voice-over, spoken as the souls of the dead march across the screen**

Despite the "Rainbow" moniker, it's primarily an Irish unit. One recurring joke revolves around a Jewish guy (Sammy Cohen) who calls himself Murphy. The protagonist is Jerry Plunkett (James Cagney), a tough, cocky kid who's in trouble from the moment he sets foot in Camp Mills, even before he is officially enlisted. The year is 1917 and the 69th is getting ready to ship out to France.

Three key supporting characters are based on real people; the regiment's commander, "Wild Bill" Donovan (George Brent); Sgt. Joyce Kilmer (Jeffrey Lynn), the poet most famous for "Trees"; and, of course, the chaplain Fr. Duffy (Pat O'Brien), a veritable saint in khaki. In a moment that's not untypical, right before the 69th is to go into battle for the first time, Donovan falls to his knees before Fr. Duffy and asks his blessing for the regiment. As director William Keighley blocks the scene, the characters could be re-creating a pose from a medieval tapestry, with a king in armor kneeling before a pope.

But that is not the film's central issue. Plunkett's transformation from bad boy to hero is the point, and it is accomplished through unusual, if dubious, plot turns in a swiftly paced script. Plunkett's transit is a bumpy ride, but Cagney makes it believable . . . well, believable enough. As an actor, he was just hitting his feisty stride, and he simply powers through the more incredulous stretches of an emotional-psychological roller-coaster ride. His performance alone is enough to recommend the film, but both the training sequences and the combat scenes are extremely well done for the most part. Not surprisingly, in the big no-man's-land finish, heroics overpower common sense. That's also when the religious and sacrificial elements are taken to such flamboyant extremes that more skeptical and irreverent viewers may not be able to contain themselves. (See accompanying quote.)

See also
The Red Badge of Courage
Paths of Glory
Sergeant York

Jerry Plunkett (James Cagney) learns how to be a soldier in *The Fighting 69th*. The Kobal Collection

Cast: James Cagney (Jerry Plunkett), Pat O'Brien (Fr. Duffy), George Brent (Wild Bill Donovan), Jeffrey Lynn (Joyce Kilmer), Alan Hale (Sgt. Big Mike Wynn), Frank McHugh ("Crepe Hanger" Burke), Dennis (Stanley Morner) Morgan (Lt. Ames), William Lundigan (Timmy Wynn), Dick Foran (John Wynn), Guinn "Big Boy" Williams (Paddy Dolan), Henry O'Neill (The Colonel), John Litel (Capt. Mangan), George Reeves (Jack O'Keefe), Frank "Junior" Coghlan (Jimmy), Sammy Cohen (Mike Murphy), Joseph Crehan (Doctor), Eddie Dew (Regan), William Hopper (Pvt. Turner), Frank Mayo (Capt. Bootz), Herb Anderson (Casey), Byron Nelson (Soldier), Harvey Stephens (Maj. Anderson), Charles Trowbridge (Chaplain Holmes), Roland Varno (German Officer); **Written by:** Fred Niblo, Norman Reilly Raine, Dean Franklin; **Cinematography by:** Gaetano Antonio "Tony" Gaudio; **Music by:** Adolph Deutsch. **Producer:** Jack L. Warner, Hal B. Wallis, Warner Bros. **Running Time:** 90 minutes. **Format:** VHS.

THE FIGHTING 69TH

FOUR HORSEMEN OF THE APOCALYPSE

1921 Rex Ingram 🦴🦴🦴🦴

This landmark silent film will always be known first as Rudolph Valentino's breakthrough, and his star power remains undiminished. At the same time, though, his high-octane sex appeal is put in service to a fairly serious story of war and self sacrifice. Actually, June Mathis's script (based on Vicente Blasco Ibanez's novel) is a yeasty combination of soap opera and history that begins in Argentina and moves to Paris.

Young Julio Desnoyers (Valentino) is grandson of the patriarch Madariaga (Pomeroy Cannon), whose two daughters have married a Frenchman and a German. Julio is the eldest of the French side, who are viewed somewhat scornfully by the Germans. Father Karl (Alan Hale, father of Gilligan's Skipper) pompously states, "One owes his first duty to his Fatherland—that his children may grow up in allegiance with the advantages of superculture." As soon as Madariaga is out of the picture, Karl claims his half of the inheritance and moves his family back to Berlin. Julio's father Marcelo (Josef Swickard) does the same, taking wife and kids to Paris.

The first half of the film establishes Julio as the toast of the town, a bon vivant who divides his time between artistic dabbling and teaching Parisiennes how to tango. Then he falls in love with Marguerite Lurier (Alice Terry), a married woman, and just when the soapy elements threaten to overtake everything else, the Archduke Ferdinand is assassinated and the film becomes much more serious. To contemporary audiences, some of the character transformations will seem arbitrary or poorly motivated, and many of the conventions of the time are almost nonsensical. The literal personification of the title apparitions—Conquest, War, Pestilence and Death—is overused, but somehow acceptable. The appearance of cute animals (most obviously an irritating monkey) to comment on human action is intrusive.

When he turns to scenes of combat, director Rex Ingram uses a more realistic approach. Perhaps due to his service in the Canadian Royal Flying Corps, Ingram takes the subject seriously. He also brings the various threads of the complicated plot together in an unrealistically neat conclusion. Those criticisms really are unfair. Compared to other films of the times—even something as ambitious as *Birth of a Nation*—this one stands up well. If the trench warfare scenes aren't as fully realized as some that came later, they are given appropriate dramatic weight in a multi-layered story.

Even a cursory glance at the unfortunate 1962 remake, with Glenn Ford in the Valentino role, demonstrates how a genuine "star" can take over a film. It has little to do with acting, everything to do with intensity. It's widely believed that June Mathis was in love with Valentino and carefully crafted the role to play to his strengths. Director Ingram was married to Alice Terry, so both of the key people behind the camera did all they could to help their paramours on the other side.

See also

Four Horsemen of the Apocalypse (1962)
The Big Parade
All Quiet on the Western Front
War and Peace

Rudolph Valentino is playboy-turned-soldier Julio Desnoyers in *Four Horsemen of the Apocalypse*. The Kobal Collection

Cast: Rudolph Valentino (Julio Desnoyers), Alice Terry (Marguerite Lurier), Pomeroy Cannon (Madariaga), Josef Swickard (Marcelo Desnoyers), Alan Hale (Karl von Hartrott), Mabel van Buren (Elena), Nigel de Brulier (Tchernoff), Bowditch Turner (Argensola), Wallace Beery (Lt. Col. von Richthoffen), Bridgetta Clark (Dona Luisa), Virginia Warwick (Chichi), Stuart Holmes (Capt. von Hartrott), John St. Polis (Etienne), Mark Fenton (Senator Lacour), Derek Ghent (Rene Lacour); **Written by:** June Mathis; **Cinematography by:** John Seitz; **Music by:** Louis F. Gottschalk. **Producer:** Metro. **Awards:** National Film Registry '95. **Running Time:** 110 minutes. **Format:** VHS.

FOUR HORSEMEN OF THE APOCALYPSE

GALLIPOLI
1981 Peter Weir ♪♪♪♪

Before *Platoon*, before *Saving Private Ryan*, Peter Weir established the key themes and tone of the contemporary war film with *Gallipoli*. His approach is unflinchingly anti-war. In the end, he says, appeals to duty and glory are empty; destruction, waste, and futility are real. That understanding comes at a hard cost.

The entire story takes place between May and July, 1915. It begins in Western Australia—stunningly photographed (even on video) by Russell Boyd—where 18-year-old Archy Hamilton (Mark Lee) is the son of a prosperous farm family. He's also a runner, a sprinter who trains under his stern Uncle Jack (Bill Kerr). At night, Archy reads about the war in newspaper articles he has squirreled away, and he believes the breathless headlines: "Baptism of Fire," "Splendid Gallantry," "Magnificent Achievement." Though he knows his parents will never allow it, he wants to leave the bucolic countryside, and to find his own adventures in the larger world.

> "Life is cheap here, Snowy, and the women have no respect for themselves. It's the same in most foreign places."
>
> **Frank (Mel Gibson) to Snowy (David Argue) while looking at naughty postcards in an Egyptian bazaar**

At the same time, Frank Dunne (Mel Gibson) and his mates Billy (Robert Grubb), Barney (Tim McKenzie), and Snowy (David Argue) read the same papers and are tempted to play "The Greatest Game of Them All" in ANZAC, the Australian-New Zealand Army Corps. Frank goes along with his pals, but he never really intends to enlist. "It's an English war, got nothing to do with us," he says, despite considerable peer pressure.

Eventually, Frank meets Archy and they become close friends. (Think Tom and Huck down under.) After a series of episodic encounters, they find themselves in the service and training in Egypt to fight in the Dardanelles against the Ottoman Turks.

The first two-thirds of the film celebrate the heady joys of youth and discovery. Structurally, it's a classic quest story, with the green heroes undergoing various tests and experiences—from a trek across a desert to the teeming back alleys of Cairo—that prepare them for a descent into hell. That hell is the poorly planned and poorly executed engagement at Gallipoli, where the Australians cling to a beachhead beneath entrenched Turkish mortars and machine guns.

In its simplification of the details of the battle and its relative importance to the larger engagement, the film is open to criticism, but writer-director Weir is interested in characters, not tactics or history. In that respect, the film works beautifully. He gets first rate performances from his young cast. This is one of the early roles that made Mel Gibson an international star. The grace notes added by the older supporting cast are just as important.

Fact: Soldiers in the big battle scenes are played by men of Port Lincoln and Adelaide, the 18th Air Defence Regiment Cadets, and the No. 1 Recruit Training Unit, Edinburgh, South Australia.

At the end of the first act, for example, Uncle Jack reads to Archy's younger siblings from Kipling's *The Jungle Book*. It's the scene where Mowgli cries for the first time and decides to leave the jungle, ending with the line "'Now,' he said, 'Now I will go to men.'" The moment could easily be heavy-handed and obvious, but it's delicately, sadly understated. Later, Maj. Barton (played by familiar character actor Bill Hunter) takes much the same role as the only officer who realizes what he and his men are undertaking.

See also

The Lighthorsemen
Platoon
Breaker Morant
All Quiet on the Western Front

Mel Gibson is Frank in *Gallipoli*.
The Kobal Collection

Throughout, the background is filled with period details that seem absolutely authentic. In the sound-track, Wier's use of Tomaso Albinoni's "Adagio in C" strikes precisely the right emotional chord (as Oliver Stone realized when he chose Barber's "Adagio for Strings" in *Platoon*). In fact, the only incongruous note is the occasional use of electronic music, a touch borrowed from *Chariots of Fire*, the Best Picture Oscar-winner released the same year. Other than that, the film is absolutely absorbing straight through to the frozen conclusion that mirrors one of Robert Capa's most famous photographs from the Spanish Civil War.

GALLIPOLI

Seen as popular entertainment, *Gallipoli* is still a fine crowd pleaser. Its influences on the war films of the late '80s and '90s are equally important, most noticeably in its heartfelt anti-war attitudes and subtle ironies.

Cast: Mel Gibson (Frank Dunne), Mark Lee (Archy), Bill Kerr (Uncle Jack), David Argue (Snowy), Tim McKenzie (Barney), Robert Grubb (Billy), Graham Dow (Gen. Gardner), Stan Green (Sgt. Major), Heath Harris (Stockman), Harold Hopkins (Les McCann), Charles Yunupingu (Zac), Ronny Graham (Wallace Hamilton), Gerda Nicolson (Rose Hamilton), Bill Hunter (Maj. Barton); **Written by:** Peter Weir, David Williamson; **Cinematography by:** Russell Boyd; **Music by:** Brian May; **Technical Advisor:** Bill Gammage. **Producer:** Paramount Pictures, Robert Stigwood, Ben Gannon, Patricia Lovell. **Australian. Awards:** Australian Film Institute '81: Best Actor (Gibson), Best Film. **MPAA Rating:** PG. **Running Time:** 111 minutes. **Format:** VHS, Beta, LV.

Jean Renoir, son of Impressionist master Auguste Renoir, was virtually a self-taught filmmaker. He was also a veteran of World War I who began the service in the cavalry but left after he was kicked by a horse and hospitalized. After that, he enlisted in the infantry, where he took a bullet in the thigh and nearly lost the leg to gangrene. Finally he served as a pilot. If those experiences inform his brilliant war film, he did not try to re-create them on screen. Instead, Renoir chose to tell his prisoner-of-war tale without many of the conventional scenes, or the conventional conflicts. Even the film's title defies conventional interpretation. It seems to refer to a desire for peace, but that's not clear.

In 1916, before America's entry into the war, Lt. Marechal (Jean Gabin), a pilot, takes Capt. Boeldieu (Pierre Fresnay) up on an essentially pointless reconnaissance flight. They're shot down by Capt. Rauffenstein (Erich von Stroheim) who tells his aide, "Drive down by the turnip field near the sugar factory. I shot down a Caudron. If there are officers, invite them to lunch." That moment establishes Renoir's basic ideas. Though the war between France and Germany is important, so are the class differences. It immediately becomes apparent that Boeldieu and Rauffenstein have much more in common than Boeldieu and Marechal. The distance between them is heightened when they're sent to a prison camp, where they meet Lt. Rosenthal (Marcel Dalio), the son of a wealthy middle-class family.

Marechal is a rough-edged former mechanic who's been promoted to the lowest level of commissioned officers because he's a flier. Because he's Jewish, Rosenthal will never be fully accepted by Boeldieu and Rauffenstein, whose world is built around 19th century conceptions of courtliness and prejudice. But Renoir refuses to let political, social, or nationalistic stereotypes define these characters. They are fully developed individuals and they are the real point of the film.

Even though the men have been removed from the front lines of battle, the war still affects them. They put on shows; they make plans to escape; they're moved from camp to camp, finally being reunited with Rauffenstein in a remote castle. The things that they do and the events surrounding them—which would be the central focus of many prisoner-of-war films—are used to reveal the men's characters and the changes they undergo. Some of the crucial incidents aren't even shown. The initial plane crash, for example, occurs off camera because it's not important to Renoir's story. Throughout, the pace is leisurely, giving the characters time and space to develop.

As we come to know the men, we learn that there are no heroes and villains. It would be easy to turn Boeldieu and Rauffenstein into the heavies, but late in the film, they are revealed to be much more sympathetic and complex than they might seem. That's an odd approach for a war film, and it's made even odder by the subdued, naturalistic acting style of the ensemble. Though Gabin is definitely the star, every member of the cast has at least one important contribution to make. Renoir was famous for the rapport he established with his

"It's usually the clap that gets the posh people, right?"

Lt. Marechal (Jean Gabin)

"It used to be a privilege of class, but it, like all else, has been lost to the masses."

Capt. Boeldieu (Pierre Fresnay)

"We have to finish the war and let's hope that it's the last."

Lt. Marechal

"An illusion. Back to reality. If we see a patrol, what'll we do?"

Lt. Rosenthal (Marcel Dalio)

Fact:
Nazi Minister of Propaganda Josef Goebbels branded *La Grande Illusion* "Cinematographic Enemy No. 1" and banned the film. All European prints were believed to have been destroyed by the Nazis, but American troops discovered a negative in Munich in 1945. It was used to reconstruct and restore the film.

See also

Paths of Glory
Schindler's List
One Against the Wind
The Battle of Algiers
Anderson Platoon

Pierre Fresnay and Erich von Stroheim are Air Corps officers on opposite sides in the Great War, but they have more in common with each other than with the men who serve under them in *Grand Illusion.* The Kobal Collection

actors and every move, every gesture seems unforced and unpremeditated. At times, it's easy to forget that this is a fictional film.

The brutality of the fighting is only hinted at, and some might see that as a flaw, but again, that is not Renoir's point. In the end, Boeldieu and Rauffenstein are representative of a past that cannot be recovered or recreated. Marechal and Rosenthal are Europe's future, but the conclusion suggests that the future is uncertain and just as fraught with war as the present. Years later in an interview, Renoir would say, "In 1936 I made a picture named *La Grande Illusion* in which I tried to express all my deep feelings about the cause of peace. Three years later, the war broke out."

Cast: Jean Gabin (Lt. Marechal), Erich von Stroheim (Capt. von Rauffenstein), Pierre Fresnay (Capt. de Boeldieu), Marcel Dalio (Rosenthal), Julien Carette (The Actor), Gaston Modot (The Engineer), Jean Daste (The Teacher), Dita Parlo (Elsa), Georges Peclet (An Officer), Werner Florian (Arthur Kranz), Sylvain Itkine (Demolder), Jacques Becker (An English Officer); **Written by:** Jean Renoir, Charles Spaak; **Cinematography by:** Christian Matras; **Music by:** Joseph Kosma. **Producer:** RAC. **French. Awards:** New York Film Critics Awards '38: Best Foreign Film; Nominations: Academy Awards '38: Best Picture. **Running Time:** 111 minutes. **Format:** VHS, Beta, LV, DVD.

Nathan Kroll's adaptation of Barbara Tuchman's best-selling history is an adequate introduction to World War I, but that's all. It doesn't show the human, individual side of that horrible war. In fairness, it doesn't try to. Instead, the relatively brief running time is devoted to an explanation of the tangled roots of the war and an overview of the tactics of the fighting itself. Graphs, diagrams and unidentified generic combat footage tell most of the story.

The film begins with these words:

The Year 1914.

Millions of peaceful and industrious people were hounded into a war by the folly of a few all-powerful leaders. This war was in no way inevitable. But the results determined the shape of the world in which we live today.

"The innocence of the people was in the streets of Europe. The guilt was in the Cabinets."

The scene then shifts to May 6, 1910 and the funeral of England's King Edward VII, son of Queen Victoria. Nine European monarchs take part in the elaborate funeral procession. They're all related by blood or by marriage and they seem to share a fondness for gaudy military uniforms. Whenever they visit, they dress up in each other's finest regalia. Those operetta costumes also pretty much define the limits of their military experience. The film gamely tries to sort out the various allegiances and treaties that had resulted in a rough alliance of Germany, Austria-Hungary, and Italy against England, France, and Russia. (Remember that at the time, Austria-Hungary and Italy were barely countries as we define them, and Russia was still ruled by the Czar.)

They moved to the brink of war several times. When the French sent an expeditionary force to aid the Moroccan government against an insurrection, the Germans sent warships into the area and the English "concentrated the fleet." The upshot was a German-British naval arms race in 1911–12, and everything finally came unraveled on June 28, 1914, when the Archduke Ferdinand was assassinated in Sarajevo, where Serbs, Croats, and Muslims were going after each other.

While a Socialist international congress was being held in Belgium and people were rising up everywhere in anti-war protests, the leaders lined up against each other and made demands. A little more than a month after the assassination, the continent was poised for a multi-faceted conflict. As the film puts it, "Fifty hours earlier, people all over Europe had held peace demonstrations. Now caught in the emotional frenzy of farewells, the same people found themselves jubilantly going off to war. Their governments, having consistently mismanaged the situation, no longer could see any alternative but to send thousands off to unknown battles."

All the nations involved seem to have shared the naive but near-universal fantasy that the war would be over quickly and they would be victorious. It would take four years and 37 and a half million casualties to decide the issues inconclusively.

The film touches all of the important events and battles—the significance of submarines, trench warfare, the Marne, Verdun, the Russian Revolution—using grainy footage of big guns firing and infantry troops going over the top. In its depiction of the war itself, the film is

See also
All Quiet on the Western Front
The Big Parade
Paths of Glory
The Civil War

Troop movements in the early days of World War I in _The Guns of August_. Del Valle Archives

definitely "history that's written by the winners." It stresses the Prussian general Clausewitz's theories of doctrine of terrorism in conquered countries and finds the first hints of the Holocaust in the German destruction of the Belgian city of Louvain. The better fictional films of "The Great War" have much more to say about its effects on individual human beings.

Producer: Nathan Kroll. **Running Time:** 110 minutes. **Format:** VHS, LV.

Millionaire Howard Hughes's directorial debut is a glorious mess. Despite an extended shooting schedule that encompassed monumental technical obstacles, it is still absurdly entertaining. When production began in 1927, the film was intended to be a silent picture. Then sound was introduced and the producers made adjustments, including the replacement of Norwegian female lead Greta Nissen with Jean Harlow. Whatever the case, Hughes wound up making a film about his two favorite subjects—fast airplanes and hot blondes.

Seen as a depiction of World War I, *Hell's Angels* doesn't compare well to the three most famous contemporaneous films. It lacks even the romanticized "realism" that *Wings* and *Dawn Patrol* brought to the air war, and it doesn't even attempt the gritty naturalism of *All Quiet on the Western Front*. Instead, it's more enjoyable today seen strictly as a "guy flick," with one incredibly sexy heroine and lots of explosions and vivid flying sequences.

The main characters are the Rutledge brothers, both students at Oxford. Roy (James Hall) is the older and steadier of the two. Monte (Ben Lyon) is a party-hearty frat boy. Roy enlists as soon as war is declared. Monte has to be persuaded, and their friend Karl (John Darrow) so prefers England to his native Germany that he doesn't want to leave when he's called home. While they're sorting things out, lusty socialite Helen (Harlow), is making her own plans to support the troops. Roy loves and wants to marry her, but Monte realizes that she has no intention of settling down. The famous scene where she invites Monte up to her apartment—and says "Would you be shocked if I put on something more comfortable"—establishes a level of sexual frankness that wouldn't be equalled for decades. It also contributed to the establishment of the Hollywood Production Code Administration of the Hays Office, under whose strict guidelines even the film's title would not have been permitted. The platinum blonde herself literally glows on screen. Her minimalist diaphanous gowns leave little to the imagination and her character's unashamed sensuality is still bracing.

When director Hughes is able to tear his cameras away from her, the aerial action is remarkable. An extended zeppelin attack on London employs such imaginative special effects that it becomes virtual science fiction with tinges of David Lynch weirdness and odd sexual imagery. The dogfights and bombing raids in the second half are more conventional WWI fare, and they're filmed with dozens of real biplanes in the sky. Today, it would be almost impossible to re-create that first-rate stunt work with real aircraft and pilots.

The romantic element and the flying element have virtually nothing to do with each other, and so the plot is loose and mostly unfocused. Because of that, the film is also totally unpredictable. It veers wildly and without transition from one extraordinary event to the next, and the conclusion is the most astonishing part of all. In the end, *Hell's Angels* may not have much to say about World War I, but it's one of the sound era's first great guilty pleasures.

See also

Wings
Dawn Patrol
The Blue Max

A German officer confronts two captured Allied pilots in *Hell's Angels.* The Kobal Collection

Cast: Jean Harlow (Helen), Ben Lyon (Monte Rutledge), James Hall (Roy Rutledge), John Darrow (Karl Armstedt), Lucien Prival (Baron Von Kranz), Frank Clarke (Lt. Von Buren), Roy "Baldy" Wilson (Baldy Maloney), Douglas Gilmore (Capt. Redfield), Jane Winton (Baroness Von Kranz), Evelyn Hall (Lady Randolph); **Written by:** Harry Behn, Howard Estabrook, Joseph Moncure March; **Cinematography by:** Elmer Dyer, Harry Perry, E. Burton Steene, Dewey Wrigley, Gaetano Antonio "Tony" Gaudio; **Music by:** Hugo Riesenfeld. **Producer:** Howard Hughes. **Awards:** Nominations: Academy Awards '30: Best Cinematography. **Budget:** 3.95M. **Running Time:** 135 minutes. **Format:** VHS.

David Lean's epic is one of the few films that legitimately deserves to be called great. It appears on virtually all "ten best" lists and reveals deeper layers of meaning with repeated viewings. It is also a film that was made for the big screen—the bigger the better—and so it loses much of its power on video. (See "Big Screen vs. Small Screen" sidebar, p. 105) The "30th Anniversary" edition is based on the 1989 Robert A. Harris restoration and captures as much of Lean's original intention as any video version can.

Structurally, the film is a standard biography, beginning with the subject's death (in a motorcycle accident), brief interviews with people who knew him, and then a chronological recitation of the high points. The first spoken line of the film is "He was the most extraordinary man I ever knew." But T.E. Lawrence (Peter O'Toole) is not an easy subject. He's a contradictory figure, and the filmmakers properly don't try to pin him down, allowing him to remain a fascinating enigma throughout. In a visual sense, Lean combines a sure sense of place with an approach to the action that he borrows from an unlikely source—John Ford. Lean turns his vast desert canvas into another Monument Valley, and when his Bedouins ride across it, they are not far removed from Ford's cavalry. In many of the early scenes, the stately gait of the camel's walk gives the film a slower pace, and this is precisely what Lean is trying to achieve. Lean even manages to surpass Ford with his understanding of the relationship between his characters and the landscape; how the desert changes those who go into it.

The complex character was created by playwright Robert Bolt in his first script, and blacklisted Michael Wilson (who also worked with Lean on *Bridge on the River Kwai*). This Lawrence is at first an ambitious, inexperienced young officer who is transformed by his immersion into the Bedouin world into a messianic hero. Later he comes to understand himself, though that knowledge comes with a large portion of self-loathing.

Lawrence's mission, largely his own creation, is to unite the feuding Bedouin tribes under the leadership of Prince Feisal (Alec Guinness), and to keep the British politicians, as personified by Mr. Dryden (Claude Rains), from putting the Arabs under their colonial thumb after World War I is over. It is accomplished through a semi-episodic series of battles and raids where Lawrence is sometimes accompanied by Ali (Omar Sharif) and Sheik Auda (Anthony Quinn), and equally difficult bureaucratic struggles he faces with Gen. Allenby (Jack Hawkins).

Those two sides of the story are clearly contrasted—the blast-furnace desert exteriors and the cool, echoing marble interiors where the army staff does its work. The initial scene of negotiation, when Lawrence has returned from the desert for the first time and meets Allenby, takes place in a courtyard, neither interior nor exterior. It's a simple device, but an effective way to set the moment apart. In the same way, changes in clothing color and style are used to reveal changes in character, and Lean none-too-subtly inserts motorcycles at odd moments to remind viewers where it is all leading.

See also

She Wore a Yellow Ribbon
The Good, the Bad and the Ugly
Bridge on the River Kwai
Gallipoli

"I find acting very difficult. I'm sure David finds directing very difficult. When it's 130 in the shade at the top of a sand dune, sitting on a camel covered in vermin doesn't make it any easier."

Peter O'Toole in *Wind, Sand and Star*, a short film about the making of *Lawrence of Arabia*

"You're the kind of creature I can't stand, Lawrence, but I suppose I might be wrong."

Gen. Murray (Donald Wolfit)

"With Maj. Lawrence, mercy is a passion. With me, it is merely good manners. You may judge which motive is the more reliable."

Prince Feisal (Alec Guinness) to Jackson Bentley (Arthur Kennedy)

"If we've told lies, you've told half-lies. And a man who tells lies, like me, merely hides the truth. But a man who tells half-lies has forgotten where he put it."

Mr. Dryden (Claude Rains) to Lawrence (Peter O'Toole)

"Young men make wars and the virtues of war are the virtues of young men—courage and hope for the future. Then old men make the peace and the vices of peace are the vices of old men—mistrust and caution. It must be so."

Prince Feisal (Alec Guinness)

T.E. Lawrence (Peter O'Toole) leads various Arab tribes against the German-backed Turkish during World War I in *Lawrence of Arabia.* The Kobal Collection

As the filmmakers see it, the central conflict within Lawrence is his simultaneous desire for adventure with his sometimes uncontrollable blood lust. He comes to love the berserk rage of battle and to detest himself for it. If they do not resolve that conflict satisfactorily, they don't cheapen it with an easy answer, either, and given the scope and power of the film, that would have been an inexcusable flaw.

Cast: Peter O'Toole (T.E. Lawrence), Omar Sharif (Sherif Ali ibn el Kharish), Anthony Quinn (Auda abu Tavi), Alec Guinness (Prince Feisal), Jack Hawkins (Gen. Allenby), Claude Rains (Mr. Dryden), Anthony Quayle (Col. Harry Brighton), Arthur Kennedy (Jackson Bentley), Jose Ferrer (Bey of Deraa), Michel Ray (Farraj), Norman Rossington (Cpl. Jenkins), John Ruddock (Elder Harith), Donald Wolfit (Gen. Murray); **Written by:** Robert Bolt, Michael Wilson; **Cinematography by:** Frederick A. (Freddie) Young; **Music by:** Maurice Jarre. **Producer:** Sam Spiegel, Columbia Pictures. **British. Awards:** Academy Awards '62: Best Art Direction/Set Decoration (Color), Best Color Cinematography, Best Director (Lean), Best Film Editing, Best Picture, Best Sound, Best Original Score; American Film Institute (AFI) '98: Top 100; British Academy Awards '62: Best Actor (O'Toole), Best Film, Best Screenplay; Directors Guild of America Awards '62: Best Director (Lean); Golden Globe Awards '63: Best Director (Lean), Best Film—Drama, Best Supporting Actor (Sharif); National Board of Review Awards '62: Best Director (Lean), National Film Registry '91; Nominations: Academy Awards '62: Best Actor (O'Toole), Best Adapted Screenplay, Best Supporting Actor (Sharif). **Budget:** 12M. **MPAA Rating:** PG. **Running Time:** 221 minutes. **Format:** VHS, Beta, LV, Letterbox, Closed Caption.

Simon Wincer's companion piece to Peter Wier's *Gallipoli* may not be as successful and as moving, but it is still an entertaining film marked by some absolutely spectacular riding sequences. Structurally, the two are almost identical. Both are about young Australian troops fighting in World War I and receiving their baptism of fire. Both begin in the Australian countryside and then move to the Middle East. Their conclusions and their larger view of war are polar opposites.

By the time Dave Mitchell (Peter Phelps) joins the 4th Regiment of the Light Horse reinforcements in April 1917, the unit has already fought in Gallipoli and other battles. The Light Horse is "mounted infantry" as opposed to cavalry, though the details of that distinction—beyond the troopers' use of rifles and bayonets—are not too important. The regiment is involved in a stalemated attack on the Turco-German army fortress at Gaza and the town of Beersheba, Palestine. It's a desert war where the availability of water is always the critical factor.

Dave arrives and becomes a D'Artagnan figure to three unlikely Musketeers—Tas Pool (John Walton), Chiller Diggs (Tim McKenzie), and Scotty Bolton (Jon Blake)—when their friend Frank (Gary Sweet) is wounded. Dave goes through an extremely mild version of the "new guy" treatment and fits right in until the regiment sees its first real action. In that engagement, the Turks immediately retreat and Dave finds that he cannot shoot at an enemy's back. Is it a question of conscience, buck fever, or cowardice? The other two central characters are Meinertzhagen (Anthony Andrews), an eccentric bird-loving intelligence officer, and Anne (Sigrid Thornton), a nurse.

The cast is certainly attractive and capable enough, though all of the characters—many of them based on real individuals—have a sketched-in lack of depth. That's the film's central problem. It isn't able to generate the emotional intensity that makes *Gallipoli* so memorable. Australian audiences might disagree with that assessment, but the film has never been the international favorite that Wier's work is. That said, the riding scenes are magnificent.

Where Wier's central image is the runner moving across a vast landscape, Wincer focuses on horses and riders, often in massed ranks sweeping across the screen. Making full use of that strong light that Australian films of the 1980s are so famous for, Wincer and cinematographer Dean Semler create striking exterior action shots. They also do their best to flatter the equine stars, and the closing credits claim that none were injured. That's astonishing, given some of the rough falls that the horses take in the final charge on Beersheba. It's a fine scene, easily the equal of the conclusion of the 1936 *Charge of the Light Brigade*. And like that film, *The Lighthorsemen* ends on a simple heroic note when it could have been much more complex.

Scotty (Jon Blake) charges ahead in *The Lighthorsemen.* The Kobal Collection

Cast: Jon Blake (Scotty), Peter Phelps (Dave), Tony Bonner (Bourchier), Bill Kerr (Chauvel), Nick Waters (Lighthorse Sergeant), John Walton (Tas), Tim McKenzie (Chiller), Sigrid Thornton (Anne), Anthony Andrews (Meinertzhagen), Shane Briant (Reichert), Gary Sweet (Frank), Gerard Kennedy (Ismet Bey); **Written by:** Ian Jones; **Cinematography by:** Dean Semler; **Music by:** Mario Millo. **Producer:** Simon Wincer, Ian Jones. **Australian. MPAA Rating:** PG-13. **Running Time:** 110 minutes. **Format:** VHS, Beta, Closed Caption.

John Ford's World War I adventure isn't much different from his westerns. In fact, the Arizona desert stands in for Mesopotamia, and these British mounted soldiers wear pith helmets and khaki instead of cavalry blue. Beyond that, the largely invisible Arabs are essentially Sioux in long robes. What is unusual for Ford, though, is the rigorously stripped-down quality of the story. Barely more than an hour long, the film contains no wasted gestures, words, or moments. All of the conflicts have been reduced to their essential elements. Questions about politics and the morality of the Great War are not even asked. If the script were produced today, doubtless, the Kafkaesque elements would be heightened and the film would be labeled "postmodern" for its detachment, but Ford is not trying to be ironic. He is trying to tell a story simply.

The setting is a sea of rolling white sand dunes that stretches to the horizon in all directions. In the opening seconds, the officer in charge of a small patrol is shot and killed, leaving the Sergeant (Victor McLaglen) in charge. But the Lieutenant did not tell the Sergeant what their objective was. He doesn't know where they are or where they're going— only that the Brigade is somewhere out "there." When the group finds a small oasis, the Sergeant doesn't know whether they should make it their camp or move on.

Fact:
The Lost Patrol was also made as a silent film in 1929 with Victor McLaglen's brother Cyril in the role of the Sergeant.

In films like this, audiences expect the unit to be made up of unusual, colorful characters and these fit that job description, though they don't exactly fit the formula. The most visible of the group is Sanders (Boris Karloff), a Bible-toting religious lunatic whose madness is bizarrely manifested at the end. Pearson (Douglas Walton) is a raw recruit who still loves Kipling and expects his army service to be a grand adventure. Brown (Reginald Denny) is the older veteran who regales the rest with stories of the golden girls in his past.

As we get to know them, the Arabs hidden in the dunes wait for the right moment to pick them off one by one, horse by horse. Ostensibly, Germans are the enemy, but they never come into play. Why are the Arabs attacking them? Does it matter why?

Ford directs with his trademarked lack of affectation. To oversimplify, he puts his camera down and lets the actors and the action handle the rest. He keeps the sentimental aspects of the characters tightly under control—though he does give Karloff a bit too much room to roam—and never lets the pace slacken.

In the end, the film has little to do with the realities of World War I. It has everything to do with the stresses that men must deal with when they're against an invisible enemy and have no place to retreat. How do they react when they can't fight and can't run?

See also

Bataan
Beau Geste
She Wore a Yellow Ribbon
The Lighthorsemen
Sahara

Many other films have dealt with variations on those questions, but they've seldom been framed with such stark simplicity.

Members of *The Lost Patrol* try to figure out who's shooting at them, and from where. Victor McLaglen second from left; Boris Karloff, far right. The Kobal Collection

Cast: Victor McLaglen (The Sergeant), Boris Karloff (Sanders), Reginald Denny (George Brown), Wallace Ford (Morelli), Alan Hale (Cook), J.M. Kerrigan (Quincannon), Billy Bevan (Herbert Hale), Brandon Hurst (Cpl. Bell), Douglas Walton (Pearson); **Written by:** Dudley Nichols, Garrett Fort; **Cinematography by:** Harold Wenstrom; **Music by:** Max Steiner. **Producer:** RKO, Cliff Reid. **Awards:** Nominations: Academy Awards '34: Best Score. **Running Time:** 66 minutes. **Format:** VHS, Beta, LV.

Stanley Kubrick's fourth feature is an anti-war masterpiece. It's a brilliant, flawed work that established his reputation as one of the world's pre-eminent filmmakers. Though the script came from an unlikely collaboration of writers—Jim Thompson, master of lurid pulp tales, and "serious" novelist Calder Willingham working from Humphrey Cobb's novel—the film's lapses highlight the flaws that would plague Kubrick's work in the following decades. The same could be said of the strengths: inspired casting, energetic pace, innovative camerawork, uncompromising attitude.

The fact-based plot was so offensive to French authorities that the film has actually been banned there. The setting is 1916, when two years of trench warfare have arrived at a stalemate where nothing of importance has been gained at the cost of thousands of lives. The lines are frozen. Gen. Broulard (Adolphe Menjou) dangles the promise of a promotion before Gen. Mireau (George Macready) if his exhausted 701st Regiment will attempt a suicidal assault on a German position called "The Anthill" and take it. Gen. Mireau orders Col. Dax (Kirk Douglas) to lead the charge. Col. Dax orders Lt. Roget (Wayne Morris) on a night reconnaissance mission which is a partial disaster, and then Dax leads the charge himself.

> "If these little sweethearts won't face German bullets, they'll face French ones!"
>
> **Gen. Mireau (George Macready) on his regiment's unenthusiastic attack against "The Anthill"**

Those scenes are some of the most immediate and harrowing depictions of the Great War ever put on film. Kubrick sets up the attack with a series of long dolly shots inside the trenches. Then when the action moves up to the surface, he follows the men at a slow pace as they make their way across the muddy, cratered landscape amid bullets and exploding shells. It's an intricate, intimate dance between the tracking camera and its subjects. After the attack fails, the commanding officers decide that an example must be made, and three soldiers are chosen at random to be court-martialed for cowardice. Col. Dax finds himself defending Cpl. Paris (Ralph Meeker), Pvt. Ferol (Timothy Carey), and Pvt. Arnaud (Joe Turkel).

> "These executions will be a perfect tonic for the entire division. There are few things more fundamentally encouraging and stimulating than seeing someone else die."
>
> **Gen. Broulard (Adolphe Menjou) on the potential sacrifice of three enlisted men**

Kubrick is able to maintain the intensity of the combat scenes in the trial by photographing the proceedings in extreme close ups and long takes that mirror the earlier tracking sequences. The cavernous rooms of a chateau where it takes place are shown in deep focus with exaggerated lighting. The various figures are arranged in contrasting groups to further delineate their differences. While the enlisted men stand at attention or sit in straight-backed chairs, the mid-level officers are behind desks, and their officers recline on stuffed chairs and couches, tastefully set apart but not too far apart.

Though the characters have a certain forced and unnatural quality due to their circumstances, they seem real at the same time because the actors do such splendid work. Menjou and Macready are particularly effective in thoroughly despicable roles. Gen. Broulard is a study in reptilian gentility and manipulation. Gen. Mireau is more craven in his ambitious self-deception that's revealed in moments both large and small. Notice, for example, his "toast" right before the attack. As the three potential sacrificial victims, Meeker, Carey, and Turkel are equally good. They react to their situation in different but wholly believable ways, one turning to God, one fatalistically accepting his lot, one raging against it.

Kirk Douglas is French Col. Dax, who must defend three soldiers chosen at random to be court-martialed for cowardice during an ill-conceived mission in *Paths of Glory*. The Kobal Collection

Though his role could easily be the thinnest and most stereotyped, Kirk Douglas is able to invest his heroic character with real emotional power. Douglas was involved in the film's production, and his personal belief in its message is evident in every frame. If he hadn't supported the film so strongly, it might well not have been made. Its anti-authoritarian message is directly at odds with the spirit of the decade. (Remember that one of the best-selling non-fiction books of the era was *The Organization Man,* which advocated the suppression of independent individual action to corporate conformity.)

The film's cynicism and moral outrage builds so steadily and deeply that any kind of conventional ending is perhaps impossible. The "hopeful" conclusion that Kubrick arrives at seems both insincere and unearned. The moment begins as a continuation of Kubrick's frosty view of humanity, taking it from the upper classes to the masses, but then it abruptly changes and seems to find redemption and reaffirmation of a sentimental idealism that has been shattered. It is the weakest part of the film. Seven years later, Kubrick would deal with the same subject and similar ideas more successfully in his black comedy, *Dr. Strangelove*.

Cast: Kirk Douglas (Col. Dax), Adolphe Menjou (Gen. Broulard), George Macready (Gen. Mireau), Ralph Meeker (Cpl. Paris), Richard Anderson (Maj. Saint-Auban), Wayne Morris (Lt. Roget), Timothy Carey (Pvt. Ferol), Susanne Christian (German singer), Bert Freed (St. Boulanger), Joe Turkel (Pvt. Arnaud), Peter Capell (Col. Judge); Written by: Stanley Kubrick, Calder Willingham, Jim Thompson; Cinematography by: Georg Krause; Music by: Gerald Fried; Technical Advisor: Baron von Waldendels. Producer: United Artists, James B. Harris. Awards: National Film Registry '92. Budget: $935,000. Running Time: 86 minutes. Format: VHS, Beta, LV, Closed Caption.

SERGEANT YORK

1941 Howard Hawks ♪♪♪♪

Hollywood's most honored piece of propaganda—and one of its most popular—is also a thoughtful, even gentle film. It can be faulted for taking a rosy view of World War I, but that's because it was part of a larger effort by the entertainment industry to prepare the country for World War II. The subject is Congressional Medal of Honor–winner Alvin York. His is an unusual tale of heroism, and, by all accounts, this is an unusually accurate version of real events. To no one's surprise, it's also uncritical. York's diary is the source of the script and he served as an advisor. The film's enduring success, though, comes from a brilliant performance by Gary Cooper, one of the best in his long career. He won his first Academy Award for it; the second came for *High Noon*.

When we first meet Alvin C. York, he is sowing his wild oats in an Arcadian rural Tennessee. (The place is so idealized that it must be close to Brigadoon.) Alvin rips around with his pals Ike (Ward Bond) and Buck (Noah Beery Jr.), getting drunk and shooting their pistols. "Satan's got you by the shirttail, Alvin," Pastor Pile (Walter Brennan) says "He's gonna yank you straight down to hell!" Alvin's saintly mother (Margaret Wycherly) agrees. (In the long history of long-suffering Hollywood mothers, she may be the longest suffering of them all and, like Cooper and Brennan, she was nominated for an Oscar.) Then Alvin meets lovely young Gracie (Joan Leslie) and thinks about changing his ways, but nothing comes easy. His conversion to the straight and narrow is finally accomplished through a particularly crazed bit of business. Somehow, though, Cooper's craggy innocence pulls off the transformation. A great actor might not be able to manage the scene, but a real movie star can.

Unfortunately for Alvin, he finds religion on the eve of America's entry into the war. As he sees it, "I ain't a-goin' to war. War is killin' and the Book's agin killin', so war is agin the Book." His draft board doesn't agree, so Alvin, who's also a deadeye shot, is faced with a second set of moral questions. And for a second time—in defiance of all dramatic logic—Cooper, director Howard Hawks and a team of writers make it work. We believe that York wrestles with his angels and comes to the right decision. That's when, at long last, the scene shifts to France, where York accomplishes his astonishing feats. Again, the filmmakers manage to make potentially absurd events seem absolutely believable, and much of the credit for that must go with Arthur Edeson, who photographed the battle sequences.

Two other aspects need mention. First, this may be the most flattering and forgiving depiction of the Army as an organization ever put on film. Officers and non-coms are shown as wise, compassionate, and forbearing men. They're probably cheerful, thrifty, brave, clean, and reverent, too. Second, though the Southern accents are pure Hollywood, with speech patterns that seem strange and forced, they're not entirely inaccurate. (For more realistic use of deep Southern accents, see Robert Duvall in *Tomorrow*, adapted by Horton Foote from a William Faulkner story.)

In the end, *Sergeant York* is unabashed, unembarrassed hero worship, and to criticize it for being effective hero worship misses the point. No, the film does not question York's rationale that he killed

See also
No Time for Sergeants
To Hell and Back

WORLD WAR I

only to prevent more killing, but it doesn't revel in his deeds, either. Instead, it tells an involving, emotional story about an admirable man who served his country well.

Sgt. York **attempts to help a fallen comrade.** The Kobal Collection

Cast: Gary Cooper (Sgt. Alvin C. York), Joan Leslie (Gracie Williams), Walter Brennan (Pastor Rosier Pile), Dickie Moore (George York), Ward Bond (Ike Botkin), George Tobias (Michael T. "Pusher" Ross), Noah Beery Jr. (Buck Lipscomb), June Lockhart (Rosie York), Stanley Ridges (Maj. Buxton), Margaret Wycherly (Ma York), James Anderson (Eb), David Bruce (Bert Thomas), Lane Chandler (Cpl. Savage), Elisha Cook Jr. (Piano player), Erville Alderson (Nate Tomkins), Howard da Silva (Lem), Donald Douglas (Capt. Tillman), Frank Faylen (Butt Boy), Pat Flaherty (Sgt. Harry Parsons), Joseph Girard (Gen. John Pershing), Creighton Hale (AP Man), Russell Hicks (General), George Irving (Harrison), Selmer Jackson (Gen. Duncan), Jack

Pennick (Cpl. Cutting), Harvey Stephens (Capt. Danforth), Kay Sutton (Saloon girl), Clem Bevans (Zeke), Charles Trowbridge (Cordell Hull), Guy Wilkerson (Tom Carver), Gig Young (Soldier); **Written by:** Abem Finkel, Harry Chandler, Howard Koch, John Huston; **Cinematography by:** Sol Polito; **Music by:** Max Steiner. **Producer:** Howard Hawks, Jesse L. Lasky, Hal B. Wallis, Warner Bros. **Awards:** Academy Awards '41: Best Actor (Cooper), Best Film Editing; New York Film Critics Awards '41: Best Actor (Cooper); Nominations: Academy Awards '41: Best Black and White Cinematography, Best Director (Hawks), Best Interior Decoration, Best Original Screenplay, Best Picture, Best Sound, Best Supporting Actor (Brennan), Best Supporting Actress (Wycherly), Best Original Dramatic Score. **Running Time:** 134 minutes. **Format:** VHS, Beta.

The first aerial combat movie mapped out the territory for all that have followed, but it's far from the best. Like so many other works of the silent era, it's slow, and contemporary audiences will probably think that it's too soft and sentimental for its grim subject. Those flaws not withstanding, some of the flying sequences have an unvarnished realism that today's films can't touch.

The first title card sets an idyllic scene: "Small town 1917—Youth and dreams of youth."

Jack Powell (Charles "Buddy" Rogers) is the archetypal boy-next-door who tinkers with cars. Mary Preston (Clara Bow) is not the archetypal girl-next-door. She loves Jack, but he's stuck on Sylvia Lewis (Jobyna Ralston), a visiting city girl. So is David Armstrong (Richard Arlen), and Sylvia's stuck on him. But, through a series of improbable misunderstandings, Jack thinks that Sylvia loves him and pays no attention to Mary. As the next big title card puts it, "So Youth laughed and wept and lived its heedless hour, while over the world hung a cloud which spread and spread until its shadow fell in some degree on every living person—WAR! And Youth answered the challenge."

David and the clueless Jack enlist in the Army Air Corps. During a brief interlude in basic training and flight school, they become friends and are sent to France. Mary, meanwhile, becomes an ambulance driver.

Once the film moves to France, it takes a two-sided approach to its subject. The air war is treated as a basically clean and chivalrous operation where pilots observe polite rules—letting an opponent fly away when he has empty machine guns, for example. The ground war is much more devastating and brutal. Director William Wellman, who had flown in the Lafayette Escadrille, makes the desolate trenches and battlefields appallingly real. There he also hints at the random destruction of The Great War. Several of the large-scale surface battle scenes are really more spectacular than their aerial counterparts, with tanks crushing machine gun nests and the like.

Unfortunately, that part of the film is marred by far too much comic relief, including Mary's incongruous adventures in Paris, which have a tacked-on feeling, and a seemingly endless drunken-leave sequence. That's a double shame because Clara Bow, the famous "It Girl," is absolutely radiant. Her vitality and sex appeal could have been much more important to the story. Wellman is interested in the relationship between Jack and David.

Finally though, all flying movies have to do one thing. No matter what else, they've got to put you, the viewer, in the airplane, in the pilot's seat. *Wings* does—eventually. Footage filmed in the bomb bay of the huge twin engine German *Gotha* is just terrific. So is the balloon burning, and several fighter crashes are so impressively edited that they seem remarkably real. In the more involved dogfights, the use of title cards to explain the action is a problem, and the grand finale, where Jack virtually wins the war singlehandedly in his Spad, is a little hard to take.

Today, viewers who can overlook the dated elements will see an expensive studio production—winner of the first Best Picture

> "His first dawn patrol! Here was the dream come true—here was the trumpet call to breathless hazards in the skies! Here—at last!"
>
> **Typically purple title card prose**

See also
The Blue Max
Dawn Patrol
Birth of a Nation
Hell's Angels
The Big Parade

Oscar—that uses its budget to create detailed images of war. If its depiction of the human element isn't as fully realized, well, the movies had to start somewhere.

Cast: Clara Bow (Mary Preston), Charles "Buddy" Rogers (John "Jack" Powell), Richard Arlen (David Armstrong), Gary Cooper (Cadet White), Jobyna Ralston (Sylvia Lewis), El Brendel (Herman Schwimpf), Richard Tucker (Air Commander), Henry B. Walthall (David's father), Roscoe Karns (Lt. Cameron), Gunboat Smith (The Sergeant), Julia Swayne Gordon (David's mother), Arlette Marchal (Celeste), Carl von Haartman (German officer), William A. Wellman (Doughboy); **Written by:** Hope Loring, John Monk Saunders, Louis D. Lighton; **Cinematography by:** Harry Perry; **Music by:** J.S. Zamecnik. **Producer:** Lucien Hubbard, Paramount Pictures. **Awards:** Academy Awards '27: Best Picture, National Film Registry '97. **Running Time:** 139 minutes. **Format:** VHS, Beta, LV.

The Hound Salutes: William Wellman

William Wellman did almost all of his work during the years when the major studios controlled the film industry, but he was never really part of the "studio system." Even when he was a contract director, he chafed at the interference of producers and executives, and was trying to get away from them. That's hardly surprising. Along with Howard Hawks and John Ford, "Wild Bill" was one of the pioneers who took the movies from silent to sound and put his own mark on the films that he cared about. Also like them, his career cannot be reduced to war films, even though he made four of the finest.

Wellman's first success was the winner of the first Best Picture Academy Award, *Wings*, in 1927. For the director, the flamboyantly plotted film actually had a degree of autobiographical realism. He had flown with the Lafayette Escadrille and been shot down as a pilot in World War I. After the war, he took advantage of a chance meeting with Douglas Fairbanks to gain a foothold in Hollywood. After trying and disliking acting, he went to work on the other side of the camera and worked his way up to directing. He had made many silent films, most of them lost now, before he got his shot with *Wings*. After it, he worked steadily on poor films that he was forced to accept by the studio. Within that crushing system that was grinding out pictures like sausages, he managed to create *The Public Enemy* (1931), which made James Cagney a star, and *A Star Is Born* (1937), with Frederic March and Janet Gaynor. (It would be remade two more times.)

Then in 1939, Wellman made one of the screen's great adventures, *Beau Geste*. Again, changes in cinematic storytelling techniques date the film somewhat, but at the core is an inventively written, terrifically acted, beautifully photographed action film.

Given Wellman's reputation with aerial pictures and escapism, he seems an odd choice to make a down-in-the-mud look at war from the point of view of a foot soldier. But remember that the scenes of trench warfare in *Wings* are as impressive as some of the aerial sequences. When he turned his attention to World War II, Wellman directed two of the best combat films of the 1940s. Structurally, both *The Story of G.I. Joe*, based on Ernie Pyle's writings, and *Battleground* are unit pictures—stories of small groups of infantrymen told with honest emotion and an indelibly vivid sense of place.

Both are terrific films that have never quite caught on with the public for odd reasons. *The Story of G.I. Joe* has been unavailable on home video, but should be soon. The title *Battleground* is too easily confused with many others. They deserve to be much more well known than they are.

After *Battleground*, Wellman's career declined. He made some memorable films with John Wayne—notably *Island in the Sky* and *The High and the Mighty*, also unavailable on video—but studio interference ruined *Lafayette Escadrille*, and he was never enthusiastic about his final film, *Darby's Rangers*. After that, he quit the business and wrote an autobiography, *A Short Time for Insanity*, before he died in 1975. Critical opinion about him has tended to be mixed, with a dismissive edge. Only in the 1990s have filmmakers of the next generation—Scorsese, Spielberg—championed his work.

The praiseful 1996 documentary, *Wild Bill, Hollywood Maverick* (Kino on Video) was produced by his son, William A. Wellman Jr.

Between the Great War and Pearl Harbor

The films in this section might have been shoehorned into the different World War II headings. But despite the fact that they were made over a 50-year span, they share an anticipation of the conflict to come, and in some cases they show the preliminary engagements.

For Americans, World War II has a definite starting point, December 7, 1941, and it is not simply hindsight that makes that historical moment so evocative. That date divides events as significantly as BC and AD. Before that moment, people thought about the world and themselves in one way. When they learned about the attack, it changed them. In many cases, things that had been massively important were made meaningless. That's the whole point of the most famous of these films, *From Here to Eternity*.

As everyone surely knows, author James Jones was there at Schofield Barracks on that Sunday morning when the Japanese attack came, and so he felt no need to emphasize its significance. Director Fred Zinnemann pays perhaps more attention to the imminence of the situation than he needs to. His leads—Burt Lancaster, Deborah Kerr, and even Montgomery Clift and Donna Reed—make the strong emotions seem absolutely right. Though Jones's massive work presents serious problems to any dramatic adaptation, this one has become a cultural touchstone.

The same cannot be said of Charlie Chaplin's admirable but disappointing *The Great Dictator* from 1940. Most moviegoers have probably seen clips from the wonderful dance that his Hitler character does with a lighted balloon globe. It's really the only memorable scene in an otherwise uncomfortable comedy.

Michael Curtiz's *Dive Bomber* is a curious piece of understated propaganda about the research that Navy aviation doctors did in the problems of high-altitude flying. That doesn't sound like gripping dramatic material, and it isn't, but the film is a fascinating look at a pre-war military that was still using open-cockpit biplanes.

John Huston, Humphrey Bogart, Sydney Greenstreet, and Mary Astor reteamed after the success of *The Maltese Falcon* with *Across the Pacific*, a neat if predictable thriller that casts Bogie as a disgraced army officer who claims to be ready to sell his expertise to the Japanese. The cast isn't able to overcome a so-so script with racist undercurrents.

For Whom the Bell Tolls is no more successful. Some have speculated that it might have been a great war film if director Howard Hawks had accepted it. For several reasons—mostly his dislike of the novel—he declined, and the result, with Sam Wood at the helm, is a turgid, slow-moving affair.

Hong Kong 1941 is a Chinese *Casablanca* about the romantic triangle that evolves among Chow Yun-Fat, Cecilia Yip, and Alex Man as the Japanese take over the city. For videophiles who have not discovered the wonders of Hong Kong films, this one is a good place to start.

Ken Loach's *Land and Freedom* is another romance, this one among the dedicated communists who fought for the Republican Army in the Spanish Civil War. The story is strongly reminiscent of George Orwell's memoir *Homage to Catalonia*. Pekka Parikka examines another "little" preview that paved the way for what would come soon in *The Winter War*. His subject is the Russian invasion of Finland in 1939, and the tough resistance that the outnumbered Finns displayed. Though this 1989 film is barely known in this country, it is one of the more realistic depictions of modern combat.

ACROSS THE PACIFIC

1942 John Huston 🦴🦴🦴

For his third feature, John Huston tries to repeat the screen chemistry that made his debut, *The Maltese Falcon*, so successful. He gets it about half right, and turns a fairly predictable piece of propaganda into a diverting, but derivative entertainment. In strictly visual terms, the film is spookily similar to other more famous films of the period. The bleary-eyed channel surfer who happens across it early one morning might for a moment think that he's stumbled across an alternative combination of *Casablanca*, *The Big Sleep*, and *The Thin Man*.

The story begins on November 17, 1941. (Those who miss the significance of the date, the month, and year will be reminded often.) Lt. Rick Leland (Humphrey Bogart) is being cashiered from the Army at Governor's Island, New York. The reasons are vague, but before five minutes have passed, Bogie is decked out in his familiar trenchcoat. Leland tries to enlist in the Canadian army, but his disgrace is so widespread that they won't have him. Wondering aloud if perhaps the Japanese will take him on, Leland buys a ticket on the *Genoa Maru* bound for Yokohama via the Panama Canal. On board the freighter, Leland meets Alberta Marlow (Mary Astor), who lies about her past, and Dr. Lorenz (Sydney Greenstreet), a sociologist with an undisguised affinity for all things Japanese.

> "Mine's bigger than yours."
>
> **Rick Leland (Humphrey Bogart) comparing his pistol to Dr. Lorenz's (Sydney Greenstreet)**

It's really not spoiling anything to reveal that Leland is engaged in counterespionage because neither Huston nor writers Robert Carson and Richard Macaulay take the material very seriously. For most of the film, they're more interested in the cutesy shipboard romance between Leland and Alberta—getting seasick, drunk, sunburned, and swapping coy banter every step of the way. The stars handle the material lightly, but none of their scenes strike the dark spark of the sexual manipulation that goes on between Sam Spade and Brigid O'Shaughnessy in *Falcon*. Similarly, the efforts of Lorenz to recruit Leland never reach the level of the verbal sparring Spade and Gutman enjoy so much.

Did you Know?

Huston left the film before it was finished to make the War Department documentary *Report from the Aleutians*. The final scenes were directed by Vincent Sherman.

As a thriller, the film doesn't really get wound up until the third act, when it has a few fine moments, most memorably a long chase scene in a Spanish-language movie theater, and a conventional conclusion. Today, the film is more interesting for its revelation of American attitudes toward Japan. Given the circumstances of the times, the "yellow peril" racism may be defensible, but it didn't begin in 1941 and it's still ugly.

See also

Casablanca
Action in the North Atlantic
The Red Badge of Courage
The African Queen

Sydney Greenstreet, Humphrey
Bogart, and Mary Astor reteam
for pre-war intrigue in *Across
the Pacific.* The Kobal Collection

Cast: Humphrey Bogart (Rick Leland), Mary Astor (Alberta Marlow), Sydney Greenstreet (Dr. Lorenz), Charles Halton (A.V. Smith), Victor Sen Yung (Joe Totsuiko), Roland Got (Sugi), Keye Luke (Steamship office clerk), Richard Loo (First Officer Miyamu), Frank Wilcox (Capt. Morrison), Paul Stanton (Col. Hart), Lester Matthews (Canadian Major), Tom Stevenson (Tall thin man), Roland Drew (Capt. Harkness), Monte Blue (Dan Morton), Rudy Robles (Filipino assassin), Lee Tung Foo (Sam Wing On), Chester Gan (Capt. Higoto), Kam Tong (T. Oki), Spencer Chan (Chief Engineer Mitsuko), Philip Ahn (Informer in theater), Frank Faylen (Sidewalk vendor), Frank Mayo (Trial Judge Advocate); **Written by:** Richard Macaulay, Robert Carson; **Cinematography by:** Arthur Edeson; **Music by:** Adolph Deutsch. **Producer:** Jerry Wald, Jack Saper, Warner Bros. **Running Time:** 97 minutes. **Format:** VHS.

DIVE BOMBER

1941 Michael Curtiz

Michael Curtiz may be the most famous "unknown" director of Hollywood's golden era. He made some of the most popular and profitable movies—*Casablanca*, *The Adventures of Robin Hood*, *Yankee Doodle Dandy*—and because they ranged so widely in subject and tone, he was never identified with his pictures in the way that Alfred Hitchcock or John Ford were. Instead, he came to epitomize the Warner Bros. school of filmmaking—good, swiftly paced escapist stories geared to energetic handsome stars. *Dive Bomber* follows the formula entertainingly enough, but it proves that no one, not even Curtiz, could make a silk purse out of this soap bubble.

It's a frivolous treatment of a serious but essentially undramatic subject, the efforts of flight doctors to prevent pilots from blacking out during high speed and high altitude flights. Today, the film is more interesting as a snapshot of the pre-World War II armed services. Some of the titular aircraft are open-cockpit biplanes and the whole film has a delightfully dated feeling.

Lt. Doug Lee (Errol Flynn) is a Harvard-educated Navy doctor who's interested in research. Cmdr. Joe Blake (Fred MacMurray) is a cocky flyboy who first meets Lee when a fellow pilot doesn't pull out of a dive and dies on the operating table. Blake blames Lee, thereby setting up a false conflict between the two. It's fairly quickly resolved when Lee learns to fly and signs on with Dr. Rogers (Ralph Bellamy) to help with his research. That's really all there is to the story. The supporting characters are built on stereotypes, and convenient coincidences keep things moving over the slow stretches. The comic relief based on an NCO dodging his wife at payday is indicative of the film's dismissal of women. All three of the female characters are avaricious parasites who would tempt men away from their more noble pursuits, if the men were paying attention.

But they're not; they're bonding. Bonding and smoking. The film makes constant references to smoking. Cigarettes are more than a part of all this bonding. They are fetishes, objects that must be touched, caressed, and shared at every decisive moment. More specifically, three gold cigarette cases, which reappear often, are totems that represent the skills of three hotshot fliers. Doubtless, there is a degree of realism to the prevalence of tobacco use in the Navy, but compared to other films of the period, the focus on smoking is still exceptional.

As for the film itself, *Dive Bomber* is less overtly propagandistic than many military-themed movies of the late 1930s and early '40s, but it is very much a film made by and for a nation about to go to war. Today, it's enjoyable mostly for the fine, if unexceptional, performances by the two leads, and the airplanes, lovingly photographed by Bert Glennon, Winston E. Hoch, Elmer Dyer, and Charles Marshall.

Fact:

Screenwriter Frank "Spig" Wead, a Navy ace pilot in World War I, was active in efforts to support the Navy air wing between the wars. He was portrayed by John Wayne in John Ford's 1957 film *The Wings of Eagles*.

See also

An Officer and a Gentleman
Thirty Seconds over Tokyo
The Right Stuff
Bataan

Fred MacMurray, Errol Flynn, and Ralph Bellamy in *Dive Bomber*. The Kobal Collection

Cast: Errol Flynn (Lt. Doug Lee), Fred MacMurray (Cmdr. Joe Blake), Ralph Bellamy (Dr. Lance Rogers), Alexis Smith (Linda Fisher), Regis Toomey (Tim Griffin), Robert Armstrong (Art Lyons), Allen Jenkins ('Lucky Dice'), Craig Stevens (John Thomas Anthony), Herb Anderson (Chubby), Moroni Olsen (Senior Flight Surgeon-San Diego), Dennie Moore (Mrs. James), Louis Jean Heydt (Swede Larson), Cliff Nazarro (Corps Man), Tod Andrews (Telephone Man), Ann Doran (Helen), Charles Drake (Pilot), Alan Hale Jr. (Pilot), William Forrest (Commander), Creighton Hale (Hospital attendant), Howard Hickman (Admiral), Russell Hicks (Admiral), George Meeker (Commander), Richard Travis (C.O.), Addison Richards (Senior Flight Surgeon); **Written by:** Frank Wead, Robert Buckner; **Cinematography by:** Bert Glennon, Winton C. Hoch, Elmer Dyer, Charles A. Marshall; **Music by:** Max Steiner. **Producer:** Hal B. Wallis, Warner Bros. **Awards:** Nominations: Academy Awards '41: Best Color Cinematography. **Running Time:** 130 minutes. **Format:** VHS, Closed Caption.

DIVE BOMBER

FOR WHOM THE BELL TOLLS

1943 Sam Wood 🦴🦴🦴

Someone once said of writer Henry James that he chews much more than he bites off. That also applies to Sam Wood's adaptation of Ernest Hemingway's famous novel. It's a simple story of a commando raid that could have been a fine adventure tale. (Remade under the title *The Guns of Navarone*, that's exactly what it is.) But Wood overinflates every aspect, dragging out scenes that should be quick and sharply pointed. The 1995 restored edition compounds the problem by adding a musical overture and intermission, complete with production stills.

Robert Jordan (Gary Cooper), an American schoolteacher turned demolitions expert, is sent behind enemy lines by the Republican Army during the Spanish Civil War. As part of a major offensive, he is to join a group of resistance fighters and blow up a bridge spanning a mountain pass. But Pablo (Akim Tamiroff), the group's leader, thinks the mission is too dangerous and refuses to help. Pilar (Katina Paxinou) then challenges Pablo's authority and takes over. Further roiling the already stormy emotional waters, beautiful Maria (Ingrid Bergman) immediately falls for the American.

"Surely you know how rumors fly. The officers talk in the cafes and the waiters listen. The rumors come running."

Fernando (Fortunio Bonanova)

"They don't shoot you for being a Republican in America."

Robert Jordan (Gary Cooper)

Much of the first half is set inside a cave, where the group dynamics shift, and various loyalties are questioned as backgrounds are revealed. Several slowly paced, talky scenes—made even less palatable by broad overacting, phony accents, and forced humor—finally boil down to faith in Pablo's leadership. Do they trust him? Should they kill him? Most of the physical action occurs in the second half. There the confrontations between the Civil Guards and the Republicans are marred by dated special effects and jarring transitions between real exteriors and the sets meant to represent those exteriors. At one time, audiences may have accepted such conventions, but today they are intrusive, and neither the acting nor the slim story is compelling enough to compensate.

The once-daring sexual element doesn't make the earth move anymore, either. The goo-goo eyes that Jordan and Maria make to each other are more than a little embarrassing. As Ms. Bergman had proved so effectively a year before in *Casablanca*, with star-crossed wartime romance, less really is more.

Also, despite the film's inherent anti-fascist, pro-left point of view, director Sam Wood and star Cooper were active in the anticommunist witch-hunt of the late 1940s. In fact, a year after this film was released, Wood organized and became president of the Motion Picture Alliance for the Preservation of American Ideals. His politics have nothing to do with this film's problems. It's purely a matter of a filmmaker treating his fictional source material as holy writ when he should have tried to tell the story as efficiently as possible.

See also

The Guns of Navarone
To Have and Have Not
Casablanca

Gary Cooper and Ingrid
Bergman (far right), Akim
Tamiroff and Katrina Pakinou
(center left) and friends in *For
Whom the Bell Tolls.* The Kobal Collection

Cast: Gary Cooper (Robert Jordan), Ingrid Bergman (Maria), Akim Tamiroff (Pablo), Katina Paxinou (Pilar), Arturo de Cordova (Agustin), Vladimir Sokoloff (Anselmo), Mikhail Rasumny (Rafael), Fortunio Bonanova (Fernando), Victor Varconi (Primitivo), Joseph Calleia (El Sordo), Alexander Granach (Paco), Yakima Canutt (Young cavalryman), George Coulouris (Andre Massart), Yvonne De Carlo (Girl in cafe), Martin Garralaga (Capt. Mora), Soledad Jiminez (Guillermo's wife), Duncan Renaldo (Lt. Berrendo), Tito Renaldo (First sentry), Pedro de Cordoba (Frederico Gonzalez), Frank Puglia (Capt. Gomez), John Mylong (Col. Duval), Eric Feldary (Andres), Lilo Yarson (Joaquin), Leo Bugakov (Gen. Golz), Antonio Molina (Guillermo); **Written by:** Dudley Nichols; **Cinematography by:** Ray Rennahan; **Music by:** Victor Young. **Producer:** Sam Wood; released by Paramount Pictures. **Awards:** Academy Awards '43: Best Supporting Actress (Paxinou); Nominations: Academy Awards '43: Best Actor (Cooper), Best Actress (Bergman), Best Color Cinematography, Best Film Editing, Best Interior Decoration, Best Picture, Best Supporting Actor (Tamiroff), Best Original Dramatic Score. **Budget:** 2M. **Running Time:** 130 minutes. **Format:** VHS, DVD.

FROM HERE TO ETERNITY

1953 Fred Zinnemann ♪♪♪♪

The restrictions on popular films being what they were in the 1950s, writer Daniel Taradash and director Fred Zinnemann were forced to make massive changes in James Jones's profane, bawdy, excessive best-seller before they could bring it to the silver screen. Key character motivations were changed, the language was sanitized, the violence was discreetly veiled. But the filmmakers kept the core story of two GIs caught up in star-crossed romances on the eve of the Pearl Harbor attack, and it has become one of the most popular films ever made about the military. It won eight Academy Awards (at the time, more than any film since *Gone with the Wind*) and remains a perennial favorite on video.

Near perfect casting has much to do with the film's success. The stories about Frank Sinatra's lobbying for his Oscar-winning role are the stuff of Hollywood legend. At times, the producers also seriously considered Aldo Ray for the role of Prewitt, Eli Wallach for Maggio and Joan Crawford for Karen. But putting the right people in front of the camera cannot account for all of the film's continued popularity. From the Hawaiian locations to the uniforms (have starched, tailored khakis ever looked so good?) to the snappy dialogue (see sidebar) every element works and the balance is right.

If the film has a flaw, it comes in the repeated reminders that the setting is late 1941, and so the various individual conflicts will soon be deluged by cataclysmic global events. Viewers know these characters are standing on the brink of history—and that Jones had been there, too—they don't need to be reminded of it quite so often.

Before the bombs fall, though, Pvt. Robert E. Lee Prewitt (Montgomery Clift) joins Sgt. Milt Warden's (Burt Lancaster) outfit. Capt. Holmes (Philip Ober) wants the new man to box on the regimental team, but Prewitt refuses. He'd rather bugle. The boxers, all NCOs, then give him "the treatment," endless rounds of punishment for invented infractions. With the help of his friend Maggio (Frank Sinatra), Prewitt perseveres. At the same time, Warden puts some moves on Holmes's unhappy wife Karen (Deborah Kerr) and Prewitt meets Lorene (Donna Reed), who's a professional "conversationalist" at the Congress Club.

The relationships may be doomed, but their treatment set new standards for cinematic sexual frankness. Though it may seem tame and obvious now, Burt Lancaster and Deborah Kerr's torrid horizontal beach kiss broke down barriers concerning the depiction of sensuality. In the years that followed, it would be topped by the eating scene in *Tom Jones* (1963), the kiss in *The Thomas Crown Affair* (1968), and the wind chimes in *Body Heat* (1981), but it is still an immediately recognizable cinematic moment.

All of the romantic entanglements are worked out in the shadow of the men's duties as soldiers and their relationship to the Army. That's really what both the novel and the film are about—the responsibilities of the individual and the organization. At first, Warden and Prewitt seem to represent respectively, the good soldier and the free spirit, but that's far too simple. It's Warden who lets his

See also

Casablanca
Cool Hand Luke
Thin Red Line
Platoon
An Officer and a Gentleman

emotions overrule his sense of discipline and responsibility. Prewitt reacts to "the treatment" by obeying every order and toughing it out.

Zinnemann and Taradash don't explore the depths of character that Jones created—film doesn't work that way—but they certainly turned his work into one of Hollywood's most enjoyable entertainments.

Sgt. Warden (Burt Lancaster, center) tries to keep Sgt. "Fatso" Judson (Ernest Borgnine) and Pvt. Maggio (Frank Sinatra) from killing each other in *From Here to Eternity.* The Kobal Collection

Cast: Burt Lancaster (Sgt. Milton Warden), Montgomery Clift (Robert E. Lee "Prew" Prewitt), Frank Sinatra (Angelo Maggio), Deborah Kerr (Karen Holmes), Donna Reed (Alma Lorene), Ernest Borgnine (Sgt. "Fatso" Judson), Philip Ober (Capt. Dana Holmes), Jack Warden (Cpl. Buckley), Mickey Shaughnessy (Sgt. Leva), George Reeves (Sgt. Maylon Stark), Claude Akins (Dhom), Harry Bellaver (Mazzioli), John Dennis (Sgt. Ike Galovitch), Tim Ryan (Sgt. Pete Karelsen), John Bryant (Capt. Ross), John Cason (Cpl. Paluso), Douglas Henderson (Cpl. Champ Wilson), Robert Karnes (Sgt. Turp Thornhill), Robert J. Wilke (Sgt. Henderson), Carleton Young (Col. Ayres), Merle Travis (Sal Anderson), Arthur Keegan (Treadwell), Barbara Morrison (Mrs. Kipfer), Tyler McVey (Maj. Stern); **Written by:** Daniel Taradash; **Cinematography by:** Burnett Guffey; **Music by:** George Duning. **Producer:** Buddy Adler, Columbia Pictures. **Awards:** Academy Awards '53: Best Black and White Cinematography, Best Director (Zinnemann), Best Film Editing, Best Picture, Best Screenplay, Best Sound, Best Supporting Actor (Sinatra), Best Supporting Actress (Reed); American Film Institute (AFI) '98: Top 100; Directors Guild of America Awards '53: Best Director (Zinnemann); Golden Globe Awards '54: Best Supporting Actor (Sinatra); New York Film Critics Awards '53: Best Actor (Lancaster), Best Director (Zinnemann), Best Film; Nominations: Academy Awards '53: Best Actor (Clift), Best Actor (Lancaster), Best Actress (Kerr), Best Costume Design (B & W), Best Original Dramatic Score; Golden Globe Awards '54: Best Director (Zinnemann). **Budget:** 1.65M. **Running Time:** 118 minutes. **Format:** VHS, Beta, LV, 8mm.

FROM HERE TO ETERNITY

From Here to Eternity Quotes

Though he couldn't take the liberties with language that were open to James Jones when he wrote the original novel, writer Daniel Taradash created some memorable dialogue to tell the story on screen. Here are some examples:

"This here's a rifle company, Prewitt. You ain't supposed to enjoy yourself before sundown."

Sgt. Warden (Burt Lancaster)

"Strangle on his own spit if he didn't have me around here to swab out his throat for him."

Sgt. Warden on Capt. Holmes (Philip Ober)

"I can soldier with any man."

Pvt. Prewitt (Montgomery Clift)

"You'll fight, Prewitt. You'll fight because Capt. Holmes wants to be Maj. Holmes."

Sgt. Warden

"A man don't go his own way, he's nothing"

Pvt. Prewitt

"Maybe back in the days of the pioneers a man could go his own way, but today, you gotta play ball."

Sgt. Warden

"I know his type. He's a hardhead."

Sgt. Warden on Pvt. Prewitt

"Ain't nothing the matter with a soldier that ain't the matter with everyone else."

Pvt. Prewitt

"Only my friends call me Wop."

Maggio (Frank Sinatra) to Fatso (Ernest Borgnine)

"Killers, huh! I'd trade the pair of you for a good Campfire Girl."

Sgt. Warden to Maggio and Fatso

"Nobody ever lies about being lonely."

Prewitt to Lorene (Donna Reed)

In many ways, this is not a very good movie. But when an important filmmaker addresses an important subject with a directness that few of his contemporaries dared, attention must be paid. And despite the flaws, the resemblance between director-star Charlie Chaplin and Adolph Hitler, the target of his often heavy-handed parody, is eerie. Beyond the similarities in mustaches, facial features, and hair, the two men were born four days apart, Chaplin on April 16, Hitler on April 20, 1889. Perhaps then, the film, or something like it, was inevitable.

It begins in World War I, where Chaplin's famous Little Tramp is a German barber serving as a footsoldier. The first joke—about a massive cannon that aims at the Cathedral of Notre Dame and hits an outhouse—sets an obvious tone. After a fitful series of sight gags, Chaplin is involved in a plane crash that renders him an amnesiac. Years later, he's still in a hospital while the dictator Adenoid Hynkel (Chaplin) takes power in Tomania. The Jewish barber leaves the hospital, innocently ignorant of Nazi anti-Semitism and tries to reopen his shop. His new neighbor is Hannah (a gorgeous Paulette Goddard), who stands up to the stormtroopers. The couple spends the rest of the film getting into deeper trouble with the Nazis—though they're never called that—and their attempts at self-preservation seem tragically inadequate.

Hynkel, meanwhile, plots world domination. In an ersatz German that would be used later by Victor Borge and Danny Kaye, Chaplin re-creates the aggressive tone and pace of Hitler's public speeches. The film's most famous sequence has Hynkel dancing a graceful pas de deux with a glowing inflated globe. With one neatly done bit of reverse action, it is a small comic masterpiece. If only the rest matched its subtlety and insight. But too often, Chaplin's anger overpowers the comedy and he sets up humorous situations he cannot resolve. And what is the point of having Hynkel and his Italian counterpart Benzino Napaloni (Jack Oakie) engage in a food fight?

Admittedly, we know so much more now about the horrors of Nazism than Chaplin did in 1940 that lines meant to be funny are now monstrous. When Hynkel's henchman Herring (Billy Gilbert) gleefully says, "We've just discovered the most wonderful, the most marvelous poison gas. It'll kill everybody!" who can laugh?

Hindsight has also given the more serious scenes a quality of sorrow. Hannah's "wouldn't it be nice if they left us alone" speech is hopelessly naive and Chaplin's concluding plea for universal brotherhood is equally heartfelt but inadequate for the situation. To be fair, Chaplin was not at his best with feature-length films, and his kind of comedy did not need sound.

Inspired moments of physical humor flash briefly—spinning to smack a stormtrooper with a paintbrush, slipping into a basement window, skidding down a sidewalk—but they're surrounded by strained scenes that simply don't work.

See also
To Be or Not to Be
Duck Soup
Cartoons Go to War
Life Is Beautiful

Charlie Chaplin is a humble Jewish barber and Adenoid Hynkel in *The Great Dictator*. The Kobal Collection

Cast: Charlie Chaplin (Adenoid Hynkel/Jewish Barber), Paulette Goddard (Hannah), Jack Oakie (Benzino Napaloni), Billy Gilbert (Herring), Reginald Gardiner (Schultz), Henry Daniell (Garbitsch), Maurice Moscovich (Mr. Jaeckel), Emma Dunn (Mrs. Jaeckel), Bernard Gorcey (Mr. Mann), Paul Weigel (Mr. Agar), Chester Conklin, Grace Hayle (Mme. Napaloni), Carter DeHaven (Bacterian Ambassador); Written by: Charlie Chaplin; Cinematography by: Roland H. Totheroh, Karl Struss; Music by: Meredith Willson. Producer: RBC Films, United Artists. Awards: New York Film Critics Awards '40: Best Actor (Chaplin); National Film Registry '97; Nominations: Academy Awards '40: Best Actor (Chaplin), Best Original Screenplay, Best Picture, Best Supporting Actor (Oakie), Best Original Score. Budget: 2M. Running Time: 126 minutes. Format: VHS, Beta, LV.

The Chinese version of *Casablanca* has a hint of the flamboyant action that Hong Kong movies have become justly famous for, but at heart, it is a more conventional story of love in a time of chaos. Though a few cultural differences must be overcome, that story is built on universal cinematic themes and characters. More importantly for most videophiles, the film is a showcase for Chow Yun-Fat, a young actor on the brink of stardom.

In the opening scene, voice-over narrator Ah Nam (Cecilia Yip) remembers "the most painful time of my life in 1941." She's a beautiful teenager who suffers from some kind of violent migraine headaches or small seizures that can be alleviated only by smoking opium. Everyone knows that she hasn't got long to live and so her father, a prosperous merchant, is trying to force her into a quick, financially beneficial marriage. She's in love with her childhood friend Wong Hak Keung (Alex Man). A charismatic coolie, he has organized his fellow workers in the rice warehouse into a loose union. Yip Kim Fay (Chow Yun-Fat) is newly arrived in the city from Canton. He thinks that he's just passing through on his way to either the "Old Gold Mountain" (America) or the "New Gold Mountain" (Australia). Then he meets Ah Nam, helplessly racked by pain, in the street. As those three get to know each other, Japanese forces are gathering outside the city. The British announce that they will defend Hong Kong, but at the same time, they evacuate the families of government workers.

For roughly the first half of the film, writer Koon-Chung Chan and director [Leung Po-Chi] focus on the triangular relationship. A rough friendship quickly develops between Fay and Keung, and both of them are in love with Nam. She is less certain of her feelings. When the Japanese enter, the political eclipses the personal, though the two are never completely separate. Like all Hong Kong Chinese, the young people must walk a line between opposition to the new order and collaboration. There are also regional conflicts within the Chinese community to be dealt with, and Japanese-Chinese racism.

American viewers unfamiliar with Hong Kong films will have some trouble figuring out the familial and social nuances in the first part. But none of them are critical to understanding the three central characters, or their relationship to the foreign invaders. Then later, as riots are followed by martial law imposed by the Japanese, the story could be set in almost any war-torn city from Berlin to Paris. When the three finally make up their minds to escape, [Leung Po-Chi] ratchets up the tension with some neatly staged action sequences—one in the rice warehouse and another in a gambling den. The most memorable moment is an extended sequence involving a lit firecracker in a man's ear.

Hong Kong films may be an acquired taste, but *Hong Kong 1941* is one of the more accessible and expensively produced. It's a fine place for the uninitiated to begin.

See also

Casablanca
Land and Freedom
Three Came Home
The Deer Hunter
A Time to Love and a Time to Die

Cast: Cecilia Yip (Ah Nam), Alex Man (Wong Hak Keung), Chow Yun-Fat (Yip Kim Fay); **Written by:** Koon-Chung Chan. **Hong Kong. Running Time:** 118 minutes. **Format:** VHS, Letterbox, DVD.

LAND AND FREEDOM

1995 Ken Loach ♪♪♪

Though Ken Loach is known as a filmmaker with strong leftist leanings, his take on the Spanish Civil War is neither polemic nor propaganda. It's actually much closer in structure, plot, and emotion to Steven Spielberg's *Saving Private Ryan*, which was produced two years later. Loach, however, is more interested in politics and the sacrifices that political beliefs demand. He and writer Jim Allen tell the story as flashback. An aging Dave Carr (Ian Hart) suffers a heart attack in his cluttered apartment. Cleaning up the place, his granddaughter Kim (Suzanne Maddox) comes across a suitcase filled with newspaper clippings, photos, and letters detailing his service in the Spanish Civil War.

> "The party stinks. It's evil and corrupt. In Barcelona I saw good comrades snatched off the streets and executed. Others disappeared into torture chambers and it's still going on. Stalin is using the working men like pieces on a chessboard to be bartered, used, and sacrificed."
>
> **Dave Carr (Ian Hart)**

As a dedicated young Liverpool Communist in 1936, Dave falls under the spell of a speaker who describes the dire situation that the newly elected Republican government faces in Spain. Fascist Gen. Franco is leading a military rebellion against the fledgling worker's paradise, and he has the assistance of the church and the country's elite. Without a second thought, Dave decides to volunteer and make his way across Europe to Spain. He discovers that the anti-Fascist forces are terribly disorganized, and though he had hoped to join an official Communist organization, he signs on with a small unit of the P.O.U.M. Militia (Partido Obrero de Unificacion Marxista (Party of Marxist Unification)) on the Aragon front.

In a letter back home, he enthusiastically describes it as "socialism in action," a democratic organization that votes on every decision and treats women as men's equals, even allowing them to fight with the pitifully few rifles they manage to acquire. His enthusiasm has something to do with his attraction to comrade Blanca (Rosana Pastor), but not much. Dave is a believer. The first real action his militia sees is a house-to-house assault on a small village. Though it's not as intense or as noisy as similar scenes in Spielberg's film, the sequence is built around the same chaotic unpredictability. No one involved really understands what is happening and their halting progress is hard won.

Did you Know?
George Orwell deals with the same theater of war and his time with the P.O.U.M. in his fine memoir, *Homage to Catalonia.*

After that initial engagement, Loach turns to his central points: What do victors do with victory? Can a military unit be a democracy? As the action dissolves into gassy political discussions, it has an unscripted, spontaneous feeling that comes in part from the dialogue and in part from the realistic "non-actor" performances Loach favors. The same scene argues finer points of collectivist doctrine that have been rendered moot by history, and so will try many viewers' patience. It is necessary, though, as a preview of the larger conflicts that will erupt among Communists, anarchists, Trotskyites, and the other competing factions. All of that would be nothing more than posturing if the characters didn't ring true, and these do. The secondary figures are sketched lightly but David and Blanca are believably complex.

Loach deals with their situation honestly, and eventually comes to a realization that human values are more important than political values. He also comes to a solidly emotional graveside conclusion that's far less sentimental than the similar moment that ends *Saving Private Ryan*. This film manages, remarkably, to conclude with its ideology in tatters but its ideals intact.

See also

For Whom the Bell Tolls
Casablanca
Saving Private Ryan
A Time to Love and a Time to Die

Dave (Ian Hart, left) fights for
the Republicans in the Spanish
Civil War in *Land and Freedom*.

Cast: Ian Hart (David Carr), Rosana Pastor (Blanca), Iciar Bollain (Maite), Tom Gilroy (Lawrence), Frederic Pierrot (Bernard), Marc Martinez (Vidal), Angela Clarke (Kitty), David Allen (On the Roof); **Written by:** Jim Allen; **Cinematography by:** Barry Ackroyd; **Music by:** George Fenton. **Producer:** Rebecca O'Brien, Parallax Pictures, Messidor Films, Road Movies, Dritte Produktionen; released by Gramercy Pictures. **British, Spanish, German. Awards:** Cesar Awards '96: Best Foreign Film; Nominations: British Academy Awards '95: Best Film. **Running Time:** 109 minutes. **Format:** VHS.

THE WINTER WAR
Talvisota
1989 Pekka Parikka ♫♫♫♩

In 1939, with the Nazi-Soviet Non-Aggression Pact in effect, Stalin made territorial demands on neighboring countries. Estonia, Latvia and Lithuania were forced to cede land to Russia. Finland resisted. On Nov. 30, the Red Army attacked, and for 105 days, the outnumbered Finns held off the invaders. *The Winter War* is the Finnish version of that campaign. Based on military journals of the 23rd Infantry Regiment and the participants' memories, it is one of the most brutally realistic films ever made about a ground war fought in trenches, foxholes and craters.

Director Pekka Parikka spends the first half hour in preparation, as the citizen-soldiers form their units. The scenes are jumbled, almost formless, and focused on rumors and stories that somebody told somebody he heard on the radio about the negotiations. The guys gripe about everything from their pitiful equipment to the food, and wait for a war that they hope will not happen. The only two identifiable characters are the Hakala brothers, Martti (Taneli Makela) and Paavo (Konsta Makela), but in most important scenes, it is impossible to distinguish them from their comrades in the snow and dirt once the fighting starts.

> "Dying for freedom is pure and true! This vow will remain to remind us anew."
>
> **Finnish marching song**

That's part of Parikka's point. No single individual is the protagonist of this story. The entire army is the hero. Eisenstein used the same technique in *Battleship Potemkin*, but he did it for ideological reasons. For Parikka, a collective hero is closer to the truth of the matter, and by using it, he is able to stress the impersonal quality of military destruction. Most of the violence involves the effects of bombs and artillery fire that arrive with a quick shrieking whistle. Survival is a matter of luck, not bravery. Parika and cinematographer Kari Sohlberg seldom let their camera rise above a grunt's eye level, so the viewer has little idea of what's happening beyond the immediate range of sight and sound. Is the campaign going well or poorly? Who knows, and what difference does it make? The shells still fall. The bunker is still frozen.

Without recognizable stars or a familiar storyline to guide North American viewers, the film is absolutely unpredictable. Those same qualities, combined with subtitled dialogue, will make it unwatchable for some potential viewers, too. Then there's the matter of the abrupt conclusion. In his commitment to tell it the way it happened, Parikka is forced simply to stop the story. That, apparently, is accurate enough, though the filmmakers do not spell it out.

In March, 1940, after realizing what a terrible price the war was exacting, the Finnish government agreed to the Russians' original demands. The 15-week campaign cost the Finns 25,000 killed. The Russians lost 200,000 in a fight that was, essentially, a draw, though, as John Keegan writes in *The Second World War*, "The experience of the 'Winter War' . . . conditioned the Soviet Union's carefully modulated policy toward Finland when the issue of peace came round again." It is impossible to show "carefully modulated policy" in a mainstream movie and so, wisely, Parikka doesn't try to. *The Winter War* celebrates the bravery and tenacity of the Finnish Army without romanticizing or denying the hellish realities that the participants suffered.

See also
Cross of Iron
Saving Private Ryan
The Longest Day

Cast: Esko Nikkari (Ylli Alanen), Tomi Salmela (Matti Ylinen), Vesa Vierikko (Jussi Kantola), Samuli Edelmann (Mauri Haapasalo), Teemu Koskinen (Jussi Hakala), Esko Kovero (Juho Pernaa), Eero Maenpaa (Small Paavo Hakala), Konsta Makela (Paavo Hakala), Taneli Makela (Martti Hakala), Heikki Paavilainen (Vilho Erkkila), Antti Raivio (Erkki Somppi), Miitta Sorvali (Karjalaisemanta), Martti Suosalo (Arvi Huhtala), Timo Torikka (Pentti Saari); **Written by:** Pekka Parikka; **Cinematography by:** Kari Sohlberg; **Music by:** Jukka Haavisto, Juha Tikko. **Producer:** Marko Rohr. **Running Time:** 195 minutes. **Format:** VHS.

WORLD WAR II
Europe and North Africa

World War II: The European and North African Campaigns on Screen

Between 1942 and 1946, Hollywood produced a large number of films about the war, and the emphasis was strongly on the European and North African Theater. A quick count of the major war movies made during those years with an overseas setting reveals that the European productions outnumbered the Pacific almost two to one. No single reason explains the difference. The studios were trying to pay attention to every branch of the armed services, and equal venom was aimed at both the Japanese and the Germans. Certainly, America's connections to England and Europe account for some of the difference. In any case, for the movies, the European Theater is the most popular front of the most popular war, from *Action in the North Atlantic* to *Saving Private Ryan*.

During those first weeks of 1942, the Hollywood studios and the War Department forged a mutually advantageous relationship. The government wanted the studios to make inspirational films that portrayed their organizations in a favorable light. The studios wanted to make movies that would attract audiences and were happy to accept assistance from the armed services—including access to their men, bases, and equipment. In short, two powerful organizations made a good match.

The films produced during the war roughly follow its progress. The works focusing on Europe begin at a higher level of sophistication, mostly because the Brits had been involved earlier and had their propaganda machine in a higher gear. *In Which We Serve*, made by Noel Coward and David Lean, and *Immortal Battalion*, from Carol Reed, Eric Ambler, and Peter Ustinov, are both carefully crafted to inspire without overstatement. On the American side, *Action in the North Atlantic* and *Crash Dive* are much simpler calls to arms. Zoltan

Korda's *Sahara*, Billy Wilder's *Five Graves to Cairo*, and Hitchcock's *Lifeboat* are much more polished and enjoyable works of escapism.

When Hollywood turned its attention to the G.I. on the front line, it made steady progress, from the slapdash *The Immortal Sergeant*, through Edward G. Robinson's transformation into a soldier in *Mr. Winkle Goes to War*, to the realism of William Wellman's *Story of G.I. Joe*, about the "mud-rain-frost-and-wind boys," and Lewis Milestone's *A Walk in the Sun*.

After the war, the partnership between Hollywood and the military establishment continued. Though the films soften their partisan attitude, they remain largely uncritical of the armed services. The more complex psychological pressures created by the war are the subject of *Command Decision, 12 O'Clock High*, and *The Caine Mutiny*. The war on the ground is the setting for Audie Murphy's autobiography, *To Hell and Back*, and William Wellman's *Battleground*. For my money, Wellman's is the best combat film to come out of that theater of the war.

The German point of view provides one part of the three interconnected stories of Irwin Shaw's *The Young Lions*. It's also the subject of Douglas Sirk's underrated adaptation of Erich Maria Remarque's *A Time to Love and a Time to Die*, and *The Bridge*, a fine 1959 German Oscar nominee about young draftees at the end of the war.

With the increased artistic and creative freedom of the 1960s, dramatic changes come to the war film. The studios' affinity for elephantine, multi-star epics is responsible for *The Longest Day, The Battle of the Bulge, The Battle of Britain*, and *Is Paris Burning?*. In those same years, other producers use the war as a setting for escapist adventures: *The Guns of Navarone, The Train*, and *Where Eagles Dare*. The first hints of deviation from the "official" version of history, which cast Americans as unambiguous heroes appear then, too, and are carried on

into the '70s. Don Siegel's *Hell Is For Heroes* (1962) suggests that the command structure could be flawed, and men might be more concerned with survival than sacrifice. A year later, Carl Foreman's *The Victors* goes even farther with the same ideas on a larger scale. Perhaps the real turning point comes in 1967, with the popularity of Robert Aldrich's *The Dirty Dozen*, a brutally violent story that ended with Americans slaughtering helpless prisoners.

Opposition to the Vietnam War increased in the 1970s, and is reflected in Mike Nichols' adaptation of Joseph Heller's *Catch-22*, Sam Peckinpah's stunning and underappreciated *Cross of Iron*, and even *A Bridge Too Far*, the most expensive production ever attempted about an Allied defeat.

In the 1980s and '90s, the pendulum swings back to a more realistic middle ground, where the bloody realities of war are neither ignored nor dwelt upon. The first to take that more measured look is Sam Fuller's autobiographical *The Big Red One*, followed by the German submarine epic, *Das Boot*, and *Come and See*, a harrowing Russian film about Nazi atrocities that can be seen as a preview of *Schindler's List*. In his adaptation of William Wharton's novel *A Midnight Clear*, Keith Gordon revives the unit picture to create a tale of humanistic redemption. He does something similar with Kurt Vonnegut's fable of complicity and guilt, *Mother Night*.

At a time when war films were not in favor in theaters, the cable channel HBO produced *The Tuskegee Airmen*, the fact-based story of a squadron of black pilots who flew P-51s, and John Irvin's *When Trumpets Fade*, an admirable remake of *Hell Is for Heroes*. Then in 1998, the European Theater returned to the big screen with Steven Spielberg's *Saving Private Ryan*. His depiction of the D-Day invasion establishes new standards of realism for screen violence that will certainly be reflected in the next wave of war films.

ACTION IN THE NORTH ATLANTIC

1943 Lloyd Bacon 𝄞𝄞𝄞𝄝

Though conceived and produced as unvarnished propaganda for the Merchant Marines, this sea-going adventure is still enjoyable as nostalgic entertainment. A solid ensemble cast led by Humphrey Bogart and Raymond Massey makes up for not-particularly-special effects and a wandering script. The film's basic purpose is to show how brave the underappreciated seamen were and, in that area, it succeeds. The organization certainly thought so. At the New York premiere on May 21, 1943, a Victory flag was presented to producer Jack Warner as more than 300 sailors trooped into the theater.

On screen introduction: "Today in the face of this newest and greatest challenge of them all, we of the United Nations have cleared our decks and taken our battle stations. It is the will of the people that America shall deliver the goods. It can never be doubted that the goods will be delivered by this nation, which believes in the tradition of 'DAMN THE TORPEDOES; FULL SPEED AHEAD!'"

Franklin D. Roosevelt (original emphasis)

"We didn't ask for this war. I know I didn't. None of us did. And now all of us are in it. . . . I got faith in God, President Roosevelt, and the Brooklyn Dodgers in the order of their importance."

Sailor Chip Abrams (Sam Levene)

In the war, the job of the Merchant Marines is to run cargo between America and Europe. The slow-moving, unarmed ships are easy targets for German U-boats and aircraft. The crews have no illusions about their chances. Lt. Joe Rossi (Bogart) is second in command to the properly gruff Capt. Jarvis (Massey) and tries to ease the friction between Jarvis and the eager Cadet Parker (Dick Hogan).

Below decks, the crew (Alan Hale, Dane Clark, Peter Whitney, J.M. Kerrigan) complains and jokes and philosophizes. Their wisecracking humor is now the most quaint and dated part of the film. When the action picks up as a submarine closes in on the ship, the tension increases considerably. In those scenes, director Lloyd Bacon (with uncredited assistance from Byron Haskin and Raoul Walsh) and writers A.I. Bezzerides, W.R. Burnett, Guy Gilpatric, and John Howard Lawson, are remarkably innovative. Intercutting between the ship and the U-boat, they allow the German characters to speak German, without subtitles. The meaning and intention of the actions are made perfectly clear through inflection and the audience's familiarity with submarine movies. Even if we don't understand the words, we know the drill—the captain (Wilhelm von Brincken) looks through the periscope; we see the ship from his point of view; he barks numbers and orders; they're repeated by various crewmen; other bits of business are accomplished and then—whoosh!—the torpedoes are fired.

The film is divided into two halves that are set on different ships and separated by an interlude ashore in New York. In that short section, Bogart reprises his Sam Spade persona from *The Maltese Falcon*, and becomes a tough guy in a dark suit and snappy fedora who romances saloon chanteuse Pearl (Julie Bishop) while his Captain goes home to his wife (Ruth Gordon) in a neatly touching domestic scene. The second half is set on one of the new "liberty ships," in a convoy. The escalating attacks on the ships take on an almost comic book disregard for reality. The screen is filled with model ships, subs and planes, torpedoes, exploding shells and bombs. In one memorable process shot, a bomber attacks a freighter, and the perspective is so skewed that the model plane briefly appears to be larger than the model ship. That is not meant as a criticism. Audiences in 1943 suspended their disbelief for such scenes. And at that time, this particular sort of escapism was meant not merely to divert viewers but to inspire them.

The film served that purpose admirably, and it's still fun to see Bogie and Raymond Massey in roles that were well tailored to their strengths.

See also
Report from the Aleutians
Fighting Seabees
Lifeboat
In Which We Serve

Humphrey Bogart is Lt. Joe Rossi in *Action in the North Atlantic.* The Kobal Collection

Cast: Humphrey Bogart (Lt. Joe Rossi), Raymond Massey (Capt. Steve Jarvis), Alan Hale (Boots O'Hara), Julie Bishop (Pearl), Ruth Gordon (Mrs. Jarvis), Sam Levene (Chips Abrams), Dane Clark (Johnnie Pulaski), Peter Whitney (Whitey Lara), Minor Watson (Rear Adm. Hartridge), J.M. Kerrigan (Caviar Jinks), Dick Hogan (Cadet Robert Parker), Kane Richmond (Ens. Wright), Chick Chandler (Goldberg), Donald Douglas (The Lieutenant Commander), Creighton Hale (Sparks), Iris Adrian (Jenny O'Hara), Elliott Sullivan (Hennessy), Glenn Strange (Tex Mathews), Wilhelm von Brinken (German U-boat Captain); **Written by:** A.I. Bezzerides, W.R. Burnett, John Howard Lawson, Guy Gilpatric; **Cinematography by:** Ted D. McCord; **Music by:** Adolph Deutsch. **Producer:** Warner Bros., First National, Jerry Wald. **Awards:** Nominations: Academy Awards '43: Best Story. **Running Time:** 126 minutes. **Format:** VHS.

Visual Cliches of War Movies

Since 1941, Hollywood has produced hundreds, thousands of war films. In the process, a cinematic shorthand has developed. Certain images appear, and audiences respond so strongly—whether they realize it or not—that those images are refined and repeated, and soon they are accepted as truth. Viewers understand what they mean, and so filmmakers can use them to move the story along more quickly. In watching and re-watching the films for this book, I came to realize how often I was seeing variations on the same shot, and how much extra information was packed into these moments.

The most recognizable and universal example is the Nazi officer in the long black convertible. He is driven by a chauffeur. The top is down. The shot is often used to introduce and define the character. You've seen it dozens of times, and it applies only to Nazis. His American counterpart rides in a Jeep. As often as not, he takes the wheel himself. If he does have a driver, the American officer sits in the front seat beside him.

Now, consider what those two images are telling us. In less time than it takes to read, we know that the Nazi is arrogant and haughty. He assumes that he is superior to everyone else, and he flaunts the special privileges of his rank. The chauffeur is his servant. The long car gleams. The dominant color of its finish and the uniforms is black. The American officer is a common man in a common vehicle. His dominant colors (even in black and white) are olive drab and muddy brown. He's one of us.

(By the way, the one time that any character comments on this cliche is in *Schindler's List*, when Amon Goeth (Ralph Fiennes) is riding in the back of the open convertible on a snowy night. "Why is the top down?" he asks. "I'm fucking freezing.")

Here are some more of these "visual cliches." I'm sure that any true fan can name many more that I've overlooked.

- Japanese officers do not ride in cars. (The only exception occurs in *Paradise Road*.)
- Italian officers are vain and love opera. They'll switch sides without hesitation.
- An upright rifle, its bayonet stuck into the ground, with a helmet on top serves as a grave marker.
- French Resistance fighters wear black leather jackets and berets.
- Female French Resistance fighters wear tight black sweaters.
- German SS officers wear black leather trenchcoats.
- Nazi officers enjoying a glass of Pernod at a Paris sidewalk cafe will be victims of a Resistance drive-by shooting.
- A band leader interrupts a dance for a historic announcement: the Japanese have attacked Pearl Harbor; Germany has surrendered, etc.
- The hand painted signpost giving mileage to New York, Los Angeles, London, etc.
- Soldiers, sailors, airmen sharing cigarettes never light three on a match, or if they do. . . .
- The sexually voracious wife of a German officer seduces one of his subordinates. (She almost always wears a tight black dress.)
- The big board upon which models of the tanks/ships are moved around to illustrate the progress of the battle.
- The unit's pet dog.
- The parachuting Allied pilot who is killed by an enemy fighter while he's hanging helpless in his 'chute.
- The letter home that's given to a comrade by a guy who's going into battle.
- The unctuous Japanese with Coke-bottle-bottom glasses.
- People having a wonderful time on December 6, 1941.
- Tearful farewells on train platforms (usually British train platforms).
- Grease pencil writing on the foreheads of wounded men in hospitals.
- In naval films, someone always says, "Good hunting."
- A dying soldier/sailor asks for "Mother."
- Resistance fighters and escaped POWs hide in hay wagons.
- Coded radio messages are read before the news by BBC radio broadcast to Occupied France.

As long as Guy Hamilton's documentary-styled adventure stays in the air, it's near perfect. On the ground, however, the characters are such faint one-dimensional shadows that their dramatic problems barely register on the viewer's consciousness. Fortunately, the film spends most of the time aloft.

It begins in France, May 1940, as the German Blitzkrieg is driving the last of the British forces off the continent. Sir Hugh Dowding (Laurence Olivier) strongly suggests that the government reverse its decision to provide fighters and support to the French forces. It's too late for that, he says. All air power must be directed toward protection of England. He understands the size of the German forces opposing them and knows what it will take to win. "The essential arithmetic is that our young men will have to shoot down their young men at a rate of four to one if we're to keep pace at all," he says. That's the essence of the air war that will be fought over the island and, most of the time, the filmmakers show how it is played out.

The pilots, played by such familiar faces as Michael Caine, Edward Fox, and Robert Shaw, are able to regroup and train younger replacements who are rushed through the system and placed into Spitfires with minimal experience. When the German bombing raids begin, they are assisted by radar installations and a fairly sophisticated system of ground-based observers. At first, the Germans are able to put significantly larger numbers of planes in the air. But the Heinkle He111 and Messerschmitt Me110 bombers are easy targets for the quick Spitfire fighters. The Spits are also more maneuverable than the Me109 fighters. The dogfights and bombing runs are captured in some truly spectacular aerial footage. Credit for it must be distributed among aerial and second unit director David Bracknell, aerial photographers Skeets Kelly and John Jordan, director Guy Hamilton, and cinematographer Freddie Young.

They're able to put the viewer in the cockpit of both the English and German planes and to show the swiftly moving air combat from a pilot's point of view with a rare degree of realism. The live action shots, models, special effects, and archival footage are intercut so deftly that it's hard to tell one from the others. The filmmakers are not as successful at differentiating the individuals involved. Once they're in action, wearing leather flying helmets, goggles, and oxygen masks, the fliers are indistinguishable. All of the Germans—including a buffoonish Goering—are caricatures. The only significant emotional conflict occurs between Squadron Leader Harvey (Christopher Plummer) and his wife Maggie Harvey (Susannah York), who refuses to give up her position with the WAAF at his command. The entire subplot is so trifling that writers Wilfred Greatorex and James Kennaway don't even bother to resolve it. At a convenient moment, it is simply over. Their concern is with the air war, and they show it about as well as anyone ever has.

> "We're not ready. We're on our own. We've been playing for time and it's running out."
>
> **Sir David (Ralph Richardson), British ambassador to Switzerland after the retreat at Dunkirk**

See also

Tora! Tora! Tora!
Battle of Midway
Air Force
The Longest Day

Squadron Group Leader Skipper
(Robert Shaw) prepares for
takeoff in *The Battle of Britain*.

The Kobal Collection

WORLD WAR II: EUROPE AND NORTH AFRICA

Cast: Harry Andrews (Senior Civil Servant), Michael Caine (Squadron Leader Canfield), Laurence Olivier (Air Chief Marshal Sir Hugh Dowding), Trevor Howard (Air Vice Marshal Keith Park), Kenneth More (Group Captain Baker), Christopher Plummer (Squadron Leader Colin Harvey), Robert Shaw (Squadron Leader Skipper), Susannah York (Section Officer Maggie Harvey), Ralph Richardson (Sir David), Curt Jurgens (Baron von Richter), Michael Redgrave (Air Vice Marshal Evill), Nigel Patrick (Group Captian Hope), Edward Fox (Pilot Officer Archie), Ian McShane (Sgt. Pilot Andy), Patrick Wymark (Air Vice Marshal Trafford Leigh-Mallory); **Written by:** James Kennaway, Wilfred Greatorex; **Cinematography by:** Frederick A. (Freddie) Young; **Music by:** Malcolm Arnold, Ron Goodwin, William Walton; **Technical Advisor:** Adolph Galland. **Producer:** United Artists, Harry Saltzman, Benjamin Fisz. **MPAA Rating:** G. **Running Time:** 132 minutes. **Format:** VHS, Beta, LV, Letterbox, Closed Caption.

BATTLE OF THE BULGE
1965 Ken Annakin ♪♪♪♪

An archetypal studio war movie, this one is really quite faithful to the broad outlines and details of a real campaign, and then it fills out the running time with ridiculously unrealistic Hollywood heroics. The combination is somehow much more entertaining than it ought to be. Veteran director Ken Annakin knows how to keep this sort of sprawling material in line, and even if his two leads are doing a bit of slumming, they're as good as they need to be.

In December 1944, American troops and officers advancing toward Germany think that the war is over. They're on cruise control, waiting for their orders to return home. But Col. Kiley (Henry Fonda), who's a cop in civilian life, has a hunch that the enemy is up to something. On a reconnaissance flight, he spots Col. Hessler (Robert Shaw) in the back of a big black convertible with the top down, despite the freezing weather. (As we know from so many other war movies, Nazi officers always ride in the back of big black convertibles with the top down. See Visual Cliches sidebar.) Kiley also spots some Tiger tanks and thinks that he has discovered the first evidence of the counteroffensive. His superiors, Gen. Gray (Robert Ryan) and Col. Pritchard (Dana Andrews), are skeptical.

Note:
The most widely available tape version of the film is 141 minutes long. Other sources list running times of 167, 163, and 156 minutes. Given the nature of the film, the various versions are probably not significantly different.

Meanwhile, right at the point of the German attack, Maj. Wolenski's (Charles Bronson) men are hunkered in a bunker and trying to stay warm. Sgt. Duquesne (George Montgomery) keeps wet-behind-the-ears Lt. Weaver (James MacArthur) from getting himself killed, and Guffy (Telly Savalas) uses his Sherman tank to distribute black market wine, eggs, and nylons. The script by John Melson and producers Philip Yordan and Milton Sperling neatly juggles those plot elements, bringing them all together only at a wonderfully preposterous conclusion.

The various battle scenes vary widely in quality. Some of the destruction seems shockingly real, while the occasional shots of model tanks and trains are so jarring that they're unintentionally funny. Annakin realizes how important those deep, rattling, clanking sound effects are to cinematic tanks, and he uses every note in the repertoire. He also understands the importance of setting, and gives the film an appropriately bleak, muddy, snow-covered feel. Since the film was originally made for the ultra-widescreen process Cinerama, much of the scope of the big scenes is lost in the conventional pan-and-scan transfer. The tank battles in particular have almost nothing to do with the realities of war, but the filmmakers don't take as many liberties as they might have.

The Germans did time the attack to take advantage of poor weather—"night, fog and snow," as Hitler put it—to keep Allied airplanes on the ground. They hoped that stopping the Allies would give them time to take more advantage of their secret-weapons programs and V-2 attacks. The attack was led by a young tank general, and his supplies of fuel were so critically low that his forces were expected to forage for it. The filmmakers make use of all of those points. Their other exaggerations and distortions are certainly no more egregious than those made by other films which have claimed to be more truthful.

See also
A Midnight Clear
War and Peace
The Longest Day
Is Paris Burning?
The Great Escape

Henry Fonda, Dana Andrews, and Robert Ryan plan a counter attack in *Battle of the Bulge.* The Kobal Collection

Cast: Henry Fonda (Lt. Col. Kiley), Robert Shaw (Col. Hessler), Robert Ryan (Gen. Gray), Dana Andrews (Col. Pritchard), Telly Savalas (Guffy), Ty Hardin (Schumacher), Pier Angeli (Louise), George Montgomery (Sgt. Duquesne), Charles Bronson (Maj. Wolenski), Barbara Werle (Elena), Hans-Christian Blech (Conrad), James MacArthur (Lt. Weaver), Karl Otto Alberty (Von Diepel); **Written by:** Philip Yordan, John Melson, Milton Sperling; **Cinematography by:** Jack Hildyard; **Music by:** Benjamin Frankel; **Technical Advisor:** Col. Sherman Joffe, Maj. Edward King, Gen. Meinrad von Lauchbert. **Producer:** Sidney Harmon, Warner Bros., Milton Sperling, Philip Yordan. **Running Time:** 141 minutes. **Format:** VHS, Beta, LV, Letterbox, Closed Caption.

BATTLEGROUND

1949 William A. Wellman ♪♪♪♪

The Battle of the Bulge has been the basis for several films and this is one of the best—a grunt's-eye-view of war that's a worthy companion piece to *The Story of G.I. Joe*, *A Walk in the Sun*, and *Saving Private Ryan*. Director William Wellman had proven his affinity for the material with *G.I. Joe*, and again he's working with a fine semi-autobiographical script. Before the war, veteran screenwriter Robert Pirosh already had a Marx Brothers comedy, *A Day at the Races*, on his resume. During the war he served as a sergeant in the 35th Division, and though he wasn't in the Bulge, he was close enough to see what was going on and to know what the men were like. That's the film's central strength. Beyond the inevitable stereotypical characteristics, these guys are real.

With a lack of precision that will be continued throughout, the story begins "somewhere in France," 1944. Replacement Jim Layton (Marshall Thompson) is reporting to the 101st Airborne, I-company, 3rd Platoon, 2nd Squad. When he finally finds his place, the veterans casually ignore him. Tobacco-spitting Sgt. Kinnie (James Whitmore) is nominally in charge, but the group has been together for so long that everyone knows what to do. Jarvess (John Hodiak) is the small-town newspaper writer who's the brains of the outfit; "Pop" Stazak (George Murphy) thinks his arthritis may get him an early discharge; the smart-aleck Holley (Van Johnson) has an opinion about everything. All of them are looking forward to leave in Paris. Instead, they're sent back up to the front.

> "I'm getting me a private room and private bath in Paris if I have to get it at the point of a gun."
>
> **Jarvess (John Hodiak)**

Why? Who knows? That's just the way things happen in the Army. One moment, you're supposed to sew your shoulder patches on; the next moment, you've got to remove them. You're ordered to dig a foxhole on this hillside where the squad will hold a position, and when you're halfway through, the group is sent down the road. Nobody in the squad ever completely understands what is going on. As soon as one of them does think that he has it figured out, the situation changes and all of the assumptions are wrong. When the German artillery starts firing and their troops advance, it becomes even more chaotic.

Within that madness, the guys try to survive. Their griping is reflexive, common complaints they've gone through a hundred times before. They wonder about which is the best way to get sent back for medical attention: pneumonia or "a good clean flesh wound"? They'd give anything for some fresh scrambled eggs and the look on their faces when they watch a shot of brandy being poured is indescribable.

The combat scenes are filmed on some of the most authentic and evocative sets ever constructed. Art directors Cedric Gibbons and Hans Peters and cinematographer Paul C. Vogel create a heavily wooded world of snow and fog without horizon or shadow. Visibility is so limited that hearing is as important as seeing. Give them and the cast equal credit for making the atmosphere of cold desolation seem so chilling. Wellman mixes in archival footage, as most filmmakers did in those years, but few managed it so seamlessly.

Given those extreme conditions, conventional combat is impossible, but Wellman manages to draw viewers into the action scenes by focusing closely on the individual characters and on smaller

See also

A Walk in the Sun
The Story of G.I. Joe
Saving Private Ryan
A Midnight Clear
Battle of the Bulge

WORLD WAR II: EUROPE AND NORTH AFRICA

Jarvess (John Hodiak) and Holley (Van Johnson) watch for the enemy in *Battleground*. The Kobal Collection

details, like the packing and loading of .30 caliber ammunition for an M1 rifle. The first big confrontation takes place near a railroad bridge. We experience it through Layton and Holley, who are reacting in very different ways. As Jarvess says later, "Things just happen and then afterwards you try to figure out why you acted the way you did."

That's an observation that only a veteran could make, and it's a perfect example of the unvarnished truths that underlie the fiction of *Battleground*. 1949 was a big year for war films (see sidebar, pg. 278), and Wellman's film was nominated for several Academy Awards. Only Pirosh and Vogel won. Though the film was a major boxoffice hit, it has never enjoyed the reputation of its contemporaries. Any fan who's missed this sleeper should head for the video store right away.

Cast: Van Johnson (Holley), John Hodiak (Jarvess), James Whitmore (Kinnie), George Murphy (Ernest "Pop" Stazak), Ricardo Montalban (Rodriguez), Marshall Thompson (Jim Layton), Jerome Courtland (Abner Spudler), Don Taylor (Standiferd), Bruce Cowling (Wolowicz), Leon Ames (The Chaplain), Douglas Fowley (Kipp Kippton), Richard Jaeckel (Bettis), Scotty Beckett (William J. Hooper), Herb Anderson (Hansan), Thomas E. Breen (Doc), Denise Darcel (Denise), James Arness (Garby), Brett King (Lt. Teiss); Written by: Robert Pirosh; Cinematography by: Paul Vogel; Music by: Lennie Hayton; Technical Advisor: Lt. Col. H.W.O. Kinnard. Producer: MGM, Dore Schary. Awards: Academy Awards '49: Best Black and White Cinematography, Best Story & Screenplay; Golden Globe Awards '50: Best Screenplay, Best Supporting Actor (Whitmore); Nominations: Academy Awards '49: Best Director (Wellman), Best Film Editing, Best Picture, Best Supporting Actor (Whitmore). Running Time: 118 minutes. Format: VHS, Beta, LV, Closed Caption.

Though Lee Marvin won his Best Actor Academy Award for *Cat Ballou*, his performance as the Sergeant in Sam Fuller's autobiographical view of World War II may be his best work. It certainly appears to be his most comfortable role, comfortable in the sense that he is not acting but playing himself on screen. As the veteran—both a fictional and a real veteran himself—Marvin is the central figure in a small ensemble that retraces Fuller's wartime experiences.

The story actually begins at the end of World War I, where the Sergeant is part of a nightmarish three-way encounter with a shell-shocked horse and a German. The black-and-white scene takes place on a desolate plain dominated by a huge wooden statue of a hollow-eyed Christ on the Cross. That's where the Sergeant comes up with a design for a "big red one" to represent the First Infantry Division. Flash forward to 1942, off the coast of North Africa. The Sergeant is now in charge of a rifle squad of raw recruits, among them Griff (Mark Hamill), Zab (Robert Carradine), Vinci (Bobby DiCicco), and Johnson (Kelly Ward). That quintet will go from North Africa, through Sicily, to Normandy, and finally to Czechoslovakia.

The film's point of view never rises beyond their ground-level experience, whether they're hiding in a cave from advancing Germans, celebrating a rare victory on a hilltop, or creeping through a bombed out town. Zab, a cigar-chomping fledgling novelist, provides a running commentary on the action via voice-over. His deadpan observations provide one side of Fuller's views. As the men board the landing boat for their first engagement, he says, "There are four things you can hear on the boat: the waves, the engines, an occasional muffled prayer, and the sound of 50 guys heaving their guts out." Fuller fills the screen with the same kind of carefully chosen details. The men put condoms over their rifle barrels to keep out the salt water during the assault, and in every spare minute in the field, they obsessively clean and care for their weapons.

But Fuller doesn't allow his episodic story to become mired in minutiae. Never one to neglect the more lurid, pulp aspects, he fills the second half of the film with increasingly surreal scenes of sudden violence—most notably in the asylum sequence—and punctuates the action with bleak humor. "Killing insane people is not good for public relations," the Sergeant says. That comedy evaporates at the conclusion, the liberation of the concentration camp at Falkenau, where the squad faces the final dimension of the war's horror.

Budgetary limitations restrain Fuller's depiction of such crucial scenes as the D-Day invasion, but he works well with what he has and makes the fear that the men experienced seem real enough, even if he can't re-create the invasion as spectacularly as Spielberg does in *Saving Private Ryan*. That sense of emotional truth is the film's overriding strength. Some of the parallels Fuller draws between American and German soldiers may seem too blatant, but he earns the right to make those points. He also makes them swiftly and moves on. Perhaps no American filmmaker has understood the importance of a quick pace more

"You know how you smoke out a sniper? You send a guy out in the open and you see if he gets shot. They thought that one up at West Point."

Zab (Robert Carradine)

"The Bangalor Torpedo was about 50 feet long and packed with 85 pounds of TNT and you assembled it along the way. By hand. I'd love to meet the asshole that invented it."

Zab

"You sonofabitch, you're gonna live if I have to blow your brains out!"

Sergeant (Lee Marvin)

"Surviving is the only glory in war, if you know what I mean."

Zab

See also

Saving Private Ryan
A Walk in the Sun
A Midnight Clear
Pickup on South Street
Shock Corridor

The Sergeant (Lee Marvin) leads his rifle squad off the Normandy beachhead during D-Day in *The Big Red One*. The Kobal Collection

than Fuller. At times his impatience gets in his way, when a longer moment of reflection might be called for, but that is probably not a fair criticism. According to some reports, as much as 40% of the film's running time was cut before its release.

Even so, *The Big Red One* is Fuller's personal masterpiece, and one of the best films to come out of World War II.

Cast: Lee Marvin (The Sergeant), Robert Carradine (Zab), Mark Hamill (Griff), Stephane Audran (Walloon), Bobby DiCicco (Vinci), Perry Lang (Kaiser), Kelly Ward (Johnson), Siegfried Rauch (Schroeder), Serge Marquand (Rensonnet), Charles Macaulay (General/Captain), Alain Doutey (Broban), Maurice Marsac (Vichy Colonel), Colin Gilbert (Dog Face P.O.W.), Joseph Clark (Shep), Ken Campbell (Lemchek), Doug Werner (Switolski), Marthe Villalonga (Mme. Marbaise); **Written by:** Samuel Fuller; **Cinematography by:** Adam Greenberg; **Music by:** Dana Kaproff. **Producer:** Lorimar Productions, Gene Corman. **MPAA Rating:** PG. **Running Time:** 113 minutes. **Format:** VHS, Beta, LV.

The Hound Salutes: Sam Fuller

The first time Sam Fuller used a movie camera was when his platoon liberated a concentration camp in Czechoslovakia. His commanding officer, appalled by the horror they confronted, ordered Fuller to record it. For many filmmakers, that might have been the central event of their lives. But by the time that happened, Sam Fuller had already been a reporter, a cartoonist, pulp novelist, and screenwriter. And he had fought his way through North Africa, Italy, and France with the First Infantry, the famous Big Red One. All of those experiences show up in his films, many of them efficient low-budget pictures. Though he made westerns and thrillers throughout his career—23 films made between 1948 and 1989—Fuller returned frequently to war.

His first effort in the field, *The Steel Helmet*, is one of the best B-movies ever made. Reportedly written in seven days and filmed in ten, it hardly wastes a second. Though the setting is Korea—it was released six months after the "police action" began—it could just as easily have been World War II. It's bleak, tough, smart, fast-paced, and short. Fuller's next two war films—*Fixed Bayonets* with James Dean and *House of Bamboo* with Robert Ryan—are not available on video.

When Sam Fuller tried to anticipate American involvement in Vietnam, he stumbled badly. *China Gate* is one of his lesser efforts, seriously hampered by the casting of both Lee Van Cleef and Angie Dickinson as half-Chinese characters. Fuller returned to form with *Merrill's Marauders*, a relatively restrained, realistic look at a costly and little-known campaign in the Pacific Theater of World War II.

He saved his best, most autobiographical work for the end. In *The Big Red One*, Fuller found the perfect casting of Lee Marvin as a sergeant whose career begins in World War I and is continued through the European campaigns of World War II. Fuller himself was 31 years old when he joined the outfit. At the time, the average age of a rifleman was 19. (That little fact comes from *The Typewriter, the Rifle and the Movie Camera*, a fine documentary by Adam Simon about the director.) Even though *The Big Red One* that exists now is cut significantly from Fuller's original vision, it is one of the all-time greats; funny and seemingly authentic, but at the same time unpredictable with the off-beat flourishes that you find in all of Fuller's best work.

In the end, it's easy to see why Fuller was so often drawn back to the subject. In a 1962 interview, he said, "War is the oldest profession, not whoring. It is as important as breathing. It has no glamour, it is not maudlin; it is bloody and profane. I am not trying to change the world, but the reaction I would like to my pictures from an audience is: 'Only an idiot would go to war.' In war men become animals. But I don't know what effect my films have on audiences. I hear that they like them, that they are excited and so on; but I wonder because, although war has no more glamour than murder, we still talk about war."

(*Film: Book 2*, edited by Robert Hughes. Grove Press. 1962.)

In the same interview, he also said, "I hate psychological characters in war [movies] because in war really all characters are psycho. Everyone is at a nervous animal pitch; vomit is inevitable. High theatrics and adolescence are the same, in this subject." What more could a filmmaker ask for?

Samuel Fuller The Kobal Collection

Though much smaller in scope, Bernard Wicki's anti-war Oscar-nominee is a legitimate companIon piece to *All Quiet on the Western Front*. Both are concerned with the waste of German boys in pursuit of an impossible victory. *The Bridge* is set at the end of World War II. It's based on Erwin C. Dietrich's autobiographical novel and feels accurate in the early domestic scenes and the combat scenes, and at the end when the two sides overlap.

In April 1945, in an unnamed German town near the American lines, life goes on despite air raids and shortages. At first, the place seems almost normal. Mrs. Bernhardt (Edith SchultzeWestrum) still picks up laundry and Mr. Forst (Hans Elwenspoek), the local Nazi Party organizer, is busily at work. But he is virtually the only "able-bodied" man around. Mr. Horber (Klaus Hellmond) has lost a hand. Mrs. Borchert (Eva Vaitl) is running the family farm by herself, though she does have slave laborers. Most of the males are teenaged boys.

Walter (Michael Hinz) is into jazz and cigarettes. Karl (Karl Michael Balzer) has fallen in lust with his father's girlfriend. Klaus (Volker Lechtenbrink) has a girl his own age and is just discovering how complicated romance can be. Jurgen (Franz Glaubrecht) thinks that he is destined to be an officer in the Army like his father and grandfather. Siggi (Gunther Hoffmann) is the littlest of the bunch. Albert (Fritz Wepper) and Scholten (Volker Bohnet) fill out this gang of seven. (If any of those credits are incorrect, it is sometimes difficult to reconcile differences between subtitles and credits.) Actually, these are completely normal, active, curious kids. Though they understand intellectually that the war is almost over and that Germany will lose, they're still anxious to do their part. They run to get the mail every day, hoping that their enlistment orders will arrive. Their parents dread the same news.

When they are called up, each reacts differently and off they go. The veterans tolerate these eager puppies and don't make life nearly as difficult as they could. After a teacher intervenes on their behalf, one of their officers makes sure the boys will be sent somewhere away from the worst of action. He places them under the direction of Cpl. Heilmann (Gunter Pfitzmann), whose seven years of Army service have taught him one important lesson: "Keep out of the way."

> "Every square foot of land we defend is part of the heart of our fatherland. The soldier who defends that square foot to his last breath is the savior of Germany."
>
> **Col. Frolich (Siegfried Schurenberg)**

Unfortunately, that is precisely what they are not able to do. In the second half, the seven boys face the confusion of a full retreat without any adult leadership. What are they to do when they see seasoned troops bent on self-preservation passing them by? The dynamics of the group take over with frightful results. By today's standards, director Wicki spends far too much time setting the stage, but he wants viewers to know the kids as individuals and to understand the forces that have shaped them. Once the pace picks up, it moves very well, and Wicki has a strong visual sense. The first time all of the soldiers come swarming out of their barracks and moving down a flight of stairs is a wonderful moment that captures the profound changes the boys are experiencing. Then later, when they must face American troops and tanks, the level of realistically graphic violence is remarkable. In 1959, it must have been shocking.

Some have noted that the final battle in *Saving Private Ryan* owes something to the end of *The Bridge*, and there are similarities. Those

See also

Hope and Glory
Au Revoir les Enfants
A Bridge Too Far
The Red Badge of Courage

should not be taken too far, however. Wicki finds no glory or redemption in battle—only the waste of young men who never have a chance to make mature decisions about what they are doing.

Cast: Fritz Wepper (Mutz), Volker Bohnet (Scholten), Franz Glaubrecht (Borchert), Karl Michael Balzer (Karl Horber), Gunther Hoffman (Siggi Bernhardt), Michael Hinz (Forst), Cordula Trantow (Franziska), Wolfgang Stumpf (Stern), Volker Lechtenbrink (Klaus Hager), Gunter Pfitzmann (Heilmann), Edith Schultze-Westrum (Mother Bernhardt), Ruth Hausmeister (Mrs. Mutz), Eva Vaitl (Mrs. Borchert), Fritz Wepper (Albert), Siegfried Schurenberg (Col. Frolich); **Written by:** Bernhard Wicki, Michael Mansfield, Karl-Wilhelm Vivier; **Cinematography by:** Gerd Von Bonen; **Music by:** Hans-Martin Majewski. **Producer:** Hermann Schwerin. **German. Awards:** Nominations: Academy Awards '59: Best Foreign Film. **Running Time:** 102 minutes. **Format:** VHS.

Despite its reputation as the last of the dinosaurs, Richard Attenborough's epic examination of a military disaster is really a fine film. It's long, accurate, filled with sterling performances, long, demanding and, well . . . long. For anyone who appreciates the subject—a major European battle little known in America—the length is just fine; for anyone expecting conventional flagwaving, the film is an unwatchable bore.

In the fall of 1944, the Allied advance across Western Europe is progressing more swiftly than anyone had predicted. Competition is keen between Gen. Eisenhower's top commanders, Gen. Montgomery and Gen. Patton, to lead the attack into Germany. Montgomery comes up with a daring idea to leapfrog ahead through Holland, "Operation Market Garden." As Lt. Gen. Browning (Dirk Bogarde) explains it, "Actually, the plan is really very simple. We're going to take 35,000 men 300 miles and drop them behind enemy lines." American and Polish paratroopers are to take three strategic bridges while British armored units punch through the German lines and race up a road to solidify their hold on the bridges, thereby opening a way straight into Germany.

Everyone believes that the Germans have their best troops on the front, leaving the bridges lightly defended by teenagers and old men. An intelligence officer, Maj. Fuller (Frank Grimes) has contradictory information and photographs of tanks in the region, but his ideas are dismissed. Instead, Market Garden proceeds and begins with an impressive display of military organization as planes, gliders, and parachutes fill the skies and tanks line the road as far as the eye can see. Then, piece by piece, the plan slowly disintegrates.

The main players are Lt. Col. Frost (Anthony Hopkins), whose men actually manage to take one end of the bridge at Arnhem; Maj. Gen. Urquhart (Sean Connery), who lands in a glider and finds that he and his men cannot communicate with their base; Sgt. Dohun (James Caan), who refuses to believe that his Captain (Nicholas Campbell) is dead; Maj. Cook (Robert Redford), who leads an impromptu amphibious assault; and Col. Stout (Elliott Gould), who has to replace a bridge for Lt. Col. Vandeleur's (Michael Caine) tanks. On the other side, Field Marshal Model (Walter Kohut) and Lt. Gen. Bittrich (Maximilian Schell) don't believe what's happening, even when they stumble across the plans. Caught between the two forces is Dr. Spaander (Laurence Olivier) who turns Kate Ter Horst's (Liv Ullman) house into a hospital.

> "The plan, like so many plans in so many wars before it, was meant to end the fighting by Christmas and bring the boys back home."
>
> **Voice-over introduction by Liv Ullmann**

> "We shall seize the bridges—it's all a question of bridges—with thunderclap surprise and then hold them until they can be secured."
>
> **Lt. Gen. Browning (Dirk Bogarde)**

The sheer scope of the story, with key elements occurring in three different locations, leads to a curious structure. For example, Maj. Cook is first shown, asleep, at the beginning, but he doesn't reappear for two full hours. Even then, despite Redford's star billing, his heroics are brief. The central character turns out to be Col. Frost. Anthony Hopkins's performance has an effortless, off-hand believability that somehow stands out from the rest of the ensemble.

See also
The Longest Day
Tora! Tora! Tora!
Gandhi
Battle of the Bulge

Director Attenborough handles the loud, flashy, explosive side of things with the right amount of excitement, but neither he nor writer William Goldman mean to glorify this mess. Important parts of the film are about large numbers of men and pieces of equipment standing around and waiting, and that, doubtless, is much more

Maj. Gen. Sosabowski (Gene Hackman), Brig. Gen. Gavin (Ryan O'Neal), Lt. Col. Vandeleur (Michael Caine), Lt. Gen. Horrocks (Edward Fox), and Lt. Gen. Browning (Dirk Bogarde) survey the disaster at Arnhem in *A Bridge Too Far.* The Kobal Collection

realistic than most Hollywood interpretations of combat. Finally, in the last hour of the film, when the dimensions of the debacle settle in, they are careful to focus in on the human costs. The final shot is a beautifully composed moment of sadness.

Cast: Sean Connery (Maj. Gen. Urquhart), Robert Redford (Maj. Cook), James Caan (Sgt. Dohun), Michael Caine (Lt. Col. Vandeleur), Elliott Gould (Col. Stout), Gene Hackman (Maj. Gen. Sosabowski), Laurence Olivier (Dr. Spaander), Ryan O'Neal (Brig. Gen. Gavin), Liv Ullmann (Kate Ter Horst), Dirk Bogarde (Lt. Gen. Browning), Hardy Kruger (Gen. Ludwig), Arthur Hill (Colonel), Edward Fox (Lt. Gen. Horrocks), Anthony Hopkins (Lt. Col. Frost), Maximilian Schell (Lt. Gen. Bittrich), Denholm Elliott (Met. Officer), Wolfgang Preiss (Field Marshal von Rundstedt), Nicholas Campbell (Capt. Glass), Christopher Good (Maj. Carlyle), John Ratzenberger (U.S. Lieutenant), Frank Grimes (Maj. Fuller), Walter Kohut (Field Marshal Model); **Written by:** William Goldman; **Cinematography by:** Geoffrey Unsworth; **Music by:** John Addison; **Technical Advisor:** J.D. Frost, James M. Gavin, Frank A. Gregg, Brian Horrocks, Col. John Waddy. **Producer:** United Artists, Joseph E. Levine, Richard P. Levine. **British. Awards:** British Academy Awards '77: Best Supporting Actor (Fox); National Society of Film Critics Awards '77: Best Supporting Actor (Fox). **MPAA Rating:** PG. **Running Time:** 175 minutes. **Format:** VHS, Beta, LV, Letterbox, Closed Caption, DVD.

One of the first post-war examinations of the pressures of military life remains one of the most entertaining and insightful. Humphrey Bogart's brilliant cast-against-type performance is the best of the mature stage of his career, but he's part of a solid ensemble that seems to have been perfectly in tune with the material.

An extended and fairly pointless introduction defines Ensign Willie Keith (Robert Francis) as something of a mama's boy—perhaps the worst insult that could be used to describe a young man in the early 1950s. Then he's off to his first assignment on the *Caine*, "a minesweeper that has never been asked to sweep a single mine," the cynical Lt. Keefer (Fred MacMurray) says. Under the command of Capt. DeVriess (Supporting Actor nominee Tom Tully), it's part of the "junkyard Navy." Discipline and morale are scraping bottom when DeVriess finally leaves and is replaced by Capt. Philip Francis Queeg (Bogart), "a book man," as in "by the book."

Queeg demands strict adherence to regulations and soon has the ship looking much better. At the same time, though, his flaws are showing through. He's petty, obsessed by details, unwilling to accept responsibility for poor decisions or mistakes. Keefer, a smart aleck would-be novelist, begins to talk of mutiny with Lt. Maryk (Van Johnson), the executive officer. When the *Caine* goes into action, a series of increasingly serious incidents reveals the depths of Queeg's problems. Bogart's memorable interpretation of the character immediately entered the public consciousness with jokes about ball bearings and strawberries. Seen today, however, it rises above the level of stereotype.

Despite his flaws, Queeg has sympathetic qualities. At the heart of his psychosis, Bogart finds fear, not meanness. Early on, Queeg mentions having several ships shot out from under him in the Atlantic. It's fairly easy for a viewer to see Queeg as an older version of Lt. Joe Rossi, the heroic character Bogie had played 10 years before in *Action in the North Atlantic*. He's a man who has been in the war from the beginning, and now has been asked to accept one job too many.

Breaking away from his boy-next-door image, Van Johnson finds similar complexities in Maryk. He's an officer who wants to be loyal, and tries diligently to work within the established structures of the Navy to find his way out of the situation. It takes the most dangerous circumstances to force him to take action. For his part, Fred MacMurray brings hints of Walter Neff, the murderer he played so well in *Double Indemnity*, to Lt. Keefer. Remarkably, director Edward Dmytryk got the full cooperation of the Navy on the film, and the shipboard exteriors add a dimension of authenticity that's often lacking in ocean-going dramas. Dmytryk is forced to use a tank and model in one sequence. For the rest of the exteriors, he uses real ships and photographs them strikingly in "three-color" Technicolor that still looks bright and sharp on good tapes.

> "Your orders, Keith— those monstrous papers that transform ex-civilians into men without minds."
>
> Lt. Keefer (Fred MacMurray) asking for Ens. Keith's (Robert Francis) orders

On the minus side, too much is made of Keith's romantic problems with May Wynn, and at the end, a last look at Queeg would finish the story more satisfactorily. But those are quibbles. *The Caine Mutiny* is a strong story about compelling, believable characters as evidenced by its enduring popularity in print, on stage as *The Caine Mutiny Court Martial*, and on tape.

See also

Mister Roberts
From Here to Eternity
Bridge on the River Kwai
An Officer and a Gentleman

Capt. Queeg (Humphrey Bogart, right) is questioned by Lt. Greenwald (Jose Ferrer, left) as Lt. Maryk (Van Johnson) looks on in *The Caine Mutiny*. The Kobal Collection

Cast: Humphrey Bogart (Capt. Philip Francis Queeg), Jose Ferrer (Lt. Barney Greenwald), Van Johnson (Lt. Steve Maryk), Fred MacMurray (Lt. Tom Keefer), Lee Marvin (Meatball), Claude Akins (Horrible), E.G. Marshall (Lt. Cmdr. Challee), Robert Francis (Ens. Willie Keith), May Wynn (May Wynn), Tom Tully (Capt. DeVriess), Arthur Franz (Lt. Paynter), Warner Anderson (Capt. Blakely), Katherine Warren (Mrs. Keith), Jerry Paris (Ens. Harding), Steve Brodie (Chief Budge), Whit Bissell (Lt. Cmdr. Dickson), Robert Bray (Board member), Ted Cooper (Sergeant-at-Arms); **Written by:** Stanley Roberts, Michael Blankfort; **Cinematography by:** Franz Planer; **Music by:** Max Steiner; **Technical Advisor:** Cmdr. James C. Shaw. **Producer:** Columbia Pictures, Stanley Kramer. **Awards:** Nominations: Academy Awards '54: Best Actor (Bogart), Best Film Editing, Best Picture, Best Screenplay, Best Sound, Best Supporting Actor (Tully), Best Original Dramatic Score. **Running Time:** 125 minutes. **Format:** VHS, Beta, LV, 8mm, Closed Caption, DVD.

Of all the big popular novels that came out of World War II, Joseph Heller's is the most difficult to adapt to another medium. Its fragmented structure, intricate language, and grim humor work beautifully on the printed page. Translated into moving images, Heller's surreal absurdism becomes somehow more arbitrary and rigid than it is in the reader's imagination.

That, of course, is a complaint often made against movies made from best-sellers, and writer Buck Henry and director Mike Nichols probably do as well as anyone could with the book. Curiously, their version of the tale is more an anti-corporate America film, than a true antiwar film. Germans do not appear on screen and are mentioned only in passing. Their war-making activities are seen briefly as a few puffs of flak in one aerial scene. The real villains are American officers who sacrifice their men to advance their own careers within what was then referred to as "the military-industrial complex."

When the filmmakers focus on the hardware of war, they're more authentic and dynamic than the propaganda made in the early 1940s. Mexican locations become a realistic and remote Italian island where a group of B-24 bombers is based. The scenes of the huge lumbering planes rolling out onto the runway and taking off are impressive. Nichols makes the airborne interiors just as persuasive, most notably in the recurring scenes that slowly reveal Snowden's Secret. The big nighttime bombing scene is a gloriously staged bit of pyrotechnics, too. But, like any war film, *Catch-22* finally succeeds or fails on the characters.

Yossarian (Alan Arkin) is the bombardier who is being driven mad by fear as the selfserving Col. Cathcart (Martin Balsam) and Col. Korn (Buck Henry) continually raise the number of missions the men must fly before they can go home. Dobbs (Martin Sheen) is so gung-ho that he doesn't care. Orr (Bob Balaban) crashes one plane after another, so nobody wants to fly with him. The naive Natley (Art Garfunkel) is in love with a whore and doesn't want to go back. Milo Minderbinder (Jon Voight) is using the war as an excuse to form a syndicate to buy and sell military surplus, turning a profit for the soldier-shareholders. Yossarian wants Doc Daneeka (Jack Gilford) to ground him because he's crazy, but the Doc answers that concern for one's own safety is proof that he's sane. It's there in the rulebook: Catch-22. Maj. Danby (Richard Benjamin) is a clueless yes-man, and though the Chaplain (Anthony Perkins) would like to help, he can't do anything.

Those are the main characters and they're abetted by almost a dozen more who contribute cameos: The Soldier in White, McWatt's (Peter Bonerz) buzzing the beach, Nurse Duckett's (Paula Prentiss) sexy teasing, Maj. Major (Bob Newhart), the blustering Gen. Dreedle (Orson Welles). All of them make for a busy, busy movie. The film is never boring and many of the images created by Nichols and cinematographer David Watkin are staggering. But the furious action and bold visuals are at odds with Heller's verbal humor of contradiction and circular illogic. The endless discussions about what is sane and what is insane don't have the sparkle of the original lines. The filmmakers finally make their case when Milo and Yossarian discuss one character's death,

See also

*M*A*S*H*

Twelve O'Clock High

Command Decision

Art Garfunkel, Alan Arkin, and Martin Sheen in *Catch-22.* The Kobal Collection

Milo: "But he died a rich man. He had over 60 shares in the syndicate."

Yossarian: "What good is that? He's dead."

Milo: "Then his family will get it."

Yossarian: "He didn't have time to have a family."

Milo: "Then his parents will get it."

Yossarian: "They don't need it. They're rich."

Milo: "Then they'll understand."

In the end, the film defeats itself. It's not funny because it is so bleak. But the characters are so exaggerated for comic effect that the story doesn't really work as drama or tragedy, either. The conclusion, so perfect and unexpected in the novel, seems disconnected from the body of the film, following, as it does, Yossarian's long hallucinatory nightmare journey through the streets of Rome.

Still, if *Catch-22* is a failure, it is an ambitious failure that seems less dated than many films of its era.

Cast: Alan Arkin (Capt. Yossarian), Martin Balsam (Col. Cathcart), Art Garfunkel (Nately), Jon Voight (Milo Minderbinder), Richard Benjamin (Maj. Danby), Buck Henry (Col. Korn), Bob Newhart (Maj. Major), Paula Prentiss (Nurse Duckett), Martin Sheen (Dobbs), Charles Grodin (Aardvark), Anthony Perkins (Chaplain Tappman), Orson Welles (Gen. Dreedle), Jack Gilford (Doc Daneeka), Bob Balaban (Capt. Orr), Susanne Benton (Dreedle's WAC), Norman Fell (Sgt. Towswer), Austin Pendleton (Moodus), Peter Bonerz (Capt. McWatt), Jon Korkes (Snowden), Collin Wilcox Paxton (Nurse Cramer), John Brent (Cathcart's Receptionist); **Written by:** Buck Henry; **Cinematography by:** David Watkin; **Technical Advisor:** Maj. Alexander Gerry. **Producer:** Paramount Pictures, John Calley, Martin Ransohoff. **MPAA Rating:** R. **Running Time:** 121 minutes. **Format:** VHS, Beta, LV.

COME AND SEE
Idi i Smotri
Go and See
1985 Elem Klimov ♪♪♪♪

Long, flawed, absolutely harrowing, Elem Klimov's rarely seen masterpiece turns the conventional war story into horror. Though it lacks the scope and technical sophistication of *Schindler's List*, the intense reactions it provokes are the same. Klimov's subject is atrocity—true genocide, the efforts of the German Army and the Nazi Party not simply to occupy territory and gain political ends, but to eliminate entire populations of undesirable "inferior" races.

> "Inferior nations spread the microbe of communism."
> **Unidentified Nazi officer**

In Byelorussia, 1943, two peasant boys dig in the sand, surrounded by the burnt ruins of some previous engagement. The smaller boy tells Flor (Alexsei Kravchenko) that he must find a weapon if he wants to join the partisans. To the loud and emotional dismay of his mother he does just that, and finds that the guerrillas are a poorly equipped lot. He has barely been introduced to them, though, before he and a young woman, Glasha (Olga Mironova), are left behind as the others set off on a mission. At that point, the film becomes a surreal journey, an episodic story of initiation as Flor and the viewer gradually come to discover what is happening.

For Western audiences who are probably unfamiliar with what took place in Byelorussia, the action often seems inexplicable. Who are the various characters Flor and Glasha meet? What are they doing? Initially, Klimov's directorial style has certain off-putting quality for the uninitiated, too. He seems enamored of long follow shots, where his camera stays behind a group of running figures for a seemingly interminable length of time and to no apparent narrative end. In those scenes and in others that isolate Flor even farther from everything he knows, Klimov is setting up the second half of the film, when the Nazis finally emerge from the thick morning fog and Flor is trapped in a small village.

Fact:
In 1986, director Elem Klimov was elected President of the Soviet Filmmakers Union and immediately reformed the organization, declaring that from then on there would be "no forbidden subjects" and releasing dozens of films that had been banned under previous administrations. In 1988, he was the first Russian to be elected into the American Academy of Motion Picture Arts and Sciences.

Until then, the invaders have been largely invisible, seen only as airplanes high in the sky or by shells that rain down from distant guns. But once they appear in ever-increasing numbers and cajole the villagers into obeying their orders, the tenor of the film changes. Moment by moment, what had been random and remote becomes immediate. Klimov lets those events transpire at an unhurried pace at first. The soldiers are rough and brusque but businesslike. When the destruction begins and the enormity of their evil is revealed, the deliberate pace makes the horror all the more jolting and believable. And that is the film's central strength. The film is based on true accounts, written by Alex Adamovich, of German atrocities. (They destroyed more than 600 villages in their invasion.) The more significant details—posing for a photograph, the rationales used to separate people into different groups—have the unmistakable ring of truth.

Like *Schindler's List*, *Come and See* is fiction that reveals a larger truth so horrible that it is difficult to accept in any form. A black-and-white coda made of documentary footage seems a needless afterthought, but it doesn't dilute the film's power.

See also
Schindler's List
Fires on the Plain
The Seventh Cross
The Big Red One

Flor (Alexei Kravchenko) is
captured by German soldiers in
Come and See. The Kobal Collection

Cast: Alexei Kravchenko (Florya Gaishun), Olga Mironova (Glasha), Lubomiras Lauciavicus, Vladas Bagdonas, Viktor Lorents, Juris Lumiste, Kazimir Rabetsky, Yevgeni Tilicheyev; **Written by:** Elem Klimov, Alex Adamovich; **Cinematography by:** Alexei Rodionov; **Music by:** Oleg Yanchenko. **Producer:** Mosfilm, Sovexportfilm USSR. **Russian. Running
Time:** 142 minutes. **Format:** VHS.

COMMAND DECISION

As a dramatic examination of the air war in Europe, this film is a companion piece to *Twelve O'Clock High*, made a year later. Both focus on the choices made by the men who ordered the pilots and crews to fly over Germany, and on the forces that shape those choices. Though *Command Decision* also looks at the military and civilian powers that operate beyond the airfields, it remains essentially a filmed stage play.

The setting is England, 1944, a few weeks before D-Day. For two days in a row, Gen. "Casey" Dennis (Clark Gable) has ordered his B-17s to fly daylight bombing runs deep inside Germany. Both raids have resulted in massive American losses. Gen. Dennis is prepared to order a third raid when he learns that his immediate superior, Maj. Gen. Kane (Walter Pidgeon) is about to visit the base. He'll be followed by an important congressional fact-finding delegation led by the publicity-hungry Rep. Malcolm (Edward Arnold). Kane suggests that they avoid the dangerous missions while the congressmen are on hand and stick to safe runs over the French coast. Gen. Dennis answers that he doesn't know how long the good weather will hold, and he needs two more days to finish the enigmatic "Operation Stitch," and that, he claims, could be the key to the war. If he's wrong, his friendly rival Gen. Garnet (Brian Donlevy) is on hand to take his job.

> "Dennis is one of those boys whose brain is fascinated by guts. He loves this lousy war."
> **Brockhurst (Charles Bickford)**

The rest is essentially a balancing act that weighs short-term pain against long-term gain. For a time, the strong performances compensate the notable lack of physical action. Pidgeon is able to reveal the various sides of Kane's personality—conniving political animal, realist, survivor, dedicated soldier—making the man a believable contradiction. Key support is supplied by Van Johnson as the sergeant who gets things done, Cameron Mitchell as a haggard navigator, and Charles Bickford as a skeptical war correspondent. But the film belongs to Gable. It was the first film he made after the war, where he had served in the Air Force, and he brings a sense of responsibility and gravity to the role of a man who has made a difficult decision and must fight to hold onto it.

For some viewers, though, his best efforts are not enough to energize the static story. The script, by George Froeschel and William Laidlaw, doesn't break free from the limits of William Wister Haines's play. Some carefully chosen archival footage of exteriors at English airfields provides a needed break, but the film never gets off the ground, literally. None of the action takes place in the air. Director Sam Wood accepts the limits of the stage, letting his characters shuffle in and out of rooms and seldom moves his camera. The most important dramatic moments revolve around guys arguing with each other. When the subject of those arguments finally comes around to pre-war military spending levels and budget cuts, it's difficult for most viewers to care much about the outcome. That's the stuff of policy debates, not of drama.

See also
Memphis Belle
Twelve O'Clock High
Catch-22
Sink the Bismarck!
The Gallant Hours

Clark Gable (sitting) and Brian Donlevy discuss their *Command Decision.* The Kobal Collection

Cast: Clark Gable (Gen. K.C. "Casey" Dennis), Walter Pidgeon (Maj. Gen. Roland G. Kane), Van Johnson (Tech. Sgt. Immanuel T. Evans), Brian Donlevy (Gen. Clifton Garnet), Charles Bickford (Elmer Brockhurst), John Hodiak (Col. Edward R. Martin), Ray Collins (Maj. Desmond Lansing), Edward Earle (Congressman Watson), Sam Flint (Congressman), Warner Anderson (Col. Ernest Haley), Don Haggerty (Command Officer), Henry Hall (Congressman), Alvin Hammer (Sgt. Cahill), Holmes Herbert (Chairman), Edward Arnold (Congressman Malcolm), Cameron Mitchell (Lt. Ansel Goldberg), Moroni Olsen (Congressman Stone); **Written by:** George Froeschel, William Wister Haines, William R. Laidlaw; **Cinematography by:** Harold Rosson; **Music by:** Miklos Rozsa. **Producer:** MGM, Sidney Franklin. **Running Time:** 112 minutes. **Format:** VHS.

CRASH DIVE

1943 Archie Mayo

One of the industry's first efforts at pure propaganda is a confection spun from air and sugar. When it was produced in July 1942, filmmakers were still groping for the right formulas to inspire the American war effort. Though the picture was made at New London, Connecticut, with the full cooperation of the Navy, most of the military aspects are pure fantasy. They also rate less attention than an overblown and underpowered love triangle. As Bosley Crowther said in his *New York Times* review, "It leaves one wondering blankly whether Hollywood knows that we're at war."

Despite those flaws, the film does have much to tell today's audiences about the times, and the bright Technicolor image is still striking.

In the opening scene, heroic PT boat skipper Lt. Ward Stewart (Tyrone Power) rescues a raft full of survivors from an attacking U-boat. Stewart thinks that PT boats are the wave of the future for the Navy and so he's distressed when he's transferred to submarines. His new boss is Lt. Cmdr. Dewey Connors (Dana Andrews). Dewey is almost engaged to Jean Hewlett (Anne Baxter), a teacher at the local girl's school. Jean and Ward "meet cute" in the lower berth of a sleeping car en route to Washington. For most of the film, Ward and Dewey don't realize that they're in competition for the same woman. By the time they figure it out, their sub has followed a ruthless German "Q-boat" into a secret Nazi harbor, and they're embarking on a commando raid. That bit of frippery is accomplished through some moderately spectacular, Oscar-winning pyrotechnics.

More interesting than any of those plot details, though, is the appearance of Oliver Cromwell Jones (Ben Carter), a major black supporting character. For the most part in the 1930s and '40s, black characters did not appear in mainstream movies. The few who did were relegated to subservient roles or comic relief. Oliver, however, figures more prominently than any of the other supporting cast, and his is an active physical role. By the end of the movie, he's blazing away with a Tommy gun. By today's standards it may not seem like much, but in the turbulent year of 1942, it was significant.

Director Archie Mayo and writers W.R. Burnett and Jo Swerling, all veteran filmmakers, were not striking a blow for racial equality. They were trying to elevate the prestige of the Navy and to sell movie tickets.

See also

The Guns of Navarone
Das Boot
Dive Bomber
They Died with Their Boots On

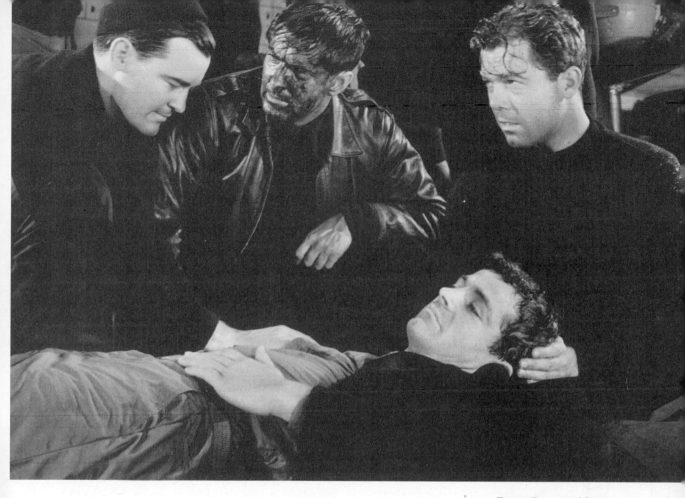

Tyrone Power and Dana Andrews in *Crash Dive*. The Kobal Collection

Cast: Tyrone Power (Lt. Ward Stewart), Anne Baxter (Jean Hewlett), Dana Andrews (Lt. Cmdr. Dewey Connors), James Gleason (McDonnell), May Whitty (Grandmother), Harry (Henry) Morgan (Brownie), Ben Carter (Oliver Cromwell Jones), Frank Conroy (Capt. Bryson), Florence Lake (Doris), John Archer (Curly), Minor Watson (Adm. Bob Stewart), Kathleen Howard (Miss Bromley), Stanley Andrews (The Captain), Thurston Hall (Senator from Texas), Trudy Marshall (Telephone operator), Charles Tannen (Seaman Hammond), Chester Gan (Lee Wong); **Written by:** Jo Swerling, W.R. Burnett; **Cinematography by:** Leon Shamroy; **Music by:** David Buttolph; **Technical Advisor:** M.K. Kirkpatrick. **Producer:** Milton Sperling, Fox. **Awards:** Academy Awards '44: Best Special Effects (Sersen). **Running Time:** 105 minutes. **Format:** VHS.

CROSS OF IRON
Steiner—Das Eiserne Kreuz
1976 Sam Peckinpah ♪♪♪♪

Sam Peckinpah's only war film is a forgotten masterpiece that has never really managed to overcome its troubled production. In many important ways, it is a variation on themes the director explored in *The Wild Bunch*, with carefully choreographed action sequences that mirror those in his great western. Both are stories of men on the wrong side who realize their position and so are loyal only to each other. In *The Wild Bunch*, they're train robbers; in *Cross of Iron*, they're German soldiers on the Russian front.

> "The German soldier no longer has any ideals. He is not fighting for the culture of the West, not for this one form of government that he wants, not for the stinking party. He's fighting for his life, God bless him."
>
> **Col. Brandt (James Mason) to Capt. Stransky (Maximilian Schell)**

> "Steiner is a myth, but men like him are our last hope and in that sense he is truly dangerous."
>
> **Capt. Kiesel (David Warner)**

> "Don't rejoice in his defeat, you men. For though the world stood up and stopped the bastard, The bitch that bore him is in heat again."
>
> **Afterword quotation from Bertold Brecht**

The year is 1943 and the Germans have begun their retreat. The opening credits emphasize the early Nazi indoctrination of children. A montage of still photographs and newsreels carries the party through its rise to power and expansion to the Wehrmacht's first defeats. Oblivious to the realities of the situation, Capt. Stransky (Maximilian Schell) arrives in Russia and immediately throws his aristocratic Prussian weight around. "I volunteered for this campaign," he boasts, "because I feel that men of quality are needed here. It is time to destroy the myth of Russian invincibility." Col. Brandt (James Mason) and his adjutant Capt. Kiesel (David Warner), both seasoned veterans, don't realize how deluded Stransky really is. (The man's madness is revealed gradually.) Instead, they advise him to rely on men like Sgt. Steiner (James Coburn), whose courage and skills as a soldier are unquestioned.

Like Col. Brandt, Steiner has been awarded an Iron Cross for bravery. Stransky covets one of the medals and is willing to do anything to get it. But how important is one madman's obsession within the larger madness? That's what the film is really about. Working from a script that he collaborated on with Julius Epstein (*Casablanca*) and veterans James Hamilton and Walter Kelley, Peckinpah shows the war as near pure chaos where women and children are recruited as soldiers along with men. He takes particular care to show the incredible destructive power of mortar and cannon shelling, and their effect on those who survive. Some of the battles are so authentic-looking that they might contain German archival footage.

The scenes of the men at rest, though, are just as important to the film. The moments in the bunker where Steiner's platoon lives have an unmistakable feeling of truth to them. A birthday where one man surprisingly cracks under the built-up pressure is the most obvious example, along with one long exchange of foxhole philosophy between Steiner and Schnurrbart (Fred Stillkrauth). Throughout, the touches of fatalistic soldier's humor are perfectly timed, and toward the end, a memorable moment redefines a fate worse than death.

Note:
Cross of Iron was severely edited in its unsuccessful American theatrical release. Several versions exist on videotape. This review is based on the 128-minute Hen's Tooth Video edition.

Peckinpah and his stars work remarkably well together. Coburn's performance is worthy of an Oscar nomination. The long, brilliantly edited hallucinatory sequence involving Steiner's stay in a hospital is some of the best work either man has ever done. Mason, usually a reserved and cool screen presence, lets real emotion show through in his role. The scenes between him and David Warner are a small balance to the conflict

See also
Grand Illusion
The Wild Bunch
Come and See
The Blue Max

WORLD WAR II: EUROPE AND NORTH AFRICA

between Steiner and Stransky. The conclusion is unusual and unexpected, but not inappropriate for such an unconventional and original war film.

James Coburn (left) and David Warner run for cover in *Cross of Iron*. The Kobal Collection

Cast: James Coburn (Sgt. Steiner), Maximilian Schell (Capt. Stransky), James Mason (Col. Brandt), David Warner (Capt. Kiesel), Senta Berger (Eva), Klaus Lowitsch (Kruger), Vadim Glowna (Kern), Roger Fritz (Triebig), Dieter Schidor (Anselm), Burkhard Driest (Maag), Fred Stillkrauth (Schnurrbart), Michael Nowka (Dietz), Veronique Vendell (Marga), Arthur Brauss (Zoll); **Written by:** Julius J. Epstein, Walter Kelley, James Hamilton; **Cinematography by:** John Coquillon; **Music by:** Ernest Gold. **Producer:** ITC Entertainment Group, Wolf C Hartwig, Arlene Sellers, Alex Winitsky. **British, German. MPAA Rating:** R. **Running Time:** 120 minutes. **Format:** VHS.

DAS BOOT
The Boat
1981 Wolfgang Petersen ♫♫♫♫

No other submarine film comes close to Wolfgang Petersen's epic. As far as undersea warfare goes, it is *Gone with the Wind*, *Citizen Kane*, and *Casablanca* combined. The 150-minute theatrical release was a commercial success, but on video, the full-length director's cut is a marvel. Based on Lothar Buchheim's autobiographical novel, the film tells the story of the final voyage of U-96.

The war is almost over, and Allied sea power has turned the tide. Where the U-boat packs once terrorized convoys, the submarines are now prey to quick destroyers with more accurate depth charges. They have suffered terrible losses—a foreword states that of the 40,000 men who served in U-boats, 30,000 were lost—and now many of the crew members are teenagers. "I feel ancient around these kids, like I'm on some Children's Crusade," the Captain (Juergen Prochnow) says. He's a veteran who tries to do his job despite the overwhelming odds.

Fact:
Das Boot was created as a mini-series and exists on tape and disc in two versions, 151 minutes and 209 minutes. The remastered director's cut looks superb. On DVD, the image is particularly sharp and crisp and so is the sound. Audio is so important to overall experience of the film, that it will test the limits of the best home theater system. Good headphones are recommended.

After a night of drunken celebrations, the boat stocks up with provisions—sausages and meats hang from every available space—and the freshly scrubbed sailors embark. It doesn't take long for all ideas of heroism to be replaced by survival. From stormy seas to relentless destroyers to crab lice, everything is out to get them. What sets the film apart from all others is the almost life-like cinematic reality it creates. For three hours, the viewer is inside that boat with the men.

That harrowing sense of claustrophobia is created by incredible sets, one built to the actual dimensions of a German sub, another mounted on a gimbal so that it could be tilted at any angle. They're complemented by superb tank shots of the conning tower in bad weather and equally believable miniature effects by Ernest Wild. All of the effects are so detailed that use of models is virtually undetectable. Most of the credit, though, must go to Petersen and director of photography Jost Vacano, whose work with a handheld camera earned an Academy Award nomination. Their efforts combine to create the physical reality of the undersea world; the actors, almost all of them unknown outside Germany, create the emotional reality, and that is just as important.

This is a film about men who are pushed to the breaking point and then beyond it. How do they deal with overpowering hopelessness? What form will their surrender or disintegration take? Petersen uses the extended running time to give the men long silent scenes which make their fear absolutely believable. With so much going on, little room is left for politics. Even so, the film has been criticized from opposing quarters for being pro-Nazi and anti-Nazi. It's neither. It is about men who are trying to sink ships and kill people while other people are trying to sink their ship and kill them. Perhaps Petersen could have made a more strident anti-fascist statement, but such revisionism is hypocritical at best, considering the factual nature of the source material. (By all accounts, like Noel Coward's *In Which We Serve*, the story is strongly based in truth.)

So, forget politics. Forget categories. *Das Boot* is simply one of the great war films.

See also
Run Silent Run Deep
In Which We Serve
All Quiet on the Western Front

Klaus Wenneman, Juergen Prochnow, and Herbert Gronemeyer in *Das Boot* The Kobal Collection

Cast: Juergen Prochnow (The Captain), Herbert Gronemeyer (Lt. Werner), Klaus Wennemann (Chief Engineer), Hubertus Bengsch (1st Lieutenant), Martin Semmelrogge (2nd Lieutenant), Bernd Tauber (Chief Quartermaster), Erwin Leder (Johann), Martin May (Ullman), Heinz Honig (Hinrich), Uwe Ochsenknecht (Chief Bosun), Claude-Oliver Rudolph (Ario), Jan Fedder (Pilgrim), Ralph Richer (Frenssen), Joachim Bernhard (Precher), Oliver Stritzel (Schwalle), Konrad Becker (Bockstiegel), Lutz Schnell (Dufte), Martin Hemme (Bruckenwilli), Rita Cadillac (Monique); **Written by:** Wolfgang Petersen; **Cinematography by:** Jost Vacano; **Music by:** Klaus Doldinger; **Technical Advisor:** Karlheinz Bohm. **Producer:** Bavaria Atelier Gmbh, Columbia Pictures, Gunter Rohrback. **German.. Awards:** Nominations: Academy Awards '82: Best Adapted Screenplay, Best Cinematography, Best Director (Petersen), Best Film Editing, Best Sound. **MPAA Rating:** R. **Running Time:** 210 minutes. **Format:** VHS, Beta, LV, DVD.

THE DIRTY DOZEN
1967 Robert Aldrich ♪♪♪♪

Director Robert Aldrich combines a 1940s look with 1960s politics to create one of the most entertaining war movies ever made. The mix of nostalgia, anti-establishment rebellion, and graphic violence was a huge commercial hit in 1967, and it has remained popular on all forms of video—tape, cable, broadcast—ever since. Yes, its morality is dubious, but the movie sure is fun.

That was a year when Hollywood was testing the limits of established genres, trying to do new things with familiar formulas: romance (*The Graduate*), gangsters (*Bonnie and Clyde*), prisons (*Cool Hand Luke*), mysteries (*In the Heat of the Night*), even true crime (*In Cold Blood*). *The Dirty Dozen* takes the same liberties with the war movie.

"I owe you an apology. I always thought you were a cold, unimaginative, and tight-lipped officer, but you're really quite . . . emotional, aren't you?"

Maj. Reisman (Lee Marvin) to Col. Breed (Robert Ryan)

"Just act mean and grunt."

Maj. Reisman to Wladislaw (Charles Bronson) on how to pass as a German officer

The premise is a Hollywood chestnut: a lovable bunch of rag-tag misfits are molded into a crack fighting unit by a officer who's tough but fair. It could describe *Sands of Iwo Jima*, *The Fighting 69th*, *Flying Leathernecks*, or a dozen others. In this case, though, the misfits are convicted rapists, murderers and thieves who range on the psychiatric scale between quick-tempered and full-blown psychotic. The more attractive ones (Jim Brown, John Cassavetes, Clint Walker, Donald Sutherland, Trini Lopez) are given enough extenuating circumstances to make them sympathetic, but they're still very bad guys facing grim punishment. (The opening execution is still a chillingly efficient sequence that heightens tension and pushes the rest of the film to a higher level.) The first two-thirds are devoted to the group's constructing its own prison compound and training. As Maj. Reisman, who's given the thankless task of leading them, Lee Marvin seems completely comfortable and at ease with the role. Even in the most ridiculous moments, he does not appear to be acting.

Fact:

Though the premise is improbable, it is not completely unrealistic. The Army did offer convicted soldiers the chance to lessen their sentences by volunteering for particularly unpleasant or hazardous duty.

The setting is another wartime favorite—England right before D-Day—and the primary villains are high-ranking American officers; a blustering Gen. Worden (Ernest Borgnine) abetted by Col. Breed (Robert Ryan at his most snide and sarcastic). By setting them up as the heavies, writers Nunnally Johnson and Lukas Heller don't need to bother with the Germans until the last act. The filmmakers are wise not to dwell on that part of the story. The group's mission is to assassinate high-ranking Nazis at a Chateau resort, and in accomplishing it, they're none-too-picky about bystanders. That kind of casual violence—cinematic "collateral damage"—would not have been tolerated in a war film of the 1940s or '50s, but it is not unusual for the times. In 1967, James Bond, with his "license to kill" set the standard for murderous escapism. Aldrich and company simply took that cool macho attitude to the next level. In escapist adventure, the body count is still climbing, and the end is not in sight.

See also

The Guns of Navarone
Where Eagles Dare
The Great Escape
Hell in the Pacific

Col. Breed (Robert Ryan) is held captive in his own Command Post by Wladislaw (Charles Bronson) during the war games in *The Dirty Dozen*. The Kobal Collection

Cast: Lee Marvin (Maj. John Reisman), Ernest Borgnine (Gen. Worden), Charles Bronson (Joseph Wladislaw), Jim Brown (Robert Jefferson), George Kennedy (Maj. Max Armbruster), John Cassavetes (Victor Franko), Clint Walker (Samson Posey), Donald Sutherland (Vernon Pinkley), Telly Savalas (Archer Maggott), Robert Ryan (Col. Everett Dasher-Breed), Ralph Meeker (Capt. Stuart Kinder), Richard Jaeckel (Sgt. Clyde Bowren), Trini Lopez (Pedro Jiminez), Robert Webber (Gen. Denton), Stuart Cooper (Rosco Lever), Robert Phillips (Cpl. Carl Morgan), Al Mancini (Tassos Bravos); **Written by:** Nunnally Johnson, Lukas Heller; **Cinematography by:** Edward Scaife; **Music by:** Frank De Vol. **Producer:** MGM, Kenneth Hyman. **Awards:** Academy Awards '67: Best Sound Effects Editing; Nominations: Academy Awards '67: Best Film Editing, Best Sound, Best Supporting Actor (Cassavetes). **MPAA Rating:** PG. **Running Time:** 149 minutes. **Format:** VHS, Beta, LV, Letterbox, DVD.

FIVE GRAVES TO CAIRO

1943 Billy Wilder ♪♪♪♪

Billy Wilder's suspense film is one of the great forgotten sleepers of World War II. He and writer-producer Charles Brackett bring out the best in each other. If this melodrama lacks the substance of *The Lost Weekend* or *Sunset Boulevard*, it is every bit as entertaining. The script is solidly built, with elements of suspense deftly laid in along with pungent acerbic humor. The casting is flawless and the actors make even the more preposterous moments seem credible.

> "If the circumstances in which we find ourselves weren't so peculiar, I might turn you over my knee and spank you—with abandon."
>
> **Cpl. Bramble (Franchot Tone) to Mouche (Anne Baxter)**

> "We have no bedbugs, I swear! Maybe one or two in the cheaper rooms, sir."
>
> **Farid (Akim Tamiroff) to Lt. Schwegler (Peter Van Eyck)**

> "The rooms immediately adjacent to the good bathroom will be occupied by the German High Command. The one with the bathroom which doesn't work goes to the Italian General."
>
> **Lt. Schwegler to Farid**

> "Can a nation that belches understand a nation that sings? . . . In fact, as we say in Milano, we are getting the end of the stick that stinks."
>
> **Gen. Sebastiano (Fortunio Bonanova) on the Germans**

After a foreword that establishes the setting—June 1942, with the British 8th Army in retreat toward Cairo after the fall of Tobruk—the film opens with an indelible image. A tank grinds slowly across an expanse of white dunes; a dead man lolls in the open hatch. Inside are more bodies. The only survivor is Cpl. John J. Bramble (Franchot Tone). Without giving away too much of the delicious plot, eventually he finds himself at the Empress of Britain Hotel, run by Farid (Akim Tamiroff), where Mouche (Anne Baxter) is the maid. The advancing Germans commandeer the place. The swaggering advance man, Lt. Schwegler (Peter Van Eyck), takes over with a terse warning: "Our complaints are brief. We make them against the nearest wall." He wants things to go smoothly for his boss, Field Marshall Erwin Rommel (Erich von Stroheim), who arrives with the key to the entire North African campaign hidden in his map case. The other two main players are Gen. Sebastiano (Fortunio Bonanova), an Italian who's not too careful with his pistol, and Paul Davoss, a dead waiter.

The rest of the story is built on hidden identities, shifting loyalties, and a hasty patchwork of extemporaneous lies. In other hands, it could have been nothing more than a featherweight mystery that exploits the war. Though the filmmakers are not above propagandistic jabs, they know that the audience shares their anti-Nazi sentiments and so those need not be hammered home. Rommel is an intriguing character, a man who can be a convivial host to a captured foe one moment, an arrogant swine the next. Though von Stroheim's work is broader, almost burlesque when compared to the similar character he played in *Grand Illusion*, it is exactly what the film calls for. Franchot Tone is every bit as good. He brings a cerebral, selfeffacing quality to his work. Perhaps because of that, he has never found the following among later generations that some his contemporaries like Humphrey Bogart and James Cagney enjoy.

In the end, the film maintains a careful balance of elements with humor, suspense, and anti-fascist politics complementing each other and arriving at a conclusion that strikes the right note of seriousness. Perhaps the film's belated arrival on video (in 1997) accounts for its relative obscurity. Whatever the reason, it is a genuine treat for any war movie fan who has missed it.

See also

The Usual Suspects
Grand Illusion
To Be or Not to Be
Casablanca
Lives of a Bengal Lancer

Cast: Franchot Tone (Cpl. John J. Bramble), Anne Baxter (Mouche), Erich von Stroheim (Field Marshall Rommel), Akim Tamiroff (Farid), Peter Van Eyck (Lt. Schwegler), Fortunio Bonanova (Gen. Sabastiano), Miles Mander (Col. Fitzhume), Konstantin Shayne (Maj. Von Buelow), Leslie Denison (British Captain), Ian Keith (Capt. St. Bride), Frederick Giermann (German Sergeant), Fred Nurney (Maj. Lamprecht); **Written by:** Billy Wilder, Charles Brackett; **Cinematography by:** John Seitz; **Music by:** Miklos Rozsa. **Producer:** Charles Brackett; released by Paramount Pictures. **Awards:** Nominations: Academy Awards '43: Best Black and White Cinematography, Best Film Editing. **Running Time:** 97 minutes. **Format:** VHS, Closed Caption.

THE GUNS OF NAVARONE

1961 J. Lee Thompson ♪♪♪♪

"Well, there's the team—pirates and cutthroats every one of 'em."

Jensen (James Robertson Justice) to Maj. Franklin (Anthony Quayle)

"Your bystanding days are over. You're in it now, up to your neck."

Capt. Mallory (Gregory Peck) to Cpl. Miller (David Niven)

The influence that this adventure has had on the action films that have come since is almost impossible to overestimate. From the James Bond series of the 1960s to the big-budget action pictures of the '80s and '90s, filmmakers have borrowed liberally from its successful mixture of character, structure, and exotic locale. Few have recreated them so well. Behind the derring-do and the often clunky mechanics of the plot lies solid craftsmanship. Journeyman director J. Lee Thompson, who has made some genuinely atrocious films, handles the story with a finer touch than he normally displays.

Most viewers certainly are familiar with the archetypal suicide-mission plot, wherein a team of British commandos sets out to destroy a brace of huge German cannon on a Greek island. Despite the patently silly nature of the premise, the introductory combination of professorial voice-over narration by James Robertson Justice with black-and-white archival footage is so persuasive that some 1961 viewers believed that the film was based on fact. Actually, the tale is a long chase. Once the details of the situation have been laid out, virtually every scene involves movement from one place to another. The motion stops only for emotional or physical confrontations.

The tank scenes, in which the small fishing boat is caught in a storm and is in danger of being smashed against rocks and cliffs, are still some of the most exciting ever filmed. That sequence is so carefully set up that it goes on for more than 14 minutes without a word of dialogue being spoken, and it mirrors the long, virtually speechless conclusion at the guns. It's a tribute to the director and the actors that they can get so much information across visually. Credit for the film's perennial popularity should be shared by production designer Geoffrey Drake, who gives the production a realistic, lived-in look that's associated more with "serious" black-and-white World War II films than with escapism.

At first blush, the cast appears to be better than the light material, but to a man, they treat it seriously. Gregory Peck's natural stiffness serves the role well, and balances David Niven's light, intelligence touch. Anthony Quinn restrains his normal flamboyance to play a glowering, vengeful Greek. Though the film was one of the major boxoffice hits of 1961, and received several Academy Award nominations, it lost out to another strong critical and commercial hit, *West Side Story*.

Two caveats: First, some older tapes appear to have been made from a less-than-perfect print and have a grainy, faded look. Also, the pan-and-scan transfer on that edition is entirely inadequate. In some conversations, both speakers are out of the frame. The widescreen version now available is far superior. Second, avoid the useless sequel, *Force Ten from Navarone*.

See also
Where Eagles Dare
Bataan
Gunga Din

Irene Papas winds up to slap
James Darren as Stanley Baker
(left), Gregory Peck, and
Anthony Quinn watch in *The
Guns of Navarone.* The Kobal Collection

Cast: Gregory Peck (Capt. Keith Mallory), David Niven (Cpl. Miller), Anthony Quinn (Col. Andrea Stavros), Richard Harris (Squadron Leader Barnsby), Stanley Baker (C.P.O. Brown), Anthony Quayle (Maj. Franklin), James Darren (Pvt. Spyros Pappadimos), Irene Papas (Maria Pappadimos), Gia Scala (Anna), James Robertson Justice (Narrator: Jensen), Bryan Forbes (Cohn), Allan Cuthbertson (Maj. Baker), Michael Trubshawe (Maj. Weaver), Percy Herbert (Grogan), Walter Gotell (Muesel), Tutte Lemkow (Nicolai); **Written by:** Carl Foreman; **Cinematography by:** Oswald Morris; **Music by:** Dimitri Tiomkin; **Technical Advisor:** Lt. Gen. Fritz Bayerlew, Lt. Col. P.J. Hands, Lt. Col. P.F. Kartemilides, Maj. N. Lazeridis, Maj. W.D. Mangham, Cmdr. John Theologitis, Brig. Gen. D.S.T. Turnbull. **Producer:** Columbia Pictures, Carl Foreman Productions. **Awards:** Academy Awards '61: Best Special Effects; Golden Globe Awards '62: Best Film—Drama, Best Score; Nominations: Academy Awards '61: Best Adapted Screenplay, Best Director (Thompson), Best Film Editing, Best Picture, Best Sound, Best Original Dramatic Score. **Budget:** 6M. **Running Time:** 159 minutes. **Format:** VHS, Beta, LV, Letterbox.

HELL IS FOR HEROES

1962 Donald Siegel 🎖🎖🎖🎖

Don Siegel's low-budget war film is tough, brutal and short. After a strangely slow introduction set in a little French town, it becomes a fast-paced, realistic look at one small battle in the last days of the European Theater. Co-writer Robert Pirosh is also responsible for the more well-known *Battleground* (1949), and this film can be seen as a sort of companion piece, with a cast of unknowns on the verge of stardom.

> "Look, dum-dum, up here this gun is your life. It's like when you were a civvie, see. It's what you own that makes you who you are."
>
> **Corby (Bobby Darin) giving Driscoll (Bob Newhart) a lesson in how to use his rifle**

Thumbnail sketches introduce Corby (Bobby Darin), the entrepreneur; Larkin (Harry Guardino), the tough-but-fair sergeant; Henshaw (James Coburn), the fix-it guy; Kolinsky (Mike Kellen), the father figure; and Homer (Nick Adams), the Polish kid who wants to be a GI. The new replacement is Reese (Steve McQueen), a loner with a troubled past. Sgt. Pike (Fess Parker) knows something of that past. Most of that information turns out to be fairly useless, because the squad that thinks it's about to go home is sent back to the front. No sooner have they taken up a position a few hundred yards away from the German Siegfried Line than the rest of their outfit is moved north, and they're left facing a much larger and better-equipped enemy. But, do the Germans know how comparatively weak they are?

The rest of the story is set on that desolate strip of dirt filled with land mines and shell craters. It's grim stuff, brightened by the appearance of Pvt. Driscoll (Bob Newhart), a typist who blunders into the wrong place. He performs one of his telephone routines, which were the hottest thing in early '60s stand-up comedy, and gives the film a needed moment of comic relief that is actually funny but does not break the bleak mood that Siegel establishes.

Everything builds to the third act. There, the pace quickens. The violence becomes truly horrifying for the first time, with men screaming helplessly. The pain and the fear they express have a visceral quality seldom seen in mainstream films. Siegel's direction becomes more fluid and experimental in those scenes, too. At key moments, his camera rises unnervingly above the action to give it a new vertiginous perspective. Overall, the young cast is excellent, though at times McQueen is too brooding for his own good. His work, though, can be seen almost as a rough draft of Jake Holman, the character he would play four years later in *The Sand Pebbles*. As the title and the synopsis suggest, *Hell Is for Heroes* has both the look and the mindset of a World War I film. The explosions, tension, and gunfire may pump up the adrenaline, but the reality is unchanged. War is about men doing terrible things to each other. Patriotism, courage, right, wrong—those are concepts that have little to do with the final outcome.

Did you Know?

Hell is for Heroes was essentially remade for HBO as the excellent *When Trumpets Fade*.

See also

The Killers
Battleground
The Sand Pebbles
Steel Helmet
The Lost Patrol

Sgt. Larkin (Harry Guardino) collects weapons from a dead soldier in *Hell is for Heroes.* The Kobal Collection

Cast: Steve McQueen (Reese), Bobby Darin (Pvt. Corby), Fess Parker (Sgt. Pike), Harry Guardino (Sgt. Larkin), James Coburn (Cpl. Henshaw), Mike Kellin (Pvt. Kolinsky), Nick Adams (Homer), Bob Newhart (Pvt. Driscoll), L.Q. (Justus E. McQueen) Jones (Sgt. Frazer), Don Haggerty (Capt. Mace), Joseph Hoover (Cpt. Loomis), Michele Montau (Monique), Bill Mullikin (Pvt. Cumberly); **Written by:** Robert Pirosh, Richard Carr; **Cinematography by:** Harold Lipstein; **Music by:** Leonard Rosenman. **Producer:** Paramount Pictures, Henry Blanke. **Running Time:** 90 minutes. **Format:** VHS, Beta, LV, Closed Caption.

HELL IS FOR HEROES

IMMORTAL BATTALION
The Way Ahead
1944 Carol Reed ♪♪♪♪

"Tommy" is the British equivalent of "GI," slang shorthand for a foot soldier. This gem of propaganda, created by an unlikely trio of filmmakers, is the English version of *The Story of G.I. Joe*, a heartfelt appreciation of the men who do the hard work of war. In terms of structure, the film takes an almost documentary approach to the familiar "unit picture" story. Its subjects are draftees.

They're quickly introduced during the last days of their civilian lives. Brewer (Stanley Halloway) tends a furnace boiler. Davenport (Raymond Huntley) is a salesman with an inflated opinion of himself. Jim Perry (David Niven) is working in a gas station. Along with several others who will become important, they meet for the first time in a railway station pub, where one of them manages to insult Sgt. Fletcher (William Hartnell). To no one's surprise, he winds up being in charge of their unit and reporting to Lt. Perry.

> "I won't be shot at merely to gratify some oafish military whim!"
>
> **Davenport (Raymond Huntley) on learning that live ammunition is used on the obstacle course**

Most of the film follows the men's basic training. The simple scenes of drills, marching, K.P., guard duty, early reveilles, running the obstacle course, and barracks bull sessions are standard stuff for the genre, but they've seldom been presented so insightfully. Novelist Eric Ambler and actor Peter Ustinov base their script on their own experiences, and that authenticity shows through in all the key moments, particularly in the smaller details of conversations. Those ring true. The group's first organized act of rebellion against their officers comes as a small surprise, but again, it's the kind of thing that probably happens often.

Once the training is over, the film becomes more intense, but still restrained when compared to similar American efforts of the period. The big scenes begin with some excellent shipboard action and continue with the battalion's first engagement with the Germans. Though some of those scenes over-rely on stock footage—one building corner must collapse four times—they're well paced and believable. Still, director Carol Reed is more interested in the characters as individuals and as a group than in pyrotechnics. There's not a single off-key note in the entire ensemble cast, and they're ably led by Niven. His big speech about the honor of the regiment could easily dissolve into a puddle of patriotic hogwash if he didn't deliver it with such unshakable conviction and passion. Though William Hartnell's role is much less showy, he brings the same rigorous believability to Sgt. Fletcher. Author George MacDonald Fraser, a veteran himself, says simply, "as for Hartnell, he doesn't play the part, he is it: the pared-to-the-bone immaculate figure, the hard eye, the cold barking voice—how you hated it, and how you missed it later on, when you realized what a good man was underneath." (*The Hollywood History of the World*. Beech Tree Books. 1988)

Did you Know?
William Hartnell originated the role of Dr. Who in the 196Ø s British television series.

Few films achieve that level of reality.

See also

In Which We Serve
The Big Red One
Five Graves to Cairo
The Dirty Dozen

A British train platform, site of many a tearful farewell in *Immortal Battalion* and other World War II films. Del Valle Archives

Cast: David Niven (Lt. Jim Perry), Stanley Holloway (Ted Brewer), Reginald Tate (The C.O.), Raymond Huntley (Herbert Davenport), William Hartnell (Sgt. Fletcher), James Donald (Lloyd), Peter Ustinov (Rispoli), John Laurie (Luke), Leslie Dwyer (Sid Beck), Hugh Burden (Bill Parson), Jimmy Hanley (Stainer), Leo Genn (Capt. Edwards), Renee Asherson (Marjorie Gillingham), Mary Jerrold (Mrs. Gillingham), Tessie O'Shea (Herself), Raymond Lovell (Mr. Jackson), A.E. Matthews (Col. Walmsley), Jack Watling (Marjorie's Boyfriend); **Written by:** Eric Ambler, Peter Ustinov; **Cinematography by:** Guy Green; **Music by:** William Alwyn; **Technical Advisor:** R. Fellowes, Brian Mayfield. **Producer:** J. Arthur Rank, 20th Century-Fox, John Sutro, Norman Walker. **British. Running Time:** 89 minutes. **Format:** VHS, Beta.

THE IMMORTAL SERGEANT

1943 John M. Stahl ♫♫♫

Before World War II was over, Hollywood would learn to make excellent propaganda. This early effort leaves much to be desired, both as entertainment and as motivation. It tells a slow, simple story that's redeemed in the second half with unrealistic but forceful desert combat scenes. Though the film's psychological premise is sound, its execution needs work.

The setting is the North African desert, where the British Eighth Army faces the Germans. Cpl. Colin Spence (Henry Fonda) is a Canadian volunteer. Though he's at best a mediocre, indecisive soldier, Sgt. Kelly (Thomas Mitchell) sees potential in the lad. A series of flashbacks to London reveals the reasons why Spence is such a weenie-wuss. He's always been something of a shy underachiever who is cowed by the presence of his colleague Benedict (Reginald Gardiner), a successful writer. When Benedict puts some heavy moves on Spence's sweetheart Valentine Lee (Maureen O'Hara), Spence does nothing. Finally, in desperation he decides to enlist to become more assertive.

> "I'm just a civilian with a couple of chevrons on my sleeve."
>
> **Cpl. Spence (Henry Fonda)**

> "You're not bad for a wartime-educated amateur."
>
> **Sgt. Kelly's (Thomas Mitchell) response**

That's how he finds himself on patrol in the middle of the trackless desert when his outfit comes under attack by German aircraft (created with uncredited special effects that are remarkably lively for the era). As the enemy engagement grows more serious and intense, so, irritatingly, do Spence's moony flashbacks. Maureen O'Hara may never have looked lovelier, but Spence and Benedict are such cartoonish caricatures that it's impossible to muster up much interest in their competition, or its predictable outcome.

Veteran character actor Mitchell fares much better with his pivotal role as the mentor who shows Spence how to transform himself. Unfortunately, those scenes are less fully developed because they're cut off when the scene shifts to an oasis. That's where the final confrontation takes place. Director John M. Stahl makes the action suspenseful enough, despite the limitations of a cliched, bare-bones soundstage. The loud pyrotechnic destruction of the set is still satisfying, though, as Spence and his outnumbered comrades sacrifice themselves to wipe out the Germans.

More troubling than the low-budget look of the production—common enough for adventure films of the day—is the star's uncomfortable performance in a poorly written role. As producer/screenwriter Lamarr Trotti creates him, Spence goes into the desert as Barney Fife and emerges as Rambo. Neither extreme is believable and it's unfair to fault Fonda. The truth is that he hated the film and didn't want to do it. According to his autobiography, *Fonda, My Life* (as told to Howard Teichmann. NAL. 1981), he had registered for the draft—despite an exemption—enlisted in the Navy, and gone to the induction center when Darryl F. Zanuck intervened. He used connections in Washington to get Fonda for this picture before he went into the service. As soon as Fonda was finished, he entered boot camp and then spent the war as an officer in Navy Air Combat Intelligence.

See also

The Lost Patrol
Sahara
An Officer and a Gentleman
Stagecoach
Once upon a Time in the West
Mister Roberts

Sgt. Kelly (Thomas Mitchell, left) transforms Cpl. Spence (Henry Fonda) into a man and a soldier, with the help of Cassity (Allyn Joslyn) in *The Immortal Sergeant*. The Kobal Collection

Cast: Henry Fonda (Cpl. Colin Spence), Thomas Mitchell (Sgt. Kelly), Maureen O'Hara (Valentine), Allyn Joslyn (Cassity), Reginald Gardiner (Benedict), Melville Cooper (Pilcher), Morton Lowry (Cottrell), Peter Lawford (Bit part), John Banner (German officer), Bud Geary (Driver), James Craven (Non-Commissioned man); **Written by:** Lamar Trotti; **Cinematography by:** Clyde De Vinna, Arthur C. Miller; **Music by:** David Buttolph. **Producer:** 20th Century-Fox, Lamar Trotti. **Running Time:** 91 minutes. **Format:** VHS, Beta, Closed Caption.

The Hound Salutes: Henry Fonda

Like so many young men of his generation, Henry Fonda was driven to enlist in the service during World War II. Many within the Hollywood acting community (David Niven, Clark Gable, James Stewart) felt the same way; others (John Wayne, Errol Flynn) did not. For Fonda, the urge was particularly strong; though at age 37, married and with two children, he was exempt from the draft. He enlisted the day after they finished shooting *The Ox-Bow Incident*, and then was incensed when studio boss Daryl Zanuck pulled strings with the Navy so that he could keep his star for one more picture after the war had started. You can see Fonda's anger and resentment in every frame of the disappointing *Immortal Sergeant*.

Fonda rose through the ranks to Lieutenant in Naval Intelligence before the war ended, and was awarded a Bronze Star and a Presidential Citation. Though he had already been nominated for an Academy Award before the war for his role in *The Grapes of Wrath*, he really hit his stride, on both stage and screen, after the war. Doubtless, his service experience had a lot to do with the success of *Mister Roberts*. He first played the title role on stage in 1948. It was a hit on Broadway, and Fonda took it on the road with the touring company. Today, it seems incredible that studio heads would even consider anyone else for the film, but that is what happened to the troubled production. (See review.) It's a part that makes the most of the essential "American" persona Fonda could project. The quality is most apparent in his political roles: *Young Mr. Lincoln*, *The Best Man*, *Advise and Consent*, *Clarence Darrow*. Though Fonda built his career on that image, he could play against it, as he did in *War and Peace* and, even more memorably, as the icy villain in *Once Upon a Time in the West*.

Despite their numbers, the rest of Fonda's war films comprise little more than a footnote to his career. He's a general in *The Longest Day*; a President trying to stop a nuclear war in *Fail Safe*; an admiral in *Midway* and *In Harm's Way*. He has more to do in *Battle of the Bulge*, and he seems to be enjoying himself more. The rest of his work in the genre consists of cameos and larger roles in lesser efforts.

As far as war films go, Henry Fonda will always be remembered as Mr. Roberts, the young officer who does a thankless job as well as he can while, at the same time, he is driven to find a more productive place for himself.

Noel Coward, a man whose name is synonymous with erudite sophisticated wit, is perhaps the last person anyone would expect to produce feature-length propaganda. But his only foray into the field is one of the finest films to come out of the war. And perhaps it's not so surprising. Throughout his long career, Coward proved to be talented in many areas—drama, comedy, song, composition—so, why shouldn't he be able to handle another popular art form? When the British government asked him to write a patriotic piece, he agreed and said that he wanted to tell a story without sentimentality but with simplicity and truth. He did just that, basing his script on the experiences of his friend Lord Louis Mountbatten on the ship *HMS Kelly*. Coward also produced the film, wrote the score, and co-directed with David Lean, who'd established his reputation as an editor.

"This is the story of a ship," Leslie Howard states in the introductory narration, and the opening montage follows *HMS Torrin* from construction to christening to commission on the eve of England's declaration of war on Germany. Immediately after, the destroyer is engaged in battle and is heavily damaged by aircraft. The crew is forced to abandon ship and, from their raft, watch the *Torrin* sink. The body of the film then is told in several layers of flashback, as members of the crew are introduced and the ship takes part in various campaigns.

At the center is Capt. Kinross (Coward), perfect archetype of the upper-class British sailing man. He's dedicated to his ship and his crew, knowing each of them by name and treating all fairly and compassionately. His wife Alix (Celia Johnson) understands that she and the children come second to him. Chief Petty Officer Walter Hardy (Bernard Miles) represents the upper middle-class. He lives in a cozy flat with his wife (Joyce Carey) and, when he's home, referees squabbles between her and her mother. Another notch or two down the social scale, Ordinary Seaman Shorty Blake (John Mills) is a younger man who meets Hardy's niece Freda (Kay Walsh) on a train and falls in love.

> ## "No War This Year"
> **Headline seen on a newspaper floating in dirty water as *HMS Torrin* is under construction**

In other hands, the interconnected lives of those three families could be the stuff of soap opera, but Coward treats them seriously. Though some have faulted the film for its flattering view of the English caste system, social criticism is hardly the point. And if Coward fails to condemn the unfairness of social strata, he does make clear the bonds that connect the classes and responsibilities that are shared.

That's really a side issue. Coward's script moves artfully through several time frames, filling in details of the lives of his characters. Despite the film's unambiguous political agenda, it is not built on conventional military heroics. The focus is relatively evenly balanced between life on the *Torrin* and fiercely British domestic scenes set in music halls, pubs, and countryside. Whether it's accurate or not, one lovely moment describes the innocence of pre-war England by showing a sailor's return home. He goes up the steps from a city street to the front door of his apartment and unlocks it with a key that's kept on a string nailed to the jamb. The rest of the film is filled with equally Capra-esque touches.

See also

Henry V (1944)
The Best Years of Our Lives
Bridge on the River Kwai

Of course, the performances are first rate. Look for a very young Richard Attenborough as a sailor who panics. As an actor, Coward is completely comfortable in a role that, at first, appears to be all

Noel Coward (center) wrote, produced, co-directed, and composed the score for *In Which We Serve*, based on the experiences of his friend, Lord Mountbatten. The Kobal Collection

wrong for him. But if he lacks the indefinable "presence" that a movie star can bring to a commanding role, he makes up for that with absolute conviction. It's impossible to watch the film even now without accepting that he believed every word that he wrote and spoke. The emotions are so honest that they make many of the American war films produced then look a bit thin.

Cast: Noel Coward (Capt. Kinross), John Mills (Ordinary Seaman Shorty Blake), Bernard Miles (C.P.O. Walter Hardy), Celia Johnson (Alix Kinross), Kay Walsh (Freda Lewis), James Donald (Doctor), Richard Attenborough (Young Sailor), Michael Wilding ("Flag"), George Carney (Mr. Blake), Gerald Case (Jasper), Joyce Carey (Mrs. Hardy); **Written by:** Noel Coward; **Cinematography by:** Ronald Neame; **Music by:** Noel Coward; **Technical Advisor:** I.T. Clark, C.R.E. Compton, T.W.J. Lawlor. **Producer:** Noel Coward. **British. Awards:** New York Film Critics Awards '42: Best Film; Nominations: Academy Awards '43: Best Original Screenplay, Best Picture. **Running Time:** 114 minutes. **Format:** VHS, Beta.

A truly international (and unconventional) collaboration of filmmakers created this companion piece to *The Longest Day*. The two films share similar defects and assets: the familiar "all-star cast" that gives good actors little to do and sprawling scope on one hand, unexpected wit and attention to individual detail on the other. The opening titles set the stage. "Paris, 1944, after four years of bitter occupation, was seething on the verge of revolt against the Nazi oppressors. With the Allies almost at the doorstep, the French Resistance in the city, composed of many divergent groups, struggled bitterly among themselves to find the way to liberation. Time was terribly short . . ." Time is short because Hitler (Billy Frick) orders Gen. Cholitz (Gert Frobe), who has never disobeyed him, to destroy the city before he allows it to fall into Allied hands. Cholitz agrees but as soon as he arrives in the city, the Swedish Consul Nordling (Orson Welles) begins to pressure him for concessions and compromise.

At the same time, the various Resistance groups squabble over strategy and worry about the tactics of the Americans. Will they enter the city or simply bypass it on their way to Germany? The people involved in the Resistance range from experienced, canny campaigners who know that the endgame must be handled carefully, to students whose enthusiasm eclipses their good sense. Most of the characters on that side of the story are portrayed by popular young French stars of the day—Jean-Paul Belmondo, Jean-Pierre Cassel, Pierre Vaneck, Alain Delon. The big American names—Kirk Douglas, Robert Stack, Glenn Ford—play generals, and their scenes tend to be clunkers.

The most interesting characters are Cholitz and Nordling. Welles, even at something less than his best, is more engaging than his more attractive co-stars. Frobe is able to make Cholitz a somewhat sympathetic and complex figure. Despite the basic good guys–bad guys plot, he's actually the protagonist of the story. He's the one character who has to make the important decisions, though that distinction tends to fade into the background of the busy action. With a script by Gore Vidal and Francis Ford Coppola (what a combination!), based on the bestseller by Larry Collins and Dominique LaPierre, with additional material by others for the French and German scenes, the overachieving plot is no surprise. Director Rene Clement manages to maintain an even semi-*cinema verite* tone throughout, and in the last hour, when the various forces come into direct contact, he does an excellent job of incorporating archival documentary footage into his own combat recreations and fiction.

Given the film's extended running time and overall lack of focus, its primary value now is as nostalgia, but it's also representative of the second wave of World War II films that toned down partisanship and attempted to view the conflict with some historical perspective. That limits the entertainment value, but on some level, you've got to like a movie that casts an actor named Billy Frick as Adolf Hitler.

See also

The Longest Day
The Great Escape
The Battle of Algiers
Goldfinger

Glenn Ford (left) and Robert
Stack ponder the question *Is
Paris Burning?* The Kobal Collection

Cast: Jean-Paul Belmondo (Pierreflot/Morandat), Charles Boyer (Docteur Monod), Leslie Caron (Francoise Labe), Jean-Pierre Cassel (Lt. Henri Karcher), George Chakiris (G.I. in tank), Claude Dauphin (Col. Lebel), Alain Delon (Jacques Chaban-Delmas), Kirk Douglas (Gen. George S. Patton), Glenn Ford (Gen. Omar Bradley), Gert Frobe (Gen. Dietrich von Cholitz), Daniel Gelin (Yves Bayet), E.G. Marshall (Intelligence Officer Powell), Yves Montand (Sgt. Tankiste), Anthony Perkins (Sgt. Warren), Claude Rich (Gen. Leclerc), Simone Signoret (Cafe proprietress), Robert Stack (Gen. Sibert), Jean-Louis Trintignant (Capt. Serge), Pierre Vaneck (Gallois), Orson Welles (Consul Nordling), Bruno Cremer (Col. Roy Tanguy), Suzy Delair (A Parisienne), Michael (Michel) Lonsdale (Debu-Bridel), Billy Frick (Adolf Hitler); **Written by:** Gore Vidal, Francis Ford Coppola; **Cinematography by:** Marcel Grignon; **Music by:** Maurice Jarre. **Producer:** Transcontinental Pictures Industries, Paramount Pictures, Paul Graetz. **French. Awards:** Nominations: Academy Awards '66: Best Art Direction/Set Decoration (B & W), Best Black and White Cinematography. **Running Time:** 173 minutes. **Format:** VHS, Closed Caption.

Alfred Hitchcock's experiment in propaganda is certainly not his finest moment, but it's still an entertaining, often suspenseful film, despite an unusually artificial structure and effects that are dated. As the title states, the entire story is told within a lifeboat. In the opening shot, the smokestack of the *Frazier* sinks beneath the surface of the ocean. Floating in the water among the debris is the corpse of a sailor from the German U-boat that attacked the ship and then was sunk itself.

Alone in a rather spacious lifeboat is Connie Porter (Tallulah Bankhead), with her mink coat, movie camera, and attitude. A prototypically liberated woman, she's some kind of correspondent or writer who views the whole war as material for her next work, current circumstances not withstanding. Her boat soon fills up with a diverse mix of survivors: "Ritt" Rittenhouse (Henry Hull), the wealthy industrialist; George "Joe" Spencer (Canada Lee), the black steward; Kovac (John Hodiak), the Southside Chicago radical; Alice MacKenzie (Mary Anderson), nurse on a mission; Gus Smith (William Bendix), jivetalking New Yorker; Mrs. Higgens (Heather Angel), desperately trying to save her infant child; Garrett (Hume Cronyn), the Brit sailor; and finally Willy (Walter Slezak), the German sub commander posing as a common sailor.

> "What good is a hep cat with one gam missing?"
>
> **Gus Smith (William Bendix)**

Once the group has been introduced, they set about squabbling about the best way to face their various logistic, health, and political problems. Given the limitations that Hitchcock places on the film, the story sometimes loses intensity in the slow moments. The script was begun by John Steinbeck and completed by Jo Swerling, with uncredited additions by Ben Hecht and, according to Hitchcock, MacKinlay Kantor. They allow each of the characters his or her moment at center stage to reveal something significant. The characters are interesting and the cast is more than capable, but the film sometimes looks and sounds like a stage play misplaced in a studio water tank.

DidyouKnow?

When it was produced, *Lifeboat* was the first film:
- to be made on one set
- without extras
- that required all the actors to be on the set at all times

Most of the film's energy is supplied by Walter Slezak, who makes Willy one of the most wonderfully evil Nazi rat-swine ever to infest the screen, as he tries to get rid of his opposition woman by woman, man by man, limb by limb. The filmmakers' political points are equally blatant. In the book *Hitchcock Truffaut* (Simon & Schuster. 1967), Hitch says that he meant to make a microcosm of the war. "We wanted to show that at that moment there were two world forces confronting each other, the democracies and the Nazis, and while the democracies were completely disorganized, all of the Germans were clearly headed in the same direction. So here was a statement telling the democracies to put their differences aside temporarily and to gather their forces to concentrate on the common enemy, whose strength was precisely derived from a spirit of unity and of determination."

See also

Hume Cronyn (left), Tallulah Bankhead, and John Hodiak are three survivors of a German U-Boat attack in *Lifeboat*. The Kobal Collection

Cast: Tallulah Bankhead (Constance Porter), John Hodiak (John Kovac), William Bendix (Gus Smith), Canada Lee (George "Joe" Spencer), Walter Slezak (Willy, the German Submarine Commander), Hume Cronyn (Stanley Garrett), Henry Hull (Charles "Ritt" Rittenhouse), Mary Anderson (Alice MacKenzie), Heather Angel (Mrs. Higgins), William Yetter Jr. (German Sailor); **Written by:** Jo Swerling; **Cinematography by:** Glen MacWilliams; **Music by:** Hugo Friedhofer; **Technical Advisor:** Thomas Fitzsimmons. **Producer:** 20th Century-Fox, Kenneth McGowan. **Awards:** New York Film Critics Awards '44: Best Actress (Bankhead); Nominations: Academy Awards '44: Best Black and White Cinematography, Best Director (Hitchcock), Best Story. **Running Time:** 96 minutes. **Format:** VHS, Beta, LV, Closed Caption.

Despite its claims to authenticity, Darryl Zanuck's D-Day epic really owes as much to Hollywood's bloated biblical pictures as it does the war films of the 1940s and '50s. It has the same "all-star" cast, elephantine structure, stilted dialogue and pretensions to high seriousness. With five directors and five writers at work behind the cameras, the finished product is decidedly mixed, with a few battle sequences that are absolutely remarkable.

Following the structure of Cornelius Ryan's best-seller, the film attempts to show the first 24 hours of D-Day as it was experienced by several of the participants, from generals to grunts to civilians. Actually, the events begin on the evening before the invasion and are followed through to the next afternoon. In the first half, much attention is focused on the weather, as the troops—American, British, and French—are poised on board their boats and ships, waiting for the rain to stop. In the key scene when Gen. Eisenhower (David Grace) makes the decision to go, the importance of time is stressed by enhancing the ticking of a clock. Such simple devices are used throughout.

> "The first 24 hours of the invasion will be decisive. For the Allies as well as the Germans, it will be the longest day."
>
> **Field Marshal Erwin Rommel (Werner Hinz)**

On the other side of the channel, the German generals, who know the invasion is imminent, see the same nasty weather and decide to take some time off for war games. French Resistance fighters receive their coded instructions from BBC radio and step up their sabotage activities. Both groups speak in their native language over clear, easy to read subtitles. Much of the early going is also devoted to some of the Allies' more unorthodox ideas, the kinds of things that make more sense cinematically than militarily: the use of metal clickers by paratroopers for identification, parachuting rubber dummies loaded with firecrackers behind German lines to sow confusion.

To their credit, the filmmakers do an excellent job of keeping the various plotlines straight despite the sheer number of them. Because so much is going on, few members of the famous cast are given enough time or material to register. Only Richard Beymer as Pvt. Schultz, who is separated from his unit in the first hours of the invasion and never really understands what's going on; Richard Burton as the fatalistic Flight Officer Campbell; Red Buttons as Pvt. Steele, who parachutes onto a church; and Hans Christian Blech as Maj. Pluskat, the first German officer to realize what is happening, make much of an impression.

American stars playing high-ranking officers have weak roles. As Brig. Gen. Theodore Roosevelt Jr., Henry Fonda limps ashore and promptly disappears. In charge of the bloody assault on Omaha Beach, Brig. Gen. Cota (Robert Mitchum) mostly chomps on his cold cigar and waves the troops onward. As Lt. Col. Vandervoort, John Wayne is almost a parody of the military roles that he played in the 1940s, a blustering bully who scowls and yells. All too often, they and the other characters recite self-important dialogue that comments on the momentous importance of what they are doing and sounds like it came out of a bad history text.

See also

Saving Private Ryan
Battleground
The Big Red One
Five Graves to Cairo
The Victors
Tora! Tora! Tora!

The film reaches its peak when the two sides in the battle are finally engaged. A long aerial shot from the point of view of a German pilot strafing Normandy Beach reveals just how much effort went

Robert Mitchum storms the beach at Normandy on *The Longest Day*, **June 6, 1944.**

into the recreation of the invasion. It pales in comparison to the French commando attack on Ouistreham. One unbelievably complex crane shot (or is it done with a helicopter?) lasts for a minute and a half.

Today it is difficult to watch the invasion scenes and not compare them to the opening of *Saving Private Ryan*, but that really is unfair. Zanuck's film is very much a product of its time. In the late '50s and early '60s, with some justification, the American military and entertainment establish-

ments thought of themselves as the saviors of the world. *The Longest Day* is the high water mark
of their self-confidence.

Cast: John Wayne (Lt. Col. Benjamin Vandervoort), Richard Burton (Flight Officer David Campbell), Red Buttons (Pvt. John Steele), Robert Mitchum (Brig. Gen. Norman Cota), Henry Fonda (Brig. Gen. Theodore Roosevelt), Robert Ryan (Brig. Gen. James Gavin), Paul Anka (U.S. Ranger), Mel Ferrer (Maj. Gen. Robert Haines), Edmond O'Brien (Gen. Raymond Barton), Fabian (U.S. Ranger), Sean Connery (Pvt. Flanagan), Roddy McDowall (Pvt. Morris), Arletty (Mme. Barrault), Curt Jurgens (Maj. Gen. Gunther Blumentritt), Rod Steiger (Destroyer Commander), Jean-Louis Barrault (Fr. Roulland), Peter Lawford (Lord Lovat), Robert Wagner (U.S. Ranger), Sal Mineo (Pvt. Martini), Leo Genn (Gen. Parker), Richard Beymer (Pvt. Dutch Schultz), Jeffrey Hunter (Sgt./Lt. Fuller), Stuart Whitman (Lt. Sheen), Eddie Albert (Col. Tom Newton), Tom Tryon (Lt. Wilson), Alexander Knox (Maj. Gen. Walter Bedell Smith), Ray Danton (Capt. Frank), Kenneth More (Capt. Colin Maud), Richard Todd (Maj. John Howard), Gert Frobe (Sgt. Kaffeklatsch), Christopher Lee, Hans-Christian Blech (Maj. Pluskat), Werner Hinz (Field Marshal Erwin Rommel), David Grace (Gen. Dwight Eisenhower); **Written by:** James Jones, David Pursall, Jack Seddon, Romain Gary, Cornelius Ryan; **Cinematography by:** Jean Bourgoin, Pierre Levent, Henri Persin, Walter Wottitz; **Music by:** Maurice Jarre. **Producer:** 20th Century-Fox, Darryl F. Zanuok, Elmo Williams. **Awards:** Academy Awards '62: Best Black and White Cinematography, Best Special Effects; Nominations: Academy Awards '62: Best Art Direction/Set Decoration (B & W), Best Film Editing, Best Picture. **Budget:** 10M. **Running Time:** 179 minutes. **Format:** VHS, Beta, LV, Letterbox.

A MIDNIGHT CLEAR

1992 Keith Gordon ♪♪♪♪

As an actor, Keith Gordon is probably best known as the young protagonist in Brian DePalma's *Dressed to Kill*. He makes an impressive debut behind the camera with a passionate, intelligent adaptation of William Wharton's novel. Though his 1990s' approach could be called revisionism, Gordon's interpretation of an isolated action within the Battle of the Bulge is legitimate. The setting is mid-December 1944, the Ardennes Forest, in France, Luxembourg, or maybe Belgium, no one's really sure which. The six surviving members of an intelligence and reconnaissance patrol know only that they've been sent to a house in the forest to see if there's anything to the rumors of a German counterattack.

Maj. Griffin (John C. McGinley), a martinet operating under the dubious assumption that military intelligence has something to do with human intelligence, has assigned the smartest young men under his command to the patrol. There used to be 12 of them, but, as our narrator, Will Knott (Ethan Hawke) says, intelligence doesn't count for much in war. Recently promoted to sergeant but refusing to wear his stripes, Knott is the nominal leader of the group. But Avakian (Kevin Dillon) really knows more about soldiering. The oldest of the group, Mother (Gary Sinese) is more than half mad. Only Stan (Arye Gross), who's Jewish, is really gungho to fight. Miller (Peter Berg) is ready for the war to be over, and Father (Frank Whaley) refuses to admit that the unit is part of the army. To underline their separateness, these six try not to curse. When they arrive at the house in the middle of the snow-covered woods, they find that the Germans are indeed in the area. But these Germans aren't the enemy they're used to fighting.

The characters and the premise make the film sound like any number of formula WWII unit pictures, but just the opposite is true. This is not the story of a group of kids from different parts of the country who are tested in battle and become a cohesive force. It's about frightened young men who have virtually no understanding of what they're doing, and only the vaguest idea about why.

The film's anti-authoritarian political slant is similar to *Catch-22*, (the novel, not the movie), and the references to *King of Hearts* are hard to miss. Gordon keeps the unusual narrative moving while giving the large ensemble cast room to work with their characters. Then, in the last third of the film, when the story becomes much more intense and unpredictable, he adds a strong religious element. Throughout, the film has an eerie, cold, dreamlike quality that creates an effective mood until it's broken by a jolting return to the realities of 1944 in the final minutes.

Viewers looking for lots of firepower and heroic action will be disappointed. Gordon uses graphic violence to shock and horrify, not to titillate. Perhaps that explains this fine film's lack of success in theatrical release and relative anonymity. It also makes *A Midnight Clear* one of the most impressive sleepers in the video store.

> "So now we've been moved north into the Ardennes Forest to await replacements. It's become a kind of front-line halfway house for straightening out our nerves. I'm not sure I can be straightened out. I'm scared all the time now."
>
> **Will Knott (Ethan Hawke) in voice-over**

> "I'm having my usual trouble—noticing how beautiful the world is just when I might be leaving it."
>
> **Will Knott walking through a snowy field on patrol**

See also

Battleground
A Walk in the Sun
Mother Night

Cast: Peter Berg (Bud Miller), Kevin Dillon (Mel Avakian), Arye Gross (Stan Shutzer), Ethan Hawke (Will Knott), Gary Sinise ("Mother" Wilkins), Frank Whaley ("Father" Mundy), John C. McGinley (Maj. Griffin), Larry Joshua (Lt. Ware), Curt Lowens (German soldier), David Jensen (Sgt. Hunt), Rachel Griffin (Janice), Tim Shoemaker (Eddie); **Written by:** Keith Gordon; **Cinematography by:** Tom Richmond; **Music by:** Mark Isham. **Producer:** Interstar Productions, Bill Borden, Dale Pollock, Marc Abraham, Armyan Bernstein, Tom Rosenberg. **Boxoffice:** 1.526M. **MPAA Rating:** PG. **Running Time:** 107 minutes. **Format:** VHS, LV, Closed Caption.

MR. WINKLE GOES TO WAR
Arms and the Woman
1944 Alfred E. Green ♪♪♪

A competent, modest addition to Hollywood's literature of propaganda, this curiosity might not be worth noting if it weren't for the sensitive and uncharacteristic performance of star Edward G. Robinson. Known best for tough gangsters and cerebral heroes, he's equally persuasive as a mild-mannered man whose midlife crisis is interrupted by the draft.

Of course, in 1944, Americans did not have "midlife crises" and so no one knows how to react to Wilbert G. Winkle's (Robinson) announcement that he has decided to follow his heart; certainly not the president of the bank where he works, and not his wife Amy (Ruth Warrick) either. She's worried that their social standing will be ruined and so is almost relieved when Wilbert receives his induction notice. Surely the Army won't take a 44-year-old man whose life revolves around the many pills he must take before and after meals. Perhaps the whole idea of the military will be enough to jolt him back to his senses.

To no one's surprise, that's not what happens. Under the tender tutelage of Sgt. "Alphabet" Czeidrowski (Richard Lane) and with the help of Tinker (Robert Armstrong, from *King Kong*), Wilbert G. eventually becomes "Rip." Prolific journeyman Alfred E. Green directs Mr. Winkle's journey through basic training as a combination of light comedy and melodrama. He doesn't make fun of the experience, and the expected Hollywood sugarcoating is applied so lightly that it's not cloying. For the most part, Green and Robinson focus squarely on the character, the changes that he's already going through and the changes brought about by the Army. As they see him, Mr. Winkle is a patriot, though he's anything but a sabre-rattler. His motivations are much more quiet and personal. "I believe the important thing is to feel that it's your community," he explains, "and see to it that it runs well, and always a little better than it did."

That statement also underlines the film's sense of civic sentimentality. It's a Depression-era attitude also found in films as diverse *Boys Town* and *The Grapes of Wrath*. The whole idea is central to understanding Hollywood's attitudes toward the war and military service. In this film, even in the concluding battle scene, virtually no mention is made of the enemy. Tinker's one reference to his desire to "strangle a Jap" is treated as something of an embarrassment. The Army is seen as a necessary evil where, with a little luck, an individual can be put into a position to do something he's good at.

That's not a particularly profound insight, but this film doesn't mean to be deep. At a time when most war movies were celebrating combat and physical courage, *Mr. Winkle Goes to War* is more interested in unashamedly middle-class pleasures and virtues. It certainly is not everyone's idea of a war film, but it makes its points eloquently, and despite Wilbert G.'s timid nature, Edward G. makes him an engaging hero.

See also
The Fighting Sullivans
Sergeant York
Fighting Seabees
The Best Years of Our Lives

Edward G. Robinson (right) goes from meek civilian to confident soldier in *Mr. Winkle Goes to War.* The Kobal Collection

Cast: Edward G. Robinson (Wilbert Winkle), Ruth Warrick (Amy Winkle), Richard Lane (Sgt. "Alphabet"), Robert Armstrong (Joe Tinker), Ted Donaldson (Barry), Richard Gaines (Ralph Westcott), Bob Haymes (Jack Pettigrew), Hugh Beaumont (Range Officer), Walter Baldwin (Plummer), Howard Freeman (Mayor Williams); **Written by:** Waldo Salt, Louis Solomon; **Cinematography by:** Joseph Walker; **Music by:** Paul Sawtell, Carmen Dragon; **Technical Advisor:** Lt. Robert Albaugh. **Producer:** Columbia Pictures, Jack Moss. **Running Time:** 80 minutes. **Format:** VHS, Beta.

MOTHER NIGHT
1996 Keith Gordon ♪♪♪♪

With any Kurt Vonnegut Jr. work—either print or film—reality is a fluid concept. Differences between what is "real" and what is imagined are finally not too important. That's the basis for *Slaughterhouse 5* and it's an important part of Keith Gordon's adaptation of *Mother Night*. On the surface, it's a simpler story, but one that is still open to several interpretations. Like Gordon's first picture, *A Midnight Clear*, it features strong acting, well-written characters, an unaffected, almost old-fashioned directorial style, and honest emotions.

Our narrator (Nick Nolte) introduces himself by stating: "I, Howard W. Campbell Jr., am an American by birth, a Nazi by reputation, and a nationless person by inclination. I am awaiting a fair trial for my war crimes by the state of Israel." As he speaks, he sits at a typewriter in a Haifa prison and writes his memoirs. His youth in New York is sketched in quickly. In 1919, General Electric transfers his father to Germany. By 1938, Howard has become a successful playwright and has married the beautiful actress Helga Noth (Sheryl Lee). When his parents decide to return to the United States, he stays. Soon after that he is approached by his "blue fairy godmother," Frank Wirtanen (John Goodman). Wirtanen is an American intelligence agent who asks Campbell to spy for his country, to ingratiate himself to the Nazi high command and report back. "To do this right," he says, "you'll have to commit nothing less than high treason."

> ## "You're obsessed
> with the notion of pure hearts and heroism. You love good and you hate evil. You sacrifice anything in the name of romance."
>
> **Frank Wirtanen (John Goodman)
> to Howard Campbell (Nick Nolte)**

> "I suppose the moral here is you must be careful about what you pretend to be because in the end you are what you pretend to be."
>
> **Howard Campbell**

> "The truth of your leader August Krapptauer and those like him will be with mankind forever as long as there are men and women like you who listen to their guts instead of their mind."
>
> **Dr. Lionel Jones (Bernard Behrens)
> to his Neo-Nazi followers**

Campbell agrees, and in 1941 becomes the creator and voice of Nazi anti-Semitic radio broadcasts, a sort of combination Lord Haw-Haw and Ezra Pound. He writes his scripts and turns them in to the ministry of propaganda. Another spy, someone he does not know, then pencils in secret editorial instructions—coughs and mispronunciations that give the weekly speeches a hidden meaning that even Campbell himself does not understand. So, is Wirtanen a real person or is he a fantasy that Campbell has created to justify his sins?

The resolution of the war and Campbell's long strange post-war odyssey to America offer few concrete answers. For the most part, Gordon handles the unconventional plot with a deadpan tone and truly bizarre black humor. Throughout, he remains completely faithful to the tone and spirit of Vonnegut's work. (The author appears in a silent cameo late in the film.) Campbell is a diffident hero, much like Billy Pilgrim in *Slaughterhouse 5*. (*Mother Night* was written two years before *Slaughterhouse 5*, and Campbell actually makes a brief appearance there, too.) Nolte's performance is one of the most careful and mannered of his career. His supporting cast could hardly be better. As a painter who befriends Campbell, Alan Arkin gives the film a lift when it's needed, and Henry Gibson (of all people!) provides the voice for an unrepentant Adolf Eichmann.

As director, Gordon seems to have allowed the material to dictate his low-key style. He uses few tricks beyond fades from black-and-white to color, and he tends to mute sounds in louder scenes. His careful visual restraint sustains an undercurrent of sorrow, which is entirely appropriate to the subject. That is an emotion that is almost never expressed in contemporary films. Gordon handles it with grace and maturity.

See also
A Midnight Clear
Slaughterhouse 5
The Last Metro
Barton Fink

Howard Campbell (Nick Nolte)
and Helga Noth (Sheryl Lee) flee
a collapsing Berlin in *Mother
Night.* The Kobal Collection

Cast: Nick Nolte (Howard Campbell), Sheryl Lee (Helga Noth), Alan Arkin (George Kraft), John Goodman (Frank Wirtanen), Kirsten Dunst (Resi Noth), David Strathairn (Bernard O'Hare), Arye Gross (Abraham Epstein), Frankie Faison (Black Fuhrer of Harlem), Bernard Behrens (Dr. Lionel Jones); **Cameo(s):** Kurt Vonnegut Jr.; **Voice(s) by:** Henry Gibson; **Written by:** Robert B. Weide; **Cinematography by:** Tom Richmond; **Music by:** Michael Convertino. **Producer:** Keith Gordon, Robert B. Weide, Ruth Vitale, Mark Ordesky, Linda Reisman, Whyaduck; released by Fine Line Features. **MPAA Rating:** R. **Running Time:** 113 minutes. **Format:** VHS.

PATTON
Patton—Lust for Glory
Patton: A Salute to a Rebel
1970 Franklin J. Schaffner 🎬🎬🎬🎬

"Ohmygod—it's George C. Scott!"

Goldie Hawn's reaction when she opened the envelope for the winner of the Best Actor at the 1970 Academy Awards ceremony is the first thing many people think of when they hear the name Patton. It's an understandable reaction, because the actor had made such an issue of his refusal to accept the award, saying, among other things, that he felt he had not done justice to the man he was portraying. Of course, by saying that, he drew even more attention to himself in a way that the real George S. Patton Jr. would have understood instinctively. The real Patton would also have understood that the tactic virtually guaranteed Scott a special place in the history of the Academy. (Quick, who won the Best Actress Award that year?)

Scott's protestations not withstanding, few actors have ever been so convincing in such a strong, colorful character. Only Peter O'Toole's T.E. Lawrence comes immediately to mind. Both he and Scott create their characters out of complementary contradictions—Lawrence detests the savagery of war but embraces it; Patton cannot separate the conduct of war from his own personal glorification—and both actors are given large canvases upon which to work.

> "NOW I want you to remember that no bastard ever won a war by dying for his country. He won it by making the other poor dumb bastard die for his country."
>
> **Gen. George S. Patton Jr. (George C. Scott)**

> "I will be proud to lead you wonderful guys into battle any time, anywhere"
>
> **Gen. George S. Patton Jr.**

> "Compared to war, all other forms of human endeavor shrink to insignificance."
>
> **Gen. George S. Patton Jr.**

Writers Francis Ford Coppola and Edmund North and director Franklin Schaffner (who also won Oscars and accepted them) introduce their hero with a risky, indelible six-minute, 15 second scene. In full uniform, his chest festooned with decorations, Patton steps up before a huge American flag and addresses an unseen gathering of soldiers, defining himself in unambiguous terms as a man who revels in war. "All real Americans love the sting of battle!" he proclaims, defining himself and daring the movie audience to disagree. Cut to a close shot of scorpions crawling across the body of a dead soldier at the Kasserine Pass. The camera then pulls back to reveal dozens of Arabs busily stripping more bodies.

The American Army has just suffered its first defeat at the hands of the Germans. Patton is put in charge of a demoralized, undisciplined force. He is, without question, as much prima donna and showman as soldier. He doesn't wear a uniform; he wears a costume, and he is never careless about it. With the help of his friend Gen. Omar Bradley (Karl Malden), he whips the men into shape and prepares to re-engage Field Marshal Rommel (Karl Michael Vogler). At the same time, his rivalry with British Field Marshal Montgomery (Michael Bates) intensifies to an almost ridiculous extreme. The rest of the film follows the two inseparable sides of Patton's career, the professional and the political. For every victory he enjoys on the battlefield, he suffers a public humiliation. Patton courts reporters, reveling in the attention they give him but rising to the bait whenever they ask delicate questions.

Did you Know?
In 1970, Glenda Jackson won the Best Actress Oscar for *Women in Love*

His most embarrassing moment comes when he slaps a soldier (Tim Considine) in a hospital. The incident occurs because Patton's views of bravery and cowardice are so severely limited. The man who has the imagination to write poetry and to believe that he has been reincarnated cannot conceive of a psychological wound that he cannot see.

See also
Lawrence of Arabia
Is Paris Burning?
Battle of the Bulge
Dr. Strangelove

Patton's tank battles are fought on broad plains. Action coordinator Joe Canutt, son of legendary stuntman Yakima Canutt, does an excellent job of illustrating the distances and forces involved, and the later battles in Europe are even more intense. Shaffner maintains that sense of large open space in the interiors. They tend to be vast, cavernous places, suggesting that Patton's personality is too big to be confined in conventional rooms, and those physical spaces diminish with Patton's state of mind when he falls from grace. The filmmakers also often turn to the Germans for comments on Patton's abilities. All of those simple devices are used to illuminate various sides of a remarkable personality. The portrait is so compelling that it's easy to overlook Patton's own final words in the film, "All glory is fleeting."

George C. Scott personifies the bigger-than-life aura of Gen. George Patton. The Kobal Collection

Cast: George C. Scott (Gen. George S. Patton), Karl Malden (Gen. Omar Bradley), Stephen Young (Capt. Chester Hansen), Michael Strong (Brig. Gen. Hobart Carver), Frank Latimore (Lt. Col. Henry Davenport), James Edwards (Sgt. William G. Meeks), Lawrence Dobkin (Col. Gaston Bell), Michael Bates (Field Marshal Sir Bernard Law Montgomery), Tim Considine (Soldier who gets slapped), Edward Binns (Maj. Gen. Walter Bedell Smith), John Doucette (Maj. Gen. Lucian K. Truscott), Morgan Paull (Capt. Richard N. Jenson), Siegfried Rauch (Capt. Oskar Steiger), Paul Stevens (Lt. Col. Charles R. Codman), Richard Muench (Col. Gen. Alfred Jodl), Karl Michael Vogler (Field Marshal Erwin Rommel); **Written by:** Francis Ford Coppola, Edmund H. North; **Cinematography by:** Fred W. Koenekamp; **Music by:** Jerry Goldsmith; **Technical Advisor:** Omar N. Bradley, Gen. Paul D. Harkins, Col. Glover S. Johns Jr., Lt. Col. Luis Martin Pozuelo. **Producer:** 20th Century-Fox, Frank McCarthy. **Awards:** Academy Awards '70: Best Actor (Scott), Best Art Direction/Set Decoration, Best Director (Schaffner), Best Film Editing, Best Picture, Best Sound, Best Story & Screenplay; American Film Institute (AFI) '98: Top 100; Directors Guild of America Awards '70: Best Director (Schaffner); Golden Globe Awards '71: Best Actor—Drama (Scott); National Board of Review Awards '70: Best Actor (Scott); New York Film Critics Awards '70: Best Actor (Scott); National Society of Film Critics Awards '70: Best Actor (Scott); Writers Guild of America '70: Best Original Screenplay; Nominations: Academy Awards '70: Best Cinematography, Best Original Score. **MPAA Rating:** PG. **Running Time:** 171 minutes. **Format:** VHS, Beta, LV, Letterbox.

SAHARA

1943 Zoltan Korda ♪♪♪♪

Early World War II propaganda films tend to suffer from a certain over-enthusiasm. They are so certain of the rightness of their cause that hatred of the enemy overpowers all other aspects. It's an understandable and easily forgivable flaw. Zoltan Korda's entry in the genre manages to avoid it—without any real loss of patriotic fervor—and remains a cracking good adventure tale that's as exciting now as it was on the day it was made.

Though the credits state that the story is based on "an incident in the Soviet film, *The Thirteen*," an equally important source is John Ford's *The Lost Patrol*. Both are about a small group of soldiers that finds itself with neither an officer nor a clear objective in the middle of a sandy wasteland, and so a sergeant is forced to make decisions to overcome a series of obstacles. In this case, it's Sgt. Joe Gunn (Humphrey Bogart), whose American tank "Lulubelle" has been assigned to the British 8th Army in Libya, 1942. Separated from the rest of his outfit, Sgt. Gunn, Waco Hoyt (Bruce Bennett), and Jimmy Doyle (Dan Duryea) are ordered to retreat south from the advancing Germans. A larger problem is water.

Before they've gone far, they come across more motley stragglers in the desert, including a Sudanese soldier, Sgt. Tambul (Rex Ingram) and his Italian prisoner (J. Carrol Naish), a French soldier (Louis Mercier), and a gaggle of Brits. Filling out the multi-national dance card is a downed German pilot (Kurt Kreuger). Dripping with new passengers, Lulubelle grinds across the dunes as the question of water becomes even more pressing and the Germans close the distance.

Did you Know?
Sahara was made in the desert east of Palm Springs, California. The German troops were played by soldiers from Camp Young.

Within that solid event-filled narrative structure, the director is able to give his cast enough time for light character development, and that's really all that's called for. When the tank finally arrives at a windswept "oasis," Korda shifts gears, slowing the pace and building suspense beautifully. The long scene at a well could have come from a Hitchcock film of the same period. It's built on the same simple techniques of closely observed details and individual reactions. That sequence, in turn, sets up the final confrontation with the Nazis, where hundreds of Germans try to take the strategic position that the Allied forces hold.

Fact:
Screenwriter John Howard Lawson was a member of the blacklisted "Hollywood Ten" who refused to cooperate with the House Un-American Activities Committee.

Though the film is very much an ensemble piece, two cast members stand out. Bogart, coming off *Casablanca*, which had cemented his status as a major star, is a tough, understated hero. The taciturn Gunn is nothing like Rick Blaine, but Bogie makes him just as effective. In at least two ways, Rex Ingram's work is even more unusual. First, it was rare for any Hollywood film of the time to feature a black character in a strong supporting role. For the character then to be depicted as intelligent, experienced, and heroic is virtually unheard of. Sgt. Tambul is all that, and Ingram makes him the most personable of the group, too. Today, it may be easy to dismiss that side of the film as tokenism, but given the widespread racism in the 1940s, even small steps should not be ignored.

That open-mindedness is just a small part of a film that transcends its origins. Over the years since it was made, *Sahara* has received Hollywood's ultimate praise in several remakes, none of them approaching the original.

See also
Lifeboat
The Lost Patrol
The Four Feathers
Lawrence of Arabia

Humphrey Bogart and Pat
O'Moore wait for approaching
Afrika Corps attackers in
Sahara. The Kobal Collection

Cast: Humphrey Bogart (Sgt. Joe Gunn), Dan Duryea (Jimmy Doyle), Bruce (Herman Brix) Bennett (Waco Hoyt), Lloyd Bridges (Fred Clarkson), Rex Ingram (Sgt. Tambul), J. Carrol Naish (Giuseppe), Richard Nugent (Capt. Jason Halliday), Pat O'Moore (Ozzie Bates), Kurt Kreuger (Capt. Von Schletow), John Wengraf (Maj. Van Falken), Carl Harbord (Marty Williams), Louis Mercier (Jean Leroux), Guy Kingsford (Peter Stegman), Peter Lawford (Bit Part); **Written by:** Zoltan Korda, John Howard Lawson, James O'Hanlon; **Cinematography by:** Rudolph Mate; **Music by:** Miklos Rozsa. **Producer:** Columbia Pictures, Harry Joe Brown. **Awards:** Nominations: Academy Awards '43: Best Black and White Cinematography, Best Sound, Best Supporting Actor (Naish). **Running Time:** 97 minutes. **Format:** VHS, Beta.

Saving Private Ryan—
The Invasion Sequence

The long opening sequence of Steven Spielberg's *Saving Private Ryan* is unlike anything in any other Hollywood depiction of war. It's 25 minutes of barely comprehensible chaos. Many veterans have stated that it's the most accurate re-creation of an amphibious assault ever put on screen, and it's easy for non-veterans to believe them. The sequence is absolutely terrifying. It's also one of the most carefully constructed action scenes in the history of the movies. In its own way it deserves comparison to the Odessa steps in *Battleship Potemkin*, the final shoot-out in *The Wild Bunch*, or the shower scene in *Psycho*.

Credit for it is shared by director of photography Janusz Kaminski, editor Michael Kahn, sound designer Gary Rydstrom, writer Robert Rodat, and director Steven Spielberg. All but Rodat won Academy Awards for their work. (Reportedly, Frank Darabont, director of *The Shawshank Redemption* and *The Green Mile,* worked on a rewrite of the scene, too.)

Together, they attempt to show the invasion as it was experienced by the American soldiers. Until the end, no German faces are shown. High angle shots from the German point of view are used sparingly to reveal the topography of the battlefield. Amazingly, the filmmakers manage to achieve two conflicting goals—first to horrify viewers with the massive violence of the invasion, while at the same time, drawing viewers into the story they're about to tell.

First, Kaminski gives the film the look of documentaries shot at the real invasion. Spielberg's DreamWorks organization had helped to restore 150 hours of color footage of D-Day, so they knew what they wanted: a faded look to the color that would recall the black and white of the "serious" '40s and '50s war movies, images seldom in sharp focus, choppy rhythm to keep viewers uncomfortable. To achieve that, Kaminski physically altered his cameras. Protective coatings were stripped from lenses, dulling the brightness of colors, and 180-degree shutters were replaced by 90-degree and 45-degree shutters. "In this way, we attained a certain staccato in the actors' movements," he said, "and a certain crispness in the explosions, which makes them slightly more realistic." To heighten that unsettling quality of movement, some scenes were shot at 12 frames per second—half of normal speed—and then each single frame was double printed. The result is a disorienting, stroboscopic effect.

Sound designer Rydstrom's Oscar-winning work loses some of its theatrical impact on most home video systems, but it still does the job. He uses ultra-realistic sound effects—the reports of World War II–era weapons were recorded and so were their bullets as they struck animal carcasses—and mixes them so that the clamor of battle actually surrounds the viewer. In the most disturbing part of the sequence, the audience goes deaf for several minutes along with Tom Hanks's character when a shell explodes close to him.

The invasion scene lasts for the first 25 pages of Rodat's screenplay, and in Hollywood scripts, a page is roughly equal to a minute of screen time, but Spielberg used Rodat's ideas as a rough guide. He shot the scenes without storyboards, keeping the spirit and tone but changing the details. Spielberg and editor Kahn worked every night after the day's shooting had been finished to create a "rough draft" of the invasion. They could handle it that way because the invasion essentially stands on its own. The sequence establishes the levels of violence that will follow but it has little to do with the rest of the plot. It has everything to do with the

The beginning of the D-Day invasion sequence from *Saving Private Ryan*. Tom Sizemore and Tom Hanks, front The Kobal Collection.

rest of the film. Without it, the audience wouldn't appreciate what the soldiers went through, and Spielberg has said unequivocally that *Saving Private Ryan* was made for those vets.

As he wrote in an article about movies for *Newsweek* magazine, "In the 1940s, realism in war movies didn't really matter. After Vietnam, it was all that mattered." In that extended opening, he manages to combine that post-Vietnam obsession with realistic violence with an appreciation of the emotional consequences of violence. The pure horror of it had never been shown that way, and the emotions are still real after more than 50 years.

SAVING PRIVATE RYAN

1998 Steven Spielberg ♪♪♪♪

Steven Spielberg wraps his combat masterpiece in the flag. Literally. The film opens and closes with sunlight pouring through a translucent, billowing Stars and Stripes. Remarkably, however, the film isn't jingoistic propaganda. Instead, it's a realistic, frightening examination of combat seen from the point of view of foot soldiers, ordinary men called upon to do extraordinary things.

The shots of the flag also reflect the film's deceptively simple mirrored plot structure. Key scenes in the first half are repeated or reflected in the second. The story begins with a prologue of an aging veteran (Harrison Young), surrounded by his attractive family, visiting a military graveyard in Normandy. As he stares at one cross in the mosaic of headstones surrounding him, the scene dissolves to a Higgins boat about to land at Omaha beach. Then perhaps the most realistic and harrowing battle scene ever filmed begins. (See sidebar.)

For more than 20 minutes, the screen is filled with chaotic violence and destruction that defy rational comprehension. The beach becomes a maelstrom of bullets and deafening explosions. When one soldier's leg is blown off, another automatically grabs an ammunition belt from him. No one understands what is going on. The American soldiers know only that to stay in the water is death and so they move ahead. That insanity is one of the main points that Spielberg and writer Robert Rodat are trying to make.

Within that chaos, the focus settles on Capt. Miller (Tom Hanks), Sgt. Horvath (Tom Sizemore), Pvt. Reiben (Edward Burns), Wade (Giovanni Ribisi) the medic, Pvt. Jackson (Barry Pepper), Pvt. Mellish (Adam Goldberg), and Pvt. Caparzo (Vin Diesel). After they've survived their harrowing hours breaking through the first line of German defense, they're given another assignment: Find Pvt. Ryan (Matt Damon), a paratrooper who's somewhere behind German lines, and bring him back to safety. Why? Because the War Department has realized that Ryan's three older brothers have just been killed in action, and Gen. George C. Marshall (Harve Presnell) will not allow an entire family to be wiped out.

The scene at the Ryan farmhouse, where the mother is told of her sons' deaths, is as solemn and as carefully composed as a Hopper or Wyeth painting. Throughout the film, Spielberg's attention to detail is astonishing. And so is his ability to use closely observed detail—the tactile sense of raindrops beading on a rifle stock, the bone-weariness of a soldier (Paul Giamatti) who simply wants to sit down in a comfortable chair—to involve the audience in the action. For all his commercial and critical success, Spielberg doesn't get nearly the credit he deserves for his use of innovative techniques to create emotional responses.

The mission itself turns out to be a relatively simple, episodic undertaking. Cpl. Upham (Jeremy Davies) joins the unit as a translator and they set off across the French countryside (actually Ireland and England), a beautiful landscape littered with the carcasses of dead horses. Those echo the dead fish washed up on the beaches along with the human bodies. As they walk, the men reveal their personalities. Reiben's the quick smartass New Yorker; Wade's the medic whose mother is a doctor; Jackson is a devoutly religious and deadly sniper; Mellish is a Jewish kid who knows his

See also

A Walk in the Sun
The Big Red One
Schindler's List
All Quiet on the Western Front
Twelve O'Clock High

Matt Damon is Pvt. James Ryan in *Saving Private Ryan*. The Kobal Collection

enemy; Upham is the bookish new guy; Horvath is the non-com who's totally devoted to his Captain. And Miller . . . nobody really knows what his story is.

Three encounters with Germans provide physical action and keep the story moving, but the more central conflicts are among the Americans; which fights they should take on, which they should avoid, what their mission really is. "We're not here to do the decent thing," Miller observes, "We're here to follow fucking orders." (That's a particularly loaded line. What would we think if a German officer spoke it?)

SAVING PRIVATE RYAN

More importantly, how do the G.I.s hold onto their humanity? Miller understands the problem when he says, "I just know that with every man I kill, the farther from home I feel." And that's finally what *Saving Private Ryan* is about. It's not about causes or politics or tactics or even the morality of war. It's about guys who want to go home. That's all. They're in a terrible place where they're doing terrible things, and they simply want to go home.

As the embodiment of a lonely man who misses his wife and his job and who must hide his fear, Tom Hanks is perfectly cast. Despite the intensity of the big action scenes, perhaps the most moving emotional moment is the brief instant when Miller is alone and is able, for a few seconds, to let down the barriers and sob uncontrollably. The scene could easily degenerate into pathos, but it's handled honestly, without the sentimentality that Spielberg is sometimes prone to.

With repeated viewings, the film's main flaw is its "have-I-lived-a-good-life?" epilogue. Given the smallest amount of objective, critical distance, the scene is far too thick and obvious. That said, the conclusion is also appropriate for a film that's so emotionally wrenching. And without that framing device, audiences might not have been able to accept the massive violence of the beginning and end. So, perhaps it's a necessary error. On video, the film loses some of the overpowering combination of surround-sound and image that it has in the best theatrical presentations, but that's unavoidable. In any medium, *Saving Private Ryan* is one of the best.

Cast: Tom Hanks (Capt. John Miller), Edward Burns (Pvt. Reiben), Tom Sizemore (Sgt. Horvath), Jeremy Davies (Cpl. Upham), Giovanni Ribisi (T/4 Medic Wade), Adam Goldberg (Pvt. Mellish), Barry Pepper (Pvt. Jackson), Vin Diesel (Pvt. Caparzo), Matt Damon (Pvt. James Ryan), Ted Danson (Capt. Hamill), Dale Dye (War Dept. Colonel), Dennis Farina (Lt. Col. Anderson), Harve Presnell (Gen. George Marshall), Paul Giamatti (Sgt. Hill), Bryan Cranston (War Dept. Colonel), David Wohl (War Dept. Captain), Leland Orser (Lt. DeWindt), Joerg Stadler (Steamboat Willie), Maximillian Martini (Cpl. Henderson), Amanda Boxer (Mrs. Margaret Ryan), Harrison Young (James Ryan as an old man); **Written by:** Robert Rodat, Frank Darabont; **Cinematography by:** Janusz Kaminski; **Music by:** John Williams; **Technical Advisor:** Dale Dye. **Producer:** Mark Gordon, Ian Bryce, Gary Levinsohn, Steven Spielberg; released by Dreamworks Pictures. **Awards:** Academy Awards '98: Best Cinematography, Best Director (Spielberg), Best Film Editing, Best Sound, Best Sound Effects Editing; British Academy Awards '98: Best Sound; Directors Guild of America Awards '98: Best Director (Spielberg); Golden Globe Awards '99: Best Director (Spielberg), Best Film—Drama; Los Angeles Film Critics Association Awards '98: Best Cinematography, Best Director (Spielberg), Best Film; New York Film Critics Awards '98: Best Film; Broadcast Film Critics Association Awards '98: Best Director (Spielberg), Best Film, Best Score; Nominations: Academy Awards '98: Best Actor (Hanks), Best Art Direction/Set Decoration, Best Makeup, Best Original Screenplay, Best Picture, Best Original Dramatic Score; British Academy Awards '98: Best Actor (Hanks), Best Cinematography, Best Director (Spielberg), Best Film, Best Film Editing, Best Score; Golden Globe Awards '99: Best Actor—Drama (Hanks), Best Screenplay, Best Score; MTV Movie Awards '99: Best Film, Best Male Performance (Hanks), Best Action Sequence; Screen Actors Guild Award '98: Best Actor (Hanks), Cast; Writers Guild of America '98: Best Screenplay. **Budget:** 70M. **Boxoffice:** 211.7M. **MPAA Rating:** R. **Running Time:** 175 minutes. **Format:** VHS.

Saving Private Ryan—The "Good" German and the "Bad" German

NOTE: This sidebar reveals an important part of the film's conclusion.

The most chilling scene in *Saving Private Ryan*—the death of Pvt. Mellish (Adam Goldberg)—is one of the most intimate. It's also a slightly confusing moment because two German characters resemble each other so strongly.

Toward the middle, a German soldier called "Steamboat Willie" (Joerg Stadler) is introduced. By the last reel, he has become the "bad" German. Later in the film, another German (possibly Martin Hub) is involved in the final battle. He takes part in an excruciating scene of hand-to-hand combat with Pvt. Mellish. The two German soldiers have similar short haircuts (revealed because they do not wear helmets) and disheveled uniforms. Because they look so much alike, many viewers have assumed that they're one character. They're not, and the distinction between the two is important.

The character who fights and kills Mellish with a knife is actually merciful. As Mellish is dying, the German tries to ease his pain and terror with a gentle whisper, saying in effect "This will soon be over. Don't fight it." I am told by Lars Wendt of Essen, Germany, that these words of comfort to the dying are referred to as "Sterbebegleitung." Understanding that, the German soldier's next action—letting a panic-stricken Cpl. Upham (Jeremy Davies) live—makes sense. Upham is not a threat to him and so he walks away.

Why then does this "good" German look so much like the "bad" German? It's probably accidental. Spielberg has said that he made up Mellish's death scene "on the spot" and so he might not have realized that audiences would confuse the two German characters. Or, perhaps unconsciously, Spielberg is making the point that, like the American soldiers, Germans were capable of every form of violence in a violent environment.

SINK THE BISMARCK!

1960 Lewis Gilbert ♫♫♫

"This is London, Ed Murrow reporting. To an American reporter there is something very special about the people of this city, this island, this nation. Never in the long and stormy history of Great Britain have her fortunes been as low as they are in this spring of 1941. Britain is fighting alone for her very existence, fighting desperately, yet her people remain steadfast and unflinching. Britain's allies have been defeated one by one as the dark stain of Nazi conquest spreads across the map of Europe. In Africa, Rommel is giving the Eighth Army a very bad time. Greece has fallen and the Luftwaffe continues to smash English cities. The worst news of all comes from the North Atlantic, where last month German U-boats and surface raiders sank six hundred thousand tons of shipping. In this battle, Britain's lifeblood is at stake. This is the battle on which depends the future course of the war, the future course of British history."

Edward R. Murrow's opening broadcast

Did you Know?

The closing credits stress the point that Capt. Shepard is not Capt. R.A.B. Edwards, who was the actual Director of Operations in charge of the hunt for the *Bismarck.*

Fact:

Johnny Horton's popular song, "Sink the Bismarck," does not appear in the film.

Veteran director Lewis Gilbert does adequate work with difficult dramatic material, but he undercuts himself with some blatant jingoism. The story of one of the most important European naval engagements of the war is inherently interesting. The *Bismarck* was the largest battleship ever built, in a time when the battleship was still considered the most dangerous ocean-going weapon. In its day, it was the equivalent of George Lucas's Death Star. The film begins with what appears to be actual archival footage of the *Bismarck*'s christening in February 1939, attended by Hitler himself.

Flash forward to Edward R. Murrow broadcasting form London in 1941, at perhaps the lowest point of the war for England. Its forces are being battered on all fronts. Naval operations are run from an Admiralty war room buried deep beneath London. Capt. John Shepard (Kenneth More) is the new boss, arriving for his first day on the job. Straightaway, he lets everyone know that he's a "by the book" guy, completely unsentimental and, as a fellow officer puts it, "as cold as a witch's heart." He pays no attention to the human costs of the conflict. For him, the war is a chess game. A map of the North Atlantic is the board. The ships are represented by pieces of wood. On hand in the war room to test his hard-heartedness is Lt. Anne Davis (Dana Wynter).

Shepard's opposite number is Adm. Lutjens (Karel Stepanek), the fleet commander who's in charge of the *Bismarck* and its sister ship, which have just left the Baltic Sea and are trying to get into the open waters. Once Shepard learns that the two ships are on the move, he frantically pulls his own ships from other positions to stop them.

In terms of plot, writer Edmund H. North (working from C.S. Forster's book) stays close to real events while compressing them. He and director Gilbert are also fairly successful at making the insular intensity of the war room seem real. A subplot involving Shepard's son is fairly predictable, and if Dana Wynter is finally reduced to little more than window dressing, she is gorgeous window dressing. Howard Lydecker's special effects are obviously model ships in tanks, but they're integrated well enough into the black-and-white action along with documentary footage of real ship's guns being loaded and fired. The action scenes of the carrier-based Swordfish fighters—open-cockpit biplanes armed with torpedoes—attacking the German ships aren't as realistic as some other sea-based war films.

A much larger flaw is the one-dimensional stereotyping of the German characters. "Never forget that you are Germans!" the Admiral bellows at one point. "Never forget that you are Nazis!" Since he and Shepard are never in the same scene, it's difficult for the viewer to become emotionally involved in their conflict. The supporting characters also lack strong personalities, and so the whole film is more interesting than enjoyable, even for the most committed fan.

See also

The Battle of Britain
Tora! Tora! Tora!
In Which We Serve

Dana Wynter, Kenneth More, and Jack Watling plot strategy in an attempt to *Sink the Bismarck!* The Kobal Collection

Cast: Kenneth More (Capt. Jonathan Shepard), Dana Wynter (Anne Davis), Karel Stepanek (Adm. Lutjens), Carl Mohner (Capt. Lindemann), Laurence Naismith (1st Sea Lord), Geoffrey Keen (A.C.N.S.), Michael Hordern (Cmdr. on King George), Maurice Denham (Cmdr. Richards), Esmond Knight (Capt. on Prince of Wales), Michael Goodliffe (Capt. Banister), Esmond Knight (Capt. on Prince of Wales), Jack Watling (Signals Officer), Jack Gwillim (Capt. on King George), Mark Dignam (Capt. on Ark Royal), Ernest Clark (Capt. on Suffolk), John Horsley (Capt. on Sheffield), Sydney Tafler (1st Workman), John Stuart (Capt. on Hood), Walter Hudd (Adm. on Hood), Sean Barrett (Able Seaman Brown), Peter Burton (Capt. on First Destroyer), Edward R. Murrow (Himself); **Written by:** Edmund H. North; **Cinematography by:** Christopher Challis; **Music by:** Clifton Parker. **Producer:** 20th Century-Fox, John Brabourne. **British. Running Time:** 97 minutes. **Format:** VHS, Beta.

SINK THE BISMARK!

THE STORY OF G.I. JOE

1945 William A. Wellman ♪♪♪♪

When this fact-based fiction was released in 1945, it was called "the least glamorous war picture ever made" (*Time* magazine) and the record still stands. The film is an honestly emotional look at an infantry company's battles in Tunisia, Sicily, and Italy. As such, it's also about the transformation of young American men into veterans. That's a story that's been told many times, but seldom with such grace and poetry. The grace comes from a combination of William Wellman's direction, and editing by Albrecht Joseph and Otho Lovering that deftly weaves actual combat footage into the story. The poetry comes from Ernie Pyle.

Pyle (played here by Burgess Meredith) was a war correspondent whose columns usually focused on the foot soldiers. He traveled with them all the way to the front, shared meals with them, stayed with them, and, most important, listened to them. In this film—when they talk to each other, when they gripe, when they think out loud, when they just yak—they sound right. Like Pyle, Wellman never strays from their point of view. The whole film is shown through their eyes. There are no high-level staff meetings, no aerial shots of the entire battlefield, no discussions of tactics. Wellman sets that authentic tone early with a great series of shots of the men in C Company, 18th Infantry, as they lie awake in pup tents and listen to a radio broadcasting Axis Sally and Artie Shaw's band.

Like so many other combat films of World War II, the two central characters are Lt., then Capt. Bill Walker (Robert Mitchum), and Sgt. Warnicki (Freddie Steele). Their troops make the slow, painful transformation from green young men to grim veterans in a series of bleak landscapes that reflect their growing disillusionment. Pyle called these kids his "mud-rain-frost-and-wind boys" and Wellman is careful to make that part of the campaign all too real. In a completely literal sense, this is one of the dirtiest movies ever made. Seldom has the physical discomfort of war been so palpable. Wellman was one of the first directors to make his cast undergo a regime of "basic training" before the film was made. He was forced to do it because the actors are surrounded by 150 real veterans playing themselves.

The most important combat sequence concerns the company's house-to-house advancement through a bombed-out Italian town to a ruined church, where two snipers are hiding. The sequence is told virtually without dialogue. The viewer doesn't know what's going on or what the objective is until the men do. Most of the time though, these guys are either working their way toward the front, or simply waiting.

That's usually where the Hollywood professionals take over, and their work is superb. Meredith, a veteran himself, never strikes a false note, and his voice-over narration is used sparingly and effectively. Freddie Steele, a character actor whose face is more familiar than his name, is the archetypal grizzled non-com. But the film belongs to Mitchum. He was nominated for a Supporting Actor Academy Award (his only nomination) and it may be the best work he ever did. His acting here is so natural that at times you forget you're watching Robert Mitchum. He also manages to give the conclusion an emotional resonance that few war films, and even fewer films of the period, can approach.

See also

All Quiet on the Western Front
Battle of San Pietro
Saving Private Ryan
A Walk in the Sun
The Big Red One
Stalag 17

Sadly, Ernie Pyle and several of the real soldiers who play themselves were killed in the Pacific campaign before the film's release.

Burgess Meredith (second from left) is famous war correspondent Ernie Pyle in *The Story of G.I. Joe.* The Kobal Collection

Cast: Burgess Meredith (Ernie Pyle), Robert Mitchum (Lt. Bill Walker), Wally Cassell (Pvt. Dondaro), Billy Benedict (Whitey), William Murphy (Pvt. Mew), Jimmy Lloyd (Pvt. Spencer), Fred Steele (Sgt. Warnicki), William Self (Cookie Henderson), Jack Reilly (Pvt. Murphy), Tito Renaldo (Lopez), Hal Boyle (Himself), Chris Cunningham (Himself), Jack Foisie (Himself), George Lah (Himself), Bob Landry (Himself), Clete Roberts (Himself), Robert Rueben (Himself), Don Whitehead (Himself); **Written by:** Leopold Atlas, Guy Endore, Philip Stevenson, Ernie Pyle; **Cinematography by:** Russell Metty; **Music by:** Louis Applebaum, Ann Ronell; **Technical Advisor:** Ernie Pyle. **Producer:** Lester Cowan, Columbia Pictures. **Awards:** Nominations: Academy Awards '45: Best Supporting Actor (Mitchum). **Running Time:** 109 minutes.

A TIME TO LOVE AND A TIME TO DIE

1958 Douglas Sirk 🦴🦴🦴

Many contemporary viewers will have a hard time separating the substance of this romance from its style. In many ways, the film looks like a typical mid-'50s melodrama. Director Douglas Sirk was responsible for some of the better Rock Hudson pictures, and he gives the action a polished Hollywood sheen that's really at odds with the story. Based on a novel by Eric Maria Remarque (who appears in a small but crucial role), it's really a glossy companion piece to *All Quiet on the Western Front*.

It begins on the Russian Front, where Wehrmacht soldier Ernst Graeber (John Gavin) is waiting without much hope for his furlough to come through. A veteran of campaigns in France and North Africa, he's due for some time off. His depleted and dispirited squad has been reduced to reburying corpses that rise from shallow graves in the spring thaw. And Steinbrenner (Bengt Lindstrom), the one fanatical Nazi in the group, demands that they execute any civilians they encounter because they might be guerrillas. When the orders for Ernst's leave miraculously appear, he heads to Germany for the first time in years, and finds that his country and his nameless hometown are suffering.

> "Divulging troop movement or position is treason. Idle criticism is treason."
>
> **Unnamed officer to soldiers about to go on leave**

> "Enjoy the war, my friends, the peace will be awful."
>
> **Unnamed singer during air raid**

> "The war is lost, Ernst. More terrifyingly, it must be lost before a country can regain its soul."
>
> **Prof. Pohlmann (Erique Maria Remarque)**

Officials give returning soldiers boxes of fruit to fool citizens into thinking that things aren't so bad on the front, while bombing raids have reduced blocks of apartments to rubble. The paranoia of National Socialism has made everyone suspicious of everyone else. Ernst soon finds that Oscar (Thayer David), an underachieving old friend from high school, has risen to a position of such importance within the party that he can surround himself with every imaginable luxury while others sleep in the streets. The single bright spot is Elizabeth (Lilo Pulver), the daughter of his family's doctor. They fall in love with a completely believable suddenness, given the madness of their world.

Their relationship is the central thread in an episodic plot that gradually, steadily reveals the Kafkaesque horrors of fascism. Ernst, basically a decent man who believes that he is doing the right things, comes to understand that he has become part of something horrible. The film tries to decipher the degrees of complicity and responsibility of all Germans during those years, from the woman who works in a uniform factory, to the soldier who takes part in a firing squad, to the Gestapo officer who gleefully demonstrates how he burns concentration camp prisoners.

The casting is unusually strong and creative. Jock Mahoney, Don DeFore, and Keenan Wynn are very good as fellow soldiers. Jim Hutton (listed as Dana Hutton) makes a distinct impression in a small role, and in an even smaller one, Klaus Kinski gives a preview of the singular weirdness that would mark his career. Paul Frees, who provides several voices, is familiar to any fan of European films. Author Remarque's presence is more than a deferential cameo, too. His role as a quietly heroic professor provides the only real note of hope in a story that's stripped of all sugar-coating.

The leads are excellent, too. Though Gavin has a reputation as a wooden, pretty actor, he makes Ernst a sympathetic hero. Lilo Pulver's determined, often angry performance probably plays better

See also

Doctor Zhivago
All Quiet on the Western Front
Hope and Glory
White Rose

now than it did in 1958. They're not going to make anyone forget Bogart and Bergman in *Casablanca*, but their characters have depth and emotional realism that's not often associated with films of the period.

It's true that the film does go on a little too long, and it lacks subtlety, but it deserves a better reputation than it has. Given the changes in cinematic conventions and audience expectations, the story should be a prime candidate for a remake.

John Gavin and Jim Hutton in *A Time to Love and a Time to Die* The Kobal Collection

Cast: John Gavin (Ernst Graeber), Lilo (Liselotte) Pulver (Elizabeth Kruse), Jock Mahoney (Immerman), Keenan Wynn (Reuter), Klaus Kinski (Gestapo Lieutenant), Don DeFore (Hermann Boettcher), Thayer David (Oscar Binding), Dieter Borsche (Capt. Rahe), Erich Maria Remarque (Prof. Pohlmann), Barbara Rutting (Woman guerilla), Charles Regnler (Joseph), Dorothea Wieck (Frau Lieser), Kurt Meisel (Heini), Clancy Cooper (Sauer), John van Dreelen (Political officer), Dana J. [Jim] Hutton (Hirschland), Bengt Lindstrom (Steinbrenner); **Written by:** Orin Jannings; **Cinematography by:** Russell Metty; **Music by:** Miklos Rozsa. **Producer:** U-I, Robert Arthur. **Awards:** Nominations: Academy Awards '58: Best Sound. **Running Time:** 133 minutes. **Format:** VHS, Beta.

TO HELL AND BACK

1955 Jesse Hibbs 🦴🦴🦴

Audie Murphy's screen autobiography is a much better film than it has any right to be. It's dated and imperfect, but, more importantly, it is not celluloid hero-worship. The figure who emerges may be a bit too flawless, but he's not boastful and he doesn't set himself apart from his fellow dogfaces. Actually, the central theme of the film is that the Army provides a Depression-era kid from East Texas with a strong family structure that he has never really experienced.

In 1937, a young Audie Murphy (played by Gordon Gebert as a boy, by Murphy himself later) is forced to become the head of a family with an ailing mother and an absent father. He drops out of grade school and goes to work full time to provide for his brothers and sisters until, at roughly the same time, World War II starts and his mother dies. By joining up, he can provide more money for his siblings, but neither the Navy nor the Marines are interested in the small guy. In the Army, he is promoted to Acting Sergeant on the troop ship carrying him to French North Africa and the 3rd Infantry Division, B Company, 15th Regiment. It soon becomes apparent that the babyfaced kid has a genuine aptitude for soldiering.

After Africa, his outfit takes part in the invasions of Sicily, Anzio and Southern France. In every engagement, Murphy steps up and does whatever he can. At the same time, he becomes friends with Brandon (Charles Drake), Johnson (Marshall Thompson), and Kerrigan (Jack Kelly). They're the core of his platoon, and Murphy's various heroics never take place in a vacuum. He sees himself as part of a unit, and everything that he does is meant to advance the unit, not the individual. The one long scene that moves away from the military—an interlude in an Italian town where he meets Maria (Susan Kohner) and her family—is embarrassingly bad. As long as the focus stays on the platoon's activities on the battlefield, the film is in fine shape. By today's standards, the depiction of combat may seem a bit sanitized, but director Jesse Hibbs makes the cold mud and rain of the Italian campaign believably real, especially a series of scenes revolving around a farmhouse and a tank.

It's difficult to criticize someone who is playing himself, but Murphy is not the most expressive or commanding presence ever to grace the screen. In the quiet moments, he is only slightly more comfortable-looking than he is in John Huston's *The Red Badge of Courage*, though he does appear to be at ease in the action scenes. Throughout, he comes across as a likeable young man, with the emphasis on young. All of the events recounted in the film took place before Murphy was 19 years old. In that brief military career, America's most decorated soldier won more than 20 medals, including the Congressional Medal of Honor and the French Croix de Guerre, and killed more than 240 enemy soldiers.

Such an active campaign makes for a story that would be dismissed as screenwriter's fantasy if it weren't true.

See also

Sergeant York
A Walk in the Sun
The Young Lions
The Story of G.I. Joe
Battle of San Pietro
Red Badge of Courage

Audie Murphy plays himself in
To Hell and Back. The Kobal Collection

Cast: Audie Murphy (Audie Murphy), Marshall Thompson (Johnson), Jack Kelly (Kerrigan), Charles Drake (Brandon), Gregg Palmer (Lt. Manning), Paul Picerni (Valentino), David Janssen (Lt. Lee), Bruce Cowling (Capt. Marks), Paul Langton (Col. Howe), Art Aragon (Sanchez), Felix Noriego (Swope), Denver Pyle (Thompson), Brett Halsey (Saunders), Susan Kohner (Maria), Anabel Shaw (Helen), Mary Field (Mrs. Murphy), Gordon Gebert (Audie as a boy), Rand Brooks (Lt. Harris), Richard Castle (Kovak), Gen. Walter Bedell Smith (Himself); **Written by:** Gil Doud; **Cinematography by:** Maury Gertsman; **Music by:** Henry Mancini. **Producer:** Aaron Rosenberg, Universal. **Running Time:** 106 minutes. **Format:** VHS, Beta.

THE TRAIN
Le Train
Il Treno

1965 John Frankenheimer ♫♫♫♫

Though John Frankenheimer's fine suspense film doesn't have the strong cult following of *The Manchurian Candidate*, it is every bit as enjoyable, with a dirtier, more realistic atmosphere. The key plot twists are based on the physical characteristics of railroads—engines and tracks, cars and switches—all shown in enough detail to keep the viewer informed. On a purely technical level, the film deserves comparison with Hitchcock's best.

In August 1944, as the German occupation of Paris is about to end, Col. Von Waldheim (Paul Scofield) decides to appropriate dozens of Impressionist masterpieces from a museum and ship them back to Germany. Miss Villard (Suzanne Flon), the museum's curator, alerts a Resistance cell to the plan. The group's leader Labiche (Burt Lancaster) is a railway inspector and so is in a position to do something. But he states flatly, "I won't waste lives on paintings" and it is difficult to argue with him. Miss Villard claims that the paintings are part of their cultural heritage, the priceless "glory of France." Labiche is not impressed. He won't ask men to risk their lives for so much dried pigment.

> "This is 'degenerate art,' you know. As a loyal officer of the Third Reich, I should detest it. I've often wondered at the curious conceit that would attempt to determine taste and ideas by decree."
>
> **Col. Von Waldheim (Paul Schofield) to Miss Villard (Suzanne Flon)**

When a grizzled old engineer, Boule (Michel Simon), takes over on his own, Labiche is forced into some kind of action. It begins with a long sequence where an armaments train and the art train are both trying to leave the yards at Vaires. As they are being shuttled across tracks, the viewer knows that a British bombing raid is moments away. New complications are introduced whenever the pace flags, but the central conflict always returns to Labiche and Von Waldheim. The German's motivations do not change. He is obsessed by the art. Labiche is always more interested in the human cost. He'll sacrifice the paintings to save lives, though he seldom has such a simple choice.

Two forces drive the film. The first is Frankenheimer's ability to choreograph the actual trains. No miniature models were used. All of the filming was done on location with real railroad equipment. Frankenheimer and cinematographers Jean Tournier and Walter Wottitz capture the hulking size and heat of the engines, the noise and sway of the cars in motion, and the crushing power involved when the machines collide.

The second force is Burt Lancaster. At 51, he did his own stunts, and he handles them with an athletic grace that few actors of any age have ever possessed. Most of the critical action sequences are filmed in long, unforgiving takes. Notice the scene where he slides down the ladder at the Switch Tower and then later, another long single shot in the machine shops when he casts a bearing. This is certainly not his most complex dramatic work, nor does it demand the flashy gymnastics of such earlier films as *Trapeze* and *The Crimson Pirate*, but it is a physically demanding role, unusually so.

The film can be criticized for going too far with its contrived plot, but Frankenheimer and Lancaster ground the heroics so firmly in a real setting that the outlandishness of it all becomes apparent only after the closing credits have rolled. *The Train* is simply one of the best.

See also

Saboteur
The Manchurian Candidate
Seven Days in May
Is Paris Burning?
The Battle of Algiers
The General

Resistance fighter Burt
Lancaster confronts a Col. Von
Waldheim (Paul Schofield) in
The Train. The Kobal Collection

Cast: Burt Lancaster (Labiche), Paul Scofield (Col. Von Waldheim), Jeanne Moreau (Christine), Michel Simon (Papa Boule), Suzanne Flon (Miss Villard), Wolfgang Preiss (Maj. Herren), Albert Remy (Didont), Charles Millot (Pesquet), Jacques Marin (Jacques), Donald O'Brien (Schwartz), Jean-Pierre Zola (Octave), Arthur Brauss (Pilzer), Howard Vernon (Capt. Dietrich), Richard Munch (Gen. Von Lubitz), Paul Bonifas (Spinet), Jean-Claude Bercq (Major); **Written by:** Frank Davis, Walter Bernstein, Franklin Coen; **Cinematography by:** Jean Tournier, Walter Wottitz; **Music by:** Maurice Jarre. **Producer:** United Artists, Jules Bricken. **French, Italian. Awards:** Nominations: Academy Awards '65: Best Story & Screenplay. **Running Time:** 133 minutes. **Format:** VHS, LV, Letterbox, DVD.

THE TRAIN

THE TUSKEGEE AIRMEN

1995 Robert Markowitz ♫♫♫

This made-for-cable feature is a throwback to the unit pictures of the late 1940s, and it shares the same flaws and rewards. The production values are noticeably substandard, particularly in the combination of new and archival aerial footage, and the script is a collection of cliches. But cliches can be comforting, and the film is built on powerful convictions. More important, it explores a neglected chapter in the history of American race relations.

At the beginning of World War II, the armed services, like the rest of society, were strictly segregated. Some have called the system American apartheid, particularly in the South. But black leaders had pressed for change, and a few months before the war began, the Army Air Corps announced that black pilots would be trained at the newly constructed Tuskegee Air Base. Pilots are officers, and that was the cause of considerable controversy at the time. The film doesn't really deal with most of that background. Instead, it begins with one of the most familiar images of flying films: a boy in a field playing with a toy airplane; he looks up to see a biplane coming in for a landing and chases after it.

> "As God is my witness, those boys will never see combat."
>
> **Sen. Conyers (John Lithgow) on black pilots**

This time, though, the boy is black and he grows up to be Hannibal Lee Jr. (Laurence Fishburne), who boards a train in Iowa and heads south for Tuskegee, Alabama. En route, he meets Walter "Stick" Peoples (Allen Payne), a licensed pilot, and Billy "ATrain" Roberts (Cuba Gooding Jr.), the fast-talking kid. Then at the base, he meets Leroy Cappy (Malcolm Jamal Warner), the quiet serious one, and Lt. Glenn (Courtney B. Vance), the veteran who will train them to be fighter pilots. Any fan will immediately recognize them as variations on the same stereotypes introduced in *Hell's Angels* (1930) and reworked dozens of times since.

The point of the film, though, is the "other enemy" that these young men face in their development as pilots, entrenched racial prejudice at every level of the service. For every white officer with a degree of enlightenment like Col. Rogers (Daniel Hugh-Kelly), there is the openly disdainful Maj. Joy (Christopher McDonald) and Sen. Conyers (John Lithgow) who will do anything to keep black people in their place. But the filmmakers never let that side of the story take too much from the more traditional military aspects.

> **Fact:** The T-6 trainers that feature prominently in the film also double for Japanese Zeros in many other war movies.

Of course, not all of the young men make it through flight school. Even more are lost when they become the 99th Pursuit Squadron and are stationed in a North African backwater. When, at length, the 99th becomes an important part of the war in Italy, they face even more problems. Throughout, Laurence Fishburne turns in a quietly competent performance reminiscent of Jimmy Stewart or Henry Fonda. Lee doesn't swagger; he simply does his job and demands that those around him do theirs.

Unfortunately, he gets little help from the special effects department. Though a few of the flying sequences—featuring Stearmans, T-6s, and P-51 Mustangs—are handled well, the actual combat footage is so jarringly rough that the big scenes don't put the viewer in the cockpit the way the best flying films do. Perhaps if the movie had been made in black-and-white, the way its cinematic ancestors were, and given a rougher, scrappier look, it might have flown higher.

Even so, *The Tuskegee Airmen* is a good story that scratches the surface of an area that American movies have largely ignored.

Cast: Laurence "Larry" Fishburne (Hannibal Lee Jr.), Cuba Gooding Jr. (Billy Roberts), Allen Payne (Walter Derrick Peoples III), Malcolm Jamal Warner (Leroy Cappy), Courtney B. Vance (Lt. Glenn), Andre Braugher (Lt. Col. Benjamin O. Davis), John Lithgow (Sen. Conyers), Rosemary Murphy (Eleanor Roosevelt), Christopher McDonald (Maj. Sherman Joy), Vivica A. Fox (Charlene), Daniel Hugh-Kelly (Col. Noel Rogers), David Harrod (White pilot #1), Eddie Braun (Tail gunner), Bennet Guillory (Hannibal's father); **Written by:** Paris Qualles, Ron Hutchinson, Trey Ellis; **Cinematography by:** Ronald Orieux; **Music by:** Lee Holdridge. **Producer:** William C. Carraro, Frank Price, Price Ent., HBO Pictures. **MPAA Rating:** PG-13. **Running Time:** 107 minutes. **Format:** VHS.

TWELVE O'CLOCK HIGH
1949 Henry King ♪♪♪♪

Most war films that are focused on a single campaign examine it either through the eyes of a low-level combatant who's on the front lines or through the eyes of an officer who's removed from the action. This unorthodox "tale-told-from-memory" attempts to combine the two approaches. The subject is American precision daylight bombing raids by B-17s based in England. According to the film's premise, that tactic was the key to winning the war in Europe. Daylight bombing was so accurate that it destroyed German industry and so its ability to prosecute the war. Viewers of a strongly populist persuasion may be suspicious of the filmmakers' sympathetic portrayal of top-level staff officers, but no one can deny their rigorous attempts to nail down the physical and psychological details of the air war.

> "I want you to paint this name on the nose of your ship—*Leper Colony*. Because in it you're going to get every deadbeat in the outfit, every man with a penchant for head colds. If there's a bombardier who can't hit his plate with his fork, you get him. If there's a navigator who can't find the men's room, you get him because you rate him. Is that clear?"
>
> **Gen. Savage (Gregory Peck), dressing down the 918th Bomber Group**

In 1949, dapper American Harvey Stovall (Dean Jagger) visits his London haberdasher. Admiring his new hat in a store window, he spots a battered toby jug and buys it on the spot. It's the key that takes him back to his war years with the 918th Bomber Group at Archbury, England. The 918th is a "hard-luck" outfit. Under the leadership of Col. Keith Davenport (Gary Merrill), the 21 B-17s are suffering catastrophic losses every time they take off on their daytime missions. Why, Gen. Pritchard (Millard Mitchell) asks, and sends Gen. Frank Savage (Gregory Peck) to find the answer. At some length, Savage deduces that Davenport "overidentifies" with his men. He cares so much about them as individuals that the group suffers. Pritchard orders Savage to take over the 918th and turn it around.

He does. From the moment Savage sets foot on the base, he kicks ass and takes names. Nobody is safe, from the sentry (Kenneth Tobey) to Maj. Stovall. When Savage stands in front of the assembled pilots and crewmen, he thunders, "Stop making plans! Forget about going home! Consider yourselves already dead. Once you accept that idea, it won't be so tough." The men take more convincing, and that's the story of the film.

It works for several reasons. First, director Henry King, a solid journeyman filmmaker, makes the most of an excellent script by novelists Sy Bartlett and Beirne Lay Jr. Second, cinematographer Leon Shamroy uses ultra-crisp black-and-white photography to give the action a richly textured, evocative look. They also borrowed real combat aerial footage to heighten the sense of realism. In every scene—on the ground or in the air—the film seems absolutely authentic; the curving walls of the Quonset huts where the fliers live and work, ground crews riding bicycles out to meet the incoming bombers, the words painted over the waist hatch of a B17 "Where Angels and Generals Fear to Tread."

The film also gets the psychological details right, and those are infinitely more important. Early on, a pilot calmly describes how he had to scrape his own frozen blood off the windshield before he could see to land the plane, and the rest of the film shows that he was not exaggerating. These are men who are pushed to give "maximum effort" and then something more. When they have gone that far, they react in different ways, none of them easy to take. This is such heightened emotional material that it's difficult for actors to handle properly. This ensemble does a letter-perfect job.

See also

Catch-22

Patton

Memphis Belle

Command Decision

Jagger deservedly won a Supporting Actor Academy Award. (The film also won the Oscar for Sound and it was nominated for Best Picture.) Peck, also nominated, turns in one of the most carefully modulated performances in his substantial career. He lost, and had to wait through three more nominations until 1962, when he was recognized for his role as Atticus Finch in *To Kill a Mockingbird*. At heart, Frank Savage is cut from the same cloth. Peck invests both characters with a core decency that makes them compelling, sympathetic characters. No matter how abrasive Savage is, viewers know that he's trying to do the right things for the right reasons.

In that respect, he represents every major character. This is not a film about good guys and bad guys. It's about guys who are struggling desperately to find the right way to do an impossibly difficult job. The unexpected ending, reportedly based on a real incident, is altogether appropriate. Though *Twelve O'Clock High* is no more critical of the military than any of the flag-waving propaganda pieces made during the war, it does take a much closer look at the human costs. In that regard, it can be seen as a bridge between *Sands of Iwo Jima* and *The Best Years of Our Lives*.

Gregory Peck and Dean Jagger are Bomber Group officers in *Twelve O'Clock High*. The Kobal Collection

Cast: Gregory Peck (Gen. Frank Savage), Hugh Marlowe (Lt. Col. Ben Gately), Gary Merrill (Col. Keith Davenport), Millard Mitchell (Gen. Pritchard), Dean Jagger (Maj. Harvey Stovall), Paul Stewart (Capt. "Doc" Kaiser), Robert Arthur (Sgt. McIllhenny), John Kellogg (Maj. Cobb), Sam Edwards (Birdwell), Russ Conway (Operations officer), Lawrence Dobkin (Capt. Twombley), Kenneth Tobey (Sentry); **Written by:** Sy Bartlett, Beirne Lay Jr.; **Cinematography by:** Leon Shamroy; **Music by:** Alfred Newman. **Producer:** Darryl F. Zanuck. **Awards:** Academy Awards '49: Best Sound, Best Supporting Actor (Jagger), National Film Registry '98; Nominations: Academy Awards '49: Best Actor (Peck), Best Picture; New York Film Critics Awards '50: Best Actor (Peck). **Running Time:** 132 minutes. **Format:** VHS, Beta, LV.

1949

Most critics and movie fans consider 1939 to be Hollywood's high-water mark. With *The Wizard of Oz*, *Gone with the Wind*, and *Stagecoach* leading the Oscar nominees, they have a strong case. Add to that list *Mr. Smith Goes to Washington*, *Ninotchka*, *Dark Victory*, *Of Mice and Men*, *Wuthering Heights*, *Goodbye Mr. Chips*, *Beau Geste*, and *The Hunchback of Notre Dame* and you've got a formidable lineup. But for war movie fans, 1949 is hard to beat. That year, five of the best and most diverse works in the genre were released in either America or England.

In alphabetical order, they are:

William Wellman's wonderful and underappreciated *Battleground* is the story of a squad of veterans and young replacements caught up in the Battle of the Bulge. Strictly in visual terms, it's one of the most striking interpretations of World War II, with Oscar-winning contributions from black-and-white cinematographer Paul C. Vogel and writer Robert Pirosh. His one-sentence summation of a foot soldier's view of combat has never been topped: "Things just happen and then afterwards you try to figure out why you acted the way you did."

Over in the Pacific Theater, John Wayne set in cinematic concrete his military persona as Sgt. Stryker in *Sands of Iwo Jima*. It's one of the seminal roles of his career, and many of his fans still see it as the definitive World War II combat movie. He was nominated for Best Actor, but lost to Broderick Crawford in *All the King's Men*.

Wayne also starred in *She Wore a Yellow Ribbon*, the second volume of his friend John Ford's "cavalry trilogy." It is some of the best work those two ever did together. Cinematographer William Hoch took home the Oscar in the color division.

A creative team that includes director Carol Reed, writer Graham Greene, producers Alexander Korda and David O. Selznick, and co-star/writer Orson Welles turned the bomb-blasted city of Vienna into a surreal nightmare landscape for one of the finest post-war thrillers, *The Third Man*. Though it wouldn't reach America for another year, the film had its premiere in London in 1949.

Gregory Peck was also nominated in the Best Actor category for his superb performance as a driven Air Force general in *Twelve O'Clock High*. It is still one of the most insightful examinations of the psychological pressures of command.

Any fan of the genre would be hard pressed to come up with another five titles that combine intelligence, innovation, and entertainment so skillfully. And, if those weren't enough, 1949 was also the year that James Cagney made it to the top of the world in *White Heat*. Willis O'Brian and Ray Harryhausen created the original *Mighty Joe Young*, and professor Ray Milland became the great major league pitcher in the baseball fantasy *It Happens Every Spring*. Finally, in the midst of all that conflict and violence, one of the screen's greatest lovers, Pepe LePew, made his Oscar-winning debut in Chuck Jones' *For Scentimental Reasons*.

Without question, 1949 was a hell of a year.

UNDERGROUND
Once Upon a Time There Was a Country
Il Etait une Fois un Pays

1995 Emir Kusturica 𝄞𝄞𝄞

Emir Kusturica's self-indulgent "tragicomic satire" (to use the press kit's description) is such an ambitious, unconventional film that it cannot successfully bridge all cultural differences. Tastes in humor differ from culture to culture, and that transition is difficult for any comedy. A solid background in recent Central European history helps, too. Potential Western viewers who are still interested should approach *Underground* as a Felliniesque Balkan allegorical fantasy.

Title cards divide the story into three acts. The first begins in Belgrade at the beginning of World War II. That's where Marko (Miki Manojlovic) and Blacky (Lazar Ristovski) are making a handsome living as guerrilla fighters and war profiteers. They make their first entrance, grandly drunk and flinging money from a horse-drawn carriage as they're trailed by a brass band playing a theme that could have come from Nino Rota, Fellini's frequent collaborator. Though Blacky is married, he's also carrying on with a young actress, Natalija (Mirjana Jokovic). Marko is in love with her, too. Then the German bombing raids hit Belgrade. The first strike hits the zoo where Marko's brother Ivan (Slavko Stimac) works. When Blacky's home is bombed, he is really upset and becomes a hero of the underground in a series of broad slapstick scenes.

> "Marko, you lie so beautifully."
>
> **Natalija (Mirjana Jokovic)**

Kusturica and co-writer Dusan Kovacevic create a plot that caroms off into bizarre new directions at every opportunity, eventually leading to Blacky, Ivan, and several dozen others being hidden in a huge cellar. Marko and Natalija tell them that the war is still going on, and have them building small arms to help partisans against the Nazis until the mid 1960s. In rough terms, that second part of the film is about Yugoslavia under Tito, and to tell it, Kusturica uses some *Forrest Gump* effects that put Marko into real footage. The device is employed sparingly, and the tone of the film moderates a bit then. Even when the broad physical humor subsides, the satiric attitude is unchanged.

Kusturica challenges our expectations about cinematic depictions of war. He treats the destruction, the human costs, the individual sacrifices, even romance as farce. His fantasies take on darker tinges in the final act before arriving at two separate and conflicting conclusions. Obviously, this is not a film to all tastes, but it has moments of near brilliance, and the three leads do remarkable work with difficult roles. At various times, Manojlovic and Ristovski could be ringers for Richard Belzer and Robin Williams.

See also
Life Is Beautiful
The Last Metro
To Be or Not to Be
Amarcord
Sante Sangre

Even for adventurous viewers with a taste for European comedy, the film is a long haul at 192 minutes. In the end, the combination of serious purpose with playfulness and intelligence makes *Underground* worth the effort.

An *Underground* wedding. The Kobal
Collection

Cast: Miki Manojlovic (Marko), Lazar Ristovski (Petar Popara (Blacky)), Mirjana Jokovic (Natalija), Slavko Stimac (Ivan), Ernst Stotzner (Franz), Srdan Todorovic (Jovan), Mirjana Karanovic (Vera), Milena Pavlovic (Jelena), Danilo Stojkovic (Deda), Bora Todorovic (Golub), Davor Dujmovic (Bata), Branislav Lecic (Mustafa), Dragan Nikolic (Film director), Hark Bohm (Dr. Strasse); **Cameo(s):** Emir Kusturica; **Written by:** Emir Kusturica, Dusan Kovacevic; **Cinematography by:** Vilko Filac; **Music by:** Goran Bregovic. **Producer:** Pierre Spengler, CIBY 2000, Pandora Film, Novo Film; released by Miramax Films. **French, German, Hungarian. Awards:** Cannes Film Festival '95: Best Film; Nominations: Independent Spirit Awards '98: Best Foreign Film. **Running Time:** 192 minutes. **Format:** VHS.

Producer-writer-director Carl Foreman's serious examination of the war in Europe is too serious for its own good. Far too serious. As often as not, when he makes a valid, original point about the absurdity of it all, he hammers it home so heavily that he condescends to the audience. Moviegoers do not like sermons. They hate long boring sermons.

A lengthy throat-clearing introduction establishes an unfortunately pokey pace. In England, two American soldiers, Chase (George Peppard) and Trower (George Hamilton), stand guard at an army depot during a bomb raid. The scene finally shifts to Italy, where one of their comrades, Baker (Vince Edwards), falls for a local girl, Maria (Rosanna Schiaffino), and tries to teach her a lesson in tolerance. That beginning sets the tone and theme for the rest of the episodic story. Virtually all of the naive American solders attempt to show the jaded Europeans the error of their ways and they learn that the Europeans do not want to change.

Sgt. Craig (Eli Wallach) spends the night in a bombed-out house with a frightened French woman (Jeanne Moreau). Trower falls for Regine (Romy Schneider), a violinist he meets in an Italian club. Chase falls into a sweet arrangement with Magda (Melina Mercouri), a wealthy black marketeer who tempts him to desert. Weaver (an impossibly young Peter Fonda) falls for a puppy. Finally, Trower falls for Helga (Elke Sommer), a German girl who fears the Russians.

> "The war is almost over. The armies are crumbling at the edges like stale cake."
>
> **Magda (Melina Mercouri)**

Those are the longest stories but they're not the most interesting or important. One brief incident exposes the violent side of American racism. Another moment touches briefly and without comment on the horrors of the concentration camps. Neither scene is mentioned again after it's over, while the Americans' romantic illusions resonate throughout the film. Two set pieces stand out from the rest of the action. The first involves a group of Germans trying to surrender to a French patrol. It's intense, short, and beautifully photographed. The second scene is an extended execution staged on a snow-covered field to the accompaniment of Sinatra's "Have Yourself a Merry Little Christmas." But the dramatic staging and the ironic use of the music are ruined by a ham-fisted change in music at the end.

Foreman's focus is on the day-to-day realities of the war away from the battlefront, and his high-minded intentions are admirable. In many ways this can be seen as a transitional attempt to reach a level of realism and social seriousness that would never have been possible under the studio system of the 1940s and '50s. But that's not enough to overcome a fatal flaw. *The Victors* is still a long, dull, sanctimonious movie.

See also
The Big Red One
The Young Lions
Dr. Strangelove
Doctor Zhivago
Judgment at Nuremberg

George Hamilton, Vince Edwards, Jim Mitchum, and George Peppard rest after a skirmish in *The Victors*. The Kobal Collection

Cast: George Peppard (Cpl. Chase), George Hamilton (Cpl. Trower), Eli Wallach (Sgt. Craig), Vince Edwards (Baker), Jim Mitchum (Grogan), Peter Fonda (Weaver), Romy Schneider (Regine), Rosanna Schiaffino (Maria), Jeanne Moreau (French woman), Albert Finney (Russian soldier), Elke Sommer (Helga), Michael Callan (Eldridge), Mervyn Johns (Dennis), Melina Mercouri (Magda), Vanda Godsell (Nurse), Patrick Jordan (Tank Sergeant), Alf Kjellin (Priest), Albert Lieven (Herr Metzger), Peter Vaughan (Policeman), Senta Berger (Trudi), James Chase (Condemned soldier), Maurice Ronet (French Lt. Cohn); **Written by:** Carl Foreman; **Cinematography by:** Christopher Challis; **Music by:** Sol Kaplan. **Producer:** Carl Foreman. **Running Time:** 156 minutes.

Some unfortunate devices rob Lewis Milestone's second great war film of much of its power. The most obvious is a pretentious "folk song" glorifying the heroism of "common men." Had it appeared only in the theme, it might not have been so bothersome. But it is featured prominently in the introduction, which also includes reverential shots of hands opening Harry Brown's novel, and thumbnail sketches of the main characters (by a narrator who sounds like Burgess Meredith). Then the song reappears at slower moments to comment on recent action, and finally, at the conclusion, the words of the last verse appear on screen as a glorified subtitle. The black-and-white photography is also muddy and indistinct in places. Even on DVD, the film compares poorly to some other pictures of its time. Blame either the original print or the transfer to video.

Those reservations notwithstanding, this is one of the better examinations of the war in Europe. Opening on a pre-dawn landing craft somewhere off the Italian coast, the film follows a platoon that's isolated in a nameless battle. Before the men even reach the beach, the lieutenant is killed and Sgt. Porter (Herbert Rudley) is left in charge. He knows nothing of the larger battle plans. All he has been told is that the unit is to establish a position a hundred yards off the beach and then to follow a road six miles to a farmhouse. What should they expect to encounter on the way? Why is the farmhouse important? What will they find there? The sergeant doesn't know. No one does. But those are their orders and, after some discussion with Sgt. Tyne (Dana Andrews) and Sgt. Ward (Lloyd Bridges), they make their way inland.

> "That's the whole trouble with war. You never get to see nothing. You fight 'em by ear."
> **McWilliams (Sterling Holloway)**

> "It's not that I'm scared—I know I'm not—it's just that I can't figure things out."
> **Sgt. Porter (Herbert Rudley)**

As the title suggests, the rest is essentially a loose episodic road picture paced at a slow walk. The various situations that the platoon faces are really less important than the gradual revelation of the men's characters and their reactions to the war. Windy (John Ireland) is composing a long letter to his sister. Archibald (Norman Lloyd) thinks that the war will last forever and that in 1958, they'll be fighting the Battle of Tibet. Rivera (Richard Conte) is the unit's smart guy. His long conversations with Friedman (George Tyne) are almost comedy routines. The medic, McWilliams (Sterling Halloway), is too curious for his own good.

The combat scenes involve only the platoon and adversaries of similar size and power. Though the level of violence and amount of blood may seem tame by today's graphic standards, the physical action is realistic and believable. Again though, that side of the film is no more important than the less noisy moments. In those long scenes of walking and waiting and eating, the men's talk sounds absolutely authentic. Griping, dreaming, remembering food, taking care of each other—it all comes through in the words. That's where Robert Rossen's script, based on Brown's novel, is at its best. These guys are real. They're neither glorified for persevering in a tough job nor pilloried for their weaknesses. And those weaknesses are not ignored. A long, slow breakdown is revealed in telling detail, and at other times the characters make simple, critical mistakes.

See also

The Story of G.I. Joe
Saving Private Ryan
All Quiet on the Western Front
The Lost Patrol
Pork Chop Hill

The strong anti-war sentiments that director Milestone expressed in *All Quiet on the Western Front* are largely absent here, but the film cannot be accused of flag-waving jingoism, either. Essentially, Milestone praises the men for what they do. If he'd left it at that, and not

Dana Andrews watches as a young soldier tries to compose himself in *A Walk in the Sun*. The Kobal Collection

attempted to underline his points in other ways, he might have had a masterpiece. In the end, the flaws are not fatal to *A Walk in the Sun*, but everything else about the film is so outstanding that they are impossible to ignore.

Cast: Dana Andrews (Sgt. Tyne), Richard Conte (Rivera), John Ireland (Windy), Lloyd Bridges (Sgt. Ward), Sterling Holloway (McWilliams), George Tyne (Friedman), Norman Lloyd (Archibald), Herbert Rudley (Sgt. Eddie Porter), Richard Benedict (Tranella), Huntz Hall (Carraway), James B. Cardwell (Sgt. Hoskins), George Offerman Jr. (Tinker), Steve Brodie (Judson), Matt Willis (Sgt. Halverson), Alvin Hammer (Johnson), Chris Drake (Rankin), Victor Cutler (Cousins), Jay Norris (James); **Written by:** Robert Rossen, Harry Brown; **Cinematography by:** Russell Harlan; **Music by:** Freddie Rich, Earl Robinson. **Producer:** Lewis Milestone. **Running Time:** 117 minutes. **Format:** VHS, Beta, LV, 8mm, DVD.

John Irvin's fine HBO war film is essentially a remake of Don Siegel's *Hell Is for Heroes*. The films tell virtually identical stories set in the autumn of 1944 on the Siegfried Line. More importantly, both are made with the same tough, pared down, laconic style. In many ways, Irvin's film is the more successful because it begins on a strong note and never really lessens the tension.

A bizarre opening scene introduces Manning (Ron Eldard), the only survivor of his platoon to make it back from a patrol. The situation is so tense, with the Allied forces stretched so thin against Germans who are now defending their own country, that Capt. Pritchett (Martin Donovan) immediately gives Manning a battlefield promotion to sergeant. He doesn't want it and tries to explain, "In the woods . . . I've done things." But Pritchett doesn't have time. He gives Manning command of a group of untried replacements and sends them out to the snowy front. Of the new kids, Sanderson (Zak Orth), with his moon face and glasses, seems to be the weakest.

> "This is your first big chance to stay alive; don't fuck it up."
>
> Manning (Ron Eldard) to Sanderson (Zak Orth)

No one should know anything more about V.W. Vought's story. It is filled with violence—often grotesque and unsettling, never glamorous or gratuitous. Director Irvin and cinematographer Thomas Burstyn mute their colors, using brown and gray the way Siegel uses black-and-white. The Hungarian locations have a bone-chilling cold aura that's perfect for the melancholy mood of the piece. At the center of the film is a brilliant, complex performance by Ron Eldard.

Manning is faced with a series of moral questions that challenge his most basic assumptions about himself. At first, Manning claims to be a survivor. If he had any choice, he would refuse any promotion that put him in charge of another human being. He is not a coward and he is not going to ask others to take his duties. But how much does he owe to men he does not know? How separate and alienated from the others is he? As decisions and orders go down the chain of command, where does responsibility for the consequences lie? Whenever he thinks he has found a workable answer, the circumstances change and he has to reevaluate. Those are not easy emotions for an actor to work with, but Eldard is never less than completely convincing.

Though the film lacks the budget of its big-screen counterparts, that is not a concern for videophiles. It's actually an asset, because nothing is lost in the translation to video. This is a story about a few men caught up in a limited conflict. It's not about the sweeping power of mass troop movements. Scenes of that size would only distract attention from the individual emotions involved in a conflict that's no less intense on a one-to-one level. Nothing on screen here attempts to equal the opening of *Saving Private Ryan*, but the rest of the film can match it step for step. And the ending is stripped of all sentimentality.

For serious war movie fans, *When Trumpets Fade* is the film you may never have heard of but really have to see.

See also

Hell Is for Heroes
The Thin Red Line
Saving Private Ryan
Battleground

Cast: Ron Eldard (Manning), Zak Orth (Sanderson), Frank Whaley (Chamberlain), Dylan Bruno (Sgt. Talbot), Martin Donovan (Capt. Pritchett), Timothy Olyphant (Lt. Lukas), Dan Futterman (Despin), Dwight Yoakam (Lieutenant Colonel), Devon Gummersall (Replacement soldier), Jeffrey Donovan (Bobby); **Written by:** W.W. Vought; **Cinematography by:** Thomas Burstyn; **Music by:** Geoffrey Burgon. **Producer:** John Kemeny, David R. Ginsburg, Citadel Entertainment, HBO NYC Productions. **MPAA Rating:** R. **Running Time:** 93 minutes. **Format:** VHS, Closed Caption, DVD.

WHERE EAGLES DARE
1968 Brian G. Hutton 🦴🦴🦴

Give novelist Alistair MacLean credit for recognizing what works. He went back to the film version of *The Guns of Navarone* and figured out which elements were the most effective and reworked them for another piece of crackerjack escapism.

To begin with, he needed two good actors to replace Gregory Peck and David Niven as the sometimes testy protagonists. The producers chose well with Richard Burton, an established international star in 1968 when the film was made, and Clint Eastwood, fresh from the success of his trio of Sergio Leone westerns. Both of them have screen presence to burn and, remarkably, they work well together. Next, he wanted a location as scenic and exotic as the Aegean, and so he turned to the Bavarian Alps. Where the original made use of huge cannon mounted in a cave, the new film has an aerial tram ending at a castle carved into the edge of a towering mountain. At the conclusion of the first film, the Nazi villains had to laboriously break through heavy locked doors. Ditto here. The first films ends with a massive hidden bomb; this castle is filled with about a dozen of the cutest little prepackaged dynamite bundles, each complete with its own little timer, mounting strap, and tripwire. Just the thing for the commando who has everything.

> "Fascinating, very fascinating, perhaps even true."
> **Col. Turner (Patrick Wymark)**

Once those elements were in place, it was time to come up with a plot, and MacLean let his imagination run free, with little regard to realism, to create a yeasty confection. On the eve of D-Day, it appears that American Gen. Carnaby (Robert Beatty), who knows all the plans, has been captured when his plane is shot down. German intelligence has him ready for questioning (Remember the scopolamine "truth serum" from *Navarone*? It's back, too.) at Schloss Adler. The ever-alert British intelligence people whip up a crack team of agents led by Maj. Smith (Burton) and Lt. Schaffer (Eastwood) and five others, dress them up in German uniforms, put them in a German plane they just happen to have handy, and run them over to Bavaria, where they parachute out into the snow. They've barely landed before we know that at least one of them is a traitor. Much later, when it's all being explained, one German general stands up and screams "THIS IS PREPOSTEROUS!" and no one in the audience can disagree. They won't care either. It's preposterous but fun.

Journeyman director Brian G. Hutton understands how important the right pace is to this kind of story. He lets things move slowly in the first half and dwells on the nuts and bolts of the plot—planting bombs, preparing climbing gear, setting up escapes. Many contemporary action films tend to gloss over such mundane details, but they provide a much-needed appearance of reality to the adventurous fantasies.

The key scenes are set on the vertiginous aerial tram. They depend on some fair special effects and excellent stuntwork. For his part, Eastwood squints, shoots, and stabs his way through a fairly high body count. Even if Burton was slumming with the material, he seems to be having a good time with it, and with that incredible voice, he could make even a cliched radio conversation—"Broadsword, calling Danny Boy. Broadsword calling Danny Boy. Come in Danny Boy!"—sound like Shakespeare. In the second half, though, the action takes over, and on the simplest "Bang!Bang! Boom!Boom!" level, it's completely satisfactory, if predictable and derivative.

See also
The Dirty Dozen
Gunga Din
The Guns of Navarone
Kelly's Heroes

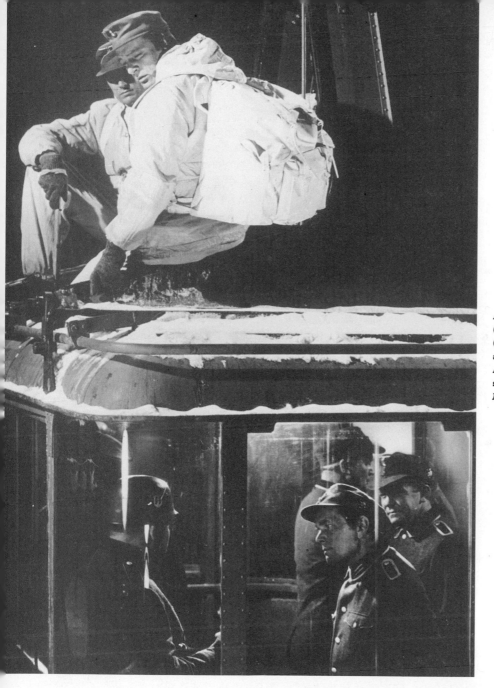

Allied commandos Smith (Richard Burton) and Schaffer (Clint Eastwood) hitch a ride on an aerial tram to rescue an American general from a Nazi stronghold in *Where Eagles Dare*. The Kobal Collection

Cast: Clint Eastwood (Lt. Morris Schaffer), Richard Burton (Maj. John Smith), Mary Ure (Mary Ellison), Michael Hordern (Vice Adm. Rolland), Anton Diffring (Col. Kramer), Ingrid Pitt (Heidi), Patrick Wymark (Wyatt Turner), Robert Beatty (Carnaby), Donald Houston (Olaf Christiansen), Derren Nesbitt (Maj. von Hapen), Ferdinand "Ferdy" Mayne (Rosemeyer), Peter Barkworth (Berkeley), William Squire (Lee Thomas), Neil McCarthy (MacPherson), Brook Williams (Sgt. Harrod), Vincent Ball (Carpenter); **Written by:** Alistair MacLean; **Cinematography by:** Arthur Ibbetson; **Music by:** Ron Goodwin. **Producer:** MGM, Elliot Kastner. **British. MPAA Rating:** PG. **Running Time:** 158 minutes. **Format:** VHS, Beta, LV, Letterbox.

THE YOUNG LIONS
1958 Edward Dmytryk 🦴🦴🦴

At one point in the transition of this story from printed page to screen, Irwin Shaw wrote a screenplay of his famous novel for an independent production company. It was a faithful adaptation that retained the triangular plot involving two American soldiers and one German. That deal fell through for lack of financing and when the novel was finally bought by 20th Century-Fox, director Edward Dmytryk decided that he wanted a new script. Then, when Marlon Brando was brought on board to play Christian Diestl, the German soldier, that role became more important and, not surprisingly, more sympathetic. Those decisions undercut several of Shaw's most important points, and turned what might have been a great war film into an overlong entertainment.

The story begins in Bavaria, New Year's Eve, 1938. That's where Margaret Freemantle (Barbara Rush) meets Christian, part-time ski instructor and budding fascist. When she asks him about it, he answers, "I'm not a Nazi; I'm not political at all, but I think that they stand for something hopeful in Germany." Flash forward to June 1940, where Lt. Diestl takes part in the occupation of Paris. By then, Margaret is back in New York where her beau, singer Michael Whiteacre (Dean Martin), has just passed his physical for the draft board. That's where he meets Noah Ackerman (Montgomery Clift), who works for Macy's, and invites him to a party where Noah meets Hope Plowman (Hope Lange).

Meanwhile, Christian's new commanding officer, Capt. Hardenberg (Maximilian Schell), explains that as a Nazi officer he "contracted for killing in all its forms" and so shouldn't be bothered by a little torture. On leave in Berlin, Christian meets Hardenberg's wife Gretchen (May Britt), a voluptuary who redefines "slinky" in her long black dress.

For the rest of its running time, the film crosscuts among the three, though the Whiteacre character gets short shrift, and all of them are pale shadows of the more fully realized characters in Shaw's fiction. Shaw's Diestl is a fairly decent young man who's transformed by brutal experience into a cold-blooded monster who kills without a second thought. His Whiteacre is a producer, a liberal intellectual who must find the courage to live up to his convictions. Ackerman, who faces anti-Semitism within the ranks of the Army, comes closest to Shaw's original.

Given that broad canvas to fill, Dmytryk sets a slow pace at the outset. As the conduct of the war intensifies, the narrative becomes more involving. The combat scenes are generally limited in scale and fairly graphic in their violence. Though some of the transitions are abrupt, the action and characters are never confusing. With the finer points of filmmaking though, Dmytryk is less consistent. While he carefully places a portrait of Franklin Roosevelt so that it looks over one character's shoulder in one key scene, he allows the shadow of a boom and microphone to become visible in another. Some interior scenes have a muddy look, though that could be due to a poor transfer from film to video.

Finally, Brando's character cannot justify the importance that is placed on him. Shaw intends for the story to be based on the contrasting personalities and experiences of the three characters. The departure from his original ending underscores the filmmakers'

See also

Judgment at Nuremberg

Career

A Time to Love and a Time to Die

The Blue Max

The Big Red One

Montgomery Clift (left) works
with another member of the Rat
Pack, Dean Martin, in *The
Young Lions*. The Kobal Collection

decision to tell a different story. Perhaps Shaw's screenplay still exists. If so, it could provide a starting point for a more faithful adaptation. Of all the "big-novel" films that came out of World War II, *The Young Lions* ought to be first in line for a remake.

THE YOUNG LIONS

Cast: Marlon Brando (Christian Diestl), Montgomery Clift (Noah Ackerman), Dean Martin (Michael Whiteacre), Hope Lange (Hope Plowman), Barbara Rush (Margaret Freemantle), Lee Van Cleef (Sgt. Rickett), Maximilian Schell (Capt. Hardenberg), May Britt (Gretchen Hardenberg), Dora Doll, Liliane Montevecchi, Parley Baer, Arthur Franz, Hal Baylor (Pvt. Burnecker), Richard Gardner (Pvt. Cowley), Herbert Rudley (Capt. Colclough), L.Q. (Justus E. McQueen) Jones (Pvt. Donnelly); **Written by:** Edward Anhalt; **Cinematography by:** Joe MacDonald; **Music by:** Hugo Friedhofer. **Producer:** TCF. **Awards:** Nominations: Academy Awards '58: Best Black and White Cinematography, Best Sound, Best Original Dramatic Score. **Running Time:** 167 minutes. **Format:** VHS, Beta, LV, Letterbox.

WORLD WAR II
Pacific Theater

World War II: The Pacific Theater on Screen

In the aftermath of the attack on Pearl Harbor, Hollywood was quick to turn out movies about the campaign in the Pacific. Like the films about the European war, they reflect the realities of the time. In the first ones, the Americans fight gallantly and manage to hold back the invading Japanese long enough for the counterattack to form. True victories do not come until later. More significantly, those first films set the formula for the "unit picture" that would become the dominant vehicle for war stories.

The formula is a simple variation on the mythic "hero's journey," familiar to all cultures and popularized by Joseph Campbell: Several men are brought together by chance or design. At first they are individuals who care more about themselves than the group or the cause. Through a course of training and combat, during which some are lost, they form a cohesive unit and are then willing to sacrifice themselves for the greater good. The transformation of that formula into entertainment is accomplished with the tools that Hollywood had on hand: good, tight writing, straightforward direction, familiar stars, special effects.

The first three examples are really terrific. *Wake Island*, which hit theater screens less than a year after the battle, is quick and tough, and it raises the bar in its graphic depictions of violence, showing the power of bombs and artillery with an unblinking clarity that was new to 1942 audiences. In *Air Force*, Howard Hawks lets the unit form around a B-17, the *Mary Ann*, as it arrives in Pearl Harbor on that fateful morning and then continues across the Pacific to a series of adventures. *Bataan* takes the formula a necessary step further by making the unit a multi-racial melting pot.

The plot of *So Proudly We Hail* roughly parallels *Air Force*, with a predominantly female cast of Army nurses (led by Paulette Goddard) heading across the Pacific at the end of 1941. *Guadalcanal Diary* is based on Richard Tregaski's non-fiction best-seller and places the unit formula in a more realistic setting than the others. The same can be said of *Thirty Seconds over Tokyo*, about the Doolittle raid.

On a more heroic note, Errol Flynn almost defeats the Japanese singlehandedly in *Objective, Burma!*. John Wayne puts on fatigues in *Fighting Seabees*. He is given a much more difficult role in John Ford's *They Were Expendable*, where the director's devotion to the Navy arrives on the screen in full flower. That film, made before the end of the war but released after it, marks the end of the unit picture. In terms of plot, the unit is established before the story begins and is slowly broken apart over the course of the action. At the end, though, the ideals of the unit—obedience, sacrifice, duty—are intact.

For a time following VJ Day, the war in the Pacific remained a popular topic for Hollywood, and the films became more complex. *Home of the Brave*, from 1949, is one of the motion picture industry's first serious attempts to deal with racial matters. *Sands of Iwo Jima*, made the same year, establishes John Wayne's reputation as a war hero, and was used by the Marines to promote the construction of the Marine Corps War Memorial at Arlington Cemetery. Wayne returns to the Corps in *Flying Leathernecks*, millionaire Howard Hughes's

attempt to incorporate real combat footage with a fictional story. The Marines also gave full cooperation to Raoul Walsh for his adaption of Leon Uris's immensely popular best-seller *Battle Cry*. It's a grand, sprawling mess of a movie that has much more to say about the 1950s than about the war.

In the post-war years, the Navy fared well with Henry Fonda as *Mister Roberts*, the role he'd made his own on stage. Burt Lancaster and Clark Gable are well matched antogonists in *Run Silent Run Deep*, still one of the best submarine adventures. If *The Gallant Hours* is a bit too pious for its own good, James Cagney is excellent as Adm. "Bull" Halsey. Of the other reality-based Pacific films, *Above and Beyond* is about the dropping of the first atomic bomb; *Merrill's Marauders* is a relatively restrained effort from Sam Fuller; and *Tora! Tora! Tora!* shows the attack on Pearl Harbor from both the Japanese and American sides.

The exotic locales of the Pacific have also given rise to less easily categorized films. Kon Ichikawa's *Fires On the Plain* views the last days of the war through the eyes of a defeated, dying Japanese soldier. It is an astonishing work. John Boorman's *Hell in the Pacific* is a two-man psychodrama, with Lee Marvin and Toshiro Mifune as combative castaways. Finally, Terrence Malick's *The Thin Red Line* turns James Jones's novel of Guadalcanal into a meditation on love, life, memory, and innocence with an incongruously star-studded cast. In the process, he apparently means to deconstruct the unit picture, but the result is an often attractive muddle.

ABOVE AND BEYOND

1953 Melvin Frank, Norman Panama ♪♪♪

> "We may have to hit Germany and Japan direct from U.S. possessions, and that means an airplane with range—real range, and Hap Arnold thinks we've got just the baby that can do it. Boeing designed it. It's called the B-29 and it'll fly higher, faster, and farther than any bomber you ever dreamed about. But there's one little hitch. The B-29 is a death trap."
>
> **Maj. Brent (Larry Keating)**

> "If enough women in enough places do enough talking, someone's going to find out something we don't want them to know."
>
> **Security officer Maj. Uanna (James Whitmore)**

> "Enola, what a funny name, I kept thinking. Enola. Backwards it spelled 'alone.' I guess that's why I thought of it. I never felt more alone in my entire life."
>
> **Lucy Tibbets's (Eleanor Parker) voice-over as she goes into labor and drives herself to the hospital**

Note:

It is somehow altogether appropriate that Jim Backus, so famous as the voice of Mr. Magoo and as Thurston Howell III on *Gilligan's Island,* should portray Gen. Curtis LeMay, George Wallace's vice-presidential running mate who, in 1968, vowed that he would "nuke North Vietnam back into the stone age" if elected.

What is it about Air Force single-mission stories that inspires directors to make films about marriage? That, inexplicably, is the case with *Thirty Seconds over Tokyo*, about the Doolittle raid, and with *Above and Beyond*, about the dropping of the first atomic bomb on Hiroshima. In both, the inner workings of the operation are no more important than the hero's domestic turmoil.

After a foreword to remind audiences of the subject, Lucy Tibbets (Eleanor Parker) explains in voice-over how worried she is about divorce. It's 1945 but she traces the problem back to 1943, when her husband Paul (Robert Taylor) is flying bombers in North Africa. That's also where and when Col. Tibbets is put in charge of "Operation Silverplate," which will deliver a new secret weapon, still under development. The first thing that he learns is the unprecedented need for secrecy concerning the project. If he forgets, he's got Maj. Uanna (James Whitmore) to remind him.

The situation is so delicate that when he is transferred to a remote air base in the high Utah desert, Lucy practically has to invite herself and their two young children to join him. Even then, her husband tells her that the scientists wearing white coveralls and lab coats are "sanitation engineers." Tibbets's mission is twofold. First, he must test fly the new B-29 bomber, and then when the atomic bomb nears completion, he is involved in determining the details of its detonation. That potentially fascinating part of the story is shown mostly in montage sequences, which are intercut with Lucy's growing dissatisfaction with her husband's refusal to tell her anything about what he does.

That marital unhappiness, however exaggerated, must reflect the emotional stresses that the war placed on many couples. But it never rings completely true—in large part because Eleanor Parker's performance is so overly dramatic. She affects precise, vaguely British diction that robs the important emotional moments of any believability. Taylor's responsibility is much easier to handle. In those same emotional moments, he is called upon to look stern and keep his mouth shut. In short, what we have here is failure to communicate. When the characters do try to talk, the script does them few favors. Punctuated with unintentional humor (see quotes), only at the very end does the writing come to terms with its subject.

The dropping of the bomb itself—that moment when the genie is unleashed—is appropriately frightening and awesome. The combination of special effects and real footage is remarkably moving, and its impact on the crew is clear. After he has returned from his successful mission, Col. Tibbets is surrounded by reporters. One demands to know what it's like. "You've just dropped a bomb that's killed 80,000 people," he says. "My readers want to now how you feel about it."

"How do they feel about it," Tibbet answers, his face revealing his own mixed emotions and the responsibility that the entire country must share. The filmmakers

See also
Thirty Seconds over Tokyo
Twelve O'Clock High
The Right Stuff

do not address the political questions that have been brought up in recent years, but, whenever they get around to it, they do deal honestly with the individual and collective emotions involved in this kind of mass destruction.

Col. Paul Tibbetts (Robert Taylor) learns of his mission in *Above and Beyond.* The Kobal Collection

Cast: Robert Taylor (Col. Paul Tibbetts), Eleanor Parker (Lucy Tibbetts), James Whitmore (Maj. Uanna), Larry Keating (Maj. Vernon C. Brent), Larry Gates (Capt. Parsons), Robert Burton (Gen. Samuel E. Roberts), Jim Backus (Gen. Curtis E. LeMay), Marilyn Erskine (Marge Bratton), Steve Dunne (Maj. Harry Bratton), John Pickard (Miller), Hayden Rorke (Dr. Ramsey), Lawrence Dobkin (Dr. Van Dyke), Jack Raine (Dr. Fiske), Jeff Richards (Thomas Ferebee), Barbara Ruick (Mary Malone), Harlan Warde (Chaplain Downey), John Close (Co-pilot), Frank Gerstle (Sgt. Wilson), Dabbs Greer (Haddock), Ewing Mitchell (Gen. Wolfe), Gregory Walcott (Burns), John Baer (Captain), Jonathon Cott (Dutch Van Kirk), Dick Simmons (Bob Lewis), John McKee (Wyatt Duzenbury), G. Pat Collins (Maj. Gen. Creston), John Hedloe (Lt. Malone), Mack Williams (Col. Bill Irvine), Dorothy Kennedy (Nurse); **Written by:** Melvin Frank, Norman Panama, Beirne Lay Jr.; **Cinematography by:** Ray June; **Music by:** Hugo Friedhofer; **Technical Advisor:** Maj. James B. Bean, Lt. Col. Charles E.H. Begg, Maj. Norman W. Ray. **Producer:** Melvin Frank, Norman Panama; released by MGM. **Awards:** Nominations: Academy Awards '53: Best Story, Best Original Dramatic Score. **Running Time:** 122 minutes. **Format:** VHS.

AIR FORCE

1943 Howard Hawks ♪♪♪♪

Though Howard Hawks's adventure opens with a quote from Lincoln's Gettysburg Address, that's not really the tone of high seriousness he's aiming for. As the title suggests, *Air Force* is a flying road movie that traces the highly improbable but fact-based adventures of one B-17 flying fortress in the first days of the war.

On December 6, 1941, the *Mary Ann* is one of nine bombers that fly from San Francisco to Hickam Field, Hawaii. In charge is Capt. "Irish" Quincannon (John Ridgely); the co-pilot is Lt. Bill Williams (Gig Young). The new guy who joins the crew just before the flight is Lt. Winocki (John Garfield), a cynic with a secret in his past who's counting the days until he can leave the Army Air Force. Lt. "Monk" Hauser (Charles Drake), the navigator, will never live up to the legacy of his father, who flew with the Lafayette Escadrille in World War I. Pvt. Chester (Ray Montgomery), the new radioman, has a teary farewell with his mother on the runway. Cpl. Weinberg (George Tobias), the obligatory New Yorker, provides comic relief. Sgt. White (Harry Carey Sr.) is the mechanic who keeps *Mary Ann* in the air no matter what. The ensemble may sound familiar—the same sort of group has certainly been brought together often enough—but before it's over, these guys become more believable than most. And before it's over, they go through a lot.

> "We all belong to this airplane."
>
> **Capt. "Irish" Quincannon (John Ridgely) to his crew**

> "Maybe the story is high-flown, maybe it overdraws a recorded fact a bit. We'd hate to think it couldn't happen—or didn't—because it certainly leaves you feeling awfully good."
>
> **Bosley Crowther, *New York Times*, February 7, 1943**

The Japanese attack while the plane is en route to Hawaii. As soon as they land, they're ordered to continue west, to Wake Island for refueling and then on to the Philippines, where the next attack is expected. Fighter jock Lt. Rader (James Brown) hitches a ride. From that moment, *Air Force* is a series of out-of-the-frying-pan-and-into-the-fire episodes as the plane and the crew become more deeply involved in the opening conflicts of the war. Though the film is more than two hours long, it never seems slow because director Howard Hawks and writers Dudley Nichols and an uncredited William Faulkner keep things moving so swiftly. The veteran Nichols (*The Lost Patrol*, *The Informer*, *Stagecoach*, *Bringing Up Baby*) and Faulkner, who's listed as dialogue director and reportedly created two scenes, keep the ensemble balanced. The script moves among the characters and reveals their quirks and conflicts gradually as tumultuous events explode around them and they are transformed from a group of individuals into a cohesive unit.

Though most of the landing and take-off scenes are accomplished with special effects that seem far too obvious today, Hawks uses real airplanes whenever he can. He also films some scenes inside a B-17, and the sets used to re-create aircraft interiors have a realistic feeling, too. Hawks had been a pilot in the first World War and had already proven himself with two of the best aviation films, *Dawn Patrol* and *Only Angels Have Wings*, before he came to this one. All that experience keeps the incredulity of the plot from overpowering the audience's disbelief, because, as silly as it sometimes seems, *Air Force* is hugely entertaining. The aerial combat scenes in the second half are superb, though again, some contemporary viewers may be bothered by the jarring difference between the actual footage and the effects.

That criticism misses the point. The film is a fantasy based on real events, and meant to uplift audiences in 1943. It still does.

See also
Thirty Seconds over Tokyo
Memphis Belle
Twelve O'Clock High
Dr. Strangelove

John Garfield struggles to get himself and an injured crew member home safely in *Air Force*. The Kobal Collection

Cast: John Garfield (Sgt. Winocki), John Ridgely (Capt. Quincannon), Gig Young (Lt. Bill Williams), Arthur Kennedy (Lt. Tommy McMartin), Charles Drake (Lt. Hauser), Harry Carey Sr. (Sgt. White), George Tobias (Cpl. Weinberg), Ray Montgomery (Pvt. Chester), James Brown (Lt. Rader), Stanley Ridges (Maj. Mallory), Willard Robertson (Colonel), Moroni Olsen (Commanding Officer), Edward Brophy (Sgt. Callahan), Richard Lane (Maj. Roberts), Faye Emerson (Susan McMartin), Addison Richards (Maj. Daniels), James Flavin (Maj. Bagley), Ann Doran (Mary Quincannon), Dorothy Peterson (Mrs. Chester), William Forrest (Cmdr. Harper), Ward Wood (Cpl. Peterson); **Written by:** Dudley Nichols, William Faulkner; **Cinematography by:** James Wong Howe, Elmer Dyer, Charles A. Marshall; **Music by:** Franz Waxman. **Producer:** Hal B. Wallis, Warner Bros. **Awards:** Academy Awards '43: Best Film Editing; Nominations: Academy Awards '43: Best Black and White Cinematography, Best Original Screenplay. **Running Time:** 124 minutes. **Format:** VHS, Closed Caption.

The Hound Salutes: Howard Hawks

When discussing the early years of Hollywood, it's easy to fall into the "There Were Giants in Those Days" way of thinking. Director Howard Hawks is the perfect example. He's one of those near-mythic figures whose life off-screen was more eventful than most of his films. Complicating matters, according to most sources, including his biographer Todd McCarthy, Hawks was a facile liar who revised his past regularly and often, particularly in his later years. Because he was such a gifted craftsman, he worked—and worked well—in almost all genres.

He made comedies (*Bringing Up Baby*), gangster movies (*Scarface*), thrillers (*The Big Sleep*), adventures (*Hatari!*), westerns (*Red River*), and science-fiction (*The Thing*). His work is so varied that his reputation is that of a generalist. Of course, for those who appreciate good Hollywood storytelling, there's nothing wrong with being a generalist. Hawks was at the top of his form in the 1930s and '40s, and so the war film is one area where his contribution is easy to see. He made three of the most important.

The first was his first sound picture, the 1930 version of *Dawn Patrol* (still unavailable on home video). During the production of it, he engaged in a series of struggles with millionaire Howard Hughes, who was retooling his own *Hell's Angels* from silent to sound at the time and didn't want to compete with Hawks at the boxoffice. When *Dawn Patrol* was remade in 1938, many of the effects from the original were simply incorporated into the new footage.

Sergeant York, his second war film, was the biggest critical and commercial success of Hawks's career. The story of a religious pacifist turned World War I hero, played by Gary Cooper, was the right film at the right time. Though the country was divided on participation in the war before Pearl Harbor, the film touched a chord. Initial reviews were all glowing; ticket-sales records were shattered. Cooper won an Academy Award; Hawks received his only nomination. Curiously, Howard Hughes figured in Hawks's participation in the film. If the millionaire hadn't fired him from *The Outlaw*, Hawks might not have been available when the other pieces of the *Sergeant York* production fell into place.

His third significant war film, *Air Force*, was another piece of propaganda. Along with such early efforts as *Bataan* and *Wake Island*, it created the formula for the World War II unit picture, the story of a group of men who subsume their individuality to form an efficient fighting force. The troubled production ran into many problems on the Florida locations, including lack of proper lighting, killer heat, and massive swarms of insects that delayed night shooting. Then, toward the end of the schedule, William Faulkner was brought in to rewrite one crucial death scene and add comic relief to another moment. Finally, Hawks's long-standing personal difficulties with producer Hal Wallis came to a head. Despite all that, the film is still one of Hawks's most entertaining works.

Hawks also worked with war and aviation themes in *Today We Live* (1933), *Road to Glory* (1936), and *Only Angels Have Wings* (1939), but his trilogy made in the 1940s is his key contribution.

Books:

Howard Hawks: The Grey Fox of Hollywood. Todd McCarthy. Grove Press. 1997.

Hawks on Hawks. Joseph McBride. University of California Press. 1982.

Howard Hawks: Storyteller. Gerald Mast. Oxford University Press. 1982.

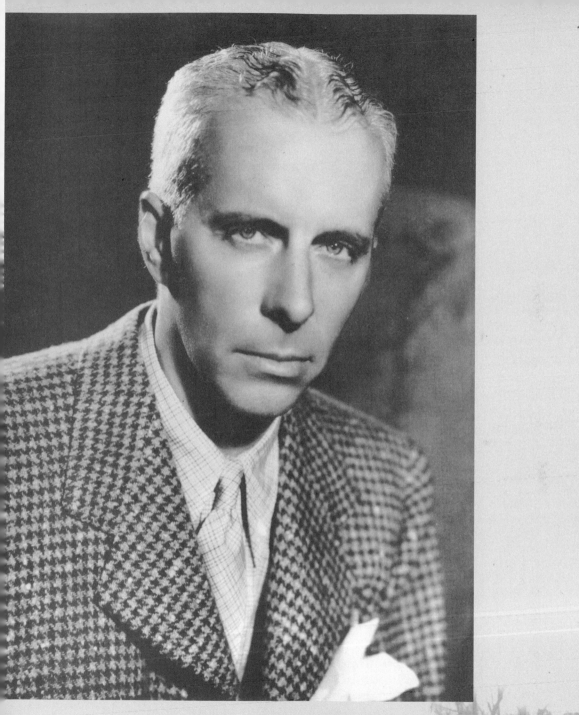

Howard Hawks The Kobal Collection

BATAAN

1943 Tay Garnett ♪♪♪♪

Today, the most surprising things about this flag-waving propaganda are the brutality of its violence and the straightforward nature of the simple story. Remember that in 1943, the fall of the Philippines following the attack on Pearl Harbor was a vivid, painful memory to American audiences. *Bataan* is an attempt—a successful attempt—to turn that military defeat into an emotional victory. From the beginning, viewers know that it's going to end badly for the brave, scrappy Americans who are valiantly holding out against the (insert derogatory racial epithet here) Japs. The dramatic questions then are: How will they die and in what order?

The makeshift group itself is a prototype of the ethnic and geographic melting pot that would become so familiar in the films of World War II. First off, there's Puckett (Robert Walker), the lanky Navy musician who inexplicably finds himself in an Army unit. Malloy (Tom Dugan) is the irascible old cook. Matowski (Barry Nelson) and Eeps (Kenneth Spencer), the lone black guy, are both demolitions experts. Hardy (Phillip Terry) is the medic. Salazar (Alex Havier), a Filipino, is a boxer. Ramirez (Desi Arnaz, yes, *that* Desi Arnaz) is a jitterbugging Los Angeleno. Cpl. Todd (Lloyd Nolan) has a guilty secret in his past. Cpl. Feingold (Thomas Mitchell) has been with Sgt.

Dane (Robert Taylor) for years. Lt. Bentley (George Murphy) is trying to get his biplane ready to fly. Capt. Lassiter (Lee Bowman) is in charge, but he's one of the first to check out, leaving Dane at the helm. Their mission is to keep the advancing Japanese from crossing a bridge over a deep vertiginous canyon as long as possible to give MacArthur's troops time to evacuate.

> "To those immortal dead, who heroically stayed the wave of barbaric conquest, this picture is reverently dedicated."
>
> **Onscreen introduction**

The bridge and the canyon are created by a few well-chosen special effects that are remarkably sophisticated for the day. Almost all of the action takes place on a set that represents a jungle clearing. It's just as effective as many of the contemporaneous jungle pictures that were made outdoors, usually on California exteriors. The film works well and has remained a perennial audience favorite for three reasons.

First, it is wonderfully cast. Though Robert Taylor is normally associated with lighter, more polished comedies and melodramas, he has all the grit and determination that the role requires. It takes a particular combination of the common touch and authority to play a convincing noncom. Burt Lancaster nails it perfectly in *From Here to Eternity*, and Taylor does almost as well here. Lloyd Nolan is fine as the black sheep who will redeem himself, and the other members of the ensemble all manage to make their characters stand out.

Second, Robert Andrews's script gives them excellent material to work with. By now everyone knows the drill. Within minutes of telling the others about life back home, or his wife, or his new baby, a guy is sure to catch a bullet. But the stories don't go on too long; they're interesting, and the stickier emotions are mostly avoided. Finally, Tay Garnett's direction crackles. A veteran of both the Navy Air Service and silent comedies, he was a respected journeyman filmmaker at the top of his game when he made *Bataan*. He handles the steadily intensifying physical violence without frills, putting the hand-to-hand combat scenes right in front of the camera. He and Andrews also give the film a dark, understated streak of humor. Notice the grim visual joke they play in the background of the film's final shot.

See also

Seven Samurai
The Dirty Dozen
From Here to Eternity
Air Force
Fires on the Plain

WORLD WAR II: PACIFIC THEATER

Robert Walker (right), Desi
Arnaz (aiming gun), and George
Murphy (left) in *Bataan*. The Kobal
Collection

Cast: Robert Taylor (Sgt. Bill Dane), George Murphy (Lt. Steve Bentley), Thomas Mitchell (Cpl. Jake Fein-gold), Desi Arnaz Sr. (Felix Ramirez), Lee Bowman (Capt. Henry Lassiter), Lloyd Nolan (Cpl. Barney Todd/Danny Burns), Robert Walker (Leonard Puckett), Barry Nelson (F.X. Matowski), Phillip Terry (Matthew Hardy), Tom Dugan (Sam Malloy), Roque Espiritu (Cpl. Juan Katigbak), Kenneth Spencer (Wesley Eeps), Alex Havier (Yankee Salazar), Donald Curtis (Lieutenant), Lynne Carver (Nurse), Bud Geary (Infantry soldier), Dorothy Morris (Nurse); **Written by:** Robert D. Andrews; **Cinematography by:** Sidney Wagner; **Music by:** Bronislau Kaper, Eric Zeisl; **Technical Advisor:** L.S. Chappelear. **Producer:** Irving Starr, MGM, Loew's, Inc. **Running Time:** 115 minutes. **Format:** VHS, Beta.

BATTLE CRY
1955 Raoul Walsh ♫♫♫

In the back seat of a convertible parked on a dark street somewhere near Hollywood, *From Here to Eternity* and *Peyton Place* were locked in a steamy embrace. Straps unstrapped, buttons unbuttoned, zippers ripped open. Nine months later, *Battle Cry* hit theaters.

Leon Uris's adaptation of his own best-selling novel is, in many ways, the perfect mid-'50s war movie. First, it is so worshipful toward the military—specifically the Marines—that it's a two and a half hour "the few, the proud" recruiting commercial. All unpleasant aspects of life in the service are ignored and the positive ones are celebrated, though they are less important than the young characters' sexual initiation. The film's coy evasiveness in sexual matters may seem dated and a little embarrassing now, but to leave it at that misses a larger point. The film struck the right note in 1955. It was a huge commercial hit, number three at the boxoffice that year, and so it was showing people something that they wanted to see. What was that?

> "You think I'm a tramp, don't you, Danny?"
> **Mrs. Yarborough (Dorothy Malone)**

> "Talk about your iron men, these kids are tougher. They're a new metal!"
> **Maj. Wellman (Carleton Young) on Maj. Huxley's (Van Heflin) Marines**

The story begins in January 1942, with new enlistees making their way west by train to basic training in San Diego. Andy Hookens (Aldo Ray) is the lady-killing lumberjack from Washington state; Ski (William Campbell) can barely stand to leave his girl back in Philadelphia; Hotchkiss (John Lupton) is the bookish guy; Forrester (Tab Hunter) is the hunky boy-next-door from Baltimore. Eventually, they (and several others) find themselves under the tough-but-fair guidance of Sgt. Mac (James Whitmore), who's also our narrator. The boss of the outfit is Maj. Sam "Highpockets" Huxley (Van Heflin), fair-but-tough.

The kids are fresh out of boot camp, which is given barely a glance by Uris and director Raoul Walsh, when the focus shifts to their after-hours activities. Danny Forrester runs into the married but eminently available Mrs. Yarborough (Dorothy Malone) at the USO and forgets about Kathy (Mona Freeman) back home. Hotchkiss runs into Rae (Anne Francis) on the Coronodo Ferry. She likes his writing so they're chaste and pure. Hookens has to wait until they ship out to New Zealand before he can meet Pat Rogers (Nancy Olson). Throughout, the acting is true to its era and to the often banal dialogue. The men tend to be stiff-backed, even in relaxed situations, and the women are breathless and dewy-eyed.

Did you Know?
Character actor Justus E. McQueen was so taken with the character he played that he adopted the name L.Q. Jones for himself. He has appeared in dozens of films, including *The Wild Bunch* and *Casino*.

As the trio of sexual relationships is being untangled, the guys march and learn radio communications. Walsh is in his element with those big outdoor scenes. Given the full cooperation of the Marines, the filmmakers had literally thousands of extras at their disposal. Walsh makes full use of them in several impressive scenes built around marching columns of men that stretch from horizon to horizon. Despite the title, the big combat scenes are reserved for the conclusion. Though they have a look of authenticity, they don't really compare to the same moments in the best of the '40s war movies—*Battleground*, *A Walk in the Sun*, *The Story of G.I. Joe*.

But then, those films shouldn't be judged against *Battle Cry*. It's a potboiler meant to turn the shared experience of World War II into light nostalgic entertainment. Underlying the various plot elements

See also
An Officer and a Gentleman
Full Metal Jacket
The Young Lions
From Here to Eternity
The Thin Red Line
Any episode of *Gomer Pyle*

is the idea that the war caused all of this behavior—good and bad—and so any indiscretion can be quickly forgiven. Besides, all of the right people wind up together, except for the guys who die, and they were brave Marines. In the end, the film ennobles the war, the military and, by extension, the audience. Seen today, it is an instructive example of time-capsule period escapism, slow but enjoyable enough for fans of the era.

Aldo Ray, Perry Lopez, Tab Hunter, and James Whitmore in *Battle Cry.* The Kobal Collection

Cast: Van Heflin (Maj. Sam Huxley), Aldo Ray (Andy Hookens), Mona Freeman (Kathy Walker), Tab Hunter (Dan Forrester), Dorothy Malone (Mrs. Elaine Yarborough), Anne Francis (Rae), James Whitmore (Sgt. Mac/Narrator), Raymond Massey (Gen. Snipes), William Campbell (Ski), John Lupton (Marion Hotchkiss), L.Q. (Justus E. McQueen) Jones (L.Q. Jones), Perry Lopez (Joe Gomez), Fess Parker (Speedy), Jonas Applegarth (Lighttower), Tommy Cook (Ziltch), Felix Noriego (Crazy Horse), Nancy Olson (Mrs. Pat Rogers), Susan Morrow (Susan), Carleton Young (Maj. Jim Wellman), Rhys Williams (Enoch Rogers), Gregory Walcott (Sgt. Jim Beller), Frank Ferguson (Mr. Hector Walker), Sarah Selby (Mrs. Forrester), Willis Bouchey (Mr. Forrester); **Written by:** Leon Uris; **Cinematography by:** Sid Hickox; **Music by:** Max Steiner; **Technical Advisor:** Lt. Col. H.P. Crowe. **Producer:** Raoul Walsh, Warner Bros. **Awards:** Nominations: Academy Awards '55: Best Original Dramatic Score. **Running Time:** 169 minutes. **Format:** VHS, Beta, LV, Letterbox, Closed Caption.

FIGHTING SEABEES

1944 Edward Ludwig 🦴🦴🦴

This furious, frivolous propagandistic potboiler has virtually nothing to do with the realities of the war in the Pacific, but it is one of John Wayne's major contributions to the cause. For that, if nothing else, it's worth a look because he turns in the familiar swaggering, bellicose performance that his fans love, and he even dances a brief jitterbug.

Wayne plays Wedge Donovan, the larger-than-life boss of a construction crew that's just finished a costly job for the Navy in the Pacific. When his men return home, he finds that several of them have been killed by the Japanese. According to Eddie Powers (William Frawley), they'd have been fine if the Navy had let them use weapons. Donovan is incensed until Lt. Cmdr. Yarrow (Dennie O'Keefe) explains why civilians in a combat zone cannot be armed. Then Yarrow asks for his assistance in creating a construction division for the Navy. Donovan agrees, but since he is "a hot-headed ape with a hair-trigger temper," it doesn't take long for him to become impatient with Navy regulations. Further complicating things between Donovan and Yarrow is reporter Connie Chesley (Susan Hayward), who's attracted to both.

Most of the plot, then, is a highly stylized version of the creation of the Navy's construction battalion, the "Seabees." Once the scene moves back to the Pacific Theater, the emphasis shifts to the "Fighting" part of the title. In that area, it is strictly a back-lot formula picture from the studio assembly line; lively enough, but not particularly involving. It's also casually racist, with moments that will set feminist teeth on edge, though it is pointless to be overly critical in that department. Virtually all of the characters—both the heroes and their enemies—are stereotypes. Donovan's men, for example, are a bunch of Irish brawlers who might have been left over from a lesser John Ford film. The exception in the group is Johnny Novasky (Leonid Kinskey, Sascha the bartender in *Casablanca*), who's tossed in for diversity. In essence, good guys are good guys and bad guys are "Tojo and his bug-eyed monkeys." Another character says, "We're not fighting men any more, we're fighting animals."

The romantic triangle is handled with the same broad brush strokes and lack of realism. The contorted plotting manages to place Donovan, Yarrow and Connie on the island in the middle of a Japanese attack, and the various "death" scenes leave no cliche unclutched. That said, liberated from the constraints of realism, writers Borden Chase and Aeneas MacKenzie manage to provide surprises right up until the end, and journeyman director Edward Ludwig never lets the pace flag. For undemanding nostalgic entertainment, *Fighting Seabees* isn't bad.

See also
Report from the Aleutians
Action in the North Atlantic
Sands of Iwo Jima

304 WORLD WAR II: PACIFIC THEATER

John Wayne (right) forms and leads a Navy construction unit in the early days of World War II in *The Fighting Seabees*. The Kobal Collection

Cast: John Wayne (Wedge Donovan), Susan Hayward (Constance Chesley), Dennis O'Keefe (Lt. Cmdr. Robert Yarrow), William Frawley (Eddie Powers), Grant Withers (Whanger Spreckles), Tom London (Johnson), Wally Wales (Seabee), Paul Fix (Ding Jacobs), William Forrest (Lt. Kerrick), J.M. Kerrigan (Sawyer Collins), Leonid Kinskey (Johnny Novasky), Duncan Renaldo (Juan), Addison Richards (Capt. Joyce), Ben Welden (Yump Lumkin), Crane Whitley (Refueling officer), Charles Trowbridge; **Written by:** Borden Chase, Aeneas MacKenzie; **Cinematography by:** William Bradford; **Music by:** Walter Scharf, Roy Webb. **Producer:** Republic. **Awards:** Nominations: Academy Awards '44: Best Original Dramatic Score. **Running Time:** 100 minutes. **Format:** VHS, Closed Caption.

THE FIGHTING SULLIVANS

The Sullivans

1942 Lloyd Bacon ♪♪♪

In many respects, this curious family drama barely qualifies as a war film. Virtually all of the action takes place in suburban Waterloo, Iowa; the Japanese attack on Pearl Harbor doesn't occur until the 90-minute mark; scenes of military service and combat are so abbreviated they seem almost an afterthought. Even so, *The Fighting Sullivans* is still an influential addition to Hollywood's mosaic of World War II.

Today, the story behind the film is known best for being a partial inspiration for Steven Spielberg's *Saving Private Ryan*. The five Sullivan brothers were all killed when their ship, the *Juneau*, was sunk off Guadalcanal. The family's loss was so extreme that the armed services decided that so many brothers would never again be assigned to the same ship or unit. Since 1944 audiences were completely familiar with the brothers' fate, the filmmakers decided to emphasize their childhood and the more sentimental aspects of their maturation.

It begins with five quick christenings as George, Matt, Joe, Frank, and Al are born to Mr. and Mrs. Sullivan (Thomas Mitchell and Selena Royle). Their boyhood is depicted as a slightly more domesticated version of the *Little Rascals*. The kids grow up in a rough suburban fantasyland where they hop fences, play around in railroad yards, and climb water towers. They're mischievous tykes whose first big adventure involves their trying to repair a junked rowboat. That overt foreshadowing is typical of director Lloyd Bacon's heavy hand with emotions. Subtle he is not.

> "A lot of people get married. Some of 'em even like it."
>
> **Al Sullivan (Edward Ryan)**

> "Before this war is over, plenty of people are going to find out that they can't always get what they want, that they gotta quit worrying about just takin' care of themselves. Like it or not."
>
> **Lt. Robinson (Ward Bond)**

When the brothers reach young manhood, the children who have been playing the roles are replaced by adults and the focus settles on the youngest, Al (Edward Ryan), and his courtship of Katherine Mary (Anne Baxter). His brothers give him a hard time about her, precipitating a minor crisis which is easily overcome. Other problems are hinted at but dropped until that fateful Sunday morning when the family is sitting around the radio and hears the news.

Veteran director Lloyd Bacon was most comfortable with middle-of-the-road escapist fare (*42nd Street*, *Knute Rockne—All American*, *It Happens Every Spring*) and that's the way he handles the material. He's right to do so. It's difficult to manage large groups of individuals in scenes that are set in small rooms, and in almost every pivotal moment, space has to be made for at least five actors and the camera. The film looks and feels like a TV sitcom, an early pilot episode for *My Three Sons* or *Ozzie and Harriet*. The story really ends when the boys leave to go into the Navy. Whatever changes they must have gone through in adapting to that larger family are left out.

The conclusion, though, comes when the Navy's Lt. Robinson (Ward Bond) delivers the news to the parents. The emotional weight of that moment doesn't seem nearly as devastating as it does in *Saving Private Ryan*, but that is the difference between then and now. Audiences in 1944 were just as moved as they were in 1998. The sentiment is simply expressed differently.

Today, the film's aggressive innocence makes it a first-rate exercise in nostalgia.

See also

Three Came Home
Guadalcanal Diary
It's a Wonderful Life

The Sullivan family listens to
the news of the Japanese attack
on Pearl Harbor in *The Fighting
Sullivans*. Anne Baxter (holding
baby) and Edward Ryan (left),
Thomas Mitchell (second center)

Cast: Anne Baxter (Katherine Mary Sullivan), Thomas Mitchell (Mr. Sullivan), Selena Royle (Mrs. Sullivan), Eddie Ryan (Al Sullivan), Trudy Marshall (Genevieve Sullivan), James B. Cardwell (George Sullivan), Roy Roberts (Father Francis), Ward Bond (Lt. Robinson), Mary McCarty (Gladys), Bobby Driscoll (Al Sullivan, as a child), Addison Richards (Naval Captain), Selmer Jackson (Damage Control Officer), Mae Marsh (Woman), Harry Strang (Chief Petty Officer), Barbara Brown (Nurse), George Offerman Jr. (Joe Sullivan), John Campbell (Frank Sullivan), John Alvin (Matt Sullivan), Patrick Curtis (Joe Sullivan as a child), Nancy June Robinson (Genevieve Sullivan as a child), Marvin Davis (Frank as a child); **Written by:** Edward Doherty, Mary C. McCall, Jules Schermer; **Cinematography by:** Lucien N. Andriot; **Music by:** Cyril Mockridge, Alfred Newman. **Producer:** 20th Century-Fox. **Running Time:** 110 minutes. **Format:** VHS.

THE FIGHTING SULLIVANS

FIRES ON THE PLAIN
Nobi
1959 Kon Ichikawa ♪♪♪♪

Kon Ichikawa translates the experience of a Japanese soldier in the last year of World War II into a harrowing horror film. Nothing quite like it exists in American or European cinema, though other stories of defeat deal with the same emotions. This defeat is so devastating, so total and, finally, so intimate that it is difficult to describe.

Near the beginning, the main character, Tamura (Eiji Funakoshi) states in deadpan voiceover, "I was told to die, and I intend to. Why run, then?" Why indeed? It's 1945, the Philippines. American shelling has reduced Tamura's brigade to platoon strength. Racked with tuberculosis, the infantryman is ordered by his commander to go to the hospital, which has already returned him to his unit once. But conditions are so extreme at the hospital that the doctors won't admit anyone who doesn't bring his own rations. Too weak to fight, he hangs around outside the hospital and vows that he will pull the pin on his last grenade when all hope is lost. But nothing works out properly and Tamura sets off on an episodic journey/retreat from Leyte to Cebu.

Ichikawa paces the action deliberately, giving the film a dreamlike atmosphere. Tamura wanders from one horror to another, often encountering huge numbers of grotesquely distorted and dismembered bodies. It's a landscape where the dead far outnumber the living, and those who are left have reached the end physically and emotionally. Toward the end, Tamura falls in with two other soldiers, Yasuda (Osamu Takizawa), who's still trying to make the best of the situation by selling tobacco, and Nagamatsu (Mickey Curtis), his helper. It's tempting to see the conflicts that develop among them as an allegory for the Japanese military failure, but that's far too simple. The film works on several levels, both realistic and symbolic, but Ichikawa's overriding point is the absolute horror of war, finally taking his characters' descent down to a level that can only be defined as subhuman. At several significant moments, he seems to acknowledge Japanese guilt for the barbarous acts and atrocities committed against Philippine civilians, but the film makes no clear-cut political statements. The title has a double meaning, referring to American shelling and to a soldier's fond memory of farmers' harvest back home.

Working with cinematographers Setsuo Kobayashi and Setsuo Shibata, Ichikawa creates a series of striking widescreen black-and-white images, often filling the center of the frame with extreme closeups, or surrounding small solitary figures with a vast nightmarish wilderness. (Other critics complain that various tape editions of the film are poorly cropped, pan-and-scan translations. This review is based on the Home Vision Cinema cassette, which is letterboxed to the original DaieiScope proportions and clearly subtitled.) In Japan, Ichikawa is also known for his comedies, and despite its subject, this film has moments of grim humor, too. One long sequence involving boots and mud is a brilliant set piece told completely without dialogue.

It is only one moment, though, and does nothing to dilute Ichikawa's indictment of war. His vision is so clear and powerful that its most potent images will linger in memory after the heroics of most combat films have been long forgotten.

See also
Bridge on the River Kwai
A Time to Love and a Time to Die
The Red Badge of Courage
Apocalypse Now
The Hidden Fortress
Bataan
Come and See

Japanese soldiers suffer through the chaos of the Phillippine retreat during the last days of World War II in *Fires on the Plain*. The Kobal Collection

Cast: Eiji Funakoshi (Tamura), Osamu Takizawa (Yasuda), Mickey Curtis (Nagamatsu), Asao Sano (Soldier), Kyu Sazanka (Army surgeon), Yoshihiro Hamaguchi (Officer), Hikaru Hoshi (Soldier), Yasushi Sugita (Soldier), Masaya Tsukida (Soldier), Mantaro Ushio (Sergeant); **Written by:** Natto Wada; **Cinematography by:** Setsuo Kobayashi, Setsuo Shibata; **Music by:** Yashushi Akutagawa. **Producer:** Masaichi Nagata. **Japanese. Running Time:** 105 minutes. **Format:** VHS, Beta.

FIRES ON THE PLAIN

FLYING LEATHERNECKS

1951 Nicholas Ray 🦴🦴🦴

As the story goes, legendary Howard Hughes had the rights to some excellent Technicolor documentary footage of ground and air combat in the Pacific. After he bought controlling interest in the RKO Studio in 1948, he had a script written to build a story around the film he already owned. *Flying Leathernecks* is the somewhat disappointing result. The main problem is that director Nicholas Ray is never able to fully incorporate the archival film with his fiction. The air combat shots, apparently taken from nose cameras, are impressive, but they obviously have nothing to do with the inserts of grimacing pilots in model cockpits. In other words, Ray never really puts the viewer in the airplane the way the best flying films do. Nothing here comes close to *The Blue Max* or even Hughes's own *Hell's Angels*.

The ground-based conflicts are more interesting. In 1942, Maj. Daniel Xavier Kirby (John Wayne) takes over Marine Flying Squadron VMF247 on the eve of its departure for Guadalcanal. Executive officer Capt. Carl "Griff" Griffin (Robert Ryan) had hoped to be promoted into the job, but his previous boss had thought him too soft for the job. Soon, Kirby shares the opinion. As he sees the situation, Griffin cares too much about the pilots as individuals to enforce the discipline necessary for survival. For his part, Griffin thinks that Kirby is needlessly tough on the men, pushing them beyond their limits. Most fans don't need to know any more to predict the ending.

Most of the aerial action involves "close air support of ground troops" with fighter planes flying at treetop level strafing and bombing enemy troops while the Americans are only a few yards away. In the film's terminology, the "fly guys" are helping out the "mud Marines." It's difficult work that threatens the ground forces with friendly fire, and the brass is not completely sold on the idea. Maj. Kirby means to persuade them, after a brief stateside visit with his wife Joan (Janis Carter) and young son (Gordon Gebert).

Throughout, the archival footage focuses on the destruction of Japanese ships and fortifications, and much of it is spectacular. But the dividing line between the new work and the old is never in doubt. Ray tells his part of the story in conventional early '50s style, never trying to emulate the handheld camera movement and grainy immediacy of the real combat film. Despite that glaring lapse, he still gets fine performances from his stars. Wayne's familiar roughhewn heroics play well against Ryan's angry intensity, even if everyone in the audience understands that they're going to wind up on the same side by the last reel. To be fair, war films were never Ray's forte; he was more comfortable with the darker shadings of *Rebel Without a Cause* and *Johnny Guitar*. That kind of complexity has no place in your basic John Wayne war movie and that's what *Flying Leathernecks* is.

See also

Dawn Patrol
Hell's Angels
Command Decision
The Blue Max

Capt. Griffin (Robert Ryan, left) forcibly restrains Lt. Malotke (Adam Williams) from taking off alone while commanding officer Maj. Kirby (John Wayne) looks on in *Flying Leathernecks*. The Kobal Collection

Cast: John Wayne (Maj. Dan Kirby), Robert Ryan (Capt. Carl "Griff" Griffin), Janis Carter (Joan Kirby), Don Taylor (Lt. "Cowboy" Blithe), James Bell (Colonel), James Dobson (Pudge McCabe), Jay C. Flippen (M. Sgt. Clancy), Gordon Gebert (Tommy Kirby), William Harrigan (Lt. Cmdr. Curan), Brett King (Lt. Ernie Stark), Adam Williams (Lt. Malotke), Carleton Young (Capt. McAllister), Dick Wessel (Mess Sergeant), Gail Davis (Virginia Blithe), Harlan Warde (Admiral's Aide), Michael (Steve Flagg) St. Angel (Lt. Jorgensen), Maurice Jara (Shorty Vegay), John Mallory (Lt. Black), Britt Nelson (Lt. Tanner), Lynn Stalmaster (Lt. Castle); **Written by:** Kenneth Gamet, James Edward Grant; **Cinematography by:** William E. Snyder; **Music by:** Roy Webb. **Producer:** Edmund Grainger, RKO. **Running Time:** 102 minutes. **Format:** VHS, Beta, LV.

The Hound Salutes: Robert Ryan

Whatever the prevailing emotion of a scene, Robert Ryan brought a spark of anger to it. Sometimes it was full-blown rage. More often it was irritation poorly masked by civility, but it was always there, adding another level of energy to whatever conflict was taking place. Because of it, Ryan often played villains or unsympathetic characters, and he was cast in many crime and war films. His career really didn't take off until after World War II, where he served with the Marines, but he made his stage debut in 1939. Before that, he'd been a heavyweight boxing champion in college at Dartmouth.

In Hollywood, he was signed to a contract by RKO studios, and a quick glance at the titles of his films in the '40s and '50s shows that he was often cast in the grittier, noir-tinged dramas: *The Crooked Road*, *Act of Violence*, *Caught*, *The Set-Up*, *The Woman on Pier 13*, *Clash by Night*, *Beware My Lovely*, *The Secret Fury*, *Born to Be Bad*, *The Naked Spur*, *Inferno*, *House of Bamboo*, *Odds Against Tomorrow*.

In war films, Ryan was the kind-hearted officer who was toughened up by John Wayne in *Flying Leathernecks*, the lieutenant trying to do the right things for his lost patrol in *Men in War*, Gen. James Gavin in *The Longest Day* (Ryan O'Neal would play the same character in *A Bridge Too Far*), and Lee Marvin's nemesis in *The Dirty Dozen*. *Men in War* is by far his best work in that group. He's also a memorable villain in *Bad Day at Black Rock*, as the leader of a town with a secret when returning veteran Spencer Tracy arrives and asks uncomfortable questions. Ryan was nominated for an Oscar for his portrayal of an anti-Semitic veteran in *Crossfire*. Toward the end of his career, he was perfectly cast in *The Wild Bunch* as Deke Thornton, the outlaw turned reluctant lawman hunting his old partner. The complex, sad role completes the film's themes of betrayal and honor.

By all accounts, Robert Ryan was intensely private off screen, though he was an active supporter of the ACLU and other liberal causes. He died in 1973.

Robert Montgomery's final feature is a cinematic hagiography. It's obvious from the opening second that he and co-producer James Cagney intend to venerate their subject, Adm. William F. "Bull" Halsey, and that's exactly what they do. Their methods, however, are so unusual as to border on the experimental. This is a war movie without battle scenes, indeed without any physical action, and yet the filmmakers still employ a voice-over narrator (Art Gilmore) to lead viewers through the simple story, commenting on individual characters and filling in the blanks.

They begin on November 22, 1945 at the Admiral's (Cagney) retirement aboard a battleship. After a brief ceremony, he goes to his quarters to change into civilian clothes, as tradition demands, and to reminisce on his career. He focuses on the early days of the war, specifically his taking command of Pacific operations during the battle of Guadalcanal. With the assistance of a few trusted aides, including his pilot (Dennis Weaver), Halsey embarks upon a risky strategy to turn the tide of the war.

As Halsey is revealed, his personal life, decision-making process, and leadership qualities are constantly compared to his Japanese counterpart, Adm. Yamamoto (James T. Goto, also a technical advisor). The parallels between the two are presented without subtlety, though the filmmakers have to alter timelines to make one important dramatic point about each side's efforts to eliminate the other leader. Montgomery and writers Frank D. Gilroy and Beirne Lay Jr. give the Japanese characters the same kid glove treatment that the Americans receive because the film is not pro-American propaganda, it is pro-military propaganda. Halsey is the subject, but Montgomery's admiration for the Navy crosses national boundaries.

The use of the omniscient narrator gives the film a false air of objectivity and accuracy. To a man, these guys are tough, intelligent, dedicated, compassionate, resourceful, and each of them gives 150% all the time. Surrounding them is one of the strangest musical scores ever used in a mainstream Hollywood film. Composed by Roger Wagner and sung by his Chorale, it sounds like it comes from the Mormon Tabernacle Choir. In this context, it gives the film a religiosity that's inappropriate, at best.

On the other side of the ledger, James Cagney—incapable of a bad performance—delivers one of the most tightly controlled of his career. Though his most strenuous activity is strolling into a bomb shelter, he is able to convey Halsey's passion for his job in more subtle ways. Most importantly, he is able to focus on any man he's talking to with total attention. That is certainly one key characteristic of leadership, and Cagney makes it the center of Halsey's character. His commitment to his men and his genuine empathy with their losses both seem absolutely believable.

See also
Twelve O'Clock High
Sink the Bismarck!
Battle of Midway

In the end, *The Gallant Hours* is too one-dimensionally praiseful and static to recommend it to most viewers. Cagney's fans and those with pleasant memories of the Navy will be more forgiving.

James Cagney (center) is Adm.
William F. Halsey, Jr. in *The
Gallant Hours.* The Kobal Collection

Cast: James Cagney (Fleet Adm. William F. Halsey Jr.), Dennis Weaver (Lt. Cmdr. Andy Lowe), Ward Costello (Capt. Harry Black), Richard Jaeckel (Lt. Cmdr. Roy Webb), Les Tremayne (Capt. Frank Enright), Robert Burton (Maj. Gen. Roy Geiger), Raymond Bailey (Maj. Gen. Archie Vandergrift), Karl Swenson (Capt. Bill Bailey), Harry Landers (Capt. Joe Foss), James T. Goto (Adm. Isoroku Yamamoto), Walter Sande (Capt. Horace Keys), Vaughn Taylor (Cmdr. Mike Pulaski), Leon Lontoc (Manuel), Carleton Young (Col. Evans Carlson), James Yagi (Rear Adm. Jiro Kobe), Carl Benton Reid (Vice Adm. Robert Ghormley), Selmer Jackson (Adm. Chester Nimitz), Nelson Leigh (Adm. Callaghan), John McKee (Lt. Harrison Ludlum), Tyler McVey (Adm. Ernest J. King), William Schallert (Capt. Tom Lamphier), John Zaremba (Maj. Gen. Harmon), Richard Carlyle (Fr. Gehring), Herbert Lytton (Adm. Murray), Sydney Smith (Adm. Scott), Art Gilmore (Narrator); **Written by:** Frank D. Gilroy, Beirne Lay Jr.; **Cinematography by:** Joe MacDonald; **Music by:** Roger Wagner; **Technical Advisor:** James T. Goto, Capt. Joseph U. Lademan, Capt. Idris B. Monahan. **Producer:** James Cagney, Robert Montgomery, United Artists. **Running Time:** 115 minutes. **Format:** VHS.

Despite changes in fashion and permissiveness, this adaptation of Richard Tregaskis's non-fiction best-seller retains its historical significance as one of Hollywood's first "realistic" World War II combat films. It is dated however, and its lapses are heightened by the less-sentimental approaches to the subject that have been made in more recent years. The film is also an intriguing counterpart to Terrence Malick's *The Thin Red Line*. Both are about the same engagement; both have a certain basis in fact, and they are flawed in opposite ways.

Writers Lamar Trotti and Jerome Cady and director Lewis Seiler follow Tregaskis's structure, opening on a troop ship "somewhere in the South Pacific" en route to an unknown destination which will turn out to be America's first land victory over the Japanese. An unnamed correspondent (Reed Hadley) appears briefly and then provides a deep brown voice-over narration. In the first scenes, the Marines are introduced, and the "melting-pot" aspect of the mix is hammered home when a Jew joins in the singing of "Rock of Ages" at a Sunday service led by a Catholic priest, Fr. Donnelly (Preston Foster). (One black character appears briefly and even has a line or two of dialogue. He is not listed in the credits.) Cpl. "Taxi" Potts (William Bendix) is the brash New Yorker. Johnny "Chicken" Anderson (Richard Jaeckel) is the beardless youth. Sgt. Hook Malone (Lloyd Nolan) is the tough, no-nonsense NCO. "Soose" Alvarez (Anthony Quinn) is the brash Latino and Butch (Lionel Stander) is the comic cook.

If they sound like cliches, they are. So is much of the dialogue. In one short scene, all of the following is heard: "Well, Sarge, it looks like this is it." "Hit the deck!" "So far, so good." "I hope it isn't a trap." "The second wave's coming in!" "Oh, for the love of. . . ." "Hey, gimme a cigarette, will ya." "Since when did you start smoking cigarettes?" "I'm starting right now."

True, the cliches were younger then than they are now, and they are delivered without humor or facetiousness, and the cast handles them earnestly. Too earnestly, and that points toward the film's other problem. In this entire shipload of Marines, there's not a single impure thought, not even a cross word, much less any profanity. While it is also true that strong language was mostly forbidden in movies of the time, the emotions and fears that inspire cursing are also lacking. The only moment that comes close to that psychological understanding is a long and finally embarrassing "no atheists in foxholes" speech delivered by Taxi. So, while the physical action (filmed at Ft. Pendleton) may be a fair dramatization of what occurred on the island, the characters of the soldiers don't share that authenticity.

The action scenes lack the graphic blood squibs and destruction so commonplace in today's war films, but they're well paced, understandable, and exciting. Because of that, they have been copied and often embroidered upon. Such flattery is the final proof of the film's enduring popularity.

> "Beer . . . strictly a middle-class beverage. The last time I was back home in Brooklyn—it was just such a night as this—we was having cocktails. The old lady brought 'em in. I took one taste and, boy, what a kick! You know what she did? She took 'em out and put in another slug of gin. What a sweet old lady."
>
> **Taxi (William Bendix)**

See also

Bataan
When Trumpets Fade
A Walk in the Sun
The Story of G.I. Joe

Marines wait out a round of shelling in a bunker in *Guadalcanal Diary*. Anthony Quinn (far left), William Bendix (fourth from left), Lionel Stander (center, top) Richard Jackal (fourth from right) The Kobal Collection

Cast: Preston Foster (Fr. Donnelly), Lloyd Nolan (Sgt. Hook Malone), William Bendix (Cpl. "Taxi" Potts), Richard Conte (Capt. Davis), Anthony Quinn (Jesus "Soose" Alvarez), Richard Jaeckel (Pvt. Johnny "Chicken" Anderson), Roy Roberts (Capt. James Cross), Minor Watson (Col. Grayson), Miles Mander (Weatherby), Ralph Byrd (Ned Rowman), Lionel Stander (Butch), Reed Hadley (War Correspondent/Narrator), John Archer (Lt. Thurmond), Eddie Acuff (Tex McIlvoy), Selmer Jackson (Col. Thompson), Paul Fung (Japanese prisoner); **Written by:** Lamar Trotti, Jerome Cady; **Cinematography by:** Charles Clarke; **Music by:** David Buttolph. **Producer:** Bryan Foy, 20th Century-Fox. **Running Time:** 93 minutes. **Format:** VHS, Beta, LV.

The Hound Salutes: William Bendix

Something about that catcher's mitt mug combined with the naive, open attitude, pugnacious spirit, and rounded, out-of-shape body spoke to American audiences of the 1940s and '50s. A fine character actor, William Bendix became the "regular guy" from Brooklyn in the melting pot of the unit picture. He played his role so well in *Wake Island*—and received a Best Supporting Actor Academy Award nomination for it—that he replayed it over and over again "for the duration" as they said then.

How much of that came from his innate everyman quality? How much of it was writers and directors learning to work with what he could contribute? Considering the way Hollywood relies on typecasting and the repetition of success, his popularity is certainly a combination of the two. The son of a conductor for the New York Metropolitan Opera Orchestra, he played minor league baseball before turning to the stage, where he made his first impression in William Saroyan's *The Time of Your Life* in 1939. A few years later, Bendix made the move to Hollywood. After his screen debut in *Woman of the Year* with Tracy and Hepburn, he landed the key supporting role in *Wake Island*—where he was teamed with Robert Preston in a piece of genuinely inspired casting—and worked steadily throughout the next decades. On the big screen, he was often paired with Alan Ladd. For most older viewers, he will always be thought of first as Chester A. Riley in the long-running '50s television series *Life of Riley*.

His most important war films are *Wake Island*, *Guadalcanal Diary* (where he outshines everyone else in the ensemble), Hitchcock's *Lifeboat*, and *A Bell for Adano*, which is not now available on home video. His other work in the genre includes *China*, *Abroad with Two Yanks*, Raymond Chandler's *The Blue Dahlia*—also with Ladd—where he plays a shell-shocked veteran, *Blaze of Noon*, *Submarine Command*, and *Deep Six*.

HELL IN THE PACIFIC

1969 John Boorman ♪♪♪

John Boorman's minimalist survival tale is recommended for fans of the two stars (who are the entire cast) and no one else. The story is told elliptically, without the background that most moviegoers and videophiles expect to see. From the first frame to the last—literally—viewers have to fill in large blanks.

It begins with sunrise over a jungle island. The lone inhabitant is a Japanese sailor (Toshiro Mifune). Judging by the scruffy beard and water-collection system he has constructed, he has been there for several weeks. As he scans the horizon, he spots something. A yellow rubber life raft has washed up on the island. An American pilot (Lee Marvin), delirious with thirst, has hidden himself in the undergrowth. The sailor is armed with a staff; the flier has a survival knife. The immediate object of their competition is the meager supply of water. Beyond that, what is worth fighting for?

Neither speaks a word of the other's language but it's obvious that each thinks of the other as a foreign devil.

Given that premise, it's easy to predict that the script by Alexander Jacobs and Eric Bercovici is about communication, cooperation, conflict, the futility of war, etc. etc. The film might never be anything more than a curious updating of Robinson Crusoe, but the stars are at their mature best and that helps considerably. Mifune's walk—as distinctive in its own way as John Wayne's—establishes his strong character in the first seconds. The American is less stable. At many decisive moments throughout, it's unclear whether he is completely sane. The language barrier is not the only the thing that separates these two, from each other and from the viewer. Director Boorman has considerable affinity for off-beat stories set in an exotic wilderness. In visual terms if no other, this film is a companion piece to *Deliverance*, *Excalibur*, and *The Emerald Forest*. Unlike them, however, it lacks a multilayered story and a conventional conclusion. In the end, then, even its admirers will admit that *Hell in the Pacific* is more interesting than entertaining.

See also
Walkabout
Point Blank
Yojimbo
Fires on the Plain
The Thin Red Line
The Black Stallion

Toshiro Mifune and Lee Marvin
are enemies stranded together
on a desert island during World
War II in *Hell in the Pacific*. The
Kobal Collection

Cast: Lee Marvin (American pilot), Toshiro Mifune (Japanese naval officer); **Written by:** Eric
Bercovici, Alexander Jacobs; **Cinematography by:** Conrad Hall; **Music by:** Lalo Schifrin. **Producer:** Reuben Bercov-
itch, Cinerama Releasing, Selmur. **MPAA Rating:** PG. **Running Time:** 101 minutes. **Format:** VHS, Beta, LV.

HOME OF THE BRAVE

1949 Mark Robson 𝄞𝄞𝄞

If this curious little drama lived up to its intentions, it might have been an important war film. But it falls far short and is now little more than a footnote in Hollywood's attempts to deal with American racism. Director Mark Robson starts out with two strikes against him. First, Carl Foreman's script is based on Arthur Laurents's curiously contrived stage play. Second, Laurents's play is about anti-Semitism, and though it is easy to say that all bigotry springs from the one source, discrimination against black people is different from discrimination against Jewish people. To claim that they are the same misunderstands both.

The action takes place on nameless islands in the Pacific. In the opening scenes, a psychiatrist (Jeff Corey) tries to find out how Peter Moss (James Edwards), a black soldier, came to be paralyzed from the waist down. Moss is also amnesiac and so can't remember what happened on his last mission. Maj. Robinson (Douglas Dick) and Mingo (Frank Lovejoy) tell the doctor what they know. They say that it was a reconnaissance patrol to an island held by the Japanese. Robinson picked Mingo, Finch (Lloyd Bridges), and T.J. Everett (Steve Brodie) to "volunteer" from his outfit. He had recruited Moss, an engineer from another division, to make maps of the island. Robinson was then surprised to learn that Moss was "colored." T.J. is openly racist, but it turns out that Finch and Moss are old pals from high school, where they played basketball together. Tensions within the group rise to the surface as soon as they're dropped on the island.

> "Dirtiest trick you can play on a man in a war is to make him think."
>
> **Mingo (Frank Lovejoy)**

> "Wonderful cooks, the coloreds—great entertainers, too."
>
> **T.J. (Steve Brodie)**

Neither the depiction of jungle warfare nor the racial attitudes are remotely believable. Men on sentry duty at night chatter away like schoolchildren and smoke cigarettes constantly. T.J.'s expressions of racism and Moss's reactions are equally simplistic and false. And when, finally, the reasons for the paralysis are revealed, audiences today will groan in disbelief. The resolution of the conflicts piles improbability upon improbability.

That said, the filmmakers do deserve credit for addressing racial issues at a time when the entertainment industry generally ignored them, and when segregation was the law of the land. The active recruitment of black soldiers, sailors, and airmen during World War II played a large part in changing that, and the stories of that change have yet to be fully told. *Home of the Brave* is a small first step.

See also

The Tuskegee Airmen
A Soldier's Story
Captain Newman, M.D.
Full Metal Jacket

James Edwards, Lloyd Bridges, and Frank Lovejoy battle the Japanese, as well as racism, in the Pacific in *Home of the Brave*.

The Kobal Collection

Cast: Lloyd Bridges (Finch), James Edwards (Peter Moss), Frank Lovejoy (Mingo), Jeff Corey (Doctor), Douglas Dick (Maj. Robinson), Steve Brodie (T.J.), Cliff Clark (Colonel); **Written by:** Carl Foreman; **Cinematography by:** Robert De Grasse; **Music by:** Dimitri Tiomkin. **Producer:** Stanley Kramer, United Artists. **Running Time:** 86 minutes. **Format:** VHS, Beta, LV.

IN HARM'S WAY

1965 Otto Preminger

This long, lumbering naval epic predates the various 1980s television mini-series about World War II. It's the same mixture of soap-opera action away from the battlefields and cheap-looking naval special effects that are no more convincing on the small screen than they were in theaters. Apparently, most of the budget was spent on a first-rate cast of actors who walk through substandard material.

A two-minute plus opening tracking shot establishes the scene as Pearl Harbor, December 6, 1941. At an officer's party, Liz (Barbara Bouchet), the drunken wife of Cmdr. Eddington (Kirk Douglas), makes a spectacle of herself. Since her husband is at sea with Capt. Rock Torrey (John Wayne), she heads off for a skinny-dip in the ocean with a pilot (Hugh O'Brien). Are they in for a nasty surprise the next morning! When the Japanese attack (depicted in brief, grainy shots of airplanes and a few explosions in the ocean), Lt. William McConnel (Tom Tryon) manages to get his destroyer out of the harbor before it's bombed. At the same time, Torrey and Eddington's ship is sent to fend off the Japanese fleet and suffers a devastating attack.

> "All battles are fought by scared men who'd rather be someplace else."
>
> **Capt. Torrey (John Wayne)**

Several plot twists later, Torrey is sailing a desk and Eddington is shipped off to a remote supply base. Enter Cmdr. Powell (Burgess Merdith), script writer turned intelligence officer; Lt. Maggie Haynes (Patricia Neal), a nurse who sets her cap for Torrey; Ens. Jere Torrey (Brandon de Wilde), Rock's estranged son; and his fiancee Ens. Annalee Dorne (Jill Haworth), Maggie's roommate. Those are the good guys. On the other side are the ineffectual Adm. Broderick (Dana Andrews) and his stooge, Cmdr. Owynn (Patrick O'Neal). The rest of the supporting cast is filled with such veterans as Henry Fonda (sporting a curious Southern accent), Franchot Tone, and many other names and faces who would become much more famous in the following decades.

Unfortunately, they're all saddled with a convoluted story that's so idiotically written it's unfair to judge the actors' work. For the most part, they do not embarrass themselves too much. More than any of the others, Wayne looks like he wishes he were somewhere else. Still, the film is not without interest as an example of the cozy working relationship that the entertainment industry and the military enjoyed in the years between World War II and Vietnam. The scenes that were filmed aboard real ships with Navy personnel look bright, shiny, and freshly ironed. Those recruitment poster excerpts stand in jarring comparison to the models used for the battle scenes and the pedestrian interiors. When the focus moves away from the fighting, as it often does, the story has much more to say about the early 1960s than the early 1940s. The sexual attitudes in particular are pure '60s, with an uncomfortable sniggering subtext that's never far from the surface. The absurd and convenient resolution of one seduction plotline is too bizarre to be described, much less believed. Throughout the film, the characters' emotions are exaggerated to unrealistic extremes.

One clue to the bad writing comes in the place names that were invented for the fictional campaign. When Torrey says, "You're gonna mop up Gavoobutu and mount the invasion of Lavoovona," it sounds even sillier than it reads. The few scenes that suggest jungle combat don't amount to anything, and though the effects used in the naval battles may have some nostalgic value, they're certainly not going to engage and persuade younger viewers, who demand a certain level of authenticity in both visual and emotional terms.

See also

The Longest Day
The Winds of War
War and Remembrance

The Bombing of Pearl Harbor puts Dana Andrews, Burgess Meredith, and John Wayne *In Harm's Way.* The Kobal Collection

Cast: John Wayne (Capt. Rockwell Torrey), Kirk Douglas (Cmdr. Paul Eddington), Tom Tryon (Lt. William McConnel), Patricia Neal (Lt. Maggie Haynes), Paula Prentiss (Bex McConnel), Brandon de Wilde (Ens. Jeremiah Torrey), Burgess Meredith (Cmdr. Egan Powell), Stanley Holloway (Clayton Canfil), Henry Fonda (Adm. Chester W. Nimitz), Dana Andrews (Adm. Broderick), Franchot Tone (CINPAC I Admiral), Jill Haworth (Ens. Annalee Dorne), George Kennedy (Col. Gregory), Carroll O'Connor (Lt. Cmdr. Burke), Patrick O'Neal (Cmdr. Neal Owynn), Slim Pickens (CPO Culpepper), Bruce Cabot (Quartermaster Quoddy), Larry Hagman (Lt. Cline), Hugh O'Brian (U.S. Army Air Corps Major), Jim Mitchum (Ens. Griggs), Barbara Bouchet (Liz Eddington), Stewart Moss (Ens. Balch), Tod Andrews (Capt. Tuthill); **Written by:** Wendell Mayes; **Cinematography by:** Loyal Griggs; **Music by:** Jerry Goldsmith. **Producer:** Otto Preminger, Paramount Pictures, Sigma. **Awards:** British Academy Awards '65: Best Actress (Neal); Nominations: Academy Awards '65: Best Black and White Cinematography. **Running Time:** 165 minutes. **Format:** VHS, Beta, LV, Closed Caption.

MERRILL'S MARAUDERS

1962 Samuel Fuller 🎬🎬🎬

The wild, unexpected touches that energize director Sam Fuller's best work are absent in this straightforward war film. By all accounts, he sticks fairly close to the broad outlines of historical fact to tell the story of a particularly grueling and little-known episode of the Pacific Theater.

A brief introduction made up of newsreel footage and animated maps sketches in the history of American involvement in Burma in the early 1940s. Gen. Stilwell's (John Hoyt) forces are run out by the Japanese in 1942. Two years later, he returns. Leading the attack is the 5307th Composite Provisional Regiment; 3,000 men strong, it undertakes the ambitious three-month assignment of marching 200 miles undetected through the jungle to attack the Japanese at Walawbaum. From there, though the men don't know it, they are to go even farther into Burma to Myitkyina.

Brig. Gen. Frank Merrill (Jeff Chandler) is in command. Much of the action is focused on one of his favorite officers, Lt. Stockton (Ty Hardin) and the men of Stockton's platoon: Bullseye (Peter Brown), Chowhound (Will Hutchins), Muley (Charlie Briggs), and Sgt. Kolowicz (Claude Akins).

Fuller is extremely imaginative with his Philippine locations, going beyond the familiar jungles to vertiginous mountain trails and a rail yard-refinery where he stages a major combat scene. The central point of the film is the exhausting nature of the campaign, the toll that long months in the field take on the men both physically and emotionally. In the film, as in reality, Merrill suffers from a serious heart condition but stays with his men every step of the way. Though Stockton and Merrill and Dr. Kolodny (Andrew Duggan) emerge as believable, if unexceptional stiff-upper-lip figures, the rest of the secondary characters lack much personality.

Fuller puts his camera right down in the mud with them, and he makes their fatigue seem real enough in extreme close-ups, but they still lack depth. Because the film is trying to show the actions of the entire unit, the relatively modest budget is stretched thin in places. The best moments here do not come close to their counterparts in *The Big Red One*, but then, that autobiographical film is a labor of love. *Merrill's Marauders* is a finely crafted story with a deliberately ambiguous conclusion. Despite the gung-ho title, this is not a film about victory, heroism, or the adrenaline rush of action. The only victory that Fuller sees is survival, and for men who have been so brutally ground down, survival comes at a high price.

See also

Bridge on the River Kwai
The Big Red One
Objective, Burma!

American commandos keep an eye out for the Japanese as they cross a river in *Merrill's Marauders*. Jeff Chandler **(center)** The Kobal Collection

Cast: Jeff Chandler (Brig. Gen. Frank D. Merrill), Ty Hardin (Lt. Lee Stockton), Peter Brown (Bullseye), Andrew Duggan (Capt. Abraham L. Kolodny, MD), Will Hutchins (Chowhound), Claude Akins (Sgt. Kolowicz), John Hoyt (Gen. Stilwell), Chuck Hicks (Cpl. Doskis), Charles Briggs (Muley), Vaughan Wilson (Bannister), Pancho Magalona (Taggy); **Written by:** Samuel Fuller, Milton Sperling, Charlton Ogburn Jr.; **Cinematography by:** William Clothier; **Music by:** Howard Jackson; **Technical Advisor:** Lt. Col. Samuel Wilson. **Producer:** Milton Sperling, Warner Bros. **Running Time:** 98 minutes. **Format:** VHS.

MISTER ROBERTS

1955 John Ford, Mervyn LeRoy, Josh Logan 🦴🦴🦴

One of the most successful World War II comedy-dramas had a rough road from stage to screen. Writer Frank Nugent and Joshua Logan had adapted Nugent's novel into a hit play with Henry Fonda in the lead, both on Broadway and with the road company. When Warner Bros. decided to turn it into a film, the producers hired John Ford to direct and considered more bankable stars like William Holden and Marlon Brando in the title role. Ford lobbied for his old friend Fonda, but from the first day of filming, the two men had serious disagreements about the nature of the film.

Ford wanted to make a brawling, raucous slapstick ensemble piece. Fonda wanted to keep his version of the character at the center of the story. At their lowest moment, they argued and Ford actually struck Fonda. The various people involved with the conflict tell slightly different versions, but it's clear that Ford was drinking heavily at the time and his health was deteriorating. Several weeks into shooting, he had to be hospitalized and he was replaced by veteran Mervyn Leroy. The difference between their work is immediately obvious.

Ford filmed the exteriors in the South Pacific. His "big" scenes are the crew's ogling newly-arrived nurses, and the men's drunken return from a wild night of liberty. Leroy shot the interiors, most of them dialogue-driven, involving the four stars. After Leroy's work had been completed, the studio brought in Joshua Logan to shoot two more scenes, the famous soap-suds and the closing confrontation. Not surprisingly then, the film is a mixed bag, but mostly an enjoyable one.

The setting is the cargo ship *Reluctant*, far from the action in the waning days of the Pacific campaign. Lt. Doug Roberts (Fonda) desperately wants to get into the "real war" before it's over. The Captain (James Cagney), an ambitious, petty man, understands that Roberts's efficient management of the crew is his own ticket to a promotion to Commander, and so he refuses to approve Roberts's repeated requests for transfer. Doc (William Powell) sympathizes but cannot help. The manic ensign Pulver (Jack Lemmon) plots elaborate pranks, but is too terrified of the Captain to follow through.

Ford's scenes have a dated quality. They are certainly lively and well staged, but changing tastes in humor have given them an exaggerated, forced jollity. They're not nearly as funny as they're trying to be. Ford, however, was also responsible for the "mail call" sequence, and that is the film's emotional highpoint. Leroy's scenes are built around Fonda's confident performance, and they seem absolutely right. Newcomer Lemmon received a Best Supporting Actor Academy Award for a performance that is somehow reminiscent of Daffy Duck. In less showy roles, his two senior co-stars are terrific. Cagney's Captain is a cagey piece of work, while Powell's Doc has a cool world-weary skepticism.

Those four characters are what people remember about the film, and they have made it a perennial favorite on video. If only the filmmakers had been allowed to leave in the line that scandalized Broadway audiences and was considered much too racy for the movies in the mid 1950s. As Fonda retells it in his autobiography, when Pulver is talking about making an elaborate firecracker out of fulminate of mercury, Roberts says to Doc, "That stuff's murder. Do you suppose he'll use it."

See also
The Caine Mutiny
Cool Hand Luke
*M*A*S*H*
South Pacific

Doc responds, "Of course not. Where would he get fulminate of mercury?"

"I dunno," Roberts answers. "He's pretty resourceful. Eighteen months at sea without liberty, where'd he get the clap?"

The Captain (James Cagney) and Mr. Roberts (Henry Fonda) on board the cargo ship *Reluctant* in *Mister Roberts*. The Kobal Collection

Cast: Henry Fonda (Lt. (jg) Douglas Roberts), James Cagney (Capt. Morion), Jack Lemmon (Ens. Frank Pulver), William Powell (Doc), Betsy Palmer (Lt. Ann Girard), Ward Bond (CPO Dawdy), Harry Carey Jr. (Stefanowski), Nick Adams (Reber), Phil Carey (Mannion), Ken Curtis (Dolan), Martin Milner (Shore Patrol officer), Jack Pennick (Marine sergeant), Perry Lopez (Rodrigues), Patrick Wayne (Bookser), Tige Andrews (Wiley), William Henry (Lt. Billings); **Written by:** Frank Nugent, Joshua Logan, Thomas Heggen; **Cinematography by:** Winton C. Hoch; **Music by:** Franz Waxman; **Technical Advisor:** Cmdr. Merle McBain, Adm. John Dale Price. **Producer:** Leland Hayward, Warner Bros. **Awards:** Academy Awards '55: Best Supporting Actor (Lemmon); Nominations: Academy Awards '55: Best Picture, Best Sound. **Running Time:** 120 minutes. **Format:** VHS, Beta.

OBJECTIVE, BURMA!

1945 Raoul Walsh ♪♪♪

"I've been a newspaperman for 30 years and I thought I'd seen or read about everything that one man can do to another, from the torture chambers of the Middle Ages to the gang wars and the lynchings of today, but this . . . this is different. This was done in cold blood by a people who . . . who claim to be civilized. Civilized? They're degenerate moral idiots! Stinking little savages! Wipe 'em out, I say! Wipe 'em out! WIPE 'EM OFF THE FACE OF THE EARTH!"

Mark Williams (Henry Hull) seeing American victims of Japanese torture

"But working on in Hollywood, Errol misguidedly accepted a series of war films in which he appeared playing highly heroic roles: *Dive Bomber*, *Edge of Darkness*, and *Objective, Burma!* to name a few. The press reacted angrily to his efforts, particularly in beleaguered England, where Zec, in the 4,000,000-circulation *Daily Mirror*, depicted Flynn in a half-page cartoon, dressed in battle dress, seated in a studio chair with his name stenciled on the back and in his hands the script of *Objective, Burma!*. On the studio grass beneath his chair was a multitude of tiny crosses and, beneath the jungle trees, stood the ghostly form of a soldier. The caption read: 'Excuse me, Mr. Flynn, but you're sitting on some graves.'"

David Niven. *Bring On the Empty Horses* (Putnam, 1975)

Though many combat adventures had been made before, director Raoul Walsh set the formula in concrete with this rousing potboiler. It has virtually nothing to do with real guerrilla warfare, and as propaganda, its chest-thumping moments are few. But those moments are memorable (see quotes) and the approach that writers Alvah Bessie, Lester Cole (who were blacklisted a few years later), and Ranald MacDougall take to the simple story has been copied and refined countless times since. *Objective, Burma!* remains one of the best "suicide mission behind enemy lines" tales ever put on film.

An introduction explains that Allied Forces have been kicked out of Burma, "the backdoor to China," by the Japanese, but now the big push to retake the country is about to begin. Capt. Nelson's (Errol Flynn) paratroopers are restless and ready for action. "We've been sittin' around so much we've all got bunions on our landing gear," says Cpl. Gordon (George Tobias) in a moment of typical bravado. Nelson is equally brash when he tells correspondent Mark Williams (Henry Hull) why his men have to be young. "Young men, all of us. We've got to be. You know why? I'll give you two good reasons. We jump out of planes and guys shoot at us. It isn't exactly healthy unless you're young enough to take it."

Then the mission is explained. Nelson and 50 men, with the aging Williams along for the ride, will parachute behind Japanese lines, where they'll be surrounded by enemy troops, blow up a secret radar installation, and make their way to a remote airfield where they'll be picked up. Easy as pie. And it is . . . for a while.

The film's success lies in its pace and attention to carefully chosen details. Director Walsh lingers on the preparation for the initial jump, noting the number of weapons each man will carry, how many thousand rounds of ammunition, how many grenades. He pays particular attention to the strapping on of the parachutes and the details of the interior of the airplane. Throughout, he repeats the map coordinates that become so important to the characters' movement. When the commandos are in the jungle, he emphasizes the "Awk! Awk! Ooo-Ooo-Ooo!" wildlife sound effects familiar to all Tarzan fans, and somehow manages to make a ranch near Pasadena appear to be an Asian jungle. More or less. Walsh gets considerable assistance from Franz Waxman's score, which has become an archetype for action films in its own right.

The real reason he's able to maintain verisimilitude is the film's carefully calculated pace. The action scenes are widely spaced in the first half, with more screen time spent on the simple business of walking cautiously through the threatening wilderness. When they do occur, the combat scenes are quick and graphic, and in the second half, they intensify to an absolutely ridiculous and far-fetched flag-waving finish.

That's not a criticism; it's the point of this particular brand of escapism.

See also

The Guns of Navarone
Where Eagles Dare
China Gate
Any James Bond movie

Errol Flynn leads a commando raid on a Japanese radar installation deep behind enemy lines in *Objective, Burma!* The Kobal Collection

Cast: Errol Flynn (Capt. Nelson), James Brown (Sgt. Treacy), William Prince (Lt. Sid Jacobs), George Tobias (Gabby Gordon), Henry Hull (Mark Williams), Warner Anderson (Col. Carter), Richard Erdman (Nebraska Hooper), Mark Stevens (Lt. Baker), Anthony Caruso (Miggleori), Hugh Beaumont (Capt. Hennessey), John Alvin (Hogan), William Hudson (Hollis), Lester Matthews (Maj. Fitzpatrick), George Tyne (Soapy Higgins), Erville Alderson (Gen. Stilwell); **Written by:** Ranald MacDougall, Lester Cole, Alvah Bessie; **Cinematography by:** James Wong Howe; **Music by:** Franz Waxman. **Producer:** Jerry Wald, Jack L. Warner, Warner Bros. **Awards:** Nominations: Academy Awards '45: Best Film Editing, Best Story, Best Original Dramatic Score. **Running Time:** 142 minutes. **Format:** VHS, Beta.

OBJECTIVE, BURMA!

RUN SILENT RUN DEEP
1958 Robert Wise 🦴🦴🦴🦴

Though this underwater action film may not have much to do with the realities of Pacific submarine warfare, it is wonderfully entertaining as a showcase for two of Hollywood's finest stars, one on the ascent, and the other near the end of his career. The special effects are less than perfect—you can actually see the wires towing torpedoes in some shots—but few movies have made the cramped, sweaty interior of a sub seem so real.

Near the beginning of the war, Cmdr. Richardson's (Clark Gable) sub is destroyed by a Japanese destroyer in the Bungo Straits. Richardson survives, but is assigned to a desk back at Pearl Harbor. For a year, the destroyer methodically sinks every American sub that dares to enter Sector Seven and the Straits, while Richardson develops a revolutionary strategy to defeat "Bungo Pete." His chance comes when the captain of another sub, the *Nerka*, reaches retirement. Richardson asks the Navy brass for another shot and is given command. The only problem is Lt. Bledsoe (Burt Lancaster), executive officer of the *Nerka*, who has every reason to expect a promotion to captain. He's also popular with the crew, making Richardson's job harder. That job becomes even more difficult when Richardson announces that the *Nerka* is going into the Straits in direct defiance of orders to avoid the area.

Writers Edward Beach and John Gay wisely stage most of the conflicts within the submarine. The competition between Richardson and Bledsoe is at the heart of the film. Later, of course, the destroyer vs. sub action reappears, but the most interesting questions arise between the two protagonists. Whatever the subject matter of his pictures, director Robert Wise has been most successful when he stresses the more emotional, human side. It's true from his science-fiction, *The Day the Earth Stood Still*, to his other fine war film, *The Sand Pebbles*, and even his musical, *West Side Story*. Because the film was produced by Lancaster's company, it makes each of the leads roughly equal in the audience's estimation. (In that regard it can be seen as a precursor to the "buddy" pictures of the '80s and '90s.)

The film was also made with the full cooperation of the Navy, and so they were able to create a high level of authenticity in the submarine interiors. The scenes with the most intense conflict between Richardson and Bledsoe are staged in the smaller rooms of the sub, where the bulkheads and ceilings literally force the two men closer together and intensify their differences. It's a simple dramatic trick, and Wise makes the most of it. Also, with the majority of the action set inside the sub, the characters wear simple khaki uniforms, denims, and T-shirts. That lack of fashion frees the film from the dated look so many films of the period have.

In the end, *Run Silent Run Deep* isn't a particularly serious film, but with Lancaster and Gable in top form—and getting strong support from Jack Warden, Don Rickles, and Lancaster's frequent sidekick Nick Cravat—it remains one of the most enjoyable movies of its time.

See also
Das Boot
The Caine Mutiny
The Crimson Pirate
Crash Dive

Burt Lancaster and Clark Gable search for Japanese destroyers in the Pacific in *Run Silent Run Deep*. The Kobal Collection

Cast: Burt Lancaster (Lt. Jim Bledsoe), Clark Gable (Cmdr. Richardson), Jack Warden (Mueller), Don Rickles (Ruby), Brad Dexter (Cartwright), Nick Cravat (Russo), Joe Maross (Kohler), Mary Laroche (Laura), Eddie Foy III (Larto), Rudy Bond (Cullen), H.M. Wynant (Hendrix), Joel Fluellen (Bragg), Ken Lynch (Frank), John Bryant (Beckman); **Written by:** John Gay, Edward Beach; **Cinematography by:** Russell Harlan; **Music by:** Franz Waxman. **Producer:** Harold Hecht, United Artists. **Running Time:** 93 minutes. **Format:** VHS, Beta.

RUN SILENT RUN DEEP

SANDS OF IWO JIMA

1949 Allan Dwan ♪♪♪♪

"Saddle Up!"

With that refrain, John Wayne solidifies the image that made him a star. He's Sgt. John Stryker, the toughest Leatherneck there ever was and, at the same time, fully believable, flawed, and sympathetic. He had played variations on the character in many of the films he made during the war, but here, for the first time, all of the pieces fit together perfectly. Solid fact-based story, capable ensemble cast, confident direction, and, at the center, Wayne in his first Academy Award–nominated performance. The combination is so effective that to many fans, *Sands of Iwo Jima* is the definitive war movie. That is an exaggeration, but it certainly is one of the best of its kind.

> "In boot camp you learned the book. Out here, you gotta remember the book and learn a thousand things that have never been printed, probably never will be. You gotta learn and you gotta learn fast. And any man that doesn't want to cooperate, I'll make him wish he hadn't been born. Before I'm through with you, you're gonna move like one man and think like one man. If you don't, you're dead."
>
> **Sgt. Stryker (John Wayne) to the new replacements in his squad**

Cpl. Dunne (Arthur Franz), our narrator, explains that his rifle squad first saw action on Guadalcanal. Only he, Pfc. Bass (James Brown), and Sgt. Stryker have come through for retraining in New Zealand, where they meet the new replacements, fresh from stateside. Among them are Cpl. Thomas (Forrest Tucker), who has a history with Stryker, the battling Flynn boys (Richard Jaeckel and William Murphy) from the City of Brotherly Love, and Pfc. Conway (John Agar). Conway is the son of Stryker's old commanding officer. His hatred toward his father matches Stryker's admiration. During a long training sequence, Conway is swept up in a whirlwind romance with a local (Adele Mara), and Stryker's troubled domestic situation is revealed.

> "If you're nervous, count your toes. I'll do the masterminding around here."
>
> **Sgt. Stryker to a panicked Marine during a beach assault**

The squad receives its baptism on Tarawa against "Japanese Marines, the best they've got. They're dug in and they're mean and they'd just as soon die as stick a nickel in a jukebox." In that engagement, director Allan Dwan establishes his ground rules for describing combat. Mixing actual combat footage with shots of his actors, he keeps the focus fairly narrow. For the most part, he stays with the squad, not letting the audience know any more than the men do, and he cares more about their reactions to the fight and to each other than about the battle itself. The archival footage is rough, but Dwan never dwells on violence. It tends to be quick and lethal. The levels of intensity may not equal what audiences have come to expect from *Platoon* and *Saving Private Ryan*, but the intention and emotion are the same.

The rest of the film follows that pattern of relatively quiet training sequences, where the personal side of the men's lives is revealed, followed by more combat. One long scene between Stryker and a woman who picks him up in a bar threatens to dissolve into complete sappiness, but Wayne's gruff sentimentality somehow saves it. His continuing conflict with Conway is less successful. From beginning to end, it is forced, false, and predictable. In context, though, that is relatively unimportant. Audiences loved this movie when it came out; it was one of the top boxoffice hits of 1950 and made John Wayne the number-one star in the country for the first time in his long career. They still love it, and rightly so.

John Wayne did have better, more complex roles—*The Shootist, The Man Who Shot Liberty Valance, True Grit, She Wore a Yellow*

See also
Heartbreak Ridge
From Here to Eternity
Guadalcanal Diary
Wake Island

Ribbon—but he may never have been as comfortable as he was with Sgt. Stryker. Though Wayne never served in the military, to most of us the real man and the fictional character are the same. That's what movies and movie stars are about.

Marines raise the flag after taking the island in *Sands of Iwo Jima*. The Kobal Collection

Cast: John Wayne (Sgt. John M. Stryker), Forrest Tucker (Cpl. Al Thomas), John Agar (Pfc. Peter Conway), Richard Jaeckel (Pfc. Frank Flynn), Adele Mara (Allison Bromley), Wally Cassell (Pfc. Benny Regazzi), James Brown (Pfc. Charlie Bass), Richard Webb (Pfc. Dan Shipley), Arthur Franz (Cpl. Robert Dunne), Julie Bishop (Mary), William Murphy (Pfc. Eddie Flynn), George Tyne (Pfc. Harris), Hal Baylor (Pvt. "Ski" Choynski), John McGuire (Capt. Joyce), Martin Milner (Pvt. Mike McHugh), William Self (Pvt. L.D. Fowler Jr.), Peter Coe (Pfc. Georgie Hellenopolis), I. Stanford Jolley (Forrestal), Col. D.M. Shoup (Himself), Lt. Col. H.P. Crowe (Himself), Capt. Harold G. Shrier (Himself), Rene A. Gagnon (Himself), Ira H. Hayes (Himself), John H. Bradley (Himself); **Written by:** Harry Brown, James Edward Grant; **Cinematography by:** Reggie Lanning; **Music by:** Victor Young. **Producer:** Herbert J. Yates, Edmund Grainger, Republic. **Awards:** Nominations: Academy Awards '49: Best Actor (Wayne), Best Film Editing, Best Sound, Best Story. **Running Time:** 109 minutes. **Format:** VHS, LV, Closed Caption, DVD.

SANDS OF IWO JIMA

The Hound Salutes: John Wayne

When most moviegoers think of war on screen, the first image that comes to mind is John Wayne as Sgt. Stryker in *Sands of Iwo Jima*. He embodies a certain kind of American film hero in a way that no other actor ever has. His importance goes beyond entertainment into patriotism and politics. The man and the image are so deeply intertwined that many people don't know or don't care that he never served in the military. The truth is that when America entered World War II, Wayne's career was at an important turning point. After years of hard work in low-budget westerns, he had finally made an impression with the public in *Stagecoach*. To leave Hollywood after Pearl Harbor could have been professional suicide. Wayne made a conscious decision to stay and to make better movies.

That's not meant as a personal criticism—many men made the same and similar decisions, and Wayne never denied it—but it's wrong to ascribe his lack of service to an old football injury or an ear infection, as some of his apologists have.

In other words, John Wayne the man was not John Wayne the movie hero, and John Wayne the movie hero has been inflated into something much larger than an "image." In his fine book *John Wayne's America: The Politics of Celebrity* (Simon & Schuster. 1997) Garry Wills carefully details the reasons behind Wayne's decision, and the ramifications that it had in later decades, specifically concerning his decision to make *The Alamo* and *The Green Berets*. Whatever one thinks of John Wayne's politics, he is the biggest star in the American film industry. According to one reputable poll, more than 15 years after his death, he was the most popular star in the country. Walk into a bar or restaurant in the Southwest and you're likely to see a portrait of Wayne on the wall.

Why? What accounts for the man's popularity in decades when easily half of his audience disagreed with his well-publicized right-wing political views?

A large part of the reason is so simple that it's easy to miss: Over a long career, John Wayne made some excellent movies. Conventional wisdom has it that he always played himself, and that's true in his later years. But Wayne was capable of expressing a wide range of emotions. Despite his "tough" image, he was also effective in softer moments, and he wasn't afraid to look silly on camera. (Don't miss his swing dancing in *Fighting Seabees*.) His best roles are complex, flawed characters whose weaknesses are not hidden. Like everyone else who has ever been successful in front of the camera, he worked with talented people, and so he often appeared in stories that were well written and well directed. As a group, his post-*Stagecoach* westerns are more successful than his war films, though he inspired more boys to become Marines than cowboys.

Tellingly, Wayne was his own worst enemy behind the camera. As producer-director he gave himself little to work with as an actor in *The Alamo* and *The Green Berets*. In both, he plays one-dimensional characters who don't come close to Sgt. Stryker or Ethan Edwards in *The Searchers* or even the Ringo Kid in *Stagecoach*. Wayne's other significant war films, both made with John Ford, deserve to be ranked with his best work. *They Were Expendable*, Ford's worshipful tribute to his friend Lt. John Bulkeley, casts Wayne as the second lead behind Robert Montgomery. In *She Wore a Yellow Ribbon*, the middle part of Ford's "cavalry trilogy," Wayne is at his absolute best as Capt. Nathan Brittles. For my money, nothing that Wayne would do in the genre in the following decades comes close to them. By the time he made the lumbering *In Harm's Way* and *The Longest Day*, Wayne was playing the military image that people expected to see, almost parodies of Stryker and Brittles. At the end of his career, he went back to the western for his best work—*True Grit*, *The Cowboys*, *The Shootist*.

Those are the roles that finally cemented John Wayne's image as the lonely, self-sacrificing American hero.

See also:

Duke: The Life and Image of John Wayne. Ronald Davis. University of Oklahoma Press. 1998.

Duke: The Life and Times of John Wayne. Donald Shepherd and Robert Slatzer with Dave Grayson. Doubleday. 1985.

It will be difficult for some contemporary viewers to appreciate the reality that the director and stars are trying to create here. Though the film is meant to be a gritty look at the horrors of the American retreat through the Philippines to Corregidor as seen through the eyes of three Army nurses, it is overly glamorous and glossy by today's standards. Beyond a few carefully smudged cheekbones, the women exhibit all of the carefully tended beauty that is the basis of the Hollywood dream factory. That may be a valid criticism, but it misses the larger point of this propaganda—that women have an important, independent role to play in the prosecution of the war.

Based on a real incident, the story is told through fairly clumsy flashbacks. On May 5, 1942, a transport plane lands in Australia carrying American nurses who have been evacuated from Corregidor. All of them have survived a harrowing experience. Their leader, Lt. Janet Davidson (Claudette Colbert), has been so traumatized that she cannot speak, and has to be carried off on a stretcher. En route home on a ship, a doctor asks the women to tell what they experienced so that he can get through to Janet. He has a letter for her from someone named "John."

Seven months before, in November 1941, the group had left San Francisco. Flirty Lt. Joan O'Doul (Paulette Goddard) is ducking out on two fiances. After the attack on Pearl Harbor, the women are diverted to Bataan and another nurse, Lt. Olivia D'Arcy (Veronica Lake) joins their unit. She's a stand-offish "frozen-faced ghoul" until she reveals her tragic secret. Meanwhile, Joan has struck up a relationship with a blond galoot named Kansas (Sonny Tufts), and Janet has done the same with the more serious John (George Reeves). When they arrive in the Philippines, they find that the Americans are retreating before a larger and determined Japanese force.

Did you **Know?**
Technical advisor Lt. Eunice Hatchitt was one of the nurses who actually escaped from Corregidor in May 1942.

Producer-director Mark Sandrich, known mostly for such lighter fare as Astaire-Rogers musicals, handles the destruction of the Japanese attack with unusual directness. He tries to make the killing power of the bombs and shells as graphic as possible, and if the hospital scenes are not as bloodily realistic as they've been in more recent films, they try to address the desperate conditions under which the doctors and nurses work. Sandrich also deals honestly with the emotional cost on the medical staff of the often-futile efforts to save lives.

On the other side of the dramatic scales, much of the romantic banter has lost its appeal, and the Veronica Lake subplot is bizarrely out of step with the rest of the film, from its opening revelation to its jaw-dropping conclusion. (In some ways, her character can be seen as a prototype of the 1980s' *Fatal Attraction–Basic Instinct* killer blonde.) Again, it's true that the three stars are consistently gorgeous, whether they're clad in coveralls, khakis or black negligees. Without discounting that side of the film, it is still a solid piece of studio propaganda, not much different from others that were made at the same time. It's built on one of the key plot devices of the day—the military unit that is going into action just before the attack on Pearl Harbor—and its central message is the same, too: In this war, everybody contributes. It then goes on to state that women can be just as tough and determined as men in hard situations.

In 1943, few mainstream films had come to that self-evident realization.

See also
*M*A*S*H*
Three Came Home
Bataan
From Here to Eternity
The Story of G.I. Joe

So Proudly We Hail pays tribute
to the nurses who served in the
Pacific Theater in World War II.
Claudette Colbert (seated) The Kobal
Collection

Cast: Claudette Colbert (Lt. Janet Davidson), Paulette Goddard (Lt. Joan O'Doul), Veronica Lake (Lt. Olivia D'Arcy), George Reeves (Lt. John Summers), Barbara Britton (Lt. Rosemary Larson), Walter Abel (Chaplain), Sonny Tufts (Kansas), John Litel (Dr. Harrison), Mary Servoss (Capt. "Ma" McGregor), Ted Hecht (Dr. Jose Bardia), Mary Treen (Lt. Sadie Schwartz), Helen Lynd (Lt. Elsie Bollenbacher), Lorna Gray (Lt. Tony Dacolli), Dorothy Adams (Lt. Irma Emerson), Ann Doran (Lt. Betty Peterson), Jean Willes (Lt. Carol Johnson), Jan Wiley (Lt. Lynne Hopkins), Lynn Walker (Lt. Fay Leonard), Joan Tours (Lt. Margaret Stevenson), Kitty Kelly (Lt. Ethel Armstrong), James Bell (Col. White), Dick Hogan (Flight Lt. Archie McGregor), Bill Goodwin (Capt. O'Rourke), James Flavin (Capt. O'Brien); **Written by:** Allan Scott; **Music by:** Miklos Rozsa; **Technical Advisor:** Lt. Eunice Hatchitt. **Producer:** Mark Sandrich, Paramount Pictures. **Awards:** Nominations: Academy Awards '43: Best Black and White Cinematography, Best Original Screenplay, Best Special Effects, Best Supporting Actress (Goddard). **Running Time:** 126 minutes. **Format:** VHS, Closed Caption.

THEY WERE EXPENDABLE

1945 John Ford 🦴🦴🦴

On one level, John Ford's film can be seen as the Navy's answer to *Air Force* and *Bataan*. All three films are about the early days of the war in the Pacific, specifically about the humiliating American retreat from the Philippines. Ford, however, takes an approach that's diametrically opposite to the other two. Where they are essentially "unit pictures" about a group of diverse individuals who are brought together and molded into a single force, Ford's film begins with the unit already established and ready to fight. The immediate problem is that Lt. Brickley's (Robert Montgomery) superiors don't believe that his PT boats are an effective weapon against the Japanese Navy.

On the eve of Pearl Harbor, Brickley's executive officer, Lt. Rusty Ryan (John Wayne) is ready to request a transfer to destroyers. Once the fighting starts, he puts his personal ambition aside and enthusiastically rejoins the group. That's what the film is really about—discipline, obedience to orders, the subjugation of self to larger goals. The theme is repeated with variations throughout the film, both in the major dramatic moments and in smaller details. Frank Wead's script is based on William White's book about Ford's friend Lt. John Bulkeley, and though the naval combat is presented with the usual Hollywood exaggeration, the characters and their reactions to the situation seem accurate.

The only flaw in that department is the romance between Ryan and Lt. Sandy Davyss (Donna Reed), a nurse. At first, it seems uncomfortably stilted—neither Ford nor Wead were at their most perceptive with female characters and never claimed to be—but the relationship develops and ends along much more realistic lines, adding depth to the film's elegiac tone. Despite Ford's friendship with Bulkeley and his undisguised affection for the Navy, the film is not flag-waving propaganda or hero worship. It does have an almost reverential attitude toward the armed services, beginning with the opening titles that read "Manila Bay in the Year of Our Lord Nineteen Hundred and Forty-one" (instead of the simple "Manila Bay—1941") and ending with "The Battle Hymn of the Republic" swelling up over the closing credits.

At the same time, though, Ford is aiming for a degree of realism that films made earlier in the war lacked. He carefully points out, for example, how young many of the sailors were. His choice of the Florida Keys for Philippine locations is a solid step up from the soundstage jungles that filmmakers had been using. Much more importantly, he gets some of the best performances he ever coaxed out of a large ensemble cast, many of them Ford regulars. If John Wayne and Donna Reed have the most emotional dramatic moments, the film rests on Robert Montgomery's understated work. When the film was made, Montgomery had just left the Navy. Perhaps that experience gives him the aura of quiet conviction that provides the balance to Wayne's louder, more bellicose character. Ford works with the difference between the two

"Let me be honest. Motor torpedo boats were no good. You couldn't get close to anything without being spotted. I suppose we attacked capital ships maybe 40 times. I think we hit a bunch of them, but whether we sank anything is questionable. I got credit for sinking a destroyer but I don't think she sank. The PT brass were the greatest con artists of all times. They got everything they wanted—the cream of everything, especially personnel. The only thing PT's were really effective at was raising War Bonds."

PT boat skipper Leonard Nikoloric, quoted in *The Search for JFK* by Joan and Clay Blair, Jr. (Berkley-Putnam. 1976)

Did you Know?

Robert Montgomery actually commanded a PT boat in the Pacific. He also served on a destroyer at D-Day, was awarded the Bronze Star, and was decorated as Chevalier of the French Legion of Honor. When Ford was injured on the set, Montgomery took over direction of *They Were Expendable*, and from then on devoted most of his energy to direction.

Jack Holt, John Wayne, Robert Montgomery, and Ward Bond discuss how to most effectively use PT boats in combat in *They Were Expendable*. The Kobal Collection

throughout, but brings it to the surface only in the final scene, where he plays against all of the audience's heroic expectations.

It's an unusual conclusion to an unusually complex film. Reportedly, Ford was always ambivalent about *They Were Expendable*, but like *The Man Who Shot Liberty Valence* and *She Wore a Yellow Ribbon*, it's one of the sleepers in his large body of work.

Cast: Robert Montgomery (Lt. John Brickley), John Wayne (Lt. Rusty Ryan), Donna Reed (Second Lt. Sandy Davyss), Jack Holt (Gen. Martin), Ward Bond (Boots Mulcahey), Cameron Mitchell (Ens. George Cross), Leon Ames (Maj. James Morton), Marshall Thompson (Ens. Snake Gardner), Paul Langton (Ens. Andy Andrews), Donald Curtis (Lt. "Shorty" Long), Jeff York (Ens. Tony Aiken), Murray Alper (Slug Mahan), Jack Pennick (Doc), Alex Havier (Benny Lecoco), Charles Trowbridge (Adm. Blackwell), Robert Barrat (Gen. Douglas MacArthur), Bruce Kellogg (Elder Tompkins), Louis Jean Heydt (Ohio), Russell Simpson (Dad Knowland), Philip Ahn (Orderly), Betty Blythe (Officer's wife), William B. Davidson (Hotel manager), Pedro de Cordoba (The Priest), Arthur Walsh (Seaman Jones), Harry Tenbrook ("Cookie" Squarehead Larson), Tim Murdock (Ens. Brant), Vernon Steele (Army doctor); **Written by:** Frank Wead; **Cinematography by:** Joseph August; **Music by:** Herbert Stothart, Eric Zeisl. **Producer:** John Ford, Cliff Reid, MGM, Loew's, Inc. **Awards:** Nominations: Academy Awards '45: Best Sound. **Running Time:** 135 minutes. **Format:** VHS, Beta.

Due to the timing of its release so close to *Saving Private Ryan*, Terrence Malick's war film will be compared to Steven Spielberg's, and that's unfair. Malick's is a bad, bloated film in its own right (possibly even more bloated on home video). It's also a curious choice for an individualistic filmmaker using it as a comeback to an industry that he has been away from for 20 years. Since he'd made the critically acclaimed *Badlands* in 1974 and *Days of Heaven* in 1978, Malick had virtually disappeared. When he announced his comeback with an adaptation of James Jones's massive novel, the hottest young actors in the business flocked to him. Perhaps then, it was a combination of unrealistically high expectations and too-many-cooks that brought about this disappointment.

The subject is the battle of Guadalcanal. Early on, its strategic importance is stressed—in a beefy John Travolta's only scene—but film's focus quickly narrows to the actions of a few poorly defined characters. The one who eventually becomes the most important is Pvt. Witt (James Caviezel). In an idyllic prologue filled with beautiful Polynesian children swimming in crystal waters, Witt is introduced as an AWOL soldier. Sgt. Welsh (Sean Penn) brings him back to the unit. Initially, it is tempting to see Witt and Welsh as variations on Prewitt and Warden in *From Here to Eternity*, but that comparison quickly breaks down. Actually, the entire structure of a conventional combat film breaks down as the script's focus wanders aimlessly among several characters, including Sgt. Keck (Woody Harrelson) and Sgt. McCron (John Savage), who goes mad.

Roughly the first half concerns the taking of a grassy ridge. An apoplectic, self-serving Col. Tall (Nick Nolte) demands a suicidal charge. Capt. Staros (Elias Koteas) is reluctant to lead it; Capt. Gaff (John Cusack) is not. When the battle is finally joined, it is presented with originality and intensity. But that intensity is watered down by Malick's penchant for pretty pictures of windblown grasses, leaves, raindrops, and tropical birds—all meant to remind us of larger concerns about fate, god, morality, nature, and such. And if the images aren't enough, Malick has several characters (at least, I think there were more than one) indulge in long voice-over meditations about the meaning of it all, not to mention Witt's woozy flashbacks about his angelic wife. These guys sound and act more like English grad students than soldiers.

The acting ranges from indifferent to effective to outrageous. When Nolte flies into a rage, it appears that every vein in his head is about to explode. But it is difficult to blame the cast of pretty boys for the lack of their characters' depth. Malick shuffles them on and off stage so quickly and without introduction that they leave no impression. They're just a bunch of guys with heavy five-o'clock shadows and steel helmets. According to pre-release publicity and a credits list that included deleted characters, a much longer version of the film exists, and Malick has hinted that the extended cut will be released on home video.

As it exists now, the film is dramatically weak and unbalanced. The single definitive moral confrontation, between Tall and Staros, is dispensed with almost as soon as it is raised. The rest meanders for another hour or so before the story comes to an appropriately inconclusive conclusion.

Bell (Ben Chaplin), Gaff (John Cusack), and Witt (Jim Caviezel) plan their next move in *The Thin Red Line.* The Kobal Collection

Cast: James Caviezel (Pvt. Witt), Adrien Brody (Cpl. Fife), Sean Penn (First Sgt. Edward Welsh), Nick Nolte (Lt. Col. Gordon Tall), John Cusack (Capt. John Gaff), George Clooney (Capt. Charles Bosche), Woody Harrelson (Sgt. Keck), Ben Chaplin (Pvt. Bell), Elias Koteas (Capt. James "Bugger" Staros), Jared Leto (Lt. Whyte), John Travolta (Brig. Gen. Quintard), Tim Blake Nelson (Pvt. Tills), John C. Reilly (Sgt. Storm), John Savage (Sgt. McCron), Arie Verveen (Pfc. Dale), David Harrod (Cpl. Queen), Thomas Jane (Pvt. Ash), Paul Gleason (First Lt. George Band), Penelope Allen (Witt's mother), Don Harvey (Becker), Shawn Hatosy (Tella), Donal Logue (Marl), Dash Mihok (Pfc. Doll), Larry Romano (Pvt. Mazzi); **Written by:** Terrence Malick; **Cinematography by:** John Toll; **Music by:** Hans Zimmer. **Producer:** Robert Michael Greisler, John Roberdeau, Grant Hill, George Stevens, Fox 2000 Pictures; released by 20th Century-Fox. **Awards:** New York Film Critics Awards '98: Best Director (Malick); National Society of Film Critics Awards '98: Best Cinematography; Nominations: Academy Awards '98: Best Adapted Screenplay, Best Cinematography, Best Director (Malick), Best Film Editing, Best Picture, Best Sound; Directors Guild of America Awards '98: Best Director (Malick). **Budget:** 52M. **MPAA Rating:** R. **Running Time:** 170 minutes. **Format:** VHS, Closed Caption, DVD.

THIRTY SECONDS OVER TOKYO

1944 Mervyn LeRoy ♫♫♫

Of all the reality-inspired films of World War II, this one really cries out for a remake. Given another chance, filmmakers could focus more intently on the bold mission and the men who flew it. They could leave out the tepid romance and I'm-going-to-be-a-father subplot that clutter up the first half. The story of the Doolittle raid is fascinating enough on its own. In April 1942, less than six months after the Japanese attack on Pearl Harbor, Col. Jimmy Doolittle (Spencer Tracy) led a bombing attack on Tokyo and Yokohama. At the time, such an operation was thought to be impossible. No bomber could fly that far, and bombers could not take off or land on an aircraft carrier. Or could they? It turned out that with the proper training, a crew could perfect a technique to get a B-25 Mitchell bomber into the air within the length of a carrier deck. Ted Lawson (Van Johnson) was one of the pilots who volunteered for the secret mission. At the time, he was newly married to Ellen (Phyllis Thaxter).

The early training scenes were filmed in Pensacola, Florida, where they really occurred. Like the other scenes involving real airplanes, they sparkle. Director Mervyn LeRoy, cinematographers Harold Rosson and Robert Surtees, and recording director Douglas Shearer turn the B-25s into key parts of the story. The sets recreating the interiors of the planes have an authentic feeling, right down to the rack where David Thatcher (Robert Walker) keeps his thermos of coffee. The sounds of the engines, the bulky appearance, and the gracefully ungainly look of the airplane in flight are also important.

The raid itself is carefully re-created and is faithful to its source material, a *Collier's* magazine article and book by Lawson and Robert Considine. LeRoy and screenwriter Dalton Trumbo show the raid as Lawson and his crew saw it. They use no music, little dialogue—just the drone of the engines, the mechanics of flying, aiming the bomb sight, actually dropping the bombs. It's fascinating stuff, told without the usual Hollywood trappings and all the more effective for it.

What happens afterward necessarily loses some focus, though it is still interesting. After all, they knew how to get a bomber off an aircraft carrier; they didn't know how to land one. It's much more emotional and conventionally adventurous material, but something of a letdown after the flying scenes. The symbolism during a key Christmas dream scene has become unfortunately and unintentionally comic. That's a small flaw, however. The special effects won an Oscar in 1944 and they stand up well today.

"Here, you suddenly realize you're gonna dump a ton of high explosives on one of the biggest cities in the world... I don't pretend to like the idea of killing a bunch of people, but it's a case of drop a bomb on them or pretty soon they'll be dropping one on Ellen."

Ted Lawson (Van Johnson), aboard the aircraft carrier *Hornet*, en route to Tokyo.

See also
Catch-22
Twelve O'Clock High
Sink the Bismarck

James Doolittle (Spencer Tracy)
addresses bomber crews just
before the famous raid on
Tokyo. The Kobal Collection

Cast: Spencer Tracy (Lt. Col. James H. "Jimmy" Doolittle), Van Johnson (Capt. Ted Lawson), Robert Walker (David Thatcher), Robert Mitchum (Bob Gray), Phyllis Thaxter (Ellen Lawson), Scott McKay (Davey Jones), Stephen McNally (Doc White), Louis Jean Heydt (Lt. Miller), Leon Ames (Lt. Juriles), Paul Langton (Capt. "Ski" York), Don DeFore (Charles McClure), Tim Murdock (Dean Davenport), Alan Napier (Mr. Parker), Dorothy Morris (Jane), Jacqueline White (Emmy York), Selena Royle (Mrs. Reynolds), Bill Phillips (Don Smith), Donald Curtis (Lt. Randall), Gordon McDonald (Bob Clever), John R. Reilly (Shorty Manch), Douglas Cowan (Brick Holstrom), Ann Shoemaker (Mrs. Parker), Steve Brodie (M.P.); **Written by:** Dalton Trumbo; **Cinematography by:** Robert L. Surtees, Harold Rosson; **Music by:** Herbert Stothart. **Producer:** Sam Zimbalist, MGM, Loew's, Inc. **Awards:** Academy Awards '44: Best Special Effects; Nominations: Academy Awards '44: Best Black and White Cinematography. **Running Time:** 138 minutes. **Format:** VHS, Beta.

Robert Aldrich's attempt to recapture the success of *The Dirty Dozen* is emblematic of the state of the war film in the late 1960s and early '70s. It begins as a standard jungle action picture along the lines of *Objective, Burma!*, but then changes course midway through to reflect the anti-war sentiments of the Vietnam era. Neither extreme is really convincing, despite some fine Philippine locations and a solid cast.

In the spring of 1942 in the Southwest Pacific, Lt. Lawson (Cliff Robertson) is doing everything he can to avoid his duties when Capt. Nolan (Henry Fonda, in a brief cameo) volunteers him for a secret mission. Lawson, who can speak Japanese, is to fly to the New Hebrides, where he will accompany a British commando unit into the enemy-controlled portion of the island and broadcast a fake radio message. It all has to do with a convoy carrying American troops, but that side of the plot is so muddled that it's never particularly believable, nor particularly important to the rest of the action. Aldrich and writers Lukas Heller and Robert Sherman might have dreamed up this loopy concoction to take advantage of existing sets and locations, which, by the way, are strikingly photographed by Joseph F. Biroc.

The mission begins in fairly standard fashion, until the leader, Capt. Hornsby (Denholm Elliott) proves to be something of a bumbler, a cold-blooded bumbler who shoots the wounded, but a bumbler nonetheless. Pvt. Hearne (Michael Caine) immediately erupts into open rebellion, but by then the group is several miles behind the lines. When Lawson chimes in to support Hearne, Hornsby says, "For all I know, you could be some long-haired conscientious objector." Soon after that anachronistic remark, some camouflage paint appears in a flowerpower psychedelic pattern, and the film makes its leftward turn.

In the second half, the handsome and compassionate Maj. Yamaguchi (Ken Takakura), speaking to the commandos via loudspeaker, tries to persuade them to surrender for the good of all concerned. At the same time, the surviving British and American characters debate their various responsibilities to the mission and to each other, creating a slow, talky pace. The filmmakers make it far too clear that they mean to advance the idea that there's no difference between the sides. The backstabbing Americans are even more bloodthirsty and treacherous than the Japanese.

No one can doubt that American war movies have portrayed the Japanese in derogatory, racist terms. But this attempt to balance the ledger is every bit as distorted and false, and it's handled so clumsily that it's not about to change anyone's mind. More importantly for audiences, the characters don't inspire enough sympathy to offset the structural weaknesses. Similar criticisms concerning improbable plotting and stereotyped villains could be leveled at *The Dirty Dozen*, but the pace moves so quickly and the performances are so good that nobody cares. An able cast cannot work the same magic twice.

Cliff Robertson (left) and Michael Caine are commandos in the very anti-war *Too Late the Hero*. The Kobal Collection

Cast: Michael Caine (Pvt. Tosh Hearne), Cliff Robertson (Lt. Lawson), Henry Fonda (Capt. John G. Nolan), Ian Bannen (Pvt. Thornton), Harry Andrews (Col. Thompson), Denholm Elliott (Capt. Hornsby), William Beckley (Pvt. Currie), Ronald Fraser (Campbell), Percy Herbert (Sgt. Johnstone), Patrick Jordan (Sergeant Major), Harvey Jason (Signalman Scott), Sam Kydd (Sergeant Major), Ken Takakura (Maj. Yamaguchi); **Written by:** Robert Aldrich, Lukas Heller, Robert B. Sherman; **Cinematography by:** Joseph Biroc; **Music by:** Gerald Fried. **Producer:** Robert Aldrich, Cinerama Releasing. **MPAA Rating:** PG. **Running Time:** 133 minutes. **Format:** VHS, Beta.

TORA! TORA! TORA!

1970 Richard Fleischer, Toshio Masuda, Kinji Fukasaku 🎵🎵🎵

From the early '60s to the mid-'70s, the large-scale historical re-creation of a key World War II engagement was a dominant sub-genre in war films. These are expensive productions with large, star-studded casts designed to appeal to an international audience. *Tora! Tora! Tora!* is among the most accurate in its depiction of the events leading up to the attack on Pearl Harbor, and the attack itself is presented with some remarkably realistic action footage. The high-priced cast is notably absent, with more than competent character actors handling the dramatic work. More unusual is the film's divided focus, which shows the event from both the American and Japanese perspectives, with directorial duties divided among Richard Fleischer, Kinji Fukasaku and Toshio Masuda.

In an excellent essay in the book *Past Imperfect* (Holt. 1995), Harvard historian Akira Iriye argues that the film is too sympathetic to the Japanese point of view, casting the Japanese Navy in a more flattering light than it deserves. But on most significant details, he gives the filmmakers high marks for truthfulness.

The first 70 minutes or so is devoted to the Japanese conception of a plan to take the American Navy out of the Pacific Theater with one blow. Japanese leaders regard that part of the world as their natural sphere of influence and see conflict with America as inevitable. When the Americans move the Pacific Fleet from San Diego to Hawaii, Prime Minister Prince Konoye (Koreya Senda) says that it is "a knife leveled at Japan's throat." Adm. Isoroku Yamamoto (Soh Yamamura) disagrees, but when ordered to come up with a theoretical battle plan, he accepts.

That part of the film is necessarily clumsy and slow as it follows Japanese diplomatic developments and the fitful preparations for war being made in Washington and Hawaii. At Hickam Field, Gen. Short (Jason Robards Jr.) makes all the wrong moves when he decides that saboteurs are a more immediate threat than an air attack and orders that all aircraft be parked close together near the runway. In D.C., Col. Bratton (E.G. Marshall) of the Army's G-2 intelligence branch and Lt. Cmdr. Kramer (Wesley Addy) of Naval Intelligence have broken the Japanese diplomatic code and are working with the Magic Intercepts of sensitive documents. On the night of Saturday, December 6, Kramer dashes around the city trying to get his superiors to pay attention to an ominous partial message. At the same time, the Japanese generals and admirals are debating the wisdom of their strategy and trying to postpone critical decisions until the last moment possible.

When the die is finally cast, the attack begins with a long, beautifully photographed sequence of the Japanese planes taking off from carrier decks into dim, predawn sky. The directors are able to make the intense anticipation and excitement of the young pilots seem real and infectious—even to American viewers. The attack on Battleship Row and the airfield begins with striking scenes of exploding airplanes and ships.

See also

The Longest Day
Thirty Seconds over Tokyo
Air Force
Battle of Midway
Dec. 7th
The Battle of Britain

"Tora! Tora! Tora!"
Translation: "Tiger! Tiger! Tiger!"

The Japanese signal for a successful attack on Pearl Harbor

"If we fight the Americans we can't stop at Hawaii or San Francisco. We'll have to march into Washington and dictate peace terms in the White House. Army hotheads who speak so lightly of war should think about that."

Adm. Yamamoto (Soh Yamamura)

"Many misinformed Japanese believe that America is a nation divided, isolationist, and that Americans are only interested in enjoying a life of luxury and are spiritually and morally corrupt. But that is a great mistake. If war becomes inevitable America would be the most formidable foe that we have ever fought."

Adm. Yamamoto

Did you Know?

Originally, *Tora! Tora! Tora!* was to be made as two films, one from the American point of view, the other from the Japanese. Director Akira Kurosawa began work on the Japanese film, but quickly became dissatisfied and either resigned or caused himself to be fired from the project.

James Whitmore (left) and Martin Balsam are two of the members of the U.S. Navy brass who were not expecting the Japanese attack on Pearl Harbor in December of 1941 in *Tora! Tora! Tora!*. The Kobal Collection

But the filmmakers do not follow through with all of the subplots that they introduce. The most important of them involve a flight of B-17s that arrive in the middle of the attack and a couple of American fighters that make it into the air. Neither is satisfactorily resolved.

Much of the dialogue has a false, "loaded" quality that sounds wrong (see Quotes), and the pyrotechnics, as impressive as they are, wear thin, too. Even so, *Tora! Tora! Tora!* casts a new light on a pivotal moment in world history, and is worth watching for that reason if no other.

Cast: Martin Balsam (Adm. Husband E. Kimmel), Soh Yamamura (Adm. Isoroku Yamamoto), Joseph Cotten (Sec. of War Henry L. Stimson), E.G. Marshall (Col. Rufus G. Bratton), Tatsuya Mihashi (Cmdr. Genda), Wesley Addy (Lt. Cmdr. Alvin D. Kramer), Jason Robards Jr. (Lt. Gen. Walter C. Short), James Whitmore (Adm. William F. Halsey, Jr.), Leon Ames (Frank Knox), George Macready (Sec. of State Cordell Hull), Takahiro Tamura (Lt. Cmdr. Mitsuo Fuchida), Eijiro Tono (Adm. Chuichi Nagumo), Shogo Shimada (Ambassador Nomura), Koreya Senda (Prince Konoye), Jun Usami (Adm. Yoshida), Richard Anderson (Capt. John Earle), Kazuo Kitamura (Foreign Minister Yosuke Matsuoka), Keith Andes (Gen. George C. Marshall), Edward Andrews (Adm. Harold R. Stark), Neville Brand (Lt. Kaminsky), Leora Dana (Mrs. Kramer), Walter Brooke (Capt. Theodore Wilkinson), Norman Alden (Maj. Truman Landon), Ron Masak (Lt. Laurence Ruff), Edmon Ryan (Rear Adm. Bellinger), Asao Uchida (Gen. Hideki Tojo), Frank Aletter (Lt. Cmdr. Thomas), Jerry Fogel (Lt. Cmdr. William Outerbridge); **Written by:** Ryuzo Kikushima, Hideo Oguni, Larry Forrester; **Cinematography by:** Sinsaku Himeda, Charles F. Wheeler, Osamu Furuya; **Music by:** Jerry Goldsmith. **Producer:** Elmo Williams, 20th Century-Fox. **Awards:** Academy Awards '70: Best Visual Effects; Nominations: Academy Awards '70: Best Art Direction/Set Decoration, Best Cinematography, Best Film Editing, Best Sound. **MPAA Rating:** G. **Running Time:** 144 minutes. **Format:** VHS, Beta, LV.

Perhaps the most astonishing thing about this early masterpiece of propaganda is not that it is so good, but that it was made so quickly. The truth-based feature premiered less than nine months after the actual events took place. It is an economically told story made on a few wellchosen locations by the Salton Sea. The facts dictate a quick pace, but the film never feels hurried or slapdash. The overall quality is so high that it received several Academy Award nominations and might have won a few had it not been up against more polished competition, including William Wyler's *Mrs. Miniver*, which pretty much swept the field in 1942.

A brief prologue set in November, 1941, introduces Maj. Caton (Brian Donlevy), the commanding officer who's arriving to take over the newly established base on a tiny, desolate island hundreds of miles west of Hawaii. "My outfit's supposed to be a defense battalion," he says, "I don't see much to defend here—matter of fact, not much to defend it with." Already on the scene are Pvt. Aloysius "Smacksie" Randall (William Bendix) and Pvt. Joe Doyle (Robert Preston), a couple of battling friends whose rough-and-tumble is genuinely funny comic relief.

Immediately after the attack on Pearl Harbor, a Japanese air and naval task force threatens the island. Though the Marines are vastly outnumbered and outgunned, they dig in and hold on. The shelling and aerial attacks are shown in all their destructiveness. Though director John Farrow aims most of his explosives and pyrotechnics at inanimate objects and the surrounding landscape, the ferocity of the assault is impressive and frightening.

The performances equal the effects. Though Donlevy was usually cast as a heavy—and won an Oscar for his villainous sergeant in *Beau Geste*—his gruff urgency is perfect for this part. He's believable in both the emotional moments and the action scenes. Co-star William Bendix received a Best Supporting Actor nomination for his role, one which he would repeat often in the following years. He and Preston really do steal the film with lines like, "On your way, bubblepuss, or I'll pat you with me shovel."

Veteran screenwriters W.R. Burnett (*Little Caesar*, *Asphalt Jungle*) and Frank Butler (*Going My Way*, several Hope and Crosby Road pictures) understand their job. In other hands, the material could have been revisionist saber-rattling. They use it to turn a recent defeat into motivation for an audience that needs hope. They do that by sticking close to the known facts and understating the onscreen heroics. (Only in the voice-over postscript do they cut loose.) The result is one of the least dated and most entertaining films of the era.

"These Marines fought a great fight. They wrote history but this is not the end. There are other Leathernecks, other fighting Americans, 140 million of them whose blood and sweat and fury will exact a just and terrible vengeance."

Closing voice-over

See also

Fighting Seabees
Air Force
Bataan
Thirty Seconds over Tokyo

Robert Preston (left) and William Bendix prepare for another Japanese attack on *Wake Island.* The Kobal Collection

Cast: Robert Preston (Joe Doyle), Brian Donlevy (Maj. Geoffrey Caton), William Bendix (Pvt. Aloysius "Smacksie" Randall), MacDonald Carey (Lt. Bruce Cameron), Albert Dekker (Shad McClosky), Walter Abel (Cmdr. Roberts), Rod Cameron (Capt. Lewis), Barbara Britton (Sally Cameron), Mikhail Rasumny (Probenzky), Bill Goodwin (Sgt. Higbee), Damian O'Flynn (Capt. Patrick), Frank Albertson (Johnny Rudd), Hugh Beaumont (Captain), Hillary Brooke (Girl at inn), James Brown (Wounded 1st Lieutenant), Don Castle (Pvt. Cunkle), Frank Faylen (Wounded marine), Mary Field (Miss Pringle), William Forrest (Maj. Johnson), Alan Hale Jr. (Sight setter), Charles Trowbridge (George Nielson), Philip Van Zandt (Cpl. Goebbels), Phillip Terry (Pvt. Warren); **Written by:** W.R. Burnett, Frank Butler; **Cinematography by:** William Mellor, Theodor Sparkuhl; **Music by:** David Buttolph. **Producer:** Joseph Sistrom, Paramount Pictures. **Awards:** New York Film Critics Awards '42: Best Director (Farrow); Nominations: Academy Awards '42: Best Director (Farrow), Best Original Screenplay, Best Picture, Best Supporting Actor (Bendix). **Running Time:** 88 minutes. **Format:** VHS, Beta.

WORLD WAR II
Documentaries

World War II:
Documentaries on Screen

Even before America entered World War II, some of Hollywood's best filmmakers were actively engaged in work against the Germans and Japanese. John Ford had been snooping unofficially with naval intelligence since the 1920s. Actually, there were no real American intelligence services between the wars, but Ford was connected to a group of officers (and with J. Edgar Hoover) who were sure that another war was coming. (*John Ford: A Biography*. Andrew Sinclair. Dial Press. 1979) Later, Ford would serve with "Wild" Bill Donovan and the O.S.S. as head of the Field Photographic Branch. During the war, he was on a PT boat at the Normandy invasion, and before then, he had directed one of the first important documentaries, *The Battle of Midway*.

In May 1942, the Navy knew that the Japanese had targeted the island. Ford flew there and shot as much color film as he could of the attack as it was happening. He then edited the "real" footage with staged scenes and added narration to tell a short inspirational story of American resistance to aggression.

In 1943, John Huston made *Report from the Aleutians*. Though it doesn't have the graphic violence and conflict of Ford's film, it's a fascinating glimpse of a remote part of the war—and the world—that few people know about. Huston found more exciting material when he went to Italy and followed the infantry as it attacked a strong German position. *The Battle of San Pietro* has existed in several different running times, and some have claimed that the shorter versions sanitize the violence and horror of the campaign. If so, what's left is an impressive piece of work.

The most famous documentary to come out of the war is William Wyler's *Memphis Belle*, the story of an American B-17 crew flying its last mission from England before going home. Like several other non-fiction films made during the war years, it was given a theatrical run, and like the others, it did not do particularly well. Then, as now, documentaries find it hard to compete with Hollywood fiction.

Perhaps the most widely-seen documentaries were the government's *Why We Fight* series. These seven films—directed by Frank Capra and Ernst Lubitsch, and written by Julius and Philip Epstein (*Casablanca*)—present a boldly propagandistic overview of recent (1920s and '30s) history and explain the reasons behind the war. The films were required viewing, literally, for every man and woman in uniform who was going overseas. How much good did that series and the other documentaries do? No one can say with any real certainty, but, hey, we won.

BATTLE OF MIDWAY
1942 John Ford ♪♪♪♪

The significance of John Ford's Oscar-winning documentary lies more in its historical importance than in its entertainment value. A commander in the Navy, Ford was on Midway Island when the Japanese attacked in 1942. As the story goes, when he learned what was about to happen, he placed 16mm cameras filled with color film in the sand and filmed as much of the action as he could. Ford also shot film himself from a water tower while he was relaying information on Japanese planes to men on the ground. Two of the cameras were destroyed and some of the footage was damaged. What survived became this no-frills version of the incident.

Ford sets the stage with images familiar from his Hollywood films—reverence for the military, marching Marines still wearing the flat World War I helmets, unashamed sentimentality with a guy softly playing "Red River Valley" on the squeeze-box at sunset. There's even a bit of voice-over dialogue from Henry Fonda. The air attack is abrupt, with planes coming in low and fast while American gunners fight back from anti-aircraft batteries. When the bombs explode, the cameras shake so violently that the film seems to be wrenched out of its sprockets and the sky is filled with heavy oily black smoke. Following the attack, a short coda of a church service at a bombed hospital casts the battle as a conflict between devout American boys and "Godless Japs."

The larger picture of what happened elsewhere is shown in the numbers of planes and ships destroyed. In short, the film is John Ford's home movie of what he saw at the battle. But in its brief running time, the film shows an aerial attack in all its mad confusion, and those images are so powerful that the film won an Academy Award for Best Documentary. (Reportedly, the President and Mrs. Roosevelt were so moved by a White House screening of the film that FDR said, "I want every mother in America to see this picture!") A year later, Ford would win another Documentary Oscar for *Dec. 7th*, his recreation of the attack on Pearl Harbor, co-directed with cinematographer Gregg Toland. In artistic and technical terms, the two films are polar opposites, and so they would make a fascinating double feature for anyone interested in the movie industry's first attempts at capturing the war on screen.

See also
Tora! Tora! Tora!
Report from the Aleutians
Dec. 7th
In Harm's Way
Midway
Thirty Seconds over Tokyo

An American fighter at the
Battle of Midway. The Kobal Collection

Written by: Dudley Nichols, James K. McGuinness, John Ford; **Cinematography by:** Jack MacKenzie, John Ford; **Music by:** Alfred Newman. **Producer:** John Ford, U.S. Navy. **Awards:** Academy Awards '42: Best Feature Documentary. **Running Time:** 18 minutes. **Format:** VHS, Beta.

The Hound Salutes: John Ford

Long recognized as one of America's first "great" film-makers, John Ford has been lionized by most critics. "Ford was among the most durable creative directors of the American cinema, with some 50 years of continual high-quality work to his credit, all of it stamped with his unmistakable signature," says Ephraim Katz in *The Film Encyclopedia*.

Given a different political and historical perspective, others have been more critical. In *A Biographical Dictionary of Film*, David Thomson writes, "Ford's male chauvinism believes in uniforms, drunken candor, fresh-faced little women (though never sexuality), a gallery of supporting players bristling with tedious eccentricity, and the elevation of these random prejudices into a near-political attitude." To a degree at least, Thomson is right. Those qualities are evident in much of Ford's work, but he created some fine films that people still watch, not out of any sense of obligation, but for enjoyment.

Though Ford will always be known first for his westerns, much of his important work—*The Grapes of Wrath*, *The Quiet Man*, *The Last Hurrah*—was outside the genre. He also made significant contributions to the war film, where his best pictures share many characteristics with his westerns. The two genres overlap in his excellent "cavalry trilogy"—*Fort Apache*, *She Wore a Yellow Ribbon*, and *Rio Grande*—and in his first sound war film, *The Lost Patrol* (1934), which tells an elemental story of desert warfare with the economical style that the filmmaker would perfect later in his career.

Ford was always attracted to the military, and in the 1930s he engaged in some kind of espionage in cooperation with Naval Intelligence, and later during the war for the O.S.S. In that capacity, his most important work came when he filmed an actual Japanese attack. *The Battle of Midway* was one of the first important film records of the war. Though it is classified as a documentary, Ford added fictional voice-overs from Henry Fonda and others to give the film its emotional punch. A year later, he and cinematographer Gregg Toland re-created the attack on Pearl Harbor in *December 7th*. The Navy objected to the many references to military unpreparedness and so the feature-length allegorical documentary was cut down to 32 minutes. Like *The Battle of Midway*, it won an Oscar. The full-length version was not available until it was restored for home video in 1991.

At the end of the war, Ford produced his best full-length fictional account of it, *They Were Expendable*, about the PT boat experiences of his friend, Cmdr. John Bulkeley. After the war, Ford channeled his military interests into veterans' activities off camera and the cavalry trilogy, where some see Indians symbolizing international communism. In his book *John Wayne's America*, Garry Wills states that "John Ford came out of World War II in love with the Navy, with military units in general, and with America's new imperial role as the asserter of freedom everywhere." Whether that's accurate or not, it is true that Ford was a conservative who celebrated the virtues of traditional institutions.

The last time he returned to World War II was with the ill-fated adaptation of *Mister Roberts*. Star Henry Fonda, who had worked closely and well with Ford in the past, wanted to stick close to the character he had created on the stage. The director wanted to make a slapstick service comedy. The two men eventually came to blows over the matter. Ford, in poor health and drinking heavily, was finally replaced, and the film reflects both approaches. He would go on to make other memorable films, but his work in the genre was over.

In the end, the extremes of praise and condemnation are both incomplete. Much of Ford's humor has aged poorly, and racist attitudes are never far from the surface, but his best films are solidly constructed, well-told stories. Perhaps David Thomson is closest to the mark when he tempers his political criticism of the director with the observation, "Ford's art was always that of a mythmaker, a wishful thinker, a man without stamina for reality—a moviemaker."

John Ford The Kobal Collection

BATTLE OF SAN PIETRO

1944 John Huston ♫♫♫♫

"The version we are now seeing is a cut down, watered, treated, packaged, hyped-up, and bled away patriotic product. It opens with Gen. Mark Clark, apparently reading off a blackboard to the right of a studio camera some place else, uglified by his life and using only the bare minimum of his body in this distasteful public relations job—one corner of his mouth. His little speech assures us about the necessity of destroying 'San Pietro, the key to the valley,' so that we won't believe the evidence of our eyes. It was a successful action, he says. To prove his point, the soundtrack has been invaded by heaving, seasick movie music, more suitable for selling Dristan, underscoring the invasion of the eight sinus cavities, than for describing this deathly struggle; the St. Brendan's Boys Choir and the Mormon Tabernacle Chorus offer further musical and religious sanction to the disaster; and the film concludes with that seasoned crotch sign modeled on Winston Churchill's two fingers, the V for Victory. "No matter. Even cut and distorted, the film is a masterpiece of experienced immediate horror."

Herb Gold on *Battle of San Pietro*, from *Film: Book 2*, edited by Robert Hughes (Grove Press. 1962), reprinted from *The New Yorker Film Notes*, Winter 60-61.

According to reference books and anecdotal sources, John Huston's documentary snapshot of one part of the Italian campaign has existed in at least three different versions. One, about five reels or 50 minutes long, was shown to American soldiers during World War II. Then a shortened, 30-minute edition with an introduction by General Mark Clark and a new musical soundtrack was released theatrically. (In a 1962 interview, Huston said that much of the deleted material concerned American casualties, and that the cuts were made primarily to gain wider distribution in theaters. Exhibitors did not want to handle a longer film.) The version now widely available on tape lacks the introduction but retains the soundtrack.

It's still grim stuff.

Using simple charts and a pointer, Huston describes the Liri Valley of Italy, an agricultural region that lay right in the path of the German retreat and the American advance through the country. As he drily notes in the voice-over narration, "Last year was a bad year for grapes and olives and the fall planting was late." From the end of October 1943, until mid-December, German and American soldiers fought in the region. The Germans were dug into the mountains. To reach them, the Americans had to make their way up unprotected slopes or to attempt flanking maneuvers on narrow twisting roads. Both routes were extremely costly.

To film the action, Huston and his camera crew moved with the soldiers using hand-held cameras loaded with black-and-white film. When shells explode nearby and the image shakes, it's not a special effect. When a G.I. creeping behind a tree suddenly falls, he's not a stuntman. The body half covered with loose dirt is not going to get up when the camera is turned off. Huston presents the slow-moving, back-and-forth tidal swings of the conflict mostly without comment. He describes what's happening, blaming no one for decisions that may have been incorrect and always referring to the Germans simply as "the enemy." Compared to other Hollywood directors who worked for the War Department, Huston is restrained. He's interested in the human cost of the conflict, not bellicose saber-rattling.

That comes into even sharper focus at the end, when the narration ceases and the haunting images speak for themselves: dead G.I.s being loaded into white body bags, an Italian woman walking carefully down a street with a coffin balanced on her head, a soldier's rough hands hammering dog tags onto makeshift wooden grave markers.

It's no surprise then that *Battle of San Pietro* has virtually no propaganda value. It will never be used as a recruiting film.

See also

Report from the Aleutians
A Walk in the Sun
Battleground

An Italian boy wanders through the rubble in *Battle of San Pietro*.

The Kobal Collection

Written by: Eric Ambler, John Huston; **Cinematography by:** Jules Buck, John Huston; **Music by:** Dimitri Tiomkin. **Producer:** U.S. Office of War Information, Frank Capra. **Awards:** National Film Registry '91. **Running Time:** 43 minutes. **Format:** VHS, Beta.

MEMPHIS BELLE: A STORY OF A FLYING FORTRESS

1944 William Wyler ♫♫♫♫

Note:

The title is in public domain, so it's available from several sources. The Video Treasures edition is recorded in the substandard EP mode, but it is watchable. It also contains a Democratic political cartoon from the 1944 Presidential campaign made by Chuck Jones, of Loony Tunes fame.

By far the best copy that I've seen is the "55th Anniversary" edition from Antiquary Video (1-800-225-0208). It's beautifully transferred from film to tape.

Fact:

Making *Memphis Belle* cost Wyler his hearing. He didn't realize how loud the engines and the machine guns were. He was discharged and sent back home almost completely deaf. As of this writing, the fate of the airplane itself is in some doubt. The Belle, still owned by the Air Force, has been on display in a pavilion at the Mud Island Park in Memphis, but the city and the *Memphis Belle* Association are at odds on its preservation. The plane has fallen into disrepair and is in need of restoration. The various parties involved cannot decide who will pay for it.

Soon after America entered World War II, director William Wyler, then age 40, joined the Army Air Corps. "I was European and Jewish," he said in an interview for the PBS *American Masters* series, "and I didn't enlist as an ordinary soldier. I enlisted as a filmmaker to see if I could make a film that would help the war effort in some small way and that's what I did." The result is this landmark documentary.

To make the film, Wyler and his crew flew in a B-17 named *Memphis Belle*, "324th Squadron, 91st Heavy Bombardment Group," on daylight bombing runs over Europe. They shot film when they could and machine guns when they had to. There are no simulations or re-creations or special effects.

It begins with the bombs being loaded in flying fortresses on a clear morning in the English countryside. At the briefing, the pilots learn that their target is the submarine pens in Wilhelmshaven, part of "the greater menace . . . the power behind the German lust for conquest." We're introduced to the crew of *Memphis Belle*, who are on their 25th and final mission. The pilot, Capt. Robert Morgan from Ashville, North Carolina; co-pilot Capt. Jim Veneris, a business administration student from the University of Connecticut; radio operator and gunner Sgt. Bob Hanson, a construction worker from Spokane, Washington; navigator Capt. Chuck Lathan, a chemistry student at Ohio Wesleyan; engineer and top turret gunner Sgt. Harold Lott from Green Bay, Wisconsin; tail gunner Sgt. John Quinlan from Yonkers, New York; ball turret gunner Sgt. Cecil Scott from Rahway, New Jersey; bombadier Capt. Vincent Evans from Fort Worth; waist gunners Sgt. Bill Winchell, who works for a paint company in Chicago; and Sgt. Tony Nastal from Detroit. If they come back from this one, they go home to train others.

Then the cameras move into the bomber with them and the mission begins. It's terrifying, but at the same time, strangely beautiful with the intense blue of the sky, numbers and symbols reflected in the scratched plexiglass, the geometric precision of the B-17s in formation, and the hypnotic drone of the engines. When you realize that the flashes coming from the fuzzy little dark specks outside are real bullets fired from real German fighters, the film achieves a striking degree of reality. It doesn't matter that the color is grainy or that the sound is off in places on the videotape. We see what the crew sees—sky, flak, distant ground, fighters that appear as specks, smoke. And we hear what they hear—the guns, the radio ("Dammit," Morgan mutters, "don't yell on that intercom.").

Memphis Belle is just a remarkable and influential piece of filmmaking. Virtually every film made about the air war since pays homage to it. Though Wyler may not have enjoyed the public recognition of some other directors of his generation, his fellow filmmakers realized how good he was, and his work was respected within the industry. Everyone knew that he had shown the European air war the way it was, and those images have been repeated and copied hundreds of times.

See also

Memphis Belle (1990)
Twelve O'Clock High
Catch-22
Command Decision

And, decades later, Hollywood gave the film its ultimate flattery with a fictional remake that's about a third as good as the original.

The *Memphis Belle* on one of its daytime bombing raids over Germany. Del Valle Archives

Producer: U.S. War Department, William Wyler. **Running Time:** 43 minutes. **Format:** VHS, Beta.

REPORT FROM THE ALEUTIANS

1943 John Huston ♫♫♫

As the first Technicolor documentary that director John Huston made for the Army Signal Corps, this film lacks a certain dramatic tension. Instead, as the title indicates, it's a valuable record of a virtually unknown and unseen part of World War II. In a voice-over introduction, Huston says, "The Aleutian Islands are situated in the North Pacific Ocean, forming a chain which extends about 1,200 miles south southwest from the Alaskan peninsula toward Siberia to form the southern boundary of the Bering Sea. The Aleutians comprise four groups—the Fox, Andreanof, Rat, and Near islands—and constitute part of the territory of Alaska, USA."

Obviously, Huston and the War Department wanted to let soldiers know what was going on there, but before they could define the action, they had to tell people where it was and to make sure that they knew it was part of their country. In June 1942, the Japanese attacked Midway—everyone knows about that—and a second part of the naval force went north and attacked the Aleutians. The raid was unsuccessful, but the Japanese did manage to acquire a foothold on the island of Kiska. The Americans established a base on Adak, one of the coldest, most barren, and stormy places on earth. "As remote as the moon and hardly more fertile," the island is "next to worthless in terms of human existence." Because of that, no one had fought a modern war there.

Fact:

Mystery writer Dashiell Hammett, who enlisted several times and was finally accepted in the Army at age 42, served on Adak, where he was the editor of the Army newspaper, *The Adakian*. In his biography of Hammett, Richard Layman writes, "There was an unusual concentration of suspected subversives stationed on Adak, and some of the men there felt the island functioned as an icy prison, where they were being held until the end of the war." (*Shadow Man*. Harcourt Brace Jovanovich. 1981)

Huston's cameras show how the place was constructed—a million and a half square-foot steel runway had to be laid down by the infantry for the Air Corps—and how the guys lived and worked there. (They were all guys; no women.) The last third of the film follows bombing runs from Adak to Kiska, where the Japanese are literally dug in underground. Compared to William Wyler's documentary, *Memphis Belle*, Huston takes a more unemotional, omniscient point of view, not looking at identified individuals but at the men as a group and the dangerous job that they're doing. The flying footage is every bit as rough, authentic, and riveting as Wyler's.

From the construction of the base, Huston goes on to show the everyday side of life there; from eating meals and washing mess kits to the loading of thousand-pound bombs and belts of ammunition. The faces of the men—and their dogs—are the same ones we've seen in the more realistic fictional films from *The Story of G.I. Joe* to *Saving Private Ryan*. The incredible amounts of rain on Adak make the place a constant quagmire. Even the runways are often flooded, giving Huston the opportunity to show some spectacular shots of a P-38 sliding in on its belly and of fighters attempting to land and take off as they kick up huge plumes of spray.

It's a corner of the war that remains virtually unexplored by other filmmakers, and so this concise, no-nonsense portrait of it should go on the viewing list of anyone who has missed it. The tape ends with some Movietone newsreels.

See also
Catch-22
From Here to Eternity
Bataan
Air Force
Fighting Seabees

Producer: U.S. Army Pictorial Service. **Running Time:** 47 minutes. **Format:** VHS, Beta.

The *Why We Fight* Documentary Series

The American film industry cooperated enthusiastically with the government during World War II for professional and political reasons. Though divided, the filmmaking community had become more quickly anti-fascist than the nation as a whole before Pearl Harbor, and once war was declared many of the best directors signed on to make films for the armed services. That's the genesis of this series. The War Department asked Frank Capra to explain to new recruits and draftees the reasons behind America's involvement. If Capra wasn't experienced at overt political propaganda, he understood the manipulative power of film, and he knew how to tell a story. He brought in Julius and Philip Epstein (*Casablanca*, *Mr. Skeffington*, *The Man Who Came to Dinner*) to write the scripts. He scoured newsreel libraries for footage, and even used some of the Nazi's own material—Leni Riefenstal's *Triumph of the Will*, for instance—along with Disney animation and a few "re-enactments" to explain how America had come to be in the war. The filmmakers' simple goal was to persuade these young soldiers, sailors, airmen, and airwomen of the rightness of their cause. The seven films were literally "required viewing." Everyone in the service had to see them before going overseas, and they proved so popular that they were given theatrical distribution to civilians.

Contemporary viewers may have a little trouble understanding why these films were necessary. Capra and the Epsteins explain it in the final chapter when they look back at American attitudes toward the wars that were developing in Europe and the Pacific in the 1930s. A 1936 Gallup Poll revealed that 95% of Americans thought that their country should not be involved in a foreign war. By January 1941, that figure had changed dramatically; 68% of the people were ready to aid England, but isolationism was still strong. So, even after the attack on Pearl Harbor, the government wanted to build a strong, lasting commitment to the war effort. These films helped to create it.

The first volume, *Prelude to War*, directed by Ernst Lubitsch, begins with opening titles that state: "The purpose of these films is to give factual information as to the causes, the events leading up to our entry into the war, and the principals for which we are fighting." The filmmakers immediately give up that even-handed "factual" pose when they quote Secretary of War Henry L. Stimson, "We are determined that before the sun sets on this terrible struggle, our flag will be recognized throughout the world as a **symbol of freedom** on the one hand . . . and of **overwhelming** power on the other." (Original emphasis) They cast the war as a conflict between the Free World and the Slave World. The beginnings of the Free World go back to Moses, Mohammed, Confucius, and Christ, while the Slave World starts with Mussolini, Hitler, and the Emperor of Japan. "In these hands," they say, "the people surrendered their liberties and their human dignity." They sketch in the rise of the dictatorships in the chaos of post World War I Europe, stressing Nazi persecution of Catholics and other Christians over persecution of Jews. The screen is filled with rank upon rank of goose-stepping soldiers as the then-recent political history of the 1920s and '30s is summarized.

The second installment, *The Nazis Strike*, uses the chilling footage of the Nuremberg rallies and an animated scene of a huge comet striking the planet to make the Germans appear sufficiently threatening. From there, directors Capra and Anatol Litvak summarize Hitler's consolidation of power and aggressive territorial expansion, along with a quick synopsis of the geopolitical theory of "The World Island" made up of Europe, Asia, and Africa. The narration is written in colloquial English—"But in the Sudatenland he found some stooges who fell for this bunk."—and is generally respectful of its audience.

Divide and Conquer, the third section, is focused on the event-filled years of 1939 and '40, "the period when the Nazi Blitzkrieg reached its highest point and Nazi treachery reached its lowest point." After the German invasion of Poland, England and France declare war and the Blitz is on.

In '39 the Germans state that they are going to leave the other neutral countries of Europe alone. Then, they strike into Belgium, Holland, Denmark, and Norway. As the filmmakers put it, "Many of these Nazi soldiers strutting as conquerors in 1940 had last seen Norway some 20 years earlier when, as refugee German children, they had been raised and cared for by kind Norwegians. Now these same Germans were back to repay that kindness with terror and destruction." A few scenes later, a cartoon shows hundreds of little swastikas crawling like termites into the walls of the castle representing France.

Part four, *The Battle of Russia*, may be the finest moment of the series. It's too biased to be considered history, but at the same time it's not as clumsy and blatant as most propaganda. Whatever it's called, the film is fascinating. The first part is a fast-paced history of Russia and the U.S.S.R. using re-creations and footage from other films, notably Eisenstein's battle scenes from *Alexander Nevsky*, to tell the story. The peace-loving Russians withstand invasion after invasion until Hitler and "the stooge Mussolini" turn the ravenous Wehrmacht toward Moscow in 1941. Then comes the counterattack, in which our valiant Soviet allies bravely regroup and kick some Nazi butt. The long sequence about the battle of Leningrad is as well edited as any theatrical film. Throughout *The Battle of Russia*, the filmmakers manage an artful tap dance of political selectivity. The word "communist" is never spoken, and "red" is used only to refer to the Red Army and Red Fleet.

In the fifth part, *The Battle of Britain*, the level of rancor is appropriately ratcheted up. As the conflict moves closer to home, the rhetoric becomes more strident. The film begins with an animated diagram of the proposed German invasion of England with Panzer divisions crossing the Channel in high-speed barges. Given that base of operations, the Nazis' next move would have been a transatlantic attack on America. But Capra's real interest is in the British civilian reaction to the intense Luftwaffe bombing attacks. Once the story really hits its stride, the narration leaps from the acceptably hyperbolic—"Invasion plans were going completely haywire! The Nazis were blind with rage! The German has never understood why free people fight on against overwhelming odds!"—to the incomprehensible—"A nation that calls on cold courage when hot courage runs thin may die but it can't be defeated."

The Battle of China, part six, takes more time with a thumbnail background on Chinese history and geography. Perhaps because the setting is more exotic and strange to many members of the target audience, the film stresses the brutality and horror of the conflicts between Japan and China. The footage of the Rape of Nanking is still shocking for its images of executions, corpses, and mutilations. Interestingly, much of the filmmakers' outrage is reserved for the Japanese bombing of Chinese cities, first Shanghai. "Thus the Japanese introduced the world to a new kind of war—a war of deliberate terrorization, of deliberate mass murder, of deliberate frightfulness." Remember that those words were written before the American bombings of Tokyo, Dresden, Hiroshima and Nagasaki.

With part seven, *The War Comes to America*, Capra is back in his element. He's dealing with events that most of his viewers would probably remember firsthand, and so he makes the connections more personal and direct:

"In 1935, about the time you had your first date, we read that strutting Mussolini had attacked far-off Ethiopia.

"In 1936, when you were running around in jalopies, we were disturbed by news from Spain. In our newsreels we saw German and Italian air forces and armies fighting in Spain and wondered what they were doing there."

From an opening of kids pledging their allegiance (the way that I learned it, without religious references: " . . . one nation, indivisible, with liberty and justice for all."), he gives us a quick golden overview of American history, emphasizing our populist immigrant roots and ignoring the Civil War. (After all, the purpose of the series is to inspire the audience. Why bring up "the recent unpleasantness"?) At the same time, Capra does not dismiss the isolationist sentiment that was so strong in the 1930s, but he stresses the cold numbers, the Gallup poll statistics about American views of war and the relative sizes of the countries involved in the fight. And, knowing that he has yet to play his strongest card, the attack on Pearl Harbor, Capra sums things up like a good preacher who tells the congregation what he just told them.

He repeats the strongest images from the first six installments and hammers home his final point that America is involved in a war of self-preservation. Throughout the series, though, the tone is never authoritarian, ordering warriors into the fight. Instead, he is persuasive, urging middle-class men and women to join the cause for reasons they can understand. And the films are undeniably a success. The entertainment business has given these films its highest praise—imitation. Virtually all of the popular video series about World War II that have followed—*Victory at Sea*, *The World at War*, etc.—have followed the formula that Capra and the Epsteins perfected in *Why We Fight*, combining carefully edited "real" footage with good music and narration. When it's done right, the audience is apparently endless.

World War II:
The Holocaust on Screen

It is almost impossible for a mainstream film to deal with the Holocaust. Movies are primarily a medium for escapism; 95% mean to do nothing more than make money for producers and entertain the viewer. The central horror of the 20th century—the deliberate, systematic slaughter of millions—is not a subject to be trivialized.

How, then, does a commercial filmmaker tell a story about that horror which is true to it, and at the same time finds enough redemption to give its audience some level of enjoyment? Only a handful of filmmakers have tried to address the subject and managed it with any success.

Francois Truffaut's *The Last Metro* handles it obliquely. He sets his story in Nazi-occupied Paris and confines much of the action to a theater. The persecution of Jews is an immediate and suffocating shadow that hangs over the events of the plot. It adds a strong dimension of sadness to an odd show business story. Louis Malle engages the matter more directly in *Au Revoir les Enfants*. His is an autobiographical story set in a Catholic school for boys in occupied France. Malle subtly explores the roots of prejudice—the distinctions people make between "us" and "them" and how they choose to act on those distinctions—while he slowly reveals the realities of life in a police state.

Made for German television, *The Wannsee Conference* is an astonishing re-creation of an actual meeting that took place in 1942. Nazi party officials, led by Reinhard Heydrich and Adolf Eichmann, called the meeting to iron out the particulars of the "final solution" to "the Jewish problem"—who qualified, how they would be transported, who'd be responsible for what. In its absolute ordinariness the film is thoroughly chilling.

The surprise hit *Life Is Beautiful* ambitiously attempts to find romance and nobility within the horror. To do that, Roberto Benigni lightly dances around certain aspects of Nazi brutality and terrorism. To my mind, he is less than completely successful.

By far the most important cinematic contribution to public understanding of the Holocaust is Steven Spielberg's *Schindler's List*. It shows as much of the barbarity as the screen can hold—and audiences can accept—and yet it still finds an honest measure of hope. The film is the work of a gifted director applying all of his talents to an important subject.

AU REVOIR LES ENFANTS
Goodbye, Children
1987 Louis Malle ♫♫♫♫

Some have criticized Louis Malle's autobiographical tale of occupied France as being unemotional, but that is a completely wrongheaded interpretation. They confuse sentimentality with emotion. Malle refuses to sugarcoat his characters. Their flaws are real, and so are their reactions to the terrible situation in which they find themselves.

In January 1944, young Julien Quentin (Gaspard Manesse) is sent back to a Catholic boarding school after Christmas vacation by his coolly beautiful mother (Francine Racette). He begs to be allowed to stay, and the train ride across a bleak winter landscape reflects his mood. Julien is a smart kid, bookish and something of a loner. But like the other rich, spoiled little brats in his class, he is self-centered and capable of casual cruelty in the right situation. Their bullying is an act, meant to camouflage the fact that they're all frightened little boys, but it's no less ugly. When a new kid, Bonnet (Raphael Fejto) arrives, he catches the brunt of it. Julien does his part to make Bonnet's life hell, but it soon becomes clear that the two are a lot alike.

They're both smart and they like *The Three Musketeers*. But something else sets Bonnet apart. He's a Jew. The monks who run the school have given him a false name and are hiding him from the Nazis. Julien, who barely understands who and what Jews are—he has to ask his older brother the meaning of the word "Yid"—is slow to realize what is at stake. His perceptions are revealed through deliberate, seemingly pointless scenes involving others in and around the school: Joseph (Francois Negret), an older kid who works in the kitchen; a trip to the public baths in town; an incident in a restaurant.

They lead to a sad and inevitable conclusion made all the more moving by the careful choices Malle makes. Most obvious to American viewers will be the limited use of music. Malle does not use the soundtrack to emphasize or explain emotions. By restricting the film to Julien's point of view, Malle denies himself many of the conventional scenes of heroism and intrigue. The only moment that comes close is a long war game that the boys play in a forest. Even then, Malle is using the scene for other purposes. It is only one piece, and not the most important of a coming-of-age story.

Malle's ideas about the war and the Nazis are held back until the finish, and then the revelations are particularly horrifying. Though the film does not show the graphic violence inherent to the situation, the viewer understands what it means. Admittedly, it is possible to mistake Malle's even tone for lack of caring, but the significance of the ending is obvious and wrenching. The absence of histrionics is absolutely necessary. Material as horrifying and sensitive as this is best handled without obvious or conventional manipulation.

It's clear that Louis Malle is telling a personal story of critical importance, and revealing himself in a way that few filmmakers would dare. Even fewer would manage it so successfully. At the moment, *Au Revoir les Enfants* is out of print. It exists on tape in both a dubbed version and one that's clearly subtitled in colloquial English. Either is well worth seeking out.

See also
Napoleon
The White Rose
If . . .
Schindler's List
Hope and Glory
Empire of the Sun
Lord of the Flies

WORLD WAR II: THE HOLOCAUST

Julien Quentin (Gaspard Manesse) is sent to boarding school during WWII in *Au Revoir les Enfants.* The Kobal Collection

Cast: Gaspard Manesse (Julien Quentin), Raphael Fejto (Jean Bonnet), Francine Racette (Mme. Quentin), Stanislas Carre de Malberg (Francois Quentin), Philippe Morier-Genoud (Pere Jean), Francois Berleand (Pere Michel), Peter Fitz (Muller), Francois Negret (Joseph), Irene Jacob (Mlle. Davenne), Pascal Rivet (Boulanger), Benoit Henriet (Ciron), Richard Leboeuf (Sagard), Xavier Legrand (Babinot), Arnaud Henriet (Negus), Jean-Sebastien Chauvin (Laviron), Luc Etienne (Moreau); **Written by:** Louis Malle; **Cinematography by:** Renato Berta; **Music by:** Camille Saint-Saens, Franz Schubert. **Producer:** Nouvelles Editions de Films, MK2, Stella, NEF, Louis Malle. **French, German. Awards:** British Academy Awards '88: Best Director (Malle); Cesar Awards '88: Best Art Direction/Set Decoration, Best Cinematography, Best Director (Malle), Best Film, Best Sound, Best Writing; Los Angeles Film Critics Association Awards '87: Best Foreign Film; Venice Film Festival '87: Best Film; Nominations: Academy Awards '87: Best Foreign Film, Best Original Screenplay. **Boxoffice:** 4.5M. **MPAA Rating:** PG. **Running Time:** 104 minutes. **Format:** VHS, Beta, LV.

THE LAST METRO
Le Dernier Metro
1980 Francois Truffaut ♪♪♪

The delicate touch that characterizes so much of Francois Truffaut's work is evident in his one war film, a subtle and complex study of the effects of Nazi occupation on a Parisian theater troupe. American audiences accustomed to more demonstrative physical action will find Truffaut's reticence off-putting. An important subplot is dealt with mostly through suggestion and implication, and incidents that would be important turning points in another version of the same story occur off camera. In terms of structure, the film is essentially a reversal of *Phantom of the Opera*. Almost all of the action takes place in and around the Montmartre Theater.

That is where Lucas Steiner (Heinz Bennent) had established a thriving little production company. But the time is September 1942. The Germans have occupied Paris for two years and their rabid anti-Semitism has forced Steiner to flee the country, leaving day-to-day operations in the care of his wife, actress Marion Steiner (Catherine Deneuve). She's involved in preparations for a new production with a new leading man, Bernard Granger (Gerard Depardieu), whom she has hired away from another theater. The newcomer is a relentless seducer who tries his smooth lines on every woman he encounters. Their director is Jean-Loup Cottins (Jean Poiret), who's working from notes that Lucas left before he escaped. Those circumstances put the Montmartre in a precarious situation.

Despite the occupation and the curfew—people have to finish their nightlife before "the last metro"—theater-going is incredibly popular among Parisians. If the new play is a success, the theater will be in good shape financially. But the government could shut them down at any time for any reason, particularly if Marion allows Jews to work there. Daxiat (Jean-Louis Richard), the leading critic, toes the party line and fills his reviews with anti-Semitic insults. The wrong word from him could put the Montmartre in serious trouble. While Nazi repression slowly increases, the sexual entanglements within the troupe become more complex, and at least one member of the group has something to hide. As a finishing touch to Marion's already complicated life, her husband is hiding out in the basement. He wasn't able to escape, after all, and until they can find the right route to get him to Spain, he must stay downstairs where he can hear everything happening above him.

Throughout, Truffaut weaves the personal and the political threads of the story until he arrives at a neat, tricky ending that is perfectly theatrical and cinematic. (It's also a conclusion that has been copied often since.) It is difficult to engage such serious issues in a lighter context, but Truffaut handles it much more skillfully than Roberto Benigni does in *Life Is Beautiful*, to cite a similar example. Truffaut may be criticized for not going into the full depth of French complicity with the occupation or the true horrors of fascism, but that is not completely fair. He chooses to deal with one facet of that difficult period, and he treats it honestly enough. In the end, *The Last Metro* is one of Truffaut's most enjoyable and accessible works, recommended for videophiles looking for a new twist on a familiar theme.

See also

To Be or Not to Be
Life Is Beautiful
The Seventh Cross
Casablanca
Get Shorty

Catherine Deneuve and Heinz
Bennent deal with the
hardships of being Jewish
during the Nazi occupation of
France in Francois Truffaut's
The Last Metro. The Kobal Collection

Cast: Catherine Deneuve (Marion Steiner), Gerard Depardieu (Bernard Granger), Heinz Bennent (Lucas Steiner), Jean-Louis Richard (Daxiat), Jean Poiret (Jean-Loup Cottins), Andrea Ferreol (Arlette Guillaume), Paulette Dubost (Germaine Fabre), Sabine Haudepin (Nadine Marsac), Maurice Risch (Raymond Boursier), Jean-Pierre Klein (Christian Leglise), Martine Simonet (Martine), Franck Pasquier (Jacquot), Jean-Jose Richer (Rene Bernardini), Laszlo Szabo (Lt. Bergen), Jessica Zucman (Rosette Goldstern); **Written by:** Francois Truffaut, Suzanne Schiffman, Jean-Claude Grumberg; **Cinematography by:** Nestor Almendros; **Music by:** Georges Delerue. **Producer:** Roissy, Francois Truffaut. **French. Awards:** Cesar Awards '81: Best Actor (Depardieu), Best Actress (Deneuve), Best Art Direction/Set Decoration, Best Cinematography, Best Director (Truffaut), Best Film, Best Sound, Best Writing, Best Score; Nominations: Academy Awards '80: Best Foreign Film. **MPAA Rating:** PG. **Running Time:** 135 minutes. **Format:** VHS, LV, DVD.

LIFE IS BEAUTIFUL
La Vita E Bella
1998 Roberto Benigni ♫♪♪

Despite its astonishing boxoffice success, Roberto Benigni's romantic comedy set during the Holocaust is a troubling film on several levels. Given his choice of genres, the film necessarily lightens its subject. The characters never really acknowledge it either, treating the terrorist acts of fascist thugs as bothersome distractions from the more important business of courtship. Only in one brief shot does the filmmaker attempt to face the reality of his subject, and then he keeps it at a distance and shrouds it in lacy fog.

The story begins in Italy, 1939, where Guido Orefice (Benigni) is trying to open a bookstore and working as a waiter in the meantime. He's a puckish, quick-witted fellow, always ready to conjure up a fanciful line of patter, particularly when he meets a pretty girl like Dora (Nicoletta Braschi, also Mrs. Benigni). He falls hard for her and is not dissuaded by the facts that she's a teacher and the daughter of a wealthy family. No, Guido pursues her with all the charm and imagination he can muster.

> "This is a simple story but not an easy one to tell."
>
> **Opening line of voice-over narration**

That side of the film takes up roughly the first half. Benigni, who also wrote and directed, plays a Chaplinesque hero, the lovable little guy who avoids direct confrontations whenever possible and deftly skates circles around his oafish foes. His pursuit of Dora is a clever construction of interlocking plot elements: a key thrown from a second floor window, a bolt of silk, a running gag about stealing his uncle's hat. All of the action is so neatly contrived that the film essentially ends when it's over and then begins again with the introduction of Guido and Dora's child Giosue (Giorgio Cantarini) a few years later.

With little fanfare, Guido and Giosue are sent off to a labor camp. Dora follows. The railway journey and the camp itself are darker than the first section, but not nearly as dark as the reality behind them. Guido concocts an elaborate fantasy about a game they are playing to keep the truth of the situation from his son. It's a tenuous premise made possible by only the most massive and intense suspension of disbelief. Particularly toward the end, when Giosue is so easily hidden from the guards, it becomes very difficult to remain involved with the film.

Also, as director and actor, Benigni is such a camera hog that he leaves little room for his co-stars. As co-writer (with Vincenzo Cerami), he does his wife few favors. Dora has almost nothing to do. In almost all of her scenes, she simply stands there looking beautiful and sad and noble. She is allowed to smile a few times, but mostly she's beautiful and sad and noble.

Since the story is in part autobiographical, Benigni defuses the issue of exploitation, but his handling of the subject is open to criticism. The Holocaust is the central tragedy of this century. The mass extermination of specific "undesirables" for racist reasons is a horror that tests our belief in our own humanity. Roberto Benigni is trying to reaffirm that belief. Charlie Chaplin attempts the same in *The Great Dictator*. Neither is completely successful.

See also

Clowns
Amarcord
The Great Dictator
Schindler's List
Come and See

Cast: Roberto Benigni (Guido Orefice), Nicoletta Braschi (Dora), Giustino Durano (Uncle Zio), Sergio Bustric (Ferruccio Orefice), Horst Buchholz (Dr. Lessing), Giorgio Cantarini (Giosue Orefice), Marisa Paredes (Dora's mother), Lidia Alfonsi (Guicciardini), Giuliana Lojodice (School principal); **Written by:** Vincenzo Cerami, Roberto Benigni; **Cinematography by:** Tonino Delli Colli; **Music by:** Nicola Piovani. **Producer:** Elda Ferri, Gianluigi Braschi; released by Miramax Films. **Italian. Awards:** Academy Awards '98: Best Actor (Benigni), Best Foreign Film, Best Original Dramatic Score; British Academy Awards '98: Best Actor (Benigni); Cannes Film Festival '98: Grand Jury Prize; Cesar Awards '99: Best Foreign Film; Screen Actors Guild Award '98: Best Actor (Benigni); Broadcast Film Critics Association Awards '98: Best Foreign Film; Nominations: Academy Awards '98: Best Director (Benigni), Best Film Editing, Best Original Screenplay, Best Picture; British Academy Awards '98: Best Foreign Film, Best Original Screenplay; Directors Guild of America Awards '98: Best Director (Benigni); Screen Actors Guild Award '98: Cast. **MPAA Rating:** PG-13. **Running Time:** 122 minutes. **Format:** VHS.

LIFE IS BEAUTIFUL

SCHINDLER'S LIST

1993 Steven Spielberg ♪♪♪♪

Any filmmaker who chooses to deal with the Holocaust faces several serious problems. The first is deciding which story to tell. Conventional heroics are impossible; a realistic look at the horror is too appalling. In Thomas Keneally's fact-based novel, Steven Spielberg found the right balance of redemption and sorrow.

Oskar Schindler (Liam Neeson) is an ambitious businessman who realizes that there is money to be made in war. In a masterful opening montage, Spielberg mixes the forced transfer of Polish Jews to cities after the Nazi occupation with Schindler making his own moves. As families register with bureaucrats who sit at folding tables and make their tidy lists, Schindler matches suits and ties, selects the right cufflinks, and pockets a hefty bankroll. The Jews are forced into their ghetto; Schindler goes to a nightclub where he wines and dines high-ranking Nazis. The two worlds come together when Schindler meets Itzhak Stern (Ben Kingsley) and offers him a deal. Since Jews cannot own businesses, they should work together. Stern's contacts can provide financial backing. Stern himself can provide the expertise to run a business. Schindler will bring "panache." "That's what I'm good at," he says. "Not to work . . . the presentation."

> "For six centuries there has been a Jewish Krakow. Think about that. By this evening, those six centuries are a rumor. They never happened. Today is history."
>
> **Amon Goeth (Ralph Fiennes) to SS men before the liquidation of the ghetto**

> "I realize that you're not a person in the strictest sense of the word."
>
> **Goeth to his housekeeper Helen Hirsch (Embeth Davidtz)**

> "The list is life."
>
> **Itzhak Stern (Ben Kingsley)**

It may not be a fair deal, but once Schindler signs contracts to provide the Wehrmacht with cooking utensils, he is able to open an enamelware factory that provides several hundred Jews with jobs. Those jobs, and the documentation that goes with them, give the men and women a measure of safety as the Nazis' plans for the "final solution" grind inexorably forward to the March 13, 1943 liquidation of the Krakow ghetto. That is one of the most harrowing series of scenes ever put on film, and it is matched by the concentration camp sequences that follow. In those scenes of mass chaos and slaughter, Spielberg uses a single spot of color to highlight one little girl. In the black-and-white world, her coat is red. It's almost the same shade as the jacket worn by the young protagonist of Spielberg's *Empire of the Sun*, in a similar situation when he's alone in a mob and trying to find his way home.

In those same scenes, Amon Goeth (Ralph Fiennes) is introduced. Goeth is a flabby sociopath who comes to embody the evils of Nazi racism. He is in charge of the camp where the workers are housed and so must be bribed and pampered if Schindler is to stay in business. Goeth's excessive cruelty is also part of the reason that Schindler is transformed from war profiteer to crusader. The exact moment of that change is not shown, and it should not be shown. Though popular films are built around such epiphanies, that scene would be out of place in this careful film. Instead, it's an accretion of layered awareness that makes Schindler what he becomes. Though he is a selfish, undisciplined man who drinks too much and sleeps with too many women, he is moved by the mounting barbarism, cruelty, and savagery that surrounds him. Neeson's performance is built on a combination of self-confidence, indecision, and doubt. Though some have criticized Steven Zaillian's script on the grounds that it makes Schindler more altruistic than he really was, it does stick closely to historical fact in the numbers of people that Schindler saved from

See also

The Wannsee Conference
Come and See
Sophie's Choice
The Battle of Algiers

the Holocaust. In the same way, the real Goeth was even more monstrous than he is in the film. But if the full scope of his atrocities had been shown, the film would have been unbalanced. As it is, Spielberg pushes the limit, showing as much of the horror as the screen will bear.

Hoping to save the life of a worker's daughter, Oskar Schindler (Liam Neeson, left) persuades an SS guard that the girl's hands are needed to polish the insides of shell casings. The Kobal Collection

That horror is alleviated, slightly, by Janusz Kaminski's stunning black-and-white cinematography. It gives the violence an abstract, dreamlike quality that no form of color could have matched. He won an Academy Award for his work, and the American Society of Cinematographers placed the film at number five on its best-shot (1950–1997) list. John Williams's somber, almost unnoticed score adds to the melancholy tone. Any viewer might be able to find shortcomings somewhere in the collaborative effort, but to what point? *Schindler's List* demonstrates the potential of

Hollywood filmmaking that is so rarely achieved. When the full financial resources of the industry and its best creative people are put in service of an important story, the results can be staggering.

Cast: Liam Neeson (Oskar Schindler), Ben Kingsley (Itzhak Stern), Ralph Fiennes (Amon Goeth), Embeth Davidtz (Helen Hirsch), Caroline Goodall (Emilie Schindler), Jonathan Sagalle (Poldek Pfefferberg), Mark Ivanir (Marcel Goldberg), Malgoscha Gebel (Victoria Klonowska), Shmulik Levy (Wilek Chilowicz), Beatrice Macola (Ingrid), Andrzej Seweryn (Julian Scherner), Friedrich von Thun (Rolf Czurda), Norbert Weisser (Albert Hujar), Michael Schneider (Juda Dresner), Anna Mucha (Danka Dresner); **Written by:** Steven Zaillian; **Cinematography by:** Janusz Kaminski; **Music by:** John Williams; **Technical Advisor:** Leopold Page. **Producer:** Steven Spielberg, Gerald R. Molen, Branko Lustig, Kathleen Kennedy, Amblin Entertainment; released by Universal. **Awards:** Academy Awards '93: Best Adapted Screenplay, Best Art Direction/Set Decoration, Best Cinematography, Best Director (Spielberg), Best Film Editing, Best Picture, Best Original Score; American Film Institute (AFI) '98: Top 100; British Academy Awards '93: Best Adapted Screenplay, Best Director (Spielberg), Best Film, Best Supporting Actor (Fiennes); Directors Guild of America Awards '93: Best Director (Spielberg); Golden Globe Awards '94: Best Director (Spielberg), Best Film—Drama, Best Screenplay; Los Angeles Film Critics Association Awards '93: Best Cinematography, Best Film; National Board of Review Awards '93: Best Film; New York Film Critics Awards '93: Best Cinematography, Best Film, Best Supporting Actor (Fiennes); National Society of Film Critics Awards '93: Best Cinematography, Best Director (Spielberg), Best Film, Best Supporting Actor (Fiennes); Writers Guild of America '93: Best Adapted Screenplay; Nominations: Academy Awards '93: Best Actor (Neeson), Best Costume Design, Best Makeup, Best Sound, Best Supporting Actor (Fiennes); British Academy Awards '94: Best Actor (Neeson), Best Adapted Screenplay, Best Supporting Actor (Kingsley), Best Score; Golden Globe Awards '94: Best Actor—Drama (Neeson), Best Supporting Actor (Fiennes), Best Score; MTV Movie Awards '94: Best Film, Breakthrough Performance (Fiennes). **Budget:** 25M. **Boxoffice:** 317.1M. **MPAA Rating:** R. **Running Time:** 195 minutes. **Format:** VHS, LV, Letterbox, Closed Caption.

The Hound Salutes: Steven Spielberg

Much of Steven Spielberg's popularity is built on two kinds of popular film—horror and war. His career in the first area can be traced back to his made-for-TV debut, *Duel*, about a man who is menaced by a monstrous truck whose driver is never seen. He followed that with *Jaws* and *Jurassic Park*, and audiences followed him. His success in war films mostly came later in his career, but he has brought the same deft understanding of his audience's taste to both genres. More specifically, he is very careful about the amount and quality of violence that he chooses to use. Both horror and war films are inherently violent, but Spielberg has never exploited or used it indiscriminately.

His first war movie is the underrated comedy *1941* (1979). Admittedly, it is far from perfect, but it is energetic, and in many important ways, it is true to the era it addresses. The plot is loosely based on events that took place in 1942, and the movie is about people who have suddenly been thrust into a new and frightening situation and react according-ly. The performances by Slim Pickens, John Belushi, Ned Beatty, Robert Stack, and particularly Dan Aykroyd, are worth another look all by themselves.

For my money, his next war film, *Empire of the Sun*, is his weakest. Spielberg admitted as much in a 1999 *New York Times Magazine* interview with Stephen J. Dubner when he said, "I was a visual opportunist—I just feel there's a patent lack of story and relationship." When he turned to similar subject matter with a stronger story, he was infinitely more successful. *Schindler's List* is one of the few genuinely important films of the 1990s. It places the central horror of the 20th century in a context that a mass audience can understand and will accept. (Watching it again was the most diffi-cult part of writing this book.)

The maturity that Spielberg displays in deal-ing with the Holocaust should have prepared audi-ences for *Saving Private Ryan*. At heart, it is a con-ventional unit picture, but Spielberg uses the stunning D-Day invasion to invest the story with a sense of realism that shatters everything that has come before it. Yes, the film is flawed toward the end, but Spielberg's attempt to show the full effects of war violence, combined with a brilliant performance by Tom Hanks in the lead, make the film one of the very best. It sets a standard of intensity and verisimilitude that future war films are going to be measured against.

THE WANNSEE CONFERENCE
Wannseekonferenz
1984 Heinz Schirk 𝄞𝄞𝄞𝄢

On Tuesday, January 20, 1942, key members of the Nazi party and the German government bureaucracy met at a house in the Berlin suburb of Wannsee. The meeting was called by Obergruppenfuhrer Reinhard Heydrich at the request of Hermann Goering. Its purpose was to discuss the logistics and particulars of the "final solution to the Jewish problem." Critical decisions about the extermination of European and Russian Jews had already been made. At Wannsee, the participants were to make sure that they understood their own responsibilities and the larger chain of command.

"The Jews have only themselves to blame. I understand why the Fuhrer is making them pay. They've amassed a huge debt. One day the world will thank us. But maybe it will wake up and listen to reason when we deport the 'Chosen People' en masse to the East. Maybe it will strike terror into the hearts of Roosevelt and Churchill. As the Fuhrer says, 'It's good if terror leads our way—the terror that we will exterminate the Jews.'"

Obergruppenfuhrer Reinhard Heydrich (Dietrich Mattausch)

"Under the cloak of war, obscured by the smoke of gunpowder, a lot of unusual things are possible."

Heydrich

"In the course of orderly execution Europe will be combed from west to east. Jews will be placed in collection camps, then load by load evacuated to the East and delivered to their proper destination."

Heydrich

Working from minutes taken at the meeting and the memories of Adolf Eichmann, writer Paul Mommertz and director Heinz Schirk re-create the event in roughly real time. Both the film and the meeting last about 90 minutes. The "banality of evil" has never been so illustrated with such quiet horror. With minor changes in costume and wording, the film could be about a board of supervisors discussing the conclusion of a particularly complex zoning issue. It concerns all of their constituents, so everyone has an opinion and a certain amount of turf to protect. Beyond that, the deal is done. How do they make sure that it is handled smoothly?

But their subject is not zoning. It is the murder of 11 million people. Eleven million—that's the goal. Heydrich sums it up by saying, "What lies ahead is an organizational task unparalleled in history."

Before the meeting starts, Heydrich (Dietrich Mattausch) calls aside his three most trusted assistants—Eichmann (Gerd Bockmann), Gruppenfuhrer Muller (Friedrioh G. Beckhaus), and Dr. Lange (Martin Luttge)—to make sure they're ready. Heydrich has three goals for the morning and he wants to make sure they are met. First, the dozen or so men in the other room must agree that he is in charge. Second, their commitment to the plan must be enthusiastic. Finally and most important, they must all feel responsible. "Shared knowledge means shared responsibility," he says. "Shared responsibility means shared liability." That liability has nothing to do with the morality of their plan. It refers more to procedural problems. If they can't get the right numbers of trains or trucks, for example, who takes the blame?

The meeting proceeds along those lines. They discuss revisions of Hitler's racial classifications. Who is a full Jew? A half Jew? A quarter Jew? How do they handle foreign Jews? What about mixed marriages? With each question, Heydrich, an impatient, organized man, allows a brief debate among the participants, then calls on one of his men for an opinion, and finally makes a decision. Everyone agrees with it. As Heydrich checks off points in his notebook, the brandy, coffee, and pastries flow freely. People make light, crude jokes. A barking dog outside disturbs the meeting until someone shuts it up. One man nods off. The word "elegant" is used often to describe solutions to new problems. Voices are seldom raised. Only one man is at all concerned with larger issues, and he repeatedly defends himself against the "Jew lover" label.

See also

Schindler's List

Fatherland

A Time to Love and a Time to Die

Judgment at Nuremberg

To most viewers, the most frightening aspect of all this is the participants' blithe acceptance of Hitler's racist ideas. Once one believes that another group is "subhuman," the decisions to eradicate those non-people come easily. That, finally, is the horror behind *The Wannsee Conference*. The people who commit these atrocities are able to convince themselves that they are doing the right thing, unpleasant but necessary and, whenever possible, elegant.

Cast: Dietrich Mattausch (Reinhard Heydrich), Gerd Brockmann (Adolf Eichmann), Friedrich Beckhaus (Muller), Robert Atzorn (Hofmann), Jochen Busse (Leibrandt), Hans-Werner Bussinger (Luther), Harald Dietl (Meyer), Peter Fitz (Wilhelm Stuckart), Reinhard Glemnitz (Josef Buhler), Dieter Groest (Neumann), Martin Luttge (Dr. Rudolf Lange), Anita Mally (The Secretary), Gerd Riegauer (Schongarth); Written by: Paul Mommertz; Cinematography by: Horst Schier. Producer: Infafilm/GmbH Munich. German.. Running Time: 87 minutes. Format: VHS, Beta, LV.

World War II:
The Homefront on Screen

Homefront stories are the calm center of World War II films. They tend to emphasize romance and tranquility, and they idealize domestic activities to an absolutely shameless degree. In that regard, William Wyler set a high standard with *Mrs. Miniver*. Seen today, it's a sincere soap opera that has nothing to do with reality. But to 1942 audiences, it touched a heartfelt emotional chord. People loved the story of a British family's quiet courage in the face of Nazi aggression. It set records at the boxoffice and at the Academy Awards.

Both *Since You Went Away* and David O. Selznick's *White Cliffs of Dover* are pitched at the same noble level. In *White Cliffs*, an American woman (Irene Dunne) marries into an English family and carries on bravely through two wars. Claudette Colbert does much the same in producer Selznick's ornate variation on the story. No sacrifice is too great for her and her daughters—and their dog!—to make while Dad is off doing his duty. The three films are notable for the polished sheen of their black-and-white cinematography, costumes, and sets.

When filmmakers turned their attention to the subject decades later, they took a different approach.

Steven Spielberg re-creates the glossy look in candy-bright neon colors for *1941*. That's the only similarity his raucous comedy has to the older homefront epics. In John Boorman's autobiographical *Hope and Glory*, the domestic upheaval of war is seen through the eyes of a child. Boorman brings a bracing sense of discovery to the story. The war transforms a boring British suburb into a magical realm of imagination and adventure. His sense of humor is bawdier and rougher than Spielberg's.

Anne Wheeler's *Bye Bye Blues* is about a young wife and mother (Rebecca Jenkins) who must deal with a husband who's missing in action and an unexpected career opportunity as a jazz singer in provincial Canada. The characters, their situation and, just as importantly, the setting are treated realistically and without the gushing sentiment of the 1940s.

Though *The Land Girls* can claim a basis in reality—young English women did go to work on farms to replace men who entered the service—director David Leland casts three glamorous actresses (Catherine McCormack, Rachel Weisz, and Anna Friel) in the leads. He also makes the rural locations as idyllic as the confections of the war years. And why not? If filmmakers are going to lionize warriors, shouldn't the quiet front receive some of the same idealized treatment? They also serve who only stand and wait.

BYE BYE BLUES

1989 Anne Wheeler ♪♪♪♪

The characters and conflicts in this story of the World War II homefront can be traced back as far as Homer's *Odyssey*, but writer-director Anne Wheeler tells it from an unusual point of view—western Canadian. That setting and a certain no-nonsense approach give a fresh quality to familiar material.

It begins in India with the arrival of a piano. Army doctor Teddy Cooper (Michael Ontkean) buys it for his wife Daisy (Rebecca Jenkins), who tries to teach herself how to play. Some months later in 1942, he is transferred to a more dangerous, secret posting. She, their two young children, and the instrument go back to the Canadian prairie. (Though the plot bears some superficial similarities to Jane Campion's *The Piano*, *Bye Bye Blues* has nothing to do with that overrated bodice-ripper.) Daisy moves back in with her parents but finds the transition troubling. India was hot and heavily populated. Canada is cold and empty. More to the point, in India, Daisy and Teddy were rich. In Canada, she's poor. Then she learns that Teddy was stationed in Singapore and it has been occupied by the Japanese. She doesn't know whether he's alive or dead, and the government can tell her nothing.

Hoping to earn a little money, she talks her way into a tryout with Slim Godfrey's (Stuart Margolin) little combo. It's not much of a band, but it's about all there is in that remote corner of the country. The same night that Daisy makes her inauspicious debut, a stranger, Max Gramley (Luke Reilly), asks to sit in on trombone. Astonishingly, their stumbling renditions of dance tunes are a hit with the crowd. The Stardusters set off on the rough road to fame and fortune. Will Daisy be a "grass widow," faithful to a far-away husband or his ghost, take care of the kids, and obey her overbearing father? Or will she be a singer who hangs out with jazz musicians, smokes cigarettes, and wears slinky spaghetti-strap gowns?

The band's side of the film follows the typical showbiz success trajectory. The unfamiliar locations make it different, and it serves as a reflection of the larger changes that the war brings to backwater Canada—the same changes that many North Americans experienced in one way or another. The band has a strong aura of authenticity, too. The musicians aren't miraculously transformed into a small, polished version of the Ellington orchestra. They sound like talented semi-professional provincials who play music that people can dance to.

That care with accuracy follows through in accents and period details. Visually, Wheeler favors soft light and she makes full use of the dramatic prairie sky and rolling landscape. Though the film was made for a modest budget, it was spent wisely. With the plot details, she is able to be more honest about the emotional, familial, sexual, and financial realities of the war than the films of the '40s were. The conclusion will strike some as overly dramatic, but that's not a significant flaw. With strong performances, evocative style, and well-drawn believable characters, *Bye Bye Blues* is a solid sleeper.

See also
Some Like It Hot
Since You Went Away
Hope and Glory
The Land Girls

Cast: Rebecca Jenkins (Daisy Cooper), Michael Ontkean (Teddy Cooper), Luke Reilly (Max Gramley), Stuart Margolin (Slim Godfrey), Robyn Stevan (Frances Cooper), Kate Reid (Mary Wright), Wayne Robson (Pete), Shiela Moore (Doreen Cooper), Leon Pownall (Bernie Blitzer), Vincent Gale (Will Wright), Susan Sneath (Joyce Kuchera); **Written by:** Anne Wheeler; **Cinematography by:** Vic Sarin; **Music by:** George Blondheim. **Producer:** Arvi Liimatainen, Anne Wheeler, Allarcom Ltd. **Canadian. Awards:** Genie Awards '90: Best Actress (Jenkins), Best Supporting Actress (Stevan). **Boxoffice:** $161,323. **MPAA Rating:** PG. **Running Time:** 110 minutes. **Format:** VHS.

HOPE AND GLORY

1987 John Boorman ♪♪♪♪

John Boorman's autobiographical look back at his childhood may be the most accurate portrait of the British homefront ever put on film. It's World War II seen through the eyes of a boy, but unlike most childhood memories, this one comes without the sentimentality. Beneath the unavoidable nostalgia is an honest understanding of the massive changes that the war brought to England and the English. Ideas of devotion to duty and noble self-sacrifice are conspicuously absent in a story of ordinary yet remarkable people who simply do what they have to do to get through a tough situation.

After a prologue showing dozens of wee tykes running amok at a Saturday matinee featuring Hopalong Cassidy, the story begins on September 3, 1939—the British equivalent of December 7, 1941. It's a beautiful Sunday in a lower middle-class London neighborhood. As our narrator Bill (Sebastian Rice-Edwards) remembers it, he's playing with his toy knights in the garden when he hears all of the lawnmowers stop. The Prime Minister has just announced that a state of war has been declared against Germany and he realizes that "nothing would be the same again." Bill's father Clive (David Hayman) enlists right away but is afraid to tell his wife Grace (Sarah Miles), and so she hears it first from the neighbors. Before long, blackouts, gas masks, air raid alarms, and bomb shelters become part of their lives, and when the bombing starts, the war comes right onto their street.

> "I'm going to miss the war and it's all your fault."
>
> **Bill (Sebastian Rice-Edwards) to his mother (Sarah Miles) when she considers sending him away**

For kids, though, war isn't hell, it's fun. After the bombs fall, the streets are full of shiny shrapnel, still warm—just the thing for a boy to add to his collection. The gutted houses are glorious places for gangs of kids to play out their joyously destructive fantasies. For Bill's older sister Dawn (Sammi Davis), a teenager in a hurry to grow up, the newly arrived Canadian troops are an answered prayer. In many ways, the disruption of the adults' world is more subtle, or at least more difficult for a child to comprehend. The complex depths of the relationship between Grace and her friend Mac (Derrick O'Connor) and his wife Molly (Susan Wooldridge) are slowly revealed. Likewise, Grace's parents (Ian Bannen and Annie Leon) don't really come into their own until the final act. Despite the familiarity of the setting and the situation, there is not a single stereotype in the group. All of these are fully realized, believable characters whose flaws are not hidden.

Boorman's suburban London is a world that is transformed from a deceptively well-ordered place to a vision of desolation that might have provided the inspiration for the memorable conclusion of *Excalibur*. (References to his interpretation of the Arthurian legends can be seen throughout this film.) The big scenes in the neighborhood—boys playing a dangerous game with live ammunition, the arrival of the German pilot (Boorman's son Charley), learning to swear, a New Year's Eve family party, the rogue barrage balloon—all resolve themselves in unexpected conclusions. Then in the third act Boorman suddenly shifts the scene to an idyllic riverfront. His honest tone remains unchanged.

In the end, it's that warts-and-all approach that makes *Hope and Glory* so successful. Boorman may be remembering his youth with affection, but that does not color his judgment. He refuses to offer us the easy comforts of nostalgia based on the lie that life was simpler then. The people were neither better nor worse than they are now, and their problems were no easier to deal with. It's a truth that few filmmakers are willing to admit.

See also
Mrs. Miniver
Amarcord
In Which We Serve
The Best Years of Our Lives

388 WORLD WAR II: HOMEFRONT

Bill (Sebastian Rice-Edwards)
and Sue Rohan (Geraldine Muir)
grow up in the excitement and
destruction of World War II
England in *Hope and Glory*. The
Kobal Collection

Cast: Sebastian Rice-Edwards (Bill), Geraldine Muir (Sue), Sarah Miles (Grace), Sammi Davis (Dawn), David Hayman (Clive), Derrick O'Connor (Mac), Susan Wooldridge (Molly), Jean-Marc Barr (Bruce), Ian Bannen (Grandfather George), Jill Baker (Faith), Charley Boorman (Luftwaffe pilot), Annie Leon (Grandma), Katrine Boorman (Charity), Gerald James (Headmaster), Amelda Brown (Hope), Colin Higgins (Clive's pal); **Written by:** John Boorman; **Cinematography by:** Philippe Rousselot; **Music by:** Peter Martin. **Producer:** John Boorman, Goldcrest Films, Columbia Pictures. **British. Awards:** British Academy Awards '87: Best Film, Best Supporting Actress (Wooldridge); Golden Globe Awards '88: Best Film—Musical/Comedy; Los Angeles Film Critics Association Awards '87: Best Director (Boorman), Best Film, Best Screenplay; National Society of Film Critics Awards '87: Best Cinematography, Best Director (Boorman), Best Film, Best Screenplay; Nominations: Academy Awards '87: Best Art Direction/Set Decoration, Best Cinematography, Best Director (Boorman), Best Original Screenplay, Best Picture. **Boxoffice:** 10M. **MPAA Rating:** PG-13. **Running Time:** 97 minutes. **Format:** VHS, Beta, LV, 8mm, Closed Caption.

"1941. Britain is at war with Germany. As farm workers leave the land to join the armed forces, women from all walks of life volunteer to take their place. They call themselves 'The Women's Land Army.'" That foreword sets the stage for three young women, played by beautiful actresses, who go to work on a farm that's even more beautiful. The episodic adventures that they encounter during their stay in the country are mostly of the romantic stripe. The style and substance of the film are so thoroughly British that only the most dedicated Anglophiles will understand all of the dialogue or realize the importance of some details.

Mr. Lawrence (Tom Georgeson), a crusty old farmer, makes it clear from the outset that he's none too happy about his new staff. Stella (Catherine McCormack) is engaged to Philip (Paul Bettany), a pilot. At 26 the oldest of the trio, Ag (Rachel Weisz) is something of an intellectual airhead, and Prue (Anna Friel) says that she's hoping to find "total fornication" in the country. The immediate object of her urges is Joe Lawrence (Steven Mackintosh), the farmer's son who is going to volunteer for Army duty any day now. Despite a weak heart, Mrs. Lawrence (Maureen O'Brien) tries to keep some order within the crowded household.

Initially, it is difficult to accept three glamour girls on one small farm, but the actresses manage to acquit themselves fairly well with manure spreaders and various other farm implements. For a time, at least, director David Leland is just as interested in the beautiful landscape. Several scenes are cinematic postcards to the Devon, Somerset, and Hertfordshire locations. He and co-writer Keith Dewhurst seem less certain in their adaptation of Angela Huth's novel. After they set up a seemingly important conflict between Lawrence and a bureaucrat over the plowing of a meadow, it is dropped inconclusively. The most important of the divergent plotlines concerns the relationship that each of the three girls forms with Joe, but he is an improbable stud muffin. Or perhaps that's the idea—that during those years any reasonably functional young man lucky enough to find himself in the right place could rise to the occasion, as it were, whenever called upon to do so.

The muddy accents are a more serious problem. Most frustratingly when characters are angry, their words tumble together so completely that repeated rewindings and careful listening are useless. Then there is the matter of Mr. Lawrence's brief obsession with mangoes. He has a long, pointless monologue about the proper handling of the fruit, and demonstrates his concerns with an example. It seems to have something to do with his being a bit pixilated by drink at the holidays, but that's not clear, either. It is funny, though, and perhaps that's all the viewer needs to know.

See also

Hope and Glory
Mrs. Miniver
The White Cliffs of Dover
Cold Comfort Farm

Still, despite the flaws, this snapshot of a little-known side of England's war is worth watching. As women's history, *The Land Girls*' outlook is much more 1990s than 1940s but it is a legitimate interpretation of life on the rural homefront.

"Women's Land Army! Not an army, just an excuse for a lark and I'm paying for it."

**Mr. Lawrence (Tom Georgeson)
scoffing at the newly arrived girls**

"The Japanese have taken Singapore, did you hear? It's the end of the British Empire as we've lived it. I'm afraid that actually I'm up to my eyeballs in gin."

**Philip's mother (Ann Bell) to Stella
(Catherine McCormack)**

Prue (Anna Friel), Stella
(Catherine McCormack), and Ag
(Rachel Weisz) work on a farm
in the English country while the
boys are off to war in *The Land
Girls*. The Kobal Collection

Cast: Catherine McCormack (Stella), Rachel Weisz (Ag), Anna Friel (Prue), Steven Mackintosh (Joe Lawrence), Tom Georgeson (Mr. Lawrence), Maureen O'Brien (Mrs. Lawrence), Paul Bettany (Philip), Lucy Akhurst (Janet), Ann Bell (Philip's mother); **Written by:** David Leland, Keith Dewhurst; **Cinematography by:** Henry Braham; **Music by:** Brian Lock. **Producer:** Simon Relph, Ruth Jackson, Greenpoint Films, Intermedia Films; released by Gramercy Pictures. **British. MPAA Rating:** R. **Running Time:** 110 minutes. **Format:** VHS.

MRS. MINIVER

1942 William Wyler ♪♪♪

The years have been less than kind to William Wyler's early World War II propaganda/soap opera, but that does not diminish its importance. Any film that achieves such widespread popularity with audiences, critics, and the industry—it won virtually all of the important Academy Awards in 1942—deserves attention.

The opening titles explain that this is the story of a typical middle-class British family in the summer of 1939. Architect Clem Miniver (Walter Pidgeon) and his wife Kay (Greer Garson) have three children—the oldest off at Oxford—maids, tutors, cooks, a charming little ivy-covered cottage in the village of Belham, a short train ride from London. Yes, just a typical middle-class family. Audiences in 1942 could accept that kind of idealized world as a setting for a "realistic" story. But conventions and viewers' expectations of cinematic "reality" have changed to the point that Wyler's bucolic England is just around the corner from Oz.

"I don't know what the country's coming to, everyone trying to be better than their betters—mink coats and no manners. No wonder Germany's arming."

Lady Beldon (Dame May Whitty)

"This is the people's war. It is our war. We are the fighters. Fight it, then! Fight it with all that is in us and may God defend the right!"

Vicar (Henry Wilcoxon)

"If I had several Germans in the film, I wouldn't mind having one decent young fellow, but I've only got one German, and if I make this picture, the one German is going to be a typical little Nazi son of a bitch."

William Wyler to producer Louis B. Mayer during production (quoted from *American Masters: Directed by William Wyler*)

Contemporaneous moviegoers didn't see it that way. They saw Anglo-American characters engaged in a valiant struggle against a rising tide of Nazi barbarism; good, decent people who are able to overcome their stuffy class system, accept each other as equals and pull together to defeat their common enemy in "the people's war." Why? What was it about the picture that made it the biggest boxoffice hit of the decade?

A large part of the reason lies in simple timing. Shooting began on November 11, 1941; the finished product opened in May 1942, neatly bracketing the cataclysmic events of December 7, 1941. Clearly, it arrived at a time when Americans were ready for the right inspirational message. Wyler, who had made six Best Picture–nominated films in the previous six years, was just the man to deliver that message.

Roughly the first half is glossy sweetness and light that turns more ominous when the air raid sirens wail. At a fairly leisurely pace, Wyler brings in the retreat from Dunkirk; the Battle of Britain; wartime romances between son Vin (Richard Ney) and Carol Beldon (Teresa Wright), granddaughter of the local gentry, and between Gladys (Brenda Forbes), the cook, and her beau Horace (Rhys Williams); even a wounded German pilot (Helmut Dantine) who lands in the garden. All of those events are positioned to reinforce the basic decency of these characters and their society. It all ends with one of the finest motivational sermons ever put on film. (The famous speech was reportedly revised the night before it was shot by Wyler and actor Henry Wilcoxon, who delivers it. The scene was a huge hit with Winston Churchill and Franklin Roosevelt, and the short piece was widely published in magazines.)

Though the acting seems arch and oddly accented today, it too struck the right note with the first audiences. In the Best Actor category, Walter Pidgeon lost to James Cagney's even more patriotic *Yankee Doodle Dandy*, but all the other key players on both sides of the camera took home Oscars. That sweep explains the film's popularity. Forget the flaws of then and now. *Mrs. Miniver* captures the emotion of the moment, and no one can argue with that.

See also
Hope and Glory
The Immortal Battalion
Three Came Home
The Best Years of Our Lives

In their backyard bomb shelter, Mr. Miniver (Walter Pidgeon) and Mrs. Miniver (Greer Garson) make the best of it in *Mrs. Miniver.* The Kobal Collection

Cast: Greer Garson (Kay Miniver), Walter Pidgeon (Clem Miniver), Teresa Wright (Carol Beldon), May Whitty (Lady Beldon), Richard Ney (Vin Miniver), Henry Travers (Mr. Ballard), Reginald Owen (Foley), Henry Wilcoxon (Vicar), Helmut Dantine (German flyer), Aubrey Mather (Innkeeper), Rhys Williams (Horace), Tom Conway (Man), Peter Lawford (Pilot), Christopher Severn (Toby Miniver), Clare Sandars (Judy Miniver), Marie De Becker (The Cook), Connie Leon (Simpson, the maid), Brenda Forbes (Gladys), John Abbott (Fred), Billy Bevan (Conductor), John Burton (Halliday), Mary Field (Miss Spriggins), Forrester Harvey (Mr. Huggins), Arthur Wimperis (Sir Henry), Ian Wolfe (Dentist); **Written by:** George Froeschel, James Hilton, Arthur Wimperis, Claudine West; **Cinematography by:** Joseph Ruttenberg; **Music by:** Herbert Stothart. **Producer:** Sidney Franklin, MGM. **Awards:** Academy Awards '42: Best Actress (Garson), Best Black and White Cinematography, Best Director (Wyler), Best Picture, Best Screenplay, Best Supporting Actress (Wright); Nominations: Academy Awards '42: Best Actor (Pidgeon), Best Film Editing, Best Sound, Best Supporting Actor (Travers), Best Supporting Actress (Whitty). **Running Time:** 134 minutes. **Format:** VHS, Beta, LV.

The Hound Salutes: William Wyler

"He was the classiest picture maker, I think, that ever lived."

Billy Wilder said that about William Wyler, and he wasn't wrong. Some critics still don't regard Wyler with the same respect they accord such directors as Hitchcock and Bergman, because he didn't have a single recognizable style. But the entertainment industry has given him all of its highest honors—three Oscars for best direction and the American Film Institute Life Achievement Award in 1976. Much more importantly, his films have found an enduring popularity on home video.

Like so many people in the early days, Wyler was brought into the business by "Uncle" Carl Laemmle, founder of Universal Studio. Wyler began as an apprentice working at a variety of jobs, including assistant director on Lon Chaney's silent *The Hunchback of Notre Dame*, and production assistant on the silent 1925 *Ben-Hur*. Before his long career was over, he would embody the Golden Age of Hollywood at its brightest. To judge by the films he had made in the late 1930s and early '40—*Jezebel*, *The Letter*, *The Little Foxes*—he would seem to be the least bellicose of filmmakers, not in the same league with his contemporaries Ford, Wellman, and Hawks. But Wyler was an early opponent of Hitler.

He made his first war film, *Mrs. Miniver*, as unalloyed propaganda, and his timing could not have been better. The production began shooting less than a month before the attack on Pearl Harbor and was released in May of 1942. If the story of English resistance to the Germans is creaky with age now, it could not have been more relevant to its immediate audience. It was a huge commercial hit and won Wyler his first Oscar. The day after he'd finished work on the film, he enlisted in the Army Air Corps.

The result was his second war film, the seminal documentary *Memphis Belle*, about a B-17 bomber in England. To make the film, Wyler and his cameramen, William Clothier and William Skall, actually flew bombing raids over Germany. It was dangerous work. The pilot, Capt. Robert Morgan said, "The man had a lot of nerve. The nerviest thing he ever did is something I would never have let my own men do. He rode in the ball turret under the belly of the plane on takeoff and landing. It was completely unsafe, totally against regulations. All you had to do was have a tire blow out and the guy in there is in bad shape, probably dead. We lost planes on takeoff that tore their bottoms off. But he wanted pictures of the wheels and the runway. You see the shots in the film." (*A Talent for Trouble*. Jan Herman. Putnam's. 1995)

Memphis Belle was so good that it was screened for an enthusiastic President Roosevelt at the White House and then released theatrically. Wyler also made another documentary, *Thunderbolt*, about the P-47, but it has never attracted an audience like his story of the B-17.

Wyler saved his best efforts for the post-war years. If *Mrs. Miniver* is a call to action against a foreign enemy, *The Best Years of Our Lives* is an even more deeply felt examination of the effects of the war on the victors. Seen together, the three films form an odd trilogy, united not by story or style but by belief in the humanity of their characters. What else would we expect from the classiest picture maker that ever lived?

See also:

William Wyler: The Authorized Biography. Axel Madsen. Thomas Y. Crowell. 1973.

1941

1979 Steven Spielberg ♫♫♫♪

Steven Spielberg's tendency toward sweetness is offset by a cheerful destructiveness in his underrated comedy. It's a far from perfect film, with some derivative moments and poorly timed scenes. But it's also glowingly photographed by William Fraker and filled with cameos by some of the best comic character actors in the business. The premise is loosely based on an incident that took place in 1942, when a Japanese submarine was sighted off the coast of Southern California and caused the "Great Los Angeles Air Raid."

This story begins on the Saturday after Pearl Harbor, with a parody of the famous opening scene of *Jaws* introducing a Japanese sub under the command of Cmdr. Mitamura (Toshiro Mifune), who is seeking something "honorable" to destroy before he heads back home. Hollywood, he decides, is the perfect target. In L.A., tensions are rising between zoot-suited teenagers and the growing ranks of soldiers. It comes to a head at the USO where Sgt. Stretch Sitarski (Treat Williams) puts the make on Betty (Dianne Kay) while her boyfriend Wally (Bobby DiCicco) tries to protect her, and Betty's friend Maxine (Wendie Jo Sperber) pursues Stretch.

> "You are going to have to smile at men you would never give a second glance to in peacetime. You are going to have to make polite conversation with men whose minds are in the gutter and you are going to have to dance and dance close with men you might find repulsive."
>
> **Miss Fitzroy (Penny Marshall) to new USO girls**

Realizing how absurd the situation is, Gen. Stilwell (Robert Stack) settles down to watch *Dumbo*, while his aide Lt. Birkhead (Tim Matheson) makes a move on the General's secretary Donna (Nancy Allen), who has a thing for airplanes. Overhead, Capt. Wild Bill Kelso (John Belushi) flies his fighter in pursuit of phantom Zeros while the equally mad Capt. Maddox (Warren Oates) thinks that Japanese airstrips are hidden In the alfalfa fields near Pamona. On the streets of downtown, Sgt. Tree (Dan Aykroyd) and his tank are not so firmly in control.

> "The Japs do not surrender and they don't take prisoners. They have only one idea in their mind. You know what that is, sailor? To kill! That's right, to kill you, to kill your families, yes, to kill your families, your mothers, your loved ones, your pets and to keep on killing until they conquer the world."
>
> **Sgt. Tree (Dan Aykroyd) addressing the mob**

Showing up in support are Christopher Lee, Dub Taylor, John Candy, Frank McRae, Elisha Cook Jr., Dick Miller, Michael McKean, Penny Marshall, Sydney Lassick, Eddie Deezen, Lionel Stander, and Murray Hamilton. If the names are not familiar, the faces are. The most memorable of them is Slim Pickens. As Christmas tree farmer Hollis Woods, he's a slightly smoother version of Maj. "King" Kong from *Dr. Strangelove* in a long series of scenes in the middle.

The leads handle their roles with the right combination of seriousness and silliness, particularly Dan Aykroyd. If Belushi and Matheson are replaying their characters from *National Lampoon's Animal House* in khaki, they're still funny, and Stack's unruffled deadpan performance is the film's stable center. Some of the most effective jokes are based on the era's racist and romantic cliches, though perhaps a familiarity with the real films of the time makes them funnier.

Even when the physical comedy doesn't work, the energy level remains high, thanks in part to John Williams's bouncy score. His main March theme has become a staple of pops orchestras everywhere, and "Swing, Swing, Swing" is a genuine showstopper based on Benny Goodman's "Sing, Sing, Sing." Finally, Spielberg and Fraker turn even the most mundane scenes into candy-colored

See also

On the Town

National Lampoon's Animal House

Jaws

Dr. Strangelove

Ghostbusters

neon-lit set pieces. No, *1941* will never be regarded among Spielberg's best, but it's a much better film than most critics think it is, and it stands up well to another viewing.

Sgt. Tree (Dan Aykroyd) asks Ward Douglas (Ned Beatty) for permission to station an anti-aircraft gun on the front lawn in *1941.* The Kobal Collection

Cast: John Belushi (Wild Bill Kelso), Dan Aykroyd (Sgt. Tree), Patti LuPone (Lydia Hedberg), Ned Beatty (Ward Douglas), Slim Pickens (Hollis Wood), Murray Hamilton (Claude), Christopher Lee (Von Kleinschmidt), Tim Matheson (Birkhead), Toshiro Mifune (Cmdr. Mitamura), Warren Oates (Maddox), Robert Stack (Gen. Stilwell), Nancy Allen (Donna), Elisha Cook Jr. (The Patron), Lorraine Gary (Joan Douglas), Treat Wllllams (Sitarski), Mickey Rourke (Reese), John Candy (Foley), Wendie Jo Sperber (Maxine), Lucille Benson (Gas Mama), Eddie Deezen (Herbie), Bobby DiCicco (Wally), Dianne Kay (Betty), Perry Lang (Dennis), Frank McRae (Ogden Johnson Jones), Lionel Stander (Scioli), Dub Taylor (Mr. Malcomb), Joe Flaherty (USO emcee), David Lander (Joe), Michael McKean (Willy), Samuel Fuller (Interceptor Cmdr.), Audrey Landers (USO girl), John Landis (Mizerany), Walter Olkewicz (Hinshaw), Donovan Scott (Kid Sailor), Penny Marshall (Miss Fitzroy), Sydney Lassick (Salesman), James Caan (Sailor in fight), Dick Miller; **Written by:** Robert Zemeckis, Bob Gale, John Milius; **Cinematography by:** William A. Fraker; **Music by:** John Williams. **Producer:** Buzz Feitshans, John Milius, A Team Productions. **Awards:** Nominations: Academy Awards '79: Best Cinematography, Best Sound. **MPAA Rating:** PG. **Running Time:** 120 minutes. **Format:** VHS, Beta, LV, DVD.

SINCE YOU WENT AWAY

1944 John Cromwell ♪♪♪♪

Producer-writer David O. Selznick's rosy view of the homefront is a transition film that stands somewhere between the genteel heroics of *Mrs. Miniver* and the uncomfortable realities of *The Best Years of Our Lives*. The flaws are undisguised—slow pace, stiff editing, transparent plot, unbridled sentimentality—but the picture is still delightful. Well acted mostly and handsomely produced, it is Golden Age Hollywood storytelling at its most lavish.

A foreword sets the patriotic tone with the words "This is a story of the Unconquerable Fortress: the American Home . . . 1943." The camera then pans from the home fire burning brightly on the hearth, to Dad's empty leather armchair, with the faithful family bulldog before it, waiting for the master's return. The house is an idealized "typical" middle-class suburban home created by Mark-Lee Kirk and Victor Gangelin on a huge soundstage. Like everyone else involved in the major creative positions on the film, Kirk and Gangelin received Academy Award nominations; only Max Steiner won for his lush score.

It's Tuesday, January 12, 1943, in an unnamed Midwestern city. Anne Hilton (Claudette Colbert) has just seen her husband off, and is only beginning to realize how seriously his decision to enlist has affected the family financially. She and her daughters Jane (Jennifer Jones) and Bridget (Shirley Temple) can no longer afford to keep the faithful family retainer Fidelia (Hattie McDaniel). They'll just have to economize and perhaps rent out a room to a boarder. Jane—18 and ready—says that their newspaper ad should specify that they want an officer. They get 60-ish Col. Smollett (Monty Woolley), gruff, golden-hearted, etc. But before Jane becomes too upset, charming "uncle" Tony (Joseph Cotten), now a Navy lieutenant, shows up at their doorstep. He's her father's best friend who carries on a mock flirtation with Anne. The other two main characters are divorcee Emily Hawkins (Agnes Moorehead), whose snotty narrow-minded arrogance makes Anne even more angelic, and Cpl. Bill Smollett (Robert Walker), disgraced grandson of the Colonel with whom Jane falls in love.

Selznick's adaptation of Margaret Buell Wilder's novel is an episodic collection of scenes, all designed to show the resilience of American womenfolk. Director and Selznick associate John Cromwell handles the material dutifully, and the action is punctuated with those odd "big" moments that are virtual trademarks of Selznick pictures. A USO dance staged in a cavernous airplane hanger is the kind of show-stopping scene most viewers expect to see. They'll be more surprised by the mystical, holy atmosphere that pervades the swearing in of the nurses' aides, the trip to the bowling alley, and the walk in the hayfield. All of them, and several others, are inflated to near-epic proportions. The one scene that everyone remembers, though, is Jane's saying goodbye to Bill. It's probably the most famous wartime train platform farewell in the history of movies. It turns up constantly in compilations of clips and was even parodied in a famous beer commercial.

> "These kids just break my heart. They're so, so eager. They expect to come back to something . . . something like they left only better. Hope they don't get too many surprises."
>
> **Lt. Tony Willett (Joseph Cotten) on a young airman about to take off**

DidyouKnow?

Since You Went Away was nominated for Academy Awards in every major category, but 1944 was a very tough year, with Double *Indemnity, Laura, Gaslight, Lifeboat, Going My Way,* and *Mr. Skeffington* in the running, too.

Fact/Rumor:

While writer-producer David O. Selznick was making this celluloid testimonial to "the Unconquerable Fortress: the American Home," he was having an affair with Jennifer Jones who, at the time, was married to her co-star Robert Walker.

See also

Three Came Home
The Immortal Battalion
The White Cliffs of Dover
Shadow of a Doubt

Though a bit overstated by today's standards, the performances are excellent. Cotten's glib charmer is precisely the kind of supporting role he was so good at. The same could be said of Agnes Moorehead and Monty Woolley. Robert Walker, however, would be much more persuasive a few years later as the psychopathic Bruno in *Strangers on a Train*. As the dutiful daughters, Jennifer Jones and Shirley Temple seem constantly on the edge of unintentional comedy, but they are effective, even in the more emotional moments. The six of them are a terrific ensemble, but the action revolves around Claudette Colbert and she, too, manages to keep the rampant sentimentality in check.

To look at the film as any form of realism misses its point. It was made as inspiration, a cinematic reminder that everyone was pulling together and an encouragement to do more. If its propaganda value has deflated, *Since You Went Away* is still one of the most entertaining examples of its kind, even with a running time of nearly three hours.

Jennifer Jones, Robert Walker, and Joseph Cotten in *Since You Went Away.* The Kobal Collection

Cast: Claudette Colbert (Anne Hilton), Jennifer Jones (Jane Hilton), Shirley Temple (Bridget Hilton), Joseph Cotten (Lt. Tony Willett), Agnes Moorehead (Emily Hawkins), Monty Woolley (Col. Smollett), Guy Madison (Harold Smith), Lionel Barrymore (Clergyman), Robert Walker (Cpl. William G. Smollett II), Hattie McDaniel (Fidelia), Keenan Wynn (Lt. Solomon), Craig Stevens (Danny Williams), Albert Basserman (Dr. Sigmund Golden), Alla Nazimova (Mrs. Koslowska), Lloyd Corrigan (Mr. Mahoney), Terry Moore (Refugee child), Florence Bates (Hungry woman on train), Ruth Roman (Envious girl), Andrew V. McLaglen (Former plowboy), Dorothy Dandridge (Officer's wife), Rhonda Fleming (Girl at dance), Addison Richards (Maj. Atkins), Jackie Moran (Johnny Mahoney); **Written by:** David O. Selznick; **Cinematography by:** Stanley Cortez, Lee Garmes; **Music by:** Max Steiner. **Producer:** David O. Selznick, United Artists. **Awards:** Academy Awards '44: Best Original Dramatic Score; Nominations: Academy Awards '44: Best Actress (Colbert), Best Black and White Cinematography, Best Film Editing, Best Interior Decoration, Best Picture, Best Supporting Actor (Woolley), Best Supporting Actress (Jones). **Budget:** 2.4M. **Running Time:** 172 minutes. **Format:** VHS, Beta, LV, Closed Caption.

THE WHITE CLIFFS OF DOVER

1944 Clarence Brown 🎬🎬🎬

From the opening credits that mirror *Mrs. Miniver*, it's obvious that this glossy propaganda is aimed at a female audience. In all senses of the term, it is a "women's picture" concerned with personal relationships, and the characters' emotional reaction to events, not the events themselves. (Only two images of combat appear on screen, and they are not fully developed scenes.) That is a completely legitimate, though rarely seen, approach to the subject of war, and the film encompasses two of them.

It begins in the "present" of 1943, where Red Cross worker Susan Dunn Ashwood (Irene Dunne) supervises a London hospital. In the early morning lull before an engagement that will result in her wards being filled, she thinks back on the morning when she first arrived in England on a vacation from America in 1916. An Anglophile's Anglophile, she is only slightly deterred by the grumpy reaction of her more patriotic father (Frank "pay no attention to that man behind the curtain" Morgan). Then, on the last night of her stay, the courtly old Col. Forsythe (C. Aubrey Smith) invites her to accompany him to a society shindig where the King and Queen will be in attendance.

> "There's another war in the making. It may come in five years, it may come in ten; but it's as inevitable as death."
>
> **Hiram Dunn (Frank Morgan)**

Susan jumps at the chance. Col. Forsythe arranges a meeting with his young friend Sir John Ashwood (Alan Marshal) and lets nature take its course. The expected complications arise, but the boy-meets-girl-boy-loses-girl-boy-gets-girl-back formula is played out with well-realized characters and a few interesting twists. Throughout, the production values are first-class, from the stuffy elegance of a British manor house to the rolling fields of the estate to a French seaside resort. No locations were used. Everything was created on the MGM backlot and sound stages.

Strict authenticity is not the aim here. Director Clarence Brown (*National Velvet*, *The Yearling*) is interested first in telling a good love story, and second in cementing Anglo-American cooperation against a common enemy. He does both. Neither Irene Dunne nor Alan Marshal is particularly emotional or demonstrative, and that lack of expressiveness is used to underscore their characters' sense of duty and self-sacrifice. Those virtues are personified in their son, initially played by Roddy McDowall, and later by Peter Lawford.

By contemporary standards, the film goes much too far, becoming heavy-handed in its affirmation of all things British: society, culture, class system. The points are hammered home, then for those who might still have missed them, a voice-over narrator reads from Alice Duer Miller's title poem, with additional lines by Robert Nathan. Seen as propaganda, the film is earnest, serious, and single-minded to a fault. The flag-waving coda may seem like overkill, but given the shamelessness of what has come before, it is somehow appropriate.

See also
Mrs. Miniver
Since You Went Away
Three Came Home

Alan Marshal and Irene Dunne
have stiff upper lips in *The
White Cliffs of Dover.* The Kobal Collection

Cast: Irene Dunne (Susan Dunn Ashwood), Alan Marshal (Sir John Ashwood), Frank Morgan (Hiram Porter Dunn), Peter Lawford (John Ashwood II), Gladys Cooper (Lady Jean Ashwood), May Whitty (Nanny), Sir C. Aubrey Smith (Colonel), Roddy McDowall (John Ashwood II as a boy), Van Johnson (Sam Bennett), Elizabeth Taylor (Young Betsy), June Lockhart (Betsy at 18), John Warburton (Reggie), Jill Esmond (Rosamund), Norma Varden (Mrs. Bland), Tom Drake (American soldier), Arthur Shields (Benson), Brenda Forbes (Gwennie), Edmund Breon (Maj. Bancroft), Clyde Cook (Jennings), Isobel Elsom (Mrs. Bancroft), Lumsden Hare (Vicar), Miles Mander (Maj. Loring), Ian Wolfe (Skipper); **Written by:** George Froeschel, Jan Lustig, Claudine West; **Cinematography by:** George Folsey; **Music by:** Herbert Stothart. **Producer:** Sidney Franklin, MGM. **Awards:** Nominations: Academy Awards '44: Best Black and White Cinematography. **Running Time:** 126 minutes. **Format:** VHS.

World War II: Prisoners of War on Screen

The POW situation turns the war film inside out. One basic tenant of the genre is that the sides are fairly evenly matched—either one could win. Even if it is a David vs. Goliath mismatch, we know that David has a chance. That's a key element of the story's dramatic tension. In the POW film, though, one side is essentially powerless, stripped of its weapons, and so is forced to find new tactics. Usually, that means escape, but not always. And because the rules are so fundamentally changed, filmmakers are forced to be more creative. The results are some of the more off beat, and often popular, war films.

Director Fred Zinnemann made his debut in 1944 with *The Seventh Cross*, a semi-noir tale set in 1936 and describing an escape from a concentration camp. The protagonist, played by Spencer Tracy, has been locked up for unspecified political reasons, and so the horrors of the Holocaust are only alluded to. Zinnemann sacrifices some suspense when he shifts his focus to ordinary Germans, two played by Hume Cronyn and Jessica Tandy, and their mixed reactions to Nazi rule. It makes for unusually thoughtful propaganda.

After the war, many POW films were based on fact. *Three Came Home*, from 1950, is an adaptation of Agnes Newton Keith's fine autobiographical book. It revolves around the relationship that develops between a writer (Claudette Colbert) and the Japanese colonel (Sessue Hayakawa), who is a fan of her work and the commandant in charge of the prison camps where she and her family are held. Again, the film refuses to cast the enemy as a one-dimensional villain. The two sides are too close, almost intimate, for that.

The events described in Robert Bresson's *A Man Escaped* (see review and sidebar) would be impossible to believe if they weren't true. Bresson uses them as the basis of an exploration of isolation, both physical and spiritual. This fine, austere film is virtually unknown in this country and deserves a larger audience.

Prison camps are the setting for two of the biggest boxoffice hits of the 1950s. Billy Wilder's dated *Stalag 17* won an Academy Award for its star William Holden. A few years later, Holden co-starred with Alec Guinness and Sessue Hayakawa in David Lean's phenomenal *Bridge on the River Kwai*, one of the most honored and profitable films to come out of World War II.

Novelist James Clavell, who was a prisoner of the Japanese for three years in Singapore, is largely responsible for two of the best POW films of the 1960s. He co-wrote and produced *The Great Escape*, arguably the best adventure film of the decade, and he adapted his autobiographical novel, *King Rat*, for director Bryan Forbes. Though this one has never achieved the popularity of *The Great Escape*, it is a more accurate portrait of day-to-day life in a camp, and a terrifically entertaining film in its own right.

Frank Sinatra fares well, essentially playing himself, in the escapist fluff of *Von Ryan's Express*. David Bowie attempts a more serious character study in Nagisa Oshima's dreamlike *Merry Christmas, Mr. Lawrence*. Oshima returns to the relationship between the captive, Bowie as an iron-willed commando, and the captor, played by Japanese pop star Ryuichi Sakamoto.

In the 1980s and '90s, the POW film goes back to its factual roots with Steven Spielberg's version of science-fiction writer J.G. Ballard's autobiographical *Empire of the Sun*. It's curiously cold, not nearly as successful as Spielberg's other work in the genre. Bruce Beresford's *Paradise Road* takes an ensemble cast through some of the same fact-based territory that Agnes Newton Keith explored in a story of women imprisoned by the Japanese. Part of the basis is the poetry of Margaret Dryburgh. Though the film is not as well known as some of the others in this group, its sense of place is as strong as any, and it does what the best do—it gives the viewer just a taste, a hint, an idea of what the real experience of being a prisoner must be like, and that's all that most of us would ever want to experience.

BRIDGE ON THE RIVER KWAI

1957 David Lean 🎬🎬🎬🎬

David Lean's best films are epics that grow from closely observed characters, or, in this case, from two characters. Col. Nicholson (Alec Guinness) and Col. Saito (Sessue Hayakawa) are reflections of each other; dedicated leaders with identical careers and identical flaws. Each views himself as a soldier and patriot, and each is so rigid in his own way that he is unable to see past immediate problems to achieve a larger goal.

> "This is war! This is not a game of cricket!"
>
> **Col. Saito (Sessue Hayakawa)**

> "I hate the British! You're defeated but you have no shame. You're stubborn but have no pride. You endure but you have no courage. I hate the British!"
>
> **Col. Saito**

> "You have survived with honor, that and more. Here in the wilderness, you have turned defeat into victory. I congratulate you. Well done!"
>
> **Col. Nicholson (Alec Guinness) to his men**

The setting is a Japanese prison camp deep in the Burmese jungle. It's so remote that guards and barbwire are unnecessary. No one can escape. The Japanese are building a railroad through the jungle and using British prisoners as labor. When Col. Nicholson and his men arrive at the camp, Col. Saito informs them that everyone, including officers, will work on the construction of a bridge. Nicholson, who carries a copy of the Geneva Convention in his breast pocket, says that is against the rules. Saito has him beaten and thrown into an oven-like outdoor metal cell. Nicholson refuses to relent and their war of wills in engaged. At the same time, a captured American, Cmdr. Shears (William Holden), attempts a desperate escape.

The rest of the film follows parallel tracks—often apparent but sometimes disguised—as, eventually, Nicholson and Saito work to build the bridge while Shears finds himself dragooned into Maj. Warden's (Jack Hawkins) commando unit to go back to the camp and destroy the bridge. Within that simple structure, the story explores questions of loyalty, duty, responsibility, command, the relationship between officers and their men, and, in a sense, even slavery. Though, in 1957, the script was credited to novelist Pierre Boulle (who did not even speak English), it was actually written by the blacklisted Carl Foreman and Michael Wilson, with more work by Calder Willingham. (The Best Screenplay Oscar was awarded to Boulle. The Academy amended its McCarthy-era "political correctness" in 1984, giving credit where it was due. By then, Wilson was already dead and Foreman died the day after the announcement.)

Fact/Rumor:
Alec Guinness was the third choice for the role of Col. Nicholson. Both Charles Laughton and Noel Coward were considered first.

The film gives a conventional 1950s Hollywood gloss to life in a Japanese prison camp, but that's not the point; the characters and the insanity of their situation are. The director and cast are attempting to make entertaining escapism with a realistic psychological dimension. After a richly layered conclusion, the film's unsubtle message is unsubtly stated by the doctor, Maj. Clipton (James Donald, who would play much the same role in *The Great Escape*) when he says, "Madness! Madness!"

The film is also one of the first post-war American attempts to depict the Japanese in a fully human, non-stereotypical role. Hayakawa and Guinness are perfectly cast. Their scenes together, and their reactions to each other, are the key moments. Don't miss the superb cut from one to the other about midway through Nicholson's moment of triumph. Also, this is a film that should be seen in a widescreen version if at all possible. Lean uses his entire frame, particularly in the two-shots where Nicholson and Saito are on screen together. The pan-and-scan tape is forced to resort to several inelegant chops to show the essential reaction shots.

See also
The General
Doctor Zhivago
Lawrence of Arabia
The Good, the Bad and the Ugly
The Victors

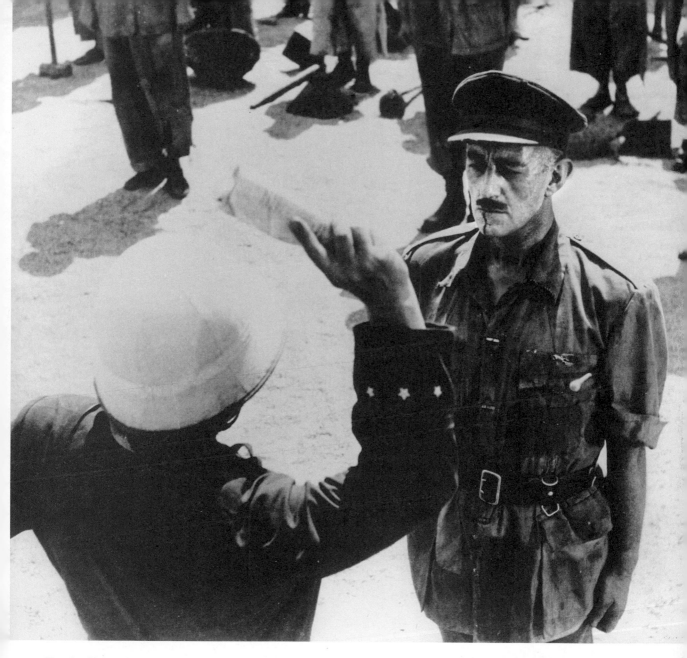

British POW Col. Nicholson
(Alec Guinness) meets Col. Saito
(Sessue Hayakawa) for the first
time in *Bridge on the River Kwai.*
The Kobal Collection

The visual image that brings the two men together is a heavy sledgehammer. It's seen first when
Nicholson is locked in the "hotbox" and then reappears later when the two men are using a similar
hammer to mount a sign on their completed bridge. Inevitably, the primary focus is on Nicholson,
but Saito is presented as an equally sympathetic and complex character. In fact, his emotional and
cultural conflicts cut more deeply than Nicholson's. (Guinness won the Best Actor Oscar for his
work; Hayakawa was nominated for Supporting Actor but lost to Red Buttons in *Sayonara*.)

The third protagonist, Shears, is the opposite of the first two. While they (and Maj. Warden)
embrace duty and devotion, Shears has to be dragged kicking and flailing every inch of the way.

BRIDGE ON THE RIVER KWAI

Finally, the jungle is almost as important as any of the characters. In the second half, several shots of a sunlit forest crossed by the shadows of thousands of huge bats are remarkable. (The film was made in Sri Lanka, then called Ceylon.) In that part, the focus of the film splits between those who are trying to build the bridge and those who would destroy it. In the end, of course, the story is much more complicated than that, and the double-edged conclusion underlines the film's several ironies. Curiously, that ending was criticized at the time for being ambiguous on one important point. Today, the ambiguity seems unimportant compared to the film's brilliant combination of conflict and character revelation.

Cast: William Holden (Shears), Alec Guinness (Col. Nicholson), Jack Hawkins (Maj. Warden), Sessue Hayakawa (Col. Saito), James Donald (Maj. Clipton), Geoffrey Horne (Lt. Joyce), Andre Morell (Col. Green), Ann Sears (Nurse), Peter Williams (Maj. Reeves), John Boxer (Maj. Hughes), Percy Herbert (Grogan), Harold Goodwin (Baker), Henry Okawa (Capt. Kanematsu), Keiichiro Katsumoto (Lt. Miura), M.R.B. Chakrabandhu (Yai); **Written by:** Carl Foreman, Michael Wilson; **Cinematography by:** Jack Hildyard; **Music by:** Malcolm Arnold. **Producer:** Sam Spiegel, Columbia Pictures. **British. Awards:** Academy Awards '57: Best Actor (Guinness), Best Adapted Screenplay, Best Cinematography, Best Director (Lean), Best Film Editing, Best Picture, Best Score; American Film Institute (AFI) '98: Top 100; British Academy Awards '57: Best Actor (Guinness), Best Film, Best Screenplay; Directors Guild of America Awards '57: Best Director (Lean); Golden Globe Awards '58: Best Actor—Drama (Guinness), Best Director (Lean), Best Film—Drama; National Board of Review Awards '57: Best Actor (Guinness), Best Director (Lean), Best Supporting Actor (Hayakawa), National Film Registry '97; New York Film Critics Awards '57: Best Actor (Guinness), Best Director (Lean), Best Film; Nominations: Academy Awards '57: Best Supporting Actor (Hayakawa). **Budget:** 3M. **Running Time:** 161 minutes. **Format:** VHS, Beta, LV, Letterbox.

The Hound Salutes: James Donald

Given his unremarkable name and face, James Donald is not an actor that many moviegoers immediately associate with war films. Even devoted fans may not realize how often they have seen him. Donald was a British character actor whose specialty was the responsible supporting role or second-in-command. He was the mid-level official who kept things on an even keel while the hero or heroes took care of the more exciting side of the plot. (Such people are as necessary in the movies as they are in real life.)

In that capacity, he was well cast as Prince Albert to Queen Victoria in a television production of *Victoria Regina*, and as Vincent Van Gogh's level-headed brother Theo in *Lust for Life*.

Watching Donald, you instinctively know that this guy is never going to attain spectacular successes, and he's not going to screw things up too badly either. You also sense that he's unshakably honest and would lie only for a worthy purpose. In short, he's the perfect military doctor. He made his first appearance in that role in Noel Coward's polished propaganda *In Which We Serve*. He followed that up with another exemplary ensemble piece, Carol Reed's *The Immortal Battalion*.

After the war, he worked steadily in the thriving British film industry, appearing in more than a dozen films. Then in 1957, he returned to work with David Lean, who had made his directorial debut with *In Which We Serve*. In *Bridge on the River Kwai*, Donald is Maj. Clipton, the prison camp doctor, who actually gets the film's significant last line. He would end his career in war films with two more prison camp stories, *The Great Escape*, where he stays behind as Richard Attenborough, Steve McQueen, and the others go traipsing across Germany, and *King Rat*, where he's the doctor again.

It's easy to understand why filmmakers from the 1940s to the '70s would be so keen to have James Donald in a film. Though actors and critics often decry typecasting, viewers do depend on it. As Alfred Hitchcock noted, when the audience sees a star, it knows who the hero is, and the director doesn't have to spend any more time explaining that. In the same way, even now, when people see James Donald, they understand that he's the trustworthy voice of reason who will likely remain somewhere between the hero and the villain, and will do the right thing.

He died in Wiltshire, England, on August 3, 1993.

EMPIRE OF THE SUN

1987 Steven Spielberg ♫♫♫

Steven Spielberg's adaptation of J.G. Ballard's autobiographical novel suffers two serious flaws. One, it's too long. Two, the protagonist is such a cocky little snot that his perilous straits never generate any real sympathy. The first problem is no surprise; Spielberg's a digressive filmmaker, for better and for worse. The second is unusual, given the idealized children who have appeared in *Close Encounters of the Third Kind*, *E.T. The Extraterrestrial*, *Poltergeist*, and so many other films that he has directed and produced. Without discounting those problems, the film also contains some memorable scenes, and its depiction of the Pacific War is strong.

Young Jamie Graham (Christian Bale) is the only child of a wealthy British couple (Emily Richard and Rupert Frazer) in Shanghai. As the film begins, it is late 1941. Japanese troops are massed outside, waiting for news of Pearl Harbor before they occupy the city. Fascinated by aviation, Jamie idolizes the Japanese pilots and keeps a small toy Zero fighter as a talisman. The opening scenes contrasting the expatriate community's affluence with Chinese squalor are obvious but effective. The two worlds collide when the invasion begins. Imperial troops march down streets clogged with panicked masses. In the crush, Jamie is separated from his parents and returns to his abandoned home. After a series of attempts to "surrender," Jamie finds himself under the none-too-tender protection of Basie (John Malkovich), a Faginesque American ne'er-do-well. Eventually, they find their way to the Soochow Creek Internment Camp, along with several hundred other Westerners.

For a boy, the camp next door to an airfield is a place of picaresque adventure and unforgiving social Darwinism. It's too artily tarted up by the filmmakers to be a believable prison camp, but it is so visually interesting that most viewers probably won't mind. They'll be more put off by the pokey pace. Spielberg often lets the action stop cold to dwell on an especially strong image—a huge poster for *Gone with the Wind*, the moment when Jamie sees his first real Zero—that means little to the narrative. Other showstopping moments, like the P-51 attack on the field, and Jamie's vision of the end of the war, have an emotional value that equals their striking presentation. Unfortunately, in all of the big moments, John Williams's score is cranked up to an intrusive level. That over-reliance on the music suggests that the filmmakers did not completely trust their characters. In Basie's case, that uncertainty is underlined visually. His face is seldom fully revealed. He hides behind sunglasses and hats.

Throughout the film, Spielberg and writer Tom Stoppard stick strictly to Jamie's adolescent point of view. That's certainly a legitimate approach to the story, one that accentuates the hallucinatory aspects. At the same time, a larger context is lost and, for all the changes he goes through, Jamie simply is not a compelling character. Spielberg's other attempts to deal seriously and lightly with World War II are much more successful.

See also

Shanghai 1941

Paradise Road

Three Came Home

Crash

Schindler's List

Raiders of the Lost Ark

Indiana Jones and the Last Crusade

Saving Private Ryan

Jamie Graham (Christian Bale), interned in a Japanese prison camp, salutes the Kamikaze pilots of the adjacent airfield in *Empire of the Sun*. The Kobal Collection

Cast: Christian Bale (Jamie Graham), John Malkovich (Basie), Miranda Richardson (Mrs. Victor), Nigel Havers (Dr. Rawlins), Joe Pantoliano (Frank Demarest), Leslie Phillips (Maxton), Rupert Frazer (Jamie's Father), Ben Stiller (Dainty), Robert Stephens (Mr. Lockwood), Burt Kwouk (Mr. Chen), Masato Ibu (Sgt. Nagata), Emily Richard (Jamie's Mother), David Neidorf (Tiptree), Ralph Seymour (Cohen), Emma Piper (Amy Matthews), Peter Gale (Mr. Victor), Zhai Nai She (Yang), Guts Ishimatsu (Sgt. Uchida), J.G. Ballard (Costume party guest); **Written by:** Tom Stoppard, Menno Meyjes; **Cinematography by:** Allen Daviau; **Music by:** John Williams. **Producer:** Steven Spielberg, Kathleen Kennedy, Amblin Entertainment. **Awards:** National Board of Review Awards '87: Best Director (Spielberg); Nominations: Academy Awards '87: Best Art Direction/Set Decoration, Best Cinematography, Best Costume Design, Best Film Editing, Best Sound, Best Original Score. **Budget:** 38M. **Boxoffice:** 22.2M. **MPAA Rating:** PG. **Running Time:** 153 minutes. **Format:** VHS, Beta, LV, 8mm, Letterbox, Closed Caption.

The French auteur theory of criticism holds that the director is responsible for all that is right or wrong in a film. That, of course, is a grotesque oversimplification, never more obviously so than with this crowd-pleaser. Stalmaster-Lister Co., which gets credit for the casting, made a huge contribution, along with Fernando Carrere and Kip Ripberger, who created the sets. So did Bert Hendrikson who designed the wardrobe, Elmer Bernstein for the score and . . . but why go on? Filmmaking is a collective art and in this case, the collaborative chemistry is close to perfect.

A foreword states: "This is a true story—although the characters are composites of real men, and time and place have been compressed—every detail of the escape is the way it really happened." Though the actual events are forced into the formula of a conventional adventure film, the key points are true enough, particularly when compared to the usual Hollywood version of history. Reportedly, writer Paul Brickhill refused to sell the film rights to his book until he was assured that the proper care would be taken with the story of a mass 1944 escape by officers from a German prison camp. Perhaps because producer-writer James Clavell had been a prisoner of war himself, he made sure that the material received that respect. (Clavell's experiences are the basis for the novel and film *King Rat*.)

As everyone knows, however, fealty to historical truth is no guarantee of boxoffice success. The right casting is much more important, and the filmmakers got it right by creating an ensemble of older, established British character actors and young Americans on the brink of stardom. Though they are familiar names now, James Coburn, Charles Bronson, James Garner, David McCallum, and Steve McQueen were less well known in 1963. (McQueen, Coburn, and Bronson had worked for director John Sturges a few years before in *The Magnificent Seven*.) They have most of the flashy scenes; their British counterparts—Richard Attenborough, James Donald, Donald Pleasence, Gordon Jackson, Angus Lennie, and Nigel Stock—do most of the dramatic heavy lifting, with assistance from Hannes Messemer as the sympathetic commandant and Hans Reiser as a fussy Gestapo officer.

The simple sets recreating a rough-hewn POW compound in the middle of a pine forest are initially forbidding. As the film progresses, the place comes to look more like a summer camp for grown-ups with arts and crafts classes in forgery, tunneling, and burglary.

Sturges is careful with the pace in the first half, letting the escape plans develop slowly and leavening the situation with a solid sense of humor. The characters are unusually well developed, and though the action is fairly evenly divided among the ensemble, one member stands out.

"We have, in effect, put all our rotten eggs in one basket, and we intend to watch this basket carefully."

Kommandant Von Luger (Hannes Messemer)

"I could tell you stories about my teeth that would make your hair stand on end."

Guard Werner "The Ferret" (Robert Graf)

This is the role that made Steve McQueen a star, despite the fact that he hardly appears in the first half of the film. He's introduced with the rest at the beginning, then disappears for 40 minutes. After returning briefly, he disappears again until the midpoint. Those scenes have relatively little to do with the rest of the action, so most viewers don't notice how maniacally McQueen mugs his way through them. He comes into his own in the third act when he gets

See also
The Dirty Dozen
The Sand Pebbles
Stalag 17
The Longest Day
The Guns of Navarone

Steve McQueen, as "Cooler King" Capt. Virgil Hilts, doesn't quite make *The Great Escape*. The Kobal Collection

on the motorcycle. That image of a regular guy in a cut-off sweatshirt and khakis outrunning (almost) the whole German army is one of the defining moments of 1960s cinema. In that long scene, combined with the conclusion which leaves him unrepentant and still defiant, McQueen defined himself as the anti-establishment hero for a generation.

Cast: Steve McQueen (Capt. Virgil Hilts, "The Cooler King"), James Garner (Hendley, "The Scrounger"), Richard Attenborough (Bartlett, "Big X"), Charles Bronson (Danny Velinski, "Tunnel King"), James Coburn (Sedgwick, "Manufacturer"), Donald Pleasence (Colin Blythe, "The Forger"), David McCallum (Ashley-Pitt, "Dispersal"), James Donald (Senior Officer Ramsey), Gordon Jackson (MacDonald, "Intelligence"), Hannes Messemer (Kommandant Von Luger), John Leyton (Willie, "Tunnel King"), Nigel Stock (Cavendish, "The Surveyor"), Jud Taylor (Goff), Hans Reiser (Kuhn), Robert Freitag (Posen), Karl Otto Alberty (Steinach), Angus Lennie (Ives, "The Mole"), Robert Graf (Werner, "The Ferret"), Harry Riebauer (Strachwitz); **Written by:** James Clavell, W.R. Burnett; **Cinematography by:** Daniel F. Fapp; **Music by:** Elmer Bernstein. **Producer:** James Clavell, John Sturges, United Artists. **Awards:** Nominations: Academy Awards '63: Best Film Editing. **Budget:** 4M. **Running Time:** 170 minutes. **Format:** VHS, Beta, LV, Letterbox, Closed Caption, DVD.

James Clavell based his novel on his experiences in a Japanese prisoner of war camp. That authenticity shows through in both physical and psychological details, making this adaptation one of the best World War II POW films. It has never equaled the boxoffice success of *The Great Escape*, which Clavell produced and co-wrote, but it is every bit as enjoyable for different reasons.

A fine, eerie opening establishes the infamous Changi Prison, 1945, home to several hundred British officers and enlisted men and a few Americans. Because it is located deep in the Malay jungle, guards and barriers are minimal. In fact, the officers live in huts outside the walls of the prison. It's a hot, hardscrabble place, and the men's gaunt appearance reflects months and years of poor nutrition. One of them, though, is in fine shape. Manicured, carefully shaven, and neatly dressed, Cpl. King (George Segal) is obviously pampered while those around him are dying by inches. He claims to be a hardworking entrepreneur who provides services as a middleman when prisoners and guards wish to make deals.

Lt. Grey (Tom Courtenay), the camp policeman, suspects otherwise and is obsessed with catching the American at something. Lt. Marlowe (James Fox) finds himself caught between the two men. Marlowe can speak Malay and so would be a useful translator for some of King's deals, but over time, the two also form a genuine friendship. Grey appeals to Marlowe's sense of duty and fair play to nail Cpl. King, but serious social and political issues divide the Brits. Grey's resentment of Marlowe's aristocratic upbringing is never far from the surface.

> "This is not a story of escape. It is a story of survival."
>
> **Onscreen foreword**

They're the central characters in a large ensemble cast. The episodic plot follows the torpid pace of life in the camp. The place is gradually revealed to function through a complex system of reward and punishment. It's a social system based on clear-cut rules that are regularly broken. Compromises must be made, but when does compromise become corruption? That's the real source of conflict as writer-director Bryan Forbes carefully lays it out. Most of the traditional devices of the POW film are missing. There are no escape attempts, no sadistic guards. The Japanese are presented as relatively unimportant supporting characters. Clavell and Forbes are much more interested in how the prisoners live from day to day, dealing with the isolation, the loneliness and, most importantly, the overpowering hunger. So much of the action revolves around the search for, production, and consumption of unconventional sources of meat that the film is contraindicated for vegetarians. Those same scenes are also some of the funniest.

Given the conventions and restrictions of the mid-60s, almost all of the violence occurs off camera. Forbes is still able to make the inherent brutality of the subject matter seem real enough, and he also uses a few visual tricks that were ahead of their time. His brief freeze-frames punctuate significant emotional moments nicely, and they're complemented by one of John Barry's best early scores. The cast of familiar character actors provides first-rate support. The unconventional plotting will keep most viewers guessing, and the film ends with a dead solid perfect closing line.

See also

The Great Escape
From Here to Eternity
Zulu
Merry Christmas, Mr. Lawrence
Three Came Home

George Segal (center, standing)
is the entrepreneurial POW Cpl.
King in *King Rat*. The Kobal Collection

Cast: George Segal (Cpl. King), Tom Courtenay (Lt. Grey), James Fox (Peter Marlowe), James Donald (Dr. Kennedy), Denholm Elliott (Lt. Col. Larkin), Patrick O'Neal (Max), John Mills (Col. Smedley-Taylor), Todd Armstrong (Tex), Gerald Sim (Col. Jones), Leonard Rossiter (Maj. McCoy), John Standing (Capt. Daven), Alan Webb (Col. Brant), Sam Reese (Kurt), Wright King (Brough), Joe Turkel (Dino), Geoffrey Bayldon (Squadron Leader Vexley), Reg Lye (Tinkerbell), Arthur Malet (Makeley), Richard Dawson (Weaver), William "Bill" Fawcett (Steinmetz), John Warburton (The Commandant), John Ronane (Capt. Hawkins), Michael Lees (Stevens), Hamilton Dyce (Chaplain Drinkwater), Hedley Mattingly (Dr. Prodhomme), Dale Ishimoto (Yoshima); **Written by:** Bryan Forbes, James Clavell; **Cinematography by:** Burnett Guffey; **Music by:** John Barry. **Producer:** James Woolf, Columbia Pictures. **Awards:** Nominations: Academy Awards '65: Best Art Direction/Set Decoration (B & W), Best Black and White Cinematography. **Running Time:** 134 minutes. **Format:** VHS, Beta.

A MAN ESCAPED

Un Condamne a Mort s'Est Echappe, Ou le Vent Souffle ou Il Vent
A Man Escaped, or the Wind Bloweth Where It Listeth
A Condemned Man Has Escaped

1957 Robert Bresson ♪♪♪♪

Robert Bresson's prisoner of war film is a cold, unsentimental examination of isolation. Forget the conventional Hollywood heroics of the genre. Bresson avoids the very scenes of action and torture that provide the emotional underpinning viewers expect to see. His rigorously fact-based black-and-white account of an escape from a German prison in Lyon, France, 1943, is pared down to the essentials of character, place, and situation.

It opens with Lt. Fontaine (Francois Leterrier) in the back seat of a moving car. The two hand-cuffed men with him have given up all hope, but Fontaine's fingers inch toward the door handle as he waits for the right moment. What follows sets the tone for the rest of the film. Though the exact charges against Fontaine are not detailed, it's clear that he is in serious trouble. Executions are part of the routine at the prison. Fontaine does not know what his future is and so he resolves to escape. It's not a dramatic declaration of his unquenchable thirst for freedom or any of the other cliched cinematic bushwa. It's simply something he must do and he sets about it quietly. The first problem: How to get out of his solitary cell?

Bresson lets the story unfold at a deliberate pace, mirroring the slow, repetitive rhythms of prison life. He keeps his camera focused tightly on Fontaine, and seldom moves beyond his immediate point of view as he makes and rejects plans, carefully hordes materials to construct tools, learns how to make his ropes, and confronts his own fears. First-person voice-over narration describes his intentions and plans as they're being formed, but most of the emotions come through Leterrier's understated, naturalistic performance, astonishingly effective for a non-professional actor. (He was a philosophy student and officer in the army.) In the same way, Bresson uses Mozart sparingly in the score, not to emphasize the big decisive moments, but to illustrate Fontaine's moods. It is an unusual technique, one that doubtlessly will put off many viewers who have been weaned on contemporary high-octane war movies.

Bresson spent a year in a German prison himself. Perhaps because of that, he knows he has nothing to prove and so can deal with the subject on a more intellectual level. Andre Devigny, whose escape is the basis for the story, served as technical advisor, and much of the film was made in the cell in Fort Montluc, where he was imprisoned. Like the other important aspects of the film, that authenticity is handled in a matter-of-fact manner.

See also

Three Came Home
Is Paris Burning?
Escape from Alcatraz
The Great Escape
The Battle of Algiers

Bresson began his career as a painter, and painterly comparisons are often applied to his work. But Bresson is also a Catholic, and the religious side of his films is as important as it is to his contemporary, Ingmar Bergman. It's strong in *A Man Escaped*, and so this is one of the most intelligent and contemplative films to come out of World War II.

Cast: Francois Leterrier (Lt. Fontaine), Charles Le Clainche (Francois Jost), Roland Monod (Le Pasteur), Maurice Beerblock (Blanchet), Jacques Ertaud (Orsini), Jean-Paul Delhumeau (Hebrard), Roger Treherne (Terry), Jean-Philippe Delamarre (Prisoner No. 110), Cesar Gattegno (Le Prisonnier X), Jacques Oerlemans (Chief Warder), Klaus Detlef Grevenhorst (German intelligence officer), Leonard Schmidt (Le Convoyeur); **Written by:** Robert Bresson; **Cinematography by:** L.H. Burel; **Technical Advisor:** Andre Devigny. **Producer:** Alain Poire, Jean Thuillier. **Awards:** Cannes Film Festival '57: Best Director (Bresson). **Running Time:** 102 minutes. **Format:** VHS.

The Hound Salutes: Andre Devigny

Andre Devigny's escape from the Montluc prison—the basis for Robert Bresson's masterful film *A Man Escaped*—is actually only a small part of this remarkable man's military career.

As a lieutenant in the French Army, Devigny was sentenced to death by a German court-martial in 1943 for, among other things, the death of the head of the Italian Fascist secret police in France. As Bresson's film shows, he was tortured and wounded during a failed escape attempt before he was sent to Montluc. There, days before his scheduled execution, he managed to break out of his cell, get through a skylight onto the roof, and then cross to another rooftop. After killing a German guard, he got out of the prison itself. That's where Bresson's film ends, but Devigny was recaptured the next day.

Almost immediately, he re-escaped, diving into the Rhone River and hiding in mud flats. After that, with the assistance of the Resistance, he made his way to Switzerland. (Shades of *The Great Escape*.) Later that year, he snuck out of the country and back into France, and then to Spain, where he was held by authorities until April 1944, when they allowed him to go to French North Africa. (Shades of *Casablanca*.) There he volunteered and was assigned to a commando unit that was sent back to Southern France, where he fought until 1945, when Gen. Charles de Gaulle awarded him the Cross of Liberation, given to only 1,036 Resistance and Free French fighters during the war.

Devigny remained in the Army until 1971, retiring as a general. His final assignment was the leadership of the Action branch of SDECE, the unit that was responsible for identifying and eliminating the Army sympathizers of the Secret Army Organization, the group that had tried to assassinate de Gaulle. (Shades of *Day of the Jackal*.)

Andre Devigny died at age 82 in February 1999.

MERRY CHRISTMAS, MR. LAWRENCE

1983 Nagisa Oshima ♫♫♫♪

Though infuriating, vague, and elliptical at times, this prisoner of war drama is a true sleeper. Imagine *Bridge on the River Kwai* refracted through the mirror of *Apocalypse Now*, with two of the leads played by pop stars. Amazingly, the combination works.

In a prison camp in Java, 1942, Col. Lawrence (Tom Conti) is the unofficial liaison between the Japanese and their British prisoners. He's bilingual, and though he has some knowledge of Japanese customs and tradition, he admits that in many ways, he does not understand his captors. Even so, he is a strong advocate for tolerance of differences, and is often able to make the situation easier for both sides. An early incident of homosexual contact between a Korean guard and a wounded prisoner reveals one area where the two cultures are poles apart.

Another guard, Sgt. Hara (Takeshi Kitano) has become fairly friendly with Lawrence. But the camp commander, Capt. Yonoi (Ryuichi Sakamoto, a Japanese singer who composed the spare, haunting score) is a warrior of the old school who views the British with scorn, and refuses to accept the slightest breach of discipline within his own ranks. The fourth player is Maj. Celliers (David Bowie), a commando who has surrendered only to save a village from destruction. Though he sees himself as "a haunted person," Celliers is as rigid and as determined as Yonoi. The two are so alike that they may even share a sexual attraction, making a clash of wills virtually inevitable. Where will it appear? How will it be resolved?

> "They're a nation of anxious people and they could do nothing individually. So they went mad en masse."
>
> **Col. Lawrence (Tom Conti) on the Japanese**

Japanese director and co-writer Nagisa Oshima does not provide all of the information that Western audiences need to understand some finer points of the conflict. An early trial seems curiously inconclusive and many parts of an extended double flashback sequence in the second half are emotionally opaque. By the end, one point is clear: Yonoi comes to see his own frailties revealed in his prisoners and to hate them for it. Oshima explores similar ideas in his much more controversial *In the Realm of the Senses*, an explicit sex film about madness and the exchange of identities. His approach here is more conventional, but he brings the same intense sense of place to the story. He's particularly good at using colored light to alter the mood of a shot, and his multinational ensemble could not be better. Bowie, whose abilities as an actor have always been undervalued, is fine in a role that's certainly cast against his androgynous "type." Sakamoto is his equal in intensity and screen presence.

The various cultural gaps inherent in the story are exacerbated by mumbled dialogue that's sometimes incomprehensible, and an ending that makes an abrupt four-year leap. Those difficulties and the frequent subtitling are enough to keep some viewers from giving the film a chance. Those who are intrigued by a new approach to familiar material, however, should give this one a try. Think of it as a challenge for the adventurous videophile.

See also
Bridge on the River Kwai
Breaker Morant
Cool Hand Luke
Fires on the Plain
Three Came Home
Apocalypse Now

David Bowie is defiant Maj. Jack Celliers in *Merry Christmas, Mr. Lawrence*. The Kobal Collection

Cast: David Bowie (Maj. Jack "Strafer" Celliers), Tom Conti (Col. John Lawrence), Ryuichi Sakamoto (Capt. Yonoi), Takeshi "Beat" Kitano (Sgt. Gengo Hara), Jack Thompson (Group Capt. Hicksley), Takashi Naitoh (Lt. Iwata), Alistair Browning (De Jong), Johnny Okura (Kanemoto), Yuya Uchida (Commandant), Ryunosuke Kaneda (President of the Court), Kan Mikami (Lt. Ito), Yuji Honma (Pfc. Yajima), Diasuke Iijima (Cpl. Ueki); **Written by:** Nagisa Oshima, Paul Mayersberg; **Cinematography by:** Toichiro Narushima; **Music by:** Ryuichi Sakamoto. **Producer:** Terry Glinwood, Jeremy Thomas, Geoffrey Nethercott, Universal. **Japanese, British. Awards:** National Board of Review Awards '83: Best Actor (Conti). **MPAA Rating:** R. **Running Time:** 124 minutes. **Format:** VHS, Beta.

PARADISE ROAD

1997 Bruce Beresford ♪♪♪♪

Bruce Beresford's ensemble film lacks the emotional power of *Breaker Morant*, but it is still an excellent examination of a little known episode of World War II—little known in America, at least. The fact-based story of a multinational group of women taken prisoner by the Japanese resorts to a few cliches and formulaic conflicts, but uniformly strong performances make up for the flaws.

A glittering crowd of Brits, Aussies, and Yanks is gathered at the Raffles Hotel in Singapore on the night of February 10, 1942. The men pooh-pooh the notion that the approaching Japanese army will actually enter the city. When artillery shells land outside, they reconsider their dismissive racial stereotypes and evacuate the women and children on a British warship. Several dozen women then embark on a halting journey that takes them on different paths to an internment camp on Sumatra.

> "Nice night for the collapse of an empire."
>
> **Topsy Merritt (Julianna Margulies) leaving the Raffles Hotel as the Japanese invade**

> "If a war has begun, it can only mean the time for rules has ended. The aim is to win."
>
> **Capt. Tanaka (Stan Egi)**

Mrs. Pargiter (Glenn Close) becomes an unofficial leader, though it takes the quiet persistence of Mrs. Drummond (Pauline Collins) to force Mrs. Pargiter into the foreground. Topsy Merritt (Julianna Margulies) is a sharp-tongued American. Susan McCarthy (Cate Blanchett) is a nurse. Mrs. Leighton-Jones (Jennifer Ehle) is the looker in the bunch. Mrs. Verstak (Frances McDormand) is a German doctor, or claims to be. Nothing suits Mrs. Tippler (Pamela Rabe) and she happily takes on the duties of camp troublemaker. Col. Hiroyo (Sab Shimono) is in charge of the camp, but he defers to the sadistic Capt. Tanaka (Stan Egi) of the secret police.

To keep the women's morale up, Mrs. Pargiter and Mrs. Drummond recruit a vocal orchestra despite strict rules against various forms of writing and assembly. Though that activity is at the center of the film, other incidents involve the women individually. Of those, the most important concerns Mrs. Pargiter and a guard (Clyde Kusatsu) and appears to have been borrowed directly from Agnes Newton Keith's *Three Came Home*. In both her book and the film based on it, the incident is described and resolved in much greater detail.

Overall, writer-director Beresford divides the focus fairly evenly among his cast. Given the film's slightly episodic structure, some moments are more successful than others. The best involve the vocal work—particularly the Dvorak—and the poems of Margaret Dryburgh, the real woman upon whom Mrs. Drummond is based. Pauline Collins, known best as *Shirley Valentine* and for her role on *Upstairs, Downstairs*, makes her one of the most memorable characters in the ensemble, and Frances McDormand's wry skeptic is the straw that stirs the drink. Though she gets top billing, Glenn Close does not do a star turn. Her work is pitched on the same emotional level as the rest. Also, these actresses allow themselves to be shown in realistically unflattering conditions. The film is probably the least glamorous work many of them will ever do.

Their accents are also realistic, and some long passages are hard for Americans to decipher. That goes for some of the colloquial English and Australian language, too. To get the joke in one early scene, you need to know that "spend a penny" means "go to the bathroom." That decorous usage is indicative of the film's carefully crafted approach to a brutal, ugly subject.

See also

Three Came Home
Empire of the Sun
Breaker Morant

Glenn Close, Johanna Ter Steege, Kitty Clinget, Tessa Humphries, Alwine Seinen, and Elizabeth Spriggs, imprisoned in a Japanese internment camp, form a chorale group to pass the time and keep spirits up in *Paradise Road.* The Kobal Collection

Cast: Glenn Close (Adrienne Pargiter), Frances McDormand (Dr. Verstak), Julianna Margulies (Topsy Merritt), Pauline Collins (Margaret Drummond), Jennifer Ehle (Rosemary Leighton-Jones), Elizabeth Spriggs (Mrs. Roberts), Tessa Humphries (Celia Roberts), Sab Shimono (Col. Hiroyo), Cate Blanchett (Susan McCarthy), Wendy Hughes (Mrs. Dickson), Johanna Ter Steege (Sister Wilhelmina), Pamela Rabe (Mrs. Tippler), Clyde Kusatsu (Snake), Stan Egi (Capt. Tanaka), Susie Porter (Oggi), Lisa Hensley (Bett), Pennie Hackforth-Jones (Mrs. Pike), Pauline Chan (Wing), Kitty Clinget (Sister Anna), Alwine Seinen (Millie); **Written by:** Bruce Beresford, David Giles, Martin Meader; **Cinematography by:** Peter James; **Music by:** Margareth Dryburgh, Ross Edwards. **Producer:** Sue Milliken, Greg Coote, Graham Burke, Village Roadshow Pictures; released by Fox Searchlight. **MPAA Rating:** R. **Running Time:** 115 minutes. **Format:** VHS, Closed Caption.

THE SEVENTH CROSS

1944 Fred Zinnemann ♪♪♪

Fred Zinnemann's earnest propaganda piece begins shakily and never really ratchets up the tension as tightly as it might. Despite persistent flaws, though, it becomes an involving tale of escape from Nazi persecution, one that takes unusually sophisticated care to explore the roots of the appeal of National Socialism to middle-class Germans. By setting the story in 1936, the filmmakers are able to give the story a dimension of historical perspective. They do not examine the true horrors of the concentration camps, but perhaps that was impossible in 1944.

George Heisler (Spencer Tracy) has been imprisoned for vaguely defined reasons. He escapes with six others. Immediately, writers Helen Deutsch and Anna Seghers separate the viewer from the action by having Wallau (Ray Collins), another escapee, comment on the action as an omniscient voice-over narrator both before and after he is killed. Though that device sounds like a precursor to film noir, the filmmakers lack a true noir sensibility. Just the opposite is true. The narrator is relentlessly, evangelically hopeful throughout, and that is the antithesis of film noir. It's also an unusually strong theme for an escape thriller, too strong at times.

> "I'd seen his face growing emptier day by day. He'd been beaten to a hollow husk, incapable of feeling, almost incapable of thinking. He'd seen too much and felt too much. His faith in people was gone, perhaps forever."
>
> **Voice-over narrator Wallau (Ray Collins) on George Heisler (Spencer Tracy)**

We follow two converging plot lines. The first, naturally, sticks to Heisler and his fellow escapees as they get away from the camp and elude the authorities. The man-on-the-run story is perennially popular, and this one is handled well. One rooftop sequence is particularly good, but when the focus falls on Heisler alone, the filmmakers over-rely on the narrator. We are told, for example, "He was dazed with despair, confused, lost. Now where?" when we can see all of that on Tracy's face. And for viewers who still haven't got the point, the music tends to swell and thicken then, too.

The second plot line concerns the activities of a fragmented resistance group that's trying to find Heisler and help him. Paul and Liesel Roeder (Hume Cronyn and Jessica Tandy in their first film work together) are old friends of Heisler who have prospered under Nazi rule. Personally apolitical, they have tried hard not to know what's going on around them. Why not? The economy is booming. They get tax breaks and extra vacation for their kids—government support for their family values. When Heisler shows up on their doorstep, they're forced to make choices. The consequences of those choices ripple outward, affecting other people, and that's where the film is at its best.

Writer Helen Deutsch, who would later adapt *Valley of the Dolls* and *The Unsinkable Molly Brown* for the screen, makes these middle-class and wealthy characters believably complex, and she takes the time to make their decisions realistic. Because so much attention is given them, the suspense isn't nearly as gripping as it could be in the later reels. Zinnemann milks every drop he can from shadowy sets filled with angular staircases and dimly lit cobblestone streets, but the slow pace prevents him from turning the film into a first-class thriller. Instead, *The Seventh Cross* is unusually complex and tolerant propaganda.

See also

Bad Day at Black Rock

Hangmen Also Die

The Third Man

A Time to Love and a Time to Die

The Fugitive

Saboteur

George Heisler (Spencer Tracy, left) and Wallau (Ray Collins) plan their escape from a German concentration camp in *The Seventh Cross*. The Kobal Collection

Cast: Spencer Tracy (George Heisler), Signe Hasso (Toni), Hume Cronyn (Paul Roeder), Jessica Tandy (Liesel Roeder), Agnes Moorehead (Mme. Marelli), Herbert Rudley (Franz Marnet), Felix Bressart (Poldi Schlamm), Ray Collins (Wallau), Alexander Granach (Zillich), George Macready (Bruno Sauer), Steve Geray (Dr. Loewenstein), Karen Verne (Leni), George Zucco (Fahrenburg), Katherine Locke (Mrs. Sauer), Paul Guilfoyle (Fiedler), Kurt Katch (Leo Hermann), Konstantin Shayne (Fuellgrabe), John Wengraf (Overkamp), Eily Malyon (Fraulein Bachmann); **Written by:** Helen Deutsch, Anna Seghers; **Cinematography by:** Karl Freund; **Music by:** Roy Webb. **Producer:** Pandro S. Berman, MGM. **Awards:** Nominations: Academy Awards '44: Best Supporting Actor (Cronyn). **Running Time:** 110 minutes. **Format:** VHS.

THE SEVENTH CROSS

STALAG 17

1953 Billy Wilder

Billy Wilder's highly honored adaptation of the play by Donald Bevan and Edmund Trzcinski really does not live up to its reputation. It's less a realistic look at life inside a German prison camp than an improbable suspense tale that depends on some clumsy contrivances. Worse yet, the moments of comic relief are appalling.

The opening overview of the camp, created through an intricate model, creates an impressive setting. After it, though, all of the important action takes place within one barracks. Stalag 17 houses 630 American airmen, all sergeants. It's a week before Christmas, 1944. The guys are tired, bored, and cold. One night, two of them attempt an escape. Sefton (William Holden), a loner who tries to turn a profit on any camp activity, bets two packs of cigarettes that the guys won't make it to the wire. When he is proved right, the others suspect that he might be a spy or a collaborator.

Their suspicions increase when a downed pilot, Lt. Dunbar (Don Taylor), is brought to their building. How do the Germans discover that he has been involved in an act of sabotage? Besides Sefton, the suspects are Price (Peter Graves), Hoffy (Richard Erdman), Blondie (Robert Shawley), "Animal" (Robert Strauss), and Shapiro (Harvey Lembeck). Someone is ratting to Sgt. Schultz (Sig Rumann) and the Commandant (Otto Preminger).

> "Now you put 630 sergeants together and, oh mother, you've got yourself a situation."
>
> **Narrator Cookie (Gil Stratton Jr.)**

Strictly on a mechanical level, the construction and revelation of the suspense elements are handled competently, so as formula escapism, the film works well enough. But that side lacks real complexity and strong characters. To fill out the running time, Robert Strauss and Harvey Lembeck engage in ridiculous and interminable physical comedy routines. They bring to mind the worst excesses of Jerry Lewis and Dean Martin. Strauss's purse-lipped mugging earned him a Supporting Actor nomination, showing how profoundly tastes in comedy have changed. In the same vein, Sig Rumann is clearly the inspiration for John Banner's Sgt. Schultz on television's *Hogan's Heroes*.

Holden won the Best Actor Academy Award for his performance, but that's a case of belated Hollywood payback for his being overlooked three years before in 1950 when he had been nominated for *Sunset Boulevard* and lost to Jose Ferrer in *Cyrano de Bergerac*. (When Holden won in '53, he displaced Burt Lancaster in *From Here to Eternity*, a much stronger performance judged by any criteria.)

In the end, *Stalag 17* is really more a Cold War film than a World War II film. Its questions about informants, loyalty, and the tyranny of the group over the individual are concerns of the 1950s, not the 1940s.

See also

To Be or Not to Be
The Great Escape
King Rat

Sefton (William Holden, right) tries to bribe Sgt. Schultz (Sig Rumann) into telling him the identity of the snitch in the barracks in *Stalag 17*. The Kobal Collection

Cast: William Holden (Sefton), Don Taylor (Lt. Dunbar), Peter Graves (Price), Otto Preminger (Oberst Von Scherbach), Harvey Lembeck (Harry Shapiro), Robert Strauss ("Animal" Stosh), Sig Rumann (Sgt. Schultz), Richard Erdman (Hoffy), Neville Brand (Duke), Gil Stratton (Cookie/Narrator), Robinson Stone (Joey), Robert Shawley (Blondie), Jay Lawrence (Bagradian); **Written by:** Billy Wilder, Edwin Blum; **Cinematography by:** Ernest Laszlo; **Music by:** Franz Waxman. **Producer:** Billy Wilder, Paramount Pictures. **Awards:** Academy Awards '53: Best Actor (Holden); Nominations: Academy Awards '53: Best Director (Wilder), Best Supporting Actor (Strauss). **Running Time:** 120 minutes. **Format:** VHS, Beta, LV.

The Hound Salutes: William Holden

William Holden's overnight success is the stuff of Hollywood myth. He actually was "discovered" by a Paramount talent scout in a school play. After a couple of bit parts, he played the violinist/boxer lead in *Golden Boy* (1939) and a star was born. Of course, in those years, the studios had virtual total control over their stars and so he worked in many less-than-stellar productions. (He did not appear on the top-ten list of boxoffice stars until 1954.)

As a popular young leading man of the 1950s, who had served in the Air Force, Holden inevitably was cast in many war films. At first, after his return to the screen in 1947, the results were ordinary, as such generic titles as *Force of Arms* and *Submarine Command* suggest. It really wasn't until Holden teamed up with director Billy Wilder, first in *Sunset Boulevard*, and then in *Stalag 17*, that he hit his stride. (He won a Best-Actor Oscar for *Stalag 17* but he really deserved it for *Sunset*.) Holden is relaxed in the uneven *Bridges at Toko-Ri*, where realistic aerial and naval scenes compete with Grace Kelly's star-turn and curiously fatalistic Cold War politics.

Holden was able to break out of the studio system, to a degree, with *Bridge on the River Kwai*, where his contract gave him partial ownership of the film and a share of its profits. After that, his only significant work in the genre is in John Ford's *The Horse Soldiers*, where his humanistic doctor easily upstages John Wayne, who plays a blustering cavalry commander. During the 1960s, Holden's war films returned to pre-*Stalag 17* levels and he saved his best work for two masterpieces. As aging outlaw Pike Bishop, he's at the center of Sam Peckinpah's elegiac *The Wild Bunch*. In Paddy Chayefksy's *Network* he's a veteran TV executive who learns late in life that he's still got some illusions to lose.

This fact-based story of imprisonment by the Japanese takes a rarely seen perspective on its subject—the main characters are women—and it attempts to be even handed. It also features two excellent performances. But more recent similar films have been grittier, and younger audiences may find the emotions overstated.

Agnes Keith (Claudette Colbert) is the wife of a government official in Sandakan, Borneo, when the Japanese invade in early 1942. The commander, Col. Suga (Sessue Hayakawa), makes it clear that, as he sees it, the lines between civilian and military are blurred. The British have ordered their people to resist passively but the authorities have wrecked machinery and burned fuel oil and gasoline. In short order, all Westerners are ordered to prison camps. Agnes and her young son George (Mark Keuning) will go to one camp, her husband Harry (Patric Knowles) to another.

But Col. Suga is a fan of Agnes's book about Borneo, *The Land Below the Wind*. He is particularly taken by her perceptive portrayal of the Japanese. Col. Suga is not the monster many had feared, and he is in charge of all of the prison camps. Though she and her family get no special treatment, acts of violence do occur.

> "Whatever the rest is, there's no difference in our hearts about our children."
>
> **Agnes Keith (Claudette Colbert) to Col. Suga (Sessue Hayakawa)**

Most of the action is set in the various compounds where Agnes and George are sent, and though the film was made on location, the camps do not seem as unpleasant as doubtless they were. That, however, is simply a reflection of the cinematic style of the time. The same criticism could be leveled at *Bridge on the River Kwai*, and to leave it at that misses the larger point. *Three Came Home* does capture the emotions of captivity. In its depiction of prison-camp life, it does not portray the guards and officers as particularly evil or depraved, focusing more on the brutality of war than on the brutality of the Japanese.

Two other important scenes—the arrival of a group of male Australian prisoners and the conclusion—will also strike some contemporary viewers as too dated and overtly sentimental to be believed, but both manage to redeem themselves. In the same way, the more important conclusion between Agnes and Col. Suga has one predictable element that slightly undercuts the genuine emotional connection that exists between them. It is a comparatively minor flaw. Throughout, Claudette Colbert and Sessue Hayakawa do excellent work, and they make the scene believable and touching.

This kind of story is so seldom told from a woman's point of view that *Three Came Home* is well worth watching. The book is excellent, too.

See also
Bridge on the River Kwai
Paradise Road
A Man Escaped

Women and children await evacuation in *Three Came Home*. Claudette Colbert (third from left, standing) The Kobal Collection

Cast: Claudette Colbert (Agnes Keith), Patric Knowles (Harry Keith), Sessue Hayakawa (Col. Suga), Florence Desmond (Betty Sommers), Sylvia Andrew (Henrietta), Mark Keuning (George), Phyllis Morris (Sister Rose), Howard Chuman (Lt. Nekata); **Written by:** Nunnally Johnson; **Cinematography by:** William H. Daniels, Milton Krasner; **Music by:** Hugo Friedhofer. **Producer:** Nunnally Johnson, 20th Century-Fox. **Running Time:** 106 minutes. **Format:** VHS.

The most popular stylistic elements of 1950s and '60s war movies are mixed together in a diverting star vehicle. As light entertainment, particularly for Frank Sinatra fans, it's enjoyable fluff, and that's all it means to be.

Sinatra is Col. Joseph Ryan, whose P-38 is shot down over Italy in August 1943. Messina has just fallen, and American forces are making their way up the boot when Ryan is brought to an Italian prisoner of war camp. Sensing that the end is underway, the Germans are preparing to withdraw, and their local allies are eager to switch sides. (The Italian troops who first find Ryan realize that he's a *paisan*, hide him from the Nazis, and give him a bottle of wine.) At the camp, he finds that the commandant Battaglia (Adolfo Celi) is a corrupt martinet while Capt. Oriani (Sergio Fantoni) has more sympathy for the men under his protection. Literally, as Col. Ryan is approaching the gates, the prisoners are burying their senior officer, and Maj. Fincham (Trevor Howard) is taking over.

Most of the prisoners are British, professional soldiers of the 9th Fusilliers, whose constant attempts to escape have led to half rations and the withholding of medicine. Compounding the problem, the Brits have been hoarding what medicine they already have to give to escapees. Even though he is one of the few Americans in the camp, Ryan is the senior officer. Before long, Ryan and Oriani find themselves united in moderation against the extremes of Battaglia and Fincham. After fairly logical plot turns, several hundred POWs are loaded into railroad cars heading north for Germany. The officers decide to take the train over and escape in it, and viewers can forget about realism from that moment on.

Director Mark Robson tries to combine the suspense of *The Great Escape* with the derring-do of *The Guns of Navarone*, and he's successful enough. The pace is quick, the Italian locations are attractive, and the physical action is neither too graphic nor too coy. In the last act, confrontations with Messerschmitts and a trainload of German troops are well handled. The only element that strikes an obviously wrong note is the appearance of a sexy collaborator (Raffaella Carra) whose tight skirt and blouse belong in a sex farce. Throughout, Howard and Fantoni acquit themselves well against their more famous co-star. By that point in his career, Sinatra was essentially playing himself in dramatic roles, and the film is built around his relaxed presence. This is far from his best work, but for featherweight entertainment, it does all that it needs to do.

See also
The Dirty Dozen
Kelly's Heroes
The Train
Ocean's Eleven
Assault on a Queen

Frank Sinatra, Trevor Howard
and Sergio Fantoni attempt to
lead a group of Allied POWs to
safety in *Von Ryan's Express.* The
Kobal Collection

Cast: Frank Sinatra (Col. Joseph Ryan), Trevor Howard (Maj. Eric Fincham), Brad Dexter (Sgt. Bostick), Raffaella Carra (Gabriella), Sergio Fantoni (Capt. Oriani), John Leyton (Orde), Vito Scotti (Italian train engineer), Edward Mulhare (Costanzo), Adolfo Celi (Battaglia), James Brolin (Pvt. Ames), James B. Sikking (American soldier), Wolfgang Preiss (Maj. Von Klemment), John van Dreelen (Col. Gortz), Richard Bakalayan (Cpl. Giannini), Michael Goodliffe (Capt. Stein), Michael St. Clair (Sgt. Dunbar), Ivan Triesault (Von Kleist); **Written by:** Wendell Mayes, Joseph Landon; **Cinematography by:** William H. Daniels; **Music by:** Jerry Goldsmith. **Producer:** Saul David, Mark Robson, 20th Century-Fox. **Running Time:** 117 minutes. **Format:** VHS, Beta, LV, Letterbox.

WORLD WAR II

The Resistance

World War II:
The Resistance on Screen

Hollywood has always loved the resistance fighter, and it's easy to understand why. The handsome young partisan who evades the authorities, the world-weary libertine whose cynicism is a pose, the plucky young woman who outwits the Nazis—they're perfect movie heroes. They were wildly romanticized during the war, but in recent years, the trend toward fact-based stories has resulted in films that re-create unforgiving realities.

Hollywood's first story of resistance to Nazi occupation is one of its finest moments. *Casablanca* can no longer be judged against other films of its kind. It exists in our collective cinematic imagination in a place by itself, where actors are no longer playing characters, and such silly contrivances as the letters of transit make perfect sense. You don't criticize it. You just play it again.

Ernst Lubitsch takes equally bold liberties in his brilliant comedy *To Be or Not to Be*. It was made at a time when Nazi power was on the rise, and so its sharp, sad humor has a gravity that few comedies can claim.

Watch on the Rhine, also made in the early days of the war, treats resistance as a sacred obligation. The filmmakers deliver their messages with a heavy hand, and their dramatic sensibility owes more to the stage than to film. Two more energetic espionage adventures made toward the end of the war, *13 Rue Madeleine* and *O.S.S.*, pave the way for the spy movies of the 1960s.

The White Rose, a Dutch film little known on this side of the Atlantic, tells a true story of German students who organize comparatively mild acts of protest against their government and learn how narrow the limits of tolerance are. Judy Davis is the spirited heroine of another fact-based story, *One Against the Wind*. The overachieving made-for-TV production has the sometimes erratic and illogical plotting of real life, and ends on a surprising note.

Except for *Casablanca*, these films have not received much attention, even among fans, and for the most part, they deserve better. They tell good stories, and even the creakier, older efforts have a nostalgic appeal.

CASABLANCA

1942 Michael Curtiz ♪♪♪♪

In the movies, as in the rest of life, timing is everything. On Monday, December 8, 1941, after he'd listened to President Franklin Delano Roosevelt the day before describing the Japanese attack on Pearl Harbor and demanding that the Congress declare war, Stephen Karnot went back to work in his cubicle. Mr. Karnot was a reader for the Warner Bros. studio. He scanned through novels and stories, anything that might be the basis for a good movie. On his desk was an unproduced play, *Everybody Comes to Rick's*. He read it and liked it. He thought that the time was right for a story about a cynical American expatriate who moves from careful neutrality to anti-fascist commitment, and he wrote an enthusiastic synopsis. Soon Hal B. Wallis, who had a new arrangement with the studio that allowed him a free hand on projects of his choice, expressed his interest, and the proverbial ball was rolling. Wallis was in the middle of his first film under the new understanding, *Now, Voyager*, but he saw the potential. First, a title change was in order. How about *Casablanca*?

Stories about the film's casting are the stuff of Hollywood legend, and they're not really as far-fetched as they sometimes sound. George Raft and James Cagney were suggested for the lead, and both of them had been popular in similar roles. But more importantly, earlier in 1941, Humphrey Bogart had found his breakthrough as Sam Spade in John Huston's version of Dashiell Hammett's *The Maltese Falcon*. His Spade is a suspicious, disillusioned man who lives in a heavily shadowed world of ominous intrigue. From bitter experience he is mistrustful of women though he's strongly attracted to them, the more mysterious the better. Spade is also a dapper dresser, heavy drinker. Hangs out with the likes of Sydney Greenstreet and Peter Lorre.

In casting the female lead, Wallis had another inspiration. He decided to recruit a new kid in town, Ingrid Bergman, who was under contract to David O. Selznick. Realizing how right she was for the part and what it would do for her career, Selznick agreed to loan her out for the film, even though the script wasn't finished.

The play, written by Murray Burnett and Joan Alison, was a one-set piece that would need to be opened up for the screen. The central characters and their conflicts were well established, and despite the contributions of several other writers, did not change much during production. The first to work on it were Julius and Philip Epstein, who wrote the first draft and gave the story many of its cynically smart lines. They had, however, already made a commitment to go to Washington to work with Frank Capra on the *Why We Fight* documentaries, and so they'd produced only about 40 pages of finished work when the cameras started rolling in May 1942. Howard Koch, who was best known then as the writer of Orson Welles's *War of the Worlds*, was already at work on the script too. Much of his contribution involved making Rick Blaine's character more mysterious. A sixth writer, Casey Robinson, was responsible for the Paris flashback scene. Somehow, that combination worked. Even though director Michael Curtiz was forced to film the script in order, and even though no one knew how it was going to end, they soldiered on. But story and casting by themselves do not explain the enduring popularity of *Casablanca*.

> "Bogart, true to the role he played, kept his 'cool.' On occasion he would invite me into his dressing room with his usual, 'Relax and have a drink.' We would talk and sometimes an idea or a line of dialogue would pop out of the whiskey bottle."
>
> **Screenwriter Howard Koch, in *As Time Goes By* (Harcourt Brace Jovanovich. 1979)**

> "It transcends the period. It seems incredible now that every major studio made a picture a week, 50 pictures a year. When we were shooting *Casablanca*, it was just one of the 50."
>
> **Screenwriter Julius Epstein, in the documentary *You Must Remember This***

See also

Across the Pacific
The Maltese Falcon
To Have and Have Not

Just as much has to do with the film's look—the black-and-white magic that was created by the seasoned Hollywood professionals who worked behind the cameras. For *Casablanca*, much of the credit goes to cinematographer Arthur Edeson. Wallis asked for him because he had created such a distinctive atmosphere when he photographed *The Maltese Falcon*, and, perhaps more importantly, he had made Bogart look so attractive. If he could do that with Bogie's world-weary mug, imagine what he could do for Ingrid Bergman. He certainly succeeded in making her a dream woman, and he got considerable help from legendary make-up artist Perc Westmore and Orry-Kelly's gowns. Art decorator Carl Jules Weyl and set decorator George James Hopkins used a few simple props and tricks to turn the Warner Bros. backlot into an exotic desert metropolis where a fantastic story can achieve the necessary degree of verisimilitude.

None of this explains why *Casablanca* has remained such a popular movie for so long. Along with a mere handful of others—*The Wizard of Oz, The Godfather*—it's a "classic" that new viewers discover and older fans rewatch again and again, year after year. Nostalgia, romance, glamour—they're part of it, but no one will ever fully explain why we love it. We simply do, and the next time you're in the video store or flipping through the channels and you come across Rick and Ilse and Capt. Renault, you could do worse than settling in for another visit. If it's after dinner, pour youself a brandy—the good stuff—and enjoy.

Rick Blaine (Humphrey Bogart, far right) double-crosses Capt. Renault (Claude Rains) for the letters of transit as Victor Laszlo (Paul Henreid) and Ilsa Lund (Ingrid Bergman) look on in *Casablanca*. The Kobal Collection

Cast: Humphrey Bogart (Richard "Rick" Blaine), Ingrid Bergman (Ilsa Lund), Paul Henreid (Victor Laszlo), Claude Rains (Capt. Louis Renault), Peter Lorre (Ugarte), Sydney Greenstreet (Senor Ferrari), Conrad Veidt (Maj. Heinrich Strasser), S.Z. Sakall (Carl, the Headwaiter), Dooley Wilson (Sam), Marcel Dalio (Emil, the croupier), John Qualen (Berger), Helmut Dantine (Jan Brandel), Madeleine LeBeau (Yvonne), Joy Page (Annina Brandel), Leonid Kinskey (Sascha, the bartender), Curt Bois (Pickpocket), Oliver Blake (German banker), Monte Blue (American), Martin Garralaga (Headwaiter), Ilka Gruning (Mrs. Leuchtag), Ludwig Stossel (Mr. Leuchtag), Frank Puglia (Arab vendor); **Written by:** Julius J. Epstein, Philip C. Epstein, Howard Koch, Casey Robinson; **Cinematography by:** Arthur Edeson; **Music by:** Max Steiner. **Producer:** Hal B. Wallis, Jack L. Warner, Warner Bros. **Awards:** Academy Awards '43: Best Director (Curtiz), Best Picture, Best Screenplay; American Film Institute (AFI) '98: Top 100, National Film Registry '89; Nominations: Academy Awards '43: Best Actor (Bogart), Best Black and White Cinematography, Best Film Editing, Best Supporting Actor (Rains), Best Original Dramatic Score. **Budget:** $950,000. **MPAA Rating:** PG. **Running Time:** 102 minutes. **Format:** VHS, Beta, LV, 8mm, Closed Caption, DVD.

Casablanca Quotes

Probably no movie in the history of Hollywood is filled with so many lines that fans know by heart. But between "I stick my neck out for nobody" and "I think this is the beginning of a beautiful friendship," are others which, while less well known, add just as much to the film's appeal. Here are some personal favorites, presented without attribution because you already know what they are and who said them. If you don't recognize them, well then, you'll have to take another look, won't you?

"With the coming of the Second World War many eyes in imprisoned Europe turned hopefully or desperately toward the freedom of the Americas. Lisbon became the great embarkation point, but not everybody could get to Lisbon directly, and so a tortuous, roundabout refugee trail sprang up. Paris to Marseilles . . . across the Mediterranean to Oran, then by train or auto or foot across the rim of Africa to Casablanca in French Morocco. Here the fortunate ones, through money or influence or luck, might obtain exit visas and scurry to Lisbon, and from Lisbon to the New World, but the others wait in Casablanca. . . . and wait. . . . and wait. . . . and wait. . . . "

My dear Rick, when will you realize that in this world today, isolationism is no longer a practical policy?"

"How extravagant you are, throwing away women like that. Someday they may be scarce."

"I've often speculated on why you don't return to America. Did you abscond with the church funds? Did you run off with a Senator's wife? I like to think that you killed a man. It's the romantic in me."

"It's a combination of all three."

"Then what in heaven's name brought you to Casablanca?"

"My health. I came to Casablanca for the waters."

"The waters? What waters? We're in the desert."

"I was misinformed."

"Let's see, the last time we met. . . . "

"Was La Belle Aurore."

"How nice. You remembered, but of course that was the day the Germans marched into Paris."

"Not an easy day to forget."

"No."

"I remember every detail. The Germans wore gray, you wore blue."

"Sit down and have a drink."

"Boss, let's get out of here."

"No, sir. I'm waiting for a lady."

"Please, boss, let's go, ain't nothing but trouble for you here."

"She's coming back. I know she's coming back."

"Sam, if it's December 1941, in Casablanca, what time is it in New York?"

"My watch stopped."

"I bet they're asleep in New York. I bet they're asleep all over America."

"As leader of all illegal activities in Casablanca, I am an influential and respected man."

"That was some going-over your men gave my place this afternoon. We just barely got cleaned up in time to open."

"Well, I told Strasser he wouldn't find the letters here, but I told my men to be especially destructive. You know how that impresses Germans."

Larry Elikann's fact-based made-for-TV film about the French Resistance is every bit as good as its big-screen counterparts. In many ways, it takes a deliberately old-fashioned approach to its subject, with solid characters and attitudes that could have come straight from the 1940s.

Countess Mary Lindell (Judy Davis), English by birth, French by marriage and choice, works for the Red Cross in German-occupied Paris. She apparently intends to remain neutral, as she did in World War I, until she spots a disheveled man (Sam Neill) in a sidewalk cafe and realizes that he is a British officer. (It's the boots that give him away.) Acting on impulse and quick wits, she saves him from the Germans. He's Maj. James Leggatt, who missed the boat at Dunkirk, was captured and then injured when he escaped. Mary agrees to help him. Her two teenaged children, Maurice (Christien Anholt) and Barbe (Kate Beckinsale), are horrified.

The act begins her relationship with British intelligence and the Underground railroad that spirits downed pilots out of France. It also brings her to the attention of SS Col. Gruber (Anthony Higgins). At the same time, Barbe is falling for Lt. Erich Von Stultsberg (Mikush Alexander), a handsome hunk of Nazi bratwurst.

Fact:
The film won a Golden Globe Best Drama award and Judy Davis won the Best Actress Award for her role.

From that premise, it's easy to see where many of the conflicts are going to arise, but writer Chris Bryant still keeps viewers guessing. As is usually the case with wartime film biographies, things begin fairly realistically. By the end, credibility has been sacrificed to the soapy heroics so common to the genre. Where does fact end and fiction begin in *Lawrence of Arabia*? In *Sergeant York*? Besides, historical truth is less important than good storytelling.

On the most basic what's-going-to-happen-next? level, the film works beautifully. It was shot in Luxembourg with top-drawer production values. The producers may have been forced to cut some corners in explosive special effects and elaborate stuntwork, but that is not a loss. Instead, Elikann keeps the camera on his star and she delivers. Judy Davis has made her career playing sharp, aggressive, abrasive women (*Absolute Power*, *Husbands and Wives*, etc.). This is one of her best and most appealing. As always, Sam Neill gives strong support and Anthony Higgins is a silky villain.

See also
Grand Illusion
Hangmen Also Die
The Seventh Cross
The Great Escape
A Man Escaped

Throughout, that attention to character sets *One Against the Wind* apart from the field. Given its non-theatrical lineage, the film has never received much promotional or critical attention. As such, it's one of the best sleepers in the video store.

Sam Neill in *One Against the Wind* The Kobal Collection

Cast: Judy Davis (Mary Lindell), Sam Neill (James Leggatt), Denholm Elliott (Fr. LeBlanc), Anthony Higgins (Herman Gruber), Christien Anholt (Maurice Lindell), Kate Beckinsale (Barbe), Frank Middlemass (Dubois), Benedick Blythe (SS Captain), Peter Cellier (Court General), Stefan Gryff (Fernand), Mark Wing-Davey (Col. Miles), John Savident (Henry Smallwood), David Ryall (Dumont), Tom Hodgkins (Big Canada), Wolf Kahler (Cmdr. Reingart), Michael Crossman (Little Canada), Terry Taplin (Von Bismarck), Mikush Alexander (Erich Von Stultsberg); **Written by:** Chris Bryant; **Cinematography by:** Denis Lewiston; **Music by:** Lee Holdridge. **MPAA Rating:** PG. **Running Time:** 96 minutes. **Format:** VHS, Closed Caption.

Today, producer Richard Maibaum's early espionage thriller can be seen as a prototype for the genre he would perfect in the 1960s. That's when he was involved with the James Bond series and either co-wrote or -produced the best early entries, from *Dr. No* to *On Her Majesty's Secret Service*. Almost all of the familiar Bond devices appear here, from the off-beat introduction, to the lethal gadgets, to the cooler-than-cool hero. Unfortunately, all the ingredients don't mesh quite as smoothly as they do in the Bond films. The primary reason is leading man Alan Ladd, who turns in a lackluster performance and fails to strike any sparks with his co-star Geraldine Fitzgerald.

Though the film claims to be based on real exploits of agents of the Office of Strategic Services, it presents them in such a fanciful light that it's impossible to take the action seriously. The plot—so loose as to be almost episodic—concerns the efforts of four O.S.S. agents parachuted into France as "Mission Applejack." The leader of the group barely makes it through his first meal, leaving Philip Masson (Ladd) in charge, with Ellen Rogers (Fitzgerald) and Bernay (Richard Benedict) in support. Their initial mission is to contact the local Resistance and then to blow up a railroad tunnel in preparation for D-Day. Their nemesis is Col. Meister (John Hoyt) who reappears throughout the film whenever the pace flags.

The big scenes—placing a bomb on a train, a confrontation with drunken Nazis in a farmhouse, and an escape from the Gestapo—are handled brightly enough by director Irving Pichel, who also co-directed *The Most Dangerous Game*. Pichel and cinematographer Lionel Lindon also pay close attention to the night scenes, where their ominous staging provides a preview of the films noir that were then beginning to appear. Those dark visuals are more memorable than the star.

Whenever Alan Ladd is forced to center stage, he seems to be going through the motions. His tough-guy persona cracks whenever he questions the role of women in this particular branch of warfare. Taking into account the differences in public attitudes between then and now, he still comes across as a chauvinistic blockhead. That, of course, is what screenwriter Maibaum means for the audience to think, but Masson is still an unsympathetic, forgettable hero.

The best scenes—and almost certainly the most realistic—involve Brink (Harold Vermilyea), a greedy Gestapo agent who can read the writing on the wall and is ready to change sides. After he departs, the film comes to an odd conclusion that belatedly attempts to invest some seriousness into an otherwise frivolous story. In the end, *O.S.S.* has considerable value as an artifact of cinematic espionage, but its entertainment value is mostly limited to Ladd's fans.

> "We're late—400 years. That's how long ago the other major powers started their O.S.S. We've only got months to build the first central intelligence agency in history."
>
> **Gen. Donovan (Joseph Crehan)**

Did you Know?
Cinematographer Lionel Lindon won an Academy Award for his work on *Around the World in 80 Days*. He was also behind the camera on John Frankenheimer's *The Manchurian Candidate*.

See also

Across the Pacific
Saboteur
The Seventh Cross
Is Paris Burning?

Philip Masson (Alan Ladd) is questioned at Gestapo headquarters while Ellen Rogers (Geraldine Fitzgerald) looks on.

The Kobal Collection

Cast: Alan Ladd (John Martin/Philip Masson), Geraldine Fitzgerald (Ellen Rogers/Elaine Duprez), Patric Knowles (Cmdr. Brady), John Hoyt (Col. Meister), Richard Benedict (Bernay), Gloria Saunders (WAC Operator Sparky), Bobby Driscoll (Gerard), Don Beddoe (Gates), Richard Webb (Partker), Gavin Muir (Col. Crawson), Onslow Stevens (Field), Joseph Crehan (Gen. Donovan), Leslie Denison (Lt. Col. Miles), Harold Vermilyea (Amadeus Brink); **Written by:** Richard Maibaum; **Cinematography by:** Lionel Linden; **Music by:** Daniele Amfitheatrof; **Technical Advisor:** Raphael G. Beugnon, John Shaheen. **Producer:** Richard Maibaum; released by Paramount Pictures. **Running Time:** 108 minutes. **Format:** VHS, Closed Caption.

Like *O.S.S.*, this early wartime thriller contains the seeds of the spy films, both serious and frivolous, that would become so hugely popular in the 1960s. To viewers who are familiar with those movies, it is an exercise in unexpected nostalgia that carefully explains the plot devices which have become accepted conventions of the genre. A ponderous introduction even goes so far as to state that Americans are decent, fair-minded people who must learn to become much more ruthless if they are to beat the Germans, who have been conniving liars for generations. The film seldom varies from that naive tone.

The subject is the establishment of an Army Intelligence operation to place several agents in Europe immediately before D-Day. Bob Sharkey (James Cagney) is the boss of the operation. He's well into the outfit's training when he learns that one of his recruits is actually a double agent for the Nazis. He suspects that it's Bill O'Connell (Richard Conte). Rather than unmask the traitor, his superiors want him to plant false information about an Allied invasion of the Low Countries and send O'Connell into the field. Their plan goes awry and Sharkey winds up parachuting behind enemy lines to repair the damage.

> " I concede nothing until they throw dirt in my face!"
>
> **Bob Sharkey (James Cagney)**

A year before in 1945, director Henry Hathaway had made the pseudo-documentary *House on 92nd St.* and so he's familiar with the landscape of espionage. But that film was set in America. The important part of this one takes place in occupied France and is more concerned with daily life under Nazi rule. The various scenes of individual heroics are kept to a fairly realistic level, and Cagney has a terrific fight scene. The performances are fine throughout, with many familiar faces—E.G. Marshall, Red Buttons, Karl Malden—(all then impossibly young) appearing in the supporting cast.

For all the film's seriousness, though, time has rendered some scenes unintentionally comedic. The most striking of those occurs when the Chief of British Intelligence deliberately sets the chain lock on the door of his office before he brings out the maps labeled "Top Secret Plans" in bold letters. It's a moment worthy of TV's *Get Smart*, but to judge the film by that scene is unfair, particularly in light of the strong, unexpected conclusion. Hathaway took considerable care in his choice of locations—Boston for London, Montreal for Paris, Washington, D.C. for itself—to create an atmosphere of authenticity that's often lacking in films of the mid-'40s.

13 Rue Madeleine is worth watching for Cagney if for nothing else. Fans of the genre will notice how neatly it fits in between the adventurous *39 Steps* and the disillusioned *Spy Who Came in from the Cold*.

See also
O.S.S.
The Seventh Cross
Hangmen Also Die
The Manchurian Candidate

E.G. Marshall, Annabella, and
Richard Conte in *13 Rue
Madeleine*. The Kobal Collection

Cast: James Cagney (Bob Sharkey), Annabella (Suzanne de Bouchard), Richard Conte (Bill O'Connell), Frank Latimore (Jeff Lassiter), Walter Abel (Charles Gibson), Sam Jaffe (Mayor Galimard), Melville Cooper (Pappy Simpson), E.G. Marshall (Emile), Karl Malden (Flight Sergeant), Red Buttons (Dispatcher), Blanche Yurka (Mme. Thillot), Peter Von Zerneck (Karl), Marcel Rousseau (Duclois), Dick Gordon (Psychiatrist), Alfred Linder (Hans Feinkl); **Written by:** Sy Bartlett, John Monks Jr.; **Cinematography by:** Norbert Brodine; **Music by:** David Buttolph. **Producer:** Warner Brothers, Louis de Rochement. **Running Time:** 95 minutes. **Format:** VHS, Beta.

The horrors of Nazism make it an almost impossible subject for comedy, but that didn't stop Ernst Lubitsch from creating a masterpiece. He translates many of his favorite themes and humorous asides—along with the famous "Lubitsch touch"—to make a romantic comedy-thriller that transcends its propagandistic roots. So many of the jokes are based on eternal truths of marriage and show business that the film remains as fresh and funny now as it was in 1942.

A complicated introduction sets the stage, both figuratively and literally, in Warsaw, Poland, 1939. A troupe of actors perform *Hamlet* on the eve of Hitler's invasion. Josef Tura (Jack Benny) is the star, though his stunning wife Maria (Carole Lombard) easily outshines him. She has caught the eye of a handsome young Polish pilot, Lt. Sobinski (Robert Stack), and has embarked on a mild flirtation with him behind her husband's back. "What a husband doesn't know won't hurt his wife," her maid Anna (Maude Eburne) notes. Before anything can really develop, the Nazis arrive. Sobinski becomes a flier for the R.A.F. while the Turas and their fellow actors are trapped in Warsaw. Then Sobinski discovers that a German spy has learned the names of the Polish underground and goes back to his homeland to prevent the revelation.

The rest of the film is a smoothly paced series of scenes involving actors impersonating Nazi officers, switched identities, more dalliance, banter and, naturally, escape. The first scene in which the three protagonists finally all confront each other is as brilliant a bit of business as anyone has ever constructed. It doesn't take place until almost the midpoint, and the participants elevate the conventional "who's been sleeping in my bed" routines to a rarified level. The supporting cast, including Lionel Atwill, who's seen most often as a villain, and the aforementioned Maude Eburne, who might have been given more to do, could not be better, and they become much more important in the second half.

Though Stack is fine as the earnest, smooth-faced juvenile, the film really belongs to Jack Benny and Carole Lombard. Sadly, it was her final appearance—she was killed in a plane crash while taking part in a war bond selling tour—and she combines beauty with intelligence and courage so well that she makes a potentially silly role seem effortless. In her silver dress, she is as sexy as any woman who ever appeared in front of a camera. For his part, Josef is equal parts shameless ham, jealous husband, and reluctant hero, and though Benny has always been most famous for his dry one-note routines, he turns in a solid, multifaceted performance. Even if he is slightly removed from his natural comedic element, his sense of timing is perfect in the punchlines.

> **"A laugh is nothing to be sneezed at."**
> — **Greenberg (Felix Bressart)**

The only criticism that can be leveled at the film is unfair. As the two Nazis who are the butt of many jokes, Col. Ehrhardt (Sig Rumann) and Capt. Schultz (Henry Victor), are the obvious models for similar caricatures on TV's *Hogan's Heroes*. *To Be or Not to Be* never stoops to such a level. It's thoughtful light humor that never takes its subject too lightly, and never lets politics get in the way of a good joke.

See also

The Seventh Cross
Hangmen Also Die
Ninotchka

Robert Stack and Jack Benny in
To Be or Not to Be The Kobal Collection

Cast: Carole Lombard (Maria Tura), Jack Benny (Josef Tura), Robert Stack (Lt. Stanislav Sobinski), Sig Rumann (Col. Ehrhardt), Lionel Atwill (Rawitch), Felix Bressart (Greenberg), Helmut Dantine (Co-pilot), Tom Dugan (Bronski), Charles Halton (Dobosh), Stanley Ridges (Prof. Alexander Siletsky), George Lynn (Actor-Adjutant), Halliwell Hobbes (Gen. Armstrong), Miles Mander (Maj. Cunningham), Henry Victor (Capt. Schultz), Leslie Denison (Captain), Frank Reicher (Polish official), John Kellogg (RAF flyer), James Finlayson (Farmer), Roland Varno (Pilot), Maude Eburne (Anna); **Written by:** Ernst Lubitsch, Edwin Justus Mayer, Melchior Lengyel; **Cinematography by:** Rudolph Mate; **Music by:** Werner R. Heymann, Miklos Rozsa. **Producer:** Alexander Korda, Ernst Lubitsch, United Artists. **Awards:** National Film Registry '96; Nominations: Academy Awards '42: Best Original Dramatic Score. **Running Time:** 102 minutes. **Format:** VHS, Beta.

Well-intentioned and seriously acted, Lillian Hellman and Dashiell Hammett's adaptation of her play never breaks free from the limitations of the stage. Other changes in acting styles further distance the work from contemporary audiences, and so now it is little more than a propagandistic curiosity.

Kurt Muller (Paul Lukas), his wife Sara (Bette Davis), and their three children nervously cross the border from Mexico into America. Though Sara is returning home, they're uneasy on the train back to her mother's estate in Virginia, near Washington. Fanny Farrelly (Lucile Watson), the domineering family matriarch, doesn't quite know what her daughter's been up to for the past 17 years, and she has problems of her own. Her houseguests, the Romanian Teck de Brancovis (George Coulouris) and his wife Marthe (Geraldine Fitzgerald), have overstayed their welcome. People are starting to gossip about her son David (Donald Woods) and Marthe, and Teck is far too chummy with the Nazis at the German embassy. At leisurely length, it is revealed that Kurt has been deeply involved with antifascist activities and is continuing his work.

> "It's unfortunate that early American liberals were such a hardy people."
>
> **Teck de Brancovis (George Coulouris)**

> "Well, we've been shaken out of the magnolias."
>
> **Fanny Farrelly (Lucile Watson) after all has been revealed**

The central problem is that none of the filmmakers were really comfortable with the medium. Director Herman Shumlin, who'd directed the play, was an established theater producer and director. (He would make only one more film, *Confidential Agent*.) Hellmann, too, had much more experience with conventional drama at that time. (She would gain more experience in screenwriting, including that wonderful '60s potboiler, *The Chase*.) Hammett's best work was done in short stories and novels. Together, they allow almost all of the action to take place in Mrs. Farrelly's living room, where the characters don't really talk to each other. Instead, they deliver a series of monologues, mostly political. Even someone who agrees with the film's politics may still find its selfrighteous "I told you so" attitude hard to stomach. Lines like "All of us haven't been so isolated as you seem to have been in this house" come across as sloganeering. Finally, the key piece of physical action—the moment that everything else builds up to—takes place off camera. In context, it's easy to see why the work would be structured that way on stage. But on screen, it's all pretty unsatisfactory.

Watch on the Rhine is also a curious counterpoint to *Casablanca*. Both are based on stage plays; both were released in the same year; and the characters even parallel each other. Kurt and Sara can be seen as older versions of Victor Laszlo and Ilse. Teck is Ugarte. The embassy Nazi Von Ramme (Henry Daniell) is Maj. Strasser, and in her more flamboyant moments, Lucile Watson could be Sidney Greenstreet in drag. Ironically, Paul Lukas won the Academy Award that should have gone to Humphrey Bogart.

See also

Casablanca
Julia

George Coulouris, Donald Woods, Lucile Watson, Bette Davis, and Paul Lukas in *Watch on the Rhine*. The Kobal Collection

Cast: Bette Davis (Sara Muller), Paul Lukas (Kurt Muller), Donald Woods (David Farrelly), Beulah Bondi (Anise), Geraldine Fitzgerald (Marthe de Brancovis), George Coulouris (Teck de Brancovis), Henry Daniell (Phili Von Ramme), Helmut Dantine (Young man), Donald Buka (Joshua), Anthony Caruso (Italian man), Clyde Fillmore (Sam Chandler), Howard Hickman (Penfield), Creighton Hale (Chauffeur), Kurt Katch (Herr Blecher), Clarence Muse (Horace), Alan Hale Jr. (Boy), Frank Reicher (Admiral), Mary Young (Mrs. Marie Sewell), Lucile Watson (Fanny Farrelly); **Written by:** Lillian Hellman, Dashiell Hammett; **Cinematography by:** Hal Mohr, Merritt B. Gerstad; **Music by:** Max Steiner. **Producer:** Hal B. Wallis, Warner Bros. **Awards:** Academy Awards '43: Best Actor (Lukas); Golden Globe Awards '44: Best Actor—Drama (Lukas); New York Film Critics Awards '43: Best Actor (Lukas), Best Film; Nominations: Academy Awards '43: Best Picture, Best Screenplay, Best Supporting Actress (Watson). **Running Time:** 114 minutes. **Format:** VHS, Beta.

Stories of the resistance movement in World War II tend to take on an heroic, almost mythic quality. That is precisely not the case with this one. It's based on fact, and every frame has the unmistakable look of truth. From an introduction that lists the names of the young protagonists and the dates of their executions, to a conclusion that stops the action abruptly at just the right moment, director Michael Verhoeven strips the action of sentimentality. He wants the viewer to appreciate the reality of what these characters did, not a glorified version of it.

In May 1942, Sophie Scholl (Lena Stolze) is a newly arrived university student in Munich. Her older brother Hans (Wulf Kessler), also a student, introduces her to his circle of friends, Christoph (Werner Stocker), Alex (Oliver Siebert), and Ulrich (Willi Graf). To all outward appearances, they are typical intelligent undergraduates, passionate about ideas, but always ready to have fun and able to change from seriousness to childlike frivolity in an instant. The guys are up to something else, too.

They type, print up, and surreptitiously distribute flyers critical of the Nazi party. At first their efforts are limited. They leave the single sheets on streetcars, in lecture halls, and tucked between the pages of public telephone books. As people begin to talk about their anonymous work, they become more ambitious and begin mailing their broadsides to specific individuals. Immediately, they face a new set of problems. That's also when Sophie discovers what they're up to and decides to join them.

To those who have grown up in a freer society, the situation that Verhoeven and writer Mario Krebs describe is almost beyond belief. In this police state, the government controls or attempts to control all forms of communication, beginning at the level of personal conversation. Sophie and Hans's father is turned in by a secretary for making unfavorable remarks about Hitler. Prof. Huber (Martin Benrath), a popular lecturer, must be careful about his references to the philosopher Spinoza, who was Jewish. Anyone who buys large amounts of postage stamps is suspect, and the same goes for paper. Even to carry the flyers on public transportation is dangerous. Officials can search baggage at any time for any reason.

Remarkably, though, as the months pass, they are not caught, and so are emboldened to make connections with other groups of dissenters and to more openly urge the army to take action against political leaders. They also argue over tactics. Should they simply urge others to action? Do they commit acts of violence themselves? Is it time to advocate cooperation with Communists and Bolsheviks? With a few changes in wording and circumstance, the arguments could take place in virtually any dormitory or student apartment during any war.

But few protesters risk as much as these kids do, and that adds a strong dimension of suspense to their simple strategies. The typical Hollywood concoction of bridges being blown up and other flamboyant acts of sabotage don't contain nearly as much tension as a deceptively simple scene revolving around the theft of a couple of reams of paper from a government office.

The lack of familiar names and faces in the cast adds even more to the film's unpredictability. Verhoeven's use of well-chosen loca-

See also
One Against the Wind
Hangmen Also Die
The Seventh Cross
The Great Dictator
The Nasty Girl

tions, and his restraint with music give the action an unusual degree of realism, too. For those who aren't dissuaded by the idea of subtitled German dialogue, *The White Rose* is an unsettling and memorable sleeper.

Cast: Lena Stolze (Sophia Scholl), Wulf Kessler (Hans Scholl), Oliver Siebert (Alex Schmorell), Ulrich Tucker (Willi Graf), Werner Stocker (Christoph Probst), Martin Benrath (Prof. Huber), Anja Kruse (Traute Lafrenz), Ulf-Jurgen Wagner (Fritz), Mechthild Reinders (Gisela Schertling), Peter Kortenbach (Falk Harnack), Gerhard Friedrich (Herr Scholl), Sabine Kretzschmar (Frau Scholl), Heinz Keller (Werner Scholl), Suzanne Seuffert (Inge Scholl), Christina Schwartz (Elisabeth Scholl); **Written by:** Michael Verhoeven, Mario Krebs; **Cinematography by:** Axel de Roche; **Music by:** Konstantin Wecker. **Producer:** Arthur Brauner, TeleCulture Films. **German. Running Time:** 108 minutes. **Format:** VHS, Beta.

KOREAN WAR

All the Young Men

Battle Circus

The Bridges at
Toko-Ri

The Hunters

The Manchurian
Candidate

M*A*S*H

Men in War

Pork Chop Hill

The Steel Helmet

Korean War on Screen

"The war has a bigger meaning. The only trouble is it came along too soon after the real big one. It's hard to sell anybody on it."

That quote from *The Hunters* is a relatively accurate assessment of Hollywood's attitude toward the Korean War—or should it be the Korean Police Action? The patriotic we're-all-in-this-together spirit of the World War II films is missing, and no single theme takes its place. Filmmakers never quite knew what they—or their audiences—thought about the Korean conflict. The anti-Communism of the Cold War is certainly evident, but it takes several forms, from rabid Red-baiting with ill-concealed racist undertones, to grudging respect for a committed enemy. In between is a wide streak of ambivalence. An equally strong apprehension runs through the films, too. Though it's seldom mentioned directly, the concept of nuclear destruction looms in the shadowy background.

Sam Fuller was the first director to tackle Korea, but his B-masterpiece, *The Steel Helmet*, is really a World War II leftover. It's a standard unit picture, with North Koreans taking the roles previously reserved for the Germans and Japanese. When Fuller addresses racial issues, he reflects his audience's immediate domestic concerns.

Battle Circus is a well-made, off-beat Humphrey Bogart vehicle that never really evokes the specifics of Korea. Again, it looks and feels like a misplaced World War II film.

The Bridges at Toko-Ri comes closer to the real issues of the war, and so it is forced into an uncomfortable political stance. As the senior officer in the piece, Frederic March spells out the offi-

KOREAN WAR

cial military position, but his defense of the war has a hollow ring, and the film's unusual ending underlines its uncertainty. The flying scenes and the footage shot on aircraft carriers are much stronger.

In *Men in War*, director Anthony Mann reduces the conflict down to its elements. The film is a "lost patrol" story where the main antagonists are two Americans—Robert Ryan and Aldo Ray—who have opposite objectives. The North Koreans are essentially background characters.

The Hunters is splendid in its aerial dogfight scenes between F-86 Saber jets and MIGs. At ground level, though, the plot is a contrived mess. Within that mixed bag are some telling observations about the war. Right after the protagonist (Robert Mitchum) makes that statement about the war being a hard sell because it follows World War II too closely, he makes another admission. He's in it simply because he's good at flying fighters. His support for the war has little to do with politics or morality. He's there because it's fun.

Lewis Milestone's *Pork Chop Hill* is not meant to be fun. He tells the fact-based story of a battle that's politically important but tactically meaningless. The combat scenes are impressive, and Milestone is able to keep the various facets of the action clear and understandable. At the same time, though, the film was made with the cooperation of the Army, and so it gently suggests and glosses over bureaucratic screw-ups that cost dozens of lives when it ought to be much angrier. Of course, that contradiction is not unusual for this contradictory war.

All the Young Men is another "lost patrol" story. With Sidney Poitier in the lead, it has a highly developed racial consciousness. This one was made in 1960, ten years after Fuller's *The Steel Helmet*, and though the film is seriously flawed, it does demonstrate the kinds of changes that were occurring in American ideas about race.

Later in the 1960s and '70s, Korea fades quickly from Hollywood's attention. By the time John Frankenheimer made *The Manchurian Candidate* in 1962, the Korean conflict is simply one plot element in a Byzantine tale of Cold War conspiracies, where political concepts of left and right are turned inside out. Then in 1970, when Robert Altman directed *M*A*S*H*, the circuit is completed. The Korean War is no longer a smaller version of World War II. It's a preview of Vietnam.

ALL THE YOUNG MEN

1960 Hall Bartlett

The story of a unit that loses its officer while in enemy territory goes back at least as far as World War I, with John Ford's *The Lost Patrol*. Hall Bartlett sets this variation in Korea with mixed results. The creative, off-beat casting virtually guarantees as much. After all, how many other films put Sidney Poitier on the screen alongside heavyweight champion Ingemar Johansson (who sings), with stand-up comedy by Mort Sahl?

In 1950, United Nations and South Korean forces mount an offensive against the Chinese and North Koreans. The second platoon of Baker Company, USMC, is sent into the snowy mountains—actually Glacier National Park, Montana—to seize and hold a farmhouse at a strategic pass. The lieutenant (Charles Quinlivan) is shot in an ambush and, with his dying breath, transfers command to Sgt. Towler (Sidney Poitier), even though Sgt. Kincaid (Alan Ladd) is the more experienced soldier. With considerable dissention in the ranks fomented by the bigoted Pvt. Bracken (Paul Richards), the Marines press on to their objective. Land mines, mortar fire, snipers, and dangerous terrain threaten every step of the way. Once they reach their goal, the conflicts within the group become more open, and pressure from the North Koreans increases.

"Don't judge us the way we are now. . . . Because we are frightened now, because we have seen too much death and we don't understand why, because we have had to bury our friends in places we can't even pronounce."

Towler's (Sidney Poitier) explanation of his unit's presence at the farmhouse owned by Maya (Ana St. Clair)

On the positive side, the acting from the leads is good enough to make up for less-thanstellar writing. Some of the action scenes are surprisingly explicit without exploitation. Images of a severed hand and a crushed foot are the most striking. Bartlett's handling of racial issues is simplistic, mostly because Bracken is such a one-dimensional caricature, but it does treat the matter seriously. On the negative side, Montana's impressive snowscapes look nothing like Korea, and the pagoda-like farmhouse is hardly more persuasive. Despite a passionate early performance by Sidney Poitier, the role really doesn't play to his strengths as an actor. When the men question his authority, he often bellows and threatens to kill anyone who gets in his face. That may be the simple reflexive reaction moviegoers expect from John Wayne or Victor McLaglen in the same situation. Poitier can handle more complex responses. He has demonstrated it dozens of times.

Though co-producer Alan Ladd gets equal billing with Poitier, his role is less important. His one big rescue scene is inventive, suspenseful and, improbable. The confrontation, where Kincaid accuses Towler of wanting to become a black martyr, is simply impossible to believe.

Seen as a war film, *All the Young Men* has little of significance to say about the Korean conflict, beyond Towler's expression of ambivalence about being there. (See quote.) In that respect, like so many films of the 1950s, it's a sad preview of Vietnam.

See also

China Gate
The Steel Helmet
The Immortal Sergeant
Sahara

Cast: Alan Ladd (Kincaid), Sidney Poitier (Towler), James Darren (Cotton), Glenn Corbett (Wade), Mort
Sahl (Crane), Ana St. Clair (Maya), Paul Richards (Bracken), Richard Davalos (Casey), Lee Kinsolving (Dean), Joseph Gallison (Jackson), Paul Baxley
(Lazitech), Charles Quinlivan (The Lieutenant), Michael Davis (Cho), Ingemar Johannson (Torgil); **Written by:** Hall Bartlett; **Cinematography by:** Daniel F. Fapp; **Music by:** George Duning. **Producer:** Columbia Pictures, Hall Bartlett. **Running Time:** 86
minutes. **Format:** VHS, Beta.

BATTLE CIRCUS

Robert Altman's *M*A*S*H* uses the Korean "police action" to comment on Vietnam. Richard Brooks's film, set in the same kind of Mobile Army Surgical Hospital, is understandably less sharply focused, reflecting America's less passionate feelings about that war. It's a curious film—flawed, but more good than bad—which treats the subject of medicine in a time of war seriously and makes no comment on the morality or political necessity of the conflict. It benefits immeasurably from the presence of Humphrey Bogart in an understated, easy-going performance.

He plays Maj. Jed Webbe, a surgeon who has a highly developed appreciation for whiskey and blondes, perhaps too highly developed. At least, that's how his boss, Lt. Col. Whalters (Robert Keith) sees it. He's not too enthusiastic about Webbe's penchant for impulsive behavior, either, particularly when it involves helicopter flights into fire zones. Webbe's attention, though, has been diverted by newly arrived nurse Ruth McGara (June Allyson), an innocent who fell right off the turnip truck. She moronically stands up and looks around when everyone else hits the ground during a mortar attack. One true love and flag-waving patriotism are also high on her list.

As an object for Webbe's affection and/or lust, she's an unlikely candidate, and she's the film's main flaw. Her wide-eyed "golly-gee whiz" line delivery and perpetually smiling perkiness are completely insufferable. To be fair, the part is so transparently written that all the blame cannot be laid on her. Actually, the most interesting woman in the cast is Lt. Franklin (Adele Longmire), a cynical brunette who has some sharp oneliners in the early going but then disappears into the background.

Director Brooks is more in his element when the film lives up to its title and pays attention to the mobile characteristics of the unit. The long scenes of striking the huge tents, packing them up and transporting them to a new location have a whiff of nuts-and-bolts realism. The operating room scenes try to achieve that same level of verisimilitude, but viewer expectations in that regard have been raised considerably since 1953, and so the surgery seems tame and bloodless. The other personal conflicts are less than compelling, too. The story finally comes into its own in the third act, with a forced move of the hospital and patients in the face of quickly advancing North Korean troops. Despite California locations that don't look much like Korea, Brooks makes the desperation of the doctors and the wounded seem real.

On its own, *Battle Circus* is unlikely to make any top-ten lists. It's still fine for Bogie's fans, and its real importance lies in the changing attitudes that it reveals. By 1953, Americans could no longer luxuriate in the role of simple, humble savior of civilization. The world had become too complicated for that, even in Hollywood. The props and John Alton's superb black-and-white cinematography recall the first wave of World War II propaganda films, but the sense of grim determination that comes from being forced into a war for survival is noticeably absent.

See also

M*A*S*H
Casablanca
Action in the North Atlantic
Doctor Zhivago

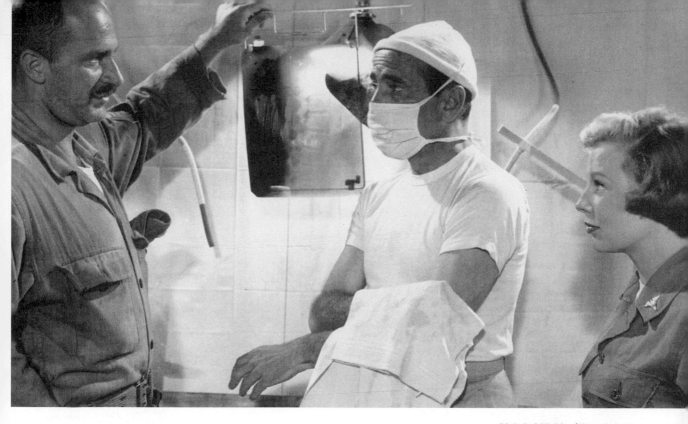

Maj. Jed Webbe (Humphrey Bogart, center) runs a M*A*S*H unit during the Korean War with the help of Sgt. Orvil Statt (Keenan Wynn) and Lt. Ruth McGara (June Allyson) in *Battle Circus*. The Kobal Collection

Cast: Humphrey Bogart (Maj. Jed Webbe), June Allyson (Lt. Ruth McGara), Keenan Wynn (Sgt. Orvil Statt), Robert Keith (Lt. Col. Hillary Whalters), William Campbell (Capt. John Rustford), Perry Sheehan (Lt. Laurence), Patricia Tiernan (Lt. Rose Ashland), Adele Longmire (Lt. Jane Franklin), Jonathon Cott (Adjutant), Ann Morrison (Lt. Edith Edwards), Helen Winston (Lt. Graciano), Sarah Selby (Capt. Dobbs), Danny Chang (Koren Child), Philip Ahn (Koren Prisoner), Steve Forrest (The Sergeant), Jeff Richards (The Lieutenant), Dick Simmons (Capt. Norson); **Written by:** Richard Brooks; **Cinematography by:** John Alton; **Music by:** Lennie Hayton; **Technical Advisor:** Mary Couch, K.E. Van Buskirk. **Producer:** Pandro S. Berman, MGM. **Running Time:** 90 minutes. **Format:** VHS, Closed Caption.

The Hound Salutes: Humphrey Bogart

Humphrey Bogart will always be thought of first as a tough guy. His interpretations of Dashiell Hammett's Sam Spade in *The Maltese Falcon* and of Raymond Chandler's Philip Marlowe in *The Big Sleep* are the definitive images of the screen private detective. But the role that first made people pay attention to him was Duke Mantee, the escaped gangster in *Petrified Forest* (1936). Though Bogart was almost 40 years old when those roles came to him, his timing could not have been better. He was the right actor in the right place to play Rick Blaine in *Casablanca* (1942). After that, the movie-going public was ready to watch just about anything he did.

Bogart had served in the Navy in World War I, where an explosion injured his face and gave him that slight but distinctive lisp that could be so menacing and so expressive. By the time he became a star, he had served a long apprenticeship, playing all sorts of roles on stage and screen—westerns, horror, comedy, whatever—mostly with Warner Bros., a studio that specialized in solid mid-budget escapism. After December 7, 1941, he worked steadily, and made four of his best war films right out of the gate. Following *The Maltese Falcon*, he teamed up with some of the same people—director John Huston and co-stars Mary Astor and Sydney Greenstreet—for the fair thriller *Across the Pacific*. *Casablanca* was released less than two months later in 1942. After it, Bogart gave the Merchant Marines a shot with *Action in the North Atlantic*, and he finished out 1943 with *Sahara*, one of the finest adventures to come out the war. A year later, he re-teamed with his *Casablanca* pals—director Michael Curtiz, co-stars Claude Rains, Sydney Greenstreet, and Peter Lorre—for the less successful *Passage to Marseilles*.

Later in his career, he and Katherine Hepburn were unlikely lovers who battled Germans in World War I in *The African Queen*. Bogie was almost two decades ahead of *M*A*S*H* with his interpretation of an Army doctor in Korea who spends too much time chasing booze and blondes in *Battle Circus*. He saved his most serious, if not his best performance, for the tortured Capt. Queeg in *The Caine Mutiny*.

So, if Bogart is not known for his war films, it is only because so many others (including *Key Largo* and *To Have and Have Not* and . . .) are so good, too. It may not be fair to give him all the credit—the Hollywood studio system was built around writers, directors, and cinematographers who knew how to accentuate the strengths of actors and actresses to get the most out of them—but the war certainly brought out the best in Bogart. From the "misinformed" cafe owner who steps out into the foggy night to join the Free French garrison, to the ship's captain who cannot deal with the pressures of command, Bogart is World War II's most unconventional screen hero.

Though the subject is the Korean conflict, this is really a Cold War film, perhaps the archetypal Cold War film, with Red-baiting politics, a strongly pro-military agenda, and an absolute blindness to the situation it addresses. To a degree, that attitude has to be expected from a film made with the full cooperation of the Navy—including liberal access to aircraft carriers at sea—but seen in the light of history, the film reveals the prejudices of its time with unforgiving clarity.

In 1952, Lt. Harry Brubaker (William Holden) is flying jet fighters from a carrier off the coast of Korea. Though the script is a little vague on the point, his participation in the war is less than completely voluntary. He had expected another reserve unit to be called up before his, or something to that effect. Whatever the circumstances, he finds himself involved in the dangerous business of taking off from and landing on a floating postage stamp in the middle of a roiling ocean. He's good at his work, though the helicopter rescue team of Forney (Mickey Rooney) and Gamidge (Earl Holliman) has had to fish him out of the drink. To his boss, Rear Adm. Tarrant (Fredric March), Brubaker is almost a surrogate son.

The best parts of the film are the flying and carrier scenes. Both have a degree of authenticity that Hollywood seldom achieves. Comparatively few models and special effects were used. The bombing runs and the landings have a strong you-are-there quality, and the filmmakers handle them with loving attention to details. That side of the film could not be better.

The same cannot be said of the long central section when the carrier docks in Japan. There, Brubaker spends his time with perfect blonde wife Nancy (Grace Kelly) and his freshly scrubbed children, while Forney and Gamidge get into the kind of trouble that enlisted men on leave always get into in war movies. Given that extended pause in the action, Adm. Tarrant takes the opportunity to hold forth on Cold War politics. "If we don't stop the Koreans here," he sagely states, "they'll be in Japan, Indochina, and the Philippines" and then on to Mississippi. "Like most people at home, you've been protected," he tells Nancy "You're ignorant and defenseless." The same patronizing superiority comes into play when he explains why women just can't seem to understand why men have to do what men have to do in war.

To underscore those points for contemporary audiences, the last act eerily anticipates the kind of action that would become far too common more than a decade later in Vietnam.

Hindsight gives the whole film, particularly the conclusion, a horrible inevitability. At the risk of belaboring one of this book's central points, war movies contain emotional truths, not historical truths. In this case, the filmmakers reveal a rigid us-vs.-them mentality that was widely accepted at the time. As a snapshot of mid-1950s American attitudes and their consequences, *The Bridges of Toko-Ri* has few equals.

See also
The Gallant Hours
Top Gun
Bat-21
Apocalypse Now
Full Metal Jacket

William Hoden (left) and Mickey
Rooney try to hold off the
enemy while waiting for a
rescue chopper in *The Bridges at
Toko-Ri.* The Kobal Collection

Cast: William Holden (Lt. Harry Brubaker), Grace Kelly (Nancy Brubaker), Fredric March (Rear Adm.
George Tarrant), Mickey Rooney (Mike Forney), Robert Strauss (Beer Barrel), Earl Holliman (Nestor Gamidge), Keiko Awaji (Kimiko), Charles McGraw (Cmdr.
Wayne Lee), Richard Shannon (Lt. Olds), Willis Bouchey (Capt. Evans); **Written by:** Valentine Davies; **Cinematography by:**
Loyal Griggs; **Music by:** Lyn Murray. **Producer:** Paramount Pictures, George Seaton, William Perlberg. **Awards:** Academy Awards
'55: Best Special Effects; Nominations: Academy Awards '55: Best Film Editing. **Running Time:** 103 minutes. **Format:** VHS, Beta, LV.

The F-86 Saberjet is a very cool airplane, beautifully designed with sleek lines that somehow recall the great World War II fighters. Hollywood didn't make nearly enough movies about it. In fact, this lumbering soap opera is probably the F-86's finest hour. Aerial photographer Tom Tutwiler makes it look as quick, graceful, and agile as any plane that ever graced the screen. His work is by far the best part of an otherwise routine formula '50s picture.

Robert Mitchum is Maj. Cleve Saville, a World War II ace who still refuses to fly a desk, despite his seniority. In Japan, on his way to his first posting in Korea, he meets Lt. Carl Abbott (Lee Philips), a young pilot who fears that he doesn't have the right stuff. With 30 missions and no kills, he tries to hide his fears in bourbon. His wife Kris (May Britt) doesn't know what to do with him. Maj. Saville sympathizes with her, perhaps more than he should. Filling out the roster when they finally arrive in Korea are the Fighter Group's boss, Col. Dutch Emil (Richard Egan) and Lt. Ed Pell (Robert Wagner), a jive fighter jock who spouts ersatz hipster lingo, as embarrassing now as the day it was written. Their nemesis is the dreaded North Korean ace Casey Jones (Leon Lontoc).

> "The war has a bigger meaning. The only trouble is it came along too soon after the real big one. It's hard to sell anybody on it."
>
> **Maj. Seville (Robert Mitchum) explaining the importance of the Korean conflict to Kris Abbott (May Britt)**

> "The war permits me to do the one thing I can do better than anything else—fight planes."
>
> **Maj. Seville**

Overall, the film shares the flaws of the big-budget pictures of its era: slow pace, sugary romance, a penchant for postcard scenery, ponderous script, and a coy, uncomfortable attitude toward adultery, though it's an important subplot. Along with those, one crash scene attempts—unsuccessfully—to incorporate archival footage of a similar but obviously different fighter. Then there is the plot. Wendell Mayes's screenplay, based on James Salter's novel, proceeds along fairly realistic lines until it reaches the third act. Then it inexplicably loses control. Really, if the Loch Ness Monster and Liberace were to make a late entrance, it would be no more unrealistic than what actually happens. Actor turned producer-director Dick Powell boldly glides right over that bit of fantasy, and the film pushes on to a conventional conclusion, but whatever illusions he had created are lost.

The flying scenes are enough to recommend the film to aviation fans. All others are on their own.

See also

The Bridges at Toko-Ri
Top Gun
From Here to Eternity
Star Wars

Robert Wagner (standing) and
Robert Mitchum and Lee Philips
are three of the *The Hunters.* The
Kobal Collection

Cast: Robert Mitchum (Maj. Cleve Saville), Robert Wagner (Lt. Ed Pell), Richard Egan (Col. Dutch Imil), May Britt (Kristina Abbott), Lee Philips (Lt. Carl Abbott), John Gabriel (Lt. Corona), Stacy Harris (Col. Monk Moncavage), John Doucette (The Sergeant), Jay Jostyn (Maj. Dark), Leon Lontoc (Casey Jones), Ralph Manza (Gifford), Alena Murray (Mrs. Mason), Robert Reed (Jackson), Victor Sen Yung (Korean man), Candace Lee (Korean child); **Written by:** Wendell Mayes; **Cinematography by:** Charles Clarke; **Music by:** Paul Sawtell. **Producer:** Dick Powell, 20th Century-Fox. **Running Time:** 108 minutes. **Format:** VHS.

THE MANCHURIAN CANDIDATE
1962 John Frankenheimer 🎞🎞🎞🎞

In their adaptation of Richard Condon's brilliant novel, John Frankenheimer and George Axelrod invent the post-World War II thriller. The form had traditionally been a matter of heroism and suspense built around an innocent man caught in the wrong place. Condon and the filmmakers move to a deeper, darker level of paranoia where all of the fears and hatreds of the Cold War coalesce. In their funhouse mirrors, every political idea is actually its opposite: the red-baiting senator is a tool of the communists, the hero is almost completely ineffectual, the villain is the most cheerful and intelligent character in the piece, and his plans are mostly successful.

Despite the story's bizarre premise and shaky narrative structure, its influence has increased steadily over the decades. Doubtless, some of that importance is due to timing. Political assassination was unimaginable in the America of the late 1950s and early '60s. The prophetic elements give the more fantastic conspiratorial fantasies a degree of believability that still resonates. The plot is so familiar now that it needs little comment. In the Korean War, a night patrol is captured by North Korean and Chinese troops. The men are brainwashed by the jovial Yen Lo (Khigh Deigh) into believing that Sgt. Raymond Shaw (Laurence Harvey) singlehandedly wiped out their captors and brought them back to safety. After the war, Maj. Marco (Frank Sinatra) and Cpl. Melvin (James Edwards) suffer nightmares that gradually reveal the truth. Meanwhile, Raymond's arch-conservative mother (Angela Lansbury) positions her husband, Sen. John Iselin (James Gregory) for higher office.

The realistic blocks upon which Condon's story is built are obvious. Iselin—superbly played by familiar character actor Gregory—is a boozy, only slightly exaggerated parody of Sen. Joseph McCarthy. The symptoms that Marco and Melvin suffer mirror what was then called "battle fatigue," A.K.A. shell shock, or post-traumatic stress syndrome. Frankenheimer, who had come to film from television, sets the action squarely in the everyday world of cluttered apartments and self-important politicians. The real subject—the corrosive bitterness of extremist politics—is made clear in his twisted ironic use of American symbols of liberty: the eagle, the flag, Lincoln.

Some of Frankenheimer's techniques are showy, most notably the 360-degree pan during Yen Lo's demonstration, while others—like the hand-held camera that follows Raymond and family into the backseat of a limo—are simply the most effective way to get close to the characters. Though the big fight scene between Sinatra and Henry Silva may not measure up to expectations of today's more jaded martial arts fans, it's still one of the best furniture-smashing hand-to-hand sequences ever put on film.

So much background information has to be delivered that important characters are not even mentioned, much less introduced, until the almost the midpoint. The romantic relationship involving Janet Leigh has almost nothing to do with the rest of the action, and several transitions are rough and poorly explained. But the film works so smoothly on the elemental what's-

"You did this, Mother!"
Raymond Shaw (Laurence Harvey)

"One of your mother's more endearing traits is her tendency to refer to anyone who disagrees with her about anything as a communist."
Sen. Jordan (John McGiver)

"We set out to do Dick Condon's book and that's what we did."
John Frankenheimer, commenting on the making of *The Manchurian Candidate*

Did you Know?
The opening narration is provided by an uncredited Paul Frees, who performed the same function in *War of the Worlds, The Monolith Monsters,* and several other science-fiction films of the era, setting the same ominous tone.

See also
The Best Man
Seconds
The Train
Psycho
Ronin

Bennett Marco (Frank Sinatra, left) discovers the extent of the Communists' control over Shaw (Laurence Harvey) in *The Manchurian Candidate*. The Kobal Collection

going-to-happen-next? level that the flaws evaporate. Also, the ensemble performances, led by Angela Lansbury, Laurence Harvey, and Sinatra, never strike a false note. The same can be said of David Amram's somber score.

The pieces all fit together perfectly. Along with *Dr. Strangelove*, *The Manchurian Candidate* is a masterpiece of the Cold War.

Cast: Frank Sinatra (Bennett Marco), Laurence Harvey (Raymond Shaw), Angela Lansbury (Mrs. Iselin), Janet Leigh (Rosie), James Gregory (Sen. John Iselin), Leslie Parrish (Jocie Jordon), John McGiver (Sen. Thomas Jordon), Henry Silva (Chunjin), Khigh Deigh (Yen Lo), James Edwards (Cpl. Melvin), Douglas Henderson (The Colonel), Albert Paulsen (Zilkov), Barry Kelley (Secretary of Defense), Lloyd Corrigan (Holborn Gaines), Whit Bissell (Medical officer), Joe Adams (Psychiatrist), Madame Spivy (Berezovo), Mimi Dillard (Melvin's wife), John Lawrence (Grossfeld), Tom Lowell (Lembeck); **Written by:** John Frankenheimer, George Axelrod; **Cinematography by:** Lionel Lindon; **Music by:** David Amram. **Producer:** M.C. Productions, George Axelrod, John Frankenheimer. **Awards:** American Film Institute (AFI) '98: Top 100; Golden Globe Awards '63: Best Supporting Actress (Lansbury); National Board of Review Awards '62: Best Supporting Actress (Lansbury), National Film Registry '94; Nominations: Academy Awards '62: Best Film Editing, Best Supporting Actress (Lansbury). **Running Time:** 126 minutes. **Format:** VHS, Beta, LV, Closed Caption, DVD.

M*A*S*H

1970 Robert Altman ♪♪♪

The long-running television series is so deeply imbedded in the public imagination that the true nature of Robert Altman's anarchic film has been largely forgotten. Younger viewers who have not seen it and expect a longer version of the sitcom are going to be shocked, because in these more politically sensitive times, *M*A*S*H* could not be made. What studio executive would give the green light to a film with a black character named "Spearchucker," a priest named "Dago Red," and a dentist who attempts suicide because he thinks that he's becoming "a fairy"?

> "This isn't a hospital! It's an insane asylum!"
> **Maj. Houlihan (Sally Kellerman)**

Seen with some historical context, Altman's scathing anti-establishment comedy is far from perfect, but the best moments are riotously funny (for all the wrong reasons) and the film expresses the rebellious mood of America in 1970 with absolute accuracy. It manages to do that without ever commenting directly on the war. Though the setting is Korea, it's really Vietnam. The only time Altman and writer Ring Lardner come close to making an overt political statement is in their funniest one liner. When by-the-book Maj. Margaret Houlihan (Sally Kellerman) says of Dr. Hawkeye Pierce (Donald Sutherland), "I wonder how a degenerated person like that could have reached a position of responsibility in the Army Medical Corps."

"He was drafted," is the deadpan answer. In 1970, the line brought down the house.

War itself is really not a subject. The only gunshot in the film is used to end the climactic football game. The nameless broken bodies that are flown in to the hospital are the only evidence of the conflict. Altman shows war's destructiveness in those graphic wounds and the bloody operating rooms. Those moments had never been presented so realistically on screen. Audiences were horrified, and so any further comment would have been irrelevant. Altman's real targets are closer to home—organized religion and the military, both seen by the filmmakers as close-minded institutions, inimical to genuine human values. They're personified in the characters of Maj. Houlihan and Maj. Frank Burns (Robert Duvall), both far removed from their TV incarnations.

Did you Know?
The football sequence was directed by Andy Sidaris, who has gone on to become famous for his inimitable softcore action/sex comedies: *Hard Ticket to Hawaii, Picasso Trigger, Savage Beach* and many others.

As interpreted by Duvall, Burns is a more serious and sinister figure. He is such a forceful character that he would upset the shaky comic balance of the film if he didn't make such an early exit. "Hotlips" Houlihan is more troubling. She is transformed, presumably by the embarrassment of the shower scene, from a competent if narrow-minded nurse into a brainless cheerleader. The change may be due to over-enthusiastic improvisation on Sally Kellerman's part during the football sequence.

The protagonists are stronger characters, too. In the operating room, they're accomplished professionals. Outside, they're lecherous, sophomoric pranksters with a wide mean streak. Altman's direction is completely in tune with the doctors' knockabout attitude. He uses filters to give a rougher texture to the already rough surfaces of the MASH unit; long lenses that allow him to keep the camera at a distance to encourage ensemble improvisation; dialogue from one scene extended into the next; semilinear narrative. And within that often chaotic structure, the big scenes are

See also
McCabe and Mrs. Miller
Nashville
Mister Roberts
Patton
Good Morning, Vietnam
Battle Circus

masterful—the unforgettable microphone under the bed, the extended "suicide" sequence, complete with The Last Supper tableau, the use of the public address system as a cracked Greek chorus, even the nonsensical football game.

If, in hindsight, *M*A*S*H* seems harsher than it once did, it's still funny and original, and its anger is not misplaced.

Donald Sutherland (left) and Elliott Gould are Army surgeons Hawkeye Pierce and Trapper John McIntyre in *M*A*S*H*. The Kobal Collection

Cast: Donald Sutherland (Capt. Benjamin Franklin "Hawkeye" Pierce), Elliott Gould (Capt. John Francis Xavier "Trapper John" McIntyre), Tom Skerritt (Capt. Augustus Bedford "Duke" Forrest), Sally Kellerman (Maj. Margaret "Hot Lips" Houlihan), JoAnn Pflug (Lt. Maria "Hot Dish" Schneider), Robert Duvall (Maj. Frank Burns), Rene Auberjonois (Fr. John Patrick "Dago Red" Mulcahy), Roger Bowen (Lt. Col. Henry Blake), Gary Burghoff (Cpl. Walter "Radar" O'Reilly), Fred Williamson (Capt. Oliver Harmon "Spearchucker" Jones), John Schuck (Capt. Walter "Painless Pole" Waldowski), Bud Cort (Pvt. Lorenzo Boone), G. Wood (Gen. Hammond), David Arkin (Staff Sgt. Vollmer), Michael Murphy (Capt. Ezekiel "Me Lay" Marston), Indus Arthur (Lt. Leslie), Ken Prymus (Pfc. Seidman), Bobby Troup (Sgt. Gorman), Kim Atwood (Ho-Jon), Timothy Brown (Cpl. Judson); **Written by:** Ring Lardner Jr.; **Cinematography by:** Harold E. Stine; **Music by:** Johnny Mandel. **Producer:** 20th Century-Fox, Aspen, Ingo Preminger. **Awards:** Academy Awards '70: Best Adapted Screenplay; American Film Institute (AFI) '98: Top 100; Cannes Film Festival '70: Best Film; Golden Globe Awards '71: Best Film—Musical/Comedy, National Film Registry '96; National Society of Film Critics Awards '70: Best Film; Writers Guild of America '70: Best Adapted Screenplay; Nominations: Academy Awards '70: Best Director (Altman), Best Film Editing, Best Picture, Best Supporting Actress (Kellerman). **MPAA Rating:** R. **Running Time:** 116 minutes. **Format:** VHS, Beta, LV, Letterbox.

The Hound Salutes: Aldo Ray

With his bulky body, thick neck, and gruff, commanding voice, Aldo Ray was immediately typecast by Hollywood as an American primitive. Putting that character into a military setting was a natural step. Ray had been a Navy frogman in World War II, and after it, he'd worked as sheriff in his hometown of Crockett, California. He was actually considered for the role of Prewitt (eventually played by Montgomery Clift) in *From Here to Eternity*, and though he certainly would have given the film a different dramatic balance, in some ways, he is closer to James Jones's version of the character.

In Hollywood, Ray's career peaked early when he played the rough but sensitive Andy Hookens, a lumberjack who joins the Marines in *Battle Cry*. The adaptation of Leon Uris's best-seller was a huge commercial hit. Two years later, Ray played a much tougher character in a much tougher film, Anthony Mann's *Men in War*. Ray's a sergeant who engages a lieutenant, played by Robert Ryan, in a battle of wills over the direction a lost patrol will take. Both actors do fine work with roles that are tailored to their strengths.

Ray didn't fare as well in the troubled film version of Norman Mailer's *The Naked and the Dead*. His next work in the genre came with Blake Edwards's semi-comic *What Did You Do in the War, Daddy?* In 1968, he provided suitable support for John Wayne in his propagandistic misfire *The Green Berets*. After that, a combination of health and financial problems forced Ray to accept work anywhere he could find it, and so he appeared in numerous B-movies. His career bottomed out with his participation in a hardcore skin flick (*Sweet Savage*) but not in sex scenes. In 1986, he was kicked out of the Screen Actor's Guild for appearing in non-union films. Ray died of throat cancer and pneumonia in 1991.

Anthony Mann's war film is a bleak piece of work. The conventional elements used by Hollywood to put an entertaining gloss on grim subjects are missing—no romantic interests, no humor, no folksy characters, no real sentiment until almost the end. In their place are two actors playing flinty, combative opponents. Lt. Benson (Robert Ryan) has been ordered to lead his patrol to a distant objective, Hill 465. Sgt. Montana (Aldo Ray) means to get his shell-shocked Colonel (Robert Keith) back to safety. Montana has a Jeep; Benson wants it.

When Lt. Benson's platoon is introduced, the men are already at a low ebb. Their truck has been wrecked beyond repair and they've lost radio contact with their battalion. Montana's Jeep is their only chance to complete their mission, and they're not even sure about that. They know that the North Koreans have pushed their forces back and so they find themselves surrounded by snipers and other dangers. Baby-faced Cpl. Zwickley (Vic Morrow) has the shakes, either from disease or terror. Riordan (Phillip Pine) refuses to give up on the radio. Sergeants Killian (James Edwards) and Davis (L.Q. Jones) are the other veterans. Lt. Benson comandeers the Jeep at gunpoint and gets grudging support from Montana, the most experienced and lethal of the group.

Direct contact with the North Koreans is limited to a few short, deadly encounters. The conflict between Benson and Montana is more important. Benson cannot hide his uncertainty about the best way to proceed—if they should proceed at all—while Montana makes it clear that his only goal is to protect his catatonic Colonel. The two men despise and need each other in equal measures, and those are the only emotions that are revealed. These guys are names and ranks and little more. The viewer also sees a couple of pictures of families and a pin-up torn from a magazine. That's it; no conversations about sweethearts back home, no flashbacks. The focus is strictly limited to the war as these guys see it on the ground.

The details of combat are less certain. Would a veteran who knows that he is surrounded by snipers and that his companions are all ahead of him really stop to pick flowers? That's the most glaring example of dubious tactics, but not the only one. Even so, it is not a serious error because Ray and Ryan are both in top form. Ray's thick-bodied, swaggering bravado is a perfect counterpoint to Ryan's dark intelligence and perseverance in the face of his own indecision. Even when the rest of the action is slogging at a slow pace, their divided loyalties are sharp.

Working with cinematographer Ernest Haller, who shared an Oscar for *Gone with the Wind*, Mann makes the unforgiving landscape an important part of the story. They give the film the same somber tone that Mann achieves so often in his westerns. That fatalism will never be as popular as Hollywood's conventional escapism, but for this kind of war film, it is a perfect approach.

> "Tell me the story of the foot soldier and I will tell you the story of all wars."
>
> **Onscreen foreword**

> "God help us if it takes your kind to win this war."
>
> **Lt. Benson (Robert Ryan) on Sgt. Montana (Aldo Ray)**

> "Before you fight, you gotta think, and I can't think any more."
>
> **Lt. Benson**

See also

A Walk in the Sun
The Lost Patrol
The Steel Helmet
All the Young Men
Full Metal Jacket

American G.I.s with a North
Korean prisoner in *Men in War*.

Cast: Robert Ryan (Lt. Benson), Robert Keith (The Colonel), Aldo Ray (Sgt. Montana), Vic Morrow (Cpl. Zwickley), Phillip Pine (Sgt. Riordan), Nehemiah Persoff (Sgt. Lewis), James Edwards (Sgt. Killian), L.Q. (Justus E. McQueen) Jones (Sgt. Davis), Scott Marlowe (Pvt. Meredith), Adam Kennedy (Pvt. Maslow), Race Gentry (Pvt. Haines), Walter Kelley (Pvt. Ackerman), Anthony Ray (Pvt. Penelli), Robert Normand (Pvt. Christensen), Michael Miller (Pvt. Lynch), Victor Sen Yung (Korean sniper); **Written by:** Phillip Yordan, Ben Maddow; **Cinematography by:** Ernest Haller; **Music by:** Elmer Bernstein; **Technical Advisor:** John Dickson. **Producer:** Security, Sidney Harmon. **Running Time:** 100 minutes. **Format:** VHS, Beta.

Some see Lewis Milestone's Korean War film as an anti-war companion piece to *All Quiet on the Western Front*. Others note the onscreen introductory statement of grateful thanks for the cooperation of the United States Army and see it as an apology for military-political bungling. Milestone himself claimed that studio interference altered his original conception of the story. Who's right? An objective viewer can find arguments for both interpretations, though one isolated moment near the end tips the balance toward the hawkish side.

The setting is 1953, and the peace talks between the North Korean and the United Nations provide a framework for the battlefield action. In the language of diplomacy, the discussions are "frank"—neither side is moving an inch. During a break away from the table, one of the high-ranking Americans mutters, "These aren't just Orientals, they're Communists!" Those six words are a perfect summation of all the racial and political biases of the 1950s that are played out in other scenes, too. In context, the sentiment seems serious, not facetious or ironic, and the concluding patriotic rhetoric about preserving freedom for millions underscores that reading.

Whatever Milestone's intention, the body of the film is a well-made, visceral look at updated trench warfare.

Lt. Joe Clemons (Gregory Peck, who's considerably older than most lieutenants) is ordered to lead the 135 men of King Company up a strategically unimportant hill and to take it. Believing that he has reinforcements from Love Company to protect his flank, Clemons takes two platoons up the slope in a night attack and holds one platoon in reserve. What is supposed to be a piece of cake turns into a hard-fought assault where progress is measured in inches. Communications are so fouled up from the beginning that the generals actually think that Clemons is having no trouble. Later, for unclear reasons, the same commanders choose not to send in more men.

Milestone is most comfortable in the heaviest action, showing how desperately the men fight over this ugly patch of dry dirt. He and veteran cinematographer Sam Leavitt tell the story through a series of sharply defined and textured black-and-white images. James Webb's script, based on a book by Brig. Gen. S.L.A. Marshall (USAR), creates memorable characters with a few bold strokes. Franklin (Woody Strode) is the black soldier who seriously questions the necessity of the action. Lt. O'Hashi (George Shibata) is more committed. The supporting cast is filled with familiar faces—Rip Torn, George Peppard, Martin Landau, James Edwards, Norman Fell, Robert Blake, Gavin MacLeod, Bert Remsen—but the three leads are the most memorable and completely realistic. Each reacts to the situation differently. Clemons desperately tries to explain the truth of it to his superiors while caring for his men. O'Hashi supports him without question, while Franklin is looking for a way out of a fight that means nothing to him.

The soldiers' frustration at the lack of coordination and commitment of their senior leadership is emotionally wrenching. In the middle of the first wave of the attack, their own forces mistakenly turn searchlights on them. Concertina wire that was supposed to be flat-

> "Welcome to the meatgrinder."
>
> **North Korean propagandist**

> "What do I care about this stinkin' hill?"
>
> **Franklin (Woody Strode)**

See also

Twelve O'Clock High
All Quiet on the Western Front
A Walk in the Sun
Zulu
The Siege of Firebase Gloria
Hamburger Hill

Marines struggle to keep the high ground in Korea in *Pork Chop Hill*. Woody Strade (left) and Gregory Peck (second from right). The Kobal Collection

tened by shelling is still there when they approach it, and those are only the beginning. But every SNAFU is answered or explained until finally, it's all the fault of those Oriental Communists.

Given the cozy relationship that existed between Hollywood and the military in the post-war years, perhaps such equivocation is inevitable. Still, the outrage at the Army's mistakes is so strong and heartfelt that a more definitive conclusion is called for.

Cast: Gregory Peck (Lt. Joe Clemons), Harry Guardino (Forstman), Rip Torn (Lt. Russell), George Peppard (Fedderson), James Edwards (Cpl. Jurgens), Bob Steele (Kern), Woody Strode (Franklin), Robert (Bobby) Blake (Velie), Martin Landau (Marshall), Norman Fell (Sgt. Coleman), Bert Remsen (Lt. Cummings), George Shibata (Lt. O'Hashi), Biff Elliot (Boven), Barry Atwater (Davis), Martin Garth (S-2 officer), Lew Gallo (PI officer), Charles Aidman (Harrold), Leonard Graves (Lt. Cook), Ken Lynch (Gen. Trudeau), Paul Comi (Sgt. Kreucheberg), Cliff Ketchum (Cpl. Payne), Abel Fernandez (Kindley), Gavin MacLeod (Saxon); **Written by:** James R. Webb; **Cinematography by:** Sam Leavitt; **Music by:** Leonard Rosenman; **Technical Advisor:** Capt. Joseph G. Clemons Jr. **Producer:** United Artists, Sy Bartlett. **Running Time:** 97 minutes. **Format:** VHS, Beta, LV, Closed Caption.

The Hound Salutes: James Edwards

From the late 1940s until the mid-'50s, James Edwards's was virtually the only black face that moviegoers saw in war films. His numerous appearances are a matter of timing and body type.

In those years, the armed services made their first serious effort to end racial segregation, and Hollywood attempted to reflect that change, albeit with the halting half-measures that it always uses in approaching something different and not immediately profitable. For his part, Edwards looked like a soldier, and he had been one during World War II. He had the slim build and military bearing that audiences had been conditioned to expect of enlisted men in all of the unit pictures they had seen in the previous decade. Due no doubt to his military experience, Edwards appeared comfortable and experienced in a helmet and fatigues.

He found his first major supporting role in 1949 with Robert Ryan in Robert Wise's fine boxing drama, *The Set-Up*, and followed it with his first war film, the ambitious but finally disappointing *Home of the Brave*. It's one of Hollywood's first films to attempt to deal with racism, though its source is a play about anti-Semitism. Edwards is fine in a flawed role. Though he was given less to work with in his next war film, Sam Fuller's B-masterpiece *The Steel Helmet*, the role was meatier. He's the medic, Cpl. Thompson, who has to defend his decision to be fighting with the United States Army in Korea while he is denied basic rights back home.

Following that, Edwards had a virtual cameo in *The Caine Mutiny*. He was promoted to sergeant (and re-teamed with Robert Ryan) in *Men in War*, and he made it all the way to lieutenant in *Battle Hymn*. In *Pork Chop Hill* he had a black co-star in Woody Strode, but until that point, he had almost always been the only black character in his films. Then, in *The Manchurian Candidate*, his character is married and he experiences a brief dream-hallucination scene that fills the screen with members of a black garden club. Beyond those two films though, Edwards was almost always called upon to represent his race whether he wanted to or not. His career ended with another tiny cameo in *Patton*.

According to film historian Donald Bogle in *Toms, Coons, Mulattoes, Mammies, & Bucks: An Interpretative History of Blacks in American Films* (Viking. 1973), Edwards's career went into decline when he refused to testify before the House Un-American Activities Committee. At about the same time, Sidney Poitier became a more "safe" choice for producers looking for a young black actor.

Curiously, though, as far as war films are concerned, Edwards's contemporaneous counterpart was not Poitier but James Donald (see sidebar), a white British character actor of similar age and appearance. The two men appeared in many war films of their time—never together—as upright supporting characters who fill a necessary role to keep the story moving. James Edwards died in San Diego, California, on January 4, 1970.

THE STEEL HELMET

1951 Samuel Fuller ♫♫♫♫

Reportedly written in one week and filmed in 10 days, Sam Fuller's war film is a low-budget marvel. It tells a simple, carefully paced story without a single wasted frame. Though Fuller takes time to comment on other social issues, he has stripped the standard combat story down to its fundamentals, eliminating extraneous details.

The film begins literally at ground level with the opening credits shown over a G.I.'s helmet with a bullet hole prominent near the front. It raises slowly to reveal Sgt. Zack's (Gene Evans) wary eyes. Wounded, his hands tied behind him, he slowly crawls forward among dead Korean soldiers. He is freed by a bright, spunky Korean kid he calls Short Round (William Chun). But Zack wants nothing to do with the boy. He's the only survivor of his unit. The war is no place for a child, even a child with a rifle. But the kid is persistent. He's still there when Zack meets Cpl. Thompson (James Edwards), a black medic who's another lone survivor. The three of them join up with Lt. Driscoll's (Steve Brodie) small patrol, which has been sent out to establish an artillery observation post. They do that at a Buddhist temple, where most of the rest of the action takes place and where at least one North Korean is hiding.

Within that simple frame, Fuller addresses several forms of racism. Most obvious is Thompson's treatment back home. Sgt. Tanaka (Richard Loo), a *nisei* (second generation Japanese-American), has suffered similar discrimination. Both of them are called upon to defend their decision to fight for America and their answers are careful. Zack's casual racism is part of a veteran's emotional armor, a flexible "us vs. them" view of the war that changes with his perception of the enemy. Zack sums up with "He's a South Korean when he's running with you, and he's a North Korean when he's running after you."

The line is a perfect example of the film's skeptical attitude toward the Korean conflict and war in general. It's grim, fatalistic, completely without patriotic fervor. It's also funny. Sgt. Tanaka's speech about his bald mother is vintage Fuller, and the incident with the live grenade must be based on a real event. The various conflicts and problems that must be addressed in the temple are handled with the same dispatch. Fuller makes his points and moves on. He didn't have the time or money to do anything else.

The limitations of the budget are apparent in the final attacks by the North Koreans. Despite one character's yelling that there's a million of 'em out there, it looks more like a dozen or so at most. In most war films that would be a serious flaw, but not here. The battle is finished quickly and indecisively. *The Steel Helmet* is meant to be a snapshot look at one part of a war that was barely six months old when the film was released. Fuller has nothing to say about Korean politics or American involvement in them. He's interested in soldiers—guys like the ones he served with in North Africa and Europe during World War II. Causes and patriotism are unimportant.

> "**I** am no gook! I am Korean!"
>
> **Short Round (William Chun) to Sgt. Zack (Gene Evans)**

> "Look, lieutenant, you got nothing out there but rice paddies crawling with Commies just waiting to slap you between big hunks of rye bread and wash you down with fish eggs and vodka! Good luck."
>
> **Sgt. Zack to Lt. Driscoll (Steve Brodie)**

> "If you die, I'll kill ya!"
>
> **Sgt. Zack to prisoner he has just shot**

> "There is something about *The Steel Helmet* that we knew as children watching it that it was the real thing. It was the emotional truth of it. There was a sensibility of somebody who was there, who knew it in his soul."
>
> **Martin Scorsese in *The Typewriter, the Rifle and the Movie Camera*, a documentary about Samuel Fuller**

Did you Know?

The character played by Ke Huy Quan in Steven Spielberg's *Indiana Jones and the Temple of Doom* is named after Short Round.

See also

The Big Red One
Battleground
The Story of G.I. Joe
Pick-up on South Street

Cast: Gene Evans (Sgt. Zack), Robert Hutton (Pvt. Bronte), Steve Brodie (Lt. Driscoll), William Chun
("Short Round"), James Edwards (Cpl. Thompson), Richard Loo (Sgt. Tanaka), Harold Fong (The Red), Neyle Morrow (1st G.I.), Sid Melton (2nd G.I.), Richard
Monahan (Pvt. Baldy), Lynn Stalmaster (2nd Lieutenant); **Written by:** Samuel Fuller; **Cinematography by:** Ernest Miller;
Music by: Paul Dunlap. **Producer:** Lippert Productions, Samuel Fuller. **Running Time:** 84 minutes, **Format:** VHS,
Beta, LV.

VIETNAM WAR

Vietnam War on Screen

Conventional wisdom holds that Vietnam is the first war America experienced through television. It's true that during the years of American involvement, the images that people saw on the news and read about in newspapers had a profound influence on public opinion. After the war, though, the movies played a more important role in expressing the emotions and questions that had not been resolved when the helicopters took off from the roof of the American embassy in Saigon.

This cross-section of Vietnam films is bracketed by two little-known excellent documentaries that approach the war from opposite ends.

The first is Pierre Schoendoerffer's Academy Award winning *Anderson Platoon*, from 1966. The director, a veteran of the French colonial wars in Indochina, returned to the country and spent six weeks with an American First Air Cavalry unit under the command of a black West Point graduate. Schoendoerffer's grainy, black-and-white film has the hand-held look of American World War II documentaries, but he tells a much less triumphant story. He sees the same mistakes being made again, and he presents them without blame or comment.

Both Sam Fuller's *China Gate* and John Wayne's *The Green Berets* are meant to appeal to right-wing fire-eaters but, in the end, they're undone by cheesy production values and cheap special effects, not politics. Others, from D.W. Griffith to Oliver Stone, have proved that a filmmaker can get away with almost anything if he's entertaining enough. The Fuller and Wayne films simply don't measure up, and, to a degree, they poisoned the well for other directors. Doubtless, public antipathy toward the war itself had much more to do with that lapse. It was ten years before another attempt was made to comment on Vietnam.

The Boys in Company C is both a unit picture and a reasonably accurate microcosm of the slow escalation of American efforts. It's R. Lee Ermey's first appearance as a poetically profane drill instructor, and filmmakers Sidney J. Furie and Rick Natkin were the first to set their story during the pivotal Tet Offensive of 1968. (Many others would follow their lead.) Made in the same year, 1978, *Go Tell the Spartans* treats the historical dimension with even more complexity, commenting on the whole war in one small engagement. It works through a typically superb performance from Burt Lancaster, and is the great "lost" film of that war.

Both *Boys* and *Spartans* are modestly budgeted productions, so they are overshadowed by the first two "big" Vietnam films that came from the studios in the late 1970s. The first, Michael Cimino's *The Deer Hunter*, was wildly overpraised in its initial release. Time has made its narrative flaws more obvious, but anyone who dismisses the overheated melodrama and silly history is ignoring the film's emotional power. It was among the first works to admit the deep wounds that the war inflicted on American society, and to suggest that they would heal. That was something that people wanted and needed to believe.

Francis Ford Coppola's monumental *Apocalypse Now* treats the war as a waking dream. By the time his hallucinatory vision finally arrived on the screen, it had overcome a mountain of well-publicized problems, and had achieved a kind of mythic status that no film could match. Because it did not live up to boxoffice expectations, it was labeled as Coppola's first flop (following *The Godfather* films and *The Conversation*). But in the years since, it has developed a devoted following on video. When Coppola returned to the war, via the Arlington National Cemetery in 1987's *Gardens of Stone*, his tone was more somber.

The made-for-cable adaptation of Philip Caputo's *A Rumor of War* marks the beginning of a change in Vietnam films. Based on Caputo's tour of duty, it focuses more sharply on the men who actually fought the war. The decision-making process at the levels above them has little to do with the reality of the war as they know it, and so they try to survive and not make too many compromises. Oliver Stone's *Platoon* deals with similar subject matter, but for the first time, a major Hollywood film depicts Vietnam with the high-caliber pyrotechnics normally reserved for action films. Here, the graphic violence is overlaid on a more serious political base.

Following the financial success of *Platoon*, the studios became more receptive to other Vietnam-themed projects. Barry Levinson turns it into a stage for Robin Williams's comedy in *Good Morning, Vietnam*. John Irvin's *Hamburger Hill* is more successful right-wing propaganda than *The Green Berets*, but that is hardly a recommendation. Stanley Kubrick's *Full Metal Jacket* is a bleak, believable portrait of Marine boot camp that falls off precipitously when the focus shifts to Vietnam.

More recently, Patrick Sheane Duncan's *84 Charlie MoPic* is a successful experiment that follows a reconnaissance team through the lens of a motion picture photographer who is accompanying the men. Brian Trenchard-Smith's *The Siege of Firebase Gloria* takes the Tet Offensive as its starting point but, unlike virtually all other films about the war, it presents the North Vietnamese side, too, and is the second great sleeper of this group.

Finally, Glenn Silber and Barry Alexander Brown use news footage and interviews to tell *The War at Home*. Their documentary about the protests at the University of Wisconsin at Madison from 1963 to 1970 could have been made in almost any American college town. They present a portrait of the anti-war movement as a loose confederacy of individuals and groups united by a few overarching issues, the opposite of the well-organized movement, somehow controlled by "outsiders" that so many of its critics claimed. As Silber and Brown show it, the people who opposed the war were doing what they thought was right, just as the war's supporters did. Both sides were passionate, angry, and often intemperate. They overstated their cases. They were insulting and rude. Finally, they became violent and people died because of it.

That was the war in Vietnam and America.

Why is this Oscar-winning Vietnam documentary so little known? Most guides give it cursory attention, if any, and it's seldom mentioned in discussions of that war. The film is a rough, unpolished, direct look at the early days of American involvement that attempts no grand statements, no conclusions about the futility of foreign intervention in civil wars. It will not appeal to anyone trying to make partisan political points on either side of the conflict, and it contains comparatively little action footage. Instead, director Pierre Schoendoerffer captures the famous definition of war as long periods of boredom broken by moments of pure terror.

Schoendoerffer, who also narrates, is a veteran of the French campaign in Indochina. That experience is the basis for his fictional look at Vietnam, *317th Platoon*. He admits a certain feeling of responsibility for the situation there. In 1966, 13 years after he'd left, he went back with cameraman Dominique Merlin and soundman Raymond Adams to spend six weeks filming an American outfit. It turns out to be a platoon from the First Air Cavalry, the same unit commanded by Robert Duvall's Col. Kilgore in *Apocalypse Now*. As this group is introduced, a Catholic religious service is being conducted over the background action of an American artillery barrage.

The platoon is led by Lt. Anderson, a 24-year-old black West Point graduate. He has 33 men, 28 of them draftees, from all parts of America. Though several of them are introduced, only Reese, the South Carolina radio man, becomes a recognizable character. Schoendoerffer follows the group and limits his comments to brief explanations of where they are and what they are doing—a howitzer emplacement that must be guarded, a village that may be a Vietcong base, an injured child who needs to be airlifted out, another village, night patrol, rain, more rain, a hot meal. After a slow, relatively uneventful beginning, the physical action becomes more dangerous, but in unexpected ways, and those should not be revealed.

The one light moment, Reese's leave in Saigon, turns out to be more serious than he'd expected. When violence does occur, it is sudden, and Schoendoerffer presents it without embellishment in grainy, imperfectly focused images. No music to heighten tension, no editorial comment. He's right to film it that way. A brief stomach-churning glimpse beneath a lifted bandage is enough to make the viewer feel the destruction caused by a real bullet. And when the platoon comes under fire, the look on a wounded man's face is more moving than Hollywood's most graphic special effects.

> "It began on a Sunday in September, 1966. On this day, the Vietnamese in their pagodas try to appease all the souls of the unburied dead—wandering souls, those of beggars, prostitutes, and soldiers."
>
> **Introductory voice-over narration by Pierre Schoendoerffer**

See also

The Battle of Algiers
Go Tell the Spartans
317th Platoon
Battle of San Pietro

The film ends with the same sad note that it begins, and while that may be unsatisfactory to some viewers, it is appropriate for 1966 and a war that still has several years to go and thousands more lives to claim. Schoendoerffer realizes that fact, but leaves it unsaid.

Cinematography by: Dominique Merlin. **Producer:** Pierre Schoendoerffer. French. **Awards:** Academy Awards '67: Best Feature Documentary. **Running Time:** 62 minutes. **Format:** VHS, Beta.

Opinion has always been divided over Francis Ford Coppola's ambitious Vietnam epic. To some, it takes inexcusable liberties with the realities of the war and the geography of the country. Others criticize the crackpot pseudo-philosophical pretensions of the final act. Finally, many reviewers and moviegoers admit those flaws and love the film anyway. Place me in the third group. Repeated viewings over the years reveal a boldly realized hallucinatory vision of war and a cast of complex, complementary characters.

That opening layered montage—helicopters, distorted sounds of rotors, a thick row of jungle palms erupting in a wall of flame, a sweaty face fading in and out, the spooky beginning of The Doors' "The End"—establishes a mood that the film never really loses. It's heightened by the next scene in a hotel room, where Capt. Willard (Martin Sheen) shatters a mirror and collapses in a drunken breakdown. (The moment is real, by the way, as Eleanor Coppola recalls it in her book *Notes* (Simon & Schuster. 1979).)

The rest of the film takes its structure from Joseph Conrad's *Heart of Darkness*. Willard is assigned to go to a place deep in the Cambodian jungle where a Col. Kurtz (Marlon Brando) has gathered a Montagnard tribe and is slaughtering everyone around him. "His ideas and methods became . . . unsound," as a General (G.D. Spradlin) puts it. Willard is to assassinate him. To get there, Willard takes a small plastic boat, a Navy PBR, upriver. Its skipper is the no-nonsense Chief (Albert Hall, the forgotten star of the supporting cast). The crew is made up of the teenaged Mr. Clean (Laurence Fishburn, a teenager himself when the film was made); Lance (Sam Bottoms), a surfer with a keenly developed taste for various drugs; and Chef (Frederic Forrest), a friendly guy from the Big Easy.

Their first stop along the way is with Col. Kilgore's First Air Cavalry. The famous helicopter attack on a village to the stirring strains of Wagner's "Ride of the Valkyries" contains some of the best aerial combat scenes ever caught on film. (Yes, that is R. Lee Ermey from *Full Metal Jacket* as a pilot.) After that long and grimly funny sequence, the film takes on a darker cast. Much of the rest of the action is set at night—note the way Coppola and cinematographer Vittorio Storaro paint the jungle with luminous blues and greens in the tiger scene—and even the daylight looks muted and gray. The nightmarish quality intensifies steadily through the Playmates show, the attack on the sampan, and the bridge under siege. Then Kurtz (Marlon Brando) finally appears and some of the air goes out of the balloon.

The stories about the film's troubled production schedule are perhaps the most famous in Hollywood history. Sets destroyed by a typhoon; one star (Harvey Keitel) fired; Sheen hired and suffering a heart attack; finances drying up and Coppola dipping into his own pocket; and, finally, Brando showing up for work looking mountainous for the first time in his career. Audiences at the time were not used to seeing him like that, and his appearance is still all wrong for this alleged "warrior-priest."

"Saigon, shit. I'm still only in Saigon."

Capt. Willard (Martin Sheen)

"I wanted a mission and for my sins they gave me one; brought it up to me like room service. It was a real choice mission and when it was over, I'd never want another."

Capt. Willard

"If I say it's safe to surf this beach, Captain, it's safe to surf this beach!"

Col. Kilgore (Robert Duvall)

Note:

Apocalypse Now is available on cassette in at least two different editions. The best available now is the remastered 1992 version, which was produced under the supervision of cinematographer Storaro and sound editor Walter Murch. (Both won well-deserved Oscars for their original work on the film.) Both tape and laserdisc look superb throughout and they end, more appropriately I think, without the final air attack on the village that was shown in some theaters.

See also

Taxi Driver

A Time to Love and a Time to Die

Come and See

To make matters worse, the script by Coppola and John Milius introduces a hyperactive photo-journalist (Dennis Hopper) who's as jittery as a squirrel on speed. It's never completely clear whether he is meant to be such a comic character. Whatever the filmmakers' purpose, he is completely out of place. His nonsensical ramblings underline the weakness of the conclusion. Kurtz's ponderous pontifications never ring true either, and because of that, he and Willard do not connect. For the film to end properly, those two need to form some kind of relationship or understanding. As it is, they seldom appear in the same frame.

Attempting to compensate, Coppola empties his bag of director's tricks in the last reels and attempts to end the film on the same note of seriousness that it begins. He is at best only marginally successful, but that matters little. Compared to his other work of the period—*Godfather II*, *The Conversation*—*Apocalypse Now* is still a flawed masterpiece. If its facts and philosophy are suspect, the film somehow looks right, and the recurring images of water—bathing, washing, baptism, drowning—add a quality of redemption to an otherwise pointless war.

Though the film was considered a commercial failure in its initial release, it has developed a strong following over the years. To moviegoers and videophiles everywhere it is *the* Vietnam film. Why else would the Vietnamese owners of a new chain of restaurant/bars, with establishments in Hanoi and Ho Chi Minh City (formerly Saigon), name their business "Apocalypse Now?"

Cast: Marlon Brando (Col. Walter E. Kurtz), Martin Sheen (Capt. Benjamin L. Willard), Robert Duvall (Lt. Col. Kilgore), Frederic Forrest (Chef), Sam Bottoms (Lance Johnson), Scott Glenn (Colby), Albert Hall (Chief Phillips), Laurence "Larry" Fishburne (Mr. Clean), Harrison Ford (Col. Lucas), G.D. Spradlin (The General), Dennis Hopper (Photographer), Cynthia Wood (Playmate of the Year), Colleen Camp (Playmate), Linda Carpenter (Playmate), Tom Mason (Supply sergeant), James Keane (Kilgore's gunner), Damien Leake (Kilgore's gunner), Jack Thibeau (Soldier in trench), R. Lee Ermey (Helicopter pilot), Vittorio Storaro (T.V. photographer), Francis Ford Coppola (T.V. director); **Written by:** John Milius, Michael Herr, Francis Ford Coppola; **Cinematography by:** Vittorio Storaro; **Music by:** Carmine Coppola. **Producer:** United Artists, Francis Ford Coppola. **Awards:** Academy Awards '79: Best Cinematography, Best Sound; British Academy Awards '79: Best Director (Coppola), Best Supporting Actor (Duvall); Cannes Film Festival '79: Best Film; Golden Globe Awards '80: Best Director (Coppola), Best Supporting Actor (Duvall), Best Score; National Society of Film Critics Awards '79: Best Supporting Actor (Forrest); American Film Institute (AFI) '98: Top 100; Nominations: Academy Awards '79: Best Adapted Screenplay, Best Art Direction/Set Decoration, Best Director (Coppola), Best Film Editing, Best Picture, Best Supporting Actor (Duvall). **Budget:** 31.5M. **Boxoffice:** 78.8M. **MPAA Rating:** R. **Running Time:** 153 minutes. **Format:** VHS, Beta, LV, CD-I, Letterbox.

THE BOYS IN COMPANY C

1977 Sidney J. Furie

If John Wayne's *The Green Berets* portrays American involvement in Vietnam as right-wing patriotic propaganda, the pendulum swings the other way in Sidney Furie's realistic, disillusioned look at the war. Structurally, it's a conventional unit picture that follows five young men from their induction into the Marines and through their first months of combat duty at a pivotal moment in history. The story ends on January 30, 1968, when the North Vietnamese Tet Offensive begins.

Voice-over narrator Alvin Foster (James Canning) keeps careful notes. He's a writer who hopes to turn his military experience into a book, and so the viewer always knows where and when the action is taking place. Alvin, from Emporia, Kansas, is one of five "boys" who take the oath on August 27, 1967, in San Diego. Joining him in Company C is Tryone Washington (Stan Shaw) from Chicago. Initially, he hopes to use his service in Vietnam to facilitate the drug business he's involved in back home. Billy Ray Pike (Andrew Stevens) is a hotshot athlete from Galveston, Texas, who has enlisted because it's the right thing to do. Long-haired peacenik Dave Bisbee (Craig Wasson), on the other hand, is brought to the induction center in handcuffs. Brooklynite Vinnie Fazio (Michael Lembeck) thinks he knows all the angles and figures to weasel his way out of combat. This mix of draftees and volunteers comes under the none-too-tender care of Sgt. Aquilla (Santos Morales) and Sgt. Loyce (R. Lee Ermey), whose paint-blistering tirades have the ring of first-hand experience.

The basic training scenes cover familiar territory, though some of the individual problems are hurriedly introduced and resolved. (Several explanatory scenes may have been left on the cutting room floor.) The intention of the scenes remains clear, though. Washington is the natural leader of the group, but it's a role that he does not want to accept. The pressures of indoctrination force him to take on the responsibility. The situation and the characters are updated World War II stereotypes, but they're handled so forcefully the cliches seem fresh. When the action progresses to Vietnam, the tone darkens.

Director Furie and co-writer Rick Natkin depict the war strictly in terms of black and white. The South Vietnamese military is corrupt; American officers are ambitious incompetents who sacrifice men to advance their careers; Vietnamese peasants are innocent children; North Vietnamese soldiers are patriots. Doubtless, there is a degree of truth in each of those simplifications, but to leave them at that is too easy. The filmmakers take more care with the five protagonists. The relationship between Washington and Pike, who quickly finds his way into a drug habit, is believably complex. In the same way, the grunt's-eye view of the war is properly confused and senseless. The guys arrive as North Vietnamese activity is intensifying in the South, and so it is completely chaotic to them. They never realize precisely who their enemy is or why they are fighting. The filmmakers' attempt to use a soccer game as a metaphor for the war is not a completely successful conclusion, but it's difficult to come up with anything that's more appropriate. Without

> "From now on you will not eat, sleep, blow your nose, or scratch your ass until someone tells you to do so."
>
> **Receiving sergeant (Stan Johns) to a bus filled with inductees**

> "Right now the casualty rate for young Marines is over 50%. If you don't pay attention, you are going to be that private in the body bag."
>
> **Sgt. Loyce (R. Lee Ermey)**

> "If you're gonna be dumb enough to pull a gun on a man, you'd better be smart enough to pull the trigger."
>
> **Washington (Stan Shaw) to Pike (Andrew Stevens)**

> "I guess we'll keep on walking into one bloody mess after another until somebody finally figures out that living has got to be more important than winning."
>
> **Foster's (James Canning) closing voice-over**

See also

Battle Cry
An Officer and a Gentleman
Full Metal Jacket
Sands of Iwo Jima

Michael Lembeck and Andrew Stevens are two of the young Marines of Company C. Del Valle Archives

dismissing the over-reliance on antiestablishment cliches, the film does present a consistent, passionate view of the war.

Though *The Boys in Company C* was released in the same year as the more expensive, ambitious, and prestigious *The Deer Hunter*, today it is clearly a much better film—more entertaining, and perhaps even more insightful.

Cast: Stan Shaw (Tyrone Washington), Andrew Stevens (Billy Ray Pike), James Canning (Alvin Foster), Michael Lembeck (Vinnie Fazio), Craig Wasson (Dave Bisbee), R. Lee Ermey (Sgt. Loyce), James Whitmore Jr. (Lt. Archer), Scott Hylands (Capt. Collins), Noble Willingham (Sgt. Curry), Santos Morales (Sgt. Aquilla), Claude Wilson (Roy Foster), Drew Michaels (Col. Metcalfe), Karen Hilger (Betsy), Peggy O'Neal (Nancy Bisbee), Stan Johns (Receiving sergeant); **Cameo(s):** Rick Natkin; **Written by:** Sidney J. Furie, Rick Natkin; **Cinematography by:** Godfret A. Godar; **Music by:** Jaime Mendoza-Nava. **Producer:** Andre Morgan. **MPAA Rating:** R. **Running Time:** 127 minutes. **Format:** VHS, Beta, LV.

Sam Fuller's worst war film is worth watching—or at least scanning—for several reasons. The most obvious is the bizarre casting. Then there is the unpersuasive attempt to recreate Vietnam on a studio backlot, which would be duplicated with not much more success years later by Stanley Kubrick in *Full Metal Jacket*. Finally, both the screw-loose plotting and the rabid Red-baiting have become unintentionally comic with the passage of time.

A voice-over introduction sets a hyperbolic tone: "With the end of the Korean War, France was left alone to hold the hottest front in the world and became the barrier between Communism and the rape of Asia." Moments later, we learn that because the dirty Reds have put the Vietnamese town of Sun Toy under siege, a little boy's (Warren Hsieh) pet puppy is about to be eaten! Presumably because 1957 American audiences did not know much about the country or the war, Fuller spends most of the first act spinning out a fanciful interpretation of the situation, blaming many of the country's problems on the Chinese Communists and their massive underground ammunition bunker at China Gate. The French Legionnaires decide to blow it up, and call in explosives expert Sgt. Brock (Gene Barry). The only person who can lead them from Sun Toy to China Gate is Lucky Legs (Angie Dickinson), who is allegedly half-Chinese. She's also Brock's ex, and if that weren't enough, the kid with the puppy is their son! That's doubly hard to believe because the stars generate all the sexual chemistry of two wet paper towels.

After that's been established, the already pokey action stops cold for Goldie (Nat "King" Cole) to sing the theme song. Then off they go, with half a dozen or so more Legionnaires and a couple of boxes of highly explosive detonators. At every opportunity, one or more of these guys bears his tortured soul, and as they get closer to the Chicoms, it becomes apparent that our girl Lucky has been a sort of one-woman welcoming committee whose mission is to boost morale in every way that she can. All the guys know her because she makes regular visits to the Chinese to deliver cognac and sex, even though her main squeeze is the commander of China Gate, Maj. Cham (Lee Van Cleef), yet another half-Chinese who is in line for a promotion to Moscow.

With only a few exceptions, the combat scenes are as phony as the rest. They were filmed on cheap-looking sets with little originality or energy. Nothing on screen comes close to Fuller's better work in *The Steel Helmet* and *The Big Red One*. Still, *China Gate* is instructive. It's a perfect example of Hollywood's attempt to turn every post-war conflict into another World War II. When the film does try to draw any distinctions, it still reduces the action to good guys vs. bad guys. If a few Americans will just go over there and blow up some stuff and shoot some guys, those benighted foreigners will see the error of their ways and everything will straighten itself out.

See also

317th Platoon
The Green Berets

That's a bit of an oversimplification, but given the loopy politics of *China Gate*, it's not too far off the mark.

Sgt. Brock (Gene Barry) gives a
puppy to a Vietnamese boy
(Warren Hsieh) in *China Gate*. The
Kobal Collection

Cast: Gene Barry (Sgt. Brock), Angie Dickinson (Lucky Legs), Nat "King" Cole (Goldie), Paul Dubov (Capt. Caumong), Lee Van Cleef (Maj. Cham), George Givot (Cpl. Pigalle), Marcel Dalio (Father Paul), Gerald Milton (Pvt. Andreades), Neyle Morrow (Leung), Maurice Marsac (Col. De Sars), Warren Hsieh (The Boy), Paul Busch (Cpl. Kruger), Sasha Hardin (Pvt. Jaszi), James Hong (Charlie), Walter Soo Hoo (Guard), Weaver Levy (Khuan); **Written by:** Samuel Fuller; **Cinematography by:** Joseph Biroc; **Music by:** Max Steiner, Victor Young. **Producer:** Fox, Samuel Fuller. **Running Time:** 97 minutes. **Format:** VHS.

The years have heightened the flaws in Hollywood's first major attempt to address the Vietnam War. It remains at times a moving film despite director Michael Cimino's excesses and lapses. The main characters are strong, with the four young leads doing very good work. Seen as any kind of serious comment on the war or the country of Vietnam, it is ludicrous at best, racist at worst.

The story opens in a Pennsylvania steel mill on the morning that Steven (John Savage) is going to get married. Just a few days later, he and his best friends Michael (Robert De Niro) and Nick (Christopher Walken) will join the Army and go to Vietnam. Nick is dating Linda (Meryl Streep), though they are not too serious, and she and Michael are also attracted to each other. The shattering experiences the guys are subjected to in Vietnam change everything. Those are the bare bones of the plot, and with a few alterations that synopsis could fit many American war films. Cimino buries that simple story beneath tons of extraneous details, often losing sight of it completely in sprawling scenes that add nothing.

In the first hour, for example, a long scene in a bar shows us how close the three male characters and their other friends are. After a quick scene describing Linda's abusive, drunken father, the Russian Orthodox wedding is played out, with full attention given to the trappings, the singing, the ritual. Then it's on to the combination wedding-farewell party, with more singing and dancing and drinking and bonding. Finally, the ritual deer hunt in the mountains is conducted, and that involves still more bonding, and what sounds like the entire Mormon Tabernacle Choir in celestial accompaniment during the holy moment when the buck is stalked.

Only then, more than an hour after the opening credits, does the scene shift to Vietnam. From that moment on, Cimino takes his cues from John Wayne's *The Green Berets*. His North Vietnamese are sadistic beasts who toss grenades into shelters filled with helpless women and children, and force American captives to play Russian roulette for their amusement. Admittedly, those scenes are staged with power, but later the appearance of Julien (Pierre Segui), a jaded cosmopolitan Frenchman, at a Russian roulette gambling den, implies that the suicidal game is meant to be a metaphor for America's seduction into Euro-Asian corruption. Whatever his intention, Cimino goes bravely forth, staging his big finish during the fall of Saigon, again using chaotic action and cacophonous sound to distract viewers from the massive narrative lapses.

That said, record-breaking audiences in 1978 ignored those flaws, and so did the Academy of Motion Picture Arts and Sciences when it gave the director and the film the top Oscars. What they understood then was that the film connected directly with the nation's ambivalent, contradictory feelings about the war and the men who fought it. In the quieter moments—from the opening notes of Stanley Myers's elegiac score, so beautifully played by guitarist John Williams, to the closing chorus of "God Bless America"—the film touches the right emotional

"One shot, that's what it's all about. A deer has to be taken with one shot. I try to tell people that, they don't listen."

Michael (Robert DeNiro) to his friends

"You know, I love Mike's car. Yeah, some cars, they just sit. I mean, you never know with a car like this where the hell it's gonna take you."

Axel (Chuck Aspegren) on Michael's Cadillac land yacht.

"What *The Deer Hunter* told me was what I already knew and believed in: No matter how horrid the notion of war, Robert De Niro would end up staring soulfully at the beautiful, long-suffering Meryl Streep."

William Goldman, *Adventures in the Screen Trade* (Warner Books. 1983)

See also

Coming Home
Taxi Driver
Heaven's Gate

Nick (Christopher Walken) begins to show the strain of his imprisonment by the Vietcong in *The Deer Hunter*. The Kobal Collection

chords. One can argue, as writer William Goldman does persuasively, that *The Deer Hunter* is a "comic book movie," but no one can deny that the film delivered a message that people were ready to accept.

Cast: Robert De Niro (Michael), Christopher Walken (Nick), Meryl Streep (Linda), John Savage (Steven), George Dzundza (John), John Cazale (Stan), Chuck Aspegren (Axel), Rutanya Alda (Angela), Shirley Stoler (Steven's mother), Amy Wright (Bridesmaid), Mady Kaplan (Axel's girl), Mary Ann Haenel (Stan's girl), Richard Kuss (Linda's father), Pierre Segui (Julien), Joe Grifasi (Bandleader), Christopher Colombi Jr. (Wedding man), Joe Strnad (Bingo caller), Paul D'Amato (The Sergeant); **Written by:** Michael Cimino, Deric Washburn, Louis Garfinkle; **Cinematography by:** Vilmos Zsigmond; **Music by:** John Williams, Stanley Myers. **Producer:** Universal, Barry Spikings, Michael Cimino, John Peverall. **Awards:** Academy Awards '78: Best Director (Cimino), Best Film Editing, Best Picture, Best Sound, Best Supporting Actor (Walken); Directors Guild of America Awards '78: Best Director (Cimino); Golden Globe Awards '79: Best Director (Cimino); Los Angeles Film Critics Association Awards '78: Best Director (Cimino), National Film Registry '96; New York Film Critics Awards '78: Best Film, Best Supporting Actor (Walken); National Society of Film Critics Awards '78: Best Supporting Actress (Streep); American Film Institute (AFI) '98: Top 100; Nominations: Academy Awards '78: Best Actor (De Niro), Best Cinematography, Best Original Screenplay, Best Supporting Actress (Streep). **MPAA Rating:** R. **Running Time:** 183 minutes. **Format:** VHS, Beta, LV, Letterbox, DVD.

Patrick Sheane Duncan's semi-experimental view of a reconnaissance patrol is not for all tastes. He takes the idea of cinema verite to a level that traditionalists may not appreciate. The premise is that all of the action is seen through the lens of a combat cameraman who's making a training film. It will be called "Lessons Learned" and it's the brainchild of Second Lt. Richard Drewry (Jonathan Emerson) who will be making his first trip out into the bush with a veteran squad. MoPic (Byron Thomas) is the guy behind the 16mm. camera.

It's August 1, 1969.

The five-man squad is led by "O.D.," Sgt. O'Donovan (Richard Brooks), "a walking razor blade" who makes it clear from the outset that he thinks the idea stinks. The last thing he needs in his life is a "cherry" second lieutenant. Easy (Nicholas Cascone), the class clown, is a short-timer with 27 days left before he goes home. Spec. 4 Baldwin, "Pretty Boy" (Jason Tomlins) is Easy's more retiring friend. Out in the field, everyone wants to be close to him because he's so lucky; never gets a scratch while other guys are blown away. Hammer (Christopher Burgard) carries the big M-60 machine gun and is the most enthusiastically violent of the group. Spec. 5 Frye, "Cracker" (Glenn Morshower) is their huge, quiet father figure.

The patrol begins slowly, with O.D. and the lieutenant working out who's in charge. It's a complex matter, with the untested officer deferring to the non-com but being forced to draw lines. As they move farther from their drop point, the presence of the Vietcong becomes more apparent, with O.D. analyzing booby traps and ambushes. But before the enemy activity takes center stage, each man takes a turn in front of the camera and explains who he is and how he came to be in Vietnam. Easy was "volunteered" by a judge. Cracker thinks the Army is an equal opportunity employer. O.D., whose anger is an important survival skill, has little to say directly. To Drewry, the Army's a corporation, "like Gulf+Western," and he's a junior executive who is using this patrol as an important stepping stone in his career.

Most of the graphic violence is held back until the second half, and even then Duncan handles it in unexpected ways. Given the strict limits he has placed on point-of-view, he cannot use many conventional devices to create suspense. He doesn't cut between faces; his jumps in time are naturalistic. A shot ends when MoPic (and director of photography Alan Caso) turns off the camera or falls down. Contact with the North Vietnamese almost always comes without preparation, giving this fiction the jolting surprises normally found in documentaries. In the most moving scenes involving casualties and prisoners, Duncan stretches the limits of his naturalistic approach, but he doesn't go too far.

Though more expensive productions contain more careful and elaborate effects, few are any more wrenching. Duncan makes the physical and mental effects of violence—violence given and violence received—all too immediate and painful. Part of that sense of

> "**Wars don't** come along very often. It's the chance of a lifetime for a career officer. Combat duty's the foundation of a successful career."
>
> **"LT" (Jonathan Emerson)**

> "We're the sanest killers the Army's got, O.D. says."
>
> **Hammer (Christopher Burgard)**

> "In the monsoon, dry socks are better than sex."
>
> **Pretty Boy (Jason Tomlins)**

> "On a good day, you can smell cigarette smoke a quarter mile away, especially menthols."
>
> **O.D. (Richard Brooks)**

See also

Come and See
Anderson Platoon
The Battle of Algiers
The Green Berets
Courage under Fire

Byron Thames, Richard Brooks, and Jonathan Emerson in *84 Charlie MoPic.* The Kobal Collection

hyperrealism comes from the fine ensemble acting and the careful use of military props that seem to be authentic. Whether it's absolutely faithful to the time and place is not so important.

From the opening image of universal leader to the final shot, *84 Charlie MoPic* looks like the real deal.

Cast: Richard Brooks (O.D.), Christopher Burgard (Hammer), Nicholas Cascone (Easy), Jonathan Emerson (L.T.), Glenn Morshower (Cracker), Jason Tomlins (Pretty Boy), Byron Thames (MoPic); **Written by:** Patrick Sheane Duncan; **Cinematography by:** Alan Caso; **Music by:** Donovan. **Producer:** The Charlie MoPic Company, Michael Nolin. **Boxoffice:** $154,264. **MPAA Rating:** R. **Running Time:** 89 minutes. **Format:** VHS, Beta, LV.

The first third of Stanley Kubrick's take on the Vietnam War is as powerful and shocking as any film ever made about the military. That's the famous Parris Island section, which made Sgt. R. Lee Ermey a star. Though he had played an essentially identical role in *The Boys in Company C*, under Kubrick's direction, the stereotypical drill instructor was raised to new heights. As Gunnery Sgt. Hartman, Ermey achieves cinematic immortality.

In the film's opening shots, we see close-ups of new Marine recruits getting their heads shaved. The next shot follows Hartman as he strides through a barracks and completes the first stage of the young men's intimidating indoctrination into the Marine Corps. The scene also establishes the measured pace that Kubrick maintains throughout. Booming, gloriously profane, and imaginative, Sgt. Hartman is a force of nature that will mold these boys into killing machines. At that point, most war films would turn to the young men, sketch out their pasts and then show their transformation into a cohesive unit. Kubrick isn't interested. These kids are names and archetypes—Joker (Matthew Modine) the smart aleck; Cowboy (Arliss Howard) from Texas; Leonard, A.K.A. "Gomer Pyle" (Vincent D'Onofrio), the screwup—who will react differently to Hartman's approach.

Kubrick makes Ermey such a mesmerizing force that one key early element is easy to overlook. From the first moment we see him in the barber's chair, before we even know his name, it is abundantly clear that Leonard is mad. He has that familiar vacant, smiling, dull-eyed expression of evil that Kubrick also uses to define Little Alex in *A Clockwork Orange* and Jack Torrance in *The Shining*. The other characters do not see it, and so the inevitable confrontation between Hartman and Leonard is all the more horrifying.

The middle section of the film establishes Joker's role as a dissatisfied writer for *Stars & Stripes*, working behind the lines during the Tet Offensive of 1968, and his desire for some "trigger time" with his old pals from basic. That's where Kubrick shapes his view of the war as a Strangelovian exercise in futility. A nameless Colonel could have been quoting Jack D. Ripper when he states, "We are here to help the Vietnamese, because inside every Gook there is an American trying to get out. It's a hardball world, son. We've got to try to keep our heads until this peace craze blows over." That part of the film stresses the sexual and moral corruption of the South Vietnamese, and distinguishes American and North Vietnamese reactions to it. As Kubrick and co-writers Gustav Hasford and Michael Herr put it, Americans indiscriminately kill civilians and cattle while the North Vietnamese specifically target important people.

> "Parris Island, South Carolina, the United States Marine Corps Recruit Depot—an eight-week college for the phony tough and the crazy brave."
>
> **Joker (Matthew Modine) in voice-over**

> "Your rifle is only a tool. It is the hard heart that kills."
>
> **Sgt. Hartman (R. Lee Ermey)**

> "I wanted to be the first kid on my block to get a confirmed kill."
>
> **Joker to a TV reporter**

In the third part, a new Kubrickian sociopath named Animal Mother (Adam Baldwin) is introduced, and the focus shifts to a patrol searching through the bombed out city of Hue to root out a sniper. That is where the filmmakers comment most pointedly on the war itself. They see it as a dead-end, winless enterprise where one strategy, based on flawed information, leads inevitably to escalation and deaths that serve no purpose. That's certainly a valid artis-

Animal Mother (Adam Baldwin) and Joker (Matthew Modine) are pinned down by a Vietcong sniper in *Full Metal Jacket.* The Kobal Collection

tic interpretation of history. Many other films have made the same points, often more eloquently. But Kubrick isn't interested in eloquence, either.

The three sections are unmistakably separated from each other. The first stands on its own, though key elements are restated at the end. Given Kubrick's creative power and the artistic freedom from studio interference that he always enjoyed, he tells the story that he wants to tell, and the "broken" structure is intentional. For the viewer expecting a "traditional" war film, the result is disconcerting, frustrating, and somehow unfinished. Most Kubrick fans will admit that *Paths of Glory* and *Dr. Strangelove* are more enjoyable, but even if their man is not in top form, *Full Metal Jacket* is challenging, and repeated viewings reveal more details and connections.

Cast: Matthew Modine (Pvt. Joker), R. Lee Ermey (Gunnery Sgt. Hartman), Vincent D'Onofrio (Pvt. Leonard "Gomer Pyle"), Adam Baldwin (Animal Mother), Dorian Harewood (Eightball), Arliss Howard (Cowboy), Kevyn Major Howard (Rafterman), Ed O'Ross (Lt. Touchdown), John Terry (Lt. Lockhart), Jon Stafford (Doc Jay), Marcus D'Amico (Hand Job), Kieron Jecchinis (Crazy Earl), Bruce Boa (Col. Pogue), Kirk Taylor (Sgt. Payback), Tim Colceri (Door Gunner), Ian Tyler (Lt. Cleves), Gary Landon Mills (Donlon), Sal Lopez (T.H.E. Rock), Ngoc Le (V.C. sniper), Peter Edmund (Snowball), Tan Hung Francione (ARVN pimp), Leanne Hong (Motorbike hooker), Costas Dino Chimona (Chili); Written by: Stanley Kubrick, Michael Herr, Gustav Hasford; Cinematography by: Doug Milsome; Music by: Abigail Mead; Technical Advisor: R. Lee Ermey. Producer: Stanley Kubrick, Warner. Awards: Nominations: Academy Awards '87: Best Adapted Screenplay. Boxoffice: 46.3M. MPAA Rating: R. Running Time: 116 minutes. Format: VHS, Beta, LV, 8mm, Closed Caption.

The Hound Salutes: Stanley Kubrick

Stanley Kubrick is the most problematic of modern film-makers. Critical reaction to him has been favorable but mixed. Though his work has sparked debate and controversy among his many admirers, his films have not made much money. From 1961, when he moved to England, until his death in 1999, he shunned Hollywood and America. In those same years, his ideas—as they are revealed in his films—became more refined and bleak. He came to pay little more than lip service to conventional characters, action, and plot, concentrating instead on pure image. Even so, he never had any trouble finding studio backing—usually from Warner Bros.—and, more surprisingly, he was given complete artistic control over any project he deigned to consider. No other mainstream filmmaker, save Steven Spielberg, has enjoyed such freedom in a competitive and hierarchical industry.

Kubrick began his career at 17 as a staff photographer for *Look* magazine. He took the plunge into short documentaries and low-budget crime films in the 1950s, and received his first recognition for *The Killing*, a tough heist thriller. A year later, he made *Paths of Glory*, an angry indictment of the military, focused on a poorly planned French offensive in World War I. In those two films, Kubrick's concerns with violence and the flawed nature of human beings are already taking shape. Those ideas would be wonderfully magnified in his comic Cold War masterpiece, *Dr. Strangelove: Or How I Learned to Stop Worrying and Love the Bomb*. Arguably his best film, it is certainly his most successful and involving narrative, one that combines first-rate ensemble acting with suspense and intelligent humor.

Kubrick continued to explore the roots of violence in *2001: A Space Odyssey*, *A Clockwork Orange*, and *The Shining*. Finally, he returned to the subject of war with *Full Metal Jacket*, a curiously divided film. The famous first act, covering Marine basic training at Parris Island, defies description. It is as fine a 40 minutes of film as Kubrick ever shot. Playing an exaggerated version of himself, Sgt. R. Lee Ermey overpowers the screen and the viewer. When the focus shifts to Vietnam—less than persuasively re-created in England—the level of intensity falls off precipitously. That's what Kubrick intended. Apparently, he did not mean for his viewers to engage in the traditional willing suspension of disbelief. Thematically, he was continuing the indictment of the military and humanity that he had begun 30 years before in *Paths of Glory* and chose to let the ideas and images speak for themselves.

That intellectual approach makes Kubrick's work easy to admire, to dissect and discuss, but difficult to enjoy. He treated the medium seriously and tried to express complex and unpopular beliefs. It's difficult and unfair, then, to be too critical of his failure to entertain. He was more than an entertainer, and if he failed to meet the expectations he raised, he was ambitious and challenging to the end.

Books:

Stanley Kubrick: A Biography. John Baxter. Carroll & Graf. 1997.

Stanley Kubrick: A Biography. Vincent LoBrutto. Donald I. Fine. 1997.

GARDENS OF STONE

1987 Francis Ford Coppola ♪♪♪♥

For his second Vietnam film, Francis Ford Coppola answers the cinematic pyrotechnics of *Apocalypse Now* with a more somber tone. The two films are closely connected with overlapping casts, but the sense of personal loss that hangs over *Gardens of Stone* is dark and palpable. It can be traced, at least in part, to the death of Coppola's son Giancarlo in a boating accident during the production. It eerily mirrors the film's plot, which begins with the funeral of Jackie Willow (D.B. Sweeney) at Arlington National Cemetery.

Flash back to Willow's arrival at Fort Myer, Virginia, in 1968 to serve with the Army's 3rd Infantry, "the Old Guard." As Sgt. "Goody" Nelson (James Earl Jones) puts it, "We are the nation's toy soldiers. We march with rifles that cannot shoot. We fix bayonets that cannot stick. We are the Kabuki theater of the profession of arms, jester in the court of Mars, god of war." The Old Guard's role is ceremonial, and Arlington National Cemetery is its stage for "drops" (the unit's colloquial term for burials) and other rituals. Willow is the son of a sergeant. He finds two father figures in Nelson and Sgt. Clell Hazard (James Caan). Hazard takes a particular interest in the younger man and helps him develop the leadership skills that will take him to Officer Candidate School.

> "There is no front in Vietnam—not like other wars. Hell, it's not even a war. Nothing to win, no way to win it."
>
> **Sgt. Clell Hazard (James Caan)**

> "Here's to us and those like us. Damn few left."
>
> **Toast used as refrain**

> "A soldier in the right place at the right time can change the world."
>
> **Sgt. Jackie Willow (D.B. Sweeney)**

At the same time, Hazard tells Jackie and everyone else not to be so enthusiastic about Vietnam. Having served there, he thinks the war is unwinnable. If it is going to be continued though, he would rather serve as an instructor at Fort Benning, where his experience might keep other soldiers alive. But his commanding officer, Capt. Homer Thomas (Dean Stockwell), knows his value and denies his requests for transfer. At the core of the film is Jackie's growth as a soldier, often revealed through the help that he gives to Pvt. Wildman (Casey Siemaszko), the platoon screw-up.

Both Hazard and Willow are involved with unpromising personal relationships. Hazard meets Samantha Davis (Anjelica Huston) in the lobby of their apartment building. Is there any future for a soldier and a reporter for *The Washington Post* in 1968? Willow is already carrying a torch for Rachel Feld (Mary Stuart Masterton), daughter of an ambitious well-connected Colonel who sees Jackie as a poor match. Those plotlines follow a predictable course. One moment of physical violence meant to demonstrate the intensity of the times comes across as forced, insincere, and too easily resolved, and a war games sequence also has an obligatory feel. Also, at times it seems that writer Ron Bass may have given each of these characters too much blatant political baggage to carry, but, well, maybe we did carry too much blatant political baggage then.

In visual terms, Coppola treats the cemetery and the Old Guard with the proper respect, and he makes inventive use of Washington locations. That attitude toward the military recalls John Ford's cavalry and World War II films, and, doubtless, the director had those in mind. If Ford had made it, he might have cast John Wayne and Ward Bond as Hazard and Nelson, and a young Henry Fonda for Willow. Like Ford, Coppola recognizes the Army as an organization—a family—that takes care of its own. Coppola, however, is not as uncritical as Ford could be. By placing Laurence

See also

Apocalypse Now
The War at Home
Born on the Fourth of July
She Wore a Yellow Ribbon

Fishburne, Sam Bottoms, and Bill Graham in supporting roles, he reminds viewers of the madness of *Apocalypse Now*. By focusing on Hazard's well-grounded opinions, he is able to balance a pro-military attitude with equally strong anti-war views and not come across as hypocritical.

True, that point of view was virtually unheard of at the time, but Coppola brings it home with sorrowful believability.

James Caan, D.B. Sweeney, and James Earl Jones share a happy moment in *Gardens of Stone*. The Kobal Collection

Cast: James Caan (Sgt. Clell Hazard), James Earl Jones (Sgt. Maj. "Goody" Nelson), D.B. Sweeney (Pvt. Jackie Willow), Anjelica Huston (Samantha Davis), Dean Stockwell (Capt. Homer Thomas), Lonette McKee (Betty Rae), Mary Stuart Masterson (Rachel Feld), Bill Graham (Don Brubaker), Sam Bottoms (Lt. Webber), Casey Siemaszko (Pvt. Wildman), Laurence "Larry" Fishburne (Cpl. Flanagan), Dick Anthony Williams (1st Sgt. Slasher Williams), Elias Koteas (Pete Deveber), Peter Masterson (Col. Feld), Carlin Glynn (Mrs. Feld), Eric Holland (Col. Godwin); **Written by:** Ronald Bass; **Cinematography by:** Jordan Cronenweth; **Music by:** Carmine Coppola. **Producer:** Tri-Star Pictures, Francis Ford Coppola, Michael Levy. **Boxoffice:** 5.2M. **MPAA Rating:** R. **Running Time:** 112 minutes. **Format:** VHS, Beta, LV, Closed Caption.

GO TELL THE SPARTANS

1978 Ted Post ♫♫♫♫

In many important ways, this is the best and most intelligent film made to date about American involvement in Vietnam. Though it lacks the cachet of more expensive productions, its understanding of the roots of the conflict and the people who fought it is more profound than Hollywood's best. It's also entertaining, exciting, funny, and features one of Burt Lancaster's better mature roles.

He is Maj. Asa Barker, in command of a small garrison of American advisors and Vietnamese mercenaries in 1964. As a professional soldier with a checkered career, he doesn't take the duty too seriously, doing as little as possible to get by, until his superior Gen. Harnitz (Dolph Sweet) orders him to occupy an abandoned French outpost at a place called Muc Wa. Why? Barker asks. It is of no importance to anyone, and the French lost their war because they had "too many static defense posts." But Harnitz is adamant. Despite the fact that Barker is understaffed, has weak air cover, even less reliable support from the local South Vietnamese Colonel, and poor communications—his contact with Harnitz is made via telegraph, not voice—he is to show the flag at Muc Wa.

Barker obeys and gives the job to the new guys. Second Lt. Hamilton (Joe Unger) is a fire-eating incompetent. "Send me into the field, sir. I feel I can kill Communists as well as any First Lieutenant, sir!" Along with his unfortunate name, Cpl. Abraham Lincoln (Dennis Howard) has a finely honed opium habit. Barker's old friend Sgt. "Oleo" Oleonowski (Jonathan Goldsmith) is a burnout case. No one quite understands what the bleeding-heart draftee Cpl. Courcey (Craig Wasson) is doing there. Though the Americans are supposedly in command, their translator, Cowboy (Evan C. Kim) is a cold-blooded killer who'll do whatever it takes to keep them alive. With a small contingent of South Vietnamese troops and farmers armed with shotguns, they head off to Muc Wa. So do the Vietcong.

Wendell Mayes's script, based on Daniel Ford's novel, presents the events at Muc Wa as a microcosm of the war. A combination of South Vietnamese infighting with American innocence and indecision is no match for North Vietnamese determination. At the same time, matters of promises, loyalty and escalation must be settled. Oleo is right when he says, "It's their war," but having become involved, the Americans cannot simply walk away. Or can they? That, finally, is the question that the film addresses. If it cannot come to a satisfactory answer, it deals with the issues honestly.

It is able to do that because the decisions fall on Maj. Barker, and Burt Lancaster makes him an incredibly appealing hero. His scenes with Wasson and with Marc Singer, as an ambitious young captain, are some of his best. Lancaster is relaxed, often poetically profane, yet completely in command, and, as always, intelligent. The long scene where he tells the story about an encounter in a gazebo will never appear in a compilation of great Lancaster moments, but it's one of the funniest monologues in his long career.

Despite his outstanding work, the film has never received the attention it deserves. Its disillusioned view of the war won't satisfy committed partisans of either the left or the right. Though the battle scenes are fairly realistically staged, most of them take place at

See also

Full Metal Jacket
All Quiet on the Western Front
Battleground
When Trumpets Fade

night and so they are not spectacular. The film was made on a modest budget, and that shows in the production values, though a restoration might look much better and is certainly in order.

Whatever the reasons, *Go Tell the Spartans* remains the great "lost" Vietnam film.

Sgt. Oleonowski (Jonathan Goldsmith), Cowboy (Evan Kim), Lt. Hamilton (Joe Unger), and Cpl. Courcey (Craig Wasson) prepare to fight their way out of a trap after their convoy is ambushed in *Go Tell the Spartans*. The Kobal Collection

Cast: Burt Lancaster (Maj. Asa Barker), Craig Wasson (Cpl. Courcey), David Clennon (Lt. Finley Wattsberg), Marc Singer (Capt. Olivetti), Jonathan Goldsmith (Sgt. Oleonowski), Joe Unger (Lt. Hamilton), Dennis Howard (Cpl. Abraham Lincoln), Evan C. Kim (Cowboy), John Megna (Cpl. Ackley), Hilly Hicks (Signalman Toffer), Dolph Sweet (Gen. Harnitz), Clyde Kusatsu (Col. Minh), James Hong (Cpl. Oldman); **Written by:** Wendell Mayes; **Cinematography by:** Harry Stradling Jr.; **Music by:** Dick Halligan. **Producer:** Spartan, Mar Vista, Mitchell Cannold, Allan F. Bodoh. **MPAA Rating:** R. **Running Time:** 114 minutes. **Format:** VHS, Beta, LV.

GOOD MORNING, VIETNAM

1987 Barry Levinson ♪♪♪♪

Though it is primarily a vehicle for star Robin Williams's rapid-fire free-association comedy, Barry Levinson's approach to the war does not ignore the serious side. Much of the humor comes out of the insanity of the conflict, and this is one of the few films that attempts to see the American presence through Vietnamese eyes. If the plot takes some arbitrary turns to make its points, they are not too forced.

Air Force disc jockey Adrian Cronauer (Williams) arrives in Saigon from Crete to work for Armed Forces Radio in 1965 as the "conflict" is beginning to intensify. One of the first wire stories he sees quotes President Johnson on raising the level of American commitment in the country from 75,000 men to 125,000. But Cronauer finds that he is not allowed to read such stories over the air. There is no freedom of the press, and the news has to go through twin censors before it is broadcast. Still, the news is only a small part of Cronauer's show. He brings mile-a-minute improvisational irreverence to his patter, along with the best "contemporary" rock.

His superiors—Sgt. Maj. Dickerson (J.T. Walsh) and Lt. Hauk (Bruno Kirby)—want none of it. They hate Cronauer's humor and prefer polkas to Martha and the Vandellas. The troops love his brash wit, and Cronauer is supported by his pals Garlick (Forest Whitaker) and Dreiwitz (Robert Wuhl). Outside the radio station, the sex-starved d.j.—he claims that all the women on Crete looked like Zorba the Greek—quickly falls for Trinh (Chintara Sukapatana). Her brother Tuan (Tung Thanh Tran) says that no relationship is possible between them and tries to explain why.

> "What's the difference between the Army and the Cub Scouts? The Cub Scouts don't have heavy artillery."
>
> **Adrian Cronauer (Robin Williams) on the air**

At first, the two sides of the story seem not to fit together comfortably. When the action moves out of the control room, it shifts gears, and about half way through, the war becomes a more significant part of the film. Levinson handles it with unusual skill. He portrays the Vietnamese as real people, individuals involved in a complex political struggle that has been going on for decades. It's not a matter of good vs. evil, and it's certainly not something that a guy fresh from Crete can comprehend. Levinson and writer Mitch Markowitz wisely leave that side of the story unresolved. More accurately, they leave it unfinished, reflecting the reality of the American experience.

In either case, they are more interested in the characters as individuals than in political statements. They have surrounded Cronauer with a deep supporting cast to provide targets for his humor. The most memorable of them is Cu Ba Nguyen, as a fey club owner who is obsessed with Walter Brennan. Bruno Kirby, an underrated character actor, is excellent as Cronauer's primary target, and Forest Whitaker, who has become more well known as a director in recent years, is just as good.

Finally, a personal note. I have always been fond of this film, at least in part because in the early 1970s I worked with the real Adrian Cronauer at a National Public Radio station. Though he'll never be mistaken for Robin Williams, he is intelligent and funny, and the film is based on his experiences in Vietnam.

See also

*M*A*S*H*

The Battle of Algiers

The Boys in Company C

Dead Poet's Society

The Enemy Within

Cast: Robin Williams (Adrian Cronauer), Forest Whitaker (Edward Garlick), Bruno Kirby (Lt. Steven Hauk),
Richard Edson (Pvt. Abersold), Robert Wuhl (Marty Lee Dreiwitz), J.T. Walsh (Sgt. Maj. Dickerson), Noble Willingham (Gen. Tayler), Floyd Vivino (Eddie Kirk),
Tung Thanh Tran (Tuan), Chintara Sukapatana (Trinh), Richard Portnow (Dan "The Man" Levitan), Juney Smith (Phil McPherson), Cu Ba Nguyen (Jimmy Wah),
Dan Stanton (Censor #1), Don Stanton (Censor #2); **Written by:** Mitch Markowitz; **Cinematography by:** Peter Sova;
Music by: Alex North. **Producer:** Touchstone Pictures, Larry Brezner, Mark Johnson. **Awards:** Golden Globe Awards '88: Best
Actor—Musical/Comedy (Williams); Nominations: Academy Awards '87: Best Actor (Williams). **Budget:** 13M. **Boxoffice:** 123.9M. **MPAA
Rating:** R. **Running Time:** 121 minutes. **Format:** VHS, Beta, LV, 8mm, Closed Caption, DVD.

THE GREEN BERETS

1968 John Wayne

In the long history of Hollywood war movies, John Wayne's bizarre Vietnam epic is unlike any other. The star and co-director falls victim to his own strongly held political beliefs in an alternative masterpiece that piles mistake upon mistake on the way to its justly famous final shot, where the sun sets in the east. All of the flaws evident in *The Alamo*, which he saw as a companion piece to this film, are magnified. As an actor, Wayne had already become a screen icon by 1968. As a director, he never completely realized how to construct a film or how to handle himself. Most of the defects in *The Green Berets* are simple things that could have easily been omitted.

Wayne is certainly up-front about his politics. The opening scene is an impromptu lecture on foreign policy by Special Forces Sgt. Muldoon (Aldo Ray) to a group of civilians and writers, including pantywaist correspondent George Beckworth (David Janssen). If people could just see what is going on, they'd support the troops, Muldoon explains, and then goes on with the familiar whining about newspapers not telling the truth. Meanwhile, Col. Mike Kirby (Wayne) is assigned to take over command of a Special Forces outpost in the northern part of the country. The rest of the usual suspects are rounded up—Sgt. Petersen (Jim Hutton) the scrounger; Doc McGee (Raymond St. Jacques); Sgt. Provo (Luke Askew)—and off they go to Vietnam.

It takes Wayne and co-director Ray Kellogg almost 45 minutes to get through all of their throat-clearing and scene-setting before anything significant actually happens, and even then, the pace remains glacial. They introduce the South Vietnamese commanders (George Takai and Jack Soo), the cute kid (Craig Jue), and his dog. When the big VC night attack finally arrives, it is less than spectacular. Unfortunately, it is also defined by two cheapjack special effects—the burning of a model helicopter and the collapse of a tiny observation tower complete with dolls—which would not have been out of place in Ed Wood's *Plan 9 from Outer Space*. They are that laughable.

> "My home is in Hanoi. I go home too someday. You'll see. First, kill all those stinking Cong, then go home."
>
> **Capt. Nim (George Takai)**

> "When Charlie knows he's got a nice box to be buried in, why he's just as brave as hell."
>
> **Sgt. Petersen (Jim Hutton)**

After that bit of business has been resolved with a massive air strike, the plot makes an abrupt turn in a new direction. Kirby and company set out with a femme fatale (Irene Tsu) to kidnap a North Vietnamese general. Clearly, the plot is not meant to comment seriously on Vietnam; it's unashamed pro-American propaganda. Individual North Vietnamese are recognizable because they're so ugly. As a group, they're presented as murderous child molesters and superstitious savages. Then they kill the kid's dog.

While it's true that Wayne's war films and westerns are not known for their subtlety, the better ones have straightforward stories, and they give the star room to portray a character with some dimension. The plot here is a careless hash of cliches, and Maj. Kirby is a cipher. Nothing about his personal life or military background is even hinted at. He's simply John Wayne with an M-16. As Garry Wills notes in *John Wayne's America: The Politics of Celebrity* (Simon & Schuster. 1997), that is the curious secret of the film's boxoffice success: "For Wayne's fans, its very unrealism may have been its selling point. People who did not want to know about the

Did you Know?

Did You Know? In 1968, *The Green Berets* was number 10 at the boxoffice, ahead of *2001: A Space Odyssey* and behind *Planet of the Apes*.

actual Vietnam War could feel that the national unity and resolve of World War II might turn around this strange new conflict in the far-off jungles of the East. Wayne was fighting World War II again, the only way he ever did, in make-believe; and that make-believe was a memory of American greatness that many still wanted to live by."

John Wayne leads a group of elite fighting troops in Vietnam in the unpopular flag-waver *The Green Berets*. The Kobal Collection

Cast: John Wayne (Col. Mike Kirby), David Janssen (George Beckworth), Jim Hutton (Sgt. Petersen), Aldo Ray (Sgt. Muldoon), George Takei (Capt. Nim), Raymond St. Jacques (Doc McGee), Bruce Cabot (Col. Morgan), Jack Soo (Col. Cai), Patrick Wayne (Lt. Jamison), Luke Askew (Sgt. Provo), Irene Tsu (Lin), Edward Faulkner (Capt. MacDaniel), Jason Evers (Capt. Coleman), Mike Henry (Sgt. Kowalski), Chuck Roberson (Sgt. Griffin), Eddy Donno (Sgt. Watson); **Cinematography by:** Winton C. Hoch; **Music by:** Miklos Rozsa. **Producer:** Warner Bros., Michael Wayne. **MPAA Rating:** G. **Running Time:** 135 minutes. **Format:** VHS, Beta, LV, Letterbox, Closed Caption, DVD.

THE GREEN BERETS

HAMBURGER HILL

1987 John Irvin

With the commercial success of such idiosyncratic depictions of the war as *Apocalypse Now*, *Platoon*, and *Full Metal Jacket*, a more conventional response was inevitable. This strangely flawed, old-fashioned picture is the result. While the film has been praised by some for its historical accuracy, the soldiers are played by the prettiest ensemble of young actors ever gathered for a Vietnam film. They strip down at the first possible moment to show off their abs and pecs. Then once the action begins, they turn into a bunch of right-wing crybabies who complain that their girlfriends don't understand them because they believe the liberal media vultures, the peaceniks, and even the Kennedys.

The jingoistic lapse is bad enough on its own, but the filmmakers choose to spend several minutes in separate scenes repeating and elaborating on the idea. They acknowledge the much more immediate and serious problem of American soldiers killed by friendly fire from helicopters in one brief, passing moment and then forget it. Their claims of historical accuracy, then, must be taken with a grain of salt. A foreword states "On 10 May 1969, troops of the 101st Airborne Division engaged the enemy at the base of Hill 937 in the Ashau Valley. Ten days and 11 bloody assaults later, the Troops who fought there called it Hamburger Hill."

Before these cinematic grunts arrive at the battlefield, though, they spend the first 30 minutes or so bickering with each other, visiting the local bordello, and taking off their shirts for any number of reasons. Though they lack strong personalities, the most important members of the group are Sgt. Frantz (Dylan McDermott), who typically wears his helmet at a jaunty angle, Sgt. Worcester (Steven Weber), Motown (Michael Boatman), and Doc (Courtney B. Vance), the medic. Their dialogue is filled with *beaucoup dinky-dou di di mow* cliches, and, as a group, their acting style explores the more emotive ends of the spectrum.

The combat scenes are well paced and unusually graphic, with exploding heads, shredded organs, and severed limbs created by in-your-face special effects. They are appropriately loud and chaotic, too, but never particularly moving because the characters are so thin. And the clean, clear, sharply focused images created by director John Irvin and cinematographer Peter Macdonald actually work against an atmosphere of urgent authenticity. Viewers expect those scenes to be blurred, grainy, and shaky. Though Irvin's grunts get down in the mud, his camera never does. In the same vein, the explosions of phosphorous bombs recall the beauty of chrysanthemum fireworks—more impressive than destructive.

As the title suggests, Irvin and writer James Carabatsos take Lewis Milestone's Korean War film *Pork Chop Hill* as a model. But where Milestone uses the battle to comment on the peace negotiations and, by extension, the war as a whole, this film cannot claim any larger significance. The real engagement between North Vietnamese regulars and American soldiers was an isolated occurrence. Carabatsos has said that the film is autobiographical. Irvin made a documentary in Vietnam, so he, too, can claim firsthand experience. Even so, they cannot add much that's original to the cinematic literature of Vietnam.

See also
A Rumor of War
84 Charlie MoPic
Pork Chop Hill
Go Tell the Spartans
The Boys in Company C

Cast: Michael Dolan (Murphy), Daniel O'Shea (Gaigin), Dylan McDermott (Frantz), Tommy Swerdlow (Bienstock), Courtney B. Vance (Doc Johnson), Anthony Barille (Languilli), Michael Boatman (Motown), Don Cheadle (Washburn), Tim Quill (Beletsky), Don James (McDaniel), Michael A. Nickles (Galvan), Harry O'Reilly (Duffy), Steven Weber (Sgt. Worcester), Tegan West (Lt. Eden), Kieu Chinh (Mama San), Doug Goodman (Lagunas), J.C. Palmore (Healy); **Written by:** Jim Carabatsos; **Cinematography by:** Peter Macdonald; **Music by:** Philip Glass; **Technical Advisor:** Kieu Chinh. **Producer:** Marcia Nasatir, James Carabatsos. **Boxoffice:** 13.8M. **MPAA Rating:** R. **Running Time:** 104 minutes. **Format:** VHS, Beta, LV.

PLATOON

1986 Oliver Stone ♪♪♪

> ## "Rejoice O young man in thy youth."
>
> **Epigraph from Ecclesiastes**

> ## "I think now, looking back, we did not fight the enemy— we fought ourselves and the enemy was in us."
>
> **Chris Taylor (Charlie Sheen) in voice-over.**

Though Oliver Stone has a well-deserved reputation as the enfant terrible of the left, his semi-autobiographical Vietnam film is more viscerally violent than any World War II propaganda. Stone does not present the conduct of the war in the flattering light of those "made with the full cooperation of the United States Army" productions, but his sympathies are with the men who fight, most of them anyway. He further distances himself from the political right by introducing the film with a epigraph from Ecclesiastes and then using Samuel Barber's elegiac "Adagio for Strings" throughout, instead of more conventionally martial music. Strip those away and what's left is one kick-ass war flick.

Though the fact is never explicitly stated on screen, the action is set before and during the North Vietnamese Tet Offensive of January 1968. A few months before it begins, college dropout and volunteer Chris Taylor (Charlie Sheen) joins Bravo Company, 25th Infantry. In sophomoric voice-over letters to his grandmother—not inappropriate for a character of his age in his situation, but embarrassing nonetheless—he describes his fears and his naive philosophical aspirations: "Maybe I've finally found it, way down here in the mud. Maybe from down here I can start up again, be something I can be proud of without having to fake it—be a fake human being. Maybe I can see something I don't yet see or learn something I don't yet know."

The first thing he learns is that going out on patrol at night is terribly frightening. He's thrown into a situation where his training is useless. If he doesn't figure it out on the job, he'll die. His guardian angel is Sgt. Elias (Willem Dafoe). The platoon's senior sergeant, Barnes (Tom Berenger), is a cold-blooded racist killer who loves the war. The differences between the two men are drawn in bold, unambiguous strokes. The beatific Elias hangs out with the "heads," who have a poster of Ho Chi Minh on the wall, smoke dope, and listen to Motown. Scarfaced Barnes is a "juicer," with a Confederate flag, Jack Daniels whiskey, and Merle Haggard on the stereo. Though Chris pretends briefly to be torn between the two father figures, the matter is quickly settled when they're out on patrol away from their base.

That central section, involving the discovery of a tunnel system and a nearby village that may be a Vietcong supply base, is the most tense and frightening part of the film. The mission goes so badly that by the time the Americans enter the village, they're a group of frightened kids who are ready to kill without reason. The sequence reaches a conclusion so gut-wrenching and horrifying that Stone backs away from the realities of Vietnam and settles into the traditional patterns of war movies. By changing a few details, the big attack scenes in the third act could have come from *Battleground*, *A Walk in the Sun*, or *Battle of the Bulge*.

Because the dramatic tension is pitched so high almost from the first frames, the acting is overstated. Dafoe and Berenger, both nominated for Best Supporting Actor, are particularly fierce. Of the grunts, Kevin Dillon as Bunny, the cheerful psycho who understands that he is in his element, makes the most lasting impression. When Stone is not filling the screen with explosions, he is able to make the jungle seem all too real, a wet place meant for bugs, leeches, and snakes, not for people. At his worst, Stone

See also

Full Metal Jacket
Hamburger Hill
Go Tell the Spartans
Anderson Platoon

turns to facile visual sloganeering—notice, for example, the appearance of a Nazi flag toward the end—and the conveniently contrived ending. In the end, though, the flaws are less important than the powerful images of violence and madness that Stone forges. On repeated viewings, *Platoon* loses some of its raw energy, but it's still a significant addition to the American war film.

Aftermath of the village massacre in *Platoon*; **William Dafoe (center, being restrained), Charlie Sheen (far left), Keith David (second from right).** The Kobal Collection

Cast: Charlie Sheen (Chris Taylor), Willem Dafoe (Sgt. Elias), Tom Berenger (Sgt. Barnes), Francesco Quinn (Rhah), Forest Whitaker (Big Harold), John C. McGinley (Sgt. O'Neill), Kevin Dillon (Bunny), Richard Edson (Sal), Reggie Johnson (Junior), Keith David (King), Johnny Depp (Lerner), Dale Dye (Capt. Harris), Mark Moses (Lt. Wolfe), Chris Pederson (Crawford), David Neidorf (Tex), Tony Todd (Warren), Ivan Kane (Tony), Paul Sanchez (Doc), Corey Glover (Francis); **Cameo(s):** Oliver Stone; **Written by:** Oliver Stone; **Cinematography by:** Robert Richardson; **Music by:** Georges Delerue; **Technical Advisor:** Dale Dye. **Producer:** Arnold Kopelson, Hemdale Films. **Awards:** Academy Awards '86: Best Director (Stone), Best Film Editing, Best Picture, Best Sound; British Academy Awards '87: Best Director (Stone); Directors Guild of America Awards '86: Best Director (Stone); Golden Globe Awards '87: Best Director (Stone), Best Film—Drama, Best Supporting Actor (Berenger); Independent Spirit Awards '87: Best Cinematography, Best Director (Stone), Best Film, Best Screenplay; American Film Institute (AFI) '98: Top 100; Nominations: Academy Awards '86: Best Cinematography, Best Original Screenplay, Best Supporting Actor (Berenger, Dafoe). **Budget:** 6M. **Boxoffice:** 137.9M. **MPAA Rating:** R. **Running Time:** 113 minutes. **Format:** VHS, Beta, LV, Closed Caption.

A RUMOR OF WAR

1980 Richard T. Heffron 🎬🎬🎬🎬

The adaptation of Philip Caputo's Pulitzer-prize winning book tells essentially the same story as Oliver Stone's *Platoon*. It lacks the adrenaline-pumping action sequences and plot contrivances. In their place are a solidly realistic atmosphere and a deeper understanding of the mistakes that were made in the early stages of the Vietnam War and the people who made those mistakes.

In 1963, Phil Caputo (Brad Davis) is a restless, dissatisfied college student who's still living at home. School bores him; the idea of going into business is no more appealing; he argues with his parents. When he enlists in the Marines, his girlfriend Carol (Gail Youngs) says, "That's the most conformist act of rebellion I've ever heard." True or not, in 1965, Second Lt. Caputo arrives in Vietnam. "We didn't know what to expect," he says in voice-over. "Rumors of screaming yellow hordes. But we were Americans, 1st Marines, 3rd Battalion, the first major force to land in Vietnam. We were ready for anything." Ready but almost completely ignorant.

With the sometimes overbearing assistance of Sgt. Coleman (Brian Dennehy), Caputo takes over the 2nd Platoon and learns, one piece at a time, about the realities of war. Snipers, heat, an invisible guerrilla enemy. His two best friends are Lt. Cohen (Michael O'Keefe) and Lt. McCloy (Keith Carradine) who share his humanistic values and disgust at the murderous insanity surrounding them. Caputo finds that he is not immune. His superiors seem obsessed with body- counts and kill-ratios and have no understanding of what really goes on in the bush. To survive the war, he must commit abhorrent acts. Where, then, does he draw the line between what is right and what is necessary?

John Sacret Young, who also created the TV series *China Beach*, turns Caputo's memoir into a memorably epigrammatic script. (See quotes.) Journeyman TV director Richard T. Heffron makes his Mexican locations an accurate-looking version of Vietnam. He's particularly good with mud and rain. One long sequence involving the unburying and reburial of Vietnamese bodies is as grotesque and surreal as any moment in American war films. The acting is superb. Davis is a believably angry and often powerless hero. Of the strong supporting cast, Lane Smith as the veteran Sgt. Holgren, and Stacey Keach as the bloodthirsty Maj. Ball, have the most to work with.

Because *A Rumor of War* was made for television and arrived in the wake of such high-powered theatrical releases as *Apocalypse Now* and *The Deer Hunter*, it lacks a strong following, even among fans of war films. It deserves better. Caputo, Young, and Heffron take the subject seriously. They refuse to accept cliches or easy answers to the questions concerning American involvement in that war. This is a strong sleeper worth seeking out.

> **"Specification One:** In that 1st Lt. Philip J. Caputo did subscribe under lawful oath a false statement. Specification Two: In that 1st Lt. Philip J. Caputo did murder with premeditation Le Dung, a citizen of the Republic of Vietnam. Specification Three: In that 1st Lt. Philip J. Caputo did murder with premeditation Tran Van Yan, a citizen of the Republic of Vietnam."
>
> **Opening voice-over court martial charges**

> **"The Marines—a man who wears that uniform is somebody. He passes the test."**
>
> **Philip J. Caputo (Brad Davis)**

> **"Before you leave leave here, lieutenant, one of the things you're going to learn is just how brutal a 19-year-old American boy can be."**
>
> **Sgt. Coleman (Brian Dennehy)**

> **"Battalion says if he's Vietnamese and he's dead, then he's VC, all right."**
>
> **Capt. Peterson (Chris Mitchum)**

Brad Davis in *A Rumor of War*.

The Kobal Collection

"We're here because this is
what we've got—a splendid
little war."

Lt. McCloy (Keith Carradine)

"I'll tell you the truth. I
don't mind zapping the
little jungle boogers—that's
what I'm paid for—but you
ride a chopper into a hot LZ
landing zone and don't tell
me your butt don't pucker."

Sgt. Holgren (Lane Smith)

"Da Nang in 1965 teemed with
refugees, armed soldiers,
whores, pimps, camp
followers, black marketeers,
maimed and peppered
survivors. You were lucky to
get out alive, crazy to ever
go in."

Philip Caputo, voice-over

"Fall, 1965, we were in a
commuter war. We kept to a
schedule like factory
workers. Chopper into the
bush for a day or two,
chopper out. But we weren't
factory workers. The war had
changed; we had changed. We
knew fear."

Philip Caputo, voice-over

"If I plead guilty, I'll be
found innocent?"

Philip Caputo's question to his attorney

Cast: Brad Davis (Phil Caputo), Keith Carradine (McCloy), Michael O'Keefe (Walter Cohen), Stacy Keach (Maj. Ball), Steve Forrest (Atherton), Richard Bradford (Rupert), Brian Dennehy (Sgt. Coleman), John Friedrich (Pascarella), Perry Lang (Woodward), Chris Mitchum (Capt. Peterson), Dan Shor (Soldier), Jeff Daniels (Soldier), Laurence "Larry" Fishburne (Soldier), Lane Smith (Sgt. Holgren), Gail Youngs (Carol), Bobby Ellerbee (Mackey); **Written by:** John Sacret Young; **Cinematography by:** Stevan Larner, Jorge Stahl Jr.; **Music by:** Charles Gross. **Producer:** David Manson, Stonehenge Productions, Charles Fries Productions. **Running Time:** 195 minutes. **Format:** VHS, Beta.

China Beach

This book is about war films, and so television series are technically off-limits. But *China Beach* made such a strong impression with its complex views of Vietnam that some mention must be made.

The series ran from 1988 to 1991, and in narrative terms it covers the years 1968 to 1985. The protagonist is Lt. Colleen McMurphy (Dana Delaney), a nurse with strong, troubled ties to her family back home in America and to her new family in Vietnam. The main supporting cast is Dr. Richard (Robert Picardo), a surgeon with his own problems; Samuel Beckett (Michael Boatman), who is in charge of sending bodies back; K.C. Koloski (Marg Helgenberger), the local madam; Dodger (Jeff Kober), the half-mad jungle fighter; and Boonie (Brian Wimmer), the tame G.I.

At its best, the series looks like a feature film, with excellent lighting, sets, and effects; fans of the genre will catch bits borrowed from *M*A*S*H*, *Apocalypse Now*, *Platoon*, and even *Battle Circus*. In the video version of the pilot film, you can hardly spot the commercial breaks. And as the various literary references suggest, *China Beach* is a serious original. Creator John Sacret Young always takes care with the characters. He and the various directors use inventive techniques to keep the action fresh—moving back and forth in time and place in some episodes, taking a documentary approach in others. They always seem to hit the right emotional note, and they're not shy about hammering it home, either.

Only the pilot is available on video, but the series is rebroadcast regularly on cable.

See www.xnet.com/~djk/ChinaBeach_2.shtml for a complete episode guide.

THE SIEGE OF FIREBASE GLORIA

1989 Brian Trenchard-Smith ♪♪♪♪

This is the film that John Wayne's *The Green Berets* might have been. When Wayne pitched the idea to President Lyndon Johnson, he said that he wanted to make *The Alamo* set in Vietnam, and to tell an honest story about the violent tactics used by both sides. Not surprisingly, the Army demanded that its role be sanitized before permission would be given to use bases and equipment, and the result is one of Hollywood's most notorious turkeys. Twenty years later, other filmmakers stuck to that basic idea, though they chose another great war film as their model: *Zulu*.

In January 1968, Sgt. Hafner (R. Lee Ermey) and Cpl. DiNardo (Wings Hauser) lead a Marine patrol to the village of An Loc. They've been told that the Vietcong have announced a cease-fire and so they do not expect the horrors they encounter. Without giving away important plot details, they make their way to Firebase Gloria, a remote outpost commanded by a madman (John Calvin). Hafner takes charge and, though he cannot persuade Saigon that a major attack is imminent, he does his best to shape the men up and to fortify the defenses. His opposite number is Cao Van (Robert Arevalo), commander of a Vietcong regiment that's taking part in the Tet Offensive. He has political problems to deal with, too. The North Vietnamese Army wants results. Though Cao Van has superior numbers, the Marines hold the high ground. The battle will not be easy for either side.

Inevitably, writers William Nagle and Tony Johnston and director Brian Trenchard-Smith fall back on some cliches. More often though, the darkly comic dialogue (see quotes) gives a new perspective to the war and the men who fought it. Trenchard-Smith's direction is fine in the big battle scenes, moving easily from hand-to-hand action on the ground to helicopter attacks. In the end, though, the actual fighting is less important than the film's attempts to present both sides fairly. As Hafner observes, "We were killing Charlie wholesale, but he didn't seem to care. Guess we'd do the same if Charlie occupied South Carolina."

Obviously, this is not a film about good guys and bad guys. There's more than enough guilt and horror and madness to go around, and the sight of American soldiers executing wounded Vietnamese in the field is still chilling. The film also succeeds on a visceral level; the battle scenes are gripping and exciting, and they end with a landscape filled with the dead and dying. Though Ermey occasionally appears uneasy in the lead, he's a natural with the physical action. More importantly, his voice can handle the subtle demands of voice-over narration, without resorting to the all-out verbal assault he delivered in *Full Metal Jacket*.

Though his role isn't nearly as large, Robert Arevalo manages to give the enemy a human face. He's presented here as a warrior who's fighting for his country and his people, against a well-equipped but outnumbered foe. That refusal to take a political point of view gives the film its unusual depth. It also heightens the tension of the battle scenes because it's so difficult for the viewer to take a convenient side. Our sympathies are manipulated in some thoughtful ways. Again, the similarities to *Zulu* are telling.

Firebreathers at both ends of the political spectrum will not find much comfort here. For everyone else, the film reveals a pivotal moment in history with intelligence, drama, courage, insight, and in the end, sadness. Despite limited theatrical release, *The Siege of Firebase Gloria* has developed a solid following on video. Any war movie fan who has missed it is in for a treat.

Cast: Wings Hauser (Cpl. "Nard" DiNardo), R. Lee Ermey (Sgt. Hafner), Mark Neely (Murphy), Gary Hershberger (Bugs Moran), Clyde Jones (Coates), Margi Gerard (Capt. Flanagan), Richard Kuhlman (Ghost), David Anderson (Co-pilot), Robert Arevalo (Cao Van), John Calvin (C.O. Williams), Albert "Poppy" Popwell (Jones); **Written by:** Tony Johnston, William Nagle; **Cinematography by:** Joe Batac; **Music by:** Paul Schutze. **Producer:** Fries Entertainment. **Running Time:** 95 minutes. **Format:** VHS, Beta, LV.

THE WAR AT HOME

1979 Barry Alexander Brown, Glenn Silber 🎞🎞🎞🎞

Directors Glenn Silber and Alexander Brown make no claims of objectivity in their documentary about opposition to the war in Vietnam, neither do they attempt to show the nationwide "big picture." Instead they focus almost entirely on one community—Madison, Wisconsin. While that college town does not have the notoriety of Berkeley or Harvard, it is a legitimate microcosm for campus resistance to the war. During most of the years that Silber and Brown describe, I was at the University of North Carolina at Chapel Hill, and the development of student involvement followed virtually the same course there.

Silber and Brown tell their story through the familiar combination of television news film, other archival footage, and interviews with key participants. They begin in 1963. John Kennedy is President and times are good in "the all-American town." Even so, anti-nuclear weapons demonstrations have already been staged at the University of Wisconsin, and on October 16, the first anti-Vietnam war activities take place. Nobody pays any real attention, but American involvement intensifies. So does public interest. By 1966, when the Midwest is still "a hotbed of lethargy," the first sit-in occupation of a university administration building occurs.

During those same years, Lyndon Johnson's campaign releases the infamous girl-with-daisy-and-mushroom-cloud ad against Barry Goldwater, and Sen. Teddy Kennedy appears on campus to defend the administration's decisions to send more men to Vietnam. The student movement is not specifically or entirely anti-war. Local problems are important to such groups as the Student Tenant Union and the Black Student Union. In '67, demonstrations against the Dow chemical company for its manufacture of napalm provide a preview of the Democratic convention in Chicago the next year, and violence becomes a more important consideration for the anti-war movement. The footage of a party on Mifflin Street that somehow becomes a confrontation could have come from almost any college town at that time. It's obvious in the sequence that neither the kids nor the local police knew exactly what they were doing. Both sides made mistakes and false assumptions, and it's remarkable that more people weren't hurt or killed sooner. The most sympathetic interviewee is Ralph Hanson, the University Police Chief who appears to have understood the true nature and intention of young demonstrators but still could not control what happened.

TO BE AGAINST THE WAR AND DO NOTHING IS INDEFENSIBLE

Slogan written on a bedsheet at a demonstration

That escalation of violence was still a couple of years away. The filmmakers follow the disorganized, make-it-up-as-we-go-along nature of the student demonstrations through the McCarthy campaign, and the more serious opposition to the Army Mathematics Research Center which, finally, was the target of a serious bomb attack that killed one person. They note national events—the Moratorium of 1969, the killings at Kent State and Jackson State in May of 1970, the mining of North Vietnamese ports in '72—but their focus stays on Madison. Local television stations and archives provided a wealth of footage, superbly edited by Chuck France. When it comes to the interviews, the filmmakers stay off camera and let all of their subjects speak for themselves. No tough questions are asked; no one is put on the spot. At the same time, nostalgia for the good old days of wild youth is absent, too. The film was produced in 1979, before warm and fuzzy '60s revisionism became a cottage

See also
Medium Cool
Born on the Fourth of July
Alice's Restaurant
The White Rose

industry. Anyone who can recall those times with any accuracy remembers the fear that the country was flying apart, that the center could not hold with such angry passion fueling the extremes.

Even today, those who are still angry at the excesses of the opposition may fault Silber and Brown for things that they have left out. On the important points, though, and on the emotions of the times, they get it right.

Producer: Barry A. Brown, Glenn Silber, Catalyst Films. **Running Time:** 100 minutes. **Format:** VHS.

COMING HOME

Coming Home and the Aftermath of War on Screen

The other sections of this book deal with specific wars or parts of wars. This one is devoted to the aftermath. What do the participants—both winners and losers—do with the peace? How do they handle the internal and external changes that war has brought about? It's a complex subject, and it has inspired some excellent films.

Two of the best were made in 1946. Edmund Goulding, who had been wounded in World War I, handles Somerset Maugham's novel, *The Razor's Edge*, with a confident touch. The idea of a veteran (Tyrone Power) going to Paris to find the meaning of life has become a cliche, but it's a cliche in large part because Maugham, Goulding, and Power make it seem so attractive. The addition of a solid ensemble cast makes this one of those perennial favorites that'll keep you up late on a weekend.

William Wyler's *The Best Years of Our Lives* is universally regarded as one of the finest films to come out of World War II. It's gotten better with age. This is popular entertainment taken to the highest level by a craftsman in complete control of his medium. The story of three returning veterans and their families is told with a complexity that reveals more of itself with every viewing. The same can be said of the post-war thriller, *The Third Man*. Beyond the famous zither score, Orson Welles's portrayal of the morally blighted Harry Lime combined with director Carol Reed's vision of a desolate Vienna and Graham Greene's perceptive script makes this one of the finest and most watchable films of the late 1940s.

Judgment at Nuremberg explores the most difficult moral questions in a courtroom setting.

The subject is the degree of guilt shared by German citizens for the atrocities of the Third Reich. Beyond the matters of who did what, the film suggests that no one's hands—not even the victors'—are perfectly clean. Again, that depth of complexity is almost never expressed in American films.

It certainly is nowhere to be found in Hal Ashby's *Coming Home*, where leftist politics preclude a reasoned view of the America that Vietnam vets returned to. Oliver Stone's *Born on the Fourth of July* can be criticized on the same grounds. He and writer Ron Kovic wear their outrage on their sleeves. Though it is impossible to deny the injustices they show, their moral certainty is not so self-evident.

In *Courage Under Fire*, Edward Zwick shows how the pressures of combat—in this case, the war with Iraq—can place individuals in situations that cannot be judged by civilian peacetime standards. Zwick and writer Patrick Sheane Duncan (*84 Charlie MoPic*) combine elements of serious drama with a flashback-heavy plot. They tell interrelated stories of an officer (Denzel Washington) racked by guilt for his own failings, real or imagined, and a dead helicopter pilot (Meg Ryan) who is either a hero or an incompetent coward.

Once the busy details of the plot have been worked out, the film is reduced to family. Do the experiences of a war destroy the family, or is the family group able to withstand the pressures? That, finally, is the story that all of these films tell. They arrive at radically different conclusions—some happy, some believable, some neither—but all of them show how the effects of war spread far beyond the battlefield into the home.

THE BEST YEARS OF OUR LIVES

1946 William Wyler ♪♪♪♪

Did you Know?

In the original version of MacKinlay Kantor's story, Homer was to be a spastic, due to combat injuries. William Wyler realized immediately "that no actor, no matter how great, could play a spastic with conviction." The filmmakers had considered eliminating the role until Wyler saw a documentary film about Harold Russell, *Diary of a Sergeant,* at a war bonds rally for disabled veterans. He arranged to meet Russell and was so impressed by his attitude that he changed the role. Russell went on to win both the Best Supporting Actor Academy Award and a Special Award "for bringing hope and courage to his fellow veterans." (*A Talent for Trouble: The Life of Hollywood's Most Acclaimed Director, William Wyler*. By Jan Herman. Putnam. 1995)

Fact:

Russell is the only actor ever to win two Oscars for the same role.

William Wyler's story of returning veterans is the most critically acclaimed film of the post-war years. Because it has been so popular with audiences, few people realize how unusual it is. For mainstream entertainment, it's a drama with few conventional confrontations or resolutions. The characters are faced with difficult situations and they resolve them realistically. Physical action is limited to one punch. (It's a good one, but it's completely out of step with the rest of the story.) All of that dubious material is developed at a leisurely pace, and it's told in a visual style that borders on the experimental. In short, *The Best Years of Our Lives* should never have been made. But it is one of those rare Hollywood films that captures the moment and expresses what large numbers of people were thinking and feeling at the time of its release. In this case, it is a country trying to decide what to do with victory and with itself.

Three returning servicemen meet in a B-17 being used for military transport on the way to Boone City, somewhere in the Midwest. Al Stephenson (Frederic March) was a sergeant with the Army in the Pacific. Homer Parrish (Harold Russell) served aboard a carrier until he lost his hands when the ship was attacked. Fred Derry (Dana Andrews) was the captain of a bomber in Europe. Each is unsure about what he's going find at home. Homer's engaged, but his fiancee Wilma (Cathy O'Donnell) has never seen the hooks he wears. Fred married Marie (Virginia Mayo) after a quickie wartime romance. She's still really a stranger to him. Al and his wife Millie (Myrna Loy) are an old married couple, but he hardly knows his kids.

Beyond the re-establishment of their personal lives, the men aren't certain about what they want to do with themselves. The sergeant was a successful banker before the war; the pilot was a soda jerk. Neither is too crazy about returning to his old job. They congregate at Butch's (Hoagy Carmichael) tavern. It takes Wyler and writers MacKinlay Kantor and Robert Sherwood almost three hours to figure out what happens to them. In cinematic terms, this is an epic film about ordinary people, but unlike most epics, it loses nothing on home video.

The film was made in 1946, before the various widescreen processes came into vogue. The dimensions of Wyler's image match today's video screens without letterboxing. That is particularly important here because Wyler and cinematographer Gregg Toland work with very deep focus in almost every shot, what Wyler called "carrying focus." Action in the background is just as clear as foreground, in essence doubling the amount of visual information that can be placed in the image. Orson Welles uses similar but much flashier techniques in *Citizen Kane*. Wyler claimed that he made his film that way for two reasons. First, he wanted the characters to inhabit a more "realistic" world than audiences see in most films. That calls for smaller interiors. By shrinking the rooms and enlarging the focus, the viewer is always aware of walls and ceilings. That's true even in the

See also

Schindler's List

Mrs. Miniver

Memphis Belle

Coming Home

COMING HOME

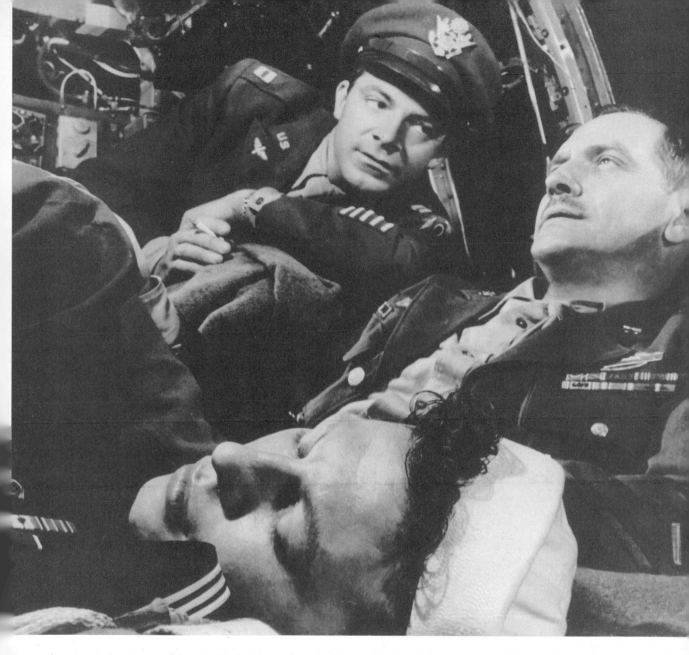

department store scenes. Second, with that deeper focus he does not have to cut between characters to show their reactions to the situation and to each other, giving the film a much smoother feel. By the time they made the film, Wyler and Toland were seasoned professionals, so the technique never calls attention to itself. As so many critics have noted, Wyler has an "invisible style." He would use anything that worked to get the emotion across, and this film contains at least three of his finest moments: Al's homecoming and Millie's reaction (said to be autobiographical, at least in setting), Homer's showing Wilma how his hooks work, and Fred's walk through the field of surplus aircraft. Those scenes have an honest poignancy that is almost never found in mainstream movies.

Fred Derry (Dana Andrews) and Al Stephenson (Fredric March) discuss their impending return to civilian life while Homer Parrish (Harold Russell) sleeps during the flight home in *The Best Years of Our Lives*. The Kobal Collection

THE BEST YEARS OF OUR LIVES

That honesty is followed through in the conclusion. It is enough of a traditional "happy ending" to please a large audience, but it doesn't sugarcoat or ignore any of the serious issues. That's the real source of the film's enduring popularity.

Cast: Fredric March (Al Stephenson), Myrna Loy (Millie Stephenson), Teresa Wright (Peggy Stephenson), Dana Andrews (Fred Derry), Virginia Mayo (Marie Derry), Harold Russell (Homer Parrish), Hoagy Carmichael (Butch Eagle), Gladys George (Hortense Derry), Roman Bohnen (Pat Derry), Steve Cochran (Cliff Scully), Charles Halton (Prew), Cathy O'Donnell (Wilma), Ray Collins (Mr. Milton), Victor Cutler (Woody), Minna Gombell (Mrs. Parrish), Walter Baldwin (Mr. Parrish), Dorothy Adams (Mrs. Cameron), Don Beddoe (Mr. Cameron), Ray Teal (Mr. Mollett), Howland Chamberlain (Mr. Thorpe); **Written by:** Robert Sherwood; **Cinematography by:** Gregg Toland; **Music by:** Hugo Friedhofer. **Producer:** Samuel Goldwyn. **Awards:** Academy Awards '46: Best Actor (March), Best Director (Wyler), Best Film Editing, Best Picture, Best Screenplay, Best Supporting Actor (Russell), Best Original Dramatic Score; British Academy Awards '47: Best Film; Golden Globe Awards '47: Best Film—Drama; National Board of Review Awards '46: Best Director (Wyler), New York Film Critics Awards '46: Best Director (Wyler), Best Film; American Film Institute (AFI) '98: Top 100; National Film Registry '89; Nominations: Academy Awards '46: Best Sound. **Running Time:** 170 minutes. **Format:** VHS, Beta, LV, DVD.

Everything that people love and detest about Oliver Stone's films is in full flower here—ambitious theme, bracing visual style, undisguised political biases. The film is also an important turning point in Tom Cruise's career, completing his transformation from rising star to serious actor. He received his first Academy Award nomination for his role as Ron Kovic. Though his autobiographical story is presented as a distillation of the political and social upheaval that America went through from the mid-'60s to the mid-'70s, the film really cannot carry that much baggage. At heart, it's propaganda.

Stone and cinematographer Robert Richardson begin the story as a twisted, tinted cinematic version of a sitcom—*Ozzie and Harriet*, perhaps—with boys playing war in suburban woods. It's Massapequa, Long Island, 1956. Ron Kovic grows up as a typical American white kid who believes in God, country, sports, and sex. His father's (Raymond J. Barry) something of a non-entity, leaving his forceful mother (Caroline Kava) as the dominant personality in the home. To Ron, she's a repressive slave driver who sets a standard he can never measure up to. That, in part, is why he enlists in the Marines, straight out of high school. Cut to the Cua Viet River, October 1967, where Sgt. Kovic is in his second tour.

The short vision of Vietnam that Stone presents here is even more surreal and horrifying than the violence in *Platoon*. An attack on a village is a disaster, and the Marines' retreat from it is even worse for Kovic. That nightmare is compounded when Kovic is seriously wounded, sent to a MASH unit, and then to a Bronx Veteran's Administration hospital. Paralyzed from the waist down, Kovic lives in a hell few can imagine. From that moment, the next hour or so is a steep downward spiral of self-pity, drunkeness, squalor and, most important, guilt over one incident for which he cannot forgive himself. It's honest, unflattering, and ugly. Then, to use the language of the times, Stone cops out. When it's time to resolve the issues that he has so passionately put forth, he hems and haws and allows the core transformation to occur off camera.

Something turns Kovic from a love-it-or-leave-it hawk into an antiwar activist who is spat upon and thrown out of the hall at the 1972 Republican National Convention, and then is received at the 1976 Democratic National Convention as an honored speaker. A throwaway moment tells the audience that he wrote a book sometime between the two events, but that is the only indication of the changes he undergoes. At the conclusion, then, the film's message is that nasty white Republicans hate anyone who looks different and challenges their cozy narrowminded beliefs, while Democrats of all colors are wise and tolerant. Such stereotyping is the stuff of campaign ads and bumper stickers. It is a lazy ending that calls into question all that has come before, and much of that is fine.

Even at his worst, Stone is never boring and, until the last reel, the action moves forcefully. That's also part of the film's undoing. If Stone had elected in the middle section to spend less time wallow-

> "God is going to punish you for this!"
>
> **Teenaged Ron Kovic's mother (Caroline Kava) when she finds a copy of *Playboy* magazine in his room**

> "Before I even got time to learn how to use it, it's gone in some jungle."
>
> **Paralyzed Ron Kovic (Tom Cruise) on his penis**

> "I'd give everything I believe in, everything I got, all my values just to have my body back again, just to be whole again. But I'm not whole. I never will and that's the way it is, isn't it?"
>
> **Ron Kovic**

See also

The Best Years of Our Lives
The War at Home
Medium Cool
Heaven and Earth
Gardens of Stone
Nixon

Tom Cruise is Vietnam war vet turned antiwar activist Ron Kovic in *Born on the Fourth of July.* The Kobal Collection

ing in Mexican fleshpots and to pay more attention to Kovic's real maturation, he might have created the antiwar epic he was aiming for, revealing the physical and psychological costs of Vietnam. He certainly could not have asked for more from his star. Cruise's performance is one of his best, capturing both the cocky, insecure young man and the haunted veteran. That, despite the political posturing, is what has made *Born on the Fourth of July* such a success at the boxoffice.

Cast: Tom Cruise (Ron Kovic), Kyra Sedgwick (Donna), Raymond J. Barry (Mr. Kovic), Jerry Levine (Steve Boyer), Tom Berenger (Recruiting Sergeant), Willem Dafoe (Charlie), Frank Whaley (Timmy), John Getz (Marine Major), Caroline Kava (Mrs. Kovic), Bryan Larkin (Young Ron), Abbie Hoffman (Strike organizer), Stephen Baldwin (Billy Vorsovich), Josh Evans (Tommy Kovic), Dale Dye (Infantry Colonel), William Baldwin (Platoon), Don "The Dragon" Wilson (Corpsman), Vivica A. Fox (Hooker), Holly Marie Combs (Jenny), Tom Sizemore (Vet), Daniel Baldwin (Vet), Ron Kovic (Veteran at parade); **Cameo(s):** Oliver Stone; **Written by:** Oliver Stone; **Cinematography by:** Robert Richardson; **Music by:** John Williams; **Technical Advisor:** Mark Ebenhoch, Dale Dye. **Producer:** Universal, Oliver Stone. **Awards:** Academy Awards '89: Best Director (Stone), Best Film Editing; Directors Guild of America Awards '89: Best Director (Stone); Golden Globe Awards '90: Best Actor—Drama (Cruise), Best Director (Stone), Best Film—Drama, Best Screenplay; Nominations: Academy Awards '89: Best Actor (Cruise), Best Adapted Screenplay, Best Cinematography, Best Picture, Best Sound, Best Original Score. **Boxoffice:** 70M. **MPAA Rating:** R. **Running Time:** 145 minutes. **Format:** VHS, Beta, LV, Letterbox, Closed Caption, DVD.

COMING HOME

Hal Ashby's film shares many of the characteristics of the other big Vietnam film of 1978, *The Deer Hunter*. Both are passionate and essentially incoherent in their view of the war. In this instance, though, the filmmakers' sharply left-of-center sensibility piles on additional political baggage. As Ashby and writers Nancy Dowd, Robert C. Jones, and Waldo Salt see it, each American who experienced the war—even for as brief a time as two weeks—came back mentally and/or physically devastated. No gray areas of doubt or disagreement are presented. Every veteran is damaged goods. But the ones who really hate the war are good in bed.

An introductory pool table conversation among several real disabled vets establishes the ground rules. Anyone who defends the war for any reason is wrong. Cut to Marine Capt. Bob Hyde (Bruce Dern) and his wife Sally (Jane Fonda) in the Officer's Club. It's 1968. The Tet Offensive has just started and Bob is looking forward to his tour of duty in Vietnam. As a career officer, he sees it primarily as an opportunity for advancement. As soon as he leaves, Sally is forced to find housing off the base and moves into a beach place with Vi Munson (Penelope Milford), whose brother Bill (Robert Carradine) is a patient at the local Veteran's Administration hospital. Physically he's fine, but "they sent him back without an ignition," Vi says. With time on her hands, Sally volunteers at the hospital and meets paraplegic Luke Martin (Jon Voight). A few years before, they had gone to the same high school, where he was the star quarterback and she was a cheerleader.

Now, paralyzed from the waist down, Luke is subject to violent, self-pitying rages, understandable but still ugly. Sally makes him her project, though from the beginning, it is obvious that her motives are partly sexual, partly altruistic. At the same time, her husband is discovering the horrors of the war.

Given that beginning, the film might have examined the war and its effects on America from three different, yet equally valid, points of view. Some have suggested that Nancy Dowd's original story worked along those lines. The final result, however, focuses almost entirely on the sexual and political radicalization of Sally and Luke, giving Bob, the hapless husband, short shrift. The filmmakers' lack of understanding and empathy for the military is obvious from the opening scenes. While the other characters have historically appropriate dress and hairstyles, Capt. Hyde's unruly curls would never have been found on a Marine in 1968, and his personal attitudes are set forth in a brusque *pro forma* manner. More importantly, his experiences in the war are alluded to only in passing, never shown or fully described. Finally, the resolution of their three-sided relationship is so pat that it insults any viewer who has taken the film seriously.

The filmmakers do deserve some credit for addressing—however inaccurately—the problems faced by returning veterans. At the time, no major film had really done that since *The Best Years of Our Lives*. Also, in visual terms, Ashby and director of photography Haskell Wexler use seemingly natural light and well-chosen locations to create that rough, lived-in realism found in the best American films of the '70s. If only they had checked their politics at the door. In practical terms, *Coming Home* and John Wayne's *The Green Berets* are opposite sides of the same coin.

> "I'm actually excited and I never thought it would get like this. I have competitive nervousness. I feel like I'm off to the Olympic Games representing the United States."
>
> **Capt. Bob Hyde (Bruce Dern) on the eve of his departure to Vietnam**

> "Now I'm here to tell you that I have killed for my country or whatever, and I don't feel good about it."
>
> **Sgt. Luke Martin (Jon Voight) addressing a high school assembly**

See also

Born on the Fourth of July
*M*A*S*H*
The Last Detail
Article 99

Luke Martin (Jon Voight) and Sally Hyde (Jane Fonda) share a tender moment in *Coming Home.* The Kobal Collection

Cast: Jane Fonda (Sally Hyde), Jon Voight (Luke Martin), Bruce Dern (Capt. Bob Hyde), Penelope Milford (Vi Munson), Robert Carradine (Bill Munson), Robert Ginty (Sgt. Dink Mobley), Mary Gregory (Martha Vickery), Kathleen Miller (Kathy Delise), Beeson Carroll (Capt. Carl Delise), Willie Tyler (Virgil), Charles Cyphers (Pee Wee), Olivia Cole (Corrine), Tresa Hughes (Nurse De Groot), Bruce French (Dr. Lincoln), Richard Lawson (Pat), Rita Taggart (Johnson), Pat Corley (Harris); **Written by:** Robert C. Jones; **Cinematography by:** Haskell Wexler. **Producer:** Jerome Hellman. **Awards:** Academy Awards '78: Best Actor (Voight), Best Actress (Fonda), Best Original Screenplay; Cannes Film Festival '78: Best Actor (Voight); Golden Globe Awards '79: Best Actor—Drama (Voight), Best Actress—Drama (Fonda); Los Angeles Film Critics Association

COMING HOME

Awards '78: Best Actor (Voight), Best Actress (Fonda), Best Film; New York Film Critics Awards '78: Best Actor (Voight); Writers Guild of America '78: Best Original Screenplay; Nominations: Academy Awards '78: Best Director (Ashby), Best Film Editing, Best Picture, Best Supporting Actor (Dern), Best Supporting Actress (Milford). MPAA Rating: R. Running Time: 130 minutes. Format: VHS, Beta, LV, Closed Caption.

COURAGE UNDER FIRE

1996 Edward Zwick ♫♫♫

Edward Zwick's second war film doesn't equal *Glory*, but it does deal fairly with complex military issues. Zwick may attempt too much in his efforts to make a serious drama entertaining on an escapist level. If so, his mistakes are ambitious, and even when it is not at its best, the film is enjoyable. It has two important assets. The first is an imaginative script by Patrick Sheane Duncan (*84 Charlie MoPic*). The second is a typically strong performance by Denzel Washington in the lead.

He is Lt. Col. Nathaniel Serling, a slightly tarnished hero of Operation Desert Storm. As the opening scenes explain, his unit of tanks was involved in an early encounter with Iraqi forces at night. In the confusion of the fighting, something went wrong and it appears that one of Serling's tanks was destroyed by friendly fire. Serling himself may have ordered the fatal shot. While that question is being officially investigated, Serling is ordered to conduct another investigation.

> "This is Captain Karen Emma Walden. She's the first woman in history to be nominated for a Medal of Honor for combat. It means this is gold. It's gold! Unfortunately, it's posthumous but I've got her little daughter."
>
> **White House aide Bruno (Bronson Pinchot), thinking about a Rose Garden ceremony**

While flying a Medevac helicopter, Capt. Karen Walden (Meg Ryan) assisted another downed chopper that was being fired upon by Iraqis. She and her crew managed to hold the attackers off for a night. During the rescue the next morning, she was killed. Do her actions justify a medal, more precisely the Medal of Honor? She would be the first woman to receive it for combat, and a cynical White House aide (Bronson Pinchot) sees a splendid photo opportunity for his boss. As Serling's friend and commanding officer Gen. Hershberg (Michael Moriarty) sees the situation, "Everybody wants it—senators, congressmen. One shining piece of something for people to believe in." If he knows what's good for him, Col. Serling will sign off on the matter quickly.

The body of the film is divided between the two investigations and Serling's reactions to both of them. Presumed guilt over the tank incident drives him to booze and away from his wife Meredith (Regina Taylor) and family. While he tries to deal with those emotional problems, Tony Gartner (Scott Glenn), a *Washington Post* reporter, wants to talk to him about the desert. Then the stories he hears about Capt. Walden don't quite add up. Were her actions those of an ingenious, resourceful hero, as Specialist Ilario (Matt Damon) claims? Or is Sgt. Monfriez (Lou Diamond Phillips) closer to the truth when he says that she was frightened and ready to surrender at the first opportunity? The truth, of course, is much more complicated than either extreme.

For the most part, director Zwick and writer Duncan handle the *Rashomon* structure deftly. Beyond the simple who-did-what revelations, their film is about the ways that people react to intense pressure and fear when there is no time for carefully reasoned responses. Is it possible or fair to judge complex split-second decisions after the fact? The filmmakers arrive at a properly mixed ending, though they try to milk the moment for more than it contains.

Seen simply as a war film, this one works fairly well. The locations look good, and though the tank battle appears a bit too clean and neat, it doesn't take many more liberties with tactics than other movies do. The helicopter material is more important, and it's handled more realistically, with a surprisingly gritty performance from

Meg Ryan. Denzel Washington's portrayal of a career soldier caught in two uncomfortable situations is completely convincing. He is able to show how Serling's love of the military and love of his family come from the same source and how important both are to him. It's a complex performance that provides a solid balance to the wilder, more melodramatic moments.

Meg Ryan and Matt Damon await rescue in *Courage Under Fire.* The Kobal Collection

Cast: Denzel Washington (Lt. Col. Nathaniel Serling), Meg Ryan (Capt. Karen Walden), Matt Damon (Ilario), Lou Diamond Phillips (Monfriez), Michael Moriarty (Gen. Hershberg), Scott Glenn (Tony Gartner), Bronson Pinchot (Bruno), Seth Gilliam (Altameyer), Sean Astin (Patella), Regina Taylor (Meredith Serling), Tim Guinee (Rady), Ken Jenkins (Joel Walden), Kathleen Widdoes (Geraldine Walden), Zeljko Ivanek (Banacek), Tim Ransom (Boylar), Ned Vaughn (Chelli); **Written by:** Patrick Sheane Duncan; **Cinematography by:** Roger Deakins; **Music by:** James Horner; **Technical Advisor:** Rory J. Aylward. **Producer:** John Davis, David T. Friendly, Joseph M. Singer, Joseph M. Caracciolo, Debra Martin Chase; released by 20th Century-Fox. **Budget:** 46M. **Boxoffice:** 61.7M. **MPAA Rating:** R. **Running Time:** 120 minutes. **Format:** VHS.

COURAGE UNDER FIRE

JUDGMENT AT NUREMBERG

1961 Stanley Kramer 𝄞𝄞𝄞𝄞

Writer Abby Mann and director Stanley Kramer use a variation on the traditional courtroom drama to examine the horrors of Nazi Germany. Though their film is long, deliberately paced, and grim, it deals honestly with a difficult subject. Unlike so many works that address Nazism, this one tries not to see it as pure evil, but instead to measure the degrees of individual and collective responsibility for acts that were committed while the Third Reich was in power. Questions of Cold War politics are brought into play, too, further complicating an already thorny situation.

The year is 1948. Top Nazi leaders have already been tried for war crimes, and the Allied tribunals have reached the lower levels. As Judge Dan Haywood (Spencer Tracy) says, "Now we're down to the business of judging the doctors, businessmen and judges. Some people think they shouldn't be judged at all." But he and two other American judges must decide the guilt or innocence of four German jurists, among them Ernst Janning (Burt Lancaster), a respected legal mind who had established an international reputation before the Nazis came to power.

> "Simple murders and atrocities do not constitute the gravamen of the charges in this indictment. Rather the charge is that of conscious participation in a nationwide government-organized system of cruelty and injustice in violation of every moral and legal principal known to civilized nations."
>
> **Judge Haywood (Spencer Tracey)**

Prosecuting him is Col. Tad Lawson (Richard Widmark), whose experiences liberating a concentration camp have made him perhaps too passionate in his desire for justice. Lawson's opposite number is defense counsel Hans Rolfe (Maximilian Schell), who is equally dedicated to his client and is willing to do whatever it takes to win his case.

Everyone involved agrees that they're dealing with "crimes committed in the name of the law" and so they are trying, in hindsight, to define acts that are legal but immoral. Two cases decided by the German judges in the 1930s become the focal points. The first concerns Rudolf Peterson (Montgomery Clift), a slightly retarded man who was subject to sterilization. The second revolves around Irene Hoffman (Judy Garland) who, as a teenager, was accused of having an affair with an older Jewish man. Outside the courtroom, Haywood sees a shamed and devastated country still rebuilding its shattered cities. Mme. Bertholt (Marlene Dietrich) is a widow whose perspective shows Haywood yet another side of the German character.

As legal dramas go, this one is notably lacking in surprises and fireworks. Instead, it doggedly sifts through the records of the past and tries to determine why decisions were made. Loud moments of anger are brief and startling, but they do lead, finally, to two separate views of the recent past. One character says bluntly, "We have to forget if we are to go on living." Another admits, "My counsel says we were not aware of the extermination of the millions. He would give you the excuse that we were only aware of the extermination of the hundreds. Does that make us any less guilty? Maybe we didn't know the details but if we didn't know, it was because we didn't want to know."

At another point, Janning delivers a reasoned explanation of the initial popularity of Nazism to average Germans, but that does not begin to explain the atrocities. By the end, the filmmakers have made a plausible explanation for a system that slowly turned normal human beings into monsters. More importantly, they do not

See also
Schindler's List
The Wannsee Conference
The Verdict
The Manchurian Candidate

settle for a conventional conclusion. Their questions are too complex for simple answers that can be reduced to fines or prison sentences. Some viewers may find the closing epilogue an unsatisfactory conclusion to the story, but no one can doubt its honesty.

Defense attorney Hans Rolfe (Maximilian Schell) questions German citizen Rudolf Peterson (Montgomery Clift) about life under the Nazis in *Judgment at Nuremburg.* The Kobal Collection

JUDGMENT AT NUREMBERG

Cast: Spencer Tracy (Judge Dan Haywood), Burt Lancaster (Ernst Janning), Richard Widmark (Col. Tad Lawson), Montgomery Clift (Rudolf Peterson), Maximilian Schell (Hans Rolfe), Judy Garland (Irene Hoffman), Marlene Dietrich (Mme. Bertholt), William Shatner (Capt. Byers), Edward Binns (Sen. Burkette), Werner Klemperer (Emil Hahn), Torben Meyer (Werner Lammpe), Martin Brandt (Friedrich Hofstetter), Kenneth MacKenna (Judge Kenneth Norris), Alan Baxter (Gen. Merrin), Ray Teal (Judge Curtiss Ives), Karl Swenson (Dr. Geuter); **Written by:** Abby Mann; **Cinematography by:** Ernest Laszlo; **Music by:** Ernest Gold. **Producer:** United Artists, Stanley Kramer. **Awards:** Academy Awards '61: Best Actor (Schell), Best Adapted Screenplay; Golden Globe Awards '62: Best Actor—Drama (Schell), Best Director (Kramer); New York Film Critics Awards '61: Best Actor (Schell), Best Screenplay; Nominations: Academy Awards '61: Best Actor (Tracy), Best Art Direction/Set Decoration (B & W), Best Black and White Cinematography, Best Costume Design (B & W), Best Director (Kramer), Best Film Editing, Best Picture, Best Supporting Actor (Clift), Best Supporting Actress (Garland). **Running Time:** 178 minutes. **Format:** VHS, Beta, LV.

The Hound Salutes: Burt Lancaster

Though John Wayne is the actor universally associated with American war movies, Burt Lancaster's work is more varied and substantial. He made six films in the genre. The five that are available on home video are uniformly excellent. As a group they're more serious than the athletic escapism he handled so gracefully, and every bit as rewarding on a second or third viewing.

Lancaster's screen career didn't begin until after World War II, where he had served with Special Services in the Fifth Army. In 1946 he made a memorable debut as the doomed boxer in Robert Siodmak's adaptation of Ernest Hemingway's *The Killers*, but he began in show business as an acrobat with his childhood friend (and later co-star) Nick Cravat. He received his first Oscar nomination in 1953 for his letter-perfect portrayal of Sgt. Milt Warden, the "top kick" in *From Here to Eternity*. He used the critical and commercial clout he earned for that work—and for a fine performance the year before in *Come Back, Little Sheba*—to form the Hecht-Lancaster production company with his agent Harold Hecht. The days of absolute studio power were disappearing then, and he was one of the first actors to take active control over his own career. He was also one of the most astute in evaluating good roles for himself. Note the popular submarine adventure, *Run Silent Run Deep*, where he plays an officer considering mutiny against a captain, Clark Gable, who's using questionable tactics. The conflict between the two larger-than-life macho stars plays particularly well within the claustrophobic interiors.

Lancaster demonstrated his remarkable range three years later when he played a German judge on trial in *Judgment at Nuremberg*. Though he has a supporting role and is upstaged by a twitchy Montgomery Clift, Lancaster really provides the emotional and intellectual center of a complex story. It's about degrees of guilt and complicity, and his understanding of a difficult character keeps the film from falling into "us vs. them" simplicity. The role also denied Lancaster the physicality that was so much a part of his work. He returned to it in John Frankenheimer's underrated thriller, *The Train*. Performing stunts that would have been daunting to actors half his age—Lancaster was 51—he plays a railway inspector who must save a trainload of French art from the Nazis as the Allies approach Paris.

In *Castle Keep*, he is the leader of a group of soldiers who occupy a French castle during World War II. The film is not available on video, and I haven't seen it since its original release in 1969. Though it is dismissed by most critics, I remember it as being slow and moody, with an introspective performance by Lancaster.

Finally, in 1978, Lancaster starred in one of the finest "lost" films of Vietnam, *Go Tell the Spartans*. In some respects, it's a modest effort, in no way comparable to the ambitions of *Apocalypse Now* or *The Deer Hunter*, but it takes a much more realistic approach to the first days of American involvement. More importantly, the film cuts straight to the moral dilemma that this country had to face after it had placed itself in the middle of a civil war without understanding the complexities of the situation.

It's a fitting end to Lancaster's contribution to the genre. After it, he would make several more of his better films—*Atlantic City*, *Local Hero*—and the "prequel" to *Zulu*, *Zulu Dawn*. In a career as richly varied as Lancaster's, one genre is not particularly important, but his war films played to his strengths as an actor and as a star. He was able to combine physical action and grace with intelligence and solid storytelling in a way that no one else has equaled.

THE RAZOR'S EDGE
1946 Edmund Goulding ♪♪♪

"This is the young man of whom I write. He is not famous. It may be that when his life at last comes to an end, he will leave no more trace of his sojourn on this earth than a stone thrown into a river leaves on the surface of the water. Yet it may be that the way of life he has chosen for himself may have an ever-growing influence over his fellow man so that long after his death, perhaps, it will be realized that there lived in this age a very remarkable creature."

So Somerset Maugham (Herbert Marshall) introduces Larry Darrell (Tyrone Power) and sets the tone for an unusually faithful adaptation. When a fiction writer becomes a character, perhaps filmmakers feel an extra sense of responsibility to the source material, but director Edmund Goulding and writer Lamar Trotti also understand exactly what the real Maugham is up to. From the opening moments, they involve the audience with the characters and then let those characters do the rest. In other hands, the plot might float away in a cloud of soap bubbles. With another cast, the whole thing might have foundered under the weight of all the dialogue. But this time that elusive screen "chemistry" works to perfection.

The story begins in the summer of 1919 in Chicago. Maugham is passing through and accepts an invitation from his old but not close friend Elliott Templeton (Clifton Webb) to attend a country club dinner party. There he meets Larry and his fiancee Isabel (Gene Tierney), Elliott's niece. He also meets their friend Sophie MacDonald (Anne Baxter), who will be more important later, and Gray Maturin (John Payne) who is also in love with Isabel. Times are good; everyone is making lots of money and the prospects for an intelligent young man like Larry seem limitless. But he wants something more. The war changed him in ways he does not understand.

He tells Isabel that on the last day of the war, the last moments, actually, his life was saved by another man who deliberately sacrificed himself. Larry can't get over the experience. "So, he's gone and I'm alive. Why? It's all so meaningless. You can't help but ask yourself what it's all about. Whether there's any sense to it or whether it's just a stupid blunder."

The marriage is delayed while he goes off in search of answers to those big questions. The routine is the stuff of cliches now—tramp steamer, boho Paris, enlightenment in India—but both the novel and the film were instrumental in the creation of those cliches, and neither loses sight of the characters. Though the romantic entanglements are important, the three male leads really have the best moments. Webb is completely within his element as the pompous, snobbish Elliott, who balances the dapper Maugham and the more passionate Larry.

The film's criticism of a particular kind of American narrow-mindedness is as fresh as it ever was. Maugham's observations about the desire among some veterans to use the transformations that they'd experienced in the war to a more productive end are accurate, and they certainly touched a chord in 1946 audiences. The film was one of the most popular of the year and was nominated for several Academy Awards. (Anne Baxter won for Best Supporting Actress.)

"Why shouldn't they be happy? They have everything in the world to make them happy—money, position, a nice house; Gray's father can't live forever."

Elliott Templeton (Clifton Webb) on the marriage between Isabel and Gray

"He's an English author. He's quite all right. In fact, he's really quite famous, so pretend that you've heard of him even if you haven't."

Elliott on Maugham (Herbert Marshall) to Louisa Bradley (Lucile Watson)

See also
The Razor's Edge (1984)
The Big Parade
The Best Years of Our Lives

The post-war idealism that Maugham addressed would fade quickly in the face of the emerging economic boom, the famous "organization man" and "good life" of the 1950s. Even so, *The Razor's Edge* remains one of the most enjoyable films of its time, and the 1984 Bill Murray remake is actually much better than its reputation.

Tyrone Power is traveler Larry Darrell in *The Razor's Edge*. The Kobal Collection

Cast: Tyrone Power (Larry Darrell), Gene Tierney (Isabel), Anne Baxter (Sophie MacDonald), Clifton Webb (Elliot Templeton), Herbert Marshall (Somerset Maugham), John Payne (Gary Maturin), Elsa Lanchester (Miss Keith), Lucile Watson (Louisa Bradley), Frank Latimore (Bob MacDonald), Cecil Humphreys (Holy Man), Harry Pilcer (Specialty dancer), Cobina Wright Sr. (Princess Novemali), Noel Cravat (Russian singer), John Wengraf (Joseph); **Written by:** Lamar Trotti; **Cinematography by:** Arthur C. Miller; **Music by:** Alfred Newman. **Producer:** Darryl F. Zanuck, 20th Century-Fox. **Awards:** Academy Awards '46: Best Supporting Actress (Baxter); Golden Globe Awards '47: Best Supporting Actor (Webb), Best Supporting Actress (Baxter); Nominations: Academy Awards '46: Best Interior Decoration, Best Picture, Best Supporting Actor (Webb). **Running Time:** 146 minutes. **Format:** VHS, Beta, LV, Closed Caption.

THE THIRD MAN
1949 Carol Reed ♪♪♪♪

"I never knew the old Vienna before the war with its Strauss music, its glamour, the easy charm. Constantinople suited me better. I really got to know it in the classic period of the black market. We'd run anything if people wanted it enough and had the money to pay. Of course, a situation like that does tempt amateurs but, well, you know, they can't stay the course like a professional."

Opening voice-over by Carol Reed

"Nobody thinks in terms of human beings. Governments don't, why should we? They talk about 'the people' and 'the proletariat.' I talk about the suckers and the mugs. It's the same thing. They have their 'five year plan' and so have I."

Harry Lime (Orson Welles)

"In Italy, for 30 years under the Borgias, they had warfare, terror, murder, and bloodshed but they produced Michelangelo, Leonardo da Vinci, and the Renaissance. In Switzerland, they had brotherly love. They had 500 years of democracy and peace and what did they produce? The cuckoo clock."

Harry Lime

Did you Know?
Assistant director Guy Hamilton and actor Bernard Lee would be reunited when Hamilton took the helm of *Goldfinger,* where Lee played the recurring character of M, James Bond's boss.

In *The Immortal Battalion*, director Carol Reed praises the patriotic spirit that united England and other countries against the evils of fascism. In *The Third Man*, he takes a cool look at the fruits of that victory and finds a moral landscape as treacherous as the bombed-out rubble of Vienna. The film is justly famous as an intelligent thriller, precursor to the American films noir that would follow in the 1950s. In its understanding of post-war Europe, it's also a companion piece to *Judgment at Nuremberg* and *The Victors*—a film about hard choices between loyalty and conscience.

Holly Martins (Joseph Cotten), hack writer of popular western novels, comes to Vienna at the invitation of his childhood friend Harry Lime (Orson Welles). Harry has promised Holly some sort of job in this "closed" city that's clumsily governed by military forces from France, England, America, and the Soviet Union. The first thing that Holly learns is that he's a day late; his friend was killed in an automobile accident. If he hurries, he can still make the funeral. That's where he is spotted by Maj. Calloway (Trevor Howard), a British security officer who tells an unbelieving Holly that his friend was involved in the black market. Harry didn't just dabble. "He was about the worst racketeer that ever made a dirty living in this city," Calloway says. Holly is insulted but his naive curiosity is aroused and he decides to learn more about Harry. Part of his motivation is sexual. He's attracted to Harry's old girlfriend Anna (Alida Valli). The more he learns, the less sense Harry's death makes and he's soon certain that it was a murder.

That's the first of Holly's mistakes. As the plot twists itself into tighter and tighter contortions, Holly makes one blunder after another. In this case, though, the story is no more important than the style in which it is told. Reed and cinematographer Robert Krasker fill the screen with canted "Dutch" angles, heavy shadows, and menace that appears in the most innocent forms. A child playing with a ball becomes an ominous figure at one of the major turning points. And all of the action is played out to the accompaniment of Anton Karas's famous zither score. The city itself, partially destroyed and dominated by the giant Ferris wheel, is as important as the human characters. An extended sequence in the middle begins with a wild taxi ride through dark streets, then turns into a foot chase, and finally becomes a descent into a rubble-strewn hell. The concluding chase through the sewers is one of the most famous sequences in the history of film, and it's still the best of its kind, with images taken straight from a dream and put on the screen.

With so much else going on, it's easy to forget the central ideas that Reed and writer Graham Greene are working with. Holly is an archetypal innocent who fundamentally misunderstands Europe and the changes that the war has caused. In one of his first scenes, he walks blithely under a ladder. Throughout the film he and the other characters get names wrong and often

See also
The Manchurian Candidate
Since You Went Away
Hangmen Also Die
The Seventh Cross
Chinatown

cannot understand what Austrian speakers are saying without translation. The famous and absolutely perfect final shot underscores how little Holly has learned. Fascism may have been defeated, but the old divisions have not been closed.

That view of post-war Europe certainly is bleak, but bleakness has never been presented in such striking, indelible images. *The Third Man* is one of the all-time greats, and in some ways, it is even better on video than it is on the big screen. The American theatrical release is 93 minutes long. The tape was made from the longer 100-minute European version with Carol Reed's voice-over narration.

Orson Welles finds himself in the middle of some dirty business in *The Third Man*. The Kobal Collection

Fact:
American Cinematographer magazine places *The Third Man* at the number nine position on its list of the 50 Best Shot Films, 1894-1949.

Cast: Joseph Cotten (Holly Martins), Orson Welles (Harry Lime), Alida Valli (Anna Schmidt), Trevor Howard (Maj. Calloway), Bernard Lee (Sgt. Paine), Wilfrid Hyde-White (Crabbin), Ernst Deutsch (Baron Kurtz), Erich Ponto (Dr. Winkel), Siegfried Breuer (Popescu), Hedwig Bleibtreu (Old woman), Paul Hoerbiger (Porter), Herbert Halbik (Hansel), Frederick Schreicker (Hansel's father), Jenny Werner (Winkel's maid), Nelly Arno (Kurtz's mother), Alexis Chesnakov (Brodsky), Leo Bieber (Barman), Paul Hardtmuth (Hall Porter), Geoffrey Keen (British policeman), Annie Rosar (Porter's wife); **Written by:** Graham Greene; **Cinematography by:** Robert Krasker; **Music by:** Anton Karas. **Producer:** British Lion, Selznick Pictures, Alexander Korda, Carol Reed, David O. Selznick. **British. Awards:** Academy Awards '50: Best Black and White Cinematography; British Academy Awards '49: Best Film; Cannes Film Festival '49: Best Film; Directors Guild of America Awards '49: Best Director (Reed); American Film Institute (AFI) '98: Top 100; Nominations: Academy Awards '50: Best Director (Reed), Best Film Editing. **Running Time:** 104 minutes. **Format:** VHS, Beta, LV, 8mm.

The "Titles Index" provides a complete list of movies reviewed in this book along with the pages on which they appear, as well as "see" references for alternative and/or translated titles. The films are listed alphabetically, and the chapter in which they appear follows each title in parentheses.

C

Casablanca (1942) (WW II: The Resistance)...............438

Catch-22 (1970) (WW II: Europe & North Africa).....213

Chapayev (1934) (Russian Wars)................................119

Charge of the Light Brigade (1936) (British Wars)..........58

Charge of the Light Brigade (1968) (British Wars)..........62

China Gate (1957) (Vietnam War) 491

The Clansman
See Birth of a Nation (1915) (American Wars)

Come and See (1985) (WW II: Europe & North Africa)................................216

Coming Home (1978) (Coming Home).........................529

Command Decision (1948) (WW II: Europe & North Africa)................................218

A Condemned Man Has Escaped
See A Man Escaped (1957) (WW II: POWs)

Courage Under Fire (1996) (Coming Home)................532

Crash Dive (1943) (WW II: Europe & North Africa).....220

Cross of Iron (1976) (WW II: Europe & North Africa).....222

D

Das Boot (1981) (WW II: Europe & North Africa).....224

Dawn Patrol (1938) (WW I)................................138

The Deer Hunter (1978) (Vietnam War).................493

Die Brucke
See The Bridge (1959) (WW II: Europe & North Africa)

Die Weisse Rose
See The White Rose (1983) (WW II: The Resistance)

The Dirty Dozen (1967) (WW II: Europe & North Africa)................................226

Dive Bomber (1941) (Between the World Wars)................................174

Dr. Strangelove, or: How I Learned to Stop Worrying and Love the Bomb (1964) (American Wars) 12

Doctor Zhivago (1965) (Russian Wars) 121

E

84 Charlie MoPic (1989) (Vietnam War)..................495

Empire of the Sun (1987) (WW II: POWs)................412

F

Fighting Seabees (1944) (WW II: Pacific) 304

The Fighting 69th (1940) (WW I)............................140

The Fighting Sullivans (1942) (WW II: Pacific).....306

Fires on the Plain (1959) (WW II: Pacific) 308

Five Graves to Cairo (1943) (WW II: Europe & North Africa)................................228

Flying Leathernecks (1951) (WW II: Pacific) 310

For Whom the Bell Tolls (1943) (Between the World Wars)................................176

The Four Feathers (1939) (British Wars) 64

Four Horsemen of the Apocalypse (1921) (WW I) 142

From Here to Eternity (1953) (Between the World Wars)................................178

Full Metal Jacket (1987) (Vietnam War)..................497

G

The Gallant Hours (1960) (WW II: Pacific) 313

Gallipoli (1981) (WW I) ...144

Gardens of Stone (1987) (Vietnam War)..................500

The General (1926) (American Wars)..........................14

Gettysburg (1993) (American Wars)................................16

Glory (1989) (American Wars)................................18

Go and See
See Come and See (1985) (WW II: Europe & North Africa)

Go Tell the Spartans (1978) (Vietnam War)..................502

Gone with the Wind (1939) (American Wars) 20

Good Morning, Vietnam (1987) (Vietnam War).......504

The Good, the Bad and the Ugly (1967) (American Wars)................................23

The "Cast Index" provides a complete listing of cast members cited within the reviews in this book. The actors' names are alphabetical by last name, and the films they appeared in are listed chronologically, from most recent film to the oldest. (Note that only the films reviewed in this book are cited.) Directors, screenwriters, cinematographers, and composers get the same treatment in their own respective indexes.

A

John Abbott
Mrs. Miniver '42 (WW II: Homefront)

Walter Abel
13 Rue Madeleine '46 (WW II: The Resistance)
So Proudly We Hail '43 (WW II: Pacific)
Wake Island '42 (WW II: Pacific)

Andrei Abrikosov
Alexander Nevsky '38 (Russian Wars)

Eddie Acuff
Guadalcanal Diary '43 (WW II: Pacific)
They Died with Their Boots On '41 (American Wars)

Claire Adams
The Big Parade '25 (WW I)

Dorothy Adams
The Best Years of Our Lives '46 (Coming Home)
So Proudly We Hail '43 (WW II: Pacific)

Joe Adams
The Manchurian Candidate '62 (Korean War)

Nick Adams
Hell Is for Heroes '62 (WW II: Europe & North Africa)
Mister Roberts '55 (WW II: Pacific)

Wesley Addy
Tora! Tora! Tora! '70 (WW II: Pacific)

Renee Adoree
The Big Parade '25 (WW I)

Iris Adrian
Action in the North Atlantic '43 (WW II: Europe & North Africa)

Max Adrian
Henry V '44 (British Wars)

John Agar
Sands of Iwo Jima '49 (WW II: Pacific)

She Wore a Yellow Ribbon '49 (American Wars)

Philip Ahn
Battle Circus '53 (Korean War)
They Were Expendable '45 (WW II: Pacific)
Across the Pacific '42 (Between the World Wars)

Charles Aidman
Pork Chop Hill '59 (Korean War)

Spottiswoode Aitken
Birth of a Nation '15 (American Wars)

Lucy Akhurst
The Land Girls '98 (WW II: Homefront)

Claude Akins
Merrill's Marauders '62 (WW II: Pacific)
The Caine Mutiny '54 (WW II: Europe & North Africa)
From Here to Eternity '53 (Between the World Wars)

Eddie Albert
The Longest Day '62 (WW II: Europe & North Africa)

Frank Albertson
Wake Island '42 (WW II: Pacific)

Karl Otto Alberty
Battle of the Bulge '65 (WW II: Europe & North Africa)
The Great Escape '63 (WW II: POWs)

Rutanya Alda
The Deer Hunter '78 (Vietnam War)

Mary Alden
Birth of a Nation '15 (American Wars)

Norman Alden
Tora! Tora! Tora! '70 (WW II: Pacific)

Erville Alderson
Objective, Burma! '45 (WW II: Pacific)
Sergeant York '41 (WW I)
America '24 (American Wars)

Frank Aletter
Tora! Tora! Tora! '70 (WW II: Pacific)

Ben Alexander
All Quiet on the Western Front '30 (WW I)

Jane Alexander
Glory '89 (American Wars)

Mikush Alexander
One Against the Wind '91 (WW II: The Resistance)

Richard Alexander
All Quiet on the Western Front '30 (WW I)

Terence Alexander
Waterloo '71 (French Wars)

Grigori Alexandrov
Battleship Potemkin '25 (Russian Wars)

Lidia Alfonsi
Life Is Beautiful '98 (WW II: The Holocaust)

Phillip Alford
Shenandoah '65 (American Wars)

David Allen
Land and Freedom '95 (Between the World Wars)

Jack Allen
The Four Feathers '39 (British Wars)

Nancy Allen
1941 '79 (WW II: Homefront)

Penelope Allen
The Thin Red Line '98 (WW II: Pacific)

June Allyson
Battle Circus '53 (Korean War)

Chelo Alonso
The Good, the Bad and the Ugly '67 (American Wars)

Murray Alper
They Were Expendable '45 (WW II: Pacific)

John Alvin
Objective, Burma! *'45 (WW II: Pacific)*
The Fighting Sullivans *'42 (WW II: Pacific)*

Leon Ames
Tora! Tora! Tora! *'70 (WW II: Pacific)*
Battleground *'49 (WW II: Europe & North Africa)*
They Were Expendable *'45 (WW II: Pacific)*
Thirty Seconds over Tokyo *'44 (WW II: Pacific)*

Paul Amiot
Napoleon *'27 (French Wars)*

David Anderson
The Siege of Firebase Gloria *'89 (Vietnam War)*

Eddie Anderson
Gone with the Wind *'39 (American Wars)*

Herb Anderson
Battleground *'49 (WW II: Europe & North Africa)*
Dive Bomber *'41 (Between the World Wars)*
The Fighting 69th *'40 (WW I)*

James Anderson
Sergeant York *'41 (WW I)*

Mary Anderson
Lifeboat *'44 (WW II: Europe & North Africa)*
Gone with the Wind *'39 (American Wars)*

Richard Anderson
Gettysburg *'93 (American Wars)*
Tora! Tora! Tora! *'70 (WW II: Pacific)*
Paths of Glory *'57 (WW I)*

Warner Anderson
The Caine Mutiny *'54 (WW II: Europe & North Africa)*
Command Decision *'48 (WW II: Europe & North Africa)*
Objective, Burma! *'45 (WW II: Pacific)*

Keith Andes
Tora! Tora! Tora! *'70 (WW II: Pacific)*

Ursula Andress
The Blue Max *'66 (WW I)*

Sylvia Andrew
Three Came Home *'50 (WW II: POWs)*

Anthony Andrews
The Lighthorsemen *'87 (WW I)*

Dana Andrews
Battle of the Bulge *'65 (WW II: Europe & North Africa)*
In Harm's Way *'65 (WW II: Pacific)*
The Best Years of Our Lives *'46 (Coming Home)*
A Walk in the Sun *'46 (WW II: Europe & North Africa)*
Crash Dive *'43 (WW II: Europe & North Africa)*

Edward Andrews
Tora! Tora! Tora! *'70 (WW II: Pacific)*

Harry Andrews
Too Late the Hero *'70 (WW II: Pacific)*
The Battle of Britain *'69 (WW II: Europe & North Africa)*
Charge of the Light Brigade *'68 (British Wars)*

Mac Andrews
Last of the Mohicans *'92 (American Wars)*

Stanley Andrews
Crash Dive *'43 (WW II: Europe & North Africa)*
Beau Geste *'39 (British Wars)*

Tige Andrews
Mister Roberts *'55 (WW II: Pacific)*

Tod Andrews
In Harm's Way *'65 (WW II: Pacific)*
Dive Bomber *'41 (Between the World Wars)*
They Died with Their Boots On *'41 (American Wars)*

Marayat Andriane
The Sand Pebbles *'66 (American Wars)*

Heather Angel
Lifeboat *'44 (WW II: Europe & North Africa)*

Pier Angeli
Battle of the Bulge *'65 (WW II: Europe & North Africa)*

Christien Anholt
One Against the Wind *'91 (WW II: The Resistance)*

Paul Anka
The Longest Day *'62 (WW II: Europe & North Africa)*

Annabella
13 Rue Madeleine *'46 (WW II: The Resistance)*
Napoleon *'27 (French Wars)*

Alexander Antonov
Battleship Potemkin *'25 (Russian Wars)*

Jonas Applegarth
Battle Cry *'55 (WW II: Pacific)*

Royce D. Applegate
Gettysburg *'93 (American Wars)*

Art Aragon
To Hell and Back *'55 (WW II: Europe & North Africa)*

John Archer
Crash Dive *'43 (WW II: Europe & North Africa)*
Guadalcanal Diary *'43 (WW II: Pacific)*

Robert Arevalo
The Siege of Firebase Gloria *'89 (Vietnam War)*

David Argue
Gallipoli *'81 (WW I)*

Ben Aris
Charge of the Light Brigade *'68 (British Wars)*

Alan Arkin
Mother Night *'96 (WW II: Europe & North Africa)*
Catch-22 *'70 (WW II: Europe & North Africa)*

David Arkin
M*A*S*H *'70 (Korean War)*

Richard Arlen
Wings *'27 (WW I)*

Arletty
The Longest Day *'62 (WW II: Europe & North Africa)*

Alun Armstrong
Braveheart *'95 (British Wars)*

Robert Armstrong
Mr. Winkle Goes to War *'44 (WW II: Europe & North Africa)*
Dive Bomber *'41 (Between the World Wars)*

Todd Armstrong
King Rat *'65 (WW II: POWs)*

Desi Arnaz, Sr.
Bataan *'43 (WW II: Pacific)*

James Arness
Battleground *'49 (WW II: Europe & North Africa)*

Nelly Arno
The Third Man *'49 (Coming Home)*

Cast Index

Edward Arnold
Command Decision '48 (WW II: Europe & North Africa)

Carlos Arruza
The Alamo '60 (American Wars)

Nikolai Arsky
Alexander Nevsky '38 (Russian Wars)

Antonin Artaud
Napoleon '27 (French Wars)

Indus Arthur
M*A*S*H '70 (Korean War)

Robert Arthur
Twelve O'Clock High '49 (WW II: Europe & North Africa)

Renee Asherson
Henry V '44 (British Wars)
Immortal Battalion '44 (WW II: Europe & North Africa)

Luke Askew
The Green Berets '68 (Vietnam War)

Chuck Aspegren
The Deer Hunter '78 (Vietnam War)

Sean Astin
Courage Under Fire '96 (Coming Home)

Mary Astor
Across the Pacific '42 (Between the World Wars)

Richard Attenborough
The Sand Pebbles '66 (American Wars)
The Great Escape '63 (WW II: POWs)
In Which We Serve '43 (WW II: Europe & North Africa)

Barry Atwater
Pork Chop Hill '59 (Korean War)

Lionel Atwill
To Be or Not to Be '42 (WW II: The Resistance)

Kim Atwood
M*A*S*H '70 (Korean War)

Robert Atzorn
The Wannsee Conference '84 (WW II: The Holocaust)

Rene Auberjonois
M*A*S*H '70 (Korean War)

Stephane Audran
The Big Red One '80 (WW II: Europe & North Africa)

Mischa Auer
Lives of a Bengal Lancer '35 (British Wars)

Frankie Avalon
The Alamo '60 (American Wars)

Keiko Awaji
The Bridges at Toko-Ri '55 (Korean War)

Dan Aykroyd
1941 '79 (WW II: Homefront)

Arthur Aylesworth
Beau Geste '39 (British Wars)

Felix Aylmer
Henry V '44 (British Wars)

Lew Ayres
All Quiet on the Western Front '30 (WW I)

B

Boris Babochkin
Chapayev '34 (Russian Wars)

Jim Backus
Above and Beyond '53 (WW II: Pacific)

John Baer
Above and Beyond '53 (WW II: Pacific)

Parley Baer
The Young Lions '58 (WW II: Europe & North Africa)

Vladas Bagdonas
Come and See '85 (WW II: Europe & North Africa)

Raymond Bailey
The Gallant Hours '60 (WW II: Pacific)

Hugh Baird
America '24 (American Wars)

Richard Bakalayan
Von Ryan's Express '65 (WW II: POWs)

Dylan Baker
Last of the Mohicans '92 (American Wars)

Jill Baker
Hope and Glory '87 (WW II: Homefront)

Stanley Baker
Zulu '64 (British Wars)

The Guns of Navarone '61 (WW II: Europe & North Africa)

William "Billy" Bakewell
Gone with the Wind '39 (American Wars)
All Quiet on the Western Front '30 (WW I)

Bob Balaban
Catch-22 '70 (WW II: Europe & North Africa)

Adam Baldwin
Full Metal Jacket '87 (Vietnam War)

Daniel Baldwin
Born on the Fourth of July '89 (Coming Home)

Stephen Baldwin
Born on the Fourth of July '89 (Coming Home)

Walter Baldwin
The Best Years of Our Lives '46 (Coming Home)
Mr. Winkle Goes to War '44 (WW II: Europe & North Africa)

William Baldwin
Born on the Fourth of July '89 (Coming Home)

Christian Bale
Henry V '89 (British Wars)
Empire of the Sun '87 (WW II: POWs)

Vincent Ball
Breaker Morant '80 (British Wars)
Where Eagles Dare '68 (WW II: Europe & North Africa)

J.G. Ballard
Empire of the Sun '87 (WW II: POWs)

Martin Balsam
Catch-22 '70 (WW II: Europe & North Africa)
Tora! Tora! Tora! '70 (WW II: Pacific)

Karl Michael Balzer
The Bridge '59 (WW II: Europe & North Africa)

Tallulah Bankhead
Lifeboat '44 (WW II: Europe & North Africa)

Dennis Banks
Last of the Mohicans '92 (American Wars)

Leslie Banks
Henry V '44 (British Wars)

Ian Bannen
Braveheart '95 (British Wars)
Hope and Glory '87 (WW II: Home-
front)
Too Late the Hero '70 (WW II:
Pacific)

John Banner
The Immortal Sergeant '43 (WW II:
Europe & North Africa)

Anthony Barille
Hamburger Hill '87 (Vietnam War)

Peter Barkworth
Where Eagles Dare '68 (WW II:
Europe & North Africa)

Frank Barnes
The General '26 (American Wars)

Jean-Marc Barr
Hope and Glory '87 (WW II: Homefront)

Robert Barrat
They Were Expendable '45 (WW II:
Pacific)
Charge of the Light Brigade '36
(British Wars)

Jean-Louis Barrault
The Longest Day '62 (WW II:
Europe & North Africa)

Sean Barrett
Sink the Bismarck! '60 (WW II:
Europe & North Africa)
War and Peace '56 (Russian Wars)

Gene Barry
China Gate '57 (Vietnam War)

Raymond J. Barry
Born on the Fourth of July '89
(Coming Home)

Lionel Barrymore
Since You Went Away '44 (WW II:
Homefront)
America '24 (American Wars)

Vladimir Barsky
Battleship Potemkin '25 (Russian
Wars)

Charles T. Barton
Beau Geste '39 (British Wars)

Albert Basserman
Since You Went Away '44 (WW II:
Homefront)

Pierre Batcheff
Napoleon '27 (French Wars)

Florence Bates
Since You Went Away '44 (WW II:
Homefront)

Michael Bates
Patton '70 (WW II: Europe & North
Africa)

Archibald Batty
The Four Feathers '39 (British
Wars)

Paul Baxley
All the Young Men '60 (Korean War)

Alan Baxter
Judgment at Nuremberg '61 (Coming Home)

Anne Baxter
The Razor's Edge '46 (Coming
Home)
Crash Dive '43 (WW II: Europe &
North Africa)
Five Graves to Cairo '43 (WW II:
Europe & North Africa)
The Fighting Sullivans '42 (WW II:
Pacific)

Clive Baxter
The Four Feathers '39 (British
Wars)

Geoffrey Bayldon
King Rat '65 (WW II: POWs)

Hal Baylor
The Young Lions '58 (WW II:
Europe & North Africa)
Sands of Iwo Jima '49 (WW II:
Pacific)

Ned Beatty
1941 '79 (WW II: Homefront)

Robert Beatty
Where Eagles Dare '68 (WW II:
Europe & North Africa)

Hugh Beaumont
Objective, Burma! '45 (WW II:
Pacific)
Mr. Winkle Goes to War '44 (WW II:
Europe & North Africa)
Wake Island '42 (WW II: Pacific)

Glenn Beck
Dr. Strangelove, or: How I Learned
to Stop Worrying and Love the
Bomb '64 (American Wars)

Jacques Becker
Grand Illusion '37 (WW I)

Konrad Becker
Das Boot '81 (WW II: Europe &
North Africa)

Scotty Beckett
Battleground '49 (WW II: Europe &
North Africa)
Charge of the Light Brigade '36
(British Wars)

Friedrich Beckhaus
The Wannsee Conference '84 (WW
II: The Holocaust)

Kate Beckinsale
One Against the Wind '91 (WW II:
The Resistance)

William Beckley
Too Late the Hero '70 (WW II:
Pacific)

Don Beddoe
The Best Years of Our Lives '46
(Coming Home)
O.S.S. '46 (WW II: The Resistance)

Maurice Beerblock
A Man Escaped '57 (WW II: POWs)

Noah Beery, Jr.
Sergeant York '41 (WW I)

Wallace Beery
Four Horsemen of the Apocalypse
'21 (WW I)

Lee Beggs
America '24 (American Wars)

Bernard Behrens
Mother Night '96 (WW II: Europe &
North Africa)

Ann Bell
The Land Girls '98 (WW II: Homefront)

James Bell
Flying Leathernecks '51 (WW II:
Pacific)
So Proudly We Hail '43 (WW II:
Pacific)

Ralph Bellamy
Dive Bomber '41 (Between the
World Wars)

Harry Bellaver
From Here to Eternity '53 (Between
the World Wars)

Jean-Paul Belmondo
Is Paris Burning? '66 (WW II:
Europe & North Africa)

John Belushi
1941 '79 (WW II: Homefront)

William Bendix
Lifeboat '44 (WW II: Europe & North
Africa)

Guadalcanal Diary '43 (WW II: Pacific)
Wake Island '42 (WW II: Pacific)

Billy Benedict
The Story of G.I. Joe '45 (WW II: Europe & North Africa)

Richard Benedict
O.S.S. '46 (WW II: The Resistance)
A Walk in the Sun '46 (WW II: Europe & North Africa)

Hubertus Bengsch
Das Boot '81 (WW II: Europe & North Africa)

Roberto Benigni
Life Is Beautiful '98 (WW II: The Holocaust)

Richard Benjamin
Catch-22 '70 (WW II: Europe & North Africa)

Heinz Bennent
The Last Metro '80 (WW II: The Holocaust)

Bruce (Herman Brix) Bennett
Sahara '43 (WW II: Europe & North Africa)

Charles Bennett
America '24 (American Wars)

Jill Bennett
Charge of the Light Brigade '68 (British Wars)

Jack Benny
To Be or Not to Be '42 (WW II: The Resistance)

Martin Benrath
The White Rose '83 (WW II: The Resistance)

Lucille Benson
1941 '79 (WW II: Homefront)

Susanne Benton
Catch-22 '70 (WW II: Europe & North Africa)

George Beranger
Birth of a Nation '15 (American Wars)

Jean-Claude Bercq
The Train '65 (WW II: Europe & North Africa)

Tom Berenger
Gettysburg '93 (American Wars)
Born on the Fourth of July '89 (Coming Home)
Platoon '86 (Vietnam War)

Peter Berg
A Midnight Clear '92 (WW II: Europe & North Africa)

Candice Bergen
The Wind and the Lion '75 (American Wars)
The Sand Pebbles '66 (American Wars)

Senta Berger
Cross of Iron '76 (WW II: Europe & North Africa)
The Victors '63 (WW II: Europe & North Africa)

Ingrid Bergman
For Whom the Bell Tolls '43 (Between the World Wars)
Casablanca '42 (WW II: The Resistance)

Francois Berleand
Au Revoir les Enfants '87 (WW II: The Holocaust)

Armand Bernard
Napoleon '27 (French Wars)

Joachim Bernhard
Das Boot '81 (WW II: Europe & North Africa)

Frank Berry
Dr. Strangelove, or: How I Learned to Stop Worrying and Love the Bomb '64 (American Wars)

James Best
Shenandoah '65 (American Wars)

Paul Bettany
The Land Girls '98 (WW II: Homefront)

Billy Bevan
Mrs. Miniver '42 (WW II: Homefront)
The Lost Patrol '34 (WW I)

Clem Bevans
Sergeant York '41 (WW I)

Richard Beymer
The Longest Day '62 (WW II: Europe & North Africa)

Suzanne Bianchetti
Napoleon '27 (French Wars)

Abner Biberman
Gunga Din '39 (British Wars)

Charles Bickford
Command Decision '48 (WW II: Europe & North Africa)

Leo Bieber
The Third Man '49 (Coming Home)

Chief John Big Tree
She Wore a Yellow Ribbon '49 (American Wars)

Stephen Billington
Braveheart '95 (British Wars)

Edward Binns
Patton '70 (WW II: Europe & North Africa)
Judgment at Nuremberg '61 (Coming Home)

Julie Bishop
Sands of Iwo Jima '49 (WW II: Pacific)
Action in the North Atlantic '43 (WW II: Europe & North Africa)

Whit Bissell
The Manchurian Candidate '62 (Korean War)
The Caine Mutiny '54 (WW II: Europe & North Africa)
The Red Badge of Courage '51 (American Wars)

Jon Blake
The Lighthorsemen '87 (WW I)

Oliver Blake
Casablanca '42 (WW II: The Resistance)

Robert (Bobby) Blake
Pork Chop Hill '59 (Korean War)

Cate Blanchett
Paradise Road '97 (WW II: POWs)

Hans-Christian Blech
Battle of the Bulge '65 (WW II: Europe & North Africa)
The Longest Day '62 (WW II: Europe & North Africa)

Hedwig Bleibtreu
The Third Man '49 (Coming Home)

Brian Blessed
Henry V '89 (British Wars)

Sergei Blinnikov
Alexander Nevsky '38 (Russian Wars)

Boris Blinov
Chapayev '34 (Russian Wars)

Monte Blue
Across the Pacific '42 (Between the World Wars)
Casablanca '42 (WW II: The Resistance)
Lives of a Bengal Lancer '35 (British Wars)

Cast Index

Benedick Blythe
One Against the Wind '91 (WW II: The Resistance)

Betty Blythe
They Were Expendable '45 (WW II: Pacific)

Bruce Boa
Full Metal Jacket '87 (Vietnam War)

Michael Boatman
Hamburger Hill '87 (Vietnam War)

Dirk Bogarde
A Bridge Too Far '77 (WW II: Europe & North Africa)

Humphrey Bogart
The Caine Mutiny '54 (WW II: Europe & North Africa)
Battle Circus '53 (Korean War)
Action in the North Atlantic '43 (WW II: Europe & North Africa)
Sahara '43 (WW II: Europe & North Africa)
Across the Pacific '42 (Between the World Wars)
Casablanca '42 (WW II: The Resistance)

Hark Bohm
Underground '95 (WW II: Europe & North Africa)

Roman Bohnen
The Best Years of Our Lives '46 (Coming Home)

Volker Bohnet
The Bridge '59 (WW II: Europe & North Africa)

Curt Bois
Casablanca '42 (WW II: The Resistance)

Iciar Bollain
Land and Freedom '95 (Between the World Wars)

Fortunio Bonanova
Five Graves to Cairo '43 (WW II: Europe & North Africa)
For Whom the Bell Tolls '43 (Between the World Wars)

Gary Bond
Zulu '64 (British Wars)

Rudy Bond
Run Silent Run Deep '58 (WW II: Pacific)

Ward Bond
Mister Roberts '55 (WW II: Pacific)

They Were Expendable '45 (WW II: Pacific)
The Fighting Sullivans '42 (WW II: Pacific)
Sergeant York '41 (WW I)
Gone with the Wind '39 (American Wars)

Beulah Bondi
Watch on the Rhine '43 (WW II: The Resistance)

Peter Bonerz
Catch-22 '70 (WW II: Europe & North Africa)

Paul Bonifas
The Train '65 (WW II: Europe & North Africa)

Tony Bonner
The Lighthorsemen '87 (WW I)

Richard Boone
The Alamo '60 (American Wars)

Charley Boorman
Hope and Glory '87 (WW II: Homefront)

Katrine Boorman
Hope and Glory '87 (WW II: Homefront)

James Booth
Zulu '64 (British Wars)

Veda Ann Borg
The Alamo '60 (American Wars)

Ernest Borgnine
The Dirty Dozen '67 (WW II: Europe & North Africa)
From Here to Eternity '53 (Between the World Wars)

Dieter Borsche
A Time to Love and a Time to Die '58 (WW II: Europe & North Africa)

Hobart Bosworth
The Big Parade '25 (WW I)

Sam Bottoms
Gardens of Stone '87 (Vietnam War)
Apocalypse Now '79 (Vietnam War)

Barbara Bouchet
In Harm's Way '65 (WW II: Pacific)

Willis Bouchey
The Horse Soldiers '59 (American Wars)
Battle Cry '55 (WW II: Pacific)
The Bridges at Toko-Ri '55 (Korean War)

Clara Bow
Wings '27 (WW I)

Roger Bowen
M*A*S*H '70 (Korean War)

David Bowie
Merry Christmas, Mr. Lawrence '83 (WW II: POWs)

Peter Bowles
Charge of the Light Brigade '68 (British Wars)

Lee Bowman
Bataan '43 (WW II: Pacific)

Amanda Boxer
Saving Private Ryan '98 (WW II: Europe & North Africa)

John Boxer
Bridge on the River Kwai '57 (WW II: POWs)

Charles Boyer
Is Paris Burning? '66 (WW II: Europe & North Africa)

Hal Boyle
The Story of G.I. Joe '45 (WW II: Europe & North Africa)

Richard Bradford
A Rumor of War '80 (Vietnam War)

John H. Bradley
Sands of Iwo Jima '49 (WW II: Pacific)

Kenneth Branagh
Henry V '89 (British Wars)

Neville Brand
Tora! Tora! Tora! '70 (WW II: Pacific)
Stalag 17 '53 (WW II: POWs)

Marlon Brando
Apocalypse Now '79 (Vietnam War)
The Young Lions '58 (WW II: Europe & North Africa)

Henry Kleinbach Brandon
Beau Geste '39 (British Wars)

Martin Brandt
Judgment at Nuremberg '61 (Coming Home)

Albert Bras
Napoleon '27 (French Wars)

Nicoletta Braschi
Life Is Beautiful '98 (WW II: The Holocaust)

Andre Braugher
The Tuskegee Airmen '95 (WW II: Europe & North Africa)

Glory '89 (American Wars)

Eddie Braun
The Tuskegee Airmen '95 (WW II:
Europe & North Africa)

Arthur Brauss
Cross of Iron '76 (WW II: Europe &
North Africa)
The Train '65 (WW II: Europe &
North Africa)

Robert Bray
The Caine Mutiny '54 (WW II:
Europe & North Africa)

Thomas E. Breen
Battleground '49 (WW II: Europe &
North Africa)

Edmund Breese
All Quiet on the Western Front '30
(WW I)

Mario Brega
The Good, the Bad and the Ugly '67
(American Wars)

El Brendel
Wings '27 (WW I)

Walter Brennan
Sergeant York '41 (WW I)

George Brent
The Fighting 69th '40 (WW I)

John Brent
Catch-22 '70 (WW II: Europe &
North Africa)

Edmund Breon
The White Cliffs of Dover '44 (WW
II: Homefront)

Felix Bressart
The Seventh Cross '44 (WW II:
POWs)
To Be or Not to Be '42 (WW II: The
Resistance)

Jeremy Brett
War and Peace '56 (Russian Wars)

Siegfried Breuer
The Third Man '49 (Coming Home)

Shane Briant
The Lighthorsemen '87 (WW I)

Lloyd Bridges
Home of the Brave '49 (WW II:
Pacific)
A Walk in the Sun '46 (WW II:
Europe & North Africa)
Sahara '43 (WW II: Europe & North
Africa)

Richard Briers
Henry V '89 (British Wars)

Charles Briggs
Merrill's Marauders '62 (WW II:
Pacific)

Adrian Brine
Waterloo '71 (French Wars)

Bo Brinkman
Gettysburg '93 (American Wars)

May Britt
The Hunters '58 (Korean War)
The Young Lions '58 (WW II:
Europe & North Africa)
War and Peace '56 (Russian Wars)

Barbara Britton
So Proudly We Hail '43 (WW II:
Pacific)
Wake Island '42 (WW II: Pacific)

I. Brobov
Battleship Potemkin '25 (Russian
Wars)

Gerd Brockmann
The Wannsee Conference '84 (WW
II: The Holocaust)

Matthew Broderick
Glory '89 (American Wars)

Steve Brodie
The Caine Mutiny '54 (WW II:
Europe & North Africa)
The Steel Helmet '51 (Korean War)
Home of the Brave '49 (WW II:
Pacific)
A Walk in the Sun '46 (WW II:
Europe & North Africa)
Thirty Seconds over Tokyo '44 (WW
II: Pacific)

Adrien Brody
The Thin Red Line '98 (WW II:
Pacific)

James Brolin
Von Ryan's Express '65 (WW II:
POWs)

Charles Bronson
The Dirty Dozen '67 (WW II: Europe
& North Africa)
Battle of the Bulge '65 (WW II:
Europe & North Africa)
The Great Escape '63 (WW II:
POWs)

Hillary Brooke
Wake Island '42 (WW II: Pacific)

Michael Brooke
Dawn Patrol '38 (WW I)

Walter Brooke
Tora! Tora! Tora! '70 (WW II: Pacific)

Rand Brooks
To Hell and Back '55 (WW II:
Europe & North Africa)
Gone with the Wind '39 (American
Wars)

Richard Brooks
84 Charlie MoPic '89 (Vietnam War)

Edward Brophy
Air Force '43 (WW II: Pacific)

Amelda Brown
Hope and Glory '87 (WW II: Homefront)

Barbara Brown
The Fighting Sullivans '42 (WW II:
Pacific)

Bryan Brown
Breaker Morant '80 (British Wars)

Dwier Brown
Gettysburg '93 (American Wars)

Everett Brown
Gone with the Wind '39 (American
Wars)

James Brown
Sands of Iwo Jima '49 (WW II:
Pacific)
Objective, Burma! '45 (WW II:
Pacific)
Air Force '43 (WW II: Pacific)
Wake Island '42 (WW II: Pacific)

Jim Brown
The Dirty Dozen '67 (WW II: Europe
& North Africa)

Peter Brown
Merrill's Marauders '62 (WW II:
Pacific)

Timothy Brown
M*A*S*H '70 (Korean War)

Alistair Browning
Merry Christmas, Mr. Lawrence '83
(WW II: POWs)

David Bruce
Sergeant York '41 (WW I)

Nigel Bruce
Charge of the Light Brigade '36
(British Wars)

Dylan Bruno
When Trumpets Fade '98 (WW II:
Europe & North Africa)

John Bryant
Run Silent Run Deep '58 (WW II: Pacific)
From Here to Eternity '53 (Between the World Wars)

Horst Buchholz
Life Is Beautiful '98 (WW II: The Holocaust)

Leo Bugakov
For Whom the Bell Tolls '43 (Between the World Wars)

Donald Buka
Watch on the Rhine '43 (WW II: The Resistance)

Peter Bull
Dr. Strangelove, or: How I Learned to Stop Worrying and Love the Bomb '64 (American Wars)

Hugh Burden
Immortal Battalion '44 (WW II: Europe & North Africa)

Christopher Burgard
84 Charlie MoPic '89 (Vietnam War)

Gary Burghoff
M*A*S*H '70 (Korean War)

James Burke
Beau Geste '39 (British Wars)
Dawn Patrol '38 (WW I)

Kathleen Burke
Lives of a Bengal Lancer '35 (British Wars)

Edward Burns
Saving Private Ryan '98 (WW II: Europe & North Africa)

Mark Burns
Charge of the Light Brigade '68 (British Wars)

John Burton
Mrs. Miniver '42 (WW II: Homefront)

Peter Burton
Sink the Bismark! '60 (WW II: Europe & North Africa)

Richard Burton
Where Eagles Dare '68 (WW II: Europe & North Africa)
The Longest Day '62 (WW II: Europe & North Africa)

Robert Burton
The Gallant Hours '60 (WW II: Pacific)
Above and Beyond '53 (WW II: Pacific)

Warren Burton
Gettysburg '93 (American Wars)

Paul Busch
China Gate '57 (Vietnam War)

Jochen Busse
The Wannsee Conference '84 (WW II: The Holocaust)

Hans-Werner Bussinger
The Wannsee Conference '84 (WW II: The Holocaust)

Sergio Bustric
Life Is Beautiful '98 (WW II: The Holocaust)

Red Buttons
The Longest Day '62 (WW II: Europe & North Africa)
13 Rue Madeleine '46 (WW II: The Resistance)

Spring Byington
Charge of the Light Brigade '36 (British Wars)

Ralph Byrd
Guadalcanal Diary '43 (WW II: Pacific)

C

James Caan
Gardens of Stone '87 (Vietnam War)
1941 '79 (WW II: Homefront)
A Bridge Too Far '77 (WW II: Europe & North Africa)

Bruce Cabot
The Green Berets '68 (Vietnam War)
In Harm's Way '65 (WW II: Pacific)

Rita Cadillac
Das Boot '81 (WW II: Europe & North Africa)

Jose Maria Caffarell
Doctor Zhivago '65 (Russian Wars)

James Cagney
The Gallant Hours '60 (WW II: Pacific)
Mister Roberts '55 (WW II: Pacific)
13 Rue Madeleine '46 (WW II: The Resistance)
The Fighting 69th '40 (WW I)

Georges Cahuzac
Napoleon '27 (French Wars)

Michael Caine
A Bridge Too Far '77 (WW II: Europe & North Africa)
Too Late the Hero '70 (WW II: Pacific)
The Battle of Britain '69 (WW II: Europe & North Africa)
Zulu '64 (British Wars)

Michael Callan
The Victors '63 (WW II: Europe & North Africa)

Joseph Calleia
The Alamo '60 (American Wars)
For Whom the Bell Tolls '43 (Between the World Wars)

John Calvin
The Siege of Firebase Gloria '89 (Vietnam War)

Rod Cameron
Wake Island '42 (WW II: Pacific)

Colleen Camp
Apocalypse Now '79 (Vietnam War)

Bill Campbell
Gettysburg '93 (American Wars)

John Campbell
The Fighting Sullivans '42 (WW II: Pacific)

Ken Campbell
The Big Red One '80 (WW II: Europe & North Africa)

Nicholas Campbell
A Bridge Too Far '77 (WW II: Europe & North Africa)

William Campbell
Battle Cry '55 (WW II: Pacific)
Battle Circus '53 (Korean War)

John Candy
1941 '79 (WW II: Homefront)

James Canning
The Boys in Company C '77 (Vietnam War)

Pomeroy Cannon
Four Horsemen of the Apocalypse '21 (WW I)

Giorgio Cantarini
Life Is Beautiful '98 (WW II: The Holocaust)

Yakima Canutt
For Whom the Bell Tolls '43 (Between the World Wars)
Gone with the Wind '39 (American Wars)

Cast
Index

Peter Capell
Paths of Glory '57 (WW I)

James B. Cardwell
A Walk in the Sun '46 (WW II:
Europe & North Africa)
The Fighting Sullivans '42 (WW II:
Pacific)

Julien Carette
Grand Illusion '37 (WW I)

Harry Carey, Sr.
Air Force '43 (WW II: Pacific)

Harry Carey, Jr.
Shenandoah '65 (American Wars)
Mister Roberts '55 (WW II: Pacific)
She Wore a Yellow Ribbon '49
(American Wars)

Joyce Carey
In Which We Serve '43 (WW II:
Europe & North Africa)

MacDonald Carey
Wake Island '42 (WW II: Pacific)

Olive Carey
The Alamo '60 (American Wars)

Phil Carey
Mister Roberts '55 (WW II: Pacific)

Timothy Carey
Paths of Glory '57 (WW I)

Richard Carlyle
The Gallant Hours '60 (WW II:
Pacific)

Hoagy Carmichael
The Best Years of Our Lives '46
(Coming Home)

Tullio Carminati
War and Peace '56 (Russian Wars)

George Carney
In Which We Serve '43 (WW II:
Europe & North Africa)

Leslie Caron
Is Paris Burning? '66 (WW II:
Europe & North Africa)

David Carpenter
Gettysburg '93 (American Wars)

Linda Carpenter
Apocalypse Now '79 (Vietnam War)

Raffaella Carra
Von Ryan's Express '65 (WW II:
POWs)

Keith Carradine
A Rumor of War '80 (Vietnam War)

Robert Carradine
The Big Red One '80 (WW II:
Europe & North Africa)
Coming Home '78 (Coming Home)

Beeson Carroll
Coming Home '78 (Coming Home)

Ben Carter
Crash Dive '43 (WW II: Europe &
North Africa)

Janis Carter
Flying Leathernecks '51 (WW II:
Pacific)

Anthony Caruso
Objective, Burma! '45 (WW II:
Pacific)
Watch on the Rhine '43 (WW II: The
Resistance)

Lynne Carver
Bataan '43 (WW II: Pacific)

Nicholas Cascone
84 Charlie MoPic '89 (Vietnam War)

Gerald Case
In Which We Serve '43 (WW II:
Europe & North Africa)

John Cason
From Here to Eternity '53 (Between
the World Wars)

John Cassavetes
The Dirty Dozen '67 (WW II: Europe
& North Africa)

Jean-Pierre Cassel
Is Paris Burning? '66 (WW II:
Europe & North Africa)

Alan Cassell
Breaker Morant '80 (British Wars)

Wally Cassell
Sands of Iwo Jima '49 (WW II:
Pacific)
The Story of G.I. Joe '45 (WW II:
Europe & North Africa)

Don Castle
Wake Island '42 (WW II: Pacific)

Richard Castle
To Hell and Back '55 (WW II:
Europe & North Africa)

Maxwell Caulfield
Gettysburg '93 (American Wars)

Glen Cavender
The General '26 (American Wars)

James Caviezel
The Thin Red Line '98 (WW II:
Pacific)

John Cazale
The Deer Hunter '78 (Vietnam War)

Aldo Cecconi
Waterloo '71 (French Wars)

Adolfo Celi
Von Ryan's Express '65 (WW II:
POWs)

Peter Cellier
One Against the Wind '91 (WW II:
The Resistance)

George Chakiris
Is Paris Burning? '66 (WW II:
Europe & North Africa)

M.R.B. Chakrabandhu
Bridge on the River Kwai '57 (WW
II: POWs)

Howland Chamberlain
The Best Years of Our Lives '46
(Coming Home)

Pauline Chan
Paradise Road '97 (WW II: POWs)

Spencer Chan
Across the Pacific '42 (Between the
World Wars)

Chick Chandler
Action in the North Atlantic '43 (WW
II: Europe & North Africa)

George Chandler
Beau Geste '39 (British Wars)

Jeff Chandler
Merrill's Marauders '62 (WW II:
Pacific)

Lane Chandler
Sergeant York '41 (WW I)

Danny Chang
Battle Circus '53 (Korean War)

Ben Chaplin
The Thin Red Line '98 (WW II:
Pacific)

Charlie Chaplin
The Great Dictator '40 (Between
the World Wars)

Geraldine Chaplin
Doctor Zhivago '65 (Russian Wars)

James Chase
The Victors '63 (WW II: Europe &
North Africa)

Jean-Sebastien Chauvin
Au Revoir les Enfants '87 (WW II:
The Holocaust)

Don Cheadle
Hamburger Hill '87 (Vietnam War)

Andrea Checchi
Waterloo '71 (French Wars)

Patrice Chereau
Last of the Mohicans '92 (American Wars)

Nikolai Cherkasov
Alexander Nevsky '38 (Russian Wars)

Alexis Chesnakov
The Third Man '49 (Coming Home)

Minoru Chiaki
The Hidden Fortress '58 (Japanese Wars)
Seven Samurai '54 (Japanese Wars)

Costas Dino Chimona
Full Metal Jacket '87 (Vietnam War)

Kieu Chinh
Hamburger Hill '87 (Vietnam War)

Boris Chirkov
Chapayev '34 (Russian Wars)

Erik Chitty
Doctor Zhivago '65 (Russian Wars)

Susanne Christian
Paths of Glory '57 (WW I)

Julie Christie
Doctor Zhivago '65 (Russian Wars)

Howard Chuman
Three Came Home '50 (WW II: POWs)

William Chun
The Steel Helmet '51 (Korean War)

Eduardo Ciannelli
Gunga Din '39 (British Wars)

Bridgetta Clark
Four Horsemen of the Apocalypse '21 (WW I)

Cliff Clark
Home of the Brave '49 (WW II: Pacific)

Dane Clark
Action in the North Atlantic '43 (WW II: Europe & North Africa)

Ernest Clark
Sink the Bismarck! '60 (WW II: Europe & North Africa)

Joseph Clark
The Big Red One '80 (WW II: Europe & North Africa)

Angela Clarke
Land and Freedom '95 (Between the World Wars)

Downing Clarke
America '24 (American Wars)

Frank Clarke
Hell's Angels '30 (WW I)

John Clements
The Four Feathers '39 (British Wars)

David Clennon
Go Tell the Spartans '78 (Vietnam War)

Richard Clifford
Henry V '89 (British Wars)

Montgomery Clift
Judgment at Nuremberg '61 (Coming Home)
The Young Lions '58 (WW II: Europe & North Africa)
From Here to Eternity '53 (Between the World Wars)

Elmer Clifton
Birth of a Nation '15 (American Wars)

Kitty Clinget
Paradise Road '97 (WW II: POWs)

E.E. Clive
Charge of the Light Brigade '36 (British Wars)

George Clooney
The Thin Red Line '98 (WW II: Pacific)

Glenn Close
Paradise Road '97 (WW II: POWs)

John Close
Above and Beyond '53 (WW II: Pacific)

James Coburn
Cross of Iron '76 (WW II: Europe & North Africa)
The Great Escape '63 (WW II: POWs)
Hell Is for Heroes '62 (WW II: Europe & North Africa)

Steve Cochran
The Best Years of Our Lives '46 (Coming Home)

Peter Coe
Sands of Iwo Jima '49 (WW II: Pacific)

Frank "Junior" Coghlan
The Fighting 69th '40 (WW I)

Sammy Cohen
The Fighting 69th '40 (WW I)

Claudette Colbert
Three Came Home '50 (WW II: POWs)
Since You Went Away '44 (WW II: Homefront)
So Proudly We Hail '43 (WW II: Pacific)

Tim Colceri
Full Metal Jacket '87 (Vietnam War)

Nat King Cole
China Gate '57 (Vietnam War)

Olivia Cole
Coming Home '78 (Coming Home)

G. Pat Collins
Above and Beyond '53 (WW II: Pacific)

Pat Collins
All Quiet on the Western Front '30 (WW I)

Pauline Collins
Paradise Road '97 (WW II: POWs)

Ray Collins
Command Decision '48 (WW II: Europe & North Africa)
The Best Years of Our Lives '46 (Coming Home)
The Seventh Cross '44 (WW II: POWs)

Christopher Colombi, Jr.
The Deer Hunter '78 (Vietnam War)

Robbie Coltrane
Henry V '89 (British Wars)

Holly Marie Combs
Born on the Fourth of July '89 (Coming Home)

Paul Comi
Pork Chop Hill '59 (Korean War)

Chester Conklin
The Great Dictator '40 (Between the World Wars)

Sean Connery
A Bridge Too Far '77 (WW II: Europe & North Africa)
The Wind and the Lion '75 (American Wars)

Jack Creley
Dr. Strangelove, or: How I Learned to Stop Worrying and Love the Bomb '64 (American Wars)

Bruno Cremer
Is Paris Burning? '66 (WW II: Europe & North Africa)
317th Platoon '65 (French Wars)

Richard Crenna
The Sand Pebbles '66 (American Wars)

Laura Hope Crews
Gone with the Wind '39 (American Wars)

Donald Crisp
Dawn Patrol '38 (WW I)
Charge of the Light Brigade '36 (British Wars)
Birth of a Nation '15 (American Wars)

Linda Cristal
The Alamo '60 (American Wars)

Richard Cromwell
Lives of a Bengal Lancer '35 (British Wars)

Hume Cronyn
Lifeboat '44 (WW II: Europe & North Africa)
The Seventh Cross '44 (WW II: POWs)

Larry Cross
The Wind and the Lion '75 (American Wars)

Michael Crossman
One Against the Wind '91 (WW II: The Resistance)

Lt. Col. H.P. Crowe
Sands of Iwo Jima '49 (WW II: Pacific)

Josephine Crowell
Birth of a Nation '15 (American Wars)

Tom Cruise
Born on the Fourth of July '89 (Coming Home)

Frederick Culley
The Four Feathers '39 (British Wars)

John Cullum
Glory '89 (American Wars)

Chris Cunningham
The Story of G.I. Joe '45 (WW II: Europe & North Africa)

Donald Curtis
They Were Expendable '45 (WW II: Pacific)
Thirty Seconds over Tokyo '44 (WW II: Pacific)
Bataan '43 (WW II: Pacific)

Ken Curtis
The Alamo '60 (American Wars)
The Horse Soldiers '59 (American Wars)
Mister Roberts '55 (WW II: Pacific)

Patrick Curtis
The Fighting Sullivans '42 (WW II: Pacific)

John Cusack
The Thin Red Line '98 (WW II: Pacific)

Mickey Custis
Fires on the Plain '59 (WW II: Pacific)

Allan Cuthbertson
The Guns of Navarone '61 (WW II: Europe & North Africa)

Victor Cutler
The Best Years of Our Lives '46 (Coming Home)
A Walk in the Sun '46 (WW II: Europe & North Africa)

Charles Cyphers
Coming Home '78 (Coming Home)

D

Howard da Silva
Sergeant York '41 (WW I)

Willem Dafoe
Born on the Fourth of July '89 (Coming Home)
Platoon '86 (Vietnam War)

Marcel Dalio
China Gate '57 (Vietnam War)
Casablanca '42 (WW II: The Resistance)
Grand Illusion '37 (WW I)

Paul D'Amato
The Deer Hunter '78 (Vietnam War)

Marcus D'Amico
Full Metal Jacket '87 (Vietnam War)

Matt Damon
Saving Private Ryan '98 (WW II: Europe & North Africa)

Courage under Fire '96 (Coming Home)

Leora Dana
Tora! Tora! Tora! '70 (WW II: Pacific)

Dorothy Dandridge
Since You Went Away '44 (WW II: Homefront)

Karl Dane
The Big Parade '25 (WW I)

Paul Daneman
Zulu '64 (British Wars)

Henry Daniell
Watch on the Rhine '43 (WW II: The Resistance)
The Great Dictator '40 (Between the World Wars)

Jeff Daniels
Gettysburg '93 (American Wars)
A Rumor of War '80 (Vietnam War)

Alexandra Danilova
Alexander Nevsky '38 (Russian Wars)

Royal Dano
The Red Badge of Courage '51 (American Wars)

Ted Danson
Saving Private Ryan '98 (WW II: Europe & North Africa)

Helmut Dantine
War and Peace '56 (Russian Wars)
Watch on the Rhine '43 (WW II: The Resistance)
Casablanca '42 (WW II: The Resistance)
Mrs. Miniver '42 (WW II: Homefront)
To Be or Not to Be '42 (WW II: The Resistance)

Ray Danton
The Longest Day '62 (WW II: Europe & North Africa)

Denise Darcel
Battleground '49 (WW II: Europe & North Africa)

Bobby Darin
Hell Is for Heroes '62 (WW II: Europe & North Africa)

James Darren
The Guns of Navarone '61 (WW II: Europe & North Africa)
All the Young Men '60 (Korean War)

John Darrow
Hell's Angels '30 (WW I)

Florence Desmond
Three Came Home '50 (WW II: POWs)

Ernst Deutsch
The Third Man '49 (Coming Home)

Andy Devine
The Red Badge of Courage '51 (American Wars)

Eddie Dew
The Fighting 69th '40 (WW I)

Arthur Dewey
America '24 (American Wars)

Brad Dexter
Von Ryan's Express '65 (WW II: POWs)
Run Silent Run Deep '58 (WW II: Pacific)

Cliff DeYoung
Glory '89 (American Wars)

Bobby DiCicco
The Big Red One '80 (WW II: Europe & North Africa)
1941 '79 (WW II: Homefront)

Douglas Dick
The Red Badge of Courage '51 (American Wars)
Home of the Brave '49 (WW II: Pacific)

Angie Dickinson
China Gate '57 (Vietnam War)

John Diehl
Gettysburg '93 (American Wars)

John Dierkes
The Alamo '60 (American Wars)
The Red Badge of Courage '51 (American Wars)

Vin Diesel
Saving Private Ryan '98 (WW II: Europe & North Africa)

Harald Dietl
The Wannsee Conference '84 (WW II: The Holocaust)

Marlene Dietrich
Judgment at Nuremberg '61 (Coming Home)

Albert Dieudonne
Napoleon '27 (French Wars)

Yvette Dieudonne
Napoleon '27 (French Wars)

Anton Diffring
Where Eagles Dare '68 (WW II: Europe & North Africa)

The Blue Max '66 (WW I)

Mark Dignam
Charge of the Light Brigade '68 (British Wars)
Sink the Bismarck! '60 (WW II: Europe & North Africa)

Mimi Dillard
The Manchurian Candidate '62 (Korean War)

Kevin Dillon
A Midnight Clear '92 (WW II: Europe & North Africa)
Platoon '86 (Vietnam War)

MacIntyre Dixon
Gettysburg '93 (American Wars)

Alan Dobie
Charge of the Light Brigade '68 (British Wars)

Lawrence Dobkin
Patton '70 (WW II: Europe & North Africa)
Above and Beyond '53 (WW II: Pacific)
Twelve O'Clock High '49 (WW II: Europe & North Africa)

James Dobson
Flying Leathernecks '51 (WW II: Pacific)

Michael Dolan
Hamburger Hill '87 (Vietnam War)

Dora Doll
The Young Lions '58 (WW II: Europe & North Africa)

James Donald
King Rat '65 (WW II: POWs)
The Great Escape '63 (WW II: POWs)
Bridge on the River Kwai '57 (WW II: POWs)
Immortal Battalion '44 (WW II: Europe & North Africa)
In Which We Serve '43 (WW II: Europe & North Africa)

Arthur Donaldson
America '24 (American Wars)

Ted Donaldson
Mr. Winkle Goes to War '44 (WW II: Europe & North Africa)

Michael Donavan
America '24 (American Wars)

Brian Donlevy
Command Decision '48 (WW II: Europe & North Africa)

Wake Island '42 (WW II: Pacific)
Beau Geste '39 (British Wars)

Mike Donlin
The General '26 (American Wars)

Donal Donnelly
Waterloo '71 (French Wars)

Eddy Donno
The Green Berets '68 (Vietnam War)

Vincent D'Onofrio
Full Metal Jacket '87 (Vietnam War)

Jeffrey Donovan
When Trumpets Fade '98 (WW II: Europe & North Africa)

Martin Donovan
When Trumpets Fade '98 (WW II: Europe & North Africa)

Terence Donovan
Breaker Morant '80 (British Wars)

Ann Doran
Air Force '43 (WW II: Pacific)
So Proudly We Hail '43 (WW II: Pacific)
Dive Bomber '41 (Between the World Wars)

Paul Doucet
America '24 (American Wars)

John Doucette
Patton '70 (WW II: Europe & North Africa)
The Hunters '58 (Korean War)

Donald Douglas
Action in the North Atlantic '43 (WW II: Europe & North Africa)
Sergeant York '41 (WW I)

Kirk Douglas
Is Paris Burning? '66 (WW II: Europe & North Africa)
In Harm's Way '65 (WW II: Pacific)
Paths of Glory '57 (WW I)

Alain Doutey
The Big Red One '80 (WW II: Europe & North Africa)

Graham Dow
Gallipoli '81 (WW I)

Patrick Doyle
Henry V '89 (British Wars)

Charles Drake
To Hell and Back '55 (WW II: Europe & North Africa)
Air Force '43 (WW II: Pacific)

Dive Bomber '41 (Between the World Wars)

Chris Drake
A Walk in the Sun '46 (WW II: Europe & North Africa)

Tom Drake
The White Cliffs of Dover '44 (WW II: Homefront)

Roland Drew
Across the Pacific '42 (Between the World Wars)

Burkhard Driest
Cross of Iron '76 (WW II: Europe & North Africa)

Bobby Driscoll
O.S.S. '46 (WW II: The Resistance)
The Fighting Sullivans '42 (WW II: Pacific)

Joanne Dru
She Wore a Yellow Ribbon '49 (American Wars)

Paulette Dubost
The Last Metro '80 (WW II: The Holocaust)

Paul Dubov
China Gate '57 (Vietnam War)

Michael Dugan
She Wore a Yellow Ribbon '49 (American Wars)

Tom Dugan
Bataan '43 (WW II: Pacific)
To Be or Not to Be '42 (WW II: The Resistance)

Andrew Duggan
Merrill's Marauders '62 (WW II: Pacific)

Davor Dujmovic
Underground '95 (WW II: Europe & North Africa)

Douglass Dumbrille
Lives of a Bengal Lancer '35 (British Wars)

Emma Dunn
The Great Dictator '40 (Between the World Wars)

Irene Dunne
The White Cliffs of Dover '44 (WW II: Homefront)

Steve Dunne
Above and Beyond '53 (WW II: Pacific)

Kirsten Dunst
Mother Night '96 (WW II: Europe & North Africa)

John Dunton
America '24 (American Wars)

June Duprez
The Four Feathers '39 (British Wars)

Giustino Durano
Life Is Beautiful '98 (WW II: The Holocaust)

Tim Durant
The Red Badge of Courage '51 (American Wars)

Dan Duryea
Sahara '43 (WW II: Europe & North Africa)

Robert Duvall
Apocalypse Now '79 (Vietnam War)
M*A*S*H '70 (Korean War)

Leslie Dwyer
Immortal Battalion '44 (WW II: Europe & North Africa)

Valentine Dyall
Henry V '44 (British Wars)

Hamilton Dyce
King Rat '65 (WW II: POWs)

Dale Dye
Saving Private Ryan '98 (WW II: Europe & North Africa)
Born on the Fourth of July '89 (Coming Home)
Platoon '86 (Vietnam War)

George Dzundza
The Deer Hunter '78 (Vietnam War)

E

Edward Earle
Command Decision '48 (WW II: Europe & North Africa)

Richard Easton
Henry V '89 (British Wars)
The Red Badge of Courage '51 (American Wars)

Clint Eastwood
Where Eagles Dare '68 (WW II: Europe & North Africa)
The Good, the Bad and the Ugly '67 (American Wars)

Maude Eburne
To Be or Not to Be '42 (WW II: The Resistance)

Samuli Edelmann
The Winter War '89 (Between the World Wars)

Mark Eden
Doctor Zhivago '65 (Russian Wars)

Peter Edmund
Full Metal Jacket '87 (Vietnam War)

Richard Edson
Good Morning, Vietnam '87 (Vietnam War)
Platoon '86 (Vietnam War)

Cliff Edwards
Gone with the Wind '39 (American Wars)

Glynn Edwards
Zulu '64 (British Wars)

James Edwards
Patton '70 (WW II: Europe & North Africa)
The Manchurian Candidate '62 (Korean War)
Pork Chop Hill '59 (Korean War)
Men in War '57 (Korean War)
The Steel Helmet '51 (Korean War)
Home of the Brave '49 (WW II: Pacific)

Sam Edwards
Twelve O'Clock High '49 (WW II: Europe & North Africa)

Vince Edwards
The Victors '63 (WW II: Europe & North Africa)

Richard Egan
The Hunters '58 (Korean War)

Stan Egi
Paradise Road '97 (WW II: POWs)

Jennifer Ehle
Paradise Road '97 (WW II: POWs)

Sergei Eisenstein
Battleship Potemkin '25 (Russian Wars)

Anita Ekberg
War and Peace '56 (Russian Wars)

Ron Eldard
When Trumpets Fade '98 (WW II: Europe & North Africa)

Bobby Ellerbee
A Rumor of War '80 (Vietnam War)

Biff Elliot
Pork Chop Hill '59 (Korean War)

Denholm Elliott
One Against the Wind '91 (WW II:
The Resistance)
A Bridge Too Far '77 (WW II:
Europe & North Africa)
Too Late the Hero '70 (WW II:
Pacific)
King Rat '65 (WW II: POWs)

Sam Elliott
Gettysburg '93 (American Wars)

Tracey Ellis
Last of the Mohicans '92 (American
Wars)

Derek Elphinstone
The Four Feathers '39 (British
Wars)

Isobel Elsom
The White Cliffs of Dover '44 (WW
II: Homefront)

Cary Elwes
Glory '89 (American Wars)

Faye Emerson
Air Force '43 (WW II: Pacific)

Jonathan Emerson
84 Charlie MoPic '89 (Vietnam War)

Roy Emerton
Henry V '44 (British Wars)

Ivor Emmanuel
Zulu '64 (British Wars)

Richard Erdman
Stalag 17 '53 (WW II: POWs)
Objective, Burma! '45 (WW II:
Pacific)

R. Lee Ermey
The Siege of Firebase Gloria '89
(Vietnam War)
Full Metal Jacket '87 (Vietnam War)
Apocalypse Now '79 (Vietnam War)
The Boys in Company C '77 (Viet-
nam War)

Marilyn Erskine
Above and Beyond '53 (WW II:
Pacific)

Jacques Ertaud
A Man Escaped '57 (WW II: POWs)

Carl Esmond
Dawn Patrol '38 (WW I)

Jill Esmond
The White Cliffs of Dover '44 (WW
II: Homefront)

Roque Espiritu
Bataan '43 (WW II: Pacific)

Luc Etienne
Au Revoir les Enfants '87 (WW II:
The Holocaust)

Gene Evans
The Steel Helmet '51 (Korean War)

Josh Evans
Born on the Fourth of July '89
(Coming Home)

Jason Evers
The Green Berets '68 (Vietnam
War)

F

Fabian
The Longest Day '62 (WW II:
Europe & North Africa)

Pierre Fabre
317th Platoon '65 (French Wars)

Douglas Fairbanks, Jr.
Gunga Din '39 (British Wars)

Frankie Faison
Mother Night '96 (WW II: Europe &
North Africa)

Sergio Fantoni
Von Ryan's Express '65 (WW II:
POWs)

Dennis Farina
Saving Private Ryan '98 (WW II:
Europe & North Africa)

Jim Farley
The General '26 (American Wars)

Edward Faulkner
The Green Berets '68 (Vietnam
War)

William "Bill" Fawcett
King Rat '65 (WW II: POWs)

Frank Faylen
Across the Pacific '42 (Between the
World Wars)
Wake Island '42 (WW II: Pacific)
Sergeant York '41 (WW I)
Gone with the Wind '39 (American
Wars)

Jan Fedder
Das Boot '81 (WW II: Europe &
North Africa)

Raphael Fejto
Au Revoir les Enfants '87 (WW II:
The Holocaust)

Eric Feldary
For Whom the Bell Tolls '43
(Between the World Wars)

Norman Fell
Catch-22 '70 (WW II: Europe &
North Africa)
Pork Chop Hill '59 (Korean War)

Lev Fenin
Alexander Nevsky '38 (Russian
Wars)

Mark Fenton
Four Horsemen of the Apocalypse
'21 (WW I)

Frank Ferguson
Battle Cry '55 (WW II: Pacific)

Abel Fernandez
Pork Chop Hill '59 (Korean War)

Andrea Ferreol
The Last Metro '80 (WW II: The
Holocaust)

Jose Ferrer
Lawrence of Arabia '62 (WW I)
The Caine Mutiny '54 (WW II:
Europe & North Africa)

Mel Ferrer
The Longest Day '62 (WW II:
Europe & North Africa)
War and Peace '56 (Russian Wars)

Maria Ferrero
War and Peace '56 (Russian Wars)

Mary Field
To Hell and Back '55 (WW II:
Europe & North Africa)
Mrs. Miniver '42 (WW II: Homefront)
Wake Island '42 (WW II: Pacific)

Ralph Fiennes
Schindler's List '93 (WW II: The
Holocaust)

Clyde Fillmore
Watch on the Rhine '43 (WW II: The
Resistance)

James Finlayson
To Be or Not to Be '42 (WW II: The
Resistance)

John Finn
Glory '89 (American Wars)

Albert Finney
The Victors '63 (WW II: Europe &
North Africa)

Cast
Index

Anne Francis
Battle Cry '55 (WW II: Pacific)

Robert Francis
The Caine Mutiny '54 (WW II: Europe & North Africa)

Arthur Franz
The Young Lions '58 (WW II: Europe & North Africa)
The Caine Mutiny '54 (WW II: Europe & North Africa)
Sands of Iwo Jima '49 (WW II: Pacific)

Ronald Fraser
Too Late the Hero '70 (WW II: Pacific)

William Frawley
Fighting Seabees '44 (WW II: Pacific)

Rupert Frazer
Empire of the Sun '87 (WW II: POWs)

Bert Freed
Paths of Glory '57 (WW I)

Howard Freeman
Mr. Winkle Goes to War '44 (WW II: Europe & North Africa)

Mona Freeman
Battle Cry '55 (WW II: Pacific)

Morgan Freeman
Glory '89 (American Wars)

Wolf Frees
Doctor Zhivago '65 (Russian Wars)

Robert Freitag
The Great Escape '63 (WW II: POWs)

Bruce French
Coming Home '78 (Coming Home)

Pierre Fresnay
Grand Illusion '37 (WW I)

Billy Frick
Is Paris Burning? '66 (WW II: Europe & North Africa)

Gerhard Friedrich
The White Rose '83 (WW II: The Resistance)

John Friedrich
A Rumor of War '80 (Vietnam War)

Anna Friel
The Land Girls '98 (WW II: Homefront)

Roger Fritz
Cross of Iron '76 (WW II: Europe & North Africa)

Gert Frobe
Is Paris Burning? '66 (WW II: Europe & North Africa)
The Longest Day '62 (WW II: Europe & North Africa)

Susumu Fujita
Yojimbo '61 (Japanese Wars)
The Hidden Fortress '58 (Japanese Wars)

Kamatari Fujiwara
Yojimbo '61 (Japanese Wars)
The Hidden Fortress '58 (Japanese Wars)
Seven Samurai '54 (Japanese Wars)

Samuel Fuller
1941 '79 (WW II: Homefront)

Eiji Funakoshi
Fires on the Plain '59 (WW II: Pacific)

Paul Fung
Guadalcanal Diary '43 (WW II: Pacific)

Joseph Fuqua
Gettysburg '93 (American Wars)

Dan Futterman
When Trumpets Fade '98 (WW II: Europe & North Africa)

G

Jean Gabin
Grand Illusion '37 (WW I)

Clark Gable
Run Silent Run Deep '58 (WW II: Pacific)
Command Decision '48 (WW II: Europe & North Africa)
Gone with the Wind '39 (American Wars)

John Gabriel
The Hunters '58 (Korean War)

Rene A. Gagnon
Sands of Iwo Jima '49 (WW II: Pacific)

Richard Gaines
Mr. Winkle Goes to War '44 (WW II: Europe & North Africa)

Peter Gale
Empire of the Sun '87 (WW II: POWs)

Vincent Gale
Bye Bye Blues '89 (WW II: Homefront)

Joseph Gallison
All the Young Men '60 (Korean War)

Lew Gallo
Pork Chop Hill '59 (Korean War)

Chester Gan
Crash Dive '43 (WW II: Europe & North Africa)
Across the Pacific '42 (Between the World Wars)

Abel Gance
Napoleon '27 (French Wars)

Marguerite Gance
Napoleon '27 (French Wars)

Reginald Gardiner
The Immortal Sergeant '43 (WW II: Europe & North Africa)
The Great Dictator '40 (Between the World Wars)

Richard Gardner
The Young Lions '58 (WW II: Europe & North Africa)

John Garfield
Air Force '43 (WW II: Pacific)

Art Garfunkel
Catch-22 '70 (WW II: Europe & North Africa)

Gianni "John" Garko
Waterloo '71 (French Wars)

Judy Garland
Judgment at Nuremberg '61 (Coming Home)

James Garner
The Great Escape '63 (WW II: POWs)

Martin Garralaga
For Whom the Bell Tolls '43 (Between the World Wars)
Casablanca '42 (WW II: The Resistance)

Ivo Garrani
Waterloo '71 (French Wars)

Greer Garson
Mrs. Miniver '42 (WW II: Homefront)

Martin Garth
Pork Chop Hill '59 (Korean War)

Cast Index

Jonathan Goldsmith
Go Tell the Spartans '78 (Vietnam War)

Minna Gombell
The Best Years of Our Lives '46 (Coming Home)

Mikhail Gomorov
Battleship Potemkin '25 (Russian Wars)

Christopher Good
A Bridge Too Far '77 (WW II: Europe & North Africa)

Caroline Goodall
Schindler's List '93 (WW II: The Holocaust)

Cuba Gooding, Jr.
The Tuskegee Airmen '95 (WW II: Europe & North Africa)

Michael Goodliffe
Von Ryan's Express '65 (WW II: POWs)
Sink the Bismarck! '60 (WW II: Europe & North Africa)

Doug Goodman
Hamburger Hill '87 (Vietnam War)

John Goodman
Mother Night '96 (WW II: Europe & North Africa)

Bill Goodwin
So Proudly We Hail '43 (WW II: Pacific)
Wake Island '42 (WW II: Pacific)

Harold Goodwin
Bridge on the River Kwai '57 (WW II: POWs)
All Quiet on the Western Front '30 (WW I)

Bernard Gorcey
The Great Dictator '40 (Between the World Wars)

C. Henry Gordon
Charge of the Light Brigade '36 (British Wars)

Dick Gordon
13 Rue Madeleine '46 (WW II: The Resistance)

Julia Swayne Gordon
Wings '27 (WW I)

Roy Gordon
The Real Glory '39 (American Wars)

Ruth Gordon
Action in the North Atlantic '43 (WW II: Europe & North Africa)

Patrick Gorman
Gettysburg '93 (American Wars)

Roland Got
Across the Pacific '42 (Between the World Wars)

Walter Gotell
The Guns of Navarone '61 (WW II: Europe & North Africa)

James T. Goto
The Gallant Hours '60 (WW II: Pacific)

Polly Gottesmann
The Wind and the Lion '75 (American Wars)

Elliott Gould
A Bridge Too Far '77 (WW II: Europe & North Africa)
M*A*S*H '70 (Korean War)

David Grace
The Longest Day '62 (WW II: Europe & North Africa)

Robert Graf
The Great Escape '63 (WW II: POWs)

Bill Graham
Gardens of Stone '87 (Vietnam War)

Ronny Graham
Gallipoli '81 (WW I)

Alexander Granach
The Seventh Cross '44 (WW II: POWs)
For Whom the Bell Tolls '43 (Between the World Wars)

Cary Grant
Gunga Din '39 (British Wars)

Charley Grapewin
They Died with Their Boots On '41 (American Wars)

Leonard Graves
Pork Chop Hill '59 (Korean War)

Peter Graves
Stalag 17 '53 (WW II: POWs)

Donald Gray
The Four Feathers '39 (British Wars)

Lorna Gray
So Proudly We Hail '43 (WW II: Pacific)

Willoughby Gray
Waterloo '71 (French Wars)

Nigel Green
Zulu '64 (British Wars)

Stan Green
Gallipoli '81 (WW I)

Sydney Greenstreet
Across the Pacific '42 (Between the World Wars)
Casablanca '42 (WW II: The Resistance)
They Died with Their Boots On '41 (American Wars)

Dabbs Greer
Shenandoah '65 (American Wars)
Above and Beyond '53 (WW II: Pacific)

James Gregory
The Manchurian Candidate '62 (Korean War)

Mary Gregory
Coming Home '78 (Coming Home)

Paul Gregory
Henry V '89 (British Wars)

Klaus Detlef Grevenhorst
A Man Escaped '57 (WW II: POWs)

Joe Grifasi
The Deer Hunter '78 (Vietnam War)

Rachel Griffin
A Midnight Clear '92 (WW II: Europe & North Africa)

Raymond Griffith
All Quiet on the Western Front '30 (WW I)

Frank Grimes
A Bridge Too Far '77 (WW II: Europe & North Africa)

Charles Grodin
Catch-22 '70 (WW II: Europe & North Africa)

Dieter Groest
The Wannsee Conference '84 (WW II: The Holocaust)

Herbert Gronemeyer
Das Boot '81 (WW II: Europe & North Africa)

Arye Gross
Mother Night '96 (WW II: Europe & North Africa)
A Midnight Clear '92 (WW II: Europe & North Africa)

Cast
Index

Lumsden Hare
The White Cliffs of Dover '44 (WW
II: Homefront)
Gunga Din '39 (British Wars)
Lives of a Bengal Lancer '35 (British
Wars)

Dorian Harewood
Full Metal Jacket '87 (Vietnam War)

Jean Harlow
Hell's Angels '30 (WW I)

Woody Harrelson
The Thin Red Line '98 (WW II:
Pacific)

William Harrigan
Flying Leathernecks '51 (WW II:
Pacific)

Heath Harris
Gallipoli '81 (WW I)

Richard Harris
The Guns of Navarone '61 (WW II:
Europe & North Africa)

Maj. Sam Harris
Lives of a Bengal Lancer '35 (British
Wars)

Stacy Harris
The Hunters '58 (Korean War)

Simon Harrison
The Wind and the Lion '75 (American Wars)

David Harrod
The Thin Red Line '98 (WW II:
Pacific)
The Tuskegee Airmen '95 (WW II:
Europe & North Africa)

Robert "Bobbie" Harron
Birth of a Nation '15 (American
Wars)

Ian Hart
Land and Freedom '95 (Between
the World Wars)

William Hartnell
Immortal Battalion '44 (WW II:
Europe & North Africa)

Alex Harvey
Gettysburg '93 (American Wars)

Don Harvey
The Thin Red Line '98 (WW II:
Pacific)

Forrester Harvey
Mrs. Miniver '42 (WW II: Homefront)

Laurence Harvey
The Manchurian Candidate '62
(Korean War)
The Alamo '60 (American Wars)

Signe Hasso
The Seventh Cross '44 (WW II:
POWs)

Riley Hatch
America '24 (American Wars)

Shawn Hatosy
The Thin Red Line '98 (WW II:
Pacific)

Sabine Haudepin
The Last Metro '80 (WW II: The
Holocaust)

Wings Hauser
The Siege of Firebase Gloria '89
(Vietnam War)

Ruth Hausmeister
The Bridge '59 (WW II: Europe &
North Africa)

Nigel Havers
Empire of the Sun '87 (WW II:
POWs)

Alex Havier
They Were Expendable '45 (WW II:
Pacific)
Bataan '43 (WW II: Pacific)

Ethan Hawke
A Midnight Clear '92 (WW II:
Europe & North Africa)

Jack Hawkins
Waterloo '71 (French Wars)
Zulu '64 (British Wars)
Lawrence of Arabia '62 (WW I)
Bridge on the River Kwai '57 (WW
II: POWs)

Jill Haworth
In Harm's Way '65 (WW II: Pacific)

Sessue Hayakawa
Bridge on the River Kwai '57 (WW
II: POWs)
Three Came Home '50 (WW II:
POWs)

Sterling Hayden
Dr. Strangelove, or: How I Learned
to Stop Worrying and Love the
Bomb '64 (American Wars)

Ira H. Hayes
Sands of Iwo Jima '49 (WW II:
Pacific)

Grace Hayle
The Great Dictator '40 (Between
the World Wars)

David Hayman
Rob Roy '95 (British Wars)
Hope and Glory '87 (WW II: Home-
front)

Bob Haymes
Mr. Winkle Goes to War '44 (WW II:
Europe & North Africa)

Susan Hayward
Fighting Seabees '44 (WW II:
Pacific)
Beau Geste '39 (British Wars)

Chris Haywood
Breaker Morant '80 (British Wars)

Ted Hecht
So Proudly We Hail '43 (WW II:
Pacific)

John Hedloe
Above and Beyond '53 (WW II:
Pacific)

Richard Heffer
Waterloo '71 (French Wars)

Van Heflin
Battle Cry '55 (WW II: Pacific)

Robert Helpmann
Henry V '44 (British Wars)

Martin Hemme
Das Boot '81 (WW II: Europe &
North Africa)

David Hemmings
Charge of the Light Brigade '68
(British Wars)

Joseph Henabery
Birth of a Nation '15 (American
Wars)

Douglas Henderson
The Manchurian Candidate '62
(Korean War)
From Here to Eternity '53 (Between
the World Wars)

Shirley Henderson
Rob Roy '95 (British Wars)

Paul Henreid
Casablanca '42 (WW II: The Resistance)

Arnaud Henriet
Au Revoir les Enfants '87 (WW II:
The Holocaust)

Cast Index

Anthony Hopkins
A Bridge Too Far '77 (WW II:
Europe & North Africa)

Harold Hopkins
Gallipoli '81 (WW I)

Dennis Hopper
Apocalypse Now '79 (Vietnam War)

William Hopper
The Fighting 69th '40 (WW I)

Michael Hordern
Where Eagles Dare '68 (WW II:
Europe & North Africa)
Sink the Bismarck! '60 (WW II:
Europe & North Africa)

Geoffrey Horne
Bridge on the River Kwai '57 (WW
II: POWs)

John Horsley
Sink the Bismarck! '60 (WW II:
Europe & North Africa)

Hikaru Hoshi
Fires on the Plain '59 (WW II:
Pacific)

Donald Houston
Where Eagles Dare '68 (WW II:
Europe & North Africa)

Arliss Howard
Full Metal Jacket '87 (Vietnam War)

Dennis Howard
Go Tell the Spartans '78 (Vietnam
War)

Kathleen Howard
Crash Dive '43 (WW II: Europe &
North Africa)

Kevyn Major Howard
Full Metal Jacket '87 (Vietnam War)

Leslie Howard
Gone with the Wind '39 (American
Wars)

Trevor Howard
The Battle of Britain '69 (WW II:
Europe & North Africa)
Charge of the Light Brigade '68
(British Wars)
Von Ryan's Express '65 (WW II:
POWs)
The Third Man '49 (Coming Home)

C. Thomas Howell
Gettysburg '93 (American Wars)

John Hoyt
Merrill's Marauders '62 (WW II:
Pacific)

O.S.S. '46 (WW II: The Resistance)

Warren Hsieh
China Gate '57 (Vietnam War)

Harold Huber
Beau Geste '39 (British Wars)

Cooper Huckabee
Gettysburg '93 (American Wars)

Walter Hudd
Sink the Bismarck! '60 (WW II:
Europe & North Africa)

William Hudson
Objective, Burma! '45 (WW II:
Pacific)

Daniel Hugh-Kelly
The Tuskegee Airmen '95 (WW II:
Europe & North Africa)

Tresa Hughes
Coming Home '78 (Coming Home)

Wendy Hughes
Paradise Road '97 (WW II: POWs)

Henry Hull
Objective, Burma! '45 (WW II:
Pacific)
Lifeboat '44 (WW II: Europe & North
Africa)

Cecil Humphreys
The Razor's Edge '46 (Coming
Home)

Tessa Humphries
Paradise Road '97 (WW II: POWs)

Arthur Hunnicutt
The Red Badge of Courage '51
(American Wars)

Bill Hunter
Gallipoli '81 (WW I)

Jeffrey Hunter
The Longest Day '62 (WW II:
Europe & North Africa)

Tab Hunter
Battle Cry '55 (WW II: Pacific)

G.P. Huntley, Jr.
They Died with Their Boots On '41
(American Wars)
Beau Geste '39 (British Wars)
Charge of the Light Brigade '36
(British Wars)

Raymond Huntley
Immortal Battalion '44 (WW II:
Europe & North Africa)

Brandon Hurst
The Lost Patrol '34 (WW I)

Paul Hurst
Gone with the Wind '39 (American
Wars)

John Hurt
Rob Roy '95 (British Wars)

Anjelica Huston
Gardens of Stone '87 (Vietnam
War)

John Huston
The Wind and the Lion '75 (American Wars)

Will Hutchins
Merrill's Marauders '62 (WW II:
Pacific)

Jim Hutton (Dana J. Hutton)
The Green Berets '68 (Vietnam
War)
A Time to Love and a Time to Die
'58 (WW II: Europe & North
Africa)

Robert Hutton
The Steel Helmet '51 (Korean War)

Wilfrid Hyde-White
The Third Man '49 (Coming Home)

Scott Hylands
The Boys in Company C '77 (Vietnam War)

I

Masato Ibu
Empire of the Sun '87 (WW II:
POWs)

Hisashi Igawa
Ran '85 (Japanese Wars)

Diasuke Iijima
Merry Christmas, Mr. Lawrence '83
(WW II: POWs)

Yoshio Inaba
Seven Samurai '54 (Japanese
Wars)

Rex Ingram
Sahara '43 (WW II: Europe & North
Africa)

Harold Innocent
Henry V '89 (British Wars)

John Ireland
A Walk in the Sun '46 (WW II:
Europe & North Africa)

George Irving
Sergeant York '41 (WW I)

Barry Jones
War and Peace '56 (Russian Wars)

Clyde Jones
The Siege of Firebase Gloria '89 (Vietnam War)

Griffith Jones
Henry V '44 (British Wars)

James Earl Jones
Gardens of Stone '87 (Vietnam War)
Dr. Strangelove, or: How I Learned to Stop Worrying and Love the Bomb '64 (American Wars)

Jennifer Jones
Since You Went Away '44 (WW II: Homefront)

L.Q. (Justus E. McQueen) Jones
Hell Is for Heroes '62 (WW II: Europe & North Africa)
The Young Lions '58 (WW II: Europe & North Africa)
Men in War '57 (Korean War)
Battle Cry '55 (WW II: Pacific)

Stan Jones
The Horse Soldiers '59 (American Wars)

W.W. Jones
America '24 (American Wars)

Patrick Jordan
Too Late the Hero '70 (WW II: Pacific)
The Victors '63 (WW II: Europe & North Africa)

Richard Jordan
Gettysburg '93 (American Wars)

Victor Jory
Gone with the Wind '39 (American Wars)

Larry Joshua
A Midnight Clear '92 (WW II: Europe & North Africa)

Allyn Joslyn
The Immortal Sergeant '43 (WW II: Europe & North Africa)

Jay Jostyn
The Hunters '58 (Korean War)

Curt Jurgens
The Battle of Britain '69 (WW II: Europe & North Africa)
The Longest Day '62 (WW II: Europe & North Africa)

James Robertson Justice
The Guns of Navarone '61 (WW II: Europe & North Africa)

K

Fawzia el Kader
The Battle of Algiers '66 (French Wars)

Wolf Kahler
One Against the Wind '91 (WW II: The Resistance)

Steve Kanaly
The Wind and the Lion '75 (American Wars)

Ivan Kane
Gettysburg '93 (American Wars)
Platoon '86 (Vietnam War)

Ryunosuke Kaneda
Merry Christmas, Mr. Lawrence '83 (WW II: POWs)

Mady Kaplan
The Deer Hunter '78 (Vietnam War)

Mirjana Karanovic
Underground '95 (WW II: Europe & North Africa)

Boris Karloff
The Lost Patrol '34 (WW I)

Robert Karnes
From Here to Eternity '53 (Between the World Wars)

Roscoe Karns
Wings '27 (WW I)

Mohamed Ben Kassen
The Battle of Algiers '66 (French Wars)

Kurt Katch
The Seventh Cross '44 (WW II: POWs)
Watch on the Rhine '43 (WW II: The Resistance)

Daisuke Kato
Yojimbo '61 (Japanese Wars)
Seven Samurai '54 (Japanese Wars)

Kazuo Kato
Ran '85 (Japanese Wars)

Takeshi Kato
Ran '85 (Japanese Wars)

Keiichiro Katsumoto
Bridge on the River Kwai '57 (WW II: POWs)

Caroline Kava
Born on the Fourth of July '89 (Coming Home)

Seizaburo Kawazu
Yojimbo '61 (Japanese Wars)

Bernard Kay
Doctor Zhivago '65 (Russian Wars)

Charles Kay
Henry V '89 (British Wars)

Dianne Kay
1941 '79 (WW II: Homefront)

Stacy Keach
A Rumor of War '80 (Vietnam War)

James Keane
Apocalypse Now '79 (Vietnam War)

Larry Keating
Above and Beyond '53 (WW II: Pacific)

Buster Keaton
The General '26 (American Wars)

Joe Keaton
The General '26 (American Wars)

Arthur Keegan
From Here to Eternity '53 (Between the World Wars)

Geoffrey Keen
Doctor Zhivago '65 (Russian Wars)
Sink the Bismarck! '60 (WW II: Europe & North Africa)
The Third Man '49 (Coming Home)

Andrew Keir
Rob Roy '95 (British Wars)

Brian Keith
The Wind and the Lion '75 (American Wars)

Ian Keith
Five Graves to Cairo '43 (WW II: Europe & North Africa)

Robert Keith
Men in War '57 (Korean War)
Battle Circus '53 (Korean War)

Cecil Kellaway
Gunga Din '39 (British Wars)

Heinz Keller
The White Rose '83 (WW II: The Resistance)

Cast
Index

The Four Feathers '39 (British
Wars)

Kuninori Kodo
Seven Samurai '54 (Japanese
Wars)

Susan Kohner
To Hell and Back '55 (WW II:
Europe & North Africa)

Walter Kohut
A Bridge Too Far '77 (WW II:
Europe & North Africa)

Nicolas Koline
Napoleon '27 (French Wars)

Scott Kolk
All Quiet on the Western Front '30
(WW I)

Henry Kolker
The Real Glory '39 (American
Wars)

Tetsu Komai
The Real Glory '39 (American
Wars)

Jon Korkes
Catch-22 '70 (WW II: Europe &
North Africa)

Korobei
Battleship Potemkin '25 (Russian
Wars)

Peter Kortenbach
The White Rose '83 (WW II: The
Resistance)

Teemu Koskinen
The Winter War '89 (Between the
World Wars)

Yoshio Kosugi
Seven Samurai '54 (Japanese
Wars)

Elias Koteas
The Thin Red Line '98 (WW II:
Pacific)
Gardens of Stone '87 (Vietnam
War)

Alexandre Koubitzky
Napoleon '27 (French Wars)

Esko Kovero
The Winter War '89 (Between the
World Wars)

Ron Kovic
Born on the Fourth of July '89
(Coming Home)

Alexei Kravchenko
Come and See '85 (WW II: Europe
& North Africa)

Sabine Kretzschmar
The White Rose '83 (WW II: The
Resistance)

Kurt Kreuger
Sahara '43 (WW II: Europe & North
Africa)

Harry Krimer
Napoleon '27 (French Wars)

Hardy Kruger
A Bridge Too Far '77 (WW II:
Europe & North Africa)

Anja Kruse
The White Rose '83 (WW II: The
Resistance)

Richard Kuhlman
The Siege of Firebase Gloria '89
(Vietnam War)

Clyde Kusatsu
Paradise Road '97 (WW II: POWs)
Go Tell the Spartans '78 (Vietnam
War)

Richard Kuss
The Deer Hunter '78 (Vietnam War)

Burt Kwouk
Empire of the Sun '87 (WW II:
POWs)

Sam Kydd
Too Late the Hero '70 (WW II:
Pacific)

L

Alan Ladd
All the Young Men '60 (Korean War)
O.S.S. '46 (WW II: The Resistance)

Ivan Lagutin
Alexander Nevsky '38 (Russian
Wars)

George Lah
The Story of G.I. Joe '45 (WW II:
Europe & North Africa)

Florence Lake
Crash Dive '43 (WW II: Europe &
North Africa)

Veronica Lake
So Proudly We Hail '43 (WW II:
Pacific)

Georges Lampin
Napoleon '27 (French Wars)

Burt Lancaster
Go Tell the Spartans '78 (Vietnam
War)
The Train '65 (WW II: Europe &
North Africa)
Judgment at Nuremberg '61 (Com-
ing Home)
Run Silent Run Deep '58 (WW II:
Pacific)
From Here to Eternity '53 (Between
the World Wars)

James Lancaster
Gettysburg '93 (American Wars)

Elsa Lanchester
The Razor's Edge '46 (Coming
Home)

Martin Landau
Pork Chop Hill '59 (Korean War)

David Lander
1941 '79 (WW II: Homefront)

Audrey Landers
1941 '79 (WW II: Homefront)

Harry Landers
The Gallant Hours '60 (WW II:
Pacific)

John Landis
1941 '79 (WW II: Homefront)

Bob Landry
The Story of G.I. Joe '45 (WW II:
Europe & North Africa)

Richard Lane
Mr. Winkle Goes to War '44 (WW II:
Europe & North Africa)
Air Force '43 (WW II: Pacific)

Perry Lang
The Big Red One '80 (WW II:
Europe & North Africa)
A Rumor of War '80 (Vietnam War)
1941 '79 (WW II: Homefront)

Stephen Lang
Gettysburg '93 (American Wars)

Hope Lange
The Young Lions '58 (WW II:
Europe & North Africa)

Jessica Lange
Rob Roy '95 (British Wars)

Paul Langton
To Hell and Back '55 (WW II:
Europe & North Africa)
They Were Expendable '45 (WW II:
Pacific)

Thirty Seconds over Tokyo '44 (WW II: Pacific)

Angela Lansbury
The Manchurian Candidate '62 (Korean War)

Bryan Larkin
Born on the Fourth of July '89 (Coming Home)

Mary Laroche
Run Silent Run Deep '58 (WW II: Pacific)

Sydney Lassick
1941 '79 (WW II: Homefront)

Frank Latimore
Patton '70 (WW II: Europe & North Africa)
The Razor's Edge '46 (Coming Home)
13 Rue Madeleine '46 (WW II: The Resistance)

Wesley Lau
The Alamo '60 (American Wars)

Lubomiras Lauciavicus
Come and See '85 (WW II: Europe & North Africa)

John Laurie
Henry V '44 (British Wars)
Immortal Battalion '44 (WW II: Europe & North Africa)
The Four Feathers '39 (British Wars)

Peter Lawford
The Longest Day '62 (WW II: Europe & North Africa)
The White Cliffs of Dover '44 (WW II: Homefront)
The Immortal Sergeant '43 (WW II: Europe & North Africa)
Sahara '43 (WW II: Europe & North Africa)
Mrs. Miniver '42 (WW II: Homefront)

Jay Lawrence
Stalag 17 '53 (WW II: POWs)

John Lawrence
The Manchurian Candidate '62 (Korean War)

Richard Lawson
Coming Home '78 (Coming Home)

Wilfred Lawson
War and Peace '56 (Russian Wars)

George Lazenby
Gettysburg '93 (American Wars)

Ngoc Le
Full Metal Jacket '87 (Vietnam War)

Charles Le Clainche
A Man Escaped '57 (WW II: POWs)

Damien Leake
Apocalypse Now '79 (Vietnam War)

Madeleine LeBeau
Casablanca '42 (WW II: The Resistance)

Richard Leboeuf
Au Revoir les Enfants '87 (WW II: The Holocaust)

Volker Lechtenbrink
The Bridge '59 (WW II: Europe & North Africa)

Branislav Lecic
Underground '95 (WW II: Europe & North Africa)

Erwin Leder
Das Boot '81 (WW II: Europe & North Africa)

Anna Lee
The Horse Soldiers '59 (American Wars)

Bernard Lee
The Third Man '49 (Coming Home)

Canada Lee
Lifeboat '44 (WW II: Europe & North Africa)

Candace Lee
The Hunters '58 (Korean War)

Christopher Lee
1941 '79 (WW II: Homefront)
The Longest Day '62 (WW II: Europe & North Africa)

Mark Lee
Gallipoli '81 (WW I)

RonReaco Lee
Glory '89 (American Wars)

Sheryl Lee
Mother Night '96 (WW II: Europe & North Africa)

Tommy Lee
The Sand Pebbles '66 (American Wars)

Andrea Leeds
The Real Glory '39 (American Wars)

Michael Lees
King Rat '65 (WW II: POWs)

Xavier Legrand
Au Revoir les Enfants '87 (WW II: The Holocaust)

Janet Leigh
The Manchurian Candidate '62 (Korean War)

Nelson Leigh
The Gallant Hours '60 (WW II: Pacific)

Vivien Leigh
Gone with the Wind '39 (American Wars)

Donovan Leitch
Glory '89 (American Wars)

Harvey Lembeck
Stalag 17 '53 (WW II: POWs)

Michael Lembeck
The Boys in Company C '77 (Vietnam War)

Tutte Lemkow
The Guns of Navarone '61 (WW II: Europe & North Africa)

Jack Lemmon
Mister Roberts '55 (WW II: Pacific)

Angus Lennie
The Great Escape '63 (WW II: POWs)

Annie Leon
Hope and Glory '87 (WW II: Homefront)

Connie Leon
Mrs. Miniver '42 (WW II: Homefront)

Joan Leslie
Sergeant York '41 (WW I)

Francois Leterrier
A Man Escaped '57 (WW II: POWs)

Jared Leto
The Thin Red Line '98 (WW II: Pacific)

Levchenko
Battleship Potemkin '25 (Russian Wars)

Sam Levene
Action in the North Atlantic '43 (WW II: Europe & North Africa)

Jerry Levine
Born on the Fourth of July '89 (Coming Home)

Alexandr Levshin
Battleship Potemkin '25 (Russian Wars)

Cast Index

Shmulik Levy
Schindler's List '93 (WW II: The Holocaust)

Weaver Levy
China Gate '57 (Vietnam War)

Geoffrey Lewis
The Wind and the Lion '75 (American Wars)

Ralph Lewis
Birth of a Nation '15 (American Wars)

John Leyton
Von Ryan's Express '65 (WW II: POWs)
The Great Escape '63 (WW II: POWs)

Albert Lieven
The Victors '63 (WW II: Europe & North Africa)

Eric Linden
Gone with the Wind '39 (American Wars)

Alfred Linder
13 Rue Madeleine '46 (WW II: The Resistance)

Bengt Lindstrom
A Time to Love and a Time to Die '58 (WW II: Europe & North Africa)

John Litel
So Proudly We Hail '43 (WW II: Pacific)
They Died with Their Boots On '41 (American Wars)
The Fighting 69th '40 (WW I)

John Lithgow
The Tuskegee Airmen '95 (WW II: Europe & North Africa)

Jimmy Lloyd
The Story of G.I. Joe '45 (WW II: Europe & North Africa)

Norman Lloyd
A Walk in the Sun '46 (WW II: Europe & North Africa)

Rollo Lloyd
Lives of a Bengal Lancer '35 (British Wars)

Katherine Locke
The Seventh Cross '44 (WW II: POWs)

Gene Lockhart
They Died with Their Boots On '41 (American Wars)

June Lockhart
The White Cliffs of Dover '44 (WW II: Homefront)
Sergeant York '41 (WW I)

Donal Logue
The Thin Red Line '98 (WW II: Pacific)
Gettysburg '93 (American Wars)

Giuliana Lojodice
Life Is Beautiful '98 (WW II: The Holocaust)

Herbert Lom
War and Peace '56 (Russian Wars)

Carole Lombard
To Be or Not to Be '42 (WW II: The Resistance)

Tom London
Fighting Seabees '44 (WW II: Pacific)

Walter Long
Birth of a Nation '15 (American Wars)

Adele Longmire
Battle Circus '53 (Korean War)

Michael (Michel) Lonsdale
Is Paris Burning? '66 (WW II: Europe & North Africa)

Leon Lontoc
The Gallant Hours '60 (WW II: Pacific)
The Hunters '58 (Korean War)

Richard Loo
The Sand Pebbles '66 (American Wars)
The Steel Helmet '51 (Korean War)
Across the Pacific '42 (Between the World Wars)

Perry Lopez
Battle Cry '55 (WW II: Pacific)
Mister Roberts '55 (WW II: Pacific)

Sal Lopez
Full Metal Jacket '87 (Vietnam War)

Trini Lopez
The Dirty Dozen '67 (WW II: Europe & North Africa)

Viktor Lorents
Come and See '85 (WW II: Europe & North Africa)

Livio Lorenzon
The Good, the Bad and the Ugly '67 (American Wars)

Peter Lorre
Casablanca '42 (WW II: The Resistance)

Jean Louis
Waterloo '71 (French Wars)

Montagu Love
Gunga Din '39 (British Wars)

Frank Lovejoy
Home of the Brave '49 (WW II: Pacific)

Raymond Lovell
Immortal Battalion '44 (WW II: Europe & North Africa)

Tom Lowell
The Manchurian Candidate '62 (Korean War)

Curt Lowens
A Midnight Clear '92 (WW II: Europe & North Africa)

Klaus Lowitsch
Cross of Iron '76 (WW II: Europe & North Africa)

Morton Lowry
The Immortal Sergeant '43 (WW II: Europe & North Africa)
Dawn Patrol '38 (WW I)

Myrna Loy
The Best Years of Our Lives '46 (Coming Home)

Arnold Lucy
All Quiet on the Western Front '30 (WW I)

Paul Lukas
Watch on the Rhine '43 (WW II: The Resistance)

Keye Luke
Across the Pacific '42 (Between the World Wars)

Juris Lumiste
Come and See '85 (WW II: Europe & North Africa)

William Lundigan
The Fighting 69th '40 (WW I)

Patti LuPone
1941 '79 (WW II: Homefront)

John Lupton
Battle Cry '55 (WW II: Pacific)

Martin Luttge
The Wannsee Conference '84 (WW II: The Holocaust)

Reg Lye
King Rat '65 (WW II: POWs)

Herbert Lylton
The Gallant Hours '60 (WW II: Pacific)

Ken Lynch
Pork Chop Hill '59 (Korean War)
Run Silent Run Deep '58 (WW II: Pacific)

Helen Lynd
So Proudly We Hail '43 (WW II: Pacific)

George Lynn
To Be or Not to Be '42 (WW II: The Resistance)

Jeffrey Lynn
The Fighting 69th '40 (WW I)

Ben Lyon
Hell's Angels '30 (WW I)

Cliff Lyons
The Horse Soldiers '59 (American Wars)
She Wore a Yellow Ribbon '49 (American Wars)

M

James MacArthur
Battle of the Bulge '65 (WW II: Europe & North Africa)

Charles Macaulay
The Big Red One '80 (WW II: Europe & North Africa)

Niall MacGinnis
Henry V '44 (British Wars)

Jack MacGowran
Doctor Zhivago '65 (Russian Wars)

Charles Mack
America '24 (American Wars)

Marion Mack
The General '26 (American Wars)

Kenneth MacKenna
Judgment at Nuremberg '61 (Coming Home)

Steven Mackintosh
The Land Girls '98 (WW II: Homefront)

Gavin MacLeod
The Sand Pebbles '66 (American Wars)
Pork Chop Hill '59 (Korean War)

Fred MacMurray
The Caine Mutiny '54 (WW II: Europe & North Africa)
Dive Bomber '41 (Between the World Wars)

Beatrice Macola
Schindler's List '93 (WW II: The Holocaust)

George Macready
Tora! Tora! Tora! '70 (WW II: Pacific)
Paths of Glory '57 (WW I)
The Seventh Cross '44 (WW II: POWs)

Peter Madden
Doctor Zhivago '65 (Russian Wars)

Guy Madison
Since You Went Away '44 (WW II: Homefront)

Eero Maenpaa
The Winter War '89 (Between the World Wars)

Pancho Magalona
Merrill's Marauders '62 (WW II: Pacific)

Patrick Magee
Zulu '64 (British Wars)

Jock Mahoney
A Time to Love and a Time to Die '58 (WW II: Europe & North Africa)

Konsta Makela
The Winter War '89 (Between the World Wars)

Taneli Makela
The Winter War '89 (Between the World Wars)

Mako
The Sand Pebbles '66 (American Wars)

Karl Malden
Patton '70 (WW II: Europe & North Africa)
13 Rue Madeleine '46 (WW II: The Resistance)

Arthur Malet
King Rat '65 (WW II: POWs)

John Malkovich
Empire of the Sun '87 (WW II: POWs)

Brian Mallon
Gettysburg '93 (American Wars)

John Mallory
Flying Leathernecks '51 (WW II: Pacific)

Anita Mally
The Wannsee Conference '84 (WW II: The Holocaust)

Dorothy Malone
Battle Cry '55 (WW II: Pacific)

Michael Maloney
Henry V '89 (British Wars)

Eily Malyon
The Seventh Cross '44 (WW II: POWs)

Alex Man
Hong Kong 1941 '84 (Between the World Wars)

Al Mancini
The Dirty Dozen '67 (WW II: Europe & North Africa)

Miles Mander
The White Cliffs of Dover '44 (WW II: Homefront)
Five Graves to Cairo '43 (WW II: Europe & North Africa)
Guadalcanal Diary '43 (WW II: Pacific)
To Be or Not to Be '42 (WW II: The Resistance)

Gina Manes
Napoleon '27 (French Wars)

Gaspard Manesse
Au Revoir les Enfants '87 (WW II: The Holocaust)

Miki Manojlovic
Underground '95 (WW II: Europe & North Africa)

Ralph Manza
The Hunters '58 (Korean War)

Adele Mara
Sands of Iwo Jima '49 (WW II: Pacific)

Sophie Marceau
Braveheart '95 (British Wars)

Fredric March
The Bridges at Toko-Ri '55 (Korean War)
The Best Years of Our Lives '46 (Coming Home)

Arlette Marchal
Wings '27 (WW I)

Stuart Margolin
Bye Bye Blues '89 (WW II: Homefront)

Julianna Margulies
Paradise Road '97 (WW II: POWs)

Jacques Marin
The Train '65 (WW II: Europe &
North Africa)

Howard Marion-Crawford
Charge of the Light Brigade '68
(British Wars)

Hugh Marlowe
Twelve O'Clock High '49 (WW II:
Europe & North Africa)

Scott Marlowe
Men in War '57 (Korean War)

Joe Maross
Run Silent Run Deep '58 (WW II:
Pacific)

Serge Marquand
The Big Red One '80 (WW II:
Europe & North Africa)

Maurice Marsac
The Big Red One '80 (WW II:
Europe & North Africa)
China Gate '57 (Vietnam War)

Mae Marsh
The Fighting Sullivans '42 (WW II:
Pacific)
Birth of a Nation '15 (American
Wars)

Alan Marshal
The White Cliffs of Dover '44 (WW
II: Homefront)

E.G. Marshall
Tora! Tora! Tora! '70 (WW II: Pacific)
Is Paris Burning? '66 (WW II:
Europe & North Africa)
The Caine Mutiny '54 (WW II:
Europe & North Africa)
13 Rue Madeleine '46 (WW II: The
Resistance)

Herbert Marshall
The Razor's Edge '46 (Coming
Home)

Penny Marshall
1941 '79 (WW II: Homefront)

Trudy Marshall
Crash Dive '43 (WW II: Europe &
North Africa)
The Fighting Sullivans '42 (WW II:
Pacific)

Rosita Marstini
The Big Parade '25 (WW I)

Dean Martin
The Young Lions '58 (WW II:
Europe & North Africa)

Gilbert Martin
Rob Roy '95 (British Wars)

Jean Martin
The Battle of Algiers '66 (French
Wars)

Strother Martin
Shenandoah '65 (American Wars)
The Horse Soldiers '59 (American
Wars)

Marc Martinez
Land and Freedom '95 (Between
the World Wars)

Maximillian Martini
Saving Private Ryan '98 (WW II:
Europe & North Africa)

Lee Marvin
The Big Red One '80 (WW II:
Europe & North Africa)
Hell in the Pacific '69 (WW II:
Pacific)
The Dirty Dozen '67 (WW II: Europe
& North Africa)
The Caine Mutiny '54 (WW II:
Europe & North Africa)

Ron Masak
Tora! Tora! Tora! '70 (WW II: Pacific)

James Mason
Cross of Iron '76 (WW II: Europe &
North Africa)
The Blue Max '66 (WW I)

Tom Mason
Apocalypse Now '79 (Vietnam War)

Varvara O. Massalitinova
Alexander Nevsky '38 (Russian
Wars)

Raymond Massey
Battle Cry '55 (WW II: Pacific)
Action in the North Atlantic '43 (WW
II: Europe & North Africa)

Vicki Masson
Rob Roy '95 (British Wars)

Mary Stuart Masterson
Gardens of Stone '87 (Vietnam
War)

Peter Masterson
Gardens of Stone '87 (Vietnam
War)

Aubrey Mather
Mrs. Miniver '42 (WW II: Homefront)

Tim Matheson
1941 '79 (WW II: Homefront)

Norio Matsui
Ran '85 (Japanese Wars)

Dietrich Mattausch
The Wannsee Conference '84 (WW
II: The Holocaust)

A.E. Matthews
Immortal Battalion '44 (WW II:
Europe & North Africa)

Lester Matthews
Objective, Burma! '45 (WW II:
Pacific)
Across the Pacific '42 (Between the
World Wars)

Hedley Mattingly
King Rat '65 (WW II: POWs)

Bill Mauldin
The Red Badge of Courage '51
(American Wars)

Max Maxudian
Napoleon '27 (French Wars)

Jodhi May
Last of the Mohicans '92 (American
Wars)

Martin May
Das Boot '81 (WW II: Europe &
North Africa)

Ferdinand "Ferdy" Mayne
Where Eagles Dare '68 (WW II:
Europe & North Africa)

Frank Mayo
Across the Pacific '42 (Between the
World Wars)
The Fighting 69th '40 (WW I)

Virginia Mayo
The Best Years of Our Lives '46
(Coming Home)

David McCallum
The Great Escape '63 (WW II:
POWs)

Brian McCardie
Rob Roy '95 (British Wars)

Neil McCarthy
Where Eagles Dare '68 (WW II:
Europe & North Africa)
Zulu '64 (British Wars)

Mary McCarty
The Fighting Sullivans '42 (WW II:
Pacific)

Cast
Index

The Story of G.I. Joe '45 (WW II: Europe & North Africa)

Gary Merrill
Twelve O'Clock High '49 (WW II: Europe & North Africa)

Hannes Messemer
The Great Escape '63 (WW II: POWs)

Torben Meyer
Judgment at Nuremberg '61 (Coming Home)

Drew Michaels
The Boys in Company C '77 (Vietnam War)

Frank Middlemass
One Against the Wind '91 (WW II: The Resistance)

Toshiro Mifune
1941 '79 (WW II: Homefront)
Hell in the Pacific '69 (WW II: Pacific)
Yojimbo '61 (Japanese Wars)
The Hidden Fortress '58 (Japanese Wars)
Seven Samurai '54 (Japanese Wars)

Tatsuya Mihashi
Tora! Tora! Tora! '70 (WW II: Pacific)

Dash Mihok
The Thin Red Line '98 (WW II: Pacific)

Kan Mikami
Merry Christmas, Mr. Lawrence '83 (WW II: POWs)

James Milady
America '24 (American Wars)

Bernard Miles
In Which We Serve '43 (WW II: Europe & North Africa)

Sarah Miles
Hope and Glory '87 (WW II: Homefront)

Penelope Milford
Coming Home '78 (Coming Home)

Ray Milland
Beau Geste '39 (British Wars)

Dick Miller
1941 '79 (WW II: Homefront)

Kathleen Miller
Coming Home '78 (Coming Home)

Michael Miller
Men in War '57 (Korean War)

Charles Millot
The Train '65 (WW II: Europe & North Africa)

Gary Landon Mills
Full Metal Jacket '87 (Vietnam War)

John Mills
King Rat '65 (WW II: POWs)
War and Peace '56 (Russian Wars)
In Which We Serve '43 (WW II: Europe & North Africa)

Martin Milner
Mister Roberts '55 (WW II: Pacific)
Sands of Iwo Jima '49 (WW II: Pacific)

Gerald Milton
China Gate '57 (Vietnam War)

Sal Mineo
The Longest Day '62 (WW II: Europe & North Africa)

Olga Mironova
Come and See '85 (WW II: Europe & North Africa)

Cameron Mitchell
Command Decision '48 (WW II: Europe & North Africa)
They Were Expendable '45 (WW II: Pacific)

Ewing Mitchell
Above and Beyond '53 (WW II: Pacific)

Millard Mitchell
Twelve O'Clock High '49 (WW II: Europe & North Africa)

Thomas Mitchell
Bataan '43 (WW II: Pacific)
The Immortal Sergeant '43 (WW II: Europe & North Africa)
The Fighting Sullivans '42 (WW II: Pacific)
Gone with the Wind '39 (American Wars)

Chris Mitchum
A Rumor of War '80 (Vietnam War)

Jim Mitchum
In Harm's Way '65 (WW II: Pacific)
The Victors '63 (WW II: Europe & North Africa)

Robert Mitchum
The Longest Day '62 (WW II: Europe & North Africa)
The Hunters '58 (Korean War)
The Story of G.I. Joe '45 (WW II: Europe & North Africa)

Thirty Seconds over Tokyo '44 (WW II: Pacific)

Koji Mitsui
The Hidden Fortress '58 (Japanese Wars)

Seiji Miyaguchi
Seven Samurai '54 (Japanese Wars)

Yoshiko Miyazaki
Ran '85 (Japanese Wars)

Eiko Miyoshi
The Hidden Fortress '58 (Japanese Wars)

Matthew Modine
Full Metal Jacket '87 (Vietnam War)

Gaston Modot
Grand Illusion '37 (WW I)

Carl Mohner
Sink the Bismarck! '60 (WW II: Europe & North Africa)

Antonio Molina
For Whom the Bell Tolls '43 (Between the World Wars)

Richard Monahan
The Steel Helmet '51 (Korean War)

Roland Monod
A Man Escaped '57 (WW II: POWs)

Ricardo Montalban
Battleground '49 (WW II: Europe & North Africa)

Yves Montand
Is Paris Burning? '66 (WW II: Europe & North Africa)

Michele Montau
Hell Is for Heroes '62 (WW II: Europe & North Africa)

Liliane Montevecchi
The Young Lions '58 (WW II: Europe & North Africa)

George Montgomery
Battle of the Bulge '65 (WW II: Europe & North Africa)

Ray Montgomery
Air Force '43 (WW II: Pacific)

Robert Montgomery
They Were Expendable '45 (WW II: Pacific)

Dennie Moore
Dive Bomber '41 (Between the World Wars)

Cast Index

N

J. Carrol Naish
Sahara '43 (WW II: Europe & North Africa)
Beau Geste '39 (British Wars)
Charge of the Light Brigade '36 (British Wars)
Lives of a Bengal Lancer '35 (British Wars)

Laurence Naismith
Sink the Bismarck! '60 (WW II: Europe & North Africa)

Takashi Naitoh
Merry Christmas, Mr. Lawrence '83 (WW II: POWs)

Tatsuya Nakadai
Ran '85 (Japanese Wars)
Yojimbo '61 (Japanese Wars)

Alan Napier
Thirty Seconds over Tokyo '44 (WW II: Pacific)

Mildred Natwick
She Wore a Yellow Ribbon '49 (American Wars)

Cliff Nazarro
Dive Bomber '41 (Between the World Wars)

Alla Nazimova
Since You Went Away '44 (WW II: Homefront)

Patricia Neal
In Harm's Way '65 (WW II: Pacific)

Mark Neely
The Siege of Firebase Gloria '89 (Vietnam War)

Liam Neeson
Rob Roy '95 (British Wars)
Schindler's List '93 (WW II: The Holocaust)

Francois Negret
Au Revoir les Enfants '87 (WW II: The Holocaust)

David Neidorf
Empire of the Sun '87 (WW II: POWs)
Platoon '86 (Vietnam War)

Sam Neill
One Against the Wind '91 (WW II: The Resistance)

Barry Nelson
Bataan '43 (WW II: Pacific)

Britt Nelson
Flying Leathernecks '51 (WW II: Pacific)

Byron Nelson
The Fighting 69th '40 (WW I)

Tim Blake Nelson
The Thin Red Line '98 (WW II: Pacific)

Tommaso Neri
The Battle of Algiers '66 (French Wars)

Derren Nesbitt
Where Eagles Dare '68 (WW II: Europe & North Africa)
The Blue Max '66 (WW I)

Derek Newark
The Blue Max '66 (WW I)

Bob Newhart
Catch-22 '70 (WW II: Europe & North Africa)
Hell Is for Heroes '62 (WW II: Europe & North Africa)

Robert Newton
Henry V '44 (British Wars)

Richard Ney
Mrs. Miniver '42 (WW II: Homefront)

Jinpachi Nezu
Ran '85 (Japanese Wars)

Cu Ba Nguyen
Good Morning, Vietnam '87 (Vietnam War)

Michael A. Nickles
Hamburger Hill '87 (Vietnam War)

Gerda Nicolson
Gallipoli '81 (WW I)

Esko Nikkari
The Winter War '89 (Between the World Wars)

Dragan Nikolic
Underground '95 (WW II: Europe & North Africa)

Ko Nishimura
Yojimbo '61 (Japanese Wars)

David Niven
The Guns of Navarone '61 (WW II: Europe & North Africa)
Immortal Battalion '44 (WW II: Europe & North Africa)
The Real Glory '39 (American Wars)
Dawn Patrol '38 (WW I)
Charge of the Light Brigade '36 (British Wars)

Lloyd Nolan
Bataan '43 (WW II: Pacific)
Guadalcanal Diary '43 (WW II: Pacific)

Nick Nolte
The Thin Red Line '98 (WW II: Pacific)
Mother Night '96 (WW II: Europe & North Africa)

Takashi Nomura
Ran '85 (Japanese Wars)

Felix Noriego
Battle Cry '55 (WW II: Pacific)
To Hell and Back '55 (WW II: Europe & North Africa)

Robert Normand
Men in War '57 (Korean War)

Jay Norris
A Walk in the Sun '46 (WW II: Europe & North Africa)

Alan North
Glory '89 (American Wars)

Vasili Novikov
Alexander Nevsky '38 (Russian Wars)

Michael Nowka
Cross of Iron '76 (WW II: Europe & North Africa)

Richard Nugent
Sahara '43 (WW II: Europe & North Africa)

Fred Nurney
Five Graves to Cairo '43 (WW II: Europe & North Africa)

Carroll Nye
Gone with the Wind '39 (American Wars)

Jack Oakie
The Great Dictator '40 (Between the World Wars)

Simon Oakland
The Sand Pebbles '66 (American Wars)

Warren Oates
1941 '79 (WW II: Homefront)
Shenandoah '65 (American Wars)

Cast Index

P

Joy Page
Casablanca '42 (WW II: The Resistance)

Nestor Paiva
Beau Geste '39 (British Wars)

Eugene Pallette
Birth of a Nation '15 (American Wars)

Betsy Palmer
Mister Roberts '55 (WW II: Pacific)

Gregg Palmer
To Hell and Back '55 (WW II: Europe & North Africa)

J.C. Palmore
Hamburger Hill '87 (Vietnam War)

Joe Pantoliano
Empire of the Sun '87 (WW II: POWs)

Irene Papas
The Guns of Navarone '61 (WW II: Europe & North Africa)

Marisa Paredes
Life Is Beautiful '98 (WW II: The Holocaust)

Jerry Paris
The Caine Mutiny '54 (WW II: Europe & North Africa)

Eleanor Parker
Above and Beyond '53 (WW II: Pacific)

Fess Parker
Hell Is for Heroes '62 (WW II: Europe & North Africa)
Battle Cry '55 (WW II: Pacific)

Dita Parlo
Grand Illusion '37 (WW I)

Leslie Parrish
The Manchurian Candidate '62 (Korean War)

Franck Pasquier
The Last Metro '80 (WW II: The Holocaust)

Rosana Pastor
Land and Freedom '95 (Between the World Wars)

Nigel Patrick
The Battle of Britain '69 (WW II: Europe & North Africa)

Morgan Paull
Patton '70 (WW II: Europe & North Africa)

Albert Paulsen
The Manchurian Candidate '62 (Korean War)

Milena Pavlovic
Underground '95 (WW II: Europe & North Africa)

Katina Paxinou
For Whom the Bell Tolls '43 (Between the World Wars)

Collin Wilcox Paxton
Catch-22 '70 (WW II: Europe & North Africa)

Allen Payne
The Tuskegee Airmen '95 (WW II: Europe & North Africa)

John Payne
The Razor's Edge '46 (Coming Home)

Gregory Peck
The Guns of Navarone '61 (WW II: Europe & North Africa)
Pork Chop Hill '59 (Korean War)
Twelve O'Clock High '49 (WW II: Europe & North Africa)

Georges Peclet
Grand Illusion '37 (WW I)

Chris Pederson
Platoon '86 (Vietnam War)

Austin Pendleton
Catch-22 '70 (WW II: Europe & North Africa)

Sean Penn
The Thin Red Line '98 (WW II: Pacific)

Jack Pennick
The Alamo '60 (American Wars)
The Horse Soldiers '59 (American Wars)
Mister Roberts '55 (WW II: Pacific)
She Wore a Yellow Ribbon '49 (American Wars)
They Were Expendable '45 (WW II: Pacific)
Sergeant York '41 (WW I)

George Peppard
The Blue Max '66 (WW I)
The Victors '63 (WW II: Europe & North Africa)
Pork Chop Hill '59 (Korean War)

Barry Pepper
Saving Private Ryan '98 (WW II: Europe & North Africa)

Anthony Perkins
Catch-22 '70 (WW II: Europe & North Africa)
Is Paris Burning? '66 (WW II: Europe & North Africa)

Jacques Perrin
317th Platoon '65 (French Wars)

Nehemiah Persoff
Men in War '57 (Korean War)

Peter
Ran '85 (Japanese Wars)

Dorothy Peterson
Air Force '43 (WW II: Pacific)

Hay Petrie
The Four Feathers '39 (British Wars)

Illarian Pevzov
Chapayev '34 (Russian Wars)

Gunter Pfitzmann
The Bridge '59 (WW II: Europe & North Africa)

JoAnn Pflug
M*A*S*H '70 (Korean War)

Peter Phelps
The Lighthorsemen '87 (WW I)

Lee Philips
The Hunters '58 (Korean War)

Barney Phillips
The Sand Pebbles '66 (American Wars)

Bill Phillips
Thirty Seconds over Tokyo '44 (WW II: Pacific)

Ethan Phillips
Glory '89 (American Wars)

Leslie Phillips
Empire of the Sun '87 (WW II: POWs)

Lou Diamond Phillips
Courage Under Fire '96 (Coming Home)

Robert Phillips
The Dirty Dozen '67 (WW II: Europe & North Africa)

Paul Picerni
To Hell and Back '55 (WW II: Europe & North Africa)

John Pickard
Above and Beyond '53 (WW II: Pacific)

Kazimir Rabetsky
Come and See '85 (WW II: Europe & North Africa)

Francine Racette
Au Revoir les Enfants '87 (WW II: The Holocaust)

Jack Raine
Above and Beyond '53 (WW II: Pacific)

Ford Rainey
The Sand Pebbles '66 (American Wars)

Claude Rains
Lawrence of Arabia '62 (WW I)
Casablanca '42 (WW II: The Resistance)

Antti Raivio
The Winter War '89 (Between the World Wars)

Jobyna Ralston
Wings '27 (WW I)

Tim Ransom
Courage Under Fire '96 (Coming Home)

Rada Rassimov
The Good, the Bad and the Ugly '67 (American Wars)

Mikhail Rasumny
For Whom the Bell Tolls '43 (Between the World Wars)
Wake Island '42 (WW II: Pacific)

Basil Rathbone
Dawn Patrol '38 (WW I)

John Ratzenberger
A Bridge Too Far '77 (WW II: Europe & North Africa)

Siegfried Rauch
The Big Red One '80 (WW II: Europe & North Africa)
Patton '70 (WW II: Europe & North Africa)

Christopher Ravenscroft
Henry V '89 (British Wars)

Aldo Ray
The Green Berets '68 (Vietnam War)
Men in War '57 (Korean War)
Battle Cry '55 (WW II: Pacific)

Anthony Ray
Men in War '57 (Korean War)

Michel Ray
Lawrence of Arabia '62 (WW I)

Robert Redford
A Bridge Too Far '77 (WW II: Europe & North Africa)

Corin Redgrave
Charge of the Light Brigade '68 (British Wars)

Michael Redgrave
The Battle of Britain '69 (WW II: Europe & North Africa)

Vanessa Redgrave
Charge of the Light Brigade '68 (British Wars)

Donna Reed
From Here to Eternity '53 (Between the World Wars)
They Were Expendable '45 (WW II: Pacific)

Robert Reed
The Hunters '58 (Korean War)

Tracy Reed
Dr. Strangelove, or: How I Learned to Stop Worrying and Love the Bomb '64 (American Wars)

Walter Reed
The Sand Pebbles '66 (American Wars)
The Horse Soldiers '59 (American Wars)

Sam Reese
King Rat '65 (WW II: POWs)

George Reeves
From Here to Eternity '53 (Between the World Wars)
So Proudly We Hail '43 (WW II: Pacific)
The Fighting 69th '40 (WW I)
Gone with the Wind '39 (American Wars)

George Regas
Beau Geste '39 (British Wars)
Gunga Din '39 (British Wars)
Charge of the Light Brigade '36 (British Wars)
Lives of a Bengal Lancer '35 (British Wars)

Charles Regnier
A Time to Love and a Time to Die '58 (WW II: Europe & North Africa)

Frank Reicher
Watch on the Rhine '43 (WW II: The Resistance)
To Be or Not to Be '42 (WW II: The Resistance)

Carl Benton Reid
The Gallant Hours '60 (WW II: Pacific)

Kate Reid
Bye Bye Blues '89 (WW II: Homefront)

Wallace Reid
Birth of a Nation '15 (American Wars)

Jack Reilly
The Story of G.I. Joe '45 (WW II: Europe & North Africa)

John C. Reilly
The Thin Red Line '98 (WW II: Pacific)

John R. Reilly
Thirty Seconds over Tokyo '44 (WW II: Pacific)

Luke Reilly
Bye Bye Blues '89 (WW II: Homefront)

Mechthild Reinders
The White Rose '83 (WW II: The Resistance)

Hans Reiser
The Great Escape '63 (WW II: POWs)

Erich Maria Remarque
A Time to Love and a Time to Die '58 (WW II: Europe & North Africa)

Bert Remsen
Pork Chop Hill '59 (Korean War)

Albert Remy
The Train '65 (WW II: Europe & North Africa)

Duncan Renaldo
Fighting Seabees '44 (WW II: Pacific)
For Whom the Bell Tolls '43 (Between the World Wars)

Tito Renaldo
The Story of G.I. Joe '45 (WW II: Europe & North Africa)
For Whom the Bell Tolls '43 (Between the World Wars)

Robert Rendel
The Four Feathers '39 (British Wars)

Repnikova
Battleship Potemkin '25 (Russian Wars)

Marjorie Reynolds
Gone with the Wind '39 *(American Wars)*

Giovanni Ribisi
Saving Private Ryan '98 *(WW II: Europe & North Africa)*

Sebastian Rice-Edwards
Hope and Glory '87 *(WW II: Homefront)*

Claude Rich
Is Paris Burning? '66 *(WW II: Europe & North Africa)*

Emily Richard
Empire of the Sun '87 *(WW II: POWs)*

Jean-Louis Richard
The Last Metro '80 *(WW II: The Holocaust)*

Addison Richards
Fighting Seabees '44 *(WW II: Pacific)*
Since You Went Away '44 *(WW II: Homefront)*
Air Force '43 *(WW II: Pacific)*
The Fighting Sullivans '42 *(WW II: Pacific)*
Dive Bomber '41 *(Between the World Wars)*

Jeff Richards
Above and Beyond '53 *(WW II: Pacific)*
Battle Circus '53 *(Korean War)*

Paul Richards
All the Young Men '60 *(Korean War)*

Joely Richardson
Charge of the Light Brigade '68 *(British Wars)*

Miranda Richardson
Empire of the Sun '87 *(WW II: POWs)*

Ralph Richardson
The Battle of Britain '69 *(WW II: Europe & North Africa)*
Doctor Zhivago '65 *(Russian Wars)*
The Four Feathers '39 *(British Wars)*

Jean-Jose Richer
The Last Metro '80 *(WW II: The Holocaust)*

Ralph Richer
Das Boot '81 *(WW II: Europe & North Africa)*

Kane Richmond
Action in the North Atlantic '43 *(WW II: Europe & North Africa)*

Don Rickles
Run Silent Run Deep '58 *(WW II: Pacific)*

John Ridgely
Air Force '43 *(WW II: Pacific)*

Stanley Ridges
Air Force '43 *(WW II: Pacific)*
To Be or Not to Be '42 *(WW II: The Resistance)*
Sergeant York '41 *(WW I)*
They Died with Their Boots On '41 *(American Wars)*

Harry Riebauer
The Great Escape '63 *(WW II: POWs)*

Gerd Riegauer
The Wannsee Conference '84 *(WW II: The Holocaust)*

Richard Riehle
Glory '89 *(American Wars)*

Shane Rimmer
Dr. Strangelove, or: How I Learned to Stop Worrying and Love the Bomb '64 *(American Wars)*

Maurice Risch
The Last Metro '80 *(WW II: The Holocaust)*

William S. Rising
America '24 *(American Wars)*

Lazar Ristovski
Underground '95 *(WW II: Europe & North Africa)*

Pascal Rivet
Au Revoir les Enfants '87 *(WW II: The Holocaust)*

Jason Robards, Jr.
Tora! Tora! Tora! '70 *(WW II: Pacific)*

Chuck Roberson
The Green Berets '68 *(Vietnam War)*

Clete Roberts
The Story of G.I. Joe '45 *(WW II: Europe & North Africa)*

Leona Roberts
Gone with the Wind '39 *(American Wars)*

Roy Roberts
Guadalcanal Diary '43 *(WW II: Pacific)*

The Fighting Sullivans '42 *(WW II: Pacific)*

Cliff Robertson
Too Late the Hero '70 *(WW II: Pacific)*

Willard Robertson
Air Force '43 *(WW II: Pacific)*

George Robey
Henry V '44 *(British Wars)*

Charles Robinson
Shenandoah '65 *(American Wars)*

Edward G. Robinson
Mr. Winkle Goes to War '44 *(WW II: Europe & North Africa)*

Nancy June Robinson
The Fighting Sullivans '42 *(WW II: Pacific)*

Rudy Robles
Across the Pacific '42 *(Between the World Wars)*
The Real Glory '39 *(American Wars)*

Wayne Robson
Bye Bye Blues '89 *(WW II: Homefront)*

Jeffrey Rockland
Doctor Zhivago '65 *(Russian Wars)*

Walter Rodgers
All Quiet on the Western Front '30 *(WW I)*

Maurice Roeves
Last of the Mohicans '92 *(American Wars)*

Charles "Buddy" Rogers
Wings '27 *(WW I)*

Naum Rogozhin
Alexander Nevsky '38 *(Russian Wars)*

Ruth Roman
Since You Went Away '44 *(WW II: Homefront)*

Larry Romano
The Thin Red Line '98 *(WW II: Pacific)*

John Ronane
King Rat '65 *(WW II: POWs)*

Maurice Ronet
The Victors '63 *(WW II: Europe & North Africa)*

Mickey Rooney
The Bridges at Toko-Ri '55 *(Korean War)*

Hayden Rorke
Above and Beyond '53 *(WW II: Pacific)*

Annie Rosar
The Third Man '49 *(Coming Home)*

Ed Roseman
America '24 *(American Wars)*

Katharine Ross
Shenandoah '65 *(American Wars)*

Norman Rossington
Charge of the Light Brigade '68 *(British Wars)*
Lawrence of Arabia '62 *(WW I)*

Leonard Rossiter
King Rat '65 *(WW II: POWs)*

Tim Roth
Rob Roy '95 *(British Wars)*

John Rothman
Gettysburg '93 *(American Wars)*

Vladimir Roudenko
Napoleon '27 *(French Wars)*

Mickey Rourke
1941 '79 *(WW II: Homefront)*

Marcel Rousseau
13 Rue Madeleine '46 *(WW II: The Resistance)*

Selena Royle
Thirty Seconds over Tokyo '44 *(WW II: Pacific)*
The Fighting Sullivans '42 *(WW II: Pacific)*

John Ruddock
Lawrence of Arabia '62 *(WW I)*

Tim Ruddy
Gettysburg '93 *(American Wars)*

Herbert Rudley
The Young Lions '58 *(WW II: Europe & North Africa)*
A Walk in the Sun '46 *(WW II: Europe & North Africa)*
The Seventh Cross '44 *(WW II: POWs)*

Claude-Oliver Rudolph
Das Boot '81 *(WW II: Europe & North Africa)*

Robert Rueben
The Story of G.I. Joe '45 *(WW II: Europe & North Africa)*

Barbara Ruick
Above and Beyond '53 *(WW II: Pacific)*

Sig Rumann
Stalag 17 '53 *(WW II: POWs)*
To Be or Not to Be '42 *(WW II: The Resistance)*

Barbara Rush
The Young Lions '58 *(WW II: Europe & North Africa)*

Bing Russell
The Horse Soldiers '59 *(American Wars)*

Harold Russell
The Best Years of Our Lives '46 *(Coming Home)*

Ann Rutherford
Gone with the Wind '39 *(American Wars)*

Barbara Rutting
A Time to Love and a Time to Die '58 *(WW II: Europe & North Africa)*

David Ryall
One Against the Wind '91 *(WW II: The Resistance)*

Eddie Ryan
The Fighting Sullivans '42 *(WW II: Pacific)*

Edmon Ryan
Tora! Tora! Tora! '70 *(WW II: Pacific)*

Meg Ryan
Courage Under Fire '96 *(Coming Home)*

Robert Ryan
The Dirty Dozen '67 *(WW II: Europe & North Africa)*
Battle of the Bulge '65 *(WW II: Europe & North Africa)*
The Longest Day '62 *(WW II: Europe & North Africa)*
Men in War '57 *(Korean War)*
Flying Leathernecks '51 *(WW II: Pacific)*

Tim Ryan
From Here to Eternity '53 *(Between the World Wars)*

Daisuke Ryu
Ran '85 *(Japanese Wars)*

S

Yacef Saadi
The Battle of Algiers '66 *(French Wars)*

Jonathan Sagalle
Schindler's List '93 *(WW II: The Holocaust)*

Mort Sahl
All the Young Men '60 *(Korean War)*

Michael (Steve Flagg) St. Angel
Flying Leathernecks '51 *(WW II: Pacific)*

Ana St. Clair
All the Young Men '60 *(Korean War)*

Michael St. Clair
Von Ryan's Express '65 *(WW II: POWs)*

Raymond St. Jacques
Glory '89 *(American Wars)*
The Green Berets '68 *(Vietnam War)*

John St. Polis
Four Horsemen of the Apocalypse '21 *(WW I)*

Keiji Sakakida
Seven Samurai '54 *(Japanese Wars)*

S.Z. Sakall
Casablanca '42 *(WW II: The Resistance)*

Ryuichi Sakamoto
Merry Christmas, Mr. Lawrence '83 *(WW II: POWs)*

Tomi Salmela
The Winter War '89 *(Between the World Wars)*

Eugene Samoilov
Waterloo '71 *(French Wars)*

Louis Sance
Napoleon '27 *(French Wars)*

Paul Sanchez
Platoon '86 *(Vietnam War)*

Clare Sandars
Mrs. Miniver '42 *(WW II: Homefront)*

Walter Sande
The Gallant Hours '60 *(WW II: Pacific)*

Jay O. Sanders
Glory '89 *(American Wars)*

Cast Index

Anabel Shaw
To Hell and Back '55 (WW II: Europe & North Africa)

Robert Shaw
The Battle of Britain '69 (WW II: Europe & North Africa)
Battle of the Bulge '65 (WW II: Europe & North Africa)

Stan Shaw
The Boys in Company C '77 (Vietnam War)

Robert Shawley
Stalag 17 '53 (WW II: POWs)

Konstantin Shayne
The Seventh Cross '44 (WW II: POWs)
Five Graves to Cairo '43 (WW II: Europe & North Africa)

Zhai Nai She
Empire of the Sun '87 (WW II: POWs)

Perry Sheehan
Battle Circus '53 (Korean War)

Charlie Sheen
Platoon '86 (Vietnam War)

Martin Sheen
Gettysburg '93 (American Wars)
Apocalypse Now '79 (Vietnam War)
Catch-22 '70 (WW II: Europe & North Africa)

Reginald Sheffield
Gunga Din '39 (British Wars)
Lives of a Bengal Lancer '35 (British Wars)

Simon Shepherd
Henry V '89 (British Wars)

Michael Shepley
Henry V '44 (British Wars)

William Morgan Sheppard
Gettysburg '93 (American Wars)

Vladek Sheybal
The Wind and the Lion '75 (American Wars)

George Shibata
Pork Chop Hill '59 (Korean War)

Arthur Shields
She Wore a Yellow Ribbon '49 (American Wars)
The White Cliffs of Dover '44 (WW II: Homefront)

Shogo Shimada
Tora! Tora! Tora! '70 (WW II: Pacific)

Gen Shimizu
Seven Samurai '54 (Japanese Wars)

Sab Shimono
Paradise Road '97 (WW II: POWs)

Takashi Shimura
Yojimbo '61 (Japanese Wars)
The Hidden Fortress '58 (Japanese Wars)
Seven Samurai '54 (Japanese Wars)

Stephan Shkurat
Chapayev '34 (Russian Wars)

Ann Shoemaker
Thirty Seconds over Tokyo '44 (WW II: Pacific)

Tim Shoemaker
A Midnight Clear '92 (WW II: Europe & North Africa)

Dan Shor
A Rumor of War '80 (Vietnam War)

Col. D.M. Shoup
Sands of Iwo Jima '49 (WW II: Pacific)

Capt. Harold G. Shrier
Sands of Iwo Jima '49 (WW II: Pacific)

Oliver Siebert
The White Rose '83 (WW II: The Resistance)

George Siegmann
Birth of a Nation '15 (American Wars)

Casey Siemaszko
Gardens of Stone '87 (Vietnam War)

Simone Signoret
Is Paris Burning? '66 (WW II: Europe & North Africa)

James B. Sikking
Von Ryan's Express '65 (WW II: POWs)

Henry Silva
The Manchurian Candidate '62 (Korean War)

Gerald Sim
King Rat '65 (WW II: POWs)

Dick Simmons
Above and Beyond '53 (WW II: Pacific)
Battle Circus '53 (Korean War)

Michel Simon
The Train '65 (WW II: Europe & North Africa)

Martine Simonet
The Last Metro '80 (WW II: The Holocaust)

Nikolai Simonov
Chapayev '34 (Russian Wars)

Russell Simpson
The Horse Soldiers '59 (American Wars)
They Were Expendable '45 (WW II: Pacific)

Frank Sinatra
Von Ryan's Express '65 (WW II: POWs)
The Manchurian Candidate '62 (Korean War)
From Here to Eternity '53 (Between the World Wars)

Marc Singer
Go Tell the Spartans '78 (Vietnam War)

Gary Sinise
A Midnight Clear '92 (WW II: Europe & North Africa)

Tom Sizemore
Saving Private Ryan '98 (WW II: Europe & North Africa)
Born on the Fourth of July '89 (Coming Home)

Tom Skerritt
M*A*S*H '70 (Korean War)

Walter Slezak
Lifeboat '44 (WW II: Europe & North Africa)

Alexis Smith
Dive Bomber '41 (Between the World Wars)

Sir C. Aubrey Smith
The White Cliffs of Dover '44 (WW II: Homefront)
The Four Feathers '39 (British Wars)
Lives of a Bengal Lancer '35 (British Wars)

Charles Smith
The General '26 (American Wars)

Gunboat Smith
Wings '27 (WW I)

Juney Smith
Good Morning, Vietnam '87 (Vietnam War)

Lane Smith
A Rumor of War '80 (Vietnam War)

Sydney Smith
The Gallant Hours '60 (WW II: Pacific)

Gen. Walter Bedell Smith
To Hell and Back '55 (WW II: Europe & North Africa)

Susan Sneath
Bye Bye Blues '89 (WW II: Home-front)

Sojin
Seven Samurai '54 (Japanese Wars)

Vladimir Sokoloff
For Whom the Bell Tolls '43 (Between the World Wars)
The Real Glory '39 (American Wars)

Elke Sommer
The Victors '63 (WW II: Europe & North Africa)

Jack Soo
The Green Berets '68 (Vietnam War)

Walter Soo Hoo
China Gate '57 (Vietnam War)

Miitta Sorvali
The Winter War '89 (Between the World Wars)

Kenneth Spencer
Bataan '43 (WW II: Pacific)

Wendie Jo Sperber
1941 '79 (WW II: Homefront)

Madame Spivy
The Manchurian Candidate '62 (Korean War)

G.D. Spradlin
Apocalypse Now '79 (Vietnam War)

Elizabeth Spriggs
Paradise Road '97 (WW II: POWs)

William Squire
Where Eagles Dare '68 (WW II: Europe & North Africa)

Robert Stack
1941 '79 (WW II: Homefront)
Is Paris Burning? '66 (WW II: Europe & North Africa)
To Be or Not to Be '42 (WW II: The Resistance)

Joerg Stadler
Saving Private Ryan '98 (WW II: Europe & North Africa)

Jon Stafford
Full Metal Jacket '87 (Vietnam War)

Lynn Stalmaster
Flying Leathernecks '51 (WW II: Pacific)
The Steel Helmet '51 (Korean War)

Lionel Stander
1941 '79 (WW II: Homefront)
Guadalcanal Diary '43 (WW II: Pacific)

Guy Standing
Lives of a Bengal Lancer '35 (British Wars)

John Standing
King Rat '65 (WW II: POWs)

Maxfield Stanley
Birth of a Nation '15 (American Wars)

Dan Stanton
Good Morning, Vietnam '87 (Vietnam War)

Don Stanton
Good Morning, Vietnam '87 (Vietnam War)

Paul Stanton
Across the Pacific '42 (Between the World Wars)

Bob Steele
Pork Chop Hill '59 (Korean War)

Fred Steele
The Story of G.I. Joe '45 (WW II: Europe & North Africa)

Rob Steele
Breaker Morant '80 (British Wars)

Vernon Steele
They Were Expendable '45 (WW II: Pacific)

Rod Steiger
Waterloo '71 (French Wars)
Doctor Zhivago '65 (Russian Wars)
The Longest Day '62 (WW II: Europe & North Africa)

Karel Stepanek
Sink the Bismarck! '60 (WW II: Europe & North Africa)

Harvey Stephens
Sergeant York '41 (WW I)
The Fighting 69th '40 (WW I)
Beau Geste '39 (British Wars)

Robert Stephens
Henry V '89 (British Wars)
Empire of the Sun '87 (WW II: POWs)

Henry Stephenson
Charge of the Light Brigade '36 (British Wars)

James Stephenson
Beau Geste '39 (British Wars)

Robyn Stevan
Bye Bye Blues '89 (WW II: Home-front)

Andrew Stevens
The Boys in Company C '77 (Vietnam War)

Charles Stevens
Lives of a Bengal Lancer '35 (British Wars)

Craig Stevens
Since You Went Away '44 (WW II: Homefront)
Dive Bomber '41 (Between the World Wars)

Mark Stevens
Objective, Burma! '45 (WW II: Pacific)

Onslow Stevens
O.S.S. '46 (WW II: The Resistance)

Paul Stevens
Patton '70 (WW II: Europe & North Africa)

Tom Stevenson
Across the Pacific '42 (Between the World Wars)

Ewan Stewart
Rob Roy '95 (British Wars)

James Stewart
Shenandoah '65 (American Wars)

Paul Stewart
Twelve O'Clock High '49 (WW II: Europe & North Africa)

Ben Stiller
Empire of the Sun '87 (WW II: POWs)

Fred Stillkrauth
Cross of Iron '76 (WW II: Europe & North Africa)

Slavko Stimac
Underground '95 (WW II: Europe & North Africa)

Nigel Stock
The Great Escape '63 (WW II: POWs)

Werner Stocker
The White Rose '83 (WW II: The Resistance)

Dean Stockwell
Gardens of Stone '87 (Vietnam War)

Danilo Stojkovic
Underground '95 (WW II: Europe & North Africa)

Shirley Stoler
The Deer Hunter '78 (Vietnam War)

Eric Stoltz
Rob Roy '95 (British Wars)

Lena Stolze
The White Rose '83 (WW II: The Resistance)

Robinson Stone
Stalag 17 '53 (WW II: POWs)

Ludwig Stossel
Casablanca '42 (WW II: The Resistance)

Ernst Stotzner
Underground '95 (WW II: Europe & North Africa)

Madeleine Stowe
Last of the Mohicans '92 (American Wars)

Harry Strang
The Fighting Sullivans '42 (WW II: Pacific)

Glenn Strange
Action in the North Atlantic '43 (WW II: Europe & North Africa)

David Strathairn
Mother Night '96 (WW II: Europe & North Africa)

Gil Stratton
Stalag 17 '53 (WW II: POWs)

Robert Strauss
The Bridges at Toko-Ri '55 (Korean War)
Stalag 17 '53 (WW II: POWs)

Meryl Streep
The Deer Hunter '78 (Vietnam War)

Oliver Stritzel
Das Boot '81 (WW II: Europe & North Africa)

Joe Strnad
The Deer Hunter '78 (Vietnam War)

Woody Strode
Pork Chop Hill '59 (Korean War)

Michael Strong
Patton '70 (WW II: Europe & North Africa)

James Patrick Stuart
Gettysburg '93 (American Wars)

John Stuart
Sink the Bismarck! '60 (WW II: Europe & North Africa)

Wes Studi
Last of the Mohicans '92 (American Wars)

Wolfgang Stumpf
The Bridge '59 (WW II: Europe & North Africa)

Yasushi Sugita
Fires on the Plain '59 (WW II: Pacific)

Chintara Sukapatana
Good Morning, Vietnam '87 (Vietnam War)

Elliott Sullivan
Action in the North Atlantic '43 (WW II: Europe & North Africa)

Slim Summerville
All Quiet on the Western Front '30 (WW I)

Martti Suosalo
The Winter War '89 (Between the World Wars)

Donald Sutherland
M*A*S*H '70 (Korean War)
The Dirty Dozen '67 (WW II: Europe & North Africa)

Kay Sutton
Sergeant York '41 (WW I)

D.B. Sweeney
Gardens of Stone '87 (Vietnam War)

Dolph Sweet
Go Tell the Spartans '78 (Vietnam War)

Gary Sweet
The Lighthorsemen '87 (WW I)

Karl Swenson
Judgment at Nuremberg '61 (Coming Home)
The Gallant Hours '60 (WW II: Pacific)

Tommy Swerdlow
Hamburger Hill '87 (Vietnam War)

Josef Swickard
Four Horsemen of the Apocalypse '21 (WW I)

Laszlo Szabo
The Last Metro '80 (WW II: The Holocaust)

T

Hiroshi Tachikawa
Yojimbo '61 (Japanese Wars)

Sydney Tafler
Sink the Bismarck! '60 (WW II: Europe & North Africa)

Amid Taftazani
The Four Feathers '39 (British Wars)

Rita Taggart
Coming Home '78 (Coming Home)

Ken Takakura
Too Late the Hero '70 (WW II: Pacific)

George Takei
The Green Berets '68 (Vietnam War)

Osamu Takizawa
Fires on the Plain '59 (WW II: Pacific)

Akim Tamiroff
Five Graves to Cairo '43 (WW II: Europe & North Africa)
For Whom the Bell Tolls '43 (Between the World Wars)
Lives of a Bengal Lancer '35 (British Wars)

Takahiro Tamura
Tora! Tora! Tora! '70 (WW II: Pacific)

Jessica Tandy
The Seventh Cross '44 (WW II: POWs)

Charles Tannen
Crash Dive '43 (WW II: Europe & North Africa)

Gordon Tanner
Dr. Strangelove, or: How I Learned to Stop Worrying and Love the Bomb '64 (American Wars)

Cast
Index

Joan Tours
So Proudly We Hail '43 (WW II:
Pacific)

Harry Towb
The Blue Max '66 (WW I)

Constance Towers
The Horse Soldiers '59 (American
Wars)

Spencer Tracy
Judgment at Nuremberg '61 (Com-
ing Home)
The Seventh Cross '44 (WW II:
POWs)
Thirty Seconds over Tokyo '44 (WW
II: Pacific)

Tung Thanh Tran
Good Morning, Vietnam '87 (Vietnam War)

Cordula Trantow
The Bridge '59 (WW II: Europe &
North Africa)

Henry Travers
Mrs. Miniver '42 (WW II: Homefront)

Merle Travis
From Here to Eternity '53 (Between
the World Wars)

Richard Travis
Dive Bomber '41 (Between the
World Wars)

John Travolta
The Thin Red Line '98 (WW II:
Pacific)

Mary Treen
So Proudly We Hail '43 (WW II:
Pacific)

Roger Treherne
A Man Escaped '57 (WW II: POWs)

Les Tremayne
The Gallant Hours '60 (WW II:
Pacific)

Ivan Triesault
Von Ryan's Express '65 (WW II:
POWs)

Gus Trikonis
The Sand Pebbles '66 (American
Wars)

Jean-Louis Trintignant
Is Paris Burning? '66 (WW II:
Europe & North Africa)

Bobby Troup
M*A*S*H '70 (Korean War)

Charles Trowbridge
They Were Expendable '45 (WW II:
Pacific)
Fighting Seabees '44 (WW II:
Pacific)
Wake Island '42 (WW II: Pacific)
Sergeant York '41 (WW I)
The Fighting 69th '40 (WW I)

Michael Trubshawe
The Guns of Navarone '61 (WW II:
Europe & North Africa)

Ralph Truman
Henry V '44 (British Wars)

Tom Tryon
In Harm's Way '65 (WW II: Pacific)
The Longest Day '62 (WW II:
Europe & North Africa)

Irene Tsu
The Green Berets '68 (Vietnam
War)

Yoshio Tsuchiya
Yojimbo '61 (Japanese Wars)
Seven Samurai '54 (Japanese
Wars)

Yoko Tsukasa
Yojimbo '61 (Japanese Wars)

Masaya Tsukida
Fires on the Plain '59 (WW II:
Pacific)

Keiko Tsushima
Seven Samurai '54 (Japanese
Wars)

Forrest Tucker
Sands of Iwo Jima '49 (WW II:
Pacific)

Richard Tucker
Wings '27 (WW I)

Ulrich Tucker
The White Rose '83 (WW II: The
Resistance)

Sonny Tufts
So Proudly We Hail '43 (WW II:
Pacific)

Tom Tully
The Caine Mutiny '54 (WW II:
Europe & North Africa)

Joe Turkel
The Sand Pebbles '66 (American
Wars)
King Rat '65 (WW II: POWs)
Paths of Glory '57 (WW I)

Bowditch Turner
Four Horsemen of the Apocalypse
'21 (WW I)

Rita Tushingham
Doctor Zhivago '65 (Russian Wars)

Ian Tyler
Full Metal Jacket '87 (Vietnam War)

Tom Tyler
She Wore a Yellow Ribbon '49
(American Wars)

Willie Tyler
Coming Home '78 (Coming Home)

George Tyne
Sands of Iwo Jima '49 (WW II:
Pacific)
A Walk in the Sun '46 (WW II:
Europe & North Africa)
Objective, Burma! '45 (WW II:
Pacific)

U

Asao Uchida
Tora! Tora! Tora! '70 (WW II: Pacific)

Yuya Uchida
Merry Christmas, Mr. Lawrence '83
(WW II: POWs)

Kichijiro Ueda
The Hidden Fortress '58 (Japanese
Wars)
Seven Samurai '54 (Japanese
Wars)

Misa Uehara
The Hidden Fortress '58 (Japanese
Wars)

Liv Ullmann
A Bridge Too Far '77 (WW II:
Europe & North Africa)

Joe Unger
Go Tell the Spartans '78 (Vietnam
War)

Mary Ure
Where Eagles Dare '68 (WW II:
Europe & North Africa)

Jun Usami
Tora! Tora! Tora! '70 (WW II: Pacific)

Mantaro Ushio
Fires on the Plain '59 (WW II:
Pacific)

Cast Index

Christopher Walken
The Deer Hunter '78 *(Vietnam War)*

Clint Walker
The Dirty Dozen '67 *(WW II: Europe & North Africa)*

Lynn Walker
So Proudly We Hail '43 *(WW II: Pacific)*

Robert Walker
Since You Went Away '44 *(WW II: Homefront)*
Thirty Seconds over Tokyo '44 *(WW II: Pacific)*
Bataan '43 *(WW II: Pacific)*

Eli Wallach
The Good, the Bad and the Ugly '67 *(American Wars)*
The Victors '63 *(WW II: Europe & North Africa)*

Arthur Walsh
They Were Expendable '45 *(WW II: Pacific)*

Frank Walsh
America '24 *(American Wars)*

J.T. Walsh
Good Morning, Vietnam '87 *(Vietnam War)*

Kay Walsh
In Which We Serve '43 *(WW II: Europe & North Africa)*

Raoul Walsh
Birth of a Nation '15 *(American Wars)*

Hal Walters
The Four Feathers '39 *(British Wars)*

Henry B. Walthall
Wings '27 *(WW I)*
Birth of a Nation '15 *(American Wars)*

Douglas Walton
The Lost Patrol '34 *(WW I)*

John Walton
The Lighthorsemen '87 *(WW I)*

John Warburton
King Rat '65 *(WW II: POWs)*
The White Cliffs of Dover '44 *(WW II: Homefront)*

Kelly Ward
The Big Red One '80 *(WW II: Europe & North Africa)*

Harlan Warde
Above and Beyond '53 *(WW II: Pacific)*
Flying Leathernecks '51 *(WW II: Pacific)*

Jack Warden
Run Silent Run Deep '58 *(WW II: Pacific)*
From Here to Eternity '53 *(Between the World Wars)*

David Warner
Cross of Iron '76 *(WW II: Europe & North Africa)*

Malcolm Jamal Warner
The Tuskegee Airmen '95 *(WW II: Europe & North Africa)*

Katherine Warren
The Caine Mutiny '54 *(WW II: Europe & North Africa)*

Ruth Warrick
Mr. Winkle Goes to War '44 *(WW II: Europe & North Africa)*

James Warwick
Lives of a Bengal Lancer '35 *(British Wars)*

Virginia Warwick
Four Horsemen of the Apocalypse '21 *(WW I)*

Denzel Washington
Courage Under Fire '96 *(Coming Home)*
Glory '89 *(American Wars)*

Craig Wasson
Go Tell the Spartans '78 *(Vietnam War)*
The Boys in Company C '77 *(Vietnam War)*

John Waters
Breaker Morant '80 *(British Wars)*

Nick Waters
The Lighthorsemen '87 *(WW I)*

Jack Watling
Sink the Bismarck! '60 *(WW II: Europe & North Africa)*
Immortal Battalion '44 *(WW II: Europe & North Africa)*

Lucile Watson
The Razor's Edge '46 *(Coming Home)*
Watch on the Rhine '43 *(WW II: The Resistance)*

Minor Watson
Action in the North Atlantic '43 *(WW II: Europe & North Africa)*
Crash Dive '43 *(WW II: Europe & North Africa)*
Guadalcanal Diary '43 *(WW II: Pacific)*
They Died with Their Boots On '41 *(American Wars)*

John Wayne
The Green Berets '68 *(Vietnam War)*
In Harm's Way '65 *(WW II: Pacific)*
The Longest Day '62 *(WW II: Europe & North Africa)*
The Alamo '60 *(American Wars)*
The Horse Soldiers '59 *(American Wars)*
Flying Leathernecks '51 *(WW II: Pacific)*
Sands of Iwo Jima '49 *(WW II: Pacific)*
She Wore a Yellow Ribbon '49 *(American Wars)*
They Were Expendable '45 *(WW II: Pacific)*
Fighting Seabees '44 *(WW II: Pacific)*

Patrick Wayne
The Green Berets '68 *(Vietnam War)*
Shenandoah '65 *(American Wars)*
The Alamo '60 *(American Wars)*
Mister Roberts '55 *(WW II: Pacific)*

Dennis Weaver
The Gallant Hours '60 *(WW II: Pacific)*

Alan Webb
King Rat '65 *(WW II: POWs)*

Clifton Webb
The Razor's Edge '46 *(Coming Home)*

Danny Webb
Henry V '89 *(British Wars)*

Richard Webb
Sands of Iwo Jima '49 *(WW II: Pacific)*
O.S.S. '46 *(WW II: The Resistance)*

Robert Webber
The Dirty Dozen '67 *(WW II: Europe & North Africa)*

Steven Weber
Hamburger Hill '87 *(Vietnam War)*

Paul Weigel
The Great Dictator '40 *(Between the World Wars)*

Norbert Weisser
Schindler's List '93 (WW II: The Holocaust)

Rachel Weisz
The Land Girls '98 (WW II: Homefront)

Ben Welden
Fighting Seabees '44 (WW II: Pacific)

Orson Welles
Waterloo '71 (French Wars)
Catch-22 '70 (WW II: Europe & North Africa)
Is Paris Burning? '66 (WW II: Europe & North Africa)
The Third Man '49 (Coming Home)

William A. Wellman
Wings '27 (WW I)

John Wengraf
The Razor's Edge '46 (Coming Home)
The Seventh Cross '44 (WW II: POWs)
Sahara '43 (WW II: Europe & North Africa)

Klaus Wennemann
Das Boot '81 (WW II: Europe & North Africa)

Fritz Wepper
The Bridge '59 (WW II: Europe & North Africa)

Barbara Werle
Battle of the Bulge '65 (WW II: Europe & North Africa)

Doug Werner
The Big Red One '80 (WW II: Europe & North Africa)

Jenny Werner
The Third Man '49 (Coming Home)

Dick Wessel
Flying Leathernecks '51 (WW II: Pacific)
They Died with Their Boots On '41 (American Wars)

Tegan West
Hamburger Hill '87 (Vietnam War)

Lucy Westmore
Doctor Zhivago '65 (Russian Wars)

Frank Whaley
When Trumpets Fade '98 (WW II: Europe & North Africa)
A Midnight Clear '92 (WW II: Europe & North Africa)

Born on the Fourth of July '89 (Coming Home)

Forest Whitaker
Good Morning, Vietnam '87 (Vietnam War)
Platoon '86 (Vietnam War)

Jacqueline White
Thirty Seconds over Tokyo '44 (WW II: Pacific)

Don Whitehead
The Story of G.I. Joe '45 (WW II: Europe & North Africa)

O.Z. Whitehead
The Horse Soldiers '59 (American Wars)

Crane Whitley
Fighting Seabees '44 (WW II: Pacific)

Stuart Whitman
The Longest Day '62 (WW II: Europe & North Africa)

James Whitmore
Tora! Tora! Tora! '70 (WW II: Pacific)
Battle Cry '55 (WW II: Pacific)
Above and Beyond '53 (WW II: Pacific)
Battleground '49 (WW II: Europe & North Africa)

James Whitmore, Jr.
The Boys in Company C '77 (Vietnam War)

Peter Whitney
Action in the North Atlantic '43 (WW II: Europe & North Africa)

May Whitty
The White Cliffs of Dover '44 (WW II: Homefront)
Crash Dive '43 (WW II: Europe & North Africa)
Mrs. Miniver '42 (WW II: Homefront)

Jeffrey Wickham
Waterloo '71 (French Wars)

Kathleen Widdoes
Courage under Fire '96 (Coming Home)

Richard Widmark
Judgment at Nuremberg '61 (Coming Home)
The Alamo '60 (American Wars)

Dorothea Wieck
A Time to Love and a Time to Die '58 (WW II: Europe & North Africa)

Frank Wilcox
Across the Pacific '42 (Between the World Wars)
They Died with Their Boots On '41 (American Wars)

Henry Wilcoxon
Mrs. Miniver '42 (WW II: Homefront)

Glenn Wilder
The Sand Pebbles '66 (American Wars)

Michael Wilding
Waterloo '71 (French Wars)
In Which We Serve '43 (WW II: Europe & North Africa)

Jan Wiley
So Proudly We Hail '43 (WW II: Pacific)

Robert J. Wilke
From Here to Eternity '53 (Between the World Wars)

Guy Wilkerson
Sergeant York '41 (WW I)

Jean Willes
So Proudly We Hail '43 (WW II: Pacific)

Peter Willes
Dawn Patrol '38 (WW I)

Adam Williams
Flying Leathernecks '51 (WW II: Pacific)

Brook Williams
Where Eagles Dare '68 (WW II: Europe & North Africa)

Dick Anthony Williams
Gardens of Stone '87 (Vietnam War)

Guinn "Big Boy" Williams
The Alamo '60 (American Wars)
The Fighting 69th '40 (WW I)

Harcourt Williams
Henry V '44 (British Wars)

Mack Williams
Above and Beyond '53 (WW II: Pacific)

Peter Williams
Bridge on the River Kwai '57 (WW II: POWs)

Rhys Williams
Battle Cry '55 (WW II: Pacific)
Mrs. Miniver '42 (WW II: Homefront)

Robin Williams
Good Morning, Vietnam '87 (Vietnam War)

Treat Williams
1941 '79 (WW II: Homefront)

Fred Williamson
M*A*S*H '70 (Korean War)

Noble Willingham
Good Morning, Vietnam '87 (Vietnam War)
The Boys in Company C '77 (Vietnam War)

Matt Willis
A Walk in the Sun '46 (WW II: Europe & North Africa)

Noel Willman
Doctor Zhivago '65 (Russian Wars)

Chill Wills
The Alamo '60 (American Wars)

Claude Wilson
The Boys in Company C '77 (Vietnam War)

Don "The Dragon" Wilson
Born on the Fourth of July '89 (Coming Home)

Dooley Wilson
Casablanca '42 (WW II: The Resistance)

Roy "Baldy" Wilson
Hell's Angels '30 (WW I)

Vaughan Wilson
Merrill's Marauders '62 (WW II: Pacific)

Arthur Wimperis
Mrs. Miniver '42 (WW II: Homefront)

Mark Wing-Davey
One Against the Wind '91 (WW II: The Resistance)

Helen Winston
Battle Circus '53 (Korean War)

Jane Winton
Hell's Angels '30 (WW I)

Grant Withers
Fighting Seabees '44 (WW II: Pacific)

David Wohl
Saving Private Ryan '98 (WW II: Europe & North Africa)

Ian Wolfe
The White Cliffs of Dover '44 (WW II: Homefront)

Mrs. Miniver '42 (WW II: Homefront)

Donald Wolfit
Charge of the Light Brigade '68 (British Wars)
Lawrence of Arabia '62 (WW I)

Louis Wolheim
All Quiet on the Western Front '30 (WW I)
America '24 (American Wars)

Cynthia Wood
Apocalypse Now '79 (Vietnam War)

G. Wood
M*A*S*H '70 (Korean War)

Ward Wood
Air Force '43 (WW II: Pacific)

Donald Woods
Watch on the Rhine '43 (WW II: The Resistance)

Harry Woods
She Wore a Yellow Ribbon '49 (American Wars)
Beau Geste '39 (British Wars)

Peter Woodthorpe
Charge of the Light Brigade '68 (British Wars)
The Blue Max '66 (WW I)

Edward Woodward
Breaker Morant '80 (British Wars)

Susan Wooldridge
Hope and Glory '87 (WW II: Homefront)

Monty Woolley
Since You Went Away '44 (WW II: Homefront)

Hank Worden
The Alamo '60 (American Wars)
The Horse Soldiers '59 (American Wars)

John Wray
All Quiet on the Western Front '30 (WW I)

Amy Wright
The Deer Hunter '78 (Vietnam War)

Cobina Wright, Sr.
The Razor's Edge '46 (Coming Home)

Teresa Wright
The Best Years of Our Lives '46 (Coming Home)
Mrs. Miniver '42 (WW II: Homefront)

Robert Wuhl
Good Morning, Vietnam '87 (Vietnam War)

Margaret Wycherly
Sergeant York '41 (WW I)

Patrick Wymark
The Battle of Britain '69 (WW II: Europe & North Africa)
Where Eagles Dare '68 (WW II: Europe & North Africa)

H.M. Wynant
Run Silent Run Deep '58 (WW II: Pacific)

Keenan Wynn
Dr. Strangelove, or: How I Learned to Stop Worrying and Love the Bomb '64 (American Wars)
A Time to Love and a Time to Die '58 (WW II: Europe & North Africa)
Battle Circus '53 (Korean War)
Since You Went Away '44 (WW II: Homefront)

May Wynn
The Caine Mutiny '54 (WW II: Europe & North Africa)

Dana Wynter
Sink the Bismarck! '60 (WW II: Europe & North Africa)

Y

James Yagi
The Gallant Hours '60 (WW II: Pacific)

Isuzu Yamada
Yojimbo '61 (Japanese Wars)

Soh Yamamura
Tora! Tora! Tora! '70 (WW II: Pacific)

Lilo Yarson
For Whom the Bell Tolls '43 (Between the World Wars)

Vladimir Yershov
Alexander Nevsky '38 (Russian Wars)

William Yetter, Jr.
Lifeboat '44 (WW II: Europe & North Africa)

Cecilia Yip
Hong Kong 1941 '84 (Between the World Wars)

The "Director Index" contains names of all directors responsible for the movies reviewed in this book. The listings for the director names follow an alphabetical sort by last name (although the names appear in a first name last name format). The movie titles are listed chronologically, starting with the most recent.

A

Robert Aldrich
Too Late the Hero '70 (WW II: Pacific)
The Dirty Dozen '67 (WW II: Europe & North Africa)

Grigori Alexandrov
Battleship Potemkin '25 (Russian Wars)

Robert Altman
M*A*S*H '70 (Korean War)

Ken Annakin
Battle of the Bulge '65 (WW II: Europe & North Africa)
The Longest Day '62 (WW II: Europe & North Africa)

Hal Ashby
Coming Home '78 (Coming Home)

Richard Attenborough
A Bridge Too Far '77 (WW II: Europe & North Africa)

B

Lloyd Bacon
Action in the North Atlantic '43 (WW II: Europe & North Africa)
The Fighting Sullivans '42 (WW II: Pacific)

Hall Bartlett
All the Young Men '60 (Korean War)

Roberto Benigni
Life Is Beautiful '98 (WW II: The Holocaust)

Bruce Beresford
Paradise Road '97 (WW II: POWs)
Breaker Morant '80 (British Wars)

Sergei Bondarchuk
Waterloo '71 (French Wars)

John Boorman
Hope and Glory '87 (WW II: Homefront)

Hell in the Pacific '69 (WW II: Pacific)

Kenneth Branagh
Henry V '89 (British Wars)

Robert Bresson
A Man Escaped '57 (WW II: POWs)

Richard Brooks
Battle Circus '53 (Korean War)

Barry Alexander Brown
The War at Home '79 (Vietnam War)

Clarence Brown
The White Cliffs of Dover '44 (WW II: Homefront)

Clyde Bruckman
The General '26 (American Wars)

C

Michael Caton-Jones
Rob Roy '95 (British Wars)

Charlie Chaplin
The Great Dictator '40 (Between the World Wars)

Michael Cimino
The Deer Hunter '78 (Vietnam War)

Rene Clement
Is Paris Burning? '66 (WW II: Europe & North Africa)

Francis Ford Coppola
Gardens of Stone '87 (Vietnam War)
Apocalypse Now '79 (Vietnam War)

Noel Coward
In Which We Serve '43 (WW II: Europe & North Africa)

John Cromwell
Since You Went Away '44 (WW II: Homefront)

Michael Curtiz
Casablanca '42 (WW II: The Resistance)

Dive Bomber '41 (Between the World Wars)
Charge of the Light Brigade '36 (British Wars)

D

Edward Dmytryk
The Young Lions '58 (WW II: Europe & North Africa)
The Caine Mutiny '54 (WW II: Europe & North Africa)

Patrick Shane Duncan
84 Charlie MoPic '89 (Vietnam War)

Allan Dwan
Sands of Iwo Jima '49 (WW II: Pacific)

E

Sergei Eisenstein
Alexander Nevsky '38 (Russian Wars)
Battleship Potemkin '25 (Russian Wars)

Larry Elikann
One Against the Wind '91 (WW II: The Resistance)

Cy Endfield
Zulu '64 (British Wars)

F

John Farrow
Wake Island '42 (WW II: Pacific)

Richard Fleischer
Tora! Tora! Tora! '70 (WW II: Pacific)

Victor Fleming
Gone with the Wind '39 (American Wars)

Bryan Forbes
King Rat '65 (WW II: POWs)

John Ford
The Horse Soldiers '59 *(American Wars)*
Mister Roberts '55 *(WW II: Pacific)*
She Wore a Yellow Ribbon '49 *(American Wars)*
They Were Expendable '45 *(WW II: Pacific)*
Battle of Midway '42 *(WW II: Documentaries)*
The Lost Patrol '34 *(WW I)*

Carl Foreman
The Victors '63 *(WW II: Europe & North Africa)*

Melvin Frank
Above and Beyond '53 *(WW II: Pacific)*

John Frankenheimer
The Train '65 *(WW II: Europe & North Africa)*
The Manchurian Candidate '62 *(Korean War)*

Kinji Fukasaku
Tora! Tora! Tora! '70 *(WW II: Pacific)*

Samuel Fuller
The Big Red One '80 *(WW II: Europe & North Africa)*
Merrill's Marauders '62 *(WW II: Pacific)*
China Gate '57 *(Vietnam War)*
The Steel Helmet '51 *(Korean War)*

Sidney J. Furie
The Boys in Company C '77 *(Vietnam War)*

G

Abel Gance
Napoleon '27 *(French Wars)*

Tay Garnett
Bataan '43 *(WW II: Pacific)*

Mel Gibson
Braveheart '95 *(British Wars)*

Lewis Gilbert
Sink the Bismarck! '60 *(WW II: Europe & North Africa)*

Keith Gordon
Mother Night '96 *(WW II: Europe & North Africa)*
A Midnight Clear '92 *(WW II: Europe & North Africa)*

Edmund Goulding
The Razor's Edge '46 *(Coming Home)*
Dawn Patrol '38 *(WW I)*

Alfred E. Green
Mr. Winkle Goes to War '44 *(WW II: Europe & North Africa)*

D.W. Griffith
America '24 *(American Wars)*
Birth of a Nation '15 *(American Wars)*

John Guillermin
The Blue Max '66 *(WW I)*

H

Guy Hamilton
The Battle of Britain '69 *(WW II: Europe & North Africa)*

Henry Hathaway
13 Rue Madeleine '46 *(WW II: The Resistance)*
The Real Glory '39 *(American Wars)*
Lives of a Bengal Lancer '35 *(British Wars)*

Howard Hawks
Air Force '43 *(WW II: Pacific)*
Sergeant York '41 *(WW I)*

Richard T. Heffron
A Rumor of War '80 *(Vietnam War)*

Jesse Hibbs
To Hell and Back '55 *(WW II: Europe & North Africa)*

Alfred Hitchcock
Lifeboat '44 *(WW II: Europe & North Africa)*

Howard Hughes
Hell's Angels '30 *(WW I)*

John Huston
The Red Badge of Courage '51 *(American Wars)*
Battle of San Pietro '44 *(WW II: Documentaries)*
Report from the Aleutians '43 *(WW II: Documentaries)*
Across the Pacific '42 *(Between the World Wars)*

Brian G. Hutton
Where Eagles Dare '68 *(WW II: Europe & North Africa)*

I

Kon Ichikawa
Fires on the Plain '59 *(WW II: Pacific)*

Rex Ingram
Four Horsemen of the Apocalypse '21 *(WW I)*

John Irvin
When Trumpets Fade '98 *(WW II: Europe & North Africa)*
Hamburger Hill '87 *(Vietnam War)*

K

Buster Keaton
The General '26 *(American Wars)*

William Keighley
The Fighting 69th '40 *(WW I)*

Henry King
Twelve O'Clock High '49 *(WW II: Europe & North Africa)*

Elem Klimov
Come and See '85 *(WW II: Europe & North Africa)*

Zoltan Korda
Sahara '43 *(WW II: Europe & North Africa)*
The Four Feathers '39 *(British Wars)*

Stanley Kramer
Judgment at Nuremberg '61 *(Coming Home)*

Nathan Kroll
The Guns of August '64 *(WW I)*

Stanley Kubrick
Full Metal Jacket '87 *(Vietnam War)*
Dr. Strangelove, or: How I Learned to Stop Worrying and Love the Bomb '64 *(American Wars)*
Paths of Glory '57 *(WW I)*

Akira Kurosawa
Ran '85 *(Japanese Wars)*
Yojimbo '61 *(Japanese Wars)*
The Hidden Fortress '58 *(Japanese Wars)*
Seven Samurai '54 *(Japanese Wars)*

Emir Kusturica
Underground '95 *(WW II: Europe & North Africa)*

L

David Lean
Doctor Zhivago '65 (Russian Wars)
Lawrence of Arabia '62 (WW I)
Bridge on the River Kwai '57 (WW II: POWs)
In Which We Serve '43 (WW II: Europe & North Africa)

David Leland
The Land Girls '98 (WW II: Homefront)

Sergio Leone
The Good, the Bad and the Ugly '67 (American Wars)

Mervyn LeRoy
Mister Roberts '55 (WW II: Pacific)
Thirty Seconds over Tokyo '44 (WW II: Pacific)

Po-Chi Leung
Hong Kong 1941 '84 (Between the World Wars)

Barry Levinson
Good Morning, Vietnam '87 (Vietnam War)

Ken Loach
Land and Freedom '95 (Between the World Wars)

Ernst Lubitsch
To Be or Not to Be '42 (WW II: The Resistance)

Edward Ludwig
Fighting Seabees '44 (WW II: Pacific)

M

Terrence Malick
The Thin Red Line '98 (WW II: Pacific)

Louis Malle
Au Revoir les Enfants '87 (WW II: The Holocaust)

Anthony Mann
Men in War '57 (Korean War)

Michael Mann
Last of the Mohicans '92 (American Wars)

Robert Markowitz
The Tuskegee Airmen '95 (WW II: Europe & North Africa)

Andrew Marton
The Longest Day '62 (WW II: Europe & North Africa)

Toshio Masuda
Tora! Tora! Tora! '70 (WW II: Pacific)

Ronald F. Maxwell
Gettysburg '93 (American Wars)

Archie Mayo
Crash Dive '43 (WW II: Europe & North Africa)

Andrew V. McLaglen
Shenandoah '65 (American Wars)

Lewis Milestone
Pork Chop Hill '59 (Korean War)
A Walk in the Sun '46 (WW II: Europe & North Africa)
All Quiet on the Western Front '30 (WW I)

John Milius
The Wind and the Lion '75 (American Wars)

Robert Montgomery
The Gallant Hours '60 (WW II: Pacific)

N

Jean Negulesco
Three Came Home '50 (WW II: POWs)

Mike Nichols
Catch-22 '70 (WW II: Europe & North Africa)

O

Laurence Olivier
Henry V '44 (British Wars)

Nagisa Oshima
Merry Christmas, Mr. Lawrence '83 (WW II: POWs)

Gerd Oswald
The Longest Day '62 (WW II: Europe & North Africa)

P

Norman Panama
Above and Beyond '53 (WW II: Pacific)

Pekka Parikka
The Winter War '89 (Between the World Wars)

Sam Peckinpah
Cross of Iron '76 (WW II: Europe & North Africa)

Wolfgang Petersen
Das Boot '81 (WW II: Europe & North Africa)

Irving Pichel
O.S.S. '46 (WW II: The Resistance)

Gillo Pontecorvo
The Battle of Algiers '66 (French Wars)

Ted Post
Go Tell the Spartans '78 (Vietnam War)

Dick Powell
The Hunters '58 (Korean War)

Otto Preminger
In Harm's Way '65 (WW II: Pacific)

R

Nicholas Ray
Flying Leathernecks '51 (WW II: Pacific)

Carol Reed
The Third Man '49 (Coming Home)
Immortal Battalion '44 (WW II: Europe & North Africa)

Jean Renoir
Grand Illusion '37 (WW I)

Tony Richardson
Charge of the Light Brigade '68 (British Wars)

Mark Robson
Von Ryan's Express '65 (WW II: POWs)
The Bridges at Toko-Ri '55 (Korean War)
Home of the Brave '49 (WW II: Pacific)

Director Index

S

Mark Sandrich
So Proudly We Hail '43 (WW II: Pacific)

Franklin J. Schaffner
Patton '70 (WW II: Europe & North Africa)

Heinz Schirk
The Wannsee Conference '84 (WW II: The Holocaust)

Pierre Schoendoerffer
Anderson Platoon '67 (Vietnam War)
317th Platoon '65 (French Wars)

Lewis Seiler
Guadalcanal Diary '43 (WW II: Pacific)

Herman Shumlin
Watch on the Rhine '43 (WW II: The Resistance)

Donald Siegel
Hell Is for Heroes '62 (WW II: Europe & North Africa)

Glenn Silber
The War at Home '79 (Vietnam War)

Douglas Sirk
A Time to Love and a Time to Die '58 (WW II: Europe & North Africa)

Steven Spielberg
Saving Private Ryan '98 (WW II: Europe & North Africa)
Schindler's List '93 (WW II: The Holocaust)
Empire of the Sun '87 (WW II: POWs)
1941 '79 (WW II: Homefront)

John M. Stahl
The Immortal Sergeant '43 (WW II: Europe & North Africa)

George Stevens
Gunga Din '39 (British Wars)

Oliver Stone
Born on the Fourth of July '89 (Coming Home)
Platoon '86 (Vietnam War)

John Sturges
The Great Escape '63 (WW II: POWs)

T

J. Lee Thompson
The Guns of Navarone '61 (WW II: Europe & North Africa)

Brian Trenchard-Smith
The Siege of Firebase Gloria '89 (Vietnam War)

Francois Truffaut
The Last Metro '80 (WW II: The Holocaust)

V

Georgy Vassiliev
Chapayev '34 (Russian Wars)

Sergei Vassiliev
Chapayev '34 (Russian Wars)

Michael Verhoeven
The White Rose '83 (WW II: The Resistance)

King Vidor
War and Peace '56 (Russian Wars)
The Big Parade '25 (WW I)

W

Raoul Walsh
Battle Cry '55 (WW II: Pacific)
Objective, Burma! '45 (WW II: Pacific)
They Died with Their Boots On '41 (American Wars)

John Wayne
The Green Berets '68 (Vietnam War)
The Alamo '60 (American Wars)

Peter Weir
Gallipoli '81 (WW I)

William A. Wellman
Battleground '49 (WW II: Europe & North Africa)
The Story of G.I. Joe '45 (WW II: Europe & North Africa)
Beau Geste '39 (British Wars)
Wings '27 (WW I)

Anne Wheeler
Bye Bye Blues '89 (WW II: Homefront)

Bernhard Wicki
The Longest Day '62 (WW II: Europe & North Africa)
The Bridge '59 (WW II: Europe & North Africa)

Billy Wilder
Stalag 17 '53 (WW II: POWs)
Five Graves to Cairo '43 (WW II: Europe & North Africa)

Simon Wincer
The Lighthorsemen '87 (WW I)

Robert Wise
The Sand Pebbles '66 (American Wars)
Run Silent Run Deep '58 (WW II: Pacific)

Sam Wood
Command Decision '48 (WW II: Europe & North Africa)
For Whom the Bell Tolls '43 (Between the World Wars)

William Wyler
The Best Years of Our Lives '46 (Coming Home)
Memphis Belle: A Story of a Flying Fortress '44 (WW II: Documentaries)
Mrs. Miniver '42 (WW II: Homefront)

Z

Darryl F. Zanuck
The Longest Day '62 (WW II: Europe & North Africa)

Fred Zinnemann
From Here to Eternity '53 (Between the World Wars)
The Seventh Cross '44 (WW II: POWs)

Edward Zwick
Courage Under Fire '96 (Coming Home)
Glory '89 (American Wars)

The "Writer Index" lists all screenwriters noted in this book. The listings for the writer names follow an alphabetical sort by last name (although the names appear in a first name, last name format). The movie titles are listed chronologically, starting with the most recent film.

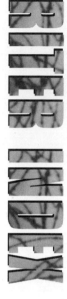

A

George Abbott
All Quiet on the Western Front '30 (WW I)

Alex Adamovich
Come and See '85 (WW II: Europe & North Africa)

Robert Aldrich
Too Late the Hero '70 (WW II: Pacific)

Jim Allen
Land and Freedom '95 (Between the World Wars)

Eric Ambler
Battle of San Pietro '44 (WW II: Documentaries)
Immortal Battalion '44 (WW II: Europe & North Africa)

Maxwell Anderson
All Quiet on the Western Front '30 (WW I)

Robert Anderson
The Sand Pebbles '66 (American Wars)

Del Andrews
All Quiet on the Western Front '30 (WW I)

Robert D. Andrews
Bataan '43 (WW II: Pacific)

Edward Anhalt
The Young Lions '58 (WW II: Europe & North Africa)

Leopold Atlas
The Story of G.I. Joe '45 (WW II: Europe & North Africa)

George Axelrod
The Manchurian Candidate '62 (Korean War)

B

John Lloyd Balderston
Lives of a Bengal Lancer '35 (British Wars)

Albert Band
The Red Badge of Courage '51 (American Wars)

James Lee Barrett
Shenandoah '65 (American Wars)

Hall Bartlett
All the Young Men '60 (Korean War)

Sy Bartlett
Twelve O'Clock High '49 (WW II: Europe & North Africa)
13 Rue Madeleine '46 (WW II: The Resistance)

Ben Barzman
The Blue Max '66 (WW I)

Ronald Bass
Gardens of Stone '87 (Vietnam War)

Edward Beach
Run Silent Run Deep '58 (WW II: Pacific)

Harry Behn
Hell's Angels '30 (WW I)
The Big Parade '25 (WW I)

Roberto Benigni
Life Is Beautiful '98 (WW II: The Holocaust)

Eric Bercovici
Hell in the Pacific '69 (WW II: Pacific)

Bruce Beresford
Paradise Road '97 (WW II: POWs)
Breaker Morant '80 (British Wars)

Walter Bernstein
The Train '65 (WW II: Europe & North Africa)

Alvah Bessie
Objective, Burma! '45 (WW II: Pacific)

A.I. Bezzerides
Action in the North Atlantic '43 (WW II: Europe & North Africa)

Lajos Biro
The Four Feathers '39 (British Wars)

Michael Blankfort
The Caine Mutiny '54 (WW II: Europe & North Africa)

Edwin Blum
Stalag 17 '53 (WW II: POWs)

Al Boasberg
The General '26 (American Wars)

Bridget Boland
War and Peace '56 (Russian Wars)

Robert Bolt
Doctor Zhivago '65 (Russian Wars)
Lawrence of Arabia '62 (WW I)

Sergei Bondarchuk
Waterloo '71 (French Wars)

Vittorio Bonicelli
Waterloo '71 (French Wars)

John Boorman
Hope and Glory '87 (WW II: Homefront)

Dallas Bower
Henry V '44 (British Wars)

Charles Brackett
Five Graves to Cairo '43 (WW II: Europe & North Africa)

Kenneth Branagh
Henry V '89 (British Wars)

Robert Bresson
A Man Escaped '57 (WW II: POWs)

Richard Brooks
Battle Circus '53 (Korean War)

Harry Brown
Sands of Iwo Jima '49 (WW II: Pacific)
A Walk in the Sun '46 (WW II: Europe & North Africa)

Clyde Bruckman
The General '26 (American Wars)

Chris Bryant
One Against the Wind '91 (WW II: The Resistance)

Robert Buckner
Dive Bomber '41 (Between the World Wars)

W.R. Burnett
The Great Escape '63 (WW II: POWs)
Action in the North Atlantic '43 (WW II: Europe & North Africa)
Crash Dive '43 (WW II: Europe & North Africa)
Wake Island '42 (WW II: Pacific)

Frank Butler
Wake Island '42 (WW II: Pacific)

C

Jerome Cady
Guadalcanal Diary '43 (WW II: Pacific)

Mario Camerini
War and Peace '56 (Russian Wars)

Jim Carabatsos
Hamburger Hill '87 (Vietnam War)

Richard Carr
Hell Is for Heroes '62 (WW II: Europe & North Africa)

Robert Carson
Across the Pacific '42 (Between the World Wars)
Beau Geste '39 (British Wars)

Vincenzo Cerami
Life Is Beautiful '98 (WW II: The Holocaust)

Robert W. Chambers
America '24 (American Wars)

Koon-Chung Chan
Hong Kong 1941 '84 (Between the World Wars)

Harry Chandler
Sergeant York '41 (WW I)

Charlie Chaplin
The Great Dictator '40 (Between the World Wars)

Borden Chase
Fighting Seabees '44 (WW II: Pacific)

Michael Cimino
The Deer Hunter '78 (Vietnam War)

James Clavell
King Rat '65 (WW II: POWs)
The Great Escape '63 (WW II: POWs)

Franklin Coen
The Train '65 (WW II: Europe & North Africa)

Lester Cole
Objective, Burma! '45 (WW II: Pacific)

Francis Ford Coppola
Apocalypse Now '79 (Vietnam War)
Patton '70 (WW II: Europe & North Africa)
Is Paris Burning? '66 (WW II: Europe & North Africa)

Noel Coward
In Which We Serve '43 (WW II: Europe & North Africa)

H.A.L. Craig
Waterloo '71 (French Wars)

Christopher Crowe
Last of the Mohicans '92 (American Wars)

D

Frank Darabont
Saving Private Ryan '98 (WW II: Europe & North Africa)

Valentine Davies
The Bridges at Toko-Ri '55 (Korean War)

Frank Davis
The Train '65 (WW II: Europe & North Africa)

Ennio de Concini
War and Peace '56 (Russian Wars)

Alan Dent
Henry V '44 (British Wars)

Helen Deutsch
The Seventh Cross '44 (WW II: POWs)

Keith Dewhurst
The Land Girls '98 (WW II: Homefront)

Edward Doherty
The Fighting Sullivans '42 (WW II: Pacific)

Sergio Donati
The Good, the Bad and the Ugly '67 (American Wars)

Gil Doud
To Hell and Back '55 (WW II: Europe & North Africa)

Patrick Sheane Duncan
Courage Under Fire '96 (Coming Home)
84 Charlie MoPic '89 (Vietnam War)

E

Sergei Eisenstein
Alexander Nevsky '38 (Russian Wars)
Battleship Potemkin '25 (Russian Wars)

Trey Ellis
The Tuskegee Airmen '95 (WW II: Europe & North Africa)

Cy Endfield
Zulu '64 (British Wars)

Guy Endore
The Story of G.I. Joe '45 (WW II: Europe & North Africa)

Julius J. Epstein
Cross of Iron '76 (WW II: Europe & North Africa)
Casablanca '42 (WW II: The Resistance)

Philip C. Epstein
Casablanca '42 (WW II: The Resistance)

Howard Estabrook
Hell's Angels '30 (WW I)

F

William Faulkner
Air Force '43 (WW II: Pacific)

Abem Finkel
Sergeant York '41 (WW I)

Bryan Forbes
King Rat '65 (WW II: POWs)

John Ford
Battle of Midway '42 (WW II: Documentaries)

Carl Foreman
The Victors '63 (WW II: Europe &
  North Africa)
The Guns of Navarone '61 (WW II:
  Europe & North Africa)
Bridge on the River Kwai '57 (WW
  II: POWs)
Home of the Brave '49 (WW II:
  Pacific)

Larry Forrester
Tora! Tora! Tora! '70 (WW II: Pacific)

Garrett Fort
The Lost Patrol '34 (WW I)

Basilio Franchina
The Blue Max '66 (WW I)

Melvin Frank
Above and Beyond '53 (WW II:
  Pacific)

John Frankenheimer
The Manchurian Candidate '62
  (Korean War)

Dean Franklin
The Fighting 69th '40 (WW I)

George Froeschel
Command Decision '48 (WW II:
  Europe & North Africa)
The White Cliffs of Dover '44 (WW
  II: Homefront)
Mrs. Miniver '42 (WW II: Homefront)

Samuel Fuller
The Big Red One '80 (WW II:
  Europe & North Africa)
Merrill's Marauders '62 (WW II:
  Pacific)
China Gate '57 (Vietnam War)
The Steel Helmet '51 (Korean War)

Sidney J. Furie
The Boys in Company C '77 (Vietnam War)

G

Bob Gale
1941 '79 (WW II: Homefront)

Kenneth Gamet
Flying Leathernecks '51 (WW II:
  Pacific)

Abel Gance
Napoleon '27 (French Wars)

Louis Garfinkle
The Deer Hunter '78 (Vietnam War)

Romain Gary
The Longest Day '62 (WW II:
  Europe & North Africa)

John Gay
Run Silent Run Deep '58 (WW II:
  Pacific)

Peter George
Dr. Strangelove, or: How I Learned
  to Stop Worrying and Love the
  Bomb '64 (American Wars)

David Giles
Paradise Road '97 (WW II: POWs)

Guy Gilpatric
Action in the North Atlantic '43 (WW
  II: Europe & North Africa)

Frank D. Gilroy
The Gallant Hours '60 (WW II:
  Pacific)

William Goldman
A Bridge Too Far '77 (WW II:
  Europe & North Africa)

Keith Gordon
A Midnight Clear '92 (WW II:
  Europe & North Africa)

James Edward Grant
The Alamo '60 (American Wars)
Flying Leathernecks '51 (WW II:
  Pacific)
Sands of Iwo Jima '49 (WW II:
  Pacific)

Wilfred Greatorex
The Battle of Britain '69 (WW II:
  Europe & North Africa)

Graham Greene
The Third Man '49 (Coming Home)

D.W. Griffith
Birth of a Nation '15 (American
  Wars)

Jean-Claude Grumberg
The Last Metro '80 (WW II: The
  Holocaust)

Fred Guiol
Gunga Din '39 (British Wars)

H

William Wister Haines
Command Decision '48 (WW II:
  Europe & North Africa)

James Hamilton
Cross of Iron '76 (WW II: Europe &
  North Africa)

Dashiell Hammett
Watch on the Rhine '43 (WW II: The
  Resistance)

Gerald Hanley
The Blue Max '66 (WW I)

Jonathon Hardy
Breaker Morant '80 (British Wars)

Gustav Hasford
Full Metal Jacket '87 (Vietnam War)

Shinobu Hashimoto
The Hidden Fortress '58 (Japanese
  Wars)
Seven Samurai '54 (Japanese
  Wars)

Ben Hecht
Gunga Din '39 (British Wars)

Thomas Heggen
Mister Roberts '55 (WW II: Pacific)

Lukas Heller
Too Late the Hero '70 (WW II:
  Pacific)
The Dirty Dozen '67 (WW II: Europe
  & North Africa)

Lillian Hellman
Watch on the Rhine '43 (WW II: The
  Resistance)

Buck Henry
Catch-22 '70 (WW II: Europe &
  North Africa)

Michael Herr
Full Metal Jacket '87 (Vietnam War)
Apocalypse Now '79 (Vietnam War)

Marshall Herskovitz
Glory '89 (American Wars)

James Hilton
Mrs. Miniver '42 (WW II: Homefront)

Sidney Howard
Gone with the Wind '39 (American
  Wars)

John Huston
Battle of San Pietro '44 (WW II:
  Documentaries)
Sergeant York '41 (WW I)

Ron Hutchinson
The Tuskegee Airmen '95 (WW II:
  Europe & North Africa)

I

Masato Ide
Ran '85 (Japanese Wars)

Agenore Incrocci
The Good, the Bad and the Ugly '67 (American Wars)

J

Alexander Jacobs
Hell in the Pacific '69 (WW II: Pacific)

Michael Jacoby
Charge of the Light Brigade '36 (British Wars)

Orin Jannings
A Time to Love and a Time to Die '58 (WW II: Europe & North Africa)

Kevin Jarre
Glory '89 (American Wars)

Nunnally Johnson
The Dirty Dozen '67 (WW II: Europe & North Africa)
Three Came Home '50 (WW II: POWs)

Tony Johnston
The Siege of Firebase Gloria '89 (Vietnam War)

Grover Jones
Lives of a Bengal Lancer '35 (British Wars)

Ian Jones
The Lighthorsemen '87 (WW I)

James Jones
The Longest Day '62 (WW II: Europe & North Africa)

Robert C. Jones
Coming Home '78 (Coming Home)

K

Buster Keaton
The General '26 (American Wars)

Walter Kelley
Cross of Iron '76 (WW II: Europe & North Africa)

James Kennaway
The Battle of Britain '69 (WW II: Europe & North Africa)

Ryuzo Kikushima
Tora! Tora! Tora! '70 (WW II: Pacific)
Yojimbo '61 (Japanese Wars)
The Hidden Fortress '58 (Japanese Wars)

Elem Klimov
Come and See '85 (WW II: Europe & North Africa)

Wally Kline
They Died with Their Boots On '41 (American Wars)

Howard Koch
Casablanca '42 (WW II: The Resistance)
Sergeant York '41 (WW I)

Zoltan Korda
Sahara '43 (WW II: Europe & North Africa)

Dusan Kovacevic
Underground '95 (WW II: Europe & North Africa)

Mario Krebs
The White Rose '83 (WW II: The Resistance)

Stanley Kubrick
Full Metal Jacket '87 (Vietnam War)
Dr. Strangelove, or: How I Learned to Stop Worrying and Love the Bomb '64 (American Wars)
Paths of Glory '57 (WW I)

Akira Kurosawa
Ran '85 (Japanese Wars)
Yojimbo '61 (Japanese Wars)
The Hidden Fortress '58 (Japanese Wars)
Seven Samurai '54 (Japanese Wars)

Emir Kusturica
Underground '95 (WW II: Europe & North Africa)

L

William R. Laidlaw
Command Decision '48 (WW II: Europe & North Africa)

Joseph Landon
Von Ryan's Express '65 (WW II: POWs)

Ring Lardner, Jr.
M*A*S*H '70 (Korean War)

John Howard Lawson
Action in the North Atlantic '43 (WW II: Europe & North Africa)
Sahara '43 (WW II: Europe & North Africa)

Beirne Lay, Jr.
The Gallant Hours '60 (WW II: Pacific)
Above and Beyond '53 (WW II: Pacific)
Twelve O'Clock High '49 (WW II: Europe & North Africa)

Rowland Leigh
Charge of the Light Brigade '36 (British Wars)

David Leland
The Land Girls '98 (WW II: Homefront)

Melchior Lengyel
To Be or Not to Be '42 (WW II: The Resistance)

Sergio Leone
The Good, the Bad and the Ugly '67 (American Wars)

Louis D. Lighton
Wings '27 (WW I)

Joshua Logan
Mister Roberts '55 (WW II: Pacific)

Hope Loring
Wings '27 (WW I)

Ernst Lubitsch
To Be or Not to Be '42 (WW II: The Resistance)

Jan Lustig
The White Cliffs of Dover '44 (WW II: Homefront)

M

Charles MacArthur
Gunga Din '39 (British Wars)

Richard Macaulay
Across the Pacific '42 (Between the World Wars)

Ranald MacDougall
Objective, Burma! '45 (WW II: Pacific)

Aeneas MacKenzie
Fighting Seabees '44 (WW II: Pacific)
They Died with Their Boots On '41 (American Wars)

Alistair MacLean
Where Eagles Dare '68 (WW II: Europe & North Africa)

Ben Maddow
Men in War '57 (Korean War)

John Lee Mahin
The Horse Soldiers '59 (American Wars)

Richard Maibaum
O.S.S. '46 (WW II: The Resistance)

Terrence Malick
The Thin Red Line '98 (WW II: Pacific)

Louis Malle
Au Revoir les Enfants '87 (WW II: The Holocaust)

Abby Mann
Judgment at Nuremberg '61 (Coming Home)

Michael Mann
Last of the Mohicans '92 (American Wars)

Michael Mansfield
The Bridge '59 (WW II: Europe & North Africa)

Joseph Moncure March
Hell's Angels '30 (WW I)

Mitch Markowitz
Good Morning, Vietnam '87 (Vietnam War)

June Mathis
Four Horsemen of the Apocalypse '21 (WW I)

Ronald F. Maxwell
Gettysburg '93 (American Wars)

Edwin Justus Mayer
To Be or Not to Be '42 (WW II: The Resistance)

Paul Mayersberg
Merry Christmas, Mr. Lawrence '83 (WW II: POWs)

Wendell Mayes
Go Tell the Spartans '78 (Vietnam War)
In Harm's Way '65 (WW II: Pacific)
Von Ryan's Express '65 (WW II: POWs)

The Hunters '58 (Korean War)

Mary C. McCall
The Fighting Sullivans '42 (WW II: Pacific)

James K. McGuinness
Battle of Midway '42 (WW II: Documentaries)

William Slavens McNutt
Lives of a Bengal Lancer '35 (British Wars)

Martin Meader
Paradise Road '97 (WW II: POWs)

John Melson
Battle of the Bulge '65 (WW II: Europe & North Africa)

Menno Meyjes
Empire of the Sun '87 (WW II: POWs)

John Milius
Apocalypse Now '79 (Vietnam War)
1941 '79 (WW II: Homefront)
The Wind and the Lion '75 (American Wars)

Seton I. Miller
Dawn Patrol '38 (WW I)

Paul Mommertz
The Wannsee Conference '84 (WW II: The Holocaust)

John Monks, Jr.
13 Rue Madeleine '46 (WW II: The Resistance)

N

William Nagle
The Siege of Firebase Gloria '89 (Vietnam War)

Rick Natkin
The Boys in Company C '77 (Vietnam War)

Fred Niblo
The Fighting 69th '40 (WW I)

Dudley Nichols
Air Force '43 (WW II: Pacific)
For Whom the Bell Tolls '43 (Between the World Wars)
Battle of Midway '42 (WW II: Documentaries)
The Lost Patrol '34 (WW I)

Edmund H. North
Patton '70 (WW II: Europe & North Africa)
Sink the Bismarck! '60 (WW II: Europe & North Africa)

Frank Nugent
Mister Roberts '55 (WW II: Pacific)
She Wore a Yellow Ribbon '49 (American Wars)

O

Charlton Ogburn, Jr.
Merrill's Marauders '62 (WW II: Pacific)

Hideo Oguni
Ran '85 (Japanese Wars)
Tora! Tora! Tora! '70 (WW II: Pacific)
Yojimbo '61 (Japanese Wars)
The Hidden Fortress '58 (Japanese Wars)
Seven Samurai '54 (Japanese Wars)

James O'Hanlon
Sahara '43 (WW II: Europe & North Africa)

Laurence Olivier
Henry V '44 (British Wars)

Nagisa Oshima
Merry Christmas, Mr. Lawrence '83 (WW II: POWs)

P

Norman Panama
Above and Beyond '53 (WW II: Pacific)

Pekka Parikka
The Winter War '89 (Between the World Wars)

Pyotr Pavlenko
Alexander Nevsky '38 (Russian Wars)

Ivo Perilli
War and Peace '56 (Russian Wars)

Wolfgang Petersen
Das Boot '81 (WW II: Europe & North Africa)

Robert Pirosh
Hell Is for Heroes '62 (WW II: Europe & North Africa)

Writer Index

Battleground '49 (WW II: Europe & North Africa)

Gillo Pontecorvo
The Battle of Algiers '66 (French Wars)

John Prebble
Zulu '64 (British Wars)

Robert Presnell
The Real Glory '39 (American Wars)

David Pursall
The Blue Max '66 (WW I)
The Longest Day '62 (WW II: Europe & North Africa)

Ernie Pyle
The Story of G.I. Joe '45 (WW II: Europe & North Africa)

Q

Paris Qualles
The Tuskegee Airmen '95 (WW II: Europe & North Africa)

R

Martin Rackin
The Horse Soldiers '59 (American Wars)

Norman Reilly Raine
The Fighting 69th '40 (WW I)

Jean Renoir
Grand Illusion '37 (WW I)

Stanley Roberts
The Caine Mutiny '54 (WW II: Europe & North Africa)

Casey Robinson
Casablanca '42 (WW II: The Resistance)

Robert Rodat
Saving Private Ryan '98 (WW II: Europe & North Africa)

Robert Rossen
A Walk in the Sun '46 (WW II: Europe & North Africa)

Cornelius Ryan
The Longest Day '62 (WW II: Europe & North Africa)

S

Waldo Salt
Mr. Winkle Goes to War '44 (WW II: Europe & North Africa)

John Monk Saunders
Wings '27 (WW I)

Joel Sayre
Gunga Din '39 (British Wars)

Furio Scarpelli
The Good, the Bad and the Ugly '67 (American Wars)

Jules Schermer
The Fighting Sullivans '42 (WW II: Pacific)

Suzanne Schiffman
The Last Metro '80 (WW II: The Holocaust)

Pierre Schoendoerffer
317th Platoon '65 (French Wars)

Allan Scott
So Proudly We Hail '43 (WW II: Pacific)

Jack Seddon
The Blue Max '66 (WW I)
The Longest Day '62 (WW II: Europe & North Africa)

Anna Seghers
The Seventh Cross '44 (WW II: POWs)

David O. Selznick
Since You Went Away '44 (WW II: Homefront)

Alan Sharp
Rob Roy '95 (British Wars)

Irwin Shaw
War and Peace '56 (Russian Wars)

Robert B. Sherman
Too Late the Hero '70 (WW II: Pacific)

R.C. Sherriff
The Four Feathers '39 (British Wars)

Robert Sherwood
The Best Years of Our Lives '46 (Coming Home)

Nina Agadzhanova Shutko
Battleship Potemkin '25 (Russian Wars)

Charles Henry Smith
The General '26 (American Wars)

Franco Solinas
The Battle of Algiers '66 (French Wars)

Louis Solomon
Mr. Winkle Goes to War '44 (WW II: Europe & North Africa)

Terry Southern
Dr. Strangelove, or: How I Learned to Stop Worrying and Love the Bomb '64 (American Wars)

Charles Spaak
Grand Illusion '37 (WW I)

Milton Sperling
Battle of the Bulge '65 (WW II: Europe & North Africa)
Merrill's Marauders '62 (WW II: Pacific)

Laurence Stallings
She Wore a Yellow Ribbon '49 (American Wars)

David Stevens
Breaker Morant '80 (British Wars)

Philip Stevenson
The Story of G.I. Joe '45 (WW II: Europe & North Africa)

Oliver Stone
Born on the Fourth of July '89 (Coming Home)
Platoon '86 (Vietnam War)

Tom Stoppard
Empire of the Sun '87 (WW II: POWs)

Jo Swerling
Lifeboat '44 (WW II: Europe & North Africa)
Crash Dive '43 (WW II: Europe & North Africa)
The Real Glory '39 (American Wars)

T

Daniel Taradash
From Here to Eternity '53 (Between the World Wars)

Jim Thompson
Paths of Glory '57 (WW I)

Dan Totheroh
Dawn Patrol '38 (WW I)

Lamar Trotti
The Razor's Edge '46 (Coming Home)

Guadalcanal Diary '43 (WW II: Pacific)
The Immortal Sergeant '43 (WW II: Europe & North Africa)

Francois Truffaut
The Last Metro '80 (WW II: The Holocaust)

Dalton Trumbo
Thirty Seconds over Tokyo '44 (WW II: Pacific)

U

Leon Uris
Battle Cry '55 (WW II: Pacific)

Peter Ustinov
Immortal Battalion '44 (WW II: Europe & North Africa)

V

Georgy Vassiliev
Chapayev '34 (Russian Wars)

Sergei Vassiliev
Chapayev '34 (Russian Wars)

Michael Verhoeven
The White Rose '83 (WW II: The Resistance)

Gore Vidal
Is Paris Burning? '66 (WW II: Europe & North Africa)

King Vidor
War and Peace '56 (Russian Wars)

Luciano Vincenzoni
The Good, the Bad and the Ugly '67 (American Wars)

Karl-Wilhelm Vivier
The Bridge '59 (WW II: Europe & North Africa)

W.W. Vought
When Trumpets Fade '98 (WW II: Europe & North Africa)

W

Natto Wada
Fires on the Plain '59 (WW II: Pacific)

Randall Wallace
Braveheart '95 (British Wars)

Deric Washburn
The Deer Hunter '78 (Vietnam War)

Frank Wead
They Were Expendable '45 (WW II: Pacific)
Dive Bomber '41 (Between the World Wars)

James R. Webb
Pork Chop Hill '59 (Korean War)

Robert B. Weide
Mother Night '96 (WW II: Europe & North Africa)

Peter Weir
Gallipoli '81 (WW I)

Claudine West
The White Cliffs of Dover '44 (WW II: Homefront)
Mrs. Miniver '42 (WW II: Homefront)

Robert Westerby
War and Peace '56 (Russian Wars)

Anne Wheeler
Bye Bye Blues '89 (WW II: Homefront)

Bernhard Wicki
The Bridge '59 (WW II: Europe & North Africa)

Billy Wilder
Stalag 17 '53 (WW II: POWs)
Five Graves to Cairo '43 (WW II: Europe & North Africa)

David Williamson
Gallipoli '81 (WW I)

Calder Willingham
Paths of Glory '57 (WW I)

Michael Wilson
Lawrence of Arabia '62 (WW I)
Bridge on the River Kwai '57 (WW II: POWs)

Arthur Wimperis
Mrs. Miniver '42 (WW II: Homefront)
The Four Feathers '39 (British Wars)

Charles Wood
Charge of the Light Brigade '68 (British Wars)

Frank E. Woods
Birth of a Nation '15 (American Wars)

Y

Philip Yordan
Battle of the Bulge '65 (WW II: Europe & North Africa)
Men in War '57 (Korean War)

John Sacret Young
A Rumor of War '80 (Vietnam War)

Waldemar Young
Lives of a Bengal Lancer '35 (British Wars)

Z

Steven Zaillian
Schindler's List '93 (WW II: The Holocaust)

Robert Zemeckis
1941 '79 (WW II: Homefront)

Writer Index

The "Cinematographer Index" lists all cinematographers, or Directors of Photography, listed in this book. Cinematographer names follow an alphabetical sort by last name (although the names appear in a first name last name format). The movie titles are listed chronologically, beginning with the most recent.

A

Barry Ackroyd
Land and Freedom '95 (Between the World Wars)

Nestor Almendros
The Last Metro '80 (WW II: The Holocaust)

John Alton
Battle Circus '53 (Korean War)

Lucien N. Andriot
The Fighting Sullivans '42 (WW II: Pacific)

John Arnold
The Big Parade '25 (WW I)

Joseph August
They Were Expendable '45 (WW II: Pacific)
Gunga Din '39 (British Wars)

B

Joe Batac
The Siege of Firebase Gloria '89 (Vietnam War)

Renato Berta
Au Revoir les Enfants '87 (WW II: The Holocaust)

Joseph Biroc
Too Late the Hero '70 (WW II: Pacific)
China Gate '57 (Vietnam War)

Billy Bitzer
America '24 (American Wars)
Birth of a Nation '15 (American Wars)

Osmond H. Borradaile
The Four Feathers '39 (British Wars)

Jean Bourgoin
The Longest Day '62 (WW II: Europe & North Africa)

Russell Boyd
Gallipoli '81 (WW I)

Charles P. Boyle
She Wore a Yellow Ribbon '49 (American Wars)

William Bradford
Fighting Seabees '44 (WW II: Pacific)

Henry Braham
The Land Girls '98 (WW II: Home-front)

Norbert Brodine
13 Rue Madeleine '46 (WW II: The Resistance)

Jules Buck
Battle of San Pietro '44 (WW II: Documentaries)

L.H. Burel
A Man Escaped '57 (WW II: POWs)
Napoleon '27 (French Wars)

Thomas Burstyn
When Trumpets Fade '98 (WW II: Europe & North Africa)

C

Jack Cardiff
War and Peace '56 (Russian Wars)
The Four Feathers '39 (British Wars)

Alan Caso
84 Charlie MoPic '89 (Vietnam War)

Christopher Challis
The Victors '63 (WW II: Europe & North Africa)
Sink the Bismarck! '60 (WW II: Europe & North Africa)

Charles Clarke
The Hunters '58 (Korean War)
Guadalcanal Diary '43 (WW II: Pacific)

William Clothier
Shenandoah '65 (American Wars)

Merrill's Marauders '62 (WW II: Pacific)
The Alamo '60 (American Wars)
The Horse Soldiers '59 (American Wars)

John Coquillon
Cross of Iron '76 (WW II: Europe & North Africa)

Stanley Cortez
Since You Went Away '44 (WW II: Homefront)

Raoul Coutard
317th Platoon '65 (French Wars)

Jordan Cronenweth
Gardens of Stone '87 (Vietnam War)

D

Stephen Dade
Zulu '64 (British Wars)

William H. Daniels
Von Ryan's Express '65 (WW II: POWs)
Three Came Home '50 (WW II: POWs)

Allen Daviau
Empire of the Sun '87 (WW II: POWs)

Robert De Grasse
Home of the Brave '49 (WW II: Pacific)

Axel de Roche
The White Rose '83 (WW II: The Resistance)

Clyde De Vinna
The Immortal Sergeant '43 (WW II: Europe & North Africa)

Roger Deakins
Courage Under Fire '96 (Coming Home)
Rob Roy '95 (British Wars)

Tonino Delli Colli
Life Is Beautiful '98 (WW II: The Holocaust)
The Good, the Bad and the Ugly '67 (American Wars)

Elmer Dyer
Air Force '43 (WW II: Pacific)
Dive Bomber '41 (Between the World Wars)
Hell's Angels '30 (WW I)

E

Arthur Edeson
Across the Pacific '42 (Between the World Wars)
Casablanca '42 (WW II: The Resistance)
All Quiet on the Western Front '30 (WW I)

F

Daniel F. Fapp
The Great Escape '63 (WW II: POWs)
All the Young Men '60 (Korean War)

Vilko Filac
Underground '95 (WW II: Europe & North Africa)

George Folsey
The White Cliffs of Dover '44 (WW II: Homefront)

John Ford
Battle of Midway '42 (WW II: Documentaries)

William A. Fraker
1941 '79 (WW II: Homefront)

Freddie Francis
Glory '89 (American Wars)

Karl Freund
The Seventh Cross '44 (WW II: POWs)
All Quiet on the Western Front '30 (WW I)

Osamu Furuya
Tora! Tora! Tora! '70 (WW II: Pacific)

G

Lee Garmes
Since You Went Away '44 (WW II: Homefront)

Marcello Gatti
The Battle of Algiers '66 (French Wars)

Gaetano Antonio "Tony" Gaudio
The Fighting 69th '40 (WW I)
Dawn Patrol '38 (WW I)
Hell's Angels '30 (WW I)

Merritt B. Gerstad
Watch on the Rhine '43 (WW II: The Resistance)

Maury Gertsman
To Hell and Back '55 (WW II: Europe & North Africa)

Bert Glennon
Dive Bomber '41 (Between the World Wars)
They Died with Their Boots On '41 (American Wars)

Godfret A. Godar
The Boys in Company C '77 (Vietnam War)

Guy Green
Immortal Battalion '44 (WW II: Europe & North Africa)

Adam Greenberg
The Big Red One '80 (WW II: Europe & North Africa)

Loyal Griggs
In Harm's Way '65 (WW II: Pacific)
The Bridges at Toko-Ri '55 (Korean War)

Marcel Grignon
Is Paris Burning? '66 (WW II: Europe & North Africa)

Burnett Guffey
King Rat '65 (WW II: POWs)
From Here to Eternity '53 (Between the World Wars)

H

Bert Haines
The General '26 (American Wars)

Conrad Hall
Hell in the Pacific '69 (WW II: Pacific)

Ernest Haller
Men in War '57 (Korean War)

Russell Harlan
Run Silent Run Deep '58 (WW II: Pacific)
A Walk in the Sun '46 (WW II: Europe & North Africa)

Sid Hickox
Battle Cry '55 (WW II: Pacific)

Jack Hildyard
Battle of the Bulge '65 (WW II: Europe & North Africa)
Bridge on the River Kwai '57 (WW II: POWs)

Sinsaku Himeda
Tora! Tora! Tora! '70 (WW II: Pacific)

Winton C. Hoch
The Green Berets '68 (Vietnam War)
Mister Roberts '55 (WW II: Pacific)
She Wore a Yellow Ribbon '49 (American Wars)
Dive Bomber '41 (Between the World Wars)

James Wong Howe
Objective, Burma! '45 (WW II: Pacific)
Air Force '43 (WW II: Pacific)

Roger Hubert
Napoleon '27 (French Wars)

John Huston
Battle of San Pietro '44 (WW II: Documentaries)

I

Arthur Ibbetson
Where Eagles Dare '68 (WW II: Europe & North Africa)

J

Peter James
Paradise Road '97 (WW II: POWs)

Devereaux Jennings
The General '26 (American Wars)

Ray June
Above and Beyond '53 (WW II: Pacific)

K

Janusz Kaminski
Saving Private Ryan '98 (WW II: Europe & North Africa)
Schindler's List '93 (WW II: The Holocaust)

Setsuo Kobayashi
Fires on the Plain '59 (WW II: Pacific)

Fred W. Koenekamp
Patton '70 (WW II: Europe & North Africa)

Robert Krasker
The Third Man '49 (Coming Home)
Henry V '44 (British Wars)

Milton Krasner
Three Came Home '50 (WW II: POWs)

Georg Krause
Paths of Glory '57 (WW I)

Jules Kruger
Napoleon '27 (French Wars)

L

Charles B(ryant) Lang
Lives of a Bengal Lancer '35 (British Wars)

Reggie Lanning
Sands of Iwo Jima '49 (WW II: Pacific)

Stevan Larner
A Rumor of War '80 (Vietnam War)

Ernest Laszlo
Judgment at Nuremberg '61 (Coming Home)
Stalag 17 '53 (WW II: POWs)

Marcel Le Picard
America '24 (American Wars)

Sam Leavitt
Pork Chop Hill '59 (Korean War)

Pierre Levent
The Longest Day '62 (WW II: Europe & North Africa)

Denis Lewiston
One Against the Wind '91 (WW II: The Resistance)

Lionel Linden
O.S.S. '46 (WW II: The Resistance)

Karl Walter Lindenlaub
Rob Roy '95 (British Wars)

Lionel Lindon
The Manchurian Candidate '62 (Korean War)

Harold Lipstein
Hell Is for Heroes '62 (WW II: Europe & North Africa)

M

Joe MacDonald
The Sand Pebbles '66 (American Wars)
The Gallant Hours '60 (WW II: Pacific)
The Young Lions '58 (WW II: Europe & North Africa)

Peter Macdonald
Hamburger Hill '87 (Vietnam War)

Jack MacKenzie
Battle of Midway '42 (WW II: Documentaries)

Kenneth Macmillan
Henry V '89 (British Wars)

Glen MacWilliams
Lifeboat '44 (WW II: Europe & North Africa)

Charles A. Marshall
Air Force '43 (WW II: Pacific)
Dive Bomber '41 (Between the World Wars)

Rudolph Mate
Sahara '43 (WW II: Europe & North Africa)
To Be or Not to Be '42 (WW II: The Resistance)
The Real Glory '39 (American Wars)

Christian Matras
Grand Illusion '37 (WW I)

Donald McAlpine
Breaker Morant '80 (British Wars)

Ted D. McCord
Action in the North Atlantio '43 (WW II: Europe & North Africa)

William Mellor
Wake Island '42 (WW II: Pacific)

Dominique Merlin
Anderson Platoon '67 (Vietnam War)

Russell Metty
A Time to Love and a Time to Die '58 (WW II: Europe & North Africa)
The Story of G.I. Joe '45 (WW II: Europe & North Africa)

Arthur C. Miller
The Razor's Edge '46 (Coming Home)
The Immortal Sergeant '43 (WW II: Europe & North Africa)

Ernest Miller
The Steel Helmet '51 (Korean War)

Doug Milsome
Full Metal Jacket '87 (Vietnam War)

Kazuo Miyagawa
Yojimbo '61 (Japanese Wars)

Hal Mohr
Watch on the Rhine '43 (WW II: The Resistance)

Oswald Morris
The Guns of Navarone '61 (WW II: Europe & North Africa)

N

Asakazu Nakai
Ran '85 (Japanese Wars)
Seven Samurai '54 (Japanese Wars)

Armando Nannuzzi
Waterloo '71 (French Wars)

Toichiro Narushima
Merry Christmas, Mr. Lawrence '83 (WW II: POWs)

Ronald Neame
In Which We Serve '43 (WW II: Europe & North Africa)

O

Ronald Orieux
The Tuskegee Airmen '95 (WW II: Europe & North Africa)

P

Georges Perinal
The Four Feathers '39 (British Wars)

Cinematographer Index

Harry Perry
Hell's Angels '30 (WW I)
Wings '27 (WW I)

Henri Persin
The Longest Day '62 (WW II:
  Europe & North Africa)

Franz Planer
The Caine Mutiny '54 (WW II:
  Europe & North Africa)

Sol Polito
Sergeant York '41 (WW I)
Charge of the Light Brigade '36
  (British Wars)

R

Ray Rennahan
For Whom the Bell Tolls '43
  (Between the World Wars)
Gone with the Wind '39 (American
  Wars)

Robert Richardson
Born on the Fourth of July '89
  (Coming Home)
Platoon '86 (Vietnam War)

Tom Richmond
Mother Night '96 (WW II: Europe &
  North Africa)
A Midnight Clear '92 (WW II:
  Europe & North Africa)

Alexei Rodionov
Come and See '85 (WW II: Europe
  & North Africa)

Nicolas Roeg
Doctor Zhivago '65 (Russian Wars)

Harold Rosson
The Red Badge of Courage '51
  (American Wars)
Command Decision '48 (WW II:
  Europe & North Africa)
Thirty Seconds over Tokyo '44 (WW
  II: Pacific)

Philippe Rousselot
Hope and Glory '87 (WW II: Homefront)

Joseph Ruttenberg
Mrs. Miniver '42 (WW II: Homefront)

S

Takao Saito
Ran '85 (Japanese Wars)

Vic Sarin
Bye Bye Blues '89 (WW II: Homefront)

Hendrik Sartov
America '24 (American Wars)

Edward Scaife
The Dirty Dozen '67 (WW II: Europe
  & North Africa)

Horst Schier
The Wannsee Conference '84 (WW
  II: The Holocaust)

John Seitz
Five Graves to Cairo '43 (WW II:
  Europe & North Africa)
Four Horsemen of the Apocalypse
  '21 (WW I)

Dean Semler
The Lighthorsemen '87 (WW I)

Leon Shamroy
Twelve O'Clock High '49 (WW II:
  Europe & North Africa)
Crash Dive '43 (WW II: Europe &
  North Africa)

Setsuo Shibata
Fires on the Plain '59 (WW II:
  Pacific)

Aleksander Sigayev
Chapayev '34 (Russian Wars)

H. Sintzenich
America '24 (American Wars)

Douglas Slocombe
The Blue Max '66 (WW I)

William E. Snyder
Flying Leathernecks '51 (WW II:
  Pacific)

Kari Sohlberg
The Winter War '89 (Between the
  World Wars)

Peter Sova
Good Morning, Vietnam '87 (Vietnam War)

Theodor Sparkuhl
Wake Island '42 (WW II: Pacific)
Beau Geste '39 (British Wars)

Dante Spinotti
Last of the Mohicans '92 (American
  Wars)

Jorge Stahl, Jr.
A Rumor of War '80 (Vietnam War)

E. Burton Steene
Hell's Angels '30 (WW I)

Harold E. Stine
M*A*S*H '70 (Korean War)

Vittorio Storaro
Apocalypse Now '79 (Vietnam War)

Louis Clyde Stouman
Beau Geste '39 (British Wars)

Archie Stout
Beau Geste '39 (British Wars)

Harry Stradling, Jr.
Go Tell the Spartans '78 (Vietnam
  War)

Karl Struss
The Great Dictator '40 (Between
  the World Wars)

Robert L. Surtees
Thirty Seconds over Tokyo '44 (WW
  II: Pacific)

T

Gilbert Taylor
Dr. Strangelove, or: How I Learned
  to Stop Worrying and Love the
  Bomb '64 (American Wars)

Eduard Tisse
Alexander Nevsky '38 (Russian
  Wars)
Battleship Potemkin '25 (Russian
  Wars)

Gregg Toland
The Best Years of Our Lives '46
  (Coming Home)

John Toll
The Thin Red Line '98 (WW II:
  Pacific)
Braveheart '95 (British Wars)

Aldo Tonti
War and Peace '56 (Russian Wars)

Roland H. Totheroh
The Great Dictator '40 (Between
  the World Wars)

Jean Tournier
The Train '65 (WW II: Europe &
  North Africa)

U

Masaharu Ueda
Ran '85 (Japanese Wars)

Geoffrey Unsworth
A Bridge Too Far '77 (WW II:
Europe & North Africa)

V

Jost Vacano
Das Boot '81 (WW II: Europe &
North Africa)

Kees Van Oostrum
Gettysburg '93 (American Wars)

Paul Vogel
Battleground '49 (WW II: Europe &
North Africa)

Gerd Von Bonen
The Bridge '59 (WW II: Europe &
North Africa)

W

Sidney Wagner
Bataan '43 (WW II: Pacific)

Joseph Walker
Mr. Winkle Goes to War '44 (WW II:
Europe & North Africa)

David Watkin
Catch-22 '70 (WW II: Europe &
North Africa)
Charge of the Light Brigade '68
(British Wars)

Harold Wenstrom
The Lost Patrol '34 (WW I)

Haskell Wexler
Coming Home '78 (Coming Home)

Charles F. Wheeler
Tora! Tora! Tora! '70 (WW II: Pacific)

Billy Williams
The Wind and the Lion '75 (American Wars)

Walter Wottitz
The Train '65 (WW II: Europe &
North Africa)
The Longest Day '62 (WW II:
Europe & North Africa)

Dewey Wrigley
Hell's Angels '30 (WW I)

X

Alexander Xenofontov
Chapayev '34 (Russian Wars)

Y

Kazuo Yamazaki
The Hidden Fortress '58 (Japanese
Wars)

Frederick A. (Freddie) Young
The Battle of Britain '69 (WW II:
Europe & North Africa)
Doctor Zhivago '65 (Russian Wars)
Lawrence of Arabia '62 (WW I)

Z

Vilmos Zsigmond
The Deer Hunter '78 (Vietnam War)

Cinematographer Index

The "Composer Index" provides a list of all composers, arrangers, lyricists, or bands that have provided an original music score for the films reviewed in this book. The listings for the composer names follow an alphabetical sort by last name (although the names appear in a first name, last name format). The movie titles are listed chronologically, beginning with the most recent film.

Benjamin Frankel
Battle of the Bulge '65 (WW II: Europe & North Africa)

Gerald Fried
Too Late the Hero '70 (WW II: Pacific)
Paths of Glory '57 (WW I)

Hugo Friedhofer
The Young Lions '58 (WW II: Europe & North Africa)
Above and Beyond '53 (WW II: Pacific)
Three Came Home '50 (WW II: POWs)
The Best Years of Our Lives '46 (Coming Home)
Lifeboat '44 (WW II: Europe & North Africa)

G

Philip Glass
Hamburger Hill '87 (Vietnam War)

Ernest Gold
Cross of Iron '76 (WW II: Europe & North Africa)
Judgment at Nuremberg '61 (Coming Home)

Jerry Goldsmith
The Wind and the Lion '75 (American Wars)
Patton '70 (WW II: Europe & North Africa)
Tora! Tora! Tora! '70 (WW II: Pacific)
The Blue Max '66 (WW I)
The Sand Pebbles '66 (American Wars)
In Harm's Way '65 (WW II: Pacific)
Von Ryan's Express '65 (WW II: POWs)

Ron Goodwin
The Battle of Britain '69 (WW II: Europe & North Africa)
Where Eagles Dare '68 (WW II: Europe & North Africa)

Louis F. Gottschalk
Four Horsemen of the Apocalypse '21 (WW I)

D.W. Griffith
Birth of a Nation '15 (American Wars)

Charles Gross
A Rumor of War '80 (Vietnam War)

H

Jukka Haavisto
The Winter War '89 (Between the World Wars)

Richard Hageman
She Wore a Yellow Ribbon '49 (American Wars)

Dick Halligan
Go Tell the Spartans '78 (Vietnam War)

Fumio Hayasaka
Seven Samurai '54 (Japanese Wars)

Lennie Hayton
Battle Circus '53 (Korean War)
Battleground '49 (WW II: Europe & North Africa)

Werner R. Heymann
To Be or Not to Be '42 (WW II: The Resistance)

Lee Holdridge
The Tuskegee Airmen '95 (WW II: Europe & North Africa)
One Against the Wind '91 (WW II: The Resistance)

Arthur Honegger
Napoleon '27 (French Wars)

James Horner
Courage Under Fire '96 (Coming Home)
Braveheart '95 (British Wars)
Glory '89 (American Wars)

I

Mark Isham
A Midnight Clear '92 (WW II: Europe & North Africa)

J

Howard Jackson
Merrill's Marauders '62 (WW II: Pacific)

Pierre Jansen
317th Platoon '65 (French Wars)

Maurice Jarre
Is Paris Burning? '66 (WW II: Europe & North Africa)
Doctor Zhivago '65 (Russian Wars)

The Train '65 (WW II: Europe & North Africa)
Lawrence of Arabia '62 (WW I)
The Longest Day '62 (WW II: Europe & North Africa)

Laurie Johnson
Dr. Strangelove, or: How I Learned to Stop Worrying and Love the Bomb '64 (American Wars)

Trevor Jones
Last of the Mohicans '92 (American Wars)

K

Bronislau Kaper
The Red Badge of Courage '51 (American Wars)
Bataan '43 (WW II: Pacific)

Sol Kaplan
The Victors '63 (WW II: Europe & North Africa)

Dana Kaproff
The Big Red One '80 (WW II: Europe & North Africa)

Anton Karas
The Third Man '49 (Coming Home)

Joseph Kosma
Grand Illusion '37 (WW I)

L

Brian Lock
The Land Girls '98 (WW II: Homefront)

M

Hans-Martin Majewski
The Bridge '59 (WW II: Europe & North Africa)

Henry Mancini
To Hell and Back '55 (WW II: Europe & North Africa)

Johnny Mandel
M*A*S*H '70 (Korean War)

Peter Martin
Hope and Glory '87 (WW II: Homefront)

Brian May
Gallipoli '81 (WW I)

Abigail Mead
Full Metal Jacket '87 (Vietnam War)

David Mendoza
The Big Parade '25 (WW I)

Jaime Mendoza-Nava
The Boys in Company C '77 (Vietnam War)

Mario Millo
The Lighthorsemen '87 (WW I)

Cyril Mockridge
The Fighting Sullivans '42 (WW II: Pacific)

Ennio Morricone
The Good, the Bad and the Ugly '67 (American Wars)
The Battle of Algiers '66 (French Wars)

Lyn Murray
The Bridges at Toko-Ri '55 (Korean War)

Stanley Myers
The Deer Hunter '78 (Vietnam War)

N

Alfred Newman
Twelve O'Clock High '49 (WW II: Europe & North Africa)
The Razor's Edge '46 (Coming Home)
Battle of Midway '42 (WW II: Documentaries)
The Fighting Sullivans '42 (WW II: Pacific)
Beau Geste '39 (British Wars)
Gunga Din '39 (British Wars)
The Real Glory '39 (American Wars)

Alex North
Good Morning, Vietnam '87 (Vietnam War)

P

Clifton Parker
Sink the Bismarck! '60 (WW II: Europe & North Africa)

Nicola Piovani
Life Is Beautiful '98 (WW II: The Holocaust)

Gillo Pontecorvo
The Battle of Algiers '66 (French Wars)

Gavriil Popov
Chapayev '34 (Russian Wars)

Sergei Prokofiev
Alexander Nevsky '38 (Russian Wars)

R

Freddie Rich
A Walk in the Sun '46 (WW II: Europe & North Africa)

Hugo Riesenfeld
Hell's Angels '30 (WW I)

Earl Robinson
A Walk in the Sun '46 (WW II: Europe & North Africa)

Milan Roder
Lives of a Bengal Lancer '35 (British Wars)

Ann Ronell
The Story of G.I. Joe '45 (WW II: Europe & North Africa)

Leonard Rosenman
Hell Is for Heroes '62 (WW II: Europe & North Africa)
Pork Chop Hill '59 (Korean War)

Nino Rota
Waterloo '71 (French Wars)
War and Peace '56 (Russian Wars)

Miklos Rozsa
The Green Berets '68 (Vietnam War)
A Time to Love and a Time to Die '58 (WW II: Europe & North Africa)
Command Decision '48 (WW II: Europe & North Africa)
Five Graves to Cairo '43 (WW II: Europe & North Africa)
Sahara '43 (WW II: Europe & North Africa)
So Proudly We Hail '43 (WW II: Pacific)
To Be or Not to Be '42 (WW II: The Resistance)
The Four Feathers '39 (British Wars)

S

Camille Saint-Saens
Au Revoir les Enfants '87 (WW II: The Holocaust)

Ryuichi Sakamoto
Merry Christmas, Mr. Lawrence '83 (WW II: POWs)

Masaru Sato
Yojimbo '61 (Japanese Wars)
The Hidden Fortress '58 (Japanese Wars)

Paul Sawtell
The Hunters '58 (Korean War)
Mr. Winkle Goes to War '44 (WW II: Europe & North Africa)

Walter Scharf
Fighting Seabees '44 (WW II: Pacific)

Lalo Schifrin
Hell in the Pacific '69 (WW II: Pacific)

Franz Schubert
Au Revoir les Enfants '87 (WW II: The Holocaust)

Paul Schutze
The Siege of Firebase Gloria '89 (Vietnam War)

Gregorio Garcia Segura
317th Platoon '65 (French Wars)

Dimitri Shostakovich
Battleship Potemkin '25 (Russian Wars)

Frank Skinner
Shenandoah '65 (American Wars)

Max Steiner
China Gate '57 (Vietnam War)
Battle Cry '55 (WW II: Pacific)
The Caine Mutiny '54 (WW II: Europe & North Africa)
Since You Went Away '44 (WW II: Homefront)
Watch on the Rhine '43 (WW II: The Resistance)
Casablanca '42 (WW II: The Resistance)
Dive Bomber '41 (Between the World Wars)
Sergeant York '41 (WW I)
They Died with Their Boots On '41 (American Wars)
Gone with the Wind '39 (American Wars)
Dawn Patrol '38 (WW I)

Composer Index

Charge of the Light Brigade '36
(British Wars)
The Lost Patrol '34 (WW I)

Herbert Stothart
They Were Expendable '45 (WW II:
Pacific)
Thirty Seconds over Tokyo '44 (WW
II: Pacific)
The White Cliffs of Dover '44 (WW
II: Homefront)
Mrs. Miniver '42 (WW II: Homefront)

T

Toru Takemitsu
Ran '85 (Japanese Wars)

Juha Tikko
The Winter War '89 (Between the
World Wars)

Dimitri Tiomkin
The Guns of Navarone '61 (WW II:
Europe & North Africa)
The Alamo '60 (American Wars)
Home of the Brave '49 (WW II:
Pacific)
Battle of San Pietro '44 (WW II:
Documentaries)

W

Roger Wagner
The Gallant Hours '60 (WW II:
Pacific)

William Walton
The Battle of Britain '69 (WW II:
Europe & North Africa)
Henry V '44 (British Wars)

Franz Waxman
Run Silent Run Deep '58 (WW II:
Pacific)
Mister Roberts '55 (WW II: Pacific)
Stalag 17 '53 (WW II: POWs)
Objective, Burma! '45 (WW II:
Pacific)
Air Force '43 (WW II: Pacific)

Roy Webb
Flying Leathernecks '51 (WW II:
Pacific)
Fighting Seabees '44 (WW II:
Pacific)
The Seventh Cross '44 (WW II:
POWs)

Paul Francis Webster
The Alamo '60 (American Wars)

Konstantin Wecker
The White Rose '83 (WW II: The
Resistance)

John Williams
Saving Private Ryan '98 (WW II:
Europe & North Africa)
Schindler's List '93 (WW II: The
Holocaust)
Born on the Fourth of July '89
(Coming Home)
Empire of the Sun '87 (WW II:
POWs)
1941 '79 (WW II: Homefront)
The Deer Hunter '78 (Vietnam War)

Meredith Willson
The Great Dictator '40 (Between
the World Wars)

Y

Oleg Yanchenko
Come and See '85 (WW II: Europe
& North Africa)

Victor Young
China Gate '57 (Vietnam War)
Sands of Iwo Jima '49 (WW II:
Pacific)
For Whom the Bell Tolls '43
(Between the World Wars)

Z

J.S. Zamecnik
Wings '27 (WW I)

Eric Zeisl
They Were Expendable '45 (WW II:
Pacific)
Bataan '43 (WW II: Pacific)

Hans Zimmer
The Thin Red Line '98 (WW II:
Pacific)

The "Category Index" includes subject terms ranging from straight genre descriptions (Comedy, Westerns, etc.) to more off-the-wall themes (Strained Suburbia, Torrid Love Scenes), from country in which the movie was produced to country in which the movie takes place, from authors of the source novels, to depictions of specific battles.

A

Adapted from a Book
See James Clavell, Richard Condon, Joseph Conrad, James Fenimore Cooper, Stephen Crane, Graham Greene, Joseph Heller, Ernest Hemingway, James Jones, Rudyard Kipling, Alistair MacLean, W. Somerset Maugham, James Michener, John Steinbeck, Leo Tolstoy, Leon Uris, Kurt Vonnegut, William Wharton, Herman Wouk

Adapted from a Play or Musical
Birth of a Nation *(American Wars)*
Casablanca *(WW II: The Resistance)*
Command Decision *(WW II: Europe & North Africa)*
Five Graves to Cairo *(WW II: Europe & North Africa)*
Henry V *(British Wars)*
Home of the Brave *(WW II: Pacific)*
Mister Roberts *(WW II: Pacific)*
Ran *(Japanese Wars)*
Watch on the Rhine *(WW II: The Resistance)*

Adapted from a Poem
Braveheart *(British Wars)*
Charge of the Light Brigade *(British Wars)*
Gunga Din *(British Wars)*
The White Cliffs of Dover *(WW II: Homefront)*

Adapted from a Story
Crash Dive *(WW II: Europe & North Africa)*
Dive Bomber *(Between the World Wars)*
Objective, Burma! *(WW II: Pacific)*

Adolescence
See Coming of Age; Teen Angst

Africa (Locale)
Casablanca *(WW II: The Resistance)*
The Lost Patrol *(WW I)*
Sahara *(WW II: Europe & North Africa)*

The Wind and the Lion *(American Wars)*
Zulu *(British Wars)*

African America
Anderson Platoon *(Vietnam War)*
Glory *(American Wars)*
Home of the Brave *(WW II: Pacific)*
The Tuskegee Airmen *(WW II: Europe & North Africa)*

Airborne
Above and Beyond *(WW II: Pacific)*
Air Force *(WW II: Pacific)*
The Battle of Britain *(WW II: Europe & North Africa)*
The Blue Max *(WW I)*
The Bridges at Toko-Ri *(Korean War)*
Dawn Patrol *(WW I)*
Dive Bomber *(Between the World Wars)*
Dr. Strangelove, or: How I Learned to Stop Worrying and Love the Bomb *(American Wars)*
Flying Leathernecks *(WW II: Pacific)*
Hell's Angels *(WW I)*
The Hunters *(Korean War)*
Memphis Belle: A Story of a Flying Fortress *(WW II: Documentaries)*
1941 *(WW II: Homefront)*
The Tuskegee Airmen *(WW II: Europe & North Africa)*
Twelve O'Clock High *(WW II: Europe & North Africa)*
Wings *(WW I)*

Airplanes
See Airborne

Algerian (Production)
The Battle of Algiers *(French Wars)*

American Indians
See Native America

American South (Locale)
See also Southern Belles
Birth of a Nation *(American Wars)*
The General *(American Wars)*
Gettysburg *(American Wars)*
Gone with the Wind *(American Wars)*

The Horse Soldiers *(American Wars)*
Shenandoah *(American Wars)*

Amnesia
See also Identity
The Great Dictator *(Between the World Wars)*
Home of the Brave *(WW II: Pacific)*
The Manchurian Candidate *(Korean War)*

Amusement Parks
1941 *(WW II: Homefront)*
The Third Man *(Coming Home)*

Anti-Heroes
See also Rebel with a Cause
Apocalypse Now *(Vietnam War)*
The Dirty Dozen *(WW II: Europe & North Africa)*
The Good, the Bad and the Ugly *(American Wars)*
Yojimbo *(Japanese Wars)*

Anti-War War Movies
See also Satire & Parody
All Quiet on the Western Front *(WW I)*
Apocalypse Now *(Vietnam War)*
The Big Parade *(WW I)*
Born on the Fourth of July *(Coming Home)*
The Bridge *(WW II: Europe & North Africa)*
The Bridges at Toko-Ri *(Korean War)*
Catch-22 *(WW II: Europe & North Africa)*
Charge of the Light Brigade (1968) *(British Wars)*
Come and See *(WW II: Europe & North Africa)*
Coming Home *(Coming Home)*
Dr. Strangelove, or: How I Learned to Stop Worrying and Love the Bomb *(American Wars)*
Fires on the Plain *(WW II: Pacific)*
Four Horsemen of the Apocalypse *(WW I)*
Gallipoli *(WW I)*
Glory *(American Wars)*
Grand Illusion *(WW I)*
Hell in the Pacific *(WW II: Pacific)*

M*A*S*H *(Korean War)*
A Midnight Clear *(WW II: Europe & North Africa)*
Paths of Glory *(WW I)*
Platoon *(Vietnam War)*
The Red Badge of Courage *(American Wars)*
The Steel Helmet *(Korean War)*
A Time to Love and a Time to Die *(WW II: Europe & North Africa)*
Too Late the Hero *(WW II: Pacific)*
The Victors *(WW II: Europe & North Africa)*
The War at Home *(Vietnam War)*
The Young Lions *(WW II: Europe & North Africa)*

Asia (Locale)
See also China; Japan
All the Young Men *(Korean War)*
Apocalypse Now *(Vietnam War)*
Battle Circus *(Korean War)*
The Boys in Company C *(Vietnam War)*
Bridge on the River Kwai *(WW II: POWs)*
The Bridges at Toko-Ri *(Korean War)*
China Gate *(Vietnam War)*
The Deer Hunter *(Vietnam War)*
84 Charlie Mopic *(Vietnam War)*
Empire of the Sun *(WW II: POWs)*
Full Metal Jacket *(Vietnam War)*
Go Tell the Spartans *(Vietnam War)*
Good Morning, Vietnam *(Vietnam War)*
The Green Berets *(Vietnam War)*
Hamburger Hill *(Vietnam War)*
The Hidden Fortress *(Japanese Wars)*
Hong Kong, 1941 *(Between the World Wars)*
The Hunters *(Korean War)*
King Rat *(WW II: POWs)*
The Manchurian Candidate *(Korean War)*
M*A*S*H *(Korean War)*
Men in War *(Korean War)*
Merry Christmas, Mr. Lawrence *(WW II: POWs)*
Paradise Road *(WW II: POWs)*
Platoon *(Vietnam War)*
Pork Chop Hill *(Korean War)*
Ran *(Japanese Wars)*
A Rumor of War *(Vietnam War)*
The Sand Pebbles *(American Wars)*
Seven Samurai *(Japanese Wars)*
The Siege of Firebase Gloria *(Vietnam War)*
The Steel Helmet *(Korean War)*
Thirty Seconds Over Tokyo *(WW II: Pacific)*

Three Came Home *(WW II: POWs)*
Yojimbo *(Japanese Wars)*

Assassinations
See also Foreign Intrigue; Hit Men; Spies & Espionage
Birth of a Nation *(American Wars)*
The Manchurian Candidate *(Korean War)*
Yojimbo *(Japanese Wars)*

Atomic Bomb
Above and Beyond *(WW II: Pacific)*
Dr. Strangelove, or: How I Learned to Stop Worrying and Love the Bomb *(American Wars)*

Australia (Locale)
See Down Under

Australian (Production)
Breaker Morant *(British Wars)*
Gallipoli *(WW I)*
The Lighthorsemen *(WW I)*

B

Battle of the Bulge
Battle of the Bulge *(WW II: Europe & North Africa)*
Battleground *(WW II: Europe & North Africa)*
The Bridge *(WW II: Europe & North Africa)*
Hell Is for Heroes *(WW II: Europe & North Africa)*
A Midnight Clear *(WW II: Europe & North Africa)*
Patton *(WW II: Europe & North Africa)*
When Trumpets Fade *(WW II: Europe & North Africa)*

Behind Bars
See Great Escapes; Men in Prison; Women in Prison

Berlin (Locale)
See also Germany
Mother Night *(WW II: Europe & North Africa)*
The Wannsee Conference *(WW II: The Holocaust)*

Big Battles
The Alamo *(American Wars)*
Alexander Nevsky *(Russian Wars)*
Apocalypse Now *(Vietnam War)*
The Battle of Britain *(WW II: Europe & North Africa)*
The Battle of Midway *(WW II: Documentaries)*

The Battle of San Pietro *(WW II: Documentaries)*
Battle of the Bulge *(WW II: Europe & North Africa)*
Battleground *(WW II: Europe & North Africa)*
Battleship Potemkin *(Russian Wars)*
The Big Parade *(WW I)*
The Big Red One *(WW II: Europe & North Africa)*
Birth of a Nation *(American Wars)*
Braveheart *(British Wars)*
A Bridge Too Far *(WW II: Europe & North Africa)*
Cross of Iron *(WW II: Europe & North Africa)*
Das Boot *(WW II: Europe & North Africa)*
The Fighting Sullivans *(WW II: Pacific)*
Gallipoli *(WW I)*
Gettysburg *(American Wars)*
Glory *(American Wars)*
Guadalcanal Diary *(WW II: Pacific)*
The Guns of Navarone *(WW II: Europe & North Africa)*
Henry V *(British Wars)*
The Lighthorsemen *(WW I)*
The Longest Day *(WW II: Europe & North Africa)*
Patton *(WW II: Europe & North Africa)*
Ran *(Japanese Wars)*
Rob Roy *(British Wars)*
The Sand Pebbles *(American Wars)*
Sands of Iwo Jima *(WW II: Pacific)*
Saving Private Ryan *(WW II: Europe & North Africa)*
The Siege of Firebase Gloria *(Vietnam War)*
They Died with Their Boots On *(American Wars)*
The Thin Red Line *(WW II: Pacific)*
To Hell and Back *(WW II: Europe & North Africa)*
Tora! Tora! Tora! *(WW II: Pacific)*
Twelve O'Clock High *(WW II: Europe & North Africa)*
War and Peace *(Russian Wars)*
Zulu *(British Wars)*

Big-Budget Bombs
Big-budget projects that didn't bring home the boxoffice bacon, regardless of critical reaction.
1941 *(WW II: Homefront)*
Tora! Tora! Tora! *(WW II: Pacific)*
Waterloo *(French Wars)*

Bikers
The Great Escape *(WW II: POWs)*

Biography
    See This Is Your Life

Black Comedy
    See also Comedy; Comedy Drama; Satire & Parody
Catch-22 *(WW II: Europe & North Africa)*
Dr. Strangelove, or: How I Learned to Stop Worrying and Love the Bomb *(American Wars)*
To Be or Not to Be *(WW II: The Resistance)*
Underground *(WW II: Europe & North Africa)*

Boating
    See Sail Away

Bosnia (Locale)
Underground *(WW II: Europe & North Africa)*

Bounty Hunters
The Good, the Bad and the Ugly *(American Wars)*

British (Production)
Bridge on the River Kwai *(WW II: POWs)*
A Bridge Too Far *(WW II: Europe & North Africa)*
Charge of the Light Brigade *(British Wars)*
Cross of Iron *(WW II: Europe & North Africa)*
Dr. Strangelove, or: How I Learned to Stop Worrying and Love the Bomb *(American Wars)*
The Four Feathers *(British Wars)*
Henry V *(British Wars)*
Hope and Glory *(WW II: Homefront)*
Immortal Battalion *(WW II: Europe & North Africa)*
In Which We Serve *(WW II: Europe & North Africa)*
Land and Freedom *(Between the World Wars)*
The Land Girls *(WW II: Homefront)*
Lawrence of Arabia *(WW I)*
Merry Christmas, Mr. Lawrence *(WW II: POWs)*
Sink the Bismarck! *(WW II: Europe & North Africa)*
The Third Man *(Coming Home)*
Where Eagles Dare *(WW II: Europe & North Africa)*

Buddies
The Alamo *(American Wars)*
The Deer Hunter *(Vietnam War)*
Gallipoli *(WW I)*
Grand Illusion *(WW I)*
Gunga Din *(British Wars)*

Hong Kong 1941 *(Between the World Wars)*
The Hunters *(Korean War)*
Lives of a Bengal Lancer *(British Wars)*
Platoon *(Vietnam War)*
The Steel Helmet *(Korean War)*

C

Canada (Locale)
    See also Cold Spots
Bye Bye Blues *(WW II: Homefront)*

Canadian (Production)
Bye Bye Blues *(WW II: Homefront)*

Childhood Visions
Au Revoir les Enfants *(WW II: The Holocaust)*
Empire of the Sun *(WW II: POWs)*
Hope and Glory *(WW II: Homefront)*

Children
    See Childhood Visions

China (Locale)
    See also Asia
Empire of the Sun *(WW II: POWs)*
The Sand Pebbles *(American Wars)*

Christmas
Merry Christmas, Mr. Lawrence *(WW II: POWs)*
A Midnight Clear *(WW II: Europe & North Africa)*
Stalag 17 *(WW II: POWs)*
The Victors *(WW II: Europe & North Africa)*

CIA
    See Spies & Espionage

City Lights
    See Berlin; London; Paris; Tokyo

Civil Rights
Birth of a Nation *(American Wars)*
Home of the Brave *(WW II: Pacific)*

Civil War
    See also American South; Southern Belles
Birth of a Nation *(American Wars)*
The General *(American Wars)*
Gettysburg *(American Wars)*
Glory *(American Wars)*
Gone with the Wind *(American Wars)*
The Good, the Bad and the Ugly *(American Wars)*

The Horse Soldiers *(American Wars)*
The Red Badge of Courage *(American Wars)*
Shenandoah *(American Wars)*

James Clavell: Books to Film
King Rat *(WW II: POWs)*

Cold Spots
Doctor Zhivago *(Russian Wars)*
Report from the Aleutians *(WW II: Documentaries)*
The Winter War *(Between the World Wars)*

Cold War
    See Red Scare

Comedy
    See also Black Comedy; Comedy Drama; Military Comedy; Satire & Parody
The General *(American Wars)*
The Great Dictator *(Between the World Wars)*
Life Is Beautiful *(WW II: The Holocaust)*
Mister Roberts *(WW II: Pacific)*
1941 *(WW II: Homefront)*

Comedy Drama
    See also Black Comedy; Comedy
Good Morning, Vietnam *(Vietnam War)*
M*A*S*H *(Korean War)*
Mr. Winkle Goes to War *(WW II: Europe & North Africa)*

Coming of Age
    See also Teen Angst
Au Revoir les Enfants *(WW II: The Holocaust)*
The Big Red One *(WW II: Europe & North Africa)*
The Boys in Company C *(Vietnam War)*
Come and See *(WW II: Europe & North Africa)*
The Deer Hunter *(Vietnam War)*
A Midnight Clear *(WW II: Europe & North Africa)*
Platoon *(Vietnam War)*
The Razor's Edge *(Coming Home)*
Sands of Iwo Jima *(WW II: Pacific)*

Concentration/Internment Camps
    See also The Holocaust; Nazis & Other Paramilitary Slugs; POW/MIA
The Big Red One *(WW II: Europe & North Africa)*
Life Is Beautiful *(WW II: The Holocaust)*

Category Index

Merry Christmas, Mr. Lawrence *(WW II: POWs)*
Paradise Road *(WW II: POWs)*
Schindler's List *(WW II: The Holocaust)*
The Seventh Cross *(WW II: POWs)*

Richard Condon: Books to Film
The Manchurian Candidate *(Korean War)*

Joseph Conrad: Books to Film
Apocalypse Now *(Vietnam War)*

Conspiracies
See It's a Conspiracy, Man!

Contemporary Noir
See also Film Noir
The Manchurian Candidate *(Korean War)*

James Fenimore Cooper: Books to Film
Last of the Mohicans *(American Wars)*

Courtroom Drama
See Order in the Court

Stephen Crane: Books to Film
The Red Badge of Courage *(American Wars)*

Crop Dusters
The Land Girls *(WW II: Homefront)*

Culture Clash
Lawrence of Arabia *(WW I)*
The Victors *(WW II: Europe and North Africa)*

D

D-Day
The Big Red One *(WW II: Europe & North Africa)*
The Longest Day *(WW II: Europe & North Africa)*
O.S.S. *(WW II: Europe & North Africa)*
Saving Private Ryan *(WW II: Europe & North Africa)*
13 Rue Madeleine *(WW II: Europe & North Africa)*

Dads
See also Monster Moms
Life Is Beautiful *(WW II: The Holocaust)*
Lives of a Bengal Lancer *(British Wars)*

Deserts
See also Foreign Legion
Beau Geste *(British Wars)*
Five Graves to Cairo *(WW II: Europe & North Africa)*
Gunga Din *(British Wars)*
Lawrence of Arabia *(WW I)*
The Lost Patrol *(WW I)*
Sahara *(WW II: Europe & North Africa)*
The Wind and the Lion *(American Wars)*

Doctors & Nurses
See also Sanity Check
Battle Circus *(Korean War)*
Dive Bomber *(Between the World Wars)*
Doctor Zhivago *(Russian Wars)*
M*A*S*H *(Korean War)*
The Real Glory *(American Wars)*
So Proudly We Hail *(WW II: Pacific)*

Docudrama
See also Documentary
The Battle of Algiers *(French Wars)*
Immortal Battalion *(WW II: Europe & North Africa)*

Documentary
See also Docudrama
Anderson Platoon *(Vietnam War)*
Battle of Midway *(WW II: Documentaries)*
Battle of San Pietro *(WW II: Documentaries)*
The Guns of August *(WW I)*
Memphis Belle: A Story of a Flying Fortress *(WW II: Documentaries)*
Report from the Aleutians *(WW II: Documentaries)*
The War at Home *(Vietnam War)*

Down Under (Locale)
Gallipoli *(WW I)*
The Lighthorsemen *(WW I)*

Drugs
See Pill Poppin'

E

Ethics & Morals
Bridge on the River Kwai *(WW II: POWs)*
Judgment at Nuremberg *(Coming Home)*
Platoon *(Vietnam War)*
Ran *(Japanese Wars)*

F

Family Ties
See also Dads; Monster Moms
Beau Geste *(British Wars)*
The Fighting Sullivans *(WW II: Pacific)*
Four Horsemen of the Apocalypse *(WW I)*
Hope and Glory *(WW II: Homefront)*
Mrs. Miniver *(WW II: Homefront)*
Ran *(Japanese Wars)*
Shenandoah *(American Wars)*
Since You Went Away *(WW II: Homefront)*
The White Cliffs of Dover *(WW II: Homefront)*

Farming
See Crop Dusters

Female Bonding
See also Women in War; Wonder Women
The Land Girls *(WW II: Homefront)*
Paradise Road *(WW II: POWs)*

Feminism
See Wonder Women

Film Noir
See also Contemporary Noir
Five Graves to Cairo *(WW II: Europe & North Africa)*
The Third Man *(Coming Home)*

Filmmaking
84 Charlie MoPic *(Vietnam War)*

Flashback
Beau Geste *(British Wars)*
Casablanca *(WW II: The Resistance)*
Courage Under Fire *(Coming Home)*
Mother Night *(WW II: Europe & North Africa)*
The Razor's Edge *(Coming Home)*

Flight
See Airborne

Foreign Films
See Algerian, Australian, British, Canadian, French, German, Hong Kong, Hungarian, Italian, Japanese, Russian, Spanish

Foreign Intrigue
See also Spies & Espionage
Mother Night *(WW II: Europe & North Africa)*
O.S.S. *(WW II: The Resistance)*
The Third Man *(Coming Home)*

The Wind and the Lion *(American Wars)*

Foreign Legion
Beau Geste *(British Wars)*
317th Platoon *(French Wars)*

France (Locale)
See also Paris

Au Revoir Les Enfants *(WW II: The Holocaust)*
Is Paris Burning? *(WW II: Europe & North Africa)*
The Last Metro *(WW II: The Holocaust)*
The Longest Day *(WW II: Europe & North Africa)*
Napoleon *(French Wars)*
One Against the Wind *(WW II: The Resistance)*
O.S.S. *(WW II: The Resistance)*
Paths of Glory *(WW I)*
Saving Private Ryan *(WW II: Europe & North Africa)*
13 Rue Madeleine *(WW II: The Resistance)*
The Train *(WW II: Europe & North Africa)*
The Victors *(WW II: Europe & North Africa)*
Waterloo *(French Wars)*

French (Production)
Anderson Platoon *(Vietnam War)*
Au Revoir les Enfants *(WW II: The Holocaust)*
Grand Illusion *(WW I)*
Is Paris Burning? *(WW II: Europe & North Africa)*
The Last Metro *(WW II: The Holocaust)*
Napoleon *(French Wars)*
Ran *(Japanese Wars)*
317th Platoon *(French Wars)*
The Train *(WW II: Europe & North Africa)*
Underground *(WW II: Europe & North Africa)*

Friendship
See Buddies

Front Page
The Green Berets *(Vietnam War)*
Objective, Burma! *(WW II: Pacific)*
The Story of G.I. Joe *(WW II: Europe & North Africa)*

Funerals
Gardens of Stone *(Vietnam War)*

G

German (Production)
Au Revoir les Enfants *(WW II: The Holocaust)*
The Bridge *(WW II: Europe & North Africa)*
Cross of Iron *(WW II: Europe & North Africa)*
Das Boot *(WW II: Europe & North Africa)*
Land and Freedom *(Between the World Wars)*
Underground *(WW II: Europe & North Africa)*
The Wannsee Conference *(WW II: The Holocaust)*
The White Rose *(WW II: The Resistance)*

Germany (Locale)
See also Berlin

All Quiet on the Western Front *(WW I)*
Battle of the Bulge *(WW II: Europe & North Africa)*
Battleground *(WW II: Europe & North Africa)*
The Blue Max *(WW I)*
The Bridge *(WW II: Europe & North Africa)*
Cross of Iron *(WW II: Europe & North Africa)*
Grand Illusion *(WW I)*
The Great Dictator *(Between the World Wars)*
The Great Escape *(WW II: POWs)*
The Guns of August *(WW I)*
Hell Is for Heroes *(WW II: Europe & North Africa)*
Mother Night *(WW II: Europe & North Africa)*
Patton *(WW II: Europe & North Africa)*
The Seventh Cross *(WW II: POWs)*
Stalag 17 *(WW II: POWs)*
A Time to Love and a Time to Die *(WW II: Europe & North Africa)*
When Trumpets Fade *(WW II: Europe & North Africa)*
The Wannsee Conference *(WW II: The Holocaust)*
The White Rose *(WW II: The Resistance)*

Going Native
Apocalypse Now *(Vietnam War)*
Hell in the Pacific *(WW II: Pacific)*
The Thin Red Line *(WW II: Pacific)*

Grand Hotel
Five Graves to Cairo *(WW II: Europe & North Africa)*

Great Britain (Locale)
See also London; Scotland
The Battle of Britain *(WW II: Europe and North Africq)*
Charge of the Light Brigade (1968) *(British Wars)*
Hope and Glory *(WW II: Homefront)*
The Land Girls *(WW II: Homefront)*
Mrs. Miniver *(WW II: Homefront)*
The White Cliffs of Dover *(WW II: Homefront)*

Great Escapes
See also Men in Prison; POW/MIA; Women in Prison
The Deer Hunter *(Vietnam War)*
The Great Escape *(WW II: POWs)*
A Man Escaped *(WW II: POWs)*
Rob Roy *(British Wars)*
The Seventh Cross *(WW II: POWs)*
Stalag 17 *(WW II: POWs)*
Von Ryan's Express *(WW II: POWs)*

Graham Greene: Books to Film
The Third Man *(Coming Home)*

Growing Older
Ran *(Japanese Wars)*

Guadalcanal
The Fighting Sullivans *(WW II: Pacific)*
The Gallant Hours *(WW II: Pacific)*
Guadalcanal Diary *(WW II: Pacific)*
The Thin Red Line *(WW II: Pacific)*

H

Hallmark Hall of Fame
One Against the Wind *(WW II: The Resistance)*

Joseph Heller: Books to Film
Catch-22 *(WW II: Europe & North Africa)*

Ernest Hemingway: Books to Film
For Whom the Bell Tolls *(Between the World Wars)*

Historical Drama
See also Medieval Romps; Period Piece
The Alamo *(American Wars)*
The Battle of Algiers *(French Wars)*
The Battle of Britain *(WW II: Europe & North Africa)*
Battle of the Bulge *(WW II: Europe & North Africa)*
Battleship Potemkin *(Russian Wars)*

Category Index

The Hidden Fortress *(Japanese Wars)*
Merry Christmas, Mr. Lawrence *(WW II: POWs)*
Ran *(Japanese Wars)*
Seven Samurai *(Japanese Wars)*
Yojimbo *(Japanese Wars)*

James Jones: Books to Film
From Here to Eternity *(Between the World Wars)*
The Thin Red Line *(WW II: Pacific)*

Journalism
See Front Page

Judaism
See also The Holocaust; Israel
Au Revoir les Enfants *(WW II: The Holocaust)*
The Last Metro *(WW II: The Holocaust)*
Schindler's List *(WW II: The Holocaust)*

Jungle Stories
Bataan *(WW II: Pacific)*
Guadalcanal Diary *(WW II: Pacific)*
Merrill's Marauders *(WW II: Pacific)*
Objective, Burma! *(WW II: Pacific)*
The Real Glory *(American Wars)*
The Thin Red Line *(WW II: Pacific)*

Justice Prevails...?
See also Order in the Court
Beau Geste *(British Wars)*
Mother Night *(WW II: Europe & North Africa)*
Paths of Glory *(WW I)*

K

Kidnapped!
The Wind and the Lion *(American Wars)*

Rudyard Kipling: Books to Film
Gunga Din *(British Wars)*

Korean War
All the Young Men *(Korean War)*
Battle Circus *(Korean War)*
The Bridges at Toko-Ri *(Korean War)*
The Hunters *(Korean War)*
The Manchurian Candidate *(Korean War)*
M*A*S*H *(Korean War)*
Men in War *(Korean War)*
Pork Chop Hill *(Korean War)*
The Steel Helmet *(Korean War)*

L

London (Locale)
See also Great Britain
The Battle of Britain *(WW II: Europe & North Africa)*
Hope and Glory *(WW II: Homefront)*
Mrs. Miniver *(WW II: Homefront)*

M

Alistair MacLean: Books to Film
The Guns of Navarone *(WW II: Europe & North Africa)*
Where Eagles Dare *(WW II: Europe & North Africa)*

Marines
All the Young Men *(Korean War)*
Bataan *(WW II: Pacific)*
Battle Cry *(WW II: Pacific)*
Born on the Fourth of July *(Vietnam War)*
The Boys in Company C *(Vietnam War)*
Flying Leathernecks *(WW II: Pacific)*
Full Metal Jacket *(Vietnam War)*
Guadalcanal Diary *(WW II: Pacific)*
Platoon *(Vietnam War)*
Pork Chop Hill *(Korean War)*
The Real Glory *(American Wars)*
A Rumor of War *(Vietnam War)*
Sands of Iwo Jima *(WW II: Pacific)*
The Siege of Firebase Gloria *(Vietnam War)*
Wake Island *(WW II: Pacific)*
The Wind and the Lion *(American Wars)*

W. Somerset Maugham: Books to Film
The Razor's Edge *(Coming Home)*

The Meaning of Life
Land and Freedom *(Between the World Wars)*
The Razor's Edge *(Coming Home)*

Medieval Romps
See also Historical Drama; Period Piece; Swashbucklers
Braveheart *(British Wars)*
Ran *(Japanese Wars)*
Seven Samurai *(Japanese Wars)*

Men in Prison
See also Great Escapes; POW/MIA; Women in Prison
Breaker Morant *(British Wars)*
The Dirty Dozen *(WW II: Europe & North Africa)*
Empire of the Sun *(WW II: POWs)*

A Man Escaped *(WW II: POWs)*

James Michener: Books to Film
The Bridges at Toko-Ri *(Korean War)*

Middle East (Locale)
See also Deserts; Foreign Legion; Israel; Persian Gulf War
Five Graves to Cairo *(WW II: Europe & North Africa)*
Lawrence of Arabia *(WW I)*
The Lighthorsemen *(WW I)*

Military: Air Force
See also Airborne
Air Force *(WW II: Pacific)*
Good Morning, Vietnam *(Vietnam War)*

Military: Army
Battle of the Bulge *(WW II: Europe & North Africa)*
Battleground *(WW II: Europe & North Africa)*
The Big Red One *(WW II: Europe & North Africa)*
Courage Under Fire *(Coming Home)*
The Dirty Dozen *(WW II: Europe & North Africa)*
The Green Berets *(Vietnam War)*
M*A*S*H *(Korean War)*
A Midnight Clear *(WW II: Europe & North Africa)*
1941 *(WW II: Homefront)*
Patton *(WW II: Europe & North Africa)*
Platoon *(Vietnam War)*
Saving Private Ryan *(WW II: Europe & North Africa)*
The Story of G.I. Joe *(WW II: Europe & North Africa)*
The Thin Red Line *(WW II: Pacific)*
When Trumpets Fade *(WW II: Europe & North Africa)*

Military: Foreign
All Quiet on the Western Front *(WW I)*
The Battle of Algiers *(French Wars)*
The Battle of Britain *(WW II: Europe & North Africa)*
Battleship Potemkin *(Russian Wars)*
Beau Geste *(British Wars)*
The Blue Max *(WW I)*
Breaker Morant *(British Wars)*
Chapayev *(Russian Wars)*
Charge of the Light Brigade (1936) *(British Wars)*
Charge of the Light Brigade (1968) *(British Wars)*

Category Index

Cross of Iron (WW II: Europe &
North Africa)
Das Boot (WW II: Europe & North
Africa)
Fires on the Plain (WW II: Pacific)
Five Graves to Cairo (WW II:
Europe & North Africa)
The Four Horsemen of the Apoca-
lypse (WW I)
Gallipoli (WW I)
Gunga Din (British Wars)
In Which We Serve (WW II: Europe
& North Africa)
Lawrence of Arabia (WW I)
The Lighthorsemen (WW I)
The Lives of a Bengal Lancer
(British Wars)
The Lost Patrol (WW I)
Napoleon (French Wars)
Paths of Glory (WW I)
317th Platoon (French Wars)
A Time to Love and a Time to Die
(WW II: Europe & North Africa)
War and Peace (Russian Wars)
Zulu (British Wars)

Missionaries
Breaker Morant (British Wars)
Paradise Road (WW II: POWs)

Mistaken Identity
See also Amnesia
Five Graves to Cairo (WW II: Europe
& North Africa)
The Great Dictator (Between the
World Wars)

Monster Moms
See also Dads
Born on the Fourth of July (Coming
Home)
The Manchurian Candidate (Korean
War)

Mystery & Suspense
Across the Pacific (Between the
World Wars)
Five Graves to Cairo (WW II:
Europe & North Africa)
The Manchurian Candidate (Korean
War)
The Third Man (Coming Home)

N

Native America
Last of the Mohicans (American
Wars)

Navy
See also Sail Away
Battleship Potemkin (Russian Wars)

The Bridges at Toko-Ri (Korean
War)
The Caine Mutiny (WW II: Europe &
North Africa)
Crash Dive (WW II: Europe & North
Africa)
Dive Bomber (Between the World
Wars)
Fighting Seabees (WW II: Pacific)
The Fighting Sullivans (WW II:
Pacific)
The Gallant Hours (WW II: Pacific)
In Harm's Way (WW II: Pacific)
Mister Roberts (WW II: Pacific)
Run Silent Run Deep (WW II:
Pacific)
The Sand Pebbles (American Wars)
They Were Expendable (WW II:
Pacific)
Tora! Tora! Tora! (WW II: Pacific)

Nazis & Other Paramilitary Slugs
See also Germany; The Holo-
caust; Judaism; World War II
Casablanca (WW II: The Resis-
tance)
The Dirty Dozen (WW II: Europe &
North Africa)
Five Graves to Cairo (WW II:
Europe & North Africa)
The Great Dictator (Between the
World Wars)
The Great Escape (WW II: POWs)
Judgment at Nuremberg (Coming
Home)
The Last Metro (WW II: The Holo-
caust)
Life Is Beautiful (WW II: The Holo-
caust)
Lifeboat (WW II: Europe & North
Africa)
The Longest Day (WW II: Europe &
North Africa)
A Man Escaped (WW II: POWs)
Mother Night (WW II: Europe &
North Africa)
O.S.S. (WW II: The Resistance)
Schindler's List (WW II: The Holo-
caust)
The Seventh Cross (WW II: POWs)
Stalag 17 (WW II: POWs)
13 Rue Madeleine (WW II: The
Resistance)
To Be or Not to Be (WW II: The
Resistance)
Watch on the Rhine (WW II: The
Resistance)
Where Eagles Dare (WW II: Europe
& North Africa)

New Zealand (Locale)
See Down Under

Newspapers
See Front Page

Nightclubs
Casablanca (WW II: The Resistance)

Normandy
See D-Day

Not-So-True Identity
Mother Night (WW II: Europe &
North Africa)

O

Oceans
See Submarines

Order in the Court
See also Justice Prevails...?
Breaker Morant (British Wars)
Judgment at Nuremberg (Coming
Home)
Paths of Glory (WW I)

Otherwise Engaged
See also Romantic Triangles
Doctor Zhivago (Russian Wars)
The Four Feathers (British Wars)
Gone with the Wind (American Wars)
Gunga Din (British Wars)
War and Peace (Russian Wars)

P

Pacific Islands (Locale)
Air Force (WW II: Pacific)
Bataan (WW II: Pacific)
Fighting Seabees (WW II: Pacific)
Flying Leathernecks (WW II: Pacific)
From Here to Eternity (Between the
World Wars)
Guadalcanal Diary (WW II: Pacific)
Hell in the Pacific (WW II: Pacific)
Home of the Brave (WW II: Pacific)
Paradise Road (WW II: POWs)
Sands of Iwo Jima (WW II: Pacific)
So Proudly We Hail (WW II: Pacific)
The Thin Red Line (WW II: Pacific)
Tora! Tora! Tora! (WW II: Pacific)
Wake Island (WW II: Pacific)

Paris (Locale)
See also France
Is Paris Burning? (WW II: Europe &
North Africa)
The Last Metro (WW II: The Holo-
caust)

One Against the Wind *(WW II: The Resistance)*
13 Rue Madeleine *(WW II: The Resistance)*

Patriotism & Paranoia
See also Propaganda
The Alamo *(American Wars)*
Born on the Fourth of July *(Coming Home)*
China Gate *(Vietnam War)*
Dr. Srangelove *American Wars)*
The Green Berets *(Vietnam War)*
Patton *(WW II: Europe & North Africa)*
So Proudly We Hail *(WW II: Pacific)*
Thirty Seconds over Tokyo *(WW II: Pacific)*

Peace
A Midnight Clear *(WW II: Europe & North Africa)*
War and Peace *(Russian Wars)*

Pearl Harbor
Air Force *(WW II: Pacific)*
From Here to Eternity *(Between the World Wars)*
The Gallant Hours *(WW II: Pacific)*
In Harm's Way *(WW II: Pacific)*
So Proudly We Hail *(WW II: Pacific)*
They Were Expendable *(WW II: Pacific)*
Tora! Tora! Tora! *(WW II: Pacific)*

Period Piece: 13th Century
Alexander Nevsky *(Russian Wars)*

Period Piece: 14th Century
Braveheart *(British Wars)*

Period Piece: 16th Century
Seven Samurai *(Japanese Wars)*

Period Piece: 18th Century
America *(American Wars)*
Last of the Mohicans *(American Wars)*
Rob Roy *(British Wars)*

Period Piece: 19th Century
The Alamo *(American Wars)*
Birth of a Nation *(American Wars)*
Charge of the Light Brigade *(British Wars)*
The Four Feathers *(British Wars)*
The General *(American Wars)*
Gettysburg *(American Wars)*
Glory *(American Wars)*
The Good, the Bad and the Ugly *(American Wars)*
Gunga Din *(British Wars)*
The Horse Soldiers *(American Wars)*
Lives of a Bengal Lancer *(British Wars)*

Napoleon *(French Wars)*
The Red Badge of Courage *(American Wars)*
She Wore a Yellow Ribbon *(American Wars)*
Shenandoah *(American Wars)*
They Died with Their Boots On *(American Wars)*
Waterloo *(French Wars)*
War and Peace *(Russian Wars)*
Zulu *(British Wars)*

Period Piece: 1900s
Battleship Potemkin *(Russian Wars)*
Breaker Morant *(British Wars)*
The Real Glory *(American Wars)*
The Wind and the Lion *(American Wars)*

Period Piece: 1910s
Stories not directly involving World War I.
Chapayev *(Russian Wars)*
Doctor Zhivago *(Russian Wars)*

Period Piece: 1940s
Stories not directly involving World War II.
Bye Bye Blues *(WW II: Homefront)*
Hong Kong 1941 *(Between the World Wars)*

Period Piece: 1960s
Stories not directly involving the Vietnam War.
Born on the Fourth of July *(Coming Home)*
The War at Home *(Vietnam War)*

Persian Gulf War
Courage Under Fire *(Coming Home)*

Philippines (Locale)
Air Force *(WW II: Pacific)*
Bataan *(WW II: Pacific)*
So Proudly We Hail *(WW II: Pacific)*
They Were Expendable *(WW II: Pacific)*

Physical Problems
The Best Years of Our Lives *(Coming Home)*
Born on the Fourth of July *(Coming Home)*
Coming Home *(Coming Home)*

Pill Poppin'
The Boys in Company C *(Vietnam War*
Platoon *(Vietnam War)*
The Third Man *(Coming Home)*

Politics
China Gate *(Vietnam War)*
Land and Freedom *(Between the World Wars)*

The Manchurian Candidate *(Korean War)*

Post-War
See also Veterans
The Best Years of Our Lives *(Coming Home)*
Born on the Fourth of July *(Coming Home)*
Courage Under Fire *(Coming Home)*
Judgment at Nuremberg *(Coming Home)*
Mother Night *(WW II: Europe & North Africa)*
The Razor's Edge *(Coming Home)*
The Third Man *(Coming Home)*

POW/MIA
See also Vietnam War; World War II
Au Revoir les Enfants *(WW II: The Holocaust)*
Bridge on the River Kwai *(WW II: POWs)*
Bye Bye Blues *(WW II: Homefront)*
The Deer Hunter *(Vietnam War)*
Empire of the Sun *(WW II: POWs)*
Grand Illusion *(WW I)*
The Great Escape *(WW II: POWs)*
King Rat *(WW II: POWs)*
A Man Escaped *(WW II: POWs)*
Merry Christmas, Mr. Lawrence *(WW II: POWs)*
Objective, Burma! *(WW II: Pacific)*
Paradise Road *(WW II: POWs)*
The Seventh Cross *(WW II: POWs)*
Stalag 17 *(WW II: POWs)*
Three Came Home *(WW II: POWs)*
Von Ryan's Express *(WW II: POWs)*

Prison
See Great Escapes; Men in Prison; POW/MIA; Women in Prison

Propaganda
See also Patriotism & Paranoia; Politics
Air Force *(WW II: Pacific)*
Alexander Nevsky *(Russian Wars)*
Bataan *(WW II: Pacific)*
Battleship Potemkin *(Russian Wars)*
Birth of a Nation *(American Wars)*
Chapayev *(Russian Wars)*
Fighting Seabees *(WW II: Pacific)*
The Fighting 69th *(WW I)*
The Green Berets *(Vietnam War)*
Guadalcanal Diary *(WW II: Pacific)*
The Immortal Battalion *(WW II: Europe & North Africa)*
Immortal Sergeant *(WW II: Europe & North Africa)*
Mrs. Miniver *(WW II: Homefront)*
Sergeant York *(WW I)*

Category Index

Wake Island *(WW II: Pacific)*

Protests
See also Rebel with a Cause
Born on the Fourth of July *(Coming Home)*
The War at Home *(Vietnam War)*

R

Radio
Good Morning, Vietnam *(Vietnam War)*
Mother Night *(WW II: Europe & North Africa)*

Rape
Rob Roy *(British Wars)*

Rebel with a Cause
See also The Resistance
Braveheart *(British Wars)*
Lawrence of Arabia *(WW I)*
Paths of Glory *(WW I)*
Rob Roy *(British Wars)*
The Sand Pebbles *(American Wars)*
The White Rose *(WW II: The Resistance)*

Red Cross
One Against the Wind *(WW II: The Resistance)*
So Proudly We Hail *(WW II: Pacific)*
The White Cliffs of Dover *(WW II: Homefront)*

Red Scare
See also Russia/USSR
Chapayev *(Russian Wars)*
China Gate *(Vietnam War)*
The Manchurian Candidate *(Korean War)*

Rescue Missions
Courage Under Fire *(Coming Home)*
The Hidden Fortress *(Japanese Wars)*
Saving Private Ryan *(WW II: Europe & North Africa)*
Seven Samurai *(Japanese Wars)*

The Resistance
See also World War II
Action in the North Atlantic *(WW II: Europe & North Africa)*
Casablanca *(WW II: The Resistance)*
The Last Metro *(WW II: The Holocaust)*
One Against the Wind *(WW II: The Resistance)*
To Be or Not to Be *(WW II: The Resistance)*

The Train *(WW II: Europe & North Africa)*
Watch on the Rhine *(WW II: The Resistance)*
The White Rose *(WW II: The Resistance)*

Restored Footage
Lawrence of Arabia *(WW I)*
Twelve O'Clock High *(WW II: Europe & North Africa)*

Revolutionary War
America *(American Wars)*

Rock Stars on Film
Merry Christmas, Mr. Lawrence *(WW II: POWs)*

Romance
See Romantic Adventures; Romantic Drama; Romantic Triangles

Romantic Adventures
Last of the Mohicans *(American Wars)*

Romantic Drama
The Big Parade *(WW I)*
Bye Bye Blues *(WW II: Homefront)*
Casablanca *(WW II: The Resistance)*
Doctor Zhivago *(Russian Wars)*
Gone with the Wind *(American Wars)*
Hong Kong 1941 *(Between the World Wars)*
The Land Girls *(WW II: Homefront)*
Rob Roy *(British Wars)*
A Time to Love and a Time to Die *(WW II: Europe & North Africa)*
War and Peace *(Russian Wars)*
The Wind and the Lion *(American Wars)*
Wings *(WW I)*

Romantic Triangles
See also Otherwise Engaged
Casablanca *(WW II: The Resistance)*
Hong Kong 1941 *(Between the World Wars)*
Last of the Mohicans *(American Wars)*

Royalty, British
See also Great Britain; Historical Drama; Medieval Romps; Period Piece
Braveheart *(British Wars)*
Henry V *(British Wars)*

Royalty, Russian
See also Historical Drama; Medieval Romps; Period Piece; Russia/USSR
Alexander Nevsky *(Russian Wars)*

Russia/USSR (Locale)
See also Red Scare
Alexander Nevsky *(Russian Wars)*
Battleship Potemkin *(Russian Wars)*
Chapayev *(Russian Wars)*
Come and See *(WW II: Europe & North Africa)*
Doctor Zhivago *(Russian Wars)*
War and Peace *(Russian Wars)*
The Winter War *(Between the World Wars)*

Russian (Production)
Alexander Nevsky *(Russian Wars)*
Battleship Potemkin *(Russian Wars)*
Chapayev *(Russian Wars)*
Come and See *(WW II: Europe & North Africa)*
Waterloo *(French Wars)*

S

Sail Away
See also Submarines
Action in the North Atlantic *(WW II: Europe & North Africa)*
Battleship Potemkin *(Russian Wars)*
The Caine Mutiny *(WW II: Europe & North Africa)*
Das Boot *(WW II: Europe & North Africa)*
The Fighting Sullivans *(WW II: Pacific)*
The Gallant Hours *(WW II: Pacific)*
In Which We Serve *(WW II: Europe & North Africa)*
Lifeboat *(WW II: Europe & North Africa)*
Mister Roberts *(WW II: Pacific)*
Run Silent Run Deep *(WW II: Pacific)*
The Sand Pebbles *(American Wars)*
Sink the Bismarck! *(WW II: Europe & North Africa)*
They Were Expendable *(WW II: Pacific)*

Sanity Check
See also Doctors & Nurses
Dr. Strangelove, or: How I Learned to Stop Worrying and Love the Bomb *(American Wars)*
1941 *(WW II: Homefront)*

Category Index

Chapayev *(Russian Wars)*
The Gallant Hours *(WW II: Pacific)*
Lawrence of Arabia *(WW I)*
Napoleon *(French Wars)*
Patton *(WW II: Europe & North Africa)*
Schindler's List *(WW II: The Holocaust)*
Three Came Home *(WW II: POWs)*
To Hell and Back *(WW II: Europe & North Africa)*

Thrillers
See Mystery & Suspense

Tokyo (Locale)
See also Japan
Thirty Seconds over Tokyo *(WW II: Pacific)*

Leo Tolstoy: Books to Film
War and Peace *(Russian Wars)*

Torrid Love Scenes
See also Sex on the Beach
From Here to Eternity *(Between the World Wars)*

Tragedy
See also Drama; Tearjerkers
The Fighting Sullivans *(WW II: Pacific)*
Hong Kong 1941 *(Between the World Wars)*
Mother Night *(WW II: Europe & North Africa)*
Ran *(Japanese Wars)*
The White Cliffs of Dover *(WW II: Homefront)*

Trains
Courage Under Fire *(Coming Home)*
The General *(American Wars)*
The Horse Soldiers *(American Wars)*
The Train *(WW II: Europe & North Africa)*
Von Ryan's Express *(WW II: POWs)*

True Stories
See also This Is Your Life
Above and Beyond *(WW II: Pacific)*
The Alamo *(American Wars)*
Au Revoir les Enfants *(WW II: The Holocaust)*
Bataan *(WW II: Pacific)*
The Big Red One *(WW II: Europe & North Africa)*
The Bridge *(WW II: Europe & North Africa)*
A Bridge Too Far *(WW II: Europe & North Africa)*
Empire of the Sun *(WW II: POWs)*
Fighting Seabees *(WW II: Pacific)*

The Fighting Sullivans *(WW II: Pacific)*
The Great Escape *(WW II: POWs)*
The Horse Soldiers *(American Wars)*
In Which We Serve *(WW II: Europe & North Africa)*
A Man Escaped *(WW II: POWs)*
One Against the Wind *(WW II: The Resistance)*
Paths of Glory *(WW I)*
Patton *(WW II: Europe & North Africa)*
A Rumor of War *(Vietnam War)*
Schindler's List *(WW II: The Holocaust)*
Sergeant York *(WW I)*
So Proudly We Hail *(WW II: Pacific)*
Thirty Seconds over Tokyo *(WW II: Pacific)*
Three Came Home *(WW II: POWs)*
The Tuskegee Airmen *(WW II: Europe & North Africa)*
The Wannsee Conference *(WW II: The Holocaust)*
The White Rose *(WW II: The Resistance)*
Zulu *(British Wars)*

U

Leon Uris: Books to Film
Battle Cry *(WW II: Pacific)*

V

Veterans
See also Post-War
The Best Years of Our Lives *(Coming Home)*
Born on the Fourth of July (Coming Home)
Coming Home *(Coming Home)*

Vietnam War
See also Post-War; POW/MIA
Anderson Platoon *(Vietnam War)*
Apocalypse Now *(Vietnam War)*
Born on the Fourth of July (Coming Home)
The Boys in Company C *(Vietnam War)*
China Gate *(Vietnam War)*
Coming Home *(Coming Home)*
The Deer Hunter *(Vietnam War)*
84 Charlie MoPic *(Vietnam War)*
Full Metal Jacket *(Vietnam War)*
Gardens of Stone *(Vietnam War)*
Go Tell the Spartans *(Vietnam War)*

Good Morning, Vietnam *(Vietnam War)*
The Green Berets *(Vietnam War)*
Hamburger Hill *(Vietnam War)*
Platoon *(Vietnam War)*
A Rumor of War *(Vietnam War)*
The Siege of Firebase Gloria *(Vietnam War)*
317th Platoon *(French Wars)*
The War at Home *(Vietnam War)*

Kurt Vonnegut: Books to Film
Mother Night *(WW II: Europe & North Africa)*

Vote for Me!
See also Capitol Capers
The Manchurian Candidate *(Korean War)*

W

War Between the Sexes
Casablanca *(WW II: The Resistance)*
Gone with the Wind *(American Wars)*

Westerns
See also Spaghetti Western
The Alamo *(American Wars)*
The Good, the Bad and the Ugly *(American Wars)*
She Wore a Yellow Ribbon *(American Wars)*
They Died with Their Boots On *(American Wars)*

William Wharton: Books to Film
A Midnight Clear *(WW II: Europe & North Africa)*

Women in Prison
See also Men in Prison
Paradise Road *(WW II: POWs)*
Three Came Home *(WW II: POWs)*

Women in War
See also Doctors & Nurses; Korean War; Vietnam War; Wonder Women; World War I; World War II
Courage Under Fire *(Coming Home)*
One Against the Wind *(WW II: The Resistance)*
Paradise Road *(WW II: POWs)*
So Proudly We Hail *(WW II: Pacific)*

Wonder Women
Courage Under Fire *(Coming Home)*
The Wind and the Lion *(American Wars)*

World War I

All Quiet on the Western Front *(WW I)*
The Big Parade *(WW I)*
The Blue Max *(WW I)*
Dawn Patrol *(WW I)*
The Fighting 69th *(WW I)*
Four Horsemen of the Apocalypse *(WW I)*
Gallipoli *(WW I)*
Grand Illusion *(WW I)*
The Guns of August *(WW I)*
Hell's Angels *(WW I)*
Lawrence of Arabia *(WW I)*
The Lighthorsemen *(WW I)*
The Lost Patrol *(WW I)*
Paths of Glory *(WW I)*
The White Cliffs of Dover *(WW II: Homefront)*
Wings *(WW I)*

World War II

See also The Holocaust; Post-War; POW/MIA; The Resistance
Above and Beyond *(WW II: Pacific)*
Across the Pacific *(Between the World Wars)*
Action in the North Atlantic *(WW II: Europe & North Africa)*
Air Force *(WW II: Pacific)*
Au Revoir les Enfants *(WW II: The Holocaust)*
Bataan *(WW II: Pacific)*
Battle Cry *(WW II: Pacific)*
The Battle of Britain *(WW II: Europe & North Africa)*
Battle of Midway *(WW II: Documentaries)*
Battle of San Pietro *(WW II: Documentaries)*
Battle of the Bulge *(WW II: Europe & North Africa)*
Battleground *(WW II: Europe & North Africa)*
The Best Years of Our Lives *(Coming Home)*
The Big Red One *(WW II: Europe & North Africa)*
The Bridge *(WW II: Europe & North Africa)*
Bridge on the River Kwai *(WW II: POWs)*
A Bridge Too Far *(WW II: Europe & North Africa)*
The Caine Mutiny *(WW II: Europe & North Africa)*
Casablanca *(WW II: The Resistance)*
Catch-22 *(WW II: Europe & North Africa)*
Come and See *(WW II: Europe & North Africa)*

Command Decision *(WW II: Europe & North Africa)*
Crash Dive *(WW II: Europe & North Africa)*
Cross of Iron *(WW II: Europe & North Africa)*
Das Boot *(WW II: Europe & North Africa)*
The Dirty Dozen *(WW II: Europe & North Africa)*
Dive Bomber *(Between the World Wars)*
Empire of the Sun *(WW II: POWs)*
Fighting Seabees *(WW II: Pacific)*
The Fighting Sullivans *(WW II: Pacific)*
Fires on the Plain *(WW II: Pacific)*
Five Graves to Cairo *(WW II: Europe & North Africa)*
Flying Leathernecks *(WW II: Pacific)*
From Here to Eternity *(Between the World Wars)*
The Gallant Hours *(WW II: Pacific)*
The Great Escape *(WW II: POWs)*
Guadalcanal Diary *(WW II: Pacific)*
The Guns of Navarone *(WW II: Europe & North Africa)*
Hell Is for Heroes *(WW II: Europe & North Africa)*
Home of the Brave *(WW II: Pacific)*
Hope and Glory *(WW II: Homefront)*
Immortal Battalion *(WW II: Europe & North Africa)*
The Immortal Sergeant *(WW II: Europe & North Africa)*
In Harm's Way *(WW II: Pacific)*
In Which We Serve *(WW II: Europe & North Africa)*
Is Paris Burning? *(WW II: Europe & North Africa)*
Judgment at Nuremberg *(Coming Home)*
King Rat *(WW II: POWs)*
The Land Girls *(WW II: Homefront)*
The Last Metro *(WW II: The Holocaust)*
Life Is Beautiful *(WW II: The Holocaust)*
Lifeboat *(WW II: Europe & North Africa)*
The Longest Day *(WW II: Europe & North Africa)*
A Man Escaped *(WW II: POWs)*
Memphis Belle: A Story of a Flying Fortress *(WW II: Documentaries)*
Merrill's Marauders *(WW II: Pacific)*
Merry Christmas, Mr. Lawrence *(WW II: POWs)*
A Midnight Clear *(WW II: Europe & North Africa)*
Mrs. Miniver *(WW II: Homefront)*

Mister Roberts *(WW II: Pacific)*
Mr. Winkle Goes to War *(WW II: Europe & North Africa)*
Mother Night *(WW II: Europe & North Africa)*
1941 *(WW II: Homefront)*
Objective, Burma! *(WW II: Pacific)*
One Against the Wind *(WW II: The Resistance)*
O.S.S. *(WW II: The Resistance)*
Paradise Road *(WW II: POWs)*
Patton *(WW II: Europe & North Africa)*
Report from the Aleutians *(WW II: Documentaries)*
Run Silent Run Deep *(WW II: Pacific)*
Sahara *(WW II: Europe & North Africa)*
Sands of Iwo Jima *(WW II: Pacific)*
Saving Private Ryan *(WW II: Europe & North Africa)*
Schindler's List *(WW II: The Holocaust)*
The Seventh Cross *(WW II: POWs)*
Since You Went Away *(WW II: Homefront)*
Sink the Bismarck! *(WW II: Europe & North Africa)*
So Proudly We Hail *(WW II: Pacific)*
Stalag 17 *(WW II: POWs)*
The Story of G.I. Joe *(WW II: Europe & North Africa)*
They Were Expendable *(WW II: Pacific)*
The Thin Red Line *(WW II: Pacific)*
13 Rue Madeleine *(WW II: The Resistance)*
Thirty Seconds over Tokyo *(WW II: Pacific)*
Three Came Home *(WW II: POWs)*
A Time to Love and a Time to Die *(WW II: Europe & North Africa)*
To Be or Not to Be *(WW II: The Resistance)*
To Hell and Back *(WW II: Europe & North Africa)*
Too Late the Hero *(WW II: Pacific)*
Tora! Tora! Tora! *(WW II: Pacific)*
The Train *(WW II: Europe & North Africa)*
The Tuskegee Airmen *(WW II: Europe & North Africa)*
Twelve O'Clock High *(WW II: Europe & North Africa)*
Underground *(WW II: Europe & North Africa)*
The Victors *(WW II: Europe & North Africa)*
Von Ryan's Express *(WW II: POWs)*
Wake Island *(WW II: Pacific)*

Category
Index

A Walk in the Sun *(WW II: Europe & North Africa)*

The Wannsee Conference *(WW II: The Holocaust)*

Watch on the Rhine *(WW II: The Resistance)*

When Trumpets Fade *(WW II: Europe & North Africa)*

Where Eagles Dare *(WW II: Europe & North Africa)*

The White Cliffs of Dover *(WW II: Homefront)*

The White Rose *(WW II: The Resistance)*

The Young Lions *(WW II: Europe & North Africa)*

Herman Wouk: Books to Film

The Caine Mutiny *(WW II: Europe & North Africa)*

Writers

See also This Is Your Life

The Big Red One *(WW II: Europe & North Africa)*

The Boys in Company C *(Vietnam War)*

The Razor's Edge *(Coming Home)*

A Rumor of War *(Vietnam War)*

The Third Man *(Coming Home)*

The Eyes Have It

VideoHound® guides keep
VCRs filled with the best movies

VideoHound's Golden Movie Retriever 2000
Complete Guide to Movies on Videocassette, Laserdisc & CD

Back and even better for the new millennium, the *Hound* has the final "woof" on what to watch and what to leave on the shelf. Our reviews never leave movie aficionados out in the cold about what to spend their leisure time watching. More than 23,000 movies, 1,000 new to this edition, are reviewed in the classic irreverent style for which the *VideoHound* has become famous. Ten indexes, from actors to screenwriters and more, make finding movies a breeze.

1999 • 1,800 pp. • ISBN 1-57859-042-6 • **$21.95**

VideoHound's Horror Show
999 Hair-Raising, Hellish, and Humorous Movies

Everyone loves big bugs, blood-sucking blobs, serial-killing creeps and alien infestations. For the die-hard fans (and the hard-to-kill monsters they love), we offer *Horror Show*. Veteran *VideoHound* author and columnist Mike Mayo offers witty critiques, fascinating sidebars and extensive credit information on 999 of the best, weirdest and most entertaining horror movies on video. On top of that, we add cast, director, category and alternative title indexes, as well as lists of horror resources in print, in organizations and on the web.

Mike Mayo • 1998 • 450 pp. • ISBN 1-57859-047-7 • **$17.95**

VideoHound's Epics
Giants of the Big Screen

Epics covers big movies in its inimitable style. Arranged in 13 subject categories for easy browsing, the book offers comprehensive information on 200 epics ready for home viewing. Entries contain a full-length description, cast and credit information, release year, running time, availability, country of origin, awards and nominations. Features include seven indexes, from actors to directors and others, quotes, sidebars, trivia and 300 photos.

Glenn Hopp • 1998 • 500 pp. • ISBN 1-57859-074-4 • **$19.95**

VISIBLE
INK
PRESS